THE War Reporter

THE ANGLO-BOER WAR THROUGH THE EYES OF THE BURGHERS

THE War Reporter

THE ANGLO-BOER WAR THROUGH THE EYES OF THE BURGHERS

J.E.H. Grobler

JONATHAN BALL PUBLISHERS
JOHANNESBURG & CAPE TOWN

The War Reporter is dedicated to the Republican Bitter-enders of the war – men, women and children. The depth of their sacrifice can never be measured.

All rights reserved. No part of this publication may be reproduced or transmitted, in any form or by any means, without prior permission from the publisher or copyright holder.

© JEH Grobler, 2004

Originally published as individual articles in *Beeld* under the title *Oorlog-Beeld*.

First published in 2004 by in large format paperback by
JONATHAN BALL PUBLISHERS
A division of Media24
PO Box 33977
Jeppestown
2043

Reprinted once in 2007, 2008, 2009, 2010, 2011, 2012 and 2013 (twice)

ISBN 978-1-86842-186-2

Typesetting and reproduction of text by Triple M Design & Advertising, Johannesburg in conjunction with Book Productions, Pretoria

Cover design and reproduction by Triple M Design & Advertising, Johannesburg

Printed and bound by CTP Printers, Cape Town

Acknowledgements

The War Reporter was translated by the author himself from *Oorlog-Beeld*, a series of 66 supplements that were originally published in the Afrikaans newspaper *Beeld* at the time of the Anglo-Boer War centennial. A number of people who were involved in the original venture deserve to be acknowledged, namely the *Beeld* editor in the initial period, Arrie Rossouw, who approved the project, his successor Peet Kruger, the journalists Jan-Jan Joubert (who acted as intermediary between *Beeld* and the author and gave the latter valuable advice), Magda Swart, Christa Smuts and Astrid Verbeek, as well as Danie van Wyk. The author's colleagues at the Department of Historical and Heritage Studies at the University of Pretoria, especially Fransjohan Pretorius, Karen Harris and Johan Bergh, as well as a number of students, including Andrew Mcleod and Ria Groenewald, provided valuable comments, advice and source references. Numerous members of the public similarly commented on the contents of *Oorlog-Beeld* as it was originally published in the newspaper and made the author aware of additional information. Names that deserve specific mention in this respect are Isak Heath, the late Gerrie Lemmer and Edwin Conroy. Other individuals who deserve special acknowledgement for their comments and advice include Arnold van Dyk and Claude Malan and the author's colleagues at Loras College in Iowa, where he spent a semester in 2001.

At Jonathan Ball Publishers the author wishes to thank Jonathan Ball himself for accepting the manuscript for publication even before it was completed, Barry Streek, Francine Blum, Eugene Ashton, Valda Strauss and Frances Perryer. The author also wishes to thank Peter Sauthoff for the initial page design and Kevin Shenton of Triple M Design & Advertising for final typesetting and reproduction of text as well as Ingrid Booysen and Nico Harmse at the University of Pretoria for their invaluable contribution. Finally the author acknowledges the support and help of all the members of his family, especially his wife Elize who typed the original *Oorlog-Beeld* as well as the translated *War Reporter*, and his mother-in-law Connie Fourie who read the whole manuscript and provided valuable comments.

The photographs that are included in *The War Reporter* were all taken at the time of the Anglo-Boer War and are no longer subject to copyright restrictions. These photographs were collected by the author from a number of private and public collections and from books and journals. The author wishes to thank the following institutions and individuals who made their photographs available for this publication:

Department of Historical and Heritage Studies, University of Pretoria
Merensky Library, University of Pretoria
Arnold van Dyk, Bloemfontein
Denise van Hoepen, Pretoria

In addition to numerous books mentioned in the bibliography, the author also sourced photographs from the following books:

Barthorp, M., *The Anglo-Boer Wars 1815-1902*. Poole (Dorset): Blandford Press, 1987.

Beevor, W., *With the Central Column in South Africa. From Belmont to Komati-Poort*. London: King and his Navy and Army, 1903.

Direko, W.I., L. Changuion & F. Jacobs. *Suffering of War. A photographic portrayal of the suffering in the Anglo-Boer War emphasising the universal elements of all wars*. Photographic editor P. Alberts. Bloemfontein: Kraal Publishers for War Museum of the Boer Republics, 2003.

Küttner, H., *Unter dem Deutschen Roten Kreuz im Südafrikanischen Kriege*. Leipzig: Verlag von S Hirzel, 1900.

Lee, E.C.G., *To the Bitter End: A Photographic History of the Boer War 1899-1902*. London, Viking, 1985.

Meintjies, J., *The Anglo-Boer War 1899-1902: A Pictorial History*. Cape Town and Johannesburg: C. Struik Publishers, 1976.

Pakenham, T., *The Boer War*. Illustrated ed. New York: Random House, 1993.

Penning, L., *De Oorlog in Zuid-Afrika. De Strijd tusschen Engeland en de verbonden Boeren-Republieken Transvaal en Oranje-Vrijstaat, in zijn verloop geschetst*. 3 vols. Rotterdam: D.A. Daamen, no date.

Contents

PREFACE vii
MAP OF SOUTH AFRICA AT THE TIME OF THE ANGLO-BOER WAR viii
CHRONOLOGY OF MAIN EVENTS REPORTED IN *THE WAR REPORTER* ix
INTRODUCTION xi

Issue	Date	Page
1	14 October 1899	1
2	21 October 1899	5
3	28 October 1899	7
4	4 November 1899	9
5	11 November 1899	11
6	18 November 1899	13
7	25 November 1899	15
8	2 December 1899	17
9	9 December 1899	19
10	16 December 1899	21
11	23 December 1899	23
12	30 December 1899	25
13	6 January 1900	27
14	13 January 1900	29
15	20 January 1900	31
16	27 January 1900	33
17	3 February 1900	37
18	10 February 1900	39
19	17 February 1900	41
20	24 February 1900	43
21	3 March 1900	45
22	10 March 1900	47
23	17 March 1900	49
24	24 March 1900	51
25	31 March 1900	53
26	7 April 1900	55
27	14 April 1900	57
28	21 April 1900	59
29	28 April 1900	61
30	5 May 1900	63
31	12 May 1900	65
32	19 May 1900	67
33	26 May 1900	69
34	2 June 1900	71
35	9 June 1900	73

Issue	Date	Page
36	16 June 1900	77
37	23 June 1900	79
38	30 June 1900	81
39	7 July 1900	83
40	14 July 1900	85
41	21 July 1900	87
42	28 July 1900	89
43	4 August 1900	91
44	1 September 1900	93
45	1 October 1900	95
46	1 November 1900	97
47	1 December 1900	99
48	1 January 1901	101
49	1 February 1901	105
50	1 March 1901	109
51	1 April 1901	111
52	1 May 1901	113
53	1 June 1901	115
54	1 July 1901	117
55	1 August 1901	119
56	1 September 1901	121
57	1 October 1901	123
58	1 November 1901	125
59	1 December 1901	127
60	1 January 1902	131
61	1 February 1902	133
62	1 March 1902	137
63	1 April 1902	139
64	1 May 1902	141
65	1 June 1902	145
66	1 July 1902	147

BIBLIOGRAPHY		151
INDEX OF PLACE NAMES		153
INDEX OF NAMES		155

Preface

In this book my colleague, Dr Jackie Grobler, has succeeded in providing a fascinating interaction between the modern reader and the Boer men, women and children who experienced the sufferings and joys of the Anglo-Boer War of 1899-1902.

In these pages we learn that, for two years and eight months, the war was the only life these Boer people knew. Their whole existence was wrapped up in the lingering war with its enforced congregation of people, its close contact with large groups as well as individuals and its various psychological experiences. There were exhilarating moments when the burghers went out to meet the enemy, the sweet taste of victory, the bitterness of defeat, the humiliation of flight. There were also long spells of inactivity and idleness. There was the dreadful experience of death and its constant presence, both on the battlefield and in the concentration camps, but also moments of relaxation, play, humour, without which nobody could have endured the struggle to the end. There was hardship, heat, cold, want, hunger, but also pleasure, gratitude for small mercies when the suffering eased for a while. There was deep concern and excruciating longing for loved ones who had been separated from them. Many of them asked themselves whether the struggle would go on forever. But when the end came it was, for those who had lived through it all, the bitter end.

I think the author of these weekly war reports has succeeded admirably in getting his message across, as if we all were there and being informed of what was happening on the spot. Read all about it!

Professor Fransjohan Pretorius
Department of Historical and Heritage Studies
University of Pretoria

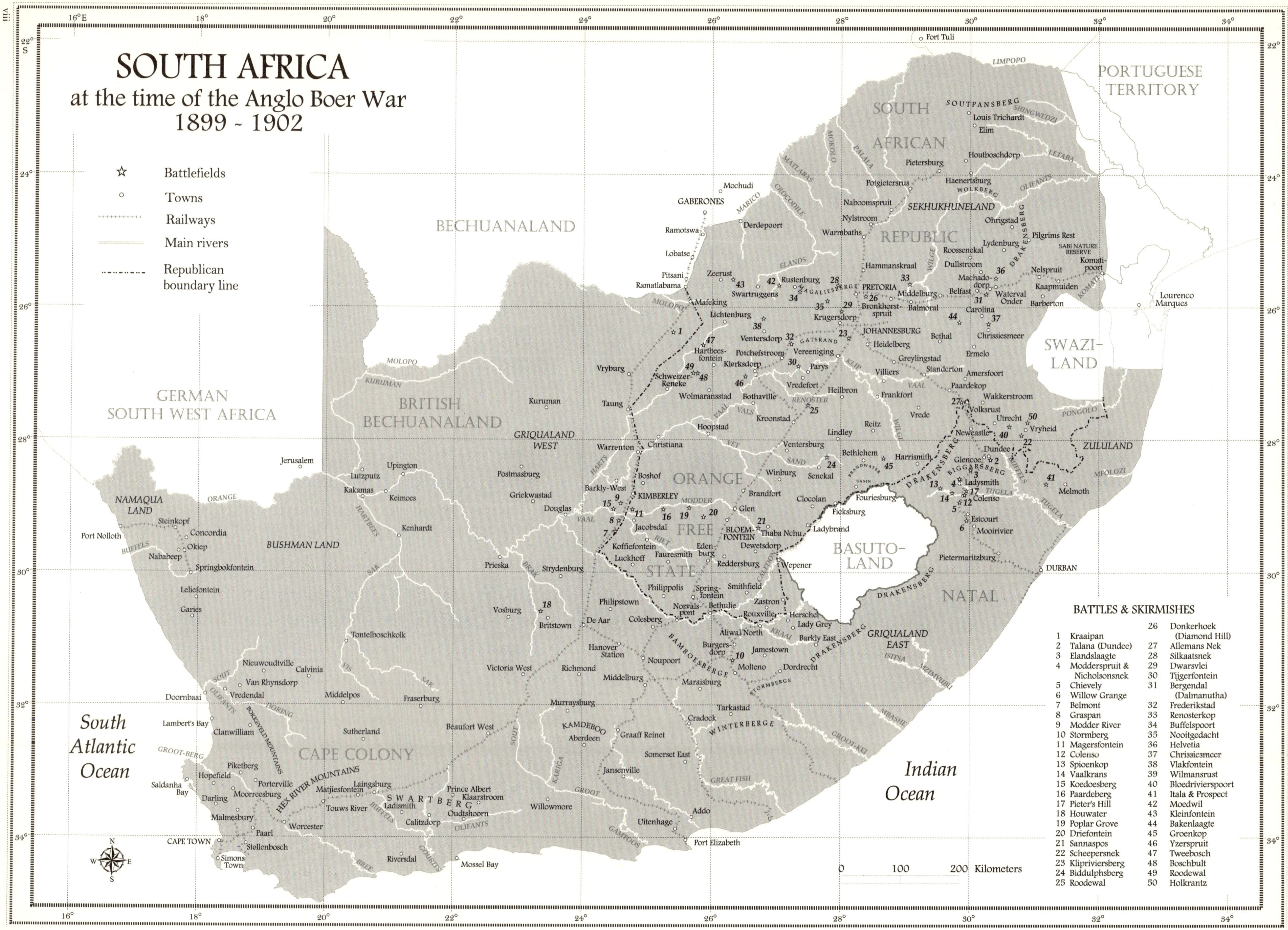

SOUTH AFRICA
at the time of the Anglo Boer War 1899 ~ 1902

Legend:
- ☆ Battlefields
- ○ Towns
- Railways
- Main rivers
- Republican boundary line

BATTLES & SKIRMISHES

#	Battle	#	Battle
1	Kraaipan	26	Donkerhoek (Diamond Hill)
2	Talana (Dundee)	27	Allemans Nek
3	Elandslaagte	28	Silkaatsnek
4	Modderspruit & Nicholsonsnek	29	Dwarsvlei
5	Chievely	30	Tigerfontein
6	Willow Grange	31	Bergendal (Dalmanutha)
7	Belmont	32	Frederikstad
8	Graspan	33	Renosterkop
9	Modder River	34	Buffelspoort
10	Stormberg	35	Nooitgedacht
11	Magersfontein	36	Helvetia
12	Colenso	37	Chrissiesmeer
13	Spioenkop	38	Vlakfontein
14	Vaalkrans	39	Wilmansrust
15	Koedoesberg	40	Bloedriviersspoort
16	Paardeberg	41	Itala & Prospect
17	Pieter's Hill	42	Moedwil
18	Houwater	43	Kleinfontein
19	Poplar Grove	44	Bakenlaagte
20	Driefontein	45	Groenkop
21	Sannaspos	46	Yzerspruit
22	Scheepersnek	47	Tweebosch
23	Kliprivierberg	48	Boschbult
24	Biddulphsberg	49	Roodewal
25	Roodewal	50	Holkrantz

Chronology
of Main Events Reported on in The War Reporter

The digits on the left refer to the issue number of the newspaper. The digits on the right are the relevant page numbers.

October 1899

1. Kruger sends ultimatum 1
   Expiry of ultimatum and outbreak of war 1
   Armoured train captured by the Boers at Kraaipan 1

2. Mafeking besieged 5
   Kimberley besieged 6
   Armoured train captured by Boers at Elandslaagte 6
   Battle of Talana Hill (Dundee) 5

3. Battle of Elandslaagte 7
   Vryburg occupied by the Boers 8
   Battle of Rietfontein 8

4. Battle of Modderspruit and Nicholson's Nek 9

5. Buller arrives in Cape Town 11

November 1899

Siege of Ladysmith begins 12

6. Aliwal North occupied by the Boers 14
   Colesberg, Burgersdorp occupied by the Boers 14
   Boers wreck armoured train between Frere and Chieveley and capture W. Churchill 13

7. Battle of Willow Grange 15
   Battle of Belmont 15

8. Battle of Graspan 17
   British forces and Bakgatla warriors attack Derdepoort 18
   Battle of Modder River 17

9. Boers destroy railway bridge at Colenso 19

December 1899

British forces attack Boer Long Tom at Ladysmith 20

10. Battle of Stormberg 21
    Battle of Magersfontein 22

11. Churchill escapes from Staats Model School in Pretoria 24
    Battle of Colenso 23

12. Boer revenge attack on Bakgatla 25
    Roberts leaves Britain to succeed Buller as Commander-in-Chief in South Africa 25
    Skirmish at Platboomfort (Game Tree Hill), Mafeking 26

13. Skirmish at Labuschagne's Nek outside Dordrecht 28

January 1900

British forces capture Douglas from the Boers 27

14. Boer attack on Platrand (Ladysmith) 29, 30
    Roberts and Kitchener arrive in Cape Town 29

15. Soldiers of Buller's force cross Upper Tugela 31
    British forces haul field gun to top of Cole's Kop (Colesberg) 32

16. Boers repulse British attack on Tabanyama (Upper Tugela) 33
    Battle of Spioenkop 33-35

17. Boers begin damming up Klip River at Ladysmith 37

February 1900

18. Battle of Vaalkrans 39, 40
    Battle of Koedoesberg 40

19. British forces begin outflanking Boers at Magersfontein 41
    Kimberley relieved 41

20. British forces launch offensive on Boer positions east of Colenso 42
    Battle of Paardeberg; Cronjés laager besieged 43

21. Cronjé surrenders at Paardeberg 45
    British breakthrough at Pieter's Hill on Natal front 46
    Ladysmith relieved 46

March 1900

22. Boers pull back from Colesberg, destroy Norvalspont railway bridge 47
    Battle of Poplar Grove 47

23. Battle of Driefontein 50
    British forces occupy Bloemfontein 49

24. Republican Council of War at Kroonstad 51

25. Boer forces occupy Ladybrand 53
    Death of Piet Joubert 53

26. Battle of Sannaspos 55

April 1900

De Wet defeats British force at Mostertshoek (Reddersburg) 56
De Villebois-Mareuil's disaster at Boshof 56

27. De Wet begins siege of British force at Jammerbergsdrif (Wepener) 57

28. British repulsed at Houwater 59

29. De Wet abandons siege of British force at Jammerbergsdrif 61

30. Battle of Toba Mountain 64

May 1900

British forces drive Boers from Brandfort 64

31. British forces occupy Winburg 65

32. British forces occupy Kroonstad 67
    Boer attack on Mafeking fails 67
    Boer forces in Natal abandon the Biggarsberg 68
    Mafeking relieved 68

33. Skirmish at Scheepersnek 69

34. Annexation of Orange Free State proclaimed 71
    Battle of Klipriviersberg 72
    President Kruger leaves Pretoria 71
    Battle of Biddulphsberg 72
    British force at Lindley overpowered 72
    British forces occupy Johannesburg 71

June 1900
35 British forces occupy Pretoria 73

36 De Wet at Roodewal Station 77
    Battle of Donkerhoek (Diamond Hill) 77
    Battle of Allemans Nek 78
    British forces occupy Volksrust 78

37 Transvaal war council meeting at Balmoral 79
    De Wet home burned down by British forces 79

38 British forces occupy Heidelberg (Transvaal) 82

July 1900
39 Boer forces briefly occupy Rustenburg 83

40 British forces occupy Bethlehem 86
    Skirmish at Tijgerpoort (Pretoria) 86
    De la Rey's success at Silkaatsnek 85
    Skirmish at Dwarsvlei (Krugersdorp) 85
    Skirmish at Onderstepoort 85

41 Steyn and De Wet leave the Brandwater Basin 87
    Roberts forces Boer women out of Pretoria 87

42 British forces begin advance from Pretoria towards Komatipoort 90

43 Prinsloo surrenders in Brandwater Basin 91

August 1900
44 De la Rey's siege of British force at
    Brakfontein (Swartruggens) 94
    Clash at Tijgerfontein 93
    De Wet's escape across the Magaliesberg 94
    Battle of Bergendal (Dalmanutha) 93
    Release of last 2 000 British prisoners of war at Nooitgedacht (Barberton) 93

September 1900
45 Formal British proclamation of annexation of Transvaal 95
    Danie Theron killed on the battlefield 95
    Kruger arrives in Lourenco Marques 95
    Boer artillerymen destroy one of their own Long Toms 96
    British forces reach Komatipoort 96

October 1900
46 Ventersburg destroyed by British forces 97
    Kruger sails for France on board the *Gelderland* 97
    Battle of Frederikstad 97

November 1900
47 De Wet defeated at Bothaville 100
    De Wet captures British garrison of Dewetsdorp 100
    Battle of Renosterkop 99
    Roberts hands over command to Kitchener 99

December 1900
48 Battle of Nooitgedacht 101
    Kritzinger enters Cape Colony 103
    Boer forces capture Helvetia post and the 'Lady Roberts' 102

January 1901
49 Hertzog occupies Vanrhynsdorp 106
    Queen Victoria dies 105
    Boer forces capture Modderfontein 107

February 1901
50 Battle of Chrissiesmeer 110
    De Wet's brief invasion of Cape Colony begins 110
    De Wet and Hertzog back in the Orange Free State 110
    Middelburg Peace Conference 109

March 1901
51 De la Rey's attempt to occupy Lichtenburg fails 111

April 1901
52 British forces occupy Pietersburg 114

May 1901
53 Meeting of Transvaal leaders at De Emigratie 115
    Battle of Vlakfontein 116
    Fourth and last Long Tom destroyed by its crew 116

June 1901
54 British forces capture women's laager at Graspan (Reitz) 118
    Battle of Wilmansrust 118
    Republican negotiations at Waterval 118

July 1901
55 President Steyn almost captured at Reitz 120
    Mrs Gezina Kruger dies 119

August 1901
56 Kitchener's proclamation of banishment for Boer readers 121

September 1901
57 Smuts's commando enters Cape Colony near Herschel 123
    Commandant Lötter's commando captured 123
    Botha defeats British force at Bloedrivier's Poort 124
    Botha attacks Forts Itala and Prospect 124
    Battle of Moedwil 124

October 1901
58 Maritz occupies Hopefield in Southwestern Cape 126
    Execution of Commandant Lötter 126
    Commandant Scheepers captured 125
    Battle of Kleinfontein 125
    Battle of Bakenlaagte 125

November 1901
59 Smuts reaches Vanrhynsdorp 127

December 1901
60 Kritzinger captured by the British 131
    De Wet defeats British force on Groenkop 131
    Smuts leads war council meeting at Soetwater 132

January 1902
61 Skirmish at Bankkop (Ermelo) 134
    Commandant Scheepers executed 133
    Beyers captures Pietersburg concentration camp 134
    General Ben Viljoen captured 134

February 1902
62 Battle of Yzerspruit 137

March 1902
63 Battle of Tweebosch 139, 140
    Death of Cecil John Rhodes 140
    Battle of Boschbult 140

April 1902
64 Boer forces capture Springbokfontein (Springbok) 142
    Boer forces begin siege of Okiep 145
    Peace negotiations begin in Klerksdorp 141
    Battle of Roodewal 141, 142

May 1902
65 Zulu attack on Holkrantz 145
    First meeting of Boer delegates at Vereeniging 145
    Boer attack on Aberdeen fails 145
    Peace of Vereeniging signed 146

June 1902
66 The bitter surrender 147

Introduction

This is not an orthodox history of the Anglo-Boer War. There is no detailed discussion of the causes or consequences of the war. There are no chapters, no introductions and conclusions, no scientific historical analysis of any specific issue. There are also no critical evaluations of the sources. Rather, it is a book about one of the most significant events in the history of South Africa, incorporating masses of historical material and photographs. As much as possible of the available published primary source material was used, and great care was taken to include only reliable information. In this sense, then, it is a history book – but it is a history book with a difference.

The War Reporter is an imaginary newspaper. There was no single Republican or Boer newspaper that was published on either a daily, weekly or monthly basis for the whole duration of the Anglo-Boer War. The 'editor', 'reporters' and 'correspondents' of *The War Reporter* never actually existed. The aim was to publish an account of the course of the war in its totality – meaning not merely the military confrontations. The format represents the way in which the war could have been reported in a pro-Boer weekly newspaper (monthly from September 1900), published in the South African Republic as the war progressed.

One of the most formidable challenges that face historians is to understand the *zeitgeist* or atmosphere of the period they write about. The same is true for readers of history books. A failure to understand the situation at the time makes it virtually impossible to understand the major events, the decisions taken by the major participants, the reactions of the ordinary people and the contradictions of the past in the context in which they occurred. This was my biggest challenge as I attempted to portray the world and the views of the Boers as the Anglo-Boer War progressed. The book is first and foremost an attempt to answer the question: how did the Boers experience the Anglo-Boer War?

The War Reporter does not claim, or aim, to be an unbiased, balanced representation of the history of the war. When reading contemporary Boer newspaper reports as well as the diaries of Boers, both men and women, who were participants in the war, one soon senses that the way in which they viewed the war constantly changed. There was no single Boer view either, but often serious disagreements on, for example, the wisdom of prolonging the war. *The War Reporter* attempts to represent the standpoints of the so-called *Bitter-enders,* who literally stuck to their guns and their hopes up to the very (and for them, bitter) end of the war.

I believe that it is impossible to fully comprehend a phenomenon such as a major war in the history of a people if one fails to understand the ways in which the participants – who did not have the luxury of hindsight – experienced the events that they were involved in. I had to divorce myself completely from knowing the eventual outcome of the war and its consequences. The 'correspondents' of *The War Reporter* similarly are not aware what the future holds for them. In each issue they 'report' on how they experienced the situation at that exact time. The challenge is to imagine how reporters and newspaper editors on the Boer side in those days would have experienced various issues. That should ideally also be the point of departure of the readers of *The War Reporter,* namely to consciously put themselves in the situation of the Boers at the specific points in time that they are reading about.

In a book of this nature there can only be one standpoint, and that is one-sided. *The War*

Reporter portrays the Boers as heroic freedom fighters and the British as brutal invaders. This was the way in which contemporary Boer newspapers portrayed the main contenders in the war and also the view reflected in Boer reports, diaries, memoirs, poems and letters.

The War Reporter attempts to illuminate the changing perceptions of the Boer society on specific war issues in the widest sense of the word. Not only military confrontations are reported on, but also life on commando, the experiences of prisoners of war in camps scattered across the globe, the activities of Boer delegates abroad whose mission it was to bring about foreign intervention on the Boer side, the activities of prominent individuals, such as President Paul Kruger and Emily Hobhouse, and the dismal fate of the women and children in the concentration camps. The reports cover Boer views on issues as diverse as the morality of propaganda, the 'treachery' of so-called joiners, the execution of traitors, of Cape Rebels and of Boer officers, British scorched earth tactics, the involvement of blacks in the war, the Boer treatment of British soldiers and officers captured by them, the Boer longing for peace and the impact of the war on Boer religion.

Numerous contemporary poems have been included – not only because poems often capture the atmosphere of a specific time and place more clearly than prose ever can, but also because newspapers at that time often included poems in their columns. The poets are acknowledged in all cases, except where it is categorically stated that the poet is not known. None of the poems were translated by the author – all are either in their original language or were translated into English by the poets themselves. Care was also taken to ensure that none of the poems were included in issues of *The War Reporter* that pre-dated the date on which the specific poems were actually written. The same is true of the photographs – they were all taken before the date of the issue of *The War Reporter* in which they are included.

What is portrayed in *The War Reporter* is an idealistic journalistic situation. Reporters of *The War Reporter* are always present when important events take place and they have immediate access to sources, including commanders with whom they have lengthy interviews. Moreover, the lines of communication from the various fronts to the editorial offices of *The War Reporter* are always open, and the news travels remarkably quickly.

The actual situation was somewhat different. At the beginning of the war there were numerous newspapers that were sympathetic towards the Republican cause. The most important ones were *De Volksstem, Standard and Diggers' News* and *De Express,* published in Pretoria, Johannesburg and Bloemfontein respectively. After the British occupation of those cities, these newspapers were closed. Indeed, according to Peter Browning (*The Changing Nature of War*, page 140), in this war the British government for the first time formally restricted war reporting.

The government of the South African Republic relocated to Machadodorp in what is now Mpumalanga after the occupation of Pretoria and kept publishing a *Staatscourant (Government Gazette)*, which included war reports, on a printing press in that rural village. The only more orthodox newspapers that were left after June 1900 – in what is often called the guerrilla phase of the war – were more in the nature of newssheets and were clandestinely and only sporadically published. These included *De Zoutpansberg Wachter* (published in Pietersburg in the northern part of the South African Republic, which was only occupied by the British forces in May 1901), and *De Brandwacht* and *De Basuin* (published in Fouriesburg in the eastern part of the Republic of the Orange Free State) on an ancient printing press. There were also small newspapers produced on the Boer side in prisoner-of-war camps. Few commandos, if any, were accompanied by reporters after the start of the so-called guerrilla phase.

A note on sources

A huge number and wide variety of sources were used in compiling this newspaper history – especially sources that reflect the Boer experience. All the sources are listed in the Bibliography (pp 151-152). They include actual newspapers published in those days, especially *De Volksstem* and the *Transvaal Government Gazette,* most of the major standard histories on the war as a whole, numerous histories on specific aspects of the war, but most importantly the journals, diaries, memoirs, autobiographies and other books by participants in the war, especially on the Boer side. Some archival material was consulted – especially published documents. Information received from numerous individuals who reacted to the publication of the original Afrikaans version of *The War Reporter* in the newspaper *Beeld* was often incorporated into the translated English version.

Source acknowledgement was a major problem, since footnotes, text notes or endnotes would not have complied with the newspaper format in which the book is written. In the Bibliography the specific number of the issue of *The War Reporter* for which a source was used is provided in brackets.

I made extensive use of the contemporary writings of people who were involved in the war. Thus excerpts from the diaries of participants are used in 'reports' to convey how the diarists experienced or felt about specific events or issues. In all cases the original authors are acknowledged in the reports themselves. Thus, for example, excerpts from General Christiaan de Wet's memoirs are used in *The War Reporter* and in the specific reports it is claimed that 'De Wet told our correspondent after the battle'; or excerpts from Jan F.E. Celliers's diary are used and in *The War Reporter* it is stated that Celliers compiled the said report for the 'newspaper'. In all 'reports' where information is given in quotation marks, the information was quoted from diaries or memoirs of original participants in the war. In many cases these 'reports' were translated into English by the author.

J.E.H. Grobler
Pretoria, 2004

…
THE War Reporter

WEEKLY EDITION

Number 1   Pretoria, South African Republic   14 October 1899

FIRST SHOTS OF THE WAR

General De la Rey captures British guns

Pretoria, 14 October – Barely 30 hours after the lapse of the Republican ultimatum, the first shots of the war rang out, soon to be followed by the first Boer victory. These events took place on the Transvaal western border near Kraaipan Railway Station. Our correspondent on that front compiled the following report:

Before midnight on the evening of 11 October, 800 men under the command of General Koos de la Rey proceeded from Mafeking southwards. According to reports, there was a British force of about 1 000 men at the railway station near Moshette's village. Our objective: to drive them off and destroy the railway line.

De la Rey and his men reached Kraaipan Station – on the main line to Vryburg some 50 kilometres south of Mafeking – at three o'clock on the afternoon of 12 October. There was no sign of any British force. The burghers cut the telegraph wire and damaged the railway line on both sides of the station. Afterwards they rested to catch up on the sleep they lost the previous evening. At that stage no shots had been fired.

The sleeping burghers were blissfully unaware that a British armoured train was approaching. From information gathered after the skirmish, it is known that Colonel R.S.S. Baden-Powell, the commander of the British garrison in Mafeking, had sent that train from Mafeking to Vryburg the previous afternoon to fetch a number of field guns designated for his forces. Those guns were only entrained late on 12 October, after the burghers had damaged the railway line at Kraaipan.

Even though the commander of the armoured train, Lieutenant Nesbit, was informed in Vryburg that the telegraph wire to Mafeking had been cut and that there were Boers on the railway near Kraaipan, he decided to return that night. He expected that the railway line would be damaged and even took some railway workers with him. At the Madibogo Pan a police sergeant informed him that the Boers had damaged the railway line and had a gun. Nesbit nevertheless decided to go ahead with his journey. He ordered the engine-driver to proceed slowly in the dark and douse the light of the train, thus ensuring that there would be a confrontation.

De la Rey and his burghers were astounded when they were awakened by their sentries shortly before 10 o'clock that evening to hear a train approaching. Moments later the locomotive derailed at the place where the burghers had destroyed the railway line. Some burghers quickly moved to the south in the dark and broke up the railway line behind the armoured train, blocking its retreat. The other burghers took up position for a battle.

The arrogant British commander obviously did not intend to turn back. His workers began repairing the railway line. That was when the first shots – indeed the first shots of this war – were fired by Field Cornet J.C. Coetzee, at about a quarter to 11 on the evening of 12 October. They were the signal for all the burghers to open fire.

The British at first returned the fire, but soon decided to seek shelter. Both Nesbit and the engine driver were lightly wounded. When day broke, the Boer artillerymen opened fire on the train with their light field guns. After the third shot the crew of the train, followed by the soldiers, surrendered. Some 40 people were captured, about half of them soldiers. There were nine wounded. The Boers suffered no casualties.

For De la Rey and his burghers the most valuable outcome of the affair was not the prisoners of war but the cargo of the train, which they seized. Their prize included three 7-pounder field guns, numerous shells, about 30 rifles with plenty of ammunition and a few cases of dynamite. Thus ended the first encounter of the war, within two days of its commencement, in a total victory for the Boers.

Kraaipan: British guns captured by the Boers

Burghers in front of the locomotive they derailed at Kraaipan

THE ULTIMATUM

Pretoria, 9 October – The ultimatum of the government of the South African Republic to the British government was issued at five o'clock this afternoon. State Secretary F.W. Reitz personally handed the envelope containing the ultimatum to the British Agent, Sir William Conyngham Greene, at his residence in Pretoria.

In the ultimatum the Transvaal authorities state unequivocally that they believe that the British government is unlawfully interfering in the internal affairs of the Republic. In order to protect the interests of the Republic, the Transvaal government feels obliged to request the British government to accede to the following four demands:

- That all points of mutual difference shall in future be settled by arbitration.
- That all British troops on the borders of the Republic shall be instantly withdrawn.
- That all reinforcements of troops that have arrived in South Africa since 1 June 1899 shall be removed from South Africa within a reasonable time.
- That the British troops that are on the sea on their way to South Africa shall not be landed in any part of South Africa.

The ultimatum ends with the statement that should the British government not give a satisfactory answer before five o'clock on the afternoon of 11 October, the South African Republic would be compelled to regard the failure of the British government to accede to the demands as a formal declaration of war.

The government (Executive Council) of the South African Republic. Front row from the left, Piet Joubert, Paul Kruger, Piet Cronjé; back row from left J.M.A. Wolmarans, F.W. Reitz, Schalk Burger and Jan Kock. J.M.A. Wolmarans died earlier this year and was replaced on the council by his brother, A.D.W. Wolmarans.

FROM THE EDITOR

War again between the Boer Republics and Britain! The first shots have been fired, and the Republican forces have scored their first victory. How many battles will be fought, nobody can guess. So far, our prospects look promising. Let us hope and pray that things will develop as they did in the Transvaal War of Independence of 1880–81, when the Republicans scored one resounding victory after the other and the British did not win a single battle.

Many amongst our countrymen seem to be excited about the war. Be assured that we in the editorial offices do not share any sense of pleasant anticipation. History teaches that war brings bloodshed and tears. As during the Transvaal War of Independence, this war will deliver its quota of grief to many families.

Since a flood of newsworthy events took place this week, we do not intend to speculate on the justification for war. Our main purpose is to keep you, our readers, accurately informed on war news. If a news item is of questionable veracity, we will make this clear. When we are certain of our facts, we will indicate that the report has been confirmed or is trustworthy.

General opinion in the two Boer Republics is that this war will follow the same pattern as the Transvaal War of Independence. In that war our burghers successfully defended our borders against a British invasion for about three months, by which time the British government had begun negotiations for a peace settlement, realising that war would be simply too costly to pursue. This time the British will probably send many more soldiers – perhaps even 100 000. The Republics can muster a good 50 000 burghers. That number should be more than sufficient to oppose the enemy. The British should realise this by the beginning of next year at the latest. Negotiations for peace will then follow. Only a very small minority of pessimists in our midst believe that the British can actually defeat us.

During the Transvaal War of Independence the government issued an occasional publication titled *Government Gazette of the Freedom War*. This was later reprinted as a book and many of our readers own copies of it. We believe that our *War Reporter* will in due course become a collector's item too. Our own correspondents, who are accompanying our brave burghers to the borders of the Republics, will give complete coverage of events there. We will also have the services of a number of independent reporters.

In addition to news of military events and related issues, we will highlight the careers of Republican military officers. Our future is entrusted to these men, who are responsible for leading our burghers to victory. Each week, for as long as the war lasts, we will feature a brief life story of a prominent Boer officer. Today's edition introduces the 69-year-old commandant-general of the South African Republic (Transvaal), Piet Joubert, who – in terms of the military pact between our two Republics – is the commander-in-chief of our combined forces.

1

THE APPROACH OF WAR

Pretoria, 10 October – Today is the 74th birthday of our elderly President, Paul Kruger. Here in the capital there are no festivities, however – the tension is much too high. The question on all lips is: will there be a war or not? Our special correspondent in Pretoria, Nicolaas Hofmeyr, compiled the following report.

WAR IS UNAVOIDABLE

'What is in store for us? Every house, every heart, each hour and each place is covered by a dark, apprehensive uncertainty. It hangs hesitatingly over the whole of South Africa. We will only know tomorrow afternoon, when the ultimatum expires, what will happen, but we have no doubt whatsoever: war is unavoidable. The English language newspapers are tirelessly fuelling the war flames. Even the most calm and quiet people are irritated and flare up in anger when they read the slanderous lies that the English newspapers dish up to the British people. It is undoubtedly the objective of the *Star*, *Transvaal Leader*, *Cape Times* and other English language papers to render a peaceful settlement impossible.'

Hofmeyr sounded out a number of public figures on the likelihood of war. 'God would not allow it,' insisted General Piet Cronjé. A peaceful solution would be found, or European developments would prevent Britain from attacking the Boer Republics.

Koos de la Rey, a prominent member of the First Volksraad (Transvaal's Parliament) and known for his clarity of opinion, had a different view. Despite being an unbending critic of President Kruger, and known as a progressive, his patriotism has never been in question. 'There is a war coming,' he predicted. 'There is nothing we can do about it. We can yield on the franchise issue, but it would not help. Our enemies want our country and our gold. If we concede on one issue, they will present a new demand. When the second has been solved, a third demand will arise. And thus it will go on until the enemy is satisfied. It is as clear as daylight: however much we humiliate ourselves, there will be war.'

Christiaan de Wet, the enigmatic and forceful Free State Volksraad member, agreed that the English want our country and our mines. War is unavoidable, no settlement is possible. 'Let it come!' was his challenge.

Hofmeyr's own conclusion is that there will be war. The war fever runs high. On the English side the calls are loud and clear: 'Majuba must be avenged.' Tragically, this war fever has spilled over from Brit to Boer. 'No more concessions,' vow burghers the length and breadth of the Transvaal. 'Enough, enough!' the Free Staters call out. The cup of humiliation of the Republican Afrikaners has been filled to the brim. Their self-respect is challenged, their national existence threatened. Their choice: to die as heroes rather than live as cowards.

President Kruger himself has no doubt about what will happen. We have learned that as early as August he telegraphed the following message to President M.T. Steyn of our sister Republic, the Orange Free State: 'Come what may, without war we would not remain independent. Don't be afraid, victory is not in the hands of kings, but in the power of God. Let us leave the issue in His hands.'

President Paul Kruger

ULTIMATUM REJECTED

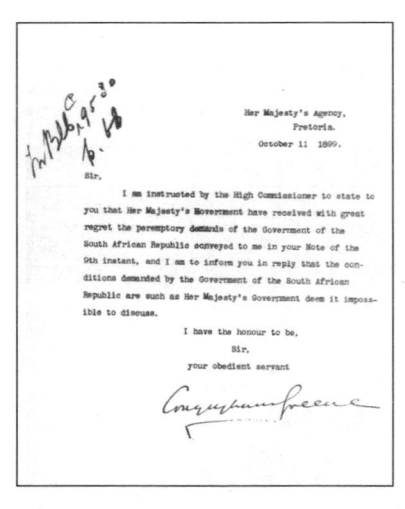

Document handed by Greene to the Transvaal government

Our correspondent in Pretoria was shown the brief note that the agent of the British government in Pretoria, Sir William Conyngham Greene, handed over personally to President Kruger at four o'clock on the afternoon of 11 October. It was addressed to the State Secretary and read as follows:

'I am instructed by the High Commissioner to state to you that Her Majesty's Government have received with great regret the peremptory demands of the Government of the South African Republic conveyed to me in your Note of the 9th instant, and I am to inform you in reply that the conditions demanded by the Government of the South African Republic are such as Her Majesty's Government deem it impossible to discuss.'

After handing over the note, Greene requested his passport and immediately left the Republic.

PRESIDENT STEYN'S MANIFESTO

Bloemfontein, 12 October – When it became known that the British had rejected the ultimatum, President Steyn issued a proclamation binding the Orange Free State to join the South African Republic in battle against British aggression. The Transvaal, it reads, 'is about to be attacked by an unscrupulous enemy, who has long looked for a pretext to annihilate the Afrikaners.' Since there are not only many historical and family ties between the people of the two republics, but also a formal treaty between their governments, the Orange Free State will stand by the Transvaal. The proclamation ends with the following exhortation: 'Burghers of the Free State, stand up as one man against the oppressor and violator of justice.'

President Steyn received a message from the British High Commissioner in South Africa, Sir Alfred Milner, yesterday evening. The latter wanted to know if Steyn condoned the actions of the South African Republic. The President answered that same evening that he regarded the unjustifiable and high-handed British intervention in the internal affairs of the Transvaal as a flagrant breach of the Convention of London and that in his opinion it constituted 'such an undoubted and unjust attack upon the independence of the South African Republic' that no other course was left to the Orange Free State 'than honourably to abide by its treaty agreements' with its sister Republic.

President Steyn

'UITLANDERS' FLEE TO SAFETY

Pretoria, 13 October – Probably the best news of the last few weeks is that most of the 'Uitlanders', as they are known, reacted to the declaration of war by fleeing headlong across the borders of our country. The Boers have little sympathy with these foreigners, who stream to the gold mines of the Witwatersrand to seek their fortune, and run to London with all their unjustifiable complaints. It is common knowledge that the Uitlanders did their utmost to force the British government into a war with the Boers in the first place, and when it became clear that they were achieving their goal, they rushed to get out of harm's way. Many of them predict that they will be back soon – within a few months, they boast, after the British army has defeated the Boers. An unpleasant surprise is in store for them!

The vast majority of the Uitlanders left the Witwatersrand by train. The exodus reached its high point last week, with special trains arranged to take the agitators to Cape Town, Port Elizabeth and Durban. Since there were not enough passenger coaches available, open cattle trucks were used, and it was quite comical to witness how they clamoured to find an open spot on a truck or a coach, hanging like bats from the windows, to ensure that they would be gone when the bullets started flying.

The biggest advantage of the flight of the obstreperous Uitlanders is that the Republican authorities need no longer fear any internal revolt on the Witwatersrand. That the troublemakers have all left is proved by the absence of enthusiasm with which the outbreak of war was greeted in Johannesburg. Apparently the mining hub is destined to be a ghost town for the remainder of the war.

Johannesburg Station: 'Uitlanders' clambering on cattle trucks to flee the Transvaal

RESTRICTIONS ON CAPE COLONISTS

Cape Town, 12 October – The British High Commissioner in South Africa, Sir Alfred Milner, issued a proclamation today in his capacity as Cape Governor in which he spelt out the duties of the inhabitants of the Cape Colony during the war. He warned the citizens of the Cape to refrain from any assistance to the Republics, to remember their loyalty to the British Queen and government and to refrain from disturbing the peace in any way. All trade with the Republics or with citizens of the Republics was immediately terminated.

This proclamation was not unexpected. Our readers will be aware that numerous Cape Afrikaners have indicated their readiness to rush to the assistance of their Republican relatives. One can only wonder what punishment Milner has in mind for Cape Afrikaners who join the Republican forces. It would not be surprising if he were to have such persons executed as rebels.

OUR MILITARY OFFICERS

Commandant-General Piet Joubert

Petrus Jacobus Joubert was born in 1831 on a Karoo farm southeast of Beaufort West in the Cape Colony. His parents were Jozua Francois Joubert and Esther Maria Gouws, whom he accompanied on the Great Trek as a little boy. In common with most children at that time, he received no formal education. His father died in Natal when he was 12 years old, and he moved to the Transvaal with his mother. He married Hendrina Johanna Susanna Botha in 1851, and they had eight children, five of whom are still living.

In 1853 Joubert and his wife settled in the Wakkerstroom district, where he is a successful farmer. Through self-study he gained sufficient legal knowledge to work as a law-agent and executor. Over the years he has been involved in several business ventures, and in the eyes of some commentators is one of the wealthiest people in the Republic.

Joubert has had a long public career. In 1855 he became a field cornet, ten years later a member of the Volksraad and in 1873 Chairman of the Volksraad. When President Burgers visited Europe in 1875–76, Joubert served as Acting President. After Burgers's return, however, he resigned as a member of the Volksraad and returned to Wakkerstroom to farm full-time.

After the annexation of Transvaal by Britain in 1877 Joubert became a leader of the resistance. In 1878 he was a member of the Boer deputation that negotiated in vain with the British government in London to restore Transvaal's independence. At the Paardekraal meeting in December 1880 he was elected Commandant-General and a member of the Triumvirate that led the Boers in the Transvaal War of Independence. He was the commander-in-chief of the Boers on the Natal front, where their victory over the British at Majuba Hill was their crowning glory.

In 1883 Joubert opposed Paul Kruger in the Transvaal presidential election, but was defeated. The same happened in 1888, 1893 and 1898, though he continued to be re-elected as Commandant-General. He is an *ex-officio* member of the Transvaal Executive Council and has participated in numerous campaigns against rebellious black communities.

Like many prominent Transvaal citizens, Joubert is opposed to the war with Great Britain. In his capacity as Commandant-General, however, he initiated countrywide preparations for the coming struggle more than two months before the official outbreak of war. He took command of the campaign in Natal upon himself. His preparations seem to indicate that in this war he intends using the same tactics as in 1880–81.

Commandant-General Piet Joubert

BOER COMMANDOS TO WESTERN BORDER
General Piet Cronjé is Commanding Officer

Boer laager outside Mafeking, 13 October – The total strength of the Boer forces on the Transvaal western border is approximately 6 000 men under the command of Assistant Commandant-General Piet Cronjé. He and his war council decided last week that they would take steps to isolate and besiege the British forces in Mafeking as soon as the war began.

Cronjé was in his main laager at Polfontein near Mafeking on the evening of 11 October when he received instructions from the government to attack the enemy. As described elsewhere in the first issue of this newspaper, he immediately dispatched General De la Rey with 800 burghers to the south, while he focused his own attention on overwhelming the British garrison in Mafeking.

Within half an hour of receiving his instructions from Pretoria, Cronjé deployed the five commandos at his disposal. Two, namely the Marico and Rustenburg Commandos, are to invest Mafeking from the north. The other three, namely the Potchefstroom Commando led by Commandant M. Wolmarans, the Lichtenburg Commando of Commandant H.C.W. Vermaas and the Wolmaransstad Commando under Commandant F.J. Potgieter, are stationed south and southeast of the town.

Abraham Stafleu, a teacher who is attached to the Red Cross section of the Marico Commando, compiled the following report on events in and around Mafeking.

STAFLEU'S REPORT

The outbreak of war came as no surprise to the Boers here in the vicinity of Zeerust and Lichtenburg. Tension had been rising since the beginning of September when the government strengthened the border police force in order to monitor British troop movements. For our people who ride transport to Mafeking it was clear that the British too were busy mobilising their forces. They were building fortifications on all sides of the town. Volunteers were given drill instruction at the police camp. The Transvaal burghers do not have much to fear from those volunteers. A visitor to Mafeking reports that the other day one of them climbed backwards on to a horse! The dumb fellow was dumped unceremoniously from the saddle by the bewildered animal and is subsequently unfit for war service.

The English also erected a camp at Ramatlabama, a railway station north of Mafeking. According to a Boer who traded farm products there, between 400 and 500 British soldiers were stationed there by the end of September. They boasted of having a large supply of ammunition and claimed that they would soon be shooting our burghers with it. We believe it is more likely that our burghers will capture that same ammunition and use it on the enemy themselves!

During a weapons demonstration in the ward of Klein Marico, Field Cornet Hansie Snyman warned all burghers between 16 and 60 years old to keep their horses and rifles, as well as 100 rounds of ammunition each and rusks and biltong for eight days' personal use, ready at all times. Assistant Field Cornet Arie Oberholzer reminded each burgher armed only with a Westley-Richards muzzle-loader to exchange that outdated rifle for a modern Mauser breech-loader. Oberholzer subsequently distributed the muzzle-loaders to people who were able to handle a rifle but who did not have to do commando duty, such as women and children, so that the farms could be defended while the burghers were away.

In mid-September our burghers received orders not to leave their wards or take out their wagons. With that, transport and trade ground to a halt. By then it was clear that the situation was critical, but even though the Transvaal Red Cross established a branch in Zeerust, there were still burghers who scoffed at indications that war was approaching.

On Friday 28 September an order from Commandant-General Piet Joubert reached Marico that all burghers with horses had to leave for Lichtenburg immediately. The Marico Commando quickly assembled and proceeded to Bultfontein on the Molopo River, a short distance east of Mafeking, where they pitched camp on 5 October. Their Commandant is Daartjie Botha. The Rustenburg Commando of Commandant P.S. Steenekamp joined them there a few days later.

Our commander on the western border is the courageous General Piet Cronjé, who, as readers of this newspaper will remember, captured the freebooter Jameson in 1896. Cronjé's disdain for the English was clearly reflected in a comment that he made the other day: 'If one hundred Boers had one hundred rounds of ammunition each, they could chase ten thousand English away!'. Well, there are many more than 100 burghers here. We hear that there are 6 000 burghers under Cronjé's command on the western border.

The precise situation of the British forces in this area is unknown. We hear all sorts of rumours of thousands of soldiers with artillery on their way here. A reliable source from within Mafeking, however, suggests that there are no soldiers on their way here, and that there are less than a thousand soldiers stationed in the town.

The burghers of Marico rejoiced on the evening of Monday 9 October when they were informed that the Transvaal government had issued an ultimatum with demands that the British had to submit to within 48 hours. They immediately held a weapon demonstration to establish how quickly they could be ready for an engagement.

From yesterday morning, 12 October, when we finally heard confirmation of the declaration of war, the sentry pickets and patrols became visibly bigger. A rumour spread like wildfire through the camp that a night attack on the British was planned. We were not sure about the target, but were surprised at the preparations when officers had picks, shovels, crowbars and dynamite loaded onto wagons.

Just before sunset a few artillerymen hauled a field gun northwards through the laager. Shortly afterwards a large number of mounted burghers followed with a fully loaded wagon. We were still kept in the dark regarding their target, but guessed that their aim was to damage the railway line.

That was indeed the case, we learned this morning. But our men returned without having achieved their objective, since they misunderstood Cronjé's orders. Fortunately we hear that Cronjé's burghers successfully broke up the railway line south of Mafeking, thus ensuring that the British would not easily receive assistance from outside.

Transvaal Boers ready for war

FREE STATE BURGHERS TO THE FRONT
War claims first casualties

Harrismith, 10 October – A memorable evening for this picturesque eastern Free State town. Several hundred burghers have passed through over the last few days, including the thoroughly drenched men of the Kroonstad Commando earlier today. The rainy weather had no marked negative impact on the excitement and self-confidence of the men. In addition a pleasant surprise awaited them, namely buckets full of steaming hot coffee, sandwiches and cake prepared for them by the ladies under the leadership of Mrs Kestell.

The Kroonstad burghers did not linger for any length of time. They had orders to proceed to the Natal border as soon as possible. There was time enough to off-saddle on the church square and hang their wet blankets and clothes on the fence to dry out. The Reverend John Kestell invited them to enter the church for a service before their departure. It was a touching ceremony. There had never been so many men in this church. It was stirring to witness them all singing together in prayer to the Almighty: 'Be with us Lord …'

One of the young Kroonstad burghers we interviewed was Chris van Niekerk, just two weeks ago a theology student at Victoria College, Stellenbosch, in the Cape Colony. By the end of September it was clear to him that war was unavoidable, and he decided to return to the Free State to fight shoulder to shoulder with his father and brothers. He had no grudge against the British, but felt he could not allow his relatives and the other burghers to fight alone for their freedom and to sacrifice their lives alone for justice. It had nothing to do with honour, Van Niekerk declared, but with our duty to defend our God-given rights and freedom.

When Van Niekerk arrived in Kroonstad on Saturday 13 September he noticed a subdued air of excitement. Though unhappy about the turn of events, people were, in his words, 'undaunted and filled with faith; every burgher determined to do his duty to protect the dear fatherland that our predecessors bought with their blood'. For the young men eager to advance to the battlefield, it made no difference if they survived or not, as long as they could make a contribution.

That Saturday morning a meeting took place in the City Hall, where final arrangements were made and numerous announcements read. Early the next morning everybody went to church, where the Reverend Van der Lingen served the Holy Communion. The first rays of the sun shone on them when they left the House of God strengthened by His Holy Sacrament.

The rest of the day was spent in preparation. For the first time that anyone could recall the shops in the Free State were opened on a Sunday to allow the burghers to buy supplies such as tobacco, clothing and food. All the farmers were in a hurry to get back to their farms for final arrangements and to pack their saddlebags and take leave of their loved ones.

The burghers of Kroonstad did not all proceed to the east. Approximately half of them went to the western border. Van Niekerk is with the eastern group led by Commandant Chris Nel, which left Kroonstad last Thursday. The next day, as they were crossing a drift near Reitz, their commando suffered its first casualty. Hermanus Grobler, a 39-year old farmer from the farm Mooiwater, was run over by a wagon that got stuck on the upward slope after crossing the drift and began rolling backwards. Grobler jumped in behind the wagon to turn on the brake, but he stumbled and the wheel rolled across him.

The Reverend Viljoen buried this unfortunate burgher at Reitz the next day. A huge crowd formed the funeral procession that followed Grobler's crushed body to the cemetery. Many tears were shed while the mourners placed flowers on his coffin and sympathised with his bereaved wife and children. The unspoken question uppermost in the minds of those present was: how many other brave burghers will be buried before the day of peace dawns?

Grobler is not the first burgher to sacrifice his life for the freedom of his country in this war. A burgher from Smithfield whose name is not known to us was struck and killed by lightning on the way to the front earlier on.

The Free State forces that are on their way to the Natal border are commanded by Marthinus Prinsloo of Winburg, who was elected chief commandant at a meeting of all the commandants held in Harrismith, in terms of the commando law. The Free State burghers are ready for whatever the freedom struggle may demand of them.

Late news, 13 October – Reports from Bloemfontein indicate that Prinsloo's burghers began occupying the mountain passes between the Orange Free State and Natal on the evening of 11 October. The passes are Oliviershoek Pass, Bezuidenhout's Pass, Tintwa Pass, Van Reenen's Pass, De Beer's Pass and Muller's Pass.

Free State burghers on their way to the front

Number 1   14 October 1899

REPUBLICAN FORCES INVADE NATAL
Large British force stationed in the Colony

Pretoria, 14 October – The most important front in this war will probably be the northern part of Natal, as was the case in the Transvaal War of Independence of 1880–81. The fact that the vast majority of British troops in South Africa are concentrated there indicates that they will again attempt to invade the Boer Republics via Natal. It is thus no wonder that the military authorities of both the Republics dispatched the larger parts of their forces to that front. We have been reliably informed that altogether 17 500 Transvaal and Free State burghers are already on the Natal border or are on their way there. The exact size of the British force in Natal is not known. A British journalist who is usually reliable states that it consists of about 16 000 men under the command of General Sir George White.

The following report on the Republican invasion of Natal reached us this morning via telegraph from Newcastle.

ASSEMBLING ON THE BORDER

By 11 October there were about 11 500 Transvaal burghers assembled on the Natal border. Commandos from six districts, including Pretoria, which was the biggest, made their first laager at Sandspruit, a railway station northwest of Volksrust. In addition there were units of the State Artillery with 23 guns, as well as foreign volunteer corps, including Dutch, German, Irish and French volunteers. The urbanites among them, to the great delight of the more experienced burghers, were introduced to the fine art of equestrian warfare by Commandant Jan Lombard – specifically how to mount and dismount quickly from a horse without making an idiot of oneself.

On 10 October, while the burghers were waiting for the British answer to the Republican ultimatum, Lieutenant-Colonel Fanie Trichard of the State Artillery stationed one of his 155 mm Creusot siege guns on Mol's Kop south of Volksrust. This French gun, nicknamed Long Tom, can fire a shell weighing 42 kilograms more than 10 kilometres. It is our best gun, and as far as we know the British have nothing that can compare with it. From Mol's Kop Trichard would have been able to fire on the railway line at Laing's Nek and on the border if the British attempted to attack. Nothing of that sort happened, but the mere presence of the Long Tom on Mol's Kop bolstered the Boers' self-confidence.

REACTION TO THE OUTBREAK OF WAR

The message that the British government had rejected the ultimatum reached Sandspruit via telegraph at six o'clock on the evening of 11 October. The news that it was war spread like wildfire through the laager. The reaction of the burghers was remarkable – grave silence. Our correspondent at Sandspruit attributes this reaction to the fact that the burghers are men of peace. They do not want war. They are not interested in glory or victory. They are taking up their rifles with the sole purpose of defending their freedom and independence.

Commandant-General Joubert immediately acknowledged receipt of the message that the British had rejected the ultimatum. His answer mirrors the deep-set religious faith that is so characteristic of the Boer leaders: 'Your telegram received at 6 o'clock. Will not be able to do anything before tomorrow. I understand I may immediately cross the border into Natal … With the assistance of God we will do what we can. The will of God will be done in heaven as well as on earth. We wait on Him; He will determine our fate. Amen.'

THE REPUBLICAN WAR PLAN

It was already dark on the evening of 11 October when all the officers gathered in Joubert's tent for a war council meeting. At this meeting, which continued until after midnight, the war plan was finalised. General Daniël Erasmus of Pretoria will lead the bulk of the Transvaal forces down the main road across Laing's Nek to Newcastle. General Jan Kock of Potchefstroom will follow the more westerly route to the same destination and General Lukas Meyer of Vryheid will proceed east of the Buffalo River to Dundee. The plan is that they will launch a combined attack on the British camp at Dundee as soon as possible and subsequently, after joining forces with the Free State commandos, attack the British forces that are at present in the vicinity of Ladysmith.

All these details became common knowledge in the Boer laagers very soon after the war council ended. The senior officers openly discussed their plans with their junior officers and the latter relayed it to the burghers. One gains the impression that Joubert is so confident that he does not regard it as either essential or valuable to keep his envisaged strategy secret.

It has been reported to Joubert that there are 6 000 Free State burghers concentrated on the border between Natal and their Republic. He was furthermore informed that the British commander on the Natal front, General White, has divided his force into two units. Some 4 000 soldiers with 18 guns are stationed in Dundee. Their commander is Major-General Sir William Symons. More than 10 000 soldiers with 30 guns are stationed 60 kilometres southwest of Dundee at Ladysmith. White himself is in command there. There are also small British units deeper in Natal at places such as Colenso and Estcourt. The Boers will certainly attempt to exploit this division of British forces.

THE INVASION OF NATAL

The Republican invasion of Natal began on the evening of 11 October, soon after it became known that the war had officially begun. Two of General Kock's commanders, Colonel Adolf Schiel and Commandant Ben Viljoen, crossed the border with patrols at Botha's Pass. Joubert's main force moved through Volksrust on 12 October, but continuous rain hindered their progress and they actually only crossed the border on 13 October. Charlestown, a small village south of the border, was the first place to be occupied. There was no sign of any British soldiers.

The Transvaal Secret Service had heard rumours that the British had placed dynamite under the railway lines. The railway tunnel at Laing's Nek was expected to be especially unsafe. Consequently the Transvaal commanders initially refrained from using the railway line. That delayed the invasion considerably, since intermittent rain had turned the road into a mud bath. In addition it was bitterly cold. The burghers were drenched and hungry, but the excitement of war kept them going down the slopes of Majuba Hill into Natal.

NEWCASTLE OCCUPIED

Beyond vociferous protests, the British authorities offered no resistance when the Transvaal vanguard, consisting of Commandant Weilbach's Heidelberg Commando, entered Newcastle this morning, 14 October. The majority of the burghers are proceeding straight through Newcastle. We understand that their next target is Dundee, where, according to the latest unconfirmed reports, a British force of 5 000 men with 30 guns is stationed.

Neatly dressed burghers ready for battle

Burghers leaving for the front from Pretoria station

Pretoria Station: Transvaal State Artillery guns entrained for war service

Pretoria burghers assembling before leaving for the front

Transvaal burghers leave for the front with a tea dealer's wagon that has been commandeered for war duty

THE War Reporter
WEEKLY EDITION

Number 2 — Pretoria, South African Republic — 21 October 1899

BLOODY BATTLE AT TALANA
Meyer's attack on British at Dundee fails

Northern Natal, 20 October – Today General Lukas Meyer's burghers launched a full-scale attack on General Symons's forces at Dundee. Apparently General Daniël Erasmus's Pretoria burghers and Commandant Weilbach's Heidelberg burghers were expected to participate, but never joined the battle. Meyer's men, who were eventually forced to fall back, are extremely unhappy about this.

The small mining village of Dundee rests between low hills. The British camp is situated right next to the town. Our correspondent reports that it was general knowledge amongst the burghers yesterday that the generals had held a war council and decided to take the offensive, Meyer attacking from the east, Erasmus from the north and Weilbach from the west. Meyer was to occupy Talana Hill east of Dundee before daybreak; Erasmus's burghers were to occupy Impati Hill with its flat crest north of Dundee at the same time. Both planned to bombard the British with their artillery.

Yesterday evening the Reverend A.P. Burger of Middelburg held a service in Meyer's laager. The burghers left for the front soon afterwards, moving in the direction of Dundee in intermittent rain. About half past two this morning they suddenly came upon a British patrol. Both sides fired a few shots, but it seems that no one was hit in the dark.

Meyer's burghers reached the top of Talana Hill soon after daybreak. He positioned some 900 men with artillery on Talana itself and another 600 on neighbouring Lennox Hill. It was misty at daybreak, but soon after five o'clock the mist on Talana and Lennox Hills lifted. Our burghers were satisfied with their position. With the sun behind them they had a clear view of the town and the British camp on its far side. Impati Hill was still covered in mist and Meyer was not sure if Erasmus and his burghers were in position.

BEGINNING OF THE BATTLE

In spite of the wet terrain the Boer artillerymen were ready with their guns by sunrise. Meyer then ordered Captain J.L. Pretorius, the artillery commander, to begin the bombardment. The first shot was fired at exactly ten minutes to six o'clock. The shell landed spot on target in the centre of the British camp, causing endless consternation. But Erasmus's burghers on Impati remained silent.

We have subsequently established that at that stage Erasmus's artillery was still at least an hour's trek from Impati's summit, not even close to its position. According to one of our senior officers, Erasmus believed that the mist was so dense on the crest of Impati that it would be senseless to occupy that hill. Neither did he do anything else to assist Meyer's burghers.

It was painful for Erasmus's burghers to hear the roaring guns and the firing of the rifles of Meyer's burghers but to be in no position to render them assistance. Our correspondent writes that they were bitterly disappointed, but powerless against the orders of their over-cautious general. For some reason that is not clear to us, Commandant Weilbach's burghers also never entered the battle.

THE BRITISH COUNTER-ATTACK

Meyer's artillerymen were extremely disappointed to note through their telescopes and binoculars from the summit of Talana Hill that the shells fired by them were not all exploding. The ground was obviously too soft after all the rain. They also noted that the British soldiers quickly regained their composure after the initial chaos. As soon as they realised that the British artillery were setting up their guns to enter the battle, the Boer artillery concentrated their bombardment. This failed to deter the enemy, who began bombarding Meyer's forces shortly after six o'clock.

For the majority of the Transvaal burghers it was their first experience of being the targets of enemy artillery. The exploding shells spread fear amongst the burghers. More than a hundred fled in panic from the battlefield. The British probably noted that some burghers were fleeing, since numerous soldiers suddenly came forward to attack us.

Since no shots were fired on the British cavalry that passed right by Impati Hill, Erasmus and his men had failed to take up position in terms of the previous day's arrangements. The result was that Meyer and his main force with their guns were forced to fall back some two kilometres to Lennox Hill to avoid the danger of encirclement. Meyer left about 400 or 500 burghers on Talana Hill. These burghers managed to pin the British soldiers down in a blue gum plantation next to a farmyard at the foot of the hill.

END OF THE BATTLE

By eleven o'clock this morning Meyer realised that the British were not going to enter into the battle at all and that he would have to disengage to avoid huge casualties. While a small rearguard covered the retreat, our burghers fell back. British soldiers immediately occupied Talana Hill.

According to our men the British artillerymen suddenly began bombarding the hill again soon afterwards. This time, they claim, the British shells exploded above their own men. The bombardment lasted a long time and probably caused heavy casualties among the soldiers.

By about half past one this afternoon, in renewed heavy rain, the British indicated with loud shouting that they were in full possession of Talana Hill. Our men had retreated quite a distance by then. Thus a long and hard day ended disappointingly for the Boers.

All our reporters agree that General Erasmus missed a golden opportunity to destroy the British forces today. Had he kept to the original plan the British would have had to surrender. But Erasmus was too cautious. Hence it was the British who scored a victory, and we suffered unnecessary casualties.

Exactly what the casualties on both sides are, we still do not know, but they were quite high. British losses include dozens of soldiers who were captured by the burghers. Some of them claim that General Symons was wounded so badly that Major-General James Yule took over the command from him.

General Meyer's burghers are tired and disappointed. They believe General Erasmus left them in the lurch. And they are extremely angry with the cowards from their own ranks who fled from the battlefield. At the same time they feel that they have proven to themselves that they will be able to stand up to the enemy, even though they had to retreat today. Many burghers state that they were impressed by the courage of the British soldiers in attack. It would be wise not to underestimate our enemies in this war.

MAFEKING BESIEGED BY THE BOERS
Cronjé implements proven tactics again

Boer laager near Mafeking, 20 October – Just after dark on Friday, the burghers are preparing their evening meal. Around the campfires laughter and violin music can be heard. In such a carnival atmosphere it is scarcely believable that we are in the midst of a war and that our men are seriously besieging an enemy garrison.

Since our previous report there has been a great deal of action here on the western front. Some 500 of our men left before daybreak on 13 October to occupy the Ramatlabama railway station north of Mafeking. The burghers damaged the railway line before turning south and destroying the railway bridge across the Mogosane River just north of the town.

Some time later the same morning, the burghers heard a train approaching from Mafeking in the south. They took up position on both sides of the railway line and prepared for battle. A locomotive pushing two cargo trucks in front of it hove into view and suddenly stopped. While our burghers looked on, men disembarked and uncoupled the two trucks. They then climbed back onto the locomotive – which, to the amazement of the burghers, steamed back to Mafeking.

The burghers immediately approached the deserted trucks. An elderly man remarked: 'To me it looks as if we have the wooden horse of Troy here. Are there not perhaps British soldiers hidden on the trucks?' Everybody, including those who knew nothing about Homer's classical tale, immediately took cover and opened fire. Moments later it was as if the Day of Judgment had dawned. Right in front of them the two trucks disintegrated in a massive explosion. It was as if ten thunderbolts hit the earth simultaneously. Pieces of metal flew through the air, fortunately not hitting anybody. Afterwards the burghers speculated that the British had loaded the trucks full of dynamite and hoped that it would explode when numbers of burghers were close by. Fortunately for us, their plan failed.

ENCIRCLEMENT COMPLETED

While these events were taking place to the north of Mafeking, about 1 000 burghers moved around the south of the town, destroying the railway line that links it to Vryburg in the south. While some burghers remained behind to ensure that the British would not repair the railway line, others moved right around the town on the western side and eventually linked up with the burghers in the north.

The British Commander in Mafeking, Colonel Baden-Powell, is an energetic figure. On his arrival here about a month ago he immediately began building fortifications and digging trenches. On 14 October General Piet Cronjé, our commander, sent him a note demanding the surrender of the town. Baden-Powell refused, whereupon Cronjé ordered the burghers to besiege the town.

Our men are confident that the British will surrender once the 'Long Tom' – one of the new Creusot heavy guns – that we have been told is on its way from Pretoria starts bombarding the town. The burghers furthermore point out that in the Transvaal War of Independence of 1880–81 Cronjé commanded the Boer forces at Potchefstroom that forced the British garrison in the fort there to surrender. They believe that their experienced commander will soon repeat his success here.

SKIRMISH AT SIGNAL HILL

The burghers almost scored a notable victory over the enemy on the very first day of the siege. The Khakis, as the Boers call the enemy, since they wear khaki-coloured uniforms, suddenly approached their entrenchments with an armoured train. While firing on the train with their light Maxim gun and their Mauser rifles, the burghers noted the approach of a unit of mounted British soldiers. In an attempt to lead those soldiers into an ambush behind a low, rocky outcrop known as Signal Hill, some burghers made as if they were fleeing in that direction. The soldiers actually pursued them, but when the Boers attacked from their hastily prepared ambush, they found safety behind the huts of black inhabitants of that vicinity. They were eventually rescued, with several casualties, by another unit of mounted British soldiers supported by artillery. Unfortunately two burghers were killed and seven wounded.

To conclude, here at Mafeking a strange situation prevails. Our burghers seem to be in control, but cannot yet overpower the British.

Boers gather for a religious service outside Mafeking

KIMBERLEY BESIEGED

Pretoria, 17 October – Our correspondent reports from Bloemfontein that some 1 500 Free State burghers crossed that Republic's western border south of Kimberley on 14 October under the leadership of Commandant Jacobus Prinsloo. Their orders are to disrupt railway and telegraphic communications between Kimberley and the south.

Prinsloo divided his men into two groups. The southern group damaged the railway line in the vicinity of Modder River Station on the morning of 15 October. The northern group broke up the railway and telegraph lines near Spytfontein that same morning. An armoured train sent by the British from Kimberley fired on the burghers, but our men repulsed the enemy with their Mauser rifles and a field gun. Nobody on the Republican side was hurt. The Free State forces now control the railway line south of Kimberley from Spytfontein almost down to Belmont Station.

North of Kimberley Free State burghers commanded by Commandant du Plessis also crossed the border on 14 October. Before daybreak the next morning they accomplished a major feat by occupying the pump station at Riverton and cutting off Kimberley's water supply.

Later that morning Du Plessis and his men were demolishing the large water pipe about ten kilometres north of Kimberley when they were suddenly attacked by a patrol of Cape policemen. In the skirmish that followed the Boers drove off the enemy. No burgher was injured, but the enemy lost one man killed and one captured.

The Free State burghers now took up position right around Kimberley. Our correspondent reports that their forces consist of 4 800 men. He has heard that President Steyn is not satisfied that that force will be strong enough to subdue or even besiege the British forces in Kimberley effectively.

Sources in Pretoria confirm that Steyn telegraphed President Kruger to request assistance from the Transvaal forces. Steyn also proposed that a combined force of Transvaal and Free State burghers cross the Orange River at Hopetown and invade the Cape Colony. According to him many Cape Afrikaners in the northern Cape would join the Republican forces.

RHODES IN KIMBERLEY

The Cape policeman captured by the Free State burghers near Riverton informed us that Colonel Robert George Kekewich is the British commander in Kimberley. He commands about 2 500 soldiers with 12 guns. The total number of inhabitants of the city is approximately 50 000 people. The policeman furthermore claims that our arch-enemy Cecil John Rhodes, the mastermind behind the notorious Jameson Raid of 1895–96, is in the city. What a glorious day it will be when the British in Kimberley surrender to our burghers!

FROM THE EDITOR

The war is now in full cry. Our burghers are besieging British garrisons in Mafeking and Kimberley and the first battle has taken place in Natal. Predictions by many burghers that the war will only last a few months already seem doubtful. The British appear determined to win and are sending thousands of troops to South Africa. A long struggle may lie ahead.

It is not our task to criticise the Boer leadership. However, we feel it is our duty to comment that communication between the military leaders leaves much to be desired. Bad communication can lead to disaster, and has probably already done so at Dundee. We must exploit technology such as the telegraph and the heliograph to our full advantage.

Another disturbing phenomenon is the reprehensible conduct of some burghers. We have heard of the plundering of shops and even houses by our people. That is of course unacceptable and indeed criminal action. We are even more disappointed by reports of cowardice and lack of patriotism. In our opinion the Republics have no hope of survival in this war if burghers do not all stand together and do their duty. In this respect our mothers and wives have a decisive role to play. Encourage your husbands day and night to remain courageous and to do their duty to defend our freedom! Always remember the motto on our coat of arms: *unity is strength.*

TRANSVAAL WESTERN BORDER IN REPUBLICAN HANDS

Pretoria, 18 October – From Warrenton in the far southwest we have received reports that the whole border south of Vryburg is now in Republican hands. The Bloemhof commando, consisting of 800 burghers under Commandant Tollie de Beer, crossed the border at Pudimoe on 14 October on orders of General Cronjé. Two days later they reached Taung. This town consists of about 2 000 black huts and a few white houses, shops and offices. The burghers occupied it unopposed.

In the meantime a Free State commando made their way westwards under orders of Chief Commandant C.J. Wessels of Boshof. On 15 October they destroyed a railway culvert on the Mafeking line at Slypklip and cut the telegraph wire in numerous places. Their objective was the village Veertien Strome. There were 270 Khakis with two guns in that town, but they departed to the south before the Boers arrived.

Commandant de Beer and his burghers reached Veertien Strome before the Free State force arrived. They occupied the town before daybreak on 17 October and destroyed the railway bridge with dynamite. They then proceeded to Warrenton, where they arrived later the same morning and hoisted the Transvaal flag. Soon after, the Free State burghers from Boshof joined them.

THE MARCH ON LADYSMITH

The Natal front, 19 October – The abundant rain on the Natal front has seriously disrupted our military plans. Traffic often bogs down on the muddy roads. Lieutenant-Colonel Trichard of the State Artillery found the going tough with his heavy guns and ammunition wagons and could not reach Newcastle before Monday 16 October. Commandant-General Joubert and his headquarters only reached Newcastle early on the morning of 17 October for the same reason.

In the meantime General Erasmus and his burghers moved from Newcastle to Dundee, approximately following the railway line. Their progress was slow, since Erasmus is the most cautious general imaginable. The closer they got to Dundee, our correspondent reports, the slower they proceeded.

Of the Free State forces we have heard that the Harrismith Commando was involved in a skirmish with a section of the Natal Carbineers near Bester Station on the railway line between Van Reenen's Pass and Ladysmith on 18 October. The burghers gained the upper hand and the Carbineers fled to Ladysmith. They deserted their camp and the burghers occupied it, as well as Bester Station. One burgher was killed in the skirmish.

Earlier today a patrol of General Jan Kock's commando occupied Elandslaagte station on the main line between Newcastle and Ladysmith and captured a British supply train. Now all contact between Ladysmith and Dundee has been disrupted. It seems certain that the Boers will attack the British force at Dundee commanded by General Symons. (See report on that attack elsewhere in this issue.)

OUR MILITARY OFFICERS

General Lukas Meyer

Lukas Johannes Meyer was born in 1846 at Sand River in Transorangia. He is the eldest son of Izaak Johannes Meijer and his wife Martha Maria Elizabeth Landman. As a young man he lived for some years in northern Natal, but in 1865 he settled in the Utrecht district in the South African Republic. In 1872 he was elected Field Cornet.

Meyer fought against the British forces in the Transvaal War of Independence of 1880–81. He was badly wounded in the Battle of Schuinshoogte in February 1881, but recovered. He served as magistrate of Utrecht from 1882 to 1884. In that year he became the District Commandant and the leader of a group of Boers who assisted Prince Dinizulu in the power struggle in Zululand.

Meyer subsequently played a leading role in the establishment of the New Republic on the land that the Boers received from Dinizulu after his victory as payment for their assistance. He became President of the Republic, but in 1888 he took a leading role in the incorporation of the New Republic into the South African Republic as the Vryheid district. In 1893 he was elected to the First Volksraad and earlier this year he became its Chairman.

Meyer is a friend and confidant of Commandant-General Joubert, who appointed him as General and commander of the southeastern commandos even before this war broke out. He is a tall, well-built man with a strong, handsome face. He is also immensely popular and is commonly referred to as the 'Lion of Vryheid'.

BULLER ON HIS WAY BACK

Cape Town, 16 October – News from London is that the 59-year-old General Sir Redvers Henry Buller has been appointed commander of the British Army Corps in South Africa. He left Southampton for South Africa on 14 October on board the *Dunottar Castle*. The ship was especially decorated for the occasion. While one part of the massive crowd that waved farewell to Buller and his thousands of soldiers solemnly sang 'God Save the Queen', a more boisterous section shouted out war cries such as 'Remember Majuba'.

Buller is a highly respected officer. He is a recipient of the highest British decoration for bravery, the Victoria Cross. Most of our readers know that he has been in South Africa before, having participated in five campaigns here, including the Anglo-Zulu War of 1879. Time will tell if he will be up to the task of commanding an army against an enemy as tough and wily as the Boers.

REDCOATS NOW KHAKIS

On the same day that Buller left Britain, some 400 men of the Yorkshire Light Infantry arrived in Table Bay on board the *HMS Powerful*. The pro-British Capetonians were there in large numbers to welcome them. They shouted the same slogan as the crowd in Southampton, 'Remember Majuba'. The British certainly seem determined to avenge that bitter defeat inflicted on them by the Boers 19 years ago.

A very notable novelty of the British soldiers is their uniforms. In the Transvaal War of Independence they still wore bright red coats and white helmets. Now they are dressed in khaki-coloured uniforms and khaki helmets. This means that our burghers will not be able to see the British as easily as in 1880–81. Khaki uniforms will obviously not stand out so brightly in the grey veld as red coats did.

On the other hand, our burghers now have more accurate rifles than the Martini-Henrys of the previous war, namely Mauser breech-loaders. The bullet of the Mauser is not as heavy as the lead slug of the Martini-Henry, but travels faster and can cover a greater distance. In addition a burgher can carry many more Mauser rounds than Martini-Henry rounds, since the new cartridges weigh less than the older ones. The British of course have new rifles too, called Lee-Metfords, but we know that the ability of an Englishman to shoot straight is limited.

General Sir Redvers Buller

THOUSANDS OF BLACK MINERS LEAVE JOHANNESBURG

On foot to Natal – shops plundered – Joubert's proclamation

Pretoria, 20 October – The flight of the Uitlanders which we reported on last week resulted in a crisis for the black mineworkers on the Witwatersrand. In addition all the Johannesburg burghers have been called up for commando duty. As a result mining activity came to a standstill virtually overnight, leaving the black miners unemployed. Consequently the government decided that they should be deported to their places of origin.

The workers who were recruited in our neighbouring countries were taken back to the borders by train. A spokesman of the Dutch South African Railway Company informed us that they transported altogether about 78 000 blacks to the borders in the period 1 September to 19 October. Thousands of others blacks left the Witwatersrand on foot.

Our correspondent on the Natal front reports that a group of about two or three thousand crossed the border into that colony in the past week. In some instances those blacks plundered shops. This happened in Charlestown, the first village on the Natal side of the border, and again when that same group of blacks moved through Newcastle.

Those blacks were not the only plunderers. We regret to report that some of our burghers also participated in the plundering, even though such activities are strictly prohibited by commando law. Commandant-General Piet Joubert was so angry when he heard of the plundering that he requested the government to send the State Attorney, Jan Smuts, to the front to halt the criminal activities of some of our burghers. In addition Joubert issued a proclamation calling upon the burghers to conduct themselves in a civilised manner and refrain from damaging the private property of any people even if it is known that those people are on the side of the enemy. This proclamation was published in a special edition of the Transvaal *Government Gazette* on 17 October.

The War Reporter
WEEKLY EDITION

Number 3 — Pretoria, South African Republic — 28 October 1899

TRAGEDY AT ELANDSLAAGTE
General Jan Kock suffers a shattering defeat

Glencoe, 23 October – The battle of 20 October at Talana had barely ended when the next major confrontation in Natal followed. Last week we reported that a patrol of the veteran General Jan Kock's commando had occupied the railroad village of Elandslaagte north of Ladysmith and captured a British supply train. We have since been informed that its cargo consisted of huge quantities of food, drink, cattle, horses and other supplies on their way to the British troops in Dundee.

Kock arrived at Elandslaagte on the 20th with about 800 burghers to strengthen his vanguard. He was delighted at the capture of the train and allowed his burghers to pillage it, to the fury of Colonel Adolf Schiel of the German Corps. Schiel also warned Kock that his scouts had spotted a British advance from Ladysmith. The old general answered that he had fought against the British in the war of 1880–81 and that they were second-rate soldiers from whom he had nothing to fear. Schiel did not have the authority to intervene and resumed his scouting in the direction of Ladysmith.

Some of the other officers, including Commandant Ben Viljoen of the Johannesburg commando, also complained to Kock about his failure to order the immediate destruction of the railway line south of Elandslaagte. 'It is unnecessary,' was the brief answer. 'The men are tired and need rest.' In the meantime it rained intermittently and most of the burghers were drenched. On Kock's orders they pitched a temporary camp two kilometres southeast of the village.

THE FIRST BRITISH ATTACK
Soon after daybreak on the morning of the 21st, while the majority of the burghers were quietly preparing their breakfast, the camp suddenly came under British fire. For many burghers it was such a frightening experience that they scampered for shelter. Kock's artillery, however, immediately replied to the British bombardment with its two Maxim-Nordenfeld 75mm field guns. These guns have a range of seven kilometres, and our gunners quickly found their targets. Through their binoculars they saw the British retreat with the loss of some wounded and of an ammunition wagon.

Kock stated that this was exactly what he had expected: the British would not press their attack. Soon afterwards his commando's supply wagons arrived and the burghers began setting up a more substantial camp – blissfully unaware that the enemy was preparing a full-scale attack.

Later, while the white flag was flying to allow our ambulance to enter the battlefield, an English war correspondent, G.W. Steevens, told us what had happened from the British viewpoint. He said that the Commander-in-Chief in Ladysmith, General White, had been furious when he heard on 19 October that the Boers had occupied Elandslaagte Station, and ordered an attacking force to drive them back again.

The Khakis left Ladysmith early yesterday morning under the command of General French. Some soldiers were mounted on horseback, but the majority travelled by train. They were off-loaded some distance south of Elandslaagte and approached the Boer camp on foot. After the first bombardment by the Boer artillery they realised that their light field guns were no match for those of the Boers and that their force was not strong enough for the task at hand. They fell back at a quarter past eight and waited for reinforcements.

THE SECOND BRITISH ATTACK
Later that morning White sent out more British soldiers by train from Ladysmith to support the vanguard. By two o'clock there were some 3 500 British soldiers with 18 field guns and six machine guns close to Elandslaagte. It was only then, according to Steevens, that French decided to resume the attack.

With Schiel and the German Volunteer Corps up front the Boers initially defended their position courageously, but in the course of the afternoon the superior British numbers forced them back. At about a quarter to five a heavy thunderstorm erupted, impairing the Boers' vision and making it impossible for them to shoot accurately. The British now attacked with new vigour. Soon they were so close that the burghers could hear them in the gloom shouting out: 'Remember Majuba!' All along the British line soldiers answered with the battle cry 'Majuba' and charged towards the Boers. Kock and H.J. Coster of the Dutch Corps did their best to rally their men. Eventually, however, they were powerless against the vast numbers of the enemy and their resistance collapsed.

THE SLAUGHTER
The real tragedy of Elandslaagte now followed. Those burghers who were able jumped on their horses and fled. The British lancers, however, were waiting for them and charged with battle cries like 'Kill the Dutchmen! Kill the Boers!' Carnage followed, since the burghers had no defence against the swords and bayonets of the soldiers.

One of the burghers, Cornelis Plokhooy of the Dutch Corps, alleged afterwards that in a few instances Khakis even bayoneted wounded Boers who were pleading for mercy. Unfortunately it did happen that while some Boers held up white flags in the form of handkerchiefs or other suitable material, others who were not aware of this kept firing on the Khakis. This naturally infuriated the latter, who concluded that the Boers were acting treacherously and attacked with anger in their hearts. Mercifully darkness soon set in and ended the slaughter.

Nobody who was on the battlefield at Elandslaagte yesterday night will ever forget the terrible scenes of misery and suffering. It was bitterly cold and rain came down intermittently. The tens of dozens wounded were crying out in the dark, wet night for assistance or groaning from pain. One of the many wounded on the Boer side was General Kock himself. We hear that he is in a critical condition and a prisoner of war. Schiel too was wounded and made prisoner and Coster was killed.

It is estimated that at least half of the burghers at Elandslaagte were killed, wounded or captured. Our correspondent has been informed that on the Boer side 38 men died on the battlefield, 113 were wounded and 185 made prisoner of war. This means a total loss of 336 men. It is but a small consolation that the British too suffered severe casualties. According to the journalist Steevens their losses were 50 men killed and 213 wounded.

EVALUATION OF KOCK'S ACTIONS
Speculation on the reasons for this defeat will go on for a long time. Perhaps it was General Kock's own fault: he was simply too reckless in his underestimation of the Khakis. He moved too far ahead into enemy territory, rendering it impossible for reinforcements from the Transvaal main force to rush to his assistance. In addition he ignored the warnings expressed by his officers.

On the other hand, the British planned their attack meticulously and carried it through with vigour. We trust that the Republican officers have learned a lesson from this defeat and will avoid future disasters of a similar nature. That the battle of Elandslaagte was a disaster cannot be doubted. We hear that Commandant-General Joubert concluded his official report to President Kruger on the engagement with the following words: 'It is a total defeat, bigger than any ever suffered by the Afrikaner people.'

Elandslaagte, before the battle: General Jan Kock and his officers; below, Boers at captured British train

Colonel Adolf Schiel

SIEGE OF KIMBERLEY
President Steyn visits the front

Kimberley, 27 October – Here on the western border of the Orange Free State the situation has hardly changed since last week. President Steyn arrived here on 23 October to discuss the best tactics to use against the British forces in Kimberley with Chief Commandant C.J. Wessels and General Koos de la Rey. Since De la Rey had not yet arrived the President left again for Bloemfontein today. While he was here he visited a number of commandos to talk to the burghers.

SKIRMISH AT DRONFELD STATION
On 24 October our men north of Kimberley clashed with the enemy. Some 600 burghers of the Boshof Commando had been stationed next to the railway line to keep the British from leaving Kimberley to relieve Riverton. A British reconnaissance party, accompanied by an armoured train, advanced right by them without noticing them. It was only when the British suddenly realised that there were Boers behind them that they attempted to retreat to Kimberley. The Boers opened fire and a heavy fight ensued at Dronfeld Station.

The burghers commanded by Field Cornet Petrus Botha initially managed to hold their positions, but when they noted that reinforcements for the Khakis were arriving by train from Kimberley, they requested assistance by heliograph. Chief Commandant Wessels was not prepared to weaken his headquarters at Olifantsfontein by sending burghers to assist Botha's men. As a result the Khakis could not be prevented from retreating to Kimberley with their armoured train at half past three that afternoon. Thus the fight ended in a hollow victory for the Free State burghers.

As for the casualties: two burghers, including Field Cornet Petrus Botha, were killed, and seven wounded, five badly. From a dependable source we have heard that three Khakis were killed and 21, including three officers, wounded.

DE LA REY ON HIS WAY HERE
From the north we have received news that General De la Rey was in Taung yesterday to arrange affairs there. Chief Molala assured him that his people would remain strictly neutral in this war. De la Rey thereupon entrusted Molala with the protection of the government offices. He then advanced to Veertien Strome, where he and his vanguard arrived earlier this afternoon.

Our readers will find it difficult to imagine how trying this expedition has been for De la Rey and his men. It is desperately dry on the western border and there is no fodder for horses or oxen. Water is extremely scarce. In addition it is unbearably hot. In terms of General Cronjé's orders, De la Rey's men were to damage the railway line at regular intervals and to destroy the railway bridge over the Vaal River. Those tasks slowed down their progress and sapped their energy. No wonder both the men and their animals are completely exhausted!

The burghers around Kimberley look forward eagerly to De la Rey's arrival. The general opinion is that if there is one Boer commander who can finish off the British, it is De la Rey. His fame after his success at Kraaipan has spread like wildfire through the Republican ranks.

DE LA REY OCCUPIES VRYBURG

Vryburg, 25 October – On 17 October General Piet Cronjé's war council decided that General Koos de la Rey, who is a member of the council, should occupy Vryburg, the biggest town in the northern Cape between Kimberley and Mafeking. De la Rey is to proceed south to assist the Free State forces at Kimberley and afterwards to join the proposed Republican invasion of the Cape Colony across the Orange River.

For De la Rey the interests of his men always come first. He gave one third of them home-leave – with specific instructions on when they should return – and advanced on Vryburg with the rest. His force consisted of 1 200 men with three guns. On 20 October he reached the outskirts of Vryburg, where dozens of Cape citizens waited on him and applied to join his forces, informing him that the town would not be defended by its British authorities. We have heard that the local Police Commissioner was so humiliated by the decision of a meeting of the citizens of Vryburg not to defend the town that he committed suicide.

De la Rey and his burghers entered Vryburg early the next morning, 21 October, accompanied by the local magistrate. After hoisting the Transvaal flag in front of the magistrate's office, the General briefly addressed the crowd. In the first place he called on all the inhabitants of Vryburg to join his commando. Secondly he expressed the opinion that Bechuanaland should be incorporated into the Transvaal and Griqualand-West into the Free State. Thirdly he assured his listeners that the Transvaal flag would fly over Vryburg forever and would only be taken down over the dead bodies of himself and his burghers. In conclusion, he assured all private individuals who conducted themselves peacefully that they would not be hindered in any way.

After his speech everybody present sang the Transvaal anthem. Thus this former capital of the Republic of Stellaland was freed from British occupation and is now, as planned when it was originally founded, again a Boer town.

This morning the officers held a war council meeting. They decided that Field Cornet J.H. Visser should remain here with 140 men to defend the town, to uphold law and order and to guard the weapons and ammunition in the powder magazine. De la Rey and the rest of his force will leave for Taung later this afternoon, from where they will advance to Kimberley.

FROM THE EDITOR

We have now entered the third week of war, without any gains to gladden a warrior's heart. Indeed, this week we report on another major Republican setback on the battlefield, namely the devastating defeat of General Jan Kock and his burghers at Elandslaagte. The question occupying every mind is: Will we ever gain the upper hand over our enemy?

It was not all bad news last week. In spite of British successes in Natal, the Khakis are in continuous retreat and are now concentrated in Ladysmith. Our heaviest siege guns, the 155mm Long Toms, are on their way there and will probably soon force the enemy even further south.

As for the British garrisons in the besieged towns of Mafeking and Kimberley, our burghers have now completely restricted their freedom of movement. The railway lines on both sides of the towns have been broken up. Skirmishes that took place at both Kimberley and Mafeking in the past week clearly indicate that the British forces there pose no threat.

From the other fronts – the Transvaal border with Rhodesia and the southern border of the Orange Free State – we have heard no news. Our readers can rest assured, however, that we will keep them informed of developments in those areas.

OUR MILITARY OFFICERS

Chief Commandant Marthinus Prinsloo

Marthinus Prinsloo was born in the Graaff-Reinet district of the Cape Colony in 1838. As a young boy he moved to Transorangia with his parents. His father, Nicolaas Frans Prinsloo, was a farmer. Like most children in the pioneer days, Prinsloo received virtually no formal education. His school was the farm and he himself became a successful and affluent farmer.

Prinsloo gained his first military experience in the wars between the Orange Free State and the Basuto of King Moshweshwe. On the battlefield, he revealed exceptional leadership qualities and a courageous fighting spirit. Consequently he was elected Field Commandant of the Winburg Commando in 1867. In recognition for his services to the Republic the Orange Free State government awarded him the farm Leeuwspruit in the district of Ladybrand after the war.

Prinsloo's stature rose even further when from time to time he served as a government official. Elected to the Free State Volksraad in 1876, he proved himself a very able public speaker, serving on numerous commissions. In 1889, however, he resigned from public life to focus his full attention on his extended farming interests.

With the outbreak of the war earlier this month, he joined the military forces of the Orange Free State in spite of his advanced age. At a war council held in Harrismith he was elected Chief Commandant in terms of Commando Law. At present he is the Commander-in-Chief of the Orange Free State forces on the Natal front.

Chief Commandant Marthinus Prinsloo

MAFEKING: THE SIEGE CONTINUES

Baden-Powell full of arrogance

Marico laager at Mafeking, 26 October – To the utter frustration of our burghers the British garrison in Mafeking is still holding out. Since our previous report last Friday evening, a lot has happened but little changed. Our men have managed to occupy most of the springs northeast of town. The British commander, Colonel Baden-Powell, reacted by sending a pious message that he regarded the occupation of the town's sources of drinking water as a breach of the peace and that he would declare war if we did not abandon them immediately. Obviously the man does not realise that we are at war already!

The burghers regarded the arrogant Englishman's threat as a joke. General Koos Snyman, however, took him seriously, and actually ordered the burghers to retreat! The next afternoon a number of burghers reoccupied the springs and dug a furrow channelling the water to our side. A strong guard was left behind, since the burghers expected British retaliation. Indeed, that very night they repulsed an attack by a Khaki patrol supported by a large number of black townsmen.

USE OF HELIOGRAPHS

One morning at about ten o'clock we spotted flickering lights far in the south. It was the heliograph of General Cronjé searching for us. Our field telegraphists immediately put up their own heliograph and thus established direct communication with headquarters. Even though there is no telegraph wire, the telegraphists can send messages by means of the movable mirrors. These work the same way as a Morse code key, the shorter or longer flickers representing the points or lines in telegraphic language.

ABUSE OF WHITE FLAGS

After the Reverend Postma held a service in the laager on Sunday 22 October, Cronjé advised Baden-Powell by letter to send the women and children out of town, since it was our intention to bombard the British on Monday with the guns captured at Kraaipan by De la Rey. Baden-Powell refused but replied that he would hoist a white flag above the place where the women and children would be assembled.

When day broke on Monday morning, there were numerous white flags waving all over the town. In addition there were Red Cross flags at two places. This annoyed our burghers tremendously – where could our artillery now aim? Mafeking is somewhat smaller than London! We regard it as extremely cowardly of the British soldiers to hide behind women and children.

While our men were still gazing in disgust at the excessive number of white flags, the British opened fire. Their target was the burghers at the water source, but no damage was done, since the shells invariably overshot or fell too short. Our artillery fired back, but we have no idea to what effect.

THE ARRIVAL OF THE LONG TOM

On 25 October the 155mm siege gun or Long Tom sent from Daspoortrand in Pretoria finally arrived. It was set up at Cronjé's laager south of Mafeking and began bombarding the enemy that same afternoon. The shells kick up huge clouds of dust in town but it is impossible to establish how effective the bombardment is in breaking down the British garrison's will to resist. Baden-Powell's reaction was another attempt at misleading us: that evening he sent a note to Cronjé threatening to fire on us with dynamite bombs if we did not end our bombardment!

We were informed that Cronjé intended to storm Mafeking today, but this did not take place. According to someone at the telegraph office in Cronjé's laager, President Kruger himself vetoed the attack, since he had heard that the British had planted dynamite bombs right around the town to blow up our men. And now, as we sit here tonight, we wonder if the siege of Mafeking will ever end.

Long Tom at Mafeking

General Piet Cronjé (whip in hand) with the Long Tom at Mafeking

EVENTS ON THE NATAL FRONT

Boer forces approach Ladysmith

Natal, north of Ladysmith, 27 October – The Transvaal forces set up camp here yesterday and the burghers are now waiting for further orders. Spirits are rather depressed in the light of the past week's tragedy and frustration at Elandslaagte and Talana. In both battles the Boer casualties were shockingly high. On the other hand, we have now heard from a reliable source that the British casualties at Talana were higher than ours, namely 51 men killed in action or mortally wounded, 203 others wounded and 246 captured by our burghers.

MISSED OPPORTUNITIES

In addition to the military setbacks, many burghers feel that their officers are not taking advantage of opportunities to defeat the British. General Erasmus's commando, for example, had already reached Glencoe, a village on the road between Newcastle and Ladysmith, on 22 October when Boer scouts reported that the British force had abandoned camp at Dundee. They had not moved out at a leisurely pace either – the same Khakis who had repulsed General Meyer's men from Talana Hill were in such a hurry that they abandoned their whole camp, with the tents still pitched, and huge stores of supplies and ammunition!

Even the British wounded were left behind, including the mortally wounded Major-General Symons, who died on 23 October. We later heard that the Khakis fell back to Ladysmith on a long detour via Helpmekaar. Most of the townspeople also fled from Dundee to Ladysmith.

In our opinion General Erasmus then lost his head. Instead of pressing on behind the fleeing Khakis and attempting to cut them off from Ladysmith, he sent his whole force back to the abandoned town to occupy the abandoned military camp. It was totally unnecessary to entrust such a minor task to a force of thousands of burghers who, when they reached Dundee, could not resist the temptation to plunder the town and the camp. The officers were simply unable to halt the unruly behaviour.

Erasmus and his burghers resumed their march to Ladysmith on 24 October, having wasted two full days. As a result, the Khakis who retreated via Helpmekaar reached Ladysmith before the Boers could overtake them. In defence of the burghers we must report that the going was tough as a result of the never-ending rain. Wagons often bogged down in the mud and the scouts of Captain Danie Theron's Bicycle Scout Corps had to carry their bicycles most of the way since the road was impassable even to them!

THE FIGHT AT RIETFONTEIN

On 23 October a Free State force of 1 500 burghers commanded by General Andries Cronjé advanced from Bester Station north of Ladysmith towards Elandslaagte at the request of Commandant-General Piet Joubert. They had one Krupp gun with them. On 24 October they reached Rietfontein, some 20 kilometres northeast of Ladysmith, where a British force attacked them. Our information indicates that General White himself commanded this force, which consisted of 5 300 soldiers with 18 field guns.

The Khakis failed to overpower the burghers, disengaged early in the afternoon and returned to Ladysmith, leaving the Free State force in full command of the battlefield. On the Republican side 11 men were killed and 19 wounded. British casualties were 13 dead and some 100 wounded. Despite grief at the losses, Chief Commandant Prinsloo is delighted with his burghers' performance against the huge enemy force.

The unification of the Transvaal and Free State forces on the Natal front eventually took place yesterday at Tintinyoni, about halfway between Elandslaagte and Ladysmith. The burghers on both sides were delighted to finally shake the hands of their comrades-in-arms. There is a new determination among the burghers to finish off the enemy as soon as possible.

THE
War Reporter
WEEKLY EDITION

Number 4 Pretoria, South African Republic 4 November 1899

'MOURNFUL MONDAY' FOR THE BRITISH

Victories for the Boers at Ladysmith

Pretoria, 2 November – After the setbacks at Talana and Elandslaagte, our burghers finally achieved success, and what fabulous success it was! One's enemies' reaction can often serve as yardstick for the successes of one's own forces. Monday 30 October, the day on which the Boers shattered the British forces at Ladysmith, has already been called 'Mournful Monday' by the British newspapers. This name spread like wildfire through the press. A devastating Monday it was indeed for our enemy.

There were actually two separate battles at Ladysmith on Mournful Monday. At Moddersspruit the Transvaal forces were involved in the successful defence of their positions against a determined British attack. At Nicholson's Nek (which some Boers, as well as British, subsequently called Little Majuba) a mixed force of Transvaal and Free State commandos defeated a huge British force and forced them to surrender. The total Republican losses on Monday were 16 men dead and 75 wounded. On the British side 106 men were killed, 374 wounded and 1 284 made prisoner of war.

BOER POSITIONS BEFORE THE BATTLE

By Sunday 29 October the Boer camps were spaced in the form of a 15-kilometre half-moon with the open side towards the south around Ladysmith. Commandant-General Joubert's headquarter camp was situated immediately northeast of Pepworth's Hill, a low, flat-topped hill northeast of Ladysmith on the farm of a Natal Member of Parliament by the name of Pepworth. That meant that the headquarters would be behind the hill to someone looking from Ladysmith.

Lieutenant-Colonel Trichard was stationed on Pepworth's Hill with seven guns, including a Long Tom siege gun that arrived at the front on the 29th. A few burghers assisted the gunners of the Transvaal State Artillery, who used a team of mules to haul that heavy gun up to the summit of the hill. The gunners worked through the night to build an emplacement to protect the Long Tom against enemy fire.

On the heights east and southeast of Pepworth's Hill was stationed the left wing of the Transvaal forces, consisting of three strong units. The first, the Lydenburg Commando of General Schalk Burger, was positioned on Long Hill directly south-southeast of Pepworth's Hill. The Heidelberg Commando of Commandant J.D. Weilbach was positioned southeast of Burger's men and General Lukas Meyer's burghers were on the extreme left flank furthest away to the southeast from headquarters. Each of these commandos was accompanied by artillerymen with one or two guns.

The right wing of the Transvaal forces included the Pretoria Commando, under General Daniël Erasmus, encamped directly north of Pepworth's Hill. There was also the Irish Corps, under the American Colonel Blake, and the Free State forces, their camps spread out on low hills stretching from Nicholson's Nek, immediately east of Erasmus's camp, all the way southeast to the railway line and the road that leads from Ladysmith to Van Reenen's Pass. By 29 October the total strength of the Boer forces near Ladysmith numbered approximately 7 000 men with about 20 guns.

BRITISH STRATEGY

British officers who are now our prisoners of war state that General White, the British commander in Ladysmith, had the Boer positions reconnoitred by mounted patrols and from an air balloon on Sunday 29 October. He then decided to go on the offensive the next day. His objective was to overrun the Boer forces in one huge effort, employing all the troops he had at his disposal, namely more than 12 000 soldiers with 60 guns, in a three-pronged attack. One British force would attack the Boer centre, the second would pressurise the Boer right wing and thus pin it down, while the third force, consisting mostly of mounted men, would outflank the Boer left wing and attack it from the rear.

JOUBERT'S PREPARATIONS

Commandant-General Joubert decided late on Sunday afternoon to move all the burghers stationed on Long Hill further to his left flank to strengthen his forces there. He reasoned that the British would bombard Long Hill in order to pin the Boer forces down, and would then try to outflank us with their mounted troops. In the opinion of our correspondent, this brilliant tactical move contributed significantly to the Republican victory the next day, since the British did exactly what Joubert expected.

October 29 certainly was Joubert's lucky day. Soon after dark that evening he received the pleasant news of the arrival of 500 men of the South African Republic Police under Commandant G.M.J. van Dam. Joubert ordered them to occupy the heights southeast of Nicholson's Nek to strengthen the Republican right flank.

According to the British officers who became our captives the next day, the Khakis were not aware of the Boer strengthening of their flanks. The British air balloon was down already and their scouts noted no movements in the dark.

BEGINNING OF THE BATTLE AT MODDERSPRUIT

The British started their advance long before daybreak on 30 October. Their artillery was already in position by dawn. A sentry of the Ermelo Commando captured a group of about 15 soldiers during the night, but never realised that a major offensive was looming.

It was Lieutenant-Colonel Trichard of the State Artillery who noticed a large group of mounted British soldiers approaching our positions soon after daybreak and fired on them. Soon afterwards the British artillery began bombarding Long Hill, under the impression that they were bombarding the main Republican force, and did not immediately realise that there were no Boers in their target area. Trichard ordered his artillery to answer the enemy's artillery. This they did so effectively that the British gunners were forced to redeploy their guns.

THE BRITISH ATTACK IN THE SOUTH

Meyer and Weilbach's men on the eastern side of the Moddersspruit and south of Long Hill entered the battle soon afterwards when a large number of British foot soldiers advanced on them. The burghers opened a determined fire on the soldiers, while their guns from the rear also fired on the enemy.

Since General Meyer had become ill early that morning, he appointed his adjutant, the Volksraad member Louis Botha, to command the burghers. Soon after six o'clock, Botha noted mounted British soldiers approaching his sector of the battlefield. Realising that it was essential to keep them from breaking through the Boer lines, Botha urged his men, including the courageous Krugersdorp burghers of Commandant F.J. Potgieter, to fight to the best of their ability. After a heavy clash the enemy fell back some distance.

THE ARTILLERY DUEL

In the meantime the British gunners had managed to move their guns closer to Pepworth's Hill and began putting the Republican artillery under heavy fire. A number of the Republican artillerymen were hit by bombshells. One of the first to be killed on Pepworth's Hill was Dr Höhls, the chief of the medical service of the State Artillery. He was directly behind our guns busy treating the wounded when shrapnel hit him.

The situation on Pepworth's Hill was becoming critical when the British fire suddenly diminished. That was because the burghers east of the Moddersspruit put so much pressure on the enemy, that the British commander had to order his artillery to redeploy to bombard the Boers in that sector. Thus the Republican gunners on Pepworth's Hill had a valuable reprieve by about eight o'clock.

THE BRITISH REPULSED

The burghers of Weilbach and Botha, supported by the Boer artillery, managed to defend their position quite easily until the British artillery began bombarding them. It soon seemed as if our men would be forced back, but the Commandant-General ordered General Burger's Lydenburg Commando to support them. At 11 o'clock the British began retreating. When our burghers noted this, they were filled with a new determination and opened a heavy fire on the Khakis, steadily pushing them back and eventually occupying their abandoned positions.

THE END OF THE BATTLE AT MODDERSPRUIT

Since the British retreat in due course became rather disorderly, we all expected that our forces would occupy Ladysmith. Joubert rejected the idea, however, even though some of his officers pleaded with him to follow up our victory. His reasons for this decision were plain: the burghers were tired after a heavy battle, and, in addition, he suspected that the British held a reserve force in Ladysmith ready to thwart such an attack from the Boers.

Joubert's belief that the enemy still had some firepower was confirmed when the British began firing with lyddite bombs on our men. We later heard that a number of British naval guns had arrived by train in Ladysmith just in time to be used in the battle against us. Our guns on Pepworth's Hill bore the brunt of the lyddite bombs and had to be moved to safer positions. Before long the firing on both sides diminished and eventually ended.

NICHOLSON'S NEK

In the battle of Nicholson's Nek on Monday 30 October the Republican forces scored an even more spectacular victory than at Moddersspruit. This included the capture of a huge number of British soldiers as prisoners of war. Their commander in the battle, Lieutenant Colonel F.R.C. Carleton, is one of the prisoners. He himself told our reporter what had happened.

Carleton had already left Ladysmith with about 1 000 soldiers on Sunday evening. They were to occupy Nicholson's Nek some 10 kilometres north of the town in order to cover the left flank of the main British assault. Initially they made good progress in the dark. Their mountain guns and reserve ammunition were transported on the backs of about 100 mules.

When Carleton and his men reached Cayingubo Hill in the course of the night, he decided to occupy it. They had almost reached the top when a group of Boer sentries heard them and fired a few shots in the dark in their direction. Some soldiers panicked and ran down the hill yelling at the top of their voices. In the chaos that followed the pack mules stampeded and were lost in the darkness. Carleton's force was consequently left with neither mountain guns nor reserve ammunition. They nevertheless occupied Cayingubo Hill. Carleton ordered his men to entrench themselves and prepare to defend their position.

THE BOER ATTACK BEGINS

The Boers on that part of the battlefield, namely General Erasmus's Pretoria commando, became aware of the British presence in the night. They prepared an attack, opening fire around five o'clock that morning, which was before daybreak.

The Free State burghers who were stationed to the east of Cayingubo heard the roaring of the guns in the dark and wondered what was going on. Acting Commandant Christiaan de Wet told our correspondent after the battle that he and Commandant Steenekamp were given permission to go out with 300 men to investigate. They arrived at the foot of Cayingubo at about sunrise and were amazed to find that there were Khakis on the hill. Their immediate reaction was the same as in the Transvaal War of Independence 19 years previously, when they noted Colley's redcoats on Majuba Hill. At that time De Wet was a Transvaal burgher and one of the Boers who stormed Majuba. This time he, Steenekamp and their valiant band of 300 Free State burghers ascended Cayingubo's northern slope without hesitation.

The battle of Majuba Hill in the war of 1880–81 and this battle at Cayingubo Hill proceeded very similarly. While the Free State burghers approached the summit from the north, Commandant van Dam and the Johannesburg Police were ascending the hill from the northeast. Both groups of burghers utilised the available covering provided by rocks and bushes to the utmost. Like Colley's force on Majuba in 1881, Carleton's force on Cayingubo never realised that the enemy was advancing. The Boers were eventually directly underneath the rim of the summit. They took their time and slowly spread around the rim. By 11 o'clock they were close enough to begin their final attack.

THE BRITISH DEFEATED

Carleton said afterwards that he had been hoping for assistance from Ladysmith, but that at about half past 11 he received a heliographic message to retreat to the town. Since he and his men were completely surrounded by Boers, however, they could not obey that command.

In the meantime, the Boers had begun a merciless attack. By 12 o'clock almost half of the British on some parts of the battlefield were either killed or wounded. Many soldiers, including full companies, attempted to flee by running down the hill. A few soldiers even dropped their rifles in panic. Upon arriving at the foot of the hill they found the opposite of the safety they were longing for. The Pretoria Commando were ready with their Mausers and chased the soldiers up the hill again.

The end was now near. Soon after one o'clock the British on the northern summit raised the white flag in the form of a white blanket attached to the barrel of a rifle. The Boers immediately stopped firing, as did the British, whose ammunition was finished anyway. The surrender did not take place on Carleton's orders, but he had to accept it. The Boers joyously approached the soldiers and waved their hats in the air as a sign of their victory.

(continued overleaf)

Boers with British field gun captured at Nicholson's Nek

(continued)

Carleton quickly burned his maps and military documents, but handed his sword and revolver to Commandant Steenekamp when the latter took him captive.

AN ENGLISHMAN'S VIEW

When our reporter reached the battlefield soon after the fight, he again met the British war correspondent, George Steevens. The latter seemed rather dejected and obviously has much more respect for our burghers now than he had after the British victory at Elandslaagte a week ago. Steevens was especially impressed by the fact that the burghers went out of their way to assist with the treatment of the British wounded; that they gave their helpless enemies water out of their own bottles; and that even though they experienced a shortage of modern rifles themselves, they gave captured Lee-Metford rifles to the British medical orderlies to use as splints to set the broken limbs of wounded soldiers. Steevens was equally surprised that the Boers did not take the British wounded prisoner of war. Neither did they celebrate their victory with excessive joy, but sat in groups under the thorn trees singing hymns of praise to the Almighty.

Thus this battle, which stifled the British attempt to defeat the Republican forces in Natal, came to an end early on the afternoon of Mournful Monday. What the British are going to do now, we do not know. We will force them to surrender Ladysmith by firing on them with our Long Tom guns, that is certain. Our men are full of self-confidence, all expecting that, as in 1881, the British political leaders in London will realise that their soldiers cannot win a war here and will negotiate for peace.

Christiaan de Wet

FROM THE EDITOR

It is with great joy that we finally report on a significant Boer victory. On Monday our burghers routed the Khakis of General White at Ladysmith. Some cynics allege that it was a hollow victory, since Commandant-General Joubert declined a golden opportunity to force White into surrender. We believe Joubert was correct not to recklessly follow up his victory by attempting to take Ladysmith itself. A Boer attack could have provided the British with the opportunity to lead our forces into an ambush and our burghers' magnificent victories at Modderspruit and Nicholson's Nek would then have been in vain.

Unfortunately we also bring bad news. General Kock died in Ladysmith as a prisoner of war a day after our victory. Rumours have it that he died of neglect rather than of the wounds he received at Elandslaagte 10 days earlier. We cannot confirm that this actually was the case. In the meantime we honour this fallen warrior by highlighting his career in the 'Our Military Officers' column.

We have at last received an extensive report on developments on the northern front. Our readers will note that the news is not positive. The course of events up north reflects a fairly general unwillingness among many burgher officers to act decisively. If these men do not immediately start doing their duty, the Republican war machine will soon grind to a complete standstill.

Nothing of immediate major interest has happened on any of the other fronts in the past week.

THE NORTHERN FRONT
Shocking rejection of orders

Pietersburg, 3 November – Even before the outbreak of hostilities, the Republican authorities were aware of a British force in Rhodesia. Not only do these troops threaten the Transvaal north and northwest border, but there is also the danger that they will persuade the black communities in that area to attack the Boers.

Under these circumstances the Transvaal government decided to send a strong force, namely the Soutpansberg and Waterberg Commandos, to the northern front under the command of Field-Cornet F.A. Grobler, who was appointed Assistant-General. His orders are to cross the northern border with his burghers, to repulse the enemy from that area and to destroy the railway line to Bulawayo.

Grobler believed that it was unnecessary and unpractical to hold a joint war council meeting of the officers of both commandos, since they were separated by a distance of more than 300 kilometres by road in an inhospitable area. On 12 October he presented his campaign plan to the war council of the Soutpansberg Commando, assembling north of Pietersburg, and was unanimously accepted. It was agreed that the Soutpansberg burghers would cross the Limpopo River, which forms the northern border, at Rhodes Drift. They would then proceed to the west and later southwest all along the border and clear that area of the enemy.

The Waterberg Commando, in terms of the plan, will cross the border where the Matlabas River joins the Limpopo. From there they are to follow the Limpopo downstream in a northeasterly direction and clear that area of enemy forces as well as destroying the railway and telegraph communication between Rhodesia and the Cape Colony in order to cut the enemy off from the outside world.

WATERBERG INSUBORDINATION

After the war council of the Soutpansberg Commando on 12 October, Grobler left for the Waterberg Commando. He reached them on 23 October at the Palala River, some 30 kilometres from the border and immediately convened a war council. He was dumbfounded when the officers informed him that they would not cross the border. Their excuse: they did not believe that the government actually wanted them to invade Rhodesia.

Grobler immediately telegraphed the authorities, who reacted by ordering the Waterberg commandant, H.S. Lombard, to Pretoria and appointing Jan du Plessis De Beer as acting commandant in his place. De Beer was personally ordered to proceed immediately with the destruction of the railway and telegraph lines on the other side of the border. He too refused to carry out this order, however, and the burghers from Waterberg remain inactive to this day.

SOUTPANSBERG IRRESOLUTION

The state of affairs in the far north is not much better. Our reporter with the Soutpansberg burghers reports that they reached the border on 18 October. There they heard a rumour that a huge enemy force with numerous guns was waiting for them in the bushes north of the Limpopo River. Acting General H.C.J. van Rensburg and his war council consequently decided it would be too dangerous to cross the river, and telegraphed for guns from Pretoria. The government immediately dispatched Captain Eloff with two pom-pom rapid-fire guns and a field gun by train to Pietersburg, with orders to assist the Soutpansberg commando.

Our reporter heard from a reliable source that the British force that seemed so threatening to the Soutpansberg officers consisted of about 500 men, including some black soldiers, with one good field gun. Their commander is Colonel H. Plumer, headquartered at Fort Tuli. From 20 October there has been sporadic fighting to and fro between our burghers and the British on the other side of the river.

SKIRMISHES ALONG THE LIMPOPO

On 23 October Field Cornet Briel crossed the Limpopo with a mounted commando and became involved in a skirmish with a British patrol. Two of Briel's burghers were wounded, while six British, including an officer, were killed and four taken prisoner. Van Rensburg, however, still refused to cross the river. On 26 and 27 October other skirmishes followed, during which the Boers lost a few horses and an unknown number of British soldiers were killed or wounded.

At the end of October Eloff arrived at the Limpopo River with his guns. Van Rensburg then decided to attack Plumer. On 2 November he crossed the Limpopo at Rhodes Drift with all his mounted burghers and guns. The burghers exhibited exemplary courage that day in their attack on the British, but the latter found cover in the dense bushes and Van Rensburg was not prepared to follow up his victory by pursuing them.

In the end Van Rensburg's commando captured ten Khakis, three of them wounded, as well as a large quantity of war supplies. These included a number of wagons loaded with provisions, an ambulance and some 60 horses, 80 mules and 18 oxen. Two of our men were killed and four slightly wounded.

STRONG LEADERSHIP NEEDED

In our opinion Grobler cannot be blamed for the refusal or inability of his commandos to carry out their original orders. It is to be blamed on those officers who either ignore their orders or are over-cautious. Grobler will either have to take strong steps to force them to obey or replace them with other officers.

Van Rensburg is clearly an unsuitable commander. According to a report we received this evening, this so-called general heard a rumour earlier today that the British were preparing an attack, and reacted by ordering his whole commando to flee back across the Limpopo in such haste that the guns were left behind. One of his officers, Danie du Preez, pulled the guns back across the river on his own initiative with the help of a few volunteers.

General F.A. Grobler

The hearse and procession at General Kock's funeral in Pretoria

OUR MILITARY OFFICERS

General Jan Kock

Johannes Hermanus Michiel Kock was born in 1835 in Graaff-Reinet in the Cape Colony. His father, Jan Kock, was a Boer commandant in Transorangia during the last phase of the Great Trek. His mother, Elsje Magdalena Smit, was the sister-in-law of former president M.W. Pretorius.

Kock travelled in the Great Trek with his parents and participated as a boy in both the battles against the British in Transorangia, namely at Swartkoppies in 1845 and Boomplaats in 1848. His parents subsequently settled north of the Vaal River in the Potchefstroom district.

Kock became a leading figure in the district. He was a well-known elder in the Dutch Reformed Church and served as a Justice of Peace in Potchefstroom before the British annexation of the Transvaal in 1877. In the War of Independence of 1880–81 he was appointed a general and participated in the siege of the British garrison in Potchefstroom.

After the war Kock again became a full-time farmer and later served as magistrate. In 1892 he became a member of the Executive Council of the South African Republic. In the meantime he participated in numerous campaigns against black communities. At the outbreak of this war he was again appointed as general. As our readers know, he was badly wounded on 21 October at Elandslaagte and taken prisoner by the British. He died in captivity 10 days later.

Jan Kock was a tall, handsome man of noble presence. The huge procession that followed his hearse to the cemetery in Pretoria this week testified to the fact that he was one of the most popular figures in the Republic. He was married to Catharina Christina Susanna Schoeman, a daughter of the late Commandant-General Stephanus Schoeman and sister of General Hendrik Schoeman.

General Jan Kock

THE War Reporter

WEEKLY EDITION

Number 5   Pretoria, South African Republic   11 November 1899

THE SIEGE OF MAFEKING

Boer laager outside Mafeking, 10 November – Here at Mafeking the siege of the British garrison proceeds unabated. The rope around the neck of the Khaki garrison is being pulled tighter every day.

On the night of 27–28 October the Boer positions northeast of the town were unexpectedly attacked by soldiers from the town. In the dark it seemed to us as if the whole front was swarming with Khakis, but we subsequently learned that there had only been about 50 attackers.

The Khakis stormed our positions yelling at the top of their voices. Our burghers fired back as rapidly as they could. Fortunately for them the British fired too high in the dark. While the enemy bullets went whistling by, Field Cornet Hans Snyman constantly moved from man to man, inspiring them with words like the following: 'Burghers! Don't be afraid! Jesus is our general. He will protect us!' On the other side we could hear the Khakis call out: 'Kill the buggers!' The Khakis carried out a bayonet charge on Field Cornet Jan Louw's burghers but fortunately it failed and by midnight the whole British force had fallen back. A total of six soldiers were killed, nine wounded and two taken prisoner. On our side one burgher was killed and one wounded.

After this attack our burghers needed no encouragement to build higher fortifications around their laagers. The Klein Marico burghers even planted a telegraph pole next to their fort and hoisted a Transvaal flag on it. Some plucky men from this commando managed the other day to capture a number of sheep right next to the town, and even removed a telephone system from a British fort.

On 30 October the war council of the Boer officers decided to attack the British fortifications at Gun Hill. The Boer artillery bombarded the target beforehand and the Rustenburg Commando attacked the town from the east to divert Khaki attention. However, the attack failed when the Boer attackers were repulsed. One burgher was killed and five wounded. We subsequently heard that eight Khakis were killed and three wounded.

Early on the morning of 7 November the Khakis unexpectedly attacked the Boer positions on the western side of Mafeking. While the burghers courageously defended their fortifications, our artillery opened a heavy bombardment on the eastern side of the town to divert the British forces. The British attack was repulsed with the loss of three wounded on our side. We have heard that the British loss was six wounded.

FATE OF BLACK TOWNSPEOPLE IN MAFEKING

Members of the Scandinavian Corps who are participating in the siege on the Republican side captured three blacks who had fled from Mafeking on 5 November. The men told their captors that some 600 black townspeople are being forced by the British to fight against the Boers. They are extremely unhappy with the state of affairs, since there is a shortage of food in the town. The Scandinavians released their captives when they promised that they would return to Mafeking and convince the others not to fight against the Boers.

DANGER OF DYNAMITE MINES

The British are still attempting to strike fear into our burghers with dynamite mines. Members of the Scandinavian Corps and German Engineers fighting as volunteers with the Boer forces destroy many of these mines each day. The enemy buries the dynamite mines underground, connecting them to each other with wires in such an ingenious way that a passer-by who is unaware of this can easily explode a bomb by disturbing the wires. The Scandinavians use the mines that they recover to further damage the railway line. Thus they use Khaki devices against Khaki.

Meanwhile the British are attempting to reach our positions by digging trenches in this direction during the night. Our men prevent this with gunfire. From our side we also attempt to put more pressure on Mafeking by building new fortifications that consist of sandbags stacked on one another ever closer to town. The Scandinavians of Captain Flygare, with their death-defying attitude, are playing a major role in this – though some Boers regard the European volunteers as foolhardy rather than brave.

'FALLING SICKNESS'

The Boers no longer fear a British bombardment. They can see from the smoke when a British gun is fired. Laughing mockingly they shout 'There it comes! There it comes!' Everybody then falls down behind their fortifications until the bomb explodes – always well in front of or behind them. The Boers call their action 'falling sickness'.

Some of the burghers turn a British bombardment into a game. As soon as they see smoke from the barrel of a British gun, they dive down behind their barricades with shouts and laughter, pinching and bumping each other. Some even have clods ready to pelt a timid comrade with when a bomb explodes, giving the poor fellow the impression that he has been hit.

At times when the burghers are bored they entice Baden-Powell's men to fire on them, using a mock-up figure consisting of a jacket and a hat mounted on a wooden frame in such a way that it looks like a human being from a distance. Every now and then this fearless being rises from the Boer fortifications to stare at the enemy. The British always react by firing for all they are worth. The 'fearless burgher' falls down after a few seconds, only to rise again at another place and draw more British fire to the great delight of the burghers.

For the Boers of the Klein Marico the highlight of the past week has been the arrival in their laager of a whole wagonload of oranges. Since for days or even weeks now we have had nothing to eat but dry bread or rusks with coffee and roasted meat, fruit is a delicacy.

At present at least six Red Cross flags are to be seen above Mafeking.

The Scandinavian Corps

A Boer fort outside Mafeking

FROM THE EDITOR

One month since the outbreak of the war, and the end is not yet in sight! Here in Pretoria the general feeling is that the war cannot continue for more than another few months. Of the eventual outcome we have no doubt: defeat is unthinkable. Sooner or later the British government will have to capitulate, since the war will totally deplete state coffers. In the meantime, everybody is speculating on British commander General Redvers Buller's strategies.

An extremely disturbing development during the past week is the increasing participation of black people in the war. Having no quarrel with any black community, we would prefer this war to remain restricted to the principal antagonists. However, both at Mafeking and at Kimberley we have found evidence that the British have been forcing the black townspeople to assist them on the battlefield. At our commandos there are also black people present, but they are merely servants who bake bread or tend the cattle and so forth. Fortunately we have been informed that the Tswana chiefs in Bechuanaland are taking up a neutral position.

The only front where there has been virtually no action yet is the southern Orange Free State. We will report on developments there next week. On all the other fronts the initiative lies with our commandos. Of course, numerous armchair strategists both at the battlefront and on the home front would like to prescribe how our authorities should approach the war. We will resist the temptation to participate in those practices, and support Commandant-General Joubert unconditionally.

BULLER IN SOUTH AFRICA

Cape Town, 31 October – The newly appointed Supreme Commander of all the British forces in South Africa, General Sir Redvers Buller, arrived in Cape Town harbour today with several thousand soldiers on board the *Dunottar Castle*. What his plans are, nobody knows. We have heard that he will probably leave Cape Town soon and launch his attack on the Republics via Durban and the Natal front.

General Buller

11

THE SIEGE OF KIMBERLEY

General de la Rey, Chief Commandant Wessels and field cornets of the Free State

Kimberley, 10 November – The highly respected Transvaal general, Koos de la Rey, arrived here on 30 October from Vryburg. He and Chief Commandant Wessels of the Free State immediately held a joint war council at Tarentaalrand. By the evening of 3 November our burghers had totally encircled Kimberley, and they are so alert at night that no living being can get out of the city. At present there are about 4 800 Free State and 2 200 Transvaal burghers positioned around the city, a total Republican force of some 7 000 men. We had previously heard that there were 13 000 white, 7 000 Coloured and Asiatic and 30 000 black people – altogether 50 000 people – within Kimberley. According to recent reports the number is closer to 55 000.

In many places the burghers are using sandbags to build fortifications. An example is what the burghers call the two 'sack-forts' of the Hoopstad Commando under Commandant I.W. du Preez at Benaauwdheidsfontein. After completing these forts, Du Preez placed his Krupp and rapid-fire guns there. His artillery then shelled the buildings that the Khakis use as stables at the Wesselton mine. The second shot was on target, scattering horses and men in all directions. The British fired back, to the alarm of the burghers, but nobody was hit.

Our men have on numerous occasions captured black people fleeing from Kimberley who say that there is a serious shortage of food in the city. Wessels sends them to Bloemfontein, from where they are taken to Basutoland, since most of them are Basuto people.

ULTIMATUM TO THE BRITISH

On 4 November Chief Commandant Wessels sent an ultimatum to the British commander in Kimberley, Colonel Kekewich. In it he demanded the immediate, unconditional surrender of Kimberley. Should Kekewich reject this, all women, children and non-combatants should be sent from Kimberley within 48 hours, since the city would subsequently be bombarded. The British rejected the ultimatum and the siege continued. When 48 hours had lapsed, our artillery began bombarding the city with nine Krupp guns from four directions.

The only people who have left Kimberley thus far are the Roos family with their three children. They say that the situation in the city is terrible. One of our bombs exploded in a bar. Another shell decapitated a servant girl. They say that there are many Boers in Kimberley who want to get out, but that Kekewich is preventing them.

KEKEWICH MISLEADS THE BESIEGED PEOPLE

Today we established that Kekewich was misleading the people in Kimberley. Our burghers caught a man leaving the city on a bicycle who alleged that he was fleeing since he wanted nothing more to do with the war. However, our men searched the bicycle and found military papers in one of the tubes. In one report it was stated that Kekewich and our arch-enemy, Cecil John Rhodes, had discussed Commandant Wessels's ultimatum and decided to publish a shortened and somewhat edited version of it in the Kimberley newspaper, the *Diamond Fields Advertiser*. According to their version only Afrikaners who intend joining the Republican forces will be allowed by the Boers to leave the city!

Wessels never included such a condition in his ultimatum to Kekewich. He realises that most of the people who find themselves in Kimberley and wish to escape the siege want nothing more to do with the war, and would certainly not join our forces. As far as we are concerned Rhodes and Kekewich are responsible from now on for all casualties of civilians in Kimberley, since they have misled those poor people.

Our men have heard a rumour that Rhodes has a huge hot air balloon in Kimberley and plans to flee in that when our forces eventually capture the city.

THE NATAL FRONT

Moddersspruit, 10 November – After their resounding victory over the British last Monday, everybody in the Boer laager is wondering if – or when – Commandant-General Joubert will order the occupation of the whole of Natal. According to our information such a venture would be easy to undertake, since our sources indicate that there are probably only about 2 000 Khakis in Natal outside Ladysmith. Of those approximately half, with eight guns, are stationed at Colenso to defend the main railway bridge over the Tugela River.

Joubert was initially not in favour of weakening the forces besieging Ladysmith by sending a large force of burghers into Natal. He expects a massive attack from Ladysmith on the Boer positions at any time, and he is not confident that his forces will be able to repulse such an attack.

One of Joubert's biggest headaches is that many burghers are leaving the front without permission. The Commandant-General himself is powerless to halt them. The Transvaal government has issued orders that deserters must return immediately, and railway officials may not transport any burgher without an official leave of absence letter, but the commandos keep melting away. Our military authorities will urgently have to take steps to end this state of affairs.

RAILWAY LINE SOUTH OF LADYSMITH DESTROYED

One of the biggest mistakes the Boers made at Ladysmith was not to destroy the railway line between Colenso and Ladysmith immediately after their victory last Monday. Consequently General White had the opportunity to send more than 1 000 soldiers to Colenso. In addition we have heard that on 31 October alone more than 10 supply trains from the south entered Ladysmith. The line was only broken up by the Free State burghers under the command of Field Cornet Jan Lyon at Pieters Station on 2 November. Free State forces subsequently occupied the hills west and southwest of Ladysmith.

BOER ATTACKS FAIL

We were under the impression that there would be a full-scale joint Boer attack on Ladysmith on 2 November. Commandant-General Joubert had indeed prepared for such an attack. In terms of the attack plan, Free State burghers would attack Ladysmith from the south. However, since the Khakis unexpectedly attacked their position that same morning, they could not honour the agreement.

On 3 November Joubert decided to act more decisively. He gave orders that a combined force of altogether some 3 000 Transvaal and Free State burghers, supported by artillery, should occupy Colenso. The Transvaal officers were eager to carry out the order, but their colleagues from the Free State were less enthusiastic, since their positions south of Ladysmith were again attacked by the Khakis that very day. The Free State forces easily repulsed the British attack, losing one man killed and nine wounded. We later heard the British loss was five men killed, 25 wounded and one missing. As a result of this skirmish, the occupation of Colenso was temporarily postponed.

A TEMPORARY ARMISTICE

On 4 November General White formally requested permission from Commandant-General Joubert to move the civilian population of Ladysmith southwards through the Boer lines so that they would no longer be subject to the Boer bombardment. Joubert rejected this request. His logical justification for this decision was that all the food supplies in the town would be available to the British military force if the civilian population left, enabling the Khakis to hold out much longer. If the Khakis are afraid of civilian losses, they must all surrender at the same time.

Joubert, however, made the following concession to White, namely that the British could establish a hospital camp outside of town that would not be bombarded. A temporary armistice was then agreed upon for this purpose. Before the armistice came into force on 4 November, there was a skirmish between sentries of Commandant Ben Viljoen and a British patrol. One burgher was killed and one wounded. On the British side there were also casualties.

OTHER BOER ATTACKS ON LADYSMITH

The temporary armistice ended at midnight on Sunday 5 November. Afterwards the Boer officers again discussed the possibility of a combined attack on Ladysmith and eventually agreed on 7 November. Both Republican forces were getting ready for the attack when the Transvaal officers decided on a postponement until 9 November, since a second Long Tom siege gun had arrived from Pretoria and they wanted it set up and ready for action on Bulwana Hill. The Orange Free State officers south of the town were not informed of the postponement and attacked on 7 November in accordance with the original agreement. When they realised that they were fighting on their own, they ended their assault. They felt angry and dejected but fortunately suffered no casualties.

The joint attack on 9 November was much better planned than that of 7 November, but failed again. The Boers attacked bravely, but the British defended equally courageously. The Republican loss was three men killed and six wounded. We have heard that the British loss was eight men killed and 23 wounded.

FREE STATE BURGHERS OCCUPY COLENSO

Earlier today we heard that on 7 November the British had abandoned Colenso and retreated to the south. Commandant De Villiers of Harrismith immediately occupied the town, including the British trenches and fortress in the vicinity. He captured a number of British wagons loaded with supplies. The Harrismith burghers then commenced destroying the railway line south of the town.

From our main laager we hear that Commandant Blake of the Irish Corps and Commandant van Dam of the Police Corps, who were both lightly wounded during the battle of Moddersspruit, are ready for action again. However, General Lukas Meyer is still not well and has returned to Pretoria for treatment. Commandant-General Joubert has appointed General Louis Botha as Meyer's successor.

BRITISH PRISONERS OF WAR IN PRETORIA

Pretoria, 6 November – One of our correspondents yesterday visited the Staats Model School here in Pretoria where all the British officers captured by the Transvaal forces are kept prisoner of war. They are doing well and are delighted with the excellent treatment they are receiving from our authorities. One of the prisoners commented that if they had been deceived about political issues in the Republics to the same extent as they had been misinformed about the military capability and the civilised nature of the Boers, he had no doubt that England as a country had been duped by her leading officials.

The officers are pleasantly surprised with all that is being done for them. Nothing surprises them more than being addressed in English by the officials. The superintendent of the Staats Model School provides all sorts of luxuries for his high-profile 'guests'. In the backyard he erected a kitchen with a stove and six burghers look after the welfare of the officers. They are granted sufficient opportunity for physical exercise on the grounds of the school.

There are already 1 400 British prisoners of war here in Pretoria. The ordinary soldiers are accommodated on the racetrack west of the centre of town. The Staats Girls School serves as the Red Cross hospital.

EXPEDITION TO BECHUANALAND

Mafeking, 31 October – One of the numerous tasks of the Transvaal commander on the western border, General Piet Cronjé, is to nullify the British threat from Bechuanaland. We do not believe that there are many British soldiers in Bechuanaland, but we do know that they have an armoured train that could be particularly troublesome. Cronjé has ordered two field cornetcies to defend the border. They are the Hex River Ward of the Rustenburg Commando and the Bushveld Ward of the Marico Commando.

Field Cornet P.D. Swart of the Bushveld Ward occupied Lobatse Railway Halt on 15 October and destroyed the railway line north of it. Assistant-Commandant Du Plessis of the Hex River Ward occupied Gaborone on 16 October. However, supported by their armoured train, named *Powerful*, the Khakis have repeatedly managed to drive the burghers off. Both Du Plessis and Swart are hampered by the fact that they have no artillery. Consequently they have urgently requested assistance from the burghers besieging Mafeking.

Realising the seriousness of the situation, Cronjé dispatched General Koos Snyman with a commando to Lobatse on 17 October. His orders were to destroy the railway line as well as the British armoured train if circumstances allowed. The burghers destroyed the huge railway bridge at Crocodile Pools with dynamite on 25 October and shot a black policeman in British service who attempted to flee.

From Crocodile Pools Snyman's force advanced on Gaborone. The British inhabitants left before their arrival and they occupied the town unopposed. Some Boers enriched themselves by plundering the hotel and private dwellings. North of the town they destroyed two more railway bridges before returning without ever making contact with the armoured train. During the expedition Snyman negotiated with a number of black chiefs who assured him that they would support neither the Boers nor the British in this war.

OUR MILITARY OFFICERS

Captain (Dr) J.O. Höhls

Johann Otto Höhls, who was killed outside Ladysmith at the end of October, was born at Hermannsburg in Natal in 1861. He was a son of the German missionary Carl Höhls and his wife Maria Gewes. After studying medicine in Germany and qualifying as a doctor at the University of Heidelberg, he practised for a short while in Natal. In 1889 he was admitted as a doctor in the South African Republic and settled in Pietersburg.

Last year Höhls moved to Pretoria, where he was appointed officer of health of the Transvaal State Artillery. After a few months he formally joined the artillery corps and was given the rank of captain. When the war broke out last month, he proceeded to the Natal front with an ambulance as the military doctor of the State Artillery and Chief of the Medical Services of the South African Republic.

Höhls's war career was destined to be brief. As related last week, he was mortally wounded in the battle of Moddersspruit while busy treating one of our wounded. His body was taken to Pretoria, where he was buried with full military honours in the German cemetery earlier this week. We honour this outstanding medical officer and wish to express our condolences to his wife, Anna Mucklenbroek, their two sons and two daughters.

Captain (Dr) J.O. Höhls

THE War Reporter
WEEKLY EDITION

Number 6 — Pretoria, South African Republic — 18 November 1899

DEEPER INTO NATAL
Republics take the initiative again

Colenso, 17 November – The Republican forces' long-awaited invasion of Natal finally began on Monday 13 November. The main objective of this expedition is to do as much damage as possible to the railway line between here and Pietermaritzburg, thus making it virtually impossible for the British authorities to provide any support to the besieged garrison in Ladysmith.

Last week we reported that Colenso was occupied on 6 November by a Free State commando under Commandant C.J. de Villiers. Subsequently De Villiers heard occasional rumours that the British were busy building up a huge force at Frere Station, about halfway between Colenso and Estcourt. By the time that Commandant-General Joubert arrived in Colenso on 13 November, reports placed 5 000 or perhaps even 7 000 Khakis with numerous guns at Frere Station.

Joubert's invasion force consists of about 2 000 burghers with two guns, so he does not want to take unnecessary risks. He sent out scouts to reconnoitre the British positions, ordered another gun from Ladysmith, and gave orders to the Republican railway authorities to prepare to blow up the railway bridge across the Tugela River so the British would not be able to use it for military purposes.

On 14 November Joubert's scouts reported that the closest British force, consisting of about 3 000 soldiers, was at Estcourt. The Commandant-General consequently decided to proceed immediately with the invasion. The first target was Estcourt and our burghers began following the railway line there that same afternoon.

ARMOURED TRAIN CAPTURED

Very early on the morning of 15 November the Wakkerstroom and Krugersdorp commandos, under the command of General Louis Botha, spotted an armoured train approaching them from Estcourt. The train consisted of five wagons, three of them armoured, in addition to a coal wagon and locomotive right in the middle.

Botha immediately decided that the Boers should attempt to capture the train. He ordered a section of his burghers to take cover at a sharp turn on the railway line some three kilometres south of Frere Station. They were to allow the train to steam past them without anybody on board noticing them, then break the railway line up behind the train and build a barricade across it. Botha himself, with the rest of the burghers, took up position with the guns near a place called Chieveley, a little distance to the north of the hidden group.

Commandant-General Piet Joubert

The armoured train steamed slowly past both groups of burghers without the British noticing anything. Soon after seven o'clock that morning it reached Chieveley Station. Having seen only a few Boers, the Khakis decided to return to Estcourt.

After the battle, the commander of the train, Captain J.A.L. Haldane, and a British war correspondent, Winston Churchill of the *Morning Post* newspaper, told us their story. There were four officers and 160 soldiers with a nine-pounder ship's gun on the train. As the train slowly steamed towards the south, the northern group of burghers suddenly opened fire with their guns and their rifles. One of the first shells exploded in the first wagon. The engine driver then did exactly what Botha hoped he would do – he increased speed in the direction of the turn where the other Boers were waiting.

Those burghers had in the meantime placed a heap of heavy rocks on the railway line. When the front wagon hit the rocks, it immediately derailed and turned over. The second wagon, the first of the armoured ones, similarly derailed and turned over and the second armoured wagon partly derailed. The rest of the train came to a sudden halt.

The burghers fired as rapidly as possible on the British, who returned fire and even fired a few shots with their 9-pounder ship's gun. Fortunately our artillery blasted it completely off the train with a direct hit and thus ended its role in the skirmish.

Subsequently the Khakis attempted to get the train going again so that they could escape. While some soldiers removed the rocks from the railway line, others fired furiously on us with their rifles. Our burghers also fired on them, but the Khakis impressed us with their valour. In the midst of our whistling bullets, they managed to uncouple the two derailed wagons from the rest of the train. We could not prevent that. Then the locomotive pulled the partly derailed wagon a little distance back.

While our men were still firing for all they were worth, the soldiers uncoupled the partly derailed wagon from the locomotive and with a mighty effort pushed it over to get it out of the way so that they could get past with the remainder of the train. However the wagon did not roll over far enough. Churchill told our reporter after the battle that they found it impossible to shift the overturned wagon far enough away for the locomotive to get past – and that while the Boers were firing on them! It was only when the locomotive's step broke off that they succeeded. By that time the Boer artillery had broken the coupling between the two wagons behind the locomotive with a direct hit. The locomotive itself was also hit, but managed to steam away towards Estcourt with a number of soldiers on the coal truck.

JOURNALIST TAKES THE LEAD IN THE FIGHT

One of our reporters, who monitored the whole fight through his binoculars, afterwards stated that the most valiant Brit at Chieveley was the reporter Churchill. It was he who made the plans and encouraged the soldiers. The latter certainly displayed admirable courage, but without Churchill's initiative, our correspondent claims, they would never have escaped with the locomotive. One wonders what the outcome might have been had one of our bullets hit Churchill early on in the encounter!

The British who did not get away on the locomotive soon afterwards surrendered. Altogether 70 Khakis, of whom 14 were wounded, fell into our hands. Four Khakis had been killed in the fight. The prisoners of war included Captain Haldane and Churchill. It is the rule not to make journalists prisoners of war, but since Churchill not only actively participated in the battle, but was dressed in khaki, Botha felt that it was his duty to have him arrested. Churchill initially refused to surrender and only gave up when Field Cornet Oosthuizen of Krugersdorp levelled his rifle at him and threatened to shoot him. He is now on his way to Pretoria with the other prisoners of war.

On our side five burghers were wounded in the engagement.

ESTCOURT OUTFLANKED

While this battle was raging, the scouts of Commandant-General Joubert reached the outskirts of Estcourt. The British fired on them from their military camp, whereupon they retreated. Two scouts of the Ermelo Commando were busy breaking up the railway line in thick mist outside Estcourt when the enemy surprised them. Both were killed.

Joubert feels that he does not have sufficient manpower to attack the British at Estcourt, but wants to proceed deeper into Natal with his reconnaissance expedition. He has divided his men into two groups with orders to find their way around the town and unite somewhere in the south to proceed with the invasion.

A British armoured train

SKIRMISHES IN THE SOUTHWEST
Free State burghers halt British approach

Bloemfontein, 16 November – Earlier this month the Free State authorities sent a commando to Belmont Station, which is on the main railway line between Kimberley and Cape Town, a short distance west of the Free State southwestern border. The task of these 350 burghers is to ensure that the British force that is gathering at Orange River Station, where the railway line from the Cape crosses the Orange River, does not relieve the besieged British garrison in Kimberley. Their commander is Commandant G. van der Merwe. His scouts report that increasing numbers of Khakis are arriving at Orange River Station on an almost daily basis and that the British patrols are becoming more and more active north of the river.

On 9 November Van der Merwe's commando clashed with a British patrol near Heuningneskloof, a few kilometres south of Belmont. The burghers fired so fiercely on the Khakis that the latter soon fled. Early the next morning a much bigger British force attacked the burghers. Van der Merwe estimates that about 700 Khakis, armed with lances and supported by artillery, participated in the attack. The Boers were stationed on a low hill approximately one hour on horseback south of Belmont. They had one gun with them, but it became unserviceable after three shots, leaving them with only their rifles to confront the enemy.

Van der Merwe allowed the Khakis to approach to within 600 metres of his position before ordering his burghers to fire. The battle that followed lasted for about three hours. The burghers remained calm and determined throughout and eventually forced the Khakis to fall back. On the Free State side two burghers were slightly wounded. On the British side, as far as we can ascertain, one officer was killed and seven soldiers wounded.

It is probably fortunate that this skirmish took place, since our authorities now realise that they will have to give priority to halting the British offensive from the southwest. President Steyn immediately ordered as many Free State burghers as possible to go to Belmont. We have learned that there were 1 600 burghers there on 16 November.

The commander of the British force at Orange River Station is General Methuen. According to our scouts he arrived there on 12 November and has a few thousand soldiers at his disposal. Many of them are obviously Scottish, since our scouts can see their uniform kilts – which to our burghers look exactly like dresses – clearly through their binoculars.

FROM THE EDITOR

Reports from Natal and the Cape Colony indicate that the British are preparing a huge offensive. General Buller is in Natal, where he will probably be in command. Thousands of Khakis are on their way to the front from Durban. We have heard that guns are being unloaded from ships in Durban harbour every day and entrained immediately. The same is happening in Cape Town, where thousands of soldiers with artillery are entraining for the Orange River. Our enemy is certainly preparing to attack.

In the meantime, our commanders are equally busy. The siege of the British garrisons in Kimberley, Mafeking and Ladysmith is being pursued less vigorously to enable burghers to leave for the other fronts. We wholeheartedly support this strategy. Transvaalers did not win the War of Independence of 1880–81 because they forced the British garrisons within the Republic to surrender. They won because they blocked the British invasion of the Transvaal. If the Republics can ward off a British invasion long enough in this war, they will win again.

The climax of military activities the past week was the capture of a British armoured train at Chieveley, south of Colenso in Natal, soon after the start of the Republican invasion deep into Natal. The pressure on the British military authorities is broadened by such invasions, since they are forced to shelve their own plans in order to take counter-measures. Consequently the initiative remains in our hands.

THE SIEGE OF LADYSMITH

Modderspruit, 17 November – Last week we reported on the start of the siege of Ladysmith and the battles between our burghers and the British up to 10 November. Since then not much has changed. Our burghers are still besieging the town, with its huge British garrison. Our commandos occupy virtually each hill in an extensive circle around the town. It takes a good nine hours on horseback to visit all the Boer laagers in this circle.

Since Commandant-General Joubert and General Botha left on their expedition into southern Natal on 13 November, it appears no Boer attacks on Ladysmith are planned. Our supreme command seems to believe that the British will eventually surrender once they run out of food and ammunition. In the meantime, our artillery is bombarding the town and the British camp every day. For this purpose we have 18 guns available at present, two of them Long Toms. We do not know how much damage this bombardment inflicts, but we believe it must be considerable, weakening the enemy's resolve. Unfortunately we do not have enough ammunition for our artillery to fire continuously and it appears that the Long Tom shells do not always explode.

On 14 November a fierce artillery duel took place here at Ladysmith when the British attacked the Free State positions at Bloubank, southwest of the town. British mounted soldiers and artillery advanced on Bloubank openly, and when their gunners began bombarding the Free State laagers, the burghers at Bloubank fired back vigorously with their two guns. Soon the Boer artillerymen from all around the town were firing merrily at the Khakis – even with the Long Toms from Pepworth's Hill and Bulwana.

By two o'clock that afternoon the Khakis who had been approaching Bloubank retreated without having sent their mounted soldiers into battle. A black man from Ladysmith who was captured by our scouts today alleges that only one Khaki was killed and three wounded. We can hardly believe that. On our side one burgher was killed and four wounded. In addition we lost a few horses.

This siege of Ladysmith may become a protracted exercise. In the meantime, an increasing number of burghers are leaving for home without permission. In addition, a new phenomenon is the arrival of dozens of women visiting their husbands in the laagers. They arrive here in oxwagons and horse carts and pitch camp in between the burghers. For the foreign journalists, this must surely be a strange sight in a war zone.

Boer officers involved in the siege of Ladysmith – second from left Commandant C. Nel, third from left General D. Erasmus, Colonel Blake in front of him, third from right Chief Commandant Prinsloo and second from right Commandant B. Viljoen

THE SOUTHERN FRONT

Boer positions on the Orange River

Bethulie, 17 November – The Free State southern border has suddenly become an increasingly important front for the Republican cause. Up until now the Boer authorities had regarded this border as unimportant. Indeed, only about 2 500 Free State burghers had been stationed at four places over the whole length of this border to protect it against British attacks. These four places are:

- Norvalspont, at the bridge across the Orange River. Burghers under the command of Chief Commandant E.R. Grobler ward off a possible attack from British troops at De Aar.
- Bethulie, at another bridge across the Orange River. The Boers there guard against a possible British attack from Noupoort.
- Aliwal North, at the most easterly bridge across the Orange River. The Boers here are defending the border against a British approach from the Stormberg mountain range. The commander of the Boer garrisons at both Bethulie and Aliwal North is Chief Commandant J.H. Olivier.
- A small commando patrols the Free State border with Basutoland.

THOUSANDS OF BURGHERS ON THEIR WAY TO THE FRONT

By the end of October reports reached us that huge numbers of British troops were assembling at the De Aar, Noupoort and Stormberg railroad junctions. Presidents Steyn and Kruger discussed this disturbing news by telegraph and decided to send a few thousand burghers to Norvalspont as soon as possible. General Hendrik Schoeman, who participated in the siege of Pretoria during the Transvaal War of Independence, was appointed their commander.

Schoeman arrived at Norvalspont at the beginning of November. His force consists of fewer than 1 000 burghers, less than half of them with horses. The majority are urbanites from Pretoria and Johannesburg.

Up to the end of October the Free State burghers who were stationed at Norvalspont, Bethulie and at Aliwal North were not particularly active. They did not even attempt to drive off the Cape Police who were guarding the bridges across the Orange River on behalf of the British authorities. Directly after Schoeman's arrival the burghers attacked those guard posts, captured 16 bridge guards and occupied all the bridges.

Schoeman told our reporter that he would enjoy invading the Cape Colony, but that he regarded his commando as too small and poorly supplied. Fewer than 300 burghers are mounted. He has four guns at his disposal, but simply not enough men.

Commandant Swanepoel shifted his camp from Bethulie to the Cape side of the Orange River on 2 November. He instructed small patrols to enter the Cape Colony and damage telegraph and railway communications. On 5 November one of his patrols destroyed two railway culverts at Van Zyl and Agtertang near Colesberg. To their surprise they were informed that the British themselves had destroyed three railway culverts, namely at Arundel, Burgersdorp and near Albert Junction – apparently to ensure that the Boers would not use the railway lines to attack them!

OCCUPATION OF CAPE BORDER DISTRICTS

During the past week the Boer commanders on the Free State southern border have received orders from Bloemfontein to start occupying the eastern districts of the Cape Colony. On 13 November the first of these occupations took place, when Chief Commandant Olivier formally annexed Aliwal North. The Free State flag was hoisted above the magistrate's office, a proclamation by President Steyn was read and martial law was proclaimed. The Cape Afrikaners who were present enthusiastically voiced their approval.

On 14 November Chief Commandant Grobler's and General Schoeman's joint commando occupied Colesberg, while a Free State commando occupied Burgersdorp. At both towns the Cape Afrikaners loudly voiced their approval of the occupations. The Free State flag is enthusiastically received and numerous volunteers are reporting for commando duty.

THE NORTHERN FRONT

Campaign cancelled – Kgama's threat – commandos regroup

Pietersburg, 17 November – Our previous report from this front covered events up to and including the skirmish north of the Limpopo River on 2 November. Even though the Soutpansberg Commando scored a convincing victory that day, General Van Rensburg and his adviser, Volksraad member Barend Vorster, were subsequently too timid to order an immediate attack on the British stronghold, Fort Tuli. This over-cautiousness utterly frustrated Captain Eloff of the State Artillery, who had been sent with a field gun and two rapid-fire guns from Pretoria to assist the Soutpansberg burghers.

On 12 November General Grobler, the Republican commander on the northern front, arrived in the Soutpansberg laager from Waterberg. He soon convinced the officers of the necessity to launch a full-scale attack on Fort Tuli in order to eliminate the British threat from the north. At the same time, however, he telegraphed a letter to Pretoria in which he argued that the whole campaign in the north was a futile undertaking: all that was necessary was a strong commando to guard the border.

One may indeed question the necessity of a campaign north of the Limpopo. The British in that area pose no real threat to the Republic. In addition we have heard that Chief Kgama of the Ngwato threatens that he will regard Boer intrusion into his territory as a declaration of war. The last thing the Republics want at this stage is a war with a black community, since such a conflict could easily spark a general conflagration.

The Transvaal government discussed the issue and decided to terminate the campaign immediately. An order was dispatched to Grobler yesterday to cancel his planned attack on Fort Tuli and to send 500 of his burghers to Pretoria for service on the southern front. The remaining burghers are to be divided into three commandos of 400 men each to guard the border and ensure that no enemy forces cross into the Republic. The commandos will be stationed at healthy, malaria-free places at the western extremity of the Soutpansberg near the Salt Pan, near or at the Palala River and between the Matlabas and the Mogol River.

THE SIEGE OF KIMBERLEY

Tarentaalrant, 17 November – All is not well with the siege of the British garrison here in Kimberley. Our artillery has often bombarded the city, but from what we learn from the statements of captured Khakis and from black townspeople who flee the city, our bombardment does little damage. General De la Rey is unhappy with the situation and has urgently requested a heavy siege gun from Pretoria, but we have learned that his request has been refused since there simply is no siege gun available.

In the meantime skirmishes regularly occur. Early on the morning of 16 November mounted British troops supported by artillery attacked a fortification of the Bloemfontein Commando. The fight that followed lasted about two hours before the British retreated to Kimberley with the loss of 11 men. This morning the British attacked the fortification of Commandant Lubbe of the Jacobsdal Commando at Alexanderfontein. The handful of young burghers who were on duty defended their position heroically, while other burghers came to their assistance. The men of the Hoopstad Commando even rushed up with their field gun, from which just a few shots were sufficient to repulse the enemy. Three burghers were wounded, one of whom died. We do not know if the British suffered any casualties.

SPY DISCLOSES BRITISH PLANS

Cronjé on his way to the southern border

Pretoria, 17 November – Our correspondent in Bloemfontein reports that the magistrate of Rouxville gained information from a British spy in a creative way. The Boers captured this spy earlier this month and detained him in the Rouxville jail.

The local magistrate's clerk, who can speak perfect English, was locked up with the spy in the same cell a few days later. Everybody, including the clerk, acted as though the latter was also suspected of spying for the British. In due course the clerk won the confidence of the real spy, whereupon the latter told him that the British were only waiting for enough soldiers to arrive before advancing from Orange River Station to Kimberley and occupying Bloemfontein.

In the past week numerous messages confirming that there is a massive buildup of British soldiers south of the Orange River have reached Pretoria and Bloemfontein. That our governments are extremely concerned about this is confirmed by the order issued earlier today to General Piet Cronjé at Mafeking to proceed immediately with the majority of his burghers to Belmont in order to stop the British.

OUR MILITARY OFFICERS

Chief Commandant E.R. Grobler

Esaias Renier Grobler was born in 1861 on the farm Grootzonderhout near Philippolis in the Free State. He is the son of Evert Nicolaas Grobler and his wife Amerancia Snyman. He briefly attended the Paarl Gymnasium, but received little formal education. As a young man he bought himself a farm in the Philippolis district and soon became a prosperous farmer.

Grobler achieved such high standing in such a brief time that he was elected as a member of the Free State Volksraad in 1886, when he was barely 25 years old. He is the youngest person so far to have achieved that honour. In 1893 he attended the World Exposition in Chicago in the United States of America as official representative of the Orange Free State. Subsequently he undertook a long journey through North America and Europe. In 1897 he was elected Deputy Chairman of the Volksraad and earlier this year he acted as occasional Chairman.

When the war broke out last month, he immediately went to the southern front as Chief Commandant of the Free State forces. It is his duty to defend that border against British attacks.

Chief Commandant Esaias Grobler

THE

War Reporter

WEEKLY EDITION

Number 7 | **Pretoria, South African Republic** | **25 November 1899**

BATTLE AT BELMONT

Khakis overrun Boer positions

Graspan Station, 24 November – British forces under the command of General Methuen scored a victory over our joint forces under the command of Chief Commandant Jacobus Prinsloo at Belmont Station yesterday. This is on the main railway line between Kimberley and the Orange River some 15 kilometres south of our present position. The masses of British infantry simply overpowered our burghers, forcing them to fall back to ensure that they would not be totally overrun.

Prinsloo had 2 950 burghers of the Boshof, Fauresmith, Jacobsdal, Hoopstad and Bloemfontein commandos at his disposal. Unfortunately he had hardly any military experience, since he was only a young man when the Free State Republic was engaged in its previous war, namely against the Basuto of King Moshweshwe in the 1860s. The only reason for his election as commander was his position as Volksraad member for Middle-Modder River. He is not popular with the burghers.

Methuen's forces began crossing the Orange River on 16 November. Five days later they reached Witteputs, the first station north of the river. A few skirmishes took place between burghers and British patrols, but no major battle ensued.

On 22 November Prinsloo was informed by his scouts that the British seemed to be preparing to attack, but ignored this warning. Instead, he and his officers discussed ways in which they themselves could assault the British. Their plan was to send a commando of 600 men to attack the Khakis from the rear. In the end nothing came of this.

When the British attack appeared inevitable, Prinsloo ordered his burghers to take up position on a ridge of low hills stretching for kilometres from Belmont Station towards the southeast. Prinsloo himself was in the centre with the Fauresmith Commando. He had two Krupp guns and a rapid-fire gun at his disposal. General De la Rey and the Transvaal burghers found themselves at the back with one gun on a hill between Belmont and Ramdam. Commandant Lubbe and the burghers of Jacobsdal were stationed to the west of De la Rey with a light gun. Commandant Van der Merwe was on a hill at the left of the left flank.

THE PRELUDE TO THE BATTLE

The vanguard of Methuen's forces openly approached the Boer positions on the morning of 22 November. The burghers could clearly see the Khakis from the low hills and sporadically fired with their rifles on soldiers who came too close. Prinsloo later on ordered Major Albrecht, the commander of the Orange Free State State Artillery, to open fire on the British. This bombardment certainly made an impression, since soon afterwards 12 British guns were rushed across the veld to answer our fire at such a pace that the poor horses drawing the gun carriages certainly became totally exhausted.

The arrival of the British guns was bad news for the burghers, since they were now subjected to a heavy bombardment. Our gunners came under such intense British fire that Albrecht decided at nightfall to remove his guns from the area. Fortunately they suffered no serious casualties.

For our burghers the night of 22–23 November was not an easy one. The burghers were only too aware of the huge force confronting them. The question was not if the British would attack, but when. Some of the Boers were extremely afraid – especially those who had never been in battle.

Before daybreak the burghers, who had remained in their positions throughout the night, could hear the enemy resuming their preparations. From the direction of the railway line they could hear the heavy iron wheels of the British guns grating on their axles and bumping over the rocky terrain. The sounds became ever louder and they soon also heard the rocking ammunition wagons and the whips of the drivers. They had no idea how many guns there were out there in the darkness, nor how many soldiers were approaching them, since the latter remained invisible and silent in the pitch-black night.

THE FIGHT BEGINS

It was the Boers on the low hills closest to Belmont Station who first saw foot soldiers directly in front of them. They were ordered to hold their fire until the Khakis were close enough to fire on them effectively. Fortunately day was breaking. The closest soldiers were only about 150 metres from the burghers when it became possible to aim accurately in the half-light. It was then that the order came: 'Fire!'

After the tension of the night the Boers eagerly began shooting for all they were worth. The British reaction, after a moment's hesitation, was to charge at our burghers. Firing as quickly as possible, the burghers managed to check the Khaki attack, but after a short while the determined soldiers resumed their advance. Our men were not able to halt them and were soon forced back.

At about this time the British artillery opened a heavy bombardment on the Boer right flank, closest to Belmont itself. They had at least 15 guns, most of them firing shrapnel. Our burghers on the right flank consequently began falling back towards a second ridge of low hills to the east. The British soldiers occupied the first ridge and obviously thought they had already won a victory, since they stood on the summit of the first ridge joyously shouting and waving their rifles in the air. The burghers, however, fired on them from their new position, and ended the attack on the Republican right flank there and then.

THE BOERS FORCED BACK

It was still very early in the morning, barely half past five, when the British units attacked the main position of the Boers in the low hills southeast of Belmont Station, where Prinsloo was in command. Huge numbers of infantry and several guns were used in this concentrated attack. Against such a force our men in the centre could not hold out. They soon began falling back to the north.

Unfortunately the retreat of the burghers in the centre soon turned more or less into a rout. Numerous burghers simply left their wagons, carts and tents behind and fled in panic. Some of those who farmed in the district departed all the way back to their farms.

On the flanks the battle ended less disastrously. There was some disorder initially when the burghers realised that the enemy was breaking through in the centre. However, the commanders convinced their men to remain in line while falling back and most of them took their wagons and guns with them. De la Rey and Lubbe fortunately managed to check the British who were pursuing Prinsloo's men and actually drove them back. Thus the battle ended.

THE SITUATION AFTER THE BATTLE

As far as we can ascertain, 15 burghers were killed and some 30 wounded in the battle at Belmont. In addition we are aware of at least 36 burghers who were taken prisoner of war by the British. One of them is Commandant Serfontein, who did not want to leave his seriously wounded son behind. At first we had no idea how many British casualties there were, but one of our scouts reported today that approximately 75 Khakis were killed and 250 wounded. Some of the wounded Khakis were treated yesterday night by our field ambulance and were handed over to their ambulance this morning.

Even though the British losses were heavier than ours, they won the battle since General Methuen occupied the battlefield. In addition the enemy captured part of our main laager. Some burghers attempted to torch the laager before falling back, but achieved only partial success. We have heard that the enemy's loot included some of our ammunition. Chief Commandant Prinsloo feels so disappointed about his defeat that he has requested President Steyn to relieve him of his responsibilities as a fighting general.

We have little doubt about the reasons for our defeat. In the first place, the British attacked courageously. Equally important is the fact that Prinsloo underestimated the resolve of the enemy and showed very little military skill. Third, there are too many weaknesses in our commando law, which does not make sufficient provision for punishment of disobedient burghers. Fourth, we saw too many burghers who were not fitted out properly, still armed with the old types of rifles such as Martini-Henry muzzle-loaders or other rifles for which we do not have ammunition. According to one Boer officer, only one third of the burghers are fully outfitted. On the positive side, many of our burghers fought with courage and defended their positions valiantly. That gives us hope for the future.

Our scouts report that the British are pitching camp at Belmont Station. Our burghers are at present busy breaking up the railway line south of Graspan. Even though they were repulsed yesterday, they still believe that they can halt the Khakis.

SIEGE OF KIMBERLEY

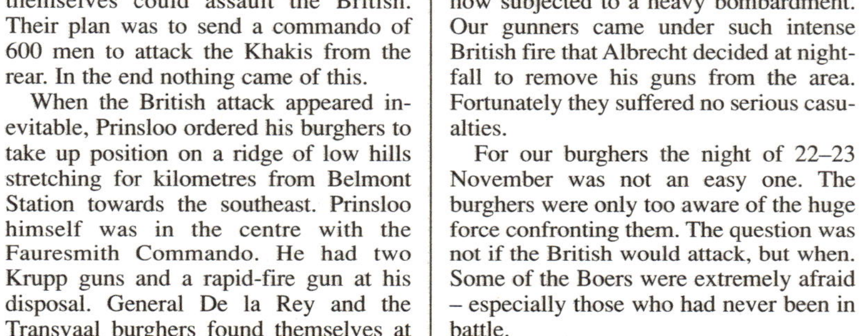

A Republican commando at Kamfer's Dam outside Kimberley

Tarentaalrant, 24 November – For most of the burghers the siege is now becoming a boring routine. Our numbers have dwindled to a frightful extent since many burghers were sent to the south to help stem the British advance across the Orange River. The burghers who are still here are immersed in the daily chores of preparing meals, washing or mending their clothes, reading, writing letters or sleeping after nocturnal sentry duty. The routine at night usually amounts to guarding a fortification or gun emplacement for one shift. In that three- or four-hour period you keep your eyes and your ears open and your rifle at the ready.

As for the British – in addition to launching sporadic attacks on Boer positions, they are sending black rustlers out of the city to capture cattle. At least that is what the blacks who are caught tell us. They say that there is a shortage of food in the city and that the British are slaughtering horses for meat. Our impression is that the blacks are fleeing from the city in their hundreds.

THE FIGHT AT WILLOW GRANGE

Colenso, 24 November – Here at Colenso we had heard no news whatsoever of Commandant-General Joubert and his 2 000 burghers who left on the expedition southwards into Natal last week until a dispatch rider arrived in our camp this afternoon. He reports that all went well but that the Commandant-General and his men are on their way back. There are tens of thousands of British on their way here, he says.

Yesterday the burghers were engaged in a battle with the Khakis at Willow Grange, south of Estcourt. The dispatch rider brought a report on that fight by Joubert's secretary, M.J. Bracht. According to the report the fighting took place on a ridge of low hills between Estcourt and Mooi River. The British attacked our position with infantry, mounted soldiers and artillery. Our men found themselves in an extended position on the grassy slopes with no rocks to use as shelter. It was horrible weather, with rain, mist and thunder. The lighting killed one of our burghers, stunned two and killed six horses; while one British soldier was also hit.

At one stage the enemy forced our burghers to retreat from a hill with the loss of one man dead. They then occupied that hill, shouting: 'Hooray, Majuba has been avenged!' Our gun was dragged up another hill to the right of Estcourt and its range set at 4 500 metres towards the hill that the Khakis had just occupied. Our artillerymen were soon firing one shell after the other into the midst of the enemy. The latter attempted to bombard us from that hill, but their shells fell short, causing no damage to us.

The Khakis soon found themselves between two fires on the occupied hill when Field Cornet Sarel Oosthuizen of Krugersdorp, whom they call the Red Bull, began attacking them from another hill. However, while those soldiers were toppling over like wheat in front of a sickle, more and more Khakis advanced on us from their camp. They were marching behind a stone wall, with the result that we could not see them until they were close to us. Fortunately our artillery soon fired a hole through that wall, ending the enemy approach.

When the battle had been going on for about two hours, the British suddenly began retreating back to Estcourt. Only then did our burghers note a group of mounted Khakis retreating from behind the first hill. Those gentlemen never even participated in the battle! Our people occupied the second hill immediately after the enemy retreat began and in the process captured Major Hobbs and his soldiers.

On this hill our men found eight dead soldiers and everywhere along the stone wall other dead Khakis. They also found 23 wounded Khakis there and 26 elsewhere. Of our people only two were killed and two wounded. The British ambulance told our people that they had already removed 111 killed and wounded soldiers from the place where we found the 23.

LIFE OUTSIDE LADYSMITH

Modderspruit, 24 November (Report by Wilhelm Mangold) – The siege is still going on and our artillery bombard the town and the British camp virtually daily. However, there is no possibility of storming the town, since Commandant-General Joubert has gone on a campaign to the south of Colenso with about 2 000 burghers.

Camp life is starting to take on a regular routine for the ordinary burghers. Each morning they rise at five o'clock at the latest. They first make coffee, and afterwards care for their horses. Then they prepare breakfast. This consists of meat cooked in a pan or roasted over the fire, with bread and coffee. In the meantime the horses are knee-haltered and left to graze in the veld where the black servants look after them.

If there is no specific task that has to be done, such as digging trenches or building gun emplacements, the burghers while away the time until lunch by cleaning their rifles or their saddles, by reading or by writing letters. Lunch is usually between 12 and two o'clock. It consists of meat and rice and sometimes potatoes and even vegetables. After lunch many burghers loiter about or visit friends in neighbouring laagers. At five o'clock the horses are fetched and tied to trees close to the laager. Each horse is given a small measure of oats or mealies.

After dinner, which usually also consists of meat, the burghers either move off to their trenches for sentry duty, or keep themselves busy in the laager. Those at the guard posts usually work on the trenches by strengthening the walls or erecting barbed-wire obstructions. Each burgher must do one hour of sentry duty each night.

Each commando sends a cart or a wagon to Modderspruit Station each morning to fetch supplies and fodder for the horses. This is supplied from Pretoria by train. Cattle are slaughtered daily and the meat is distributed to the field cornetcies according to need. Most burghers sleep in round, green tents supplied by the authorities. In many laagers there is a huge tent right in the centre where religious services are held.

There are of course many burghers who while away the time with games or even sport competitions. Thus, there are competitions in running, long jump, high jump and shot put and of course traditional sports between field cornetcies and sometimes even laagers. Tug-of-war is extremely popular. So are three-leg races, potato races, sack races, finger pulling and baboon races.

Horse racing is always a popular activity amongst the burghers and takes place regularly. Other games in which the burghers participate in teams are marbles and horseshoes. In some cases the burghers even play football, but balls are in short supply around Ladysmith. Many burghers, especially the younger ones, love to go swimming in the Modderspruit or the Klip River when the weather is fine. There are lovely swimming pools in both rivers.

One of the most important rituals here on commando is the bouncing of novices. A man is not accepted as a fully-fledged burgher before being bounced. As soon as it becomes known that a novice has arrived and has to be bounced, the hide of a recently slaughtered ox is prepared for the ritual. The hide is spread open on the ground with the hairy side up. Openings are cut around the edges of the hide. The novice lies on his back on the hide. Between 12 and 15 men take up position around him, pick up the hide by putting their hands through the openings, pull the skin tight and then begin rhythmically lifting up and down. When everybody is ready they count one, two and on three launch the novice four or five metres into the air. The poor victim lands on the tightly stretched hide, only to bounce up immediately again. If he utters no complaint, he is usually released after three bounces. Novices who protest are sometimes bounced up to 10 times. Even though it seldom happens that anybody gets hurt, it is extremely unpleasant to land on your head even though the hide gives way a little bit. Even officers are bounced, and the Reverend A.J. Louw was given this treatment at Sandspruit.

One gets the impression here in the laagers at Ladysmith that no Boer can survive without a black servant. Everywhere in and around the laagers there are servants carrying out tasks such as grooming horses, collecting firewood, making fire, and cleaning pots. Many burghers bring their own servants and the government even sends black workers here. They get the same food and clothing that the burghers do, but receive no payment. And they may of course not participate in the fighting.

Boer artillerymen with their howitzer outside Ladysmith

Boers fetching water for their morning coffee

FROM THE EDITOR

Our prediction last week that a difficult time lay ahead for the Republican forces was confirmed when the British offensive across the Orange River started in all seriousness. There is no cause for panic: we believe that had an experienced military officer – such as General Piet Cronjé or General De la Rey, or an enterprising youngster such as General Botha – been in command, our forces would have had no difficulty repulsing the British onslaught on Belmont.

The Republican military authorities' decision to unite their forces to halt the British offensive is a wise tactic. The concentration of thousands of burghers around towns like Mafeking and now even Kuruman to besiege the British garrisons there is not only a waste of energy, but also reflects bad judgement of priorities. We should concentrate our forces where the war will be either won or lost. What is essential now is to repulse the main British forces that threaten the Republics from Natal and the Cape Colony.

In this issue we bring you, in addition to our usual military reports, a description of life on commando. One of our burghers at Ladysmith, Wilhelm Mangold, drew up a lively account of the circumstances in a Boer laager near that town. The military officer whose career we highlight this week is Piet Cronjé, our commander on the western border and the victor over Rhodes's freebooter friend L.S. Jameson back in 1896.

KURUMAN BESIEGED

Vryburg, 24 November – In addition to Mafeking and Kimberley there is only one town in the northern Cape where the Boer forces are opposed. That is Kuruman, on the edge of the Kalahari Desert. General De la Rey was informed early in November that the Cape Police in Kuruman were recruiting both whites and blacks to serve as volunteers to defend the town. They had established a camp in the centre of the town and were busy erecting fortifications consisting of stone walls and sandbags.

On 9 November General Piet Cronjé ordered Field Cornet J.H. Visser, whom De la Rey had left in command of Vryburg, to occupy Kuruman. Visser immediately left with 200 men and reached Kuruman two days later. He demanded the surrender of the town from the local magistrate, but the latter refused.

When Visser and his men advanced on Kuruman on 13 November the defenders opened fire on them vigorously. Visser did not want to expose his men to unnecessary risks and disengaged. He was told by black people in the vicinity that the British had placed dynamite within their fortifications and intended to explode it should the Boers succeed in occupying the fortifications. Visser reacted by abandoning his occupation plans and sending back a dispatch rider to ask Cronjé for assistance. In the meantime he allowed his men to fire on the British defenders of the town.

Cronjé's answer arrived after about one week. Visser was told to leave Kuruman and return to Vryburg immediately to assist with halting the British advance from the south. That is now the most important task. Visser obeyed this order and immediately returned here. However, he hopes to return to Kuruman to occupy that town as soon as possible.

OUR MILITARY OFFICERS

General Piet Cronjé

Pieter Arnoldus Cronjé was born in 1836 in the Colesberg district of the Cape Colony. He is the second son of Andries Petrus Cronjé and Johanna Christina Geldenhuis and is the elder brother of Commandant Andries Cronjé of the Potchefstroom Commando. He was a mere boy when his parents moved to Transorangia and in 1848 to the Potchefstroom District in Transvaal. He attended school there for a brief period and married Hester Susanna Visser in 1857.

Cronjé became the Assistant Field Cornet of the Schoonspruit Ward in 1857. In 1865 he participated in a military campaign for the first time when he joined the Transvaal forces that rushed to the assistance of the Orange Free State in its war against the Basuto. In the meantime he was a farmer. He did not participate in political activities and stayed out of the public eye.

It was the British annexation of Transvaal in 1877 that pushed Cronjé to centre stage. In December 1879 he was elected one of the 30 Boer 'foremen' at Wonderfontein. From October 1880 he took the lead in the resistance of some Transvaal Boers against the payment of taxes to the British authorities. Two months later he attended the meeting at Paardekraal when the Transvaal Boers reinstated their Republic.

In the Transvaal War of Independence that immediately followed Cronjé served as Assistant Commandant-General. He was the commander of the Boer force that besieged the British garrison in their fort of sandbags outside Potchefstroom until the latter surrendered toward the end of the war.

In 1881 Cronjé was elected to the Volksraad. Three years later he became the Acting Commandant-General and a member of the Executive Council of the South African Republic. In 1889 he was re-elected to the Volksraad, but after 18 months resigned there. For the next six years he was the Commandant of Potchefstroom.

It was the Jameson Raid of December 1895 that made Cronjé famous. He acted quickly and decisively and on New Year's Day 1896 captured the invaders at Doornkop near Krugersdorp. Later that same year he again became a member of the Executive Council and Superintendent of Native Affairs.

Cronjé was one of the prominent Boers who hoped right up to the end that there would not be a war. When it did break out last month he was appointed Assistant Commandant-General and placed in command of the Republican forces on the western border of the Republics. It is now his task to halt the British offensive across the Orange River and to ensure that the British do not relieve the besieged garrison in Kimberley.

General Piet Cronjé

THE

War Reporter

WEEKLY EDITION

Number 8 **Pretoria, South African Republic** **2 December 1899**

BOER FORCES REPULSED AT GRASPAN AND AT MODDER RIVER

Setbacks on the Free State western border

Jacobsdal, 1 December – The Republican forces on the Free State western border suffered one setback after the other this week. Not even the most able generals could prevent the Khakis from forcing the burgher commandos back on two occasions. The only positive aspect is that the enemy in both cases suffered many more casualties than the Republican forces did.

Numerous Free State burghers expressed their dissatisfaction with the leadership of Chief Commandant Jacobus Prinsloo after the battle at Belmont Station on which we reported last week. Some of them demanded leave to return to their farms – and some simply left the front. General Koos de la Rey arrived on the western border at that stage with some 600 men. He managed to restore the morale of the Free State burghers, but their total strength is barely 2 000 burghers.

De la Rey realised that his best chance of halting General Methuen's huge forces was to deploy his burghers on a series of low hills north of Graspan Station and to damage as much as possible of the railway line south of that station. This was done early on the morning of 24 November.

Soon afterwards a British armoured train came steaming from the south. It was accompanied by a group of mounted British troops. The train stopped where the railway line was broken up, but the mounted troops pushed on right up to the low hills. The Boers saw them approaching, but waited until they were very close before opening fire with their Krupp gun on the train and their rifles on the soldiers. The British immediately fell back with the loss of at least three men, including an officer killed.

In the night the British approached again. They repaired the railway line and early on the morning of 25 November seven trains heavily loaded with troops and supplies reached Graspan Station. Thousands of other troops approached on foot or on horseback from the south. The Boers watched the British approach but could not halt them. They had to wait for a British attack. At six o'clock that morning they did fire one shot on a British armoured train with their Krupp gun, but missed the target.

THE BATTLE AT GRASPAN

The British reaction to the single shot fired by the Boer artillery was to start a bombardment. The Boer artillery answered this fire. In the meantime, mounted British troops attempted to outflank De la Rey's left flank, but our artillery drove them back with the help of the burghers of the Fauresmith Commando. This part of the battle took place on the Free State side of the border and can be regarded as the first armed confrontation within a Boer Republic during this war. Boer scouts report that a number of Khakis and their horses were killed or wounded on this part of the front.

That morning at about nine o'clock thousands of British infantry approached the Boers across the flat terrain to enter the battle. The British attack was aimed at a low hill on the left flank of the main Boer position, where the burghers of the Jacobsdal Commando under Commandant Lubbe were stationed. The British bombarded the hill with abandon, but fortunately the rocks rather than the burghers suffered under the shrapnel.

While the bombardment was still in progress, the first infantry soldiers began ascending the hill. A heavy battle followed. The brave Commandant Lubbe was wounded when a piece of shrapnel hit him in the eye, but he kept encouraging his burghers to defend their position.

De la Rey and the Transvaal burghers found themselves under attack on the low hill on the Boer right flank, from where they had a clear view of the railway line. De la Rey had dispatched a message to Jacobsdal early that morning urgently requesting reinforcements. However, no help arrived. The Transvaalers initially managed to hold out, but they saw more and more British approaching over the battlefield and realised that the huge numbers of the enemy would eventually become impossible to contain.

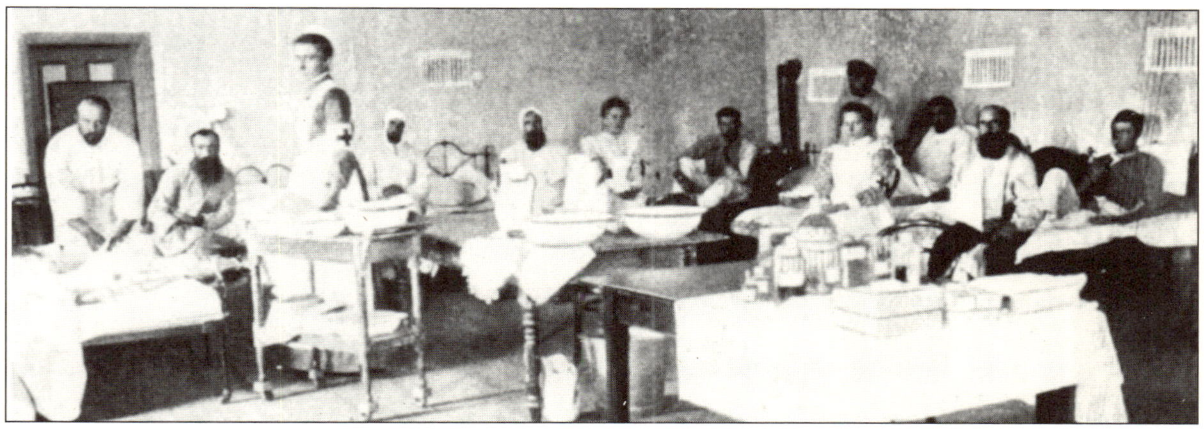

The Republican military hospital at Jacobsdal

Lubbe and his men were in a similar position. They fought with courage, but were eventually driven back by the massive number of enemy soldiers. One of their biggest problems was that they began running out of ammunition and that their ammunition wagon had earlier been withdrawn from the battlefield. In addition they noticed that the enemy was beginning to outflank them. In order to ensure that his men would not all be captured, Lubbe ordered them to retreat.

When De la Rey realised that his centre was disintegrating, he was forced to order a general retreat. This time the Boers fell back in orderly fashion and took all their guns and wagons with them. A mounted British unit attempted to outflank them, but was repulsed.

The Republican losses amount to about 20 killed and 40 wounded, while approximately 25 burghers were taken prisoner. We have no particulars on the extent of British casualties, but believe that it was much higher than ours. The tragedy is that they can again claim to have scored a victory over us.

While the Boers were retreating towards the Modder River under the command of De la Rey, they saw a huge cloud of dust in the northeast – the direction of Jacobsdal. They subsequently heard that it was the large commando under General Piet Cronjé that had arrived from Mafeking and that the latter would henceforth be in command of the campaign against the British. The arrival of Cronjé's men considerably cheered the dejected burghers.

BOERS DIG IN AT MODDER RIVER

Fortunately for our burghers the British halted for a few days after the battle of Graspan. We heard in the meantime that their losses in that battle amounted to 18 killed and about 140 wounded. In addition they are finding it difficult to procure enough fodder and water for all their horses.

De la Rey realised that the Khakis would eventually resume their advance. He and Cronjé decided to prepare defensive positions next to the railway line at the confluence of the Modder and Riet rivers some 40 kilometres south of Kimberley. The British would have to advance that way, since they were completely dependent on the railway line to transport supplies for their huge army.

The total Boer force consisted of about 2 000 burghers. They had five or six Krupp guns and four pom-poms at their disposal. On De la Rey's insistence, most of the burghers took up position on the south bank of the Riet River, where the steep riverbank, similar to a trench, provided natural cover. Cronjé's burghers were stationed on the Boer left flank with De la Rey in the centre on both sides of the railway line and Prinsloo and his Free Staters on the right flank. The Boers blew up the railway bridge with dynamite to ensure that the British would not be able to use it.

Methuen probably did not know that the Boers would oppose his soldiers at the Riet River. Our scouts took up position in the top branches of the poplar trees at the confluence of the rivers and studied the British movements from their elevated positions. They never saw any British scout near the river.

THE BATTLE OF MODDER RIVER

The British resumed their offensive on the morning of 28 November. The first soldiers approached our left flank on horseback at about six o'clock, but retreated under fire. Then, from the tops of the trees our scouts noticed hundreds of British foot soldiers and guns approaching. General Cronjé was concerned that the British would attempt to outflank us on the eastern side, so he dispatched one Krupp and one rapid-fire gun in that direction at about seven o'clock. The British artillery fired on those guns and our artillerymen were forced to retreat.

After these early manoeuvres there was a brief period of ominous silence at the river confluence. Then our scouts reported from the treetops that the British infantry was moving towards us. The burghers prepared to confront them, and were instructed to wait until the British were within 300 metres before opening fire.

The closer the British infantry came, the clearer it was that they were not expecting us at the river. By about eight o'clock they were less than 800 metres from our positions and marching towards us in the open. In spite of the order to wait, some burghers unfortunately opened fire at that time. Thus they revealed our position and lost us the element of surprise. Even so the Khakis were subjected to a murderous fire.

Most of the Khakis dived for cover right where they were, and were pinned down flat on their stomachs until sundown that evening. The Boer artillery continuously fired shells at them. The soldiers probably suffered terribly, since it was an extremely hot day. General Cronjé's secretary says that his thermometer indicated a temperature of 43° C that afternoon. Our men felt the heat too, but the difference was that there was some shade and sufficient water to drink next to the river.

UNFORTUNATE TURN OF EVENTS

By early afternoon we were confident that we had halted the Khakis and that they would have to fall back after dark. Unfortunately, they eventually discovered our weak spot, and succeeded in driving Commandant Prinsloo's burghers of the right flank back across the Modder River. We established afterwards that many of those burghers fled in panic without even being fired on by the enemy.

About 500 Khakis now occupied Rossmead village (also called Richie) on the north bank of the river. From there they attempted to attack the Boer positions from the rear. Fortunately the burghers of other commandos managed to drive them back to Rossmead in a counter-attack. Here the names of Commandant Piet Fourie of the Bloemfontein commando, Adriaan de la Rey (the brother of General Koos de la Rey), their burghers and Major Albrecht, who used his guns with great effect, deserve mention.

Even though the Boers managed to halt the British attack and to a large extent to remain in control of the battlefield until darkness ended the fighting, they subsequently decided to fall back. It was General Cronjé who gave the order that the Boers should retreat under cover of night. He argued that the Boers would not be able to hold their position on the Riet River when the British resumed their attack. The danger was that they could be surrounded. Consequently the Boers abandoned their positions.

Continued overleaf

FROM THE EDITOR

This was not a good week for the Republican forces. Indeed, some of the events on which we report today throw a dark shade over our prospects. It becomes clearer every day that the British are determined to do all in their power to defeat our forces. Both in Natal and on the Western Front more and more Khakis are arriving daily with more and more artillery. At the beginning of the war the burghers joked about the British field guns, but the naval guns that fire on us with lyddite shells are frightening. For the first time we are seriously wondering: will we be able to stop the enemy?

Even more disturbing than the Khaki offensive is the incident at Derdepoort on which we briefly report today. We have only received a brief report on the Bakgatla attack this week on that village on the western border, but from what we know it seems as if the British are inciting the blacks to attack us. Or is it perhaps the Bakgatla who are exploiting the conflict between us and the British to their own advantage? Let us hope and pray that this will prove to be an isolated incident.

We are worried about the numbers of burghers who are evading their duty. Some of our burghers simply stay away from the battlefield, while others abandon their positions rather than confront the enemy. Ongoing reports on burghers who ask for leave at any time of the day – 'leave plague', the officers call this tendency – reach us daily. Now is no time to take leave. All of us must stand together to fight for our freedom.

Continued

General De la Rey, who received a slight wound in the course of the afternoon, supported that decision. He agreed that it was essential for the Boers to ensure that they were not surrounded and forced to surrender since that would result in a British breakthrough on a major scale.

For De la Rey the forced retreat was a double blow. He blamed it on the Free State burghers who abandoned their positions on the right flank, allowing the British to cross the river and threaten our rear. De la Rey is especially angry about this since, in his opinion, this happened after the Boers had won the battle. We have been informed that he told a foreign correspondent: 'My son was killed in the battle. But that loss was not as bitter to me as the abandonment of our positions. Had we been able to hold out, the enemy would have been forced to fall back to the Orange River, since there is not sufficient water between the Modder and Orange Rivers for Methuen's mass of soldiers and animals. And had they retreated that far, we could have formed a continuous line with the forces of Generals Grobler and Schoeman along the Orange River and halted the Khakis.'

During this battle, which some burghers call the Battle of Modder River and others the Battle of Two Rivers, the British suffered far heavier losses than the Boers. The total British loss was about 70 killed and 400 wounded. On the Boer side 16 men were killed and 50 wounded.

One of the Boers who were killed was General De la Rey's eldest son, Adriaan (Adaan), hit by a bombshell on the day of his 19th birthday. Since there was no ambulance to be found, General De la Rey and a number of burghers decided to take Adriaan to the Republican field hospital at Jacobsdal, a distance of about 14 kilometres.

Since Adriaan would not have been able to stand the bumping of a horse cart, they carried him in a blanket. Adriaan was a big man and it was a difficult undertaking. Totally exhausted, they only reached their destination late that night. For Adriaan it was too late. He died about an hour later in his father's arms.

REPUBLICAN AMBULANCE PERSONNEL CAPTURED

Early this morning the British captured our ambulance personnel while they were busy treating our wounded under a Red Cross flag. We have heard that they are being taken to Cape Town as prisoners of war. Their number includes seven doctors as well as 28 ambulance ordinances.

General Cronjé is furious, since it is a contravention of the Geneva Convention to take the enemy's medical personnel prisoner. He made an official complaint to Methuen and demanded that the ambulance personnel be sent back immediately and released. We believe that the British will accede to those demands.

The only locality between the Modder River and Kimberley now left in which to set up a defence is the low hills in the area of Magersfontein, barely 20 kilometres south of Kimberley. All our burghers are retreating to Magersfontein.

MURDER AT DERDEPOORT

Black warriors attack white women

Pretoria, 30 November – One of the most scandalous events imaginable took place this week when black warriors attacked the village of Derdepoort. This small settlement is situated in the north of the Marico district, on the Transvaal side of the border with Bechuanaland. The black warriors were commanded by the Bakgatla chief Linchwe and acted in cooperation with a British force. They not only attacked the Boer commando stationed at Derdepoort on the eastern bank of the Marico River, but also killed a number of the village's inhabitants and abducted a group of white women and children.

A report on this horrendous incident by Acting Commandant Kirstein to the Transvaal government reached Pretoria today: 'On Saturday morning 25 November we were attacked at daybreak by about 300 mounted British soldiers who fired from the other side of the river on us with a machine gun and Lee-Metford rifles. At the same time we were attacked by a commando of blacks from the direction of the transport road. We do not know how many there were, but they covered the whole veld.

'The battle went on till about ten o'clock this morning, when the enemy retreated in the direction of Mochudi. Of the enemy about 50 were killed. According to a statement of one of the wounded blacks, their commando consisted of subjects of Khama, Sechele and Linchwe. They were allegedly hired to attack us and were literally driven through the river by the English and threatened with the machine gun if they did not attack.

'Helpless women were murdered by the blacks even though they hoisted white flags. The survivors were then abducted. This murder is the most barbaric ever committed in the name of a civilised authority. Our burghers courageously repulsed the attack with the help of God.'

Kirstein added a list of the Boer casualties to his report. He states that five members of the commando were killed and 14 wounded as well as nine inhabitants of Derdepoort, including two women killed. The other women and children were abducted to Mochudi, the head village of Chief Linchwe. At this stage we know nothing more than Kirstein's report, but we will keep our readers informed on any further developments.

PRESIDENT STEYN ADMONISHES FREE STATE BURGHERS

Bloemfontein, 30 November – The majority of the Free State burghers who were involved in the battle at Modder River on the 28th defended their positions admirably. However a small number dismally failed to do their duty – and have since then been severely reprimanded. Today all the Free State commandos received a telegram from President Steyn with orders that it must be read to all burghers and officers. It is absolutely clear that the Free State president has no sympathy with burghers who fail to do their duty in this war.

Even though it is not stated in the telegram, we believe Steyn's anger is aimed at the burghers who abandoned their positions in the battle at Modder River, thus allowing the British to outflank our position. In addition he is concerned that not all Free State burghers are at the front participating in the struggle. Here we publish parts of that telegram:

'We cannot express our thankfulness to God loudly enough for all the support He has provided to us thus far; and we recognise with thanks the valour revealed by our burghers in confronting the enemy forces, but it is my duty to remind you that we can only expect help from above as long as there is cooperation and love amongst our officers and burghers and if all do their duty.

'I have learned with dismay that only about 1 000 men of the Free State fought at Modder River, while the others stayed in the camp leaving their brothers to confront the enemy.

'Such conduct will have devastating effects on our freedom as a nation. Therefore I remind you that it is your duty to obey your officers and it is the duty of the officers to accompany their burghers into battle.'

We have some sympathy with the Free State burghers who fled at Modder River. These men had recently been in the front line at Belmont and at Graspan, where they were vastly outnumbered and forced to retreat. Now they had to face the murderous fire of the Khakis again. Under those circumstances one can understand that they yielded to the temptation to run for their lives.

President Steyn (seated in the centre beneath the flag of the Orange Free State) with burghers at the front

THE NATAL FRONT

Colenso, 27 November – Last week we published a report by M.J. Bracht, Commandant-General Joubert's secretary, on the battle at Willow Grange south of Estcourt on 22–23 November. Joubert and his patrol arrived here in Colenso earlier today in a bone-tired state. They told us that two Boers had been killed and two wounded during that battle. The British casualties were at least 11 killed, 60 wounded and eight captured. After the fight Joubert decided to return to the Tugela River, regarding it as the most suitable position from which to check the British advance. On 24 November he himself was badly hurt when he fell from his horse.

We have now heard that General Buller, the British supreme commander in South Africa, arrived in Durban on 25 November. This is a clear indication that the main British offensive against the Republics will take place via Natal.

The Boer chief magazine master and staff with a variety of munitions

OUR MILITARY OFFICERS

General Koos de la Rey

Jacobus Hercules de la Rey was born in 1847. He is the sixth child of Adrianus Gysbertus de la Rey popularly known as Tall Adriaan de la Rey and his wife Adriana Wilhelmina van Rooyen. His parents were farming in the Winburg district of the Orange Free State when he was born. Later they moved to the Wolmaransstad district in the Transvaal, where he spent his early life. He received virtually no formal education and was taught the basic skills at home.

After the discovery of diamonds his parents moved to Kimberley and De la Rey became a transport rider. In 1876 he married Jacoba Elizabeth Greeff, a daughter of the well-known Hendrik Adriaan Greeff, the founder of the town Lichtenburg. The young couple settled on the farm Manana and later on at Elandsfontein close to Lichtenburg. They have ten children. De la Rey became a successful farmer. His abilities quickly drew the attention of the authorities and he served occasionally as Native Commissioner and as a surveyor of farms on the Transvaal western border. In these capacities he gained an intimate knowledge of both that part of the country and its inhabitants.

De la Rey has wide military experience. As a boy he participated in the war between the Free State and the Basuto of King Moshweshwe in 1865. In 1876 he was a Field Cornet in the forces of the South African Republic that fought the Bapedi of Chief Sekhukhune. Four years later he became an officer in the Transvaal War of Independence and in 1896 he participated in the campaign against Jameson's freebooters. From 1885 to 1893 he was the commandant of Lichtenburg.

In 1893 De la Rey was elected as a member of the First Volksraad. He firmly believed that his first duty in that council was to represent the wishes and needs of his constituency. He is known as a firm supporter of the policies of Commandant-General Piet Joubert, and an outspoken critic of President Kruger's affinity to appoint Dutch officials. He is regarded as just but firm in his dealings with others, calm and moderate in his actions. His extreme loyalty to his Republic is legendary. De la Rey did his utmost to keep the Republics from entering this war, but in vain. In spite of his belief that war was the wrong option, his patriotism has never been in doubt. For that reason Commandant-General Joubert appointed him as fighting general and adviser to General Piet Cronjé, the Republican commander on the western border.

De la Rey achieved fame early in this war when he captured the British armoured train at Kraaipan. Unfortunately he has already experienced personal tragedy, since his eldest son was killed at the Modder River in the past week. As reported, he himself was lightly wounded.

De la Rey is a tall man, sinewy in build, with a dignified bearing. He has deep-set dark eyes, a prominent Roman nose and a large, dark brown beard, giving his face a strong, patrician expression.

General J.H. de la Rey

THE War Reporter
WEEKLY EDITION

Number 9   Pretoria, South African Republic   9 December 1899

JOUBERT SERIOUSLY INJURED
Louis Botha now commander at the Tugela

Colenso, 3 December – It is with regret that we have to report that our elderly commander, Commandant-General Piet Joubert, has been badly injured. As previously reported, he fell from his horse on 24 November. Initially it seemed as if Joubert was not badly hurt. He actually completed the journey back here on horseback. However, soon after his return he complained that he was constantly in pain. At the insistence of the personnel of the Republican field ambulance he received treatment, issuing orders and taking military decisions from his bed until his deteriorating condition decided the doctors to send him by train to the field hospital in Volksrust.

Before Joubert left the front he appointed his colleague on the Transvaal Executive Council, General Schalk Burger of the Lydenburg Commando, as the acting Commandant-General and commander over the siege of Ladysmith. In addition he appointed General Louis Botha of Vryheid as commander of the Republican forces on the Tugela River front.

All the burghers here at Colenso sympathise sincerely with the highly respected Joubert. At the same time they are glad that he appointed Botha, who has made a name for himself as a talented officer, filled with initiative and with the ability to lead the fight to a successful conclusion as commander on the front. It is reported from Pretoria that President Kruger has full confidence in young Botha.

FROM THE EDITOR

This week saw little military activity – perhaps the proverbial quiet before the storm. The Khakis seem to be preparing to resume their offensive on all fronts except the far north. Our burghers are just as diligently preparing to repulse the expected attacks. Even though things are quiet, we suffered a major setback with the serious injury to Commandant-General Joubert. It is our sincere hope that our wise (though at times over-cautious) supreme commander will recover soon.

The injury to Joubert was an unhappy accident; a second piece of bad news from the Natal front was brought about by negligence. The Republican authorities will have to punish those who allowed the successful British attack on one of our Long Tom siege guns at Ladysmith. On a more positive note, our correspondents on the Natal front were fortunate enough to gain information from within Ladysmith in the form of newspapers.

Fortunately there was no further involvement of black communities in the war. We hope to be able to report more fully soon on what happened at Derdepoort on 25 November.

SIEGE OF KIMBERLEY
Boer besiegers surprised twice

Tarentaalrand, 7 December – The siege of Kimberley is a low-key affair at present, since the Republican authorities have switched their attention to the front south of the city. On the morning of 25 November our burghers suffered a severe setback. Field Cornet H.J. Otto of the Bloemhof Commando and his burghers, who were on sentry duty at Carter's Ridge west of the city, fell asleep and were overwhelmed by a British unit. A skirmish followed in which nine Boers were killed, 21 wounded and 30 captured by the enemy. Otto is one of the 30. The British also captured the front section of one of our gun carriages and one of our ammunition wagons. We are ignorant of the number of British casualties.

This catastrophe could have been much worse, had General S.P. du Toit not rushed to the assistance of the Bloemhof burghers with about 100 Wolmaransstad burghers immediately he heard the Khakis were attacking Otto. After a fierce skirmish they forced the British patrol to retreat to Kimberley. Du Toit subsequently severely criticised the Bloemhof burghers in his official report: 'This fatal incident can in the first place be blamed on the culpable unpreparedness and complacency of the burghers and their refusal to carry out orders, since the enemy was on our men before they realised it.'

On 27 November the British again attempted to break the siege. We assume that they are aware that General Methuen's force is approaching, since they moved out of the city towards the south with an armoured train. However, our burghers repulsed them.

Early yesterday morning it was battle time again. This time at least 1 800 soldiers charged our fortifications south of the city. Initially our burghers were hard pressed, but Boers from other positions rushed to assist their comrades. We brought our guns into action and the attackers were repulsed. After the battle we heard from the British ambulance personnel that their casualties numbered 24 killed, including their valiant commander, Major Henry Scott Turner, and 32 wounded. On our side two men were killed and 10 wounded.

RAILWAY BRIDGE OVER TUGELA DEMOLISHED
Boers aim at rendering British advance impossible

Colenso, 8 December – Commandant-General Joubert convened a war council meeting that was attended by all the Republican officers in this vicinity immediately before he left for treatment at Volksrust. This meeting decided at the urgent request of General Louis Botha that the Tugela River with the high ridge on its northern bank would form the ideal natural fortification for the Boers to halt the British offensive from the south. The burghers are now preparing defensive positions all along the northern bank of the Tugela both east and west of the railway line. Botha personally indicated to each commando where it should dig itself in. The burghers are continually busy with the difficult task of building walls, digging trenches and camouflaging their positions.

One of the most unpleasant but unavoidable realities of war is the accompanying destruction. Since the British armies are more or less dependent on railway lines for communication and logistical purposes, the Republican forces spend a lot of energy on damaging or destroying railway lines, bridges and culverts. On 28 November we watched as our men blew up the impressive railway bridge of 154 metres across the Tugela River. An engineer placed a total of 40 loads of dynamite under the bridge and exploded them simultaneously by means of an electrical device. The bridge broke up in five places and is a total wreck.

Botha furthermore destroyed all the drifts across the river so that it would not be easy for the British to cross. His mounted patrols continuously ride up and down the river to ensure that nobody crosses unseen, while Boer scouts are permanently stationed in the heights above the river to inspect the whole southern area with their binoculars. Botha himself tirelessly moves up and down the front to support his burghers and to ensure that his orders are carried out. With the assent of Commandant-General Joubert, Botha ordered that all the burghers in Natal, with the exception of the commandos keeping up the siege of Ladysmith, must report at the Tugela. All home leave is cancelled. As many guns as possible are positioned along the Tugela to help repulse the expected British advance.

It is interesting to take note of the advice that Joubert has given Botha by telegram. He reminded him that the mainstay of Boer power is the rifle and not artillery. It is often better to have no guns at all, since they seldom trouble the enemy but always reveal our position. In the Transvaal War of Independence of 1880–81 the Boers scored their biggest victories without artillery. The same may happen in this war. The Boers must be careful not to reveal their positions to the attacking enemy before the soldiers are within easy rifle range. The closer the British are when the Boers open fire, the more accurate and deadly the Boers will be – and the more certain of victory.

Colenso railway bridge

NEWS FROM LADYSMITH

Modderspruit, 7 December – On 3 December the burghers captured a Brit who had left Ladysmith on horseback. He introduced himself as George Lynch, newspaper reporter, and said he wanted to exchange news. He offered us a few editions of the Ladysmith newspaper *Lyre*. The *Lyre* contains interesting details on everyday life in the besieged town of Ladysmith, but no military information of any value. Our military authorities allowed Lynch to proceed by train to Pretoria.

A telegraph official from Ladysmith, W.F. Mitchell, alleges that he managed to break through the British lines and eventually found his way to Pietermaritzburg. A report by him on conditions in the besieged town was published in the *Natal Mercury*. He claims that the inhabitants of Ladysmith enjoy life, notwithstanding the siege. Concerts and sports tournaments are often held. Mitchell also writes about three other newspapers published in Ladysmith. One is called the *Ladysmith Bombshell* and is illustrated by Mr Roberts, previously of the Pretoria Press. The other two are called *Daily Graphic's Own* and *Society News*.

Today our scouts captured a Natalian who attempted to flee from Ladysmith. He had numbers 1 to 3 of the above-mentioned *Ladysmith Bombshell* in his possession. It is a hand-written newssheet and contains numerous references to our officers and guns, but unfortunately hardly any particulars about conditions in the town.

PRESIDENT KRUGER'S APPEAL

Jacobsdal, 8 December – In the past week President Steyn visited the Republican laager at Magersfontein. He took a message from President Kruger with him and read it to the burghers. The elderly Transvaal leader appeals to all Republicans to remain loyal to God, country and comrades:

'All our officers and burghers must remember that if we want to defend our independence and to ensure that the enemy does not occupy our country, we will have to resist manfully and we cannot fall back.

'God has proven that he is with us, since the enemy have suffered hundreds killed and we only a few.

'I have noted that at times the absence of cooperation has been the cause of our setbacks. We must stand together to defend our country to the death.'

Number 9   9 December 1899

NEWS FROM THE SOUTHERN FRONT
Boers ready to face British onslaught

Bloemfontein, 8 December – In our previous report on developments in the north-eastern Cape Colony, we mentioned that the Boers had occupied Aliwal North, Burgersdorp, Colesberg and other smaller places. General Hendrik Schoeman has in the meantime received reports on the activities of British military units in that area. He is especially concerned about the arrival of a large British force at the Noupoort Railway Junction. Schoeman's scouts have established that the commander of that force is General French – the same British officer who inflicted defeat on General Kock's burghers at Elandslaagte in Natal in October.

The British have begun repairing the railway line north of Noupoort, which was previously damaged by our burghers. This worries Schoeman, but he is powerless to do anything about it, since he does not have a strong force at his disposal. On 22 November, moreover, he heard that the British had captured a number of outspoken pro-Republican inhabitants of the Noupoort area. The pro-Republicans in Colesberg now want to know what he intends doing to defend them. In response, he has placed a number of pro-British inhabitants of Colesberg in detention – small consolation for the Cape Afrikaners. In addition he has increased his reconnaissance patrols.

On 23 November Schoeman's concern deepened when he was told that a group of Khakis were on their way to the Stormberg Railway Junction southeast of Colesberg. His conclusion is that the British are preparing a full-scale onslaught on the southern Free State. These developments were discussed at a war council under Schoeman's chairmanship. It was decided that the best action would be to stop occupying towns in the north-eastern Cape and to unite the Republican forces and take up position at the most opportune places along the railway lines to repulse the expected British offensive.

Schoeman telegraphed these decisions to President Steyn. The latter had in the meantime received a copy of *Ons Land* of 13 November from Cape Town, in which it was reported that there were 2 000 British soldiers at Noupoort and thousands more on their way there. In the light of that news Steyn supports the war council's decisions. The President therefore ordered that all the railway lines to the south must be damaged as far as possible and that Chief Commandant Esaias Grobler and General Schoeman are to co-operate.

We have been informed that President Kruger is extremely concerned about these developments in the northeastern Cape Colony. He feels that the burghers should do all in their power to keep the British from repairing the railway lines.

Chief Commandant Grobler occupied the Stormberg Railway Junction on 26 November, and his burghers then began damaging railway lines in the vicinity. Schoeman was informed that the Khakis were approaching Colesberg from Noupoort and that his most southerly outpost, namely that of Field Cornet Coetzer at Arundel Station, was retreating towards Colesberg.

President Steyn has no doubt now that the British are concentrating on three targets, namely Kimberley, Noupoort and Stormberg. He therefore had an order signalled to Chief Commandant Olivier that the latter was to proceed to Stormberg as quickly as possible with all the Free State burghers and Cape Afrikaner volunteers he could muster, to relieve Chief Commandant Grobler, who would then proceed to Colesberg to assist General Schoeman.

Olivier was in Dordrecht on Saturday 2 December when he received this order. At that time he was busy visiting one town after the other to establish Boer control and to recruit Afrikaners to join his commando. He had already visited Rhodes, Lady Grey, Barkly East and Jamestown.

Olivier did not question the order. He dispatched Commandant De Wet with 300 burghers to Stormberg that same afternoon. Two days later he himself followed with the rest of his burghers, about 500 men. In addition he sent a message to Aliwal North that the 150 burghers who were guarding his wagon laager were to proceed to Stormberg immediately. After their arrival at Stormberg the burghers began constructing fortifications to protect their positions against a possible British attack.

Olivier himself arrived there on 6 December. Of his total force of 1 050 burghers approximately 400 are Cape Afrikaners. The force consists of a commando of Cape rebels under Commandant P. Steenkamp, the Bethulie Commando under Commandant Du Plooy, the Smithfield Commando under Commandant Swanepoel and the Rouxville Commando commanded by himself. Chief Commandant Grobler is also at Stormberg, but plans to proceed to Colesberg to join General Schoeman, who expects a British approach from Noupoort at any moment.

General Hendrik Schoeman (standing third from left) and his staff in Colesberg

OUR ELDERLY COMMANDANT-GENERAL

Pretoria, 30 November – Approximately one month ago one of our reporters on the Natal front, Nicolaas Hofmeyr, sent us this description of the daily activities of Commandant-General Piet Joubert soon after he and his burghers began besieging the British garrison in Ladysmith (that is, before he was injured):

'Day after day he is in the saddle to inspect all our fortifications. He convenes war councils, either at his own headquarters behind Pepworth's Hill or elsewhere on the front. At eight o'clock in the evening all lights must be out, but at three o'clock in the morning the restless old campaigner is up and about. Often one sees him going from tent to tent to urge on the lazy burghers in his tenor voice: "Get up! Get up! Be ready for an attack! Hurry up! The English are coming! Hurry up!"

'It is difficult to imagine more vigilance than that of General Joubert. One never sees him sleep. He is not worried about food or drink. His loyal wife, who always accompanies him on campaigns, ensures that he gets something to eat, even when he is in a hurry. We sometimes become annoyed with this energetic, tireless, scurrying old man. Why all the fuss? Why saddle up our horses in the middle of the night?

'On the other hand we deeply respect our veteran general's insight. He knows how to command a people's army. The all-seeing eye of the Archangel Gabriel, the energy of Napoleon and the patience of Job are needed to organise a troop of farmers and a mob of urbanites into an armed force. That is why the General sometimes displays the motherly care of a hen over her chickens towards the burghers. Had all the Boer officers been as caring as he is over his burghers, nothing would have been able to stop us!'

And now our elderly commander finds himself in the field hospital in Volksrust. We pray that he will soon be up and about again: a leader such as he is worth his weight in gold.

Commandant-General Piet Joubert with burghers at the front

SIEGE OF LADYSMITH
Long Tom severely damaged

Modderspruit, 8 December – Yesterday night we heard rifle fire on Lombard's Hill. Two explosions followed, then everything was silent. This morning we heard what had happened.

Some 200 Khakis had crept up on a sentry post of the Pretoria Commando, which was supposed to guard our gun emplacement on the hill in the pitch-black, moonless night. They were almost upon our men before one became aware of them. He shouted to his sleeping comrades to fire and a wild defence against the invisible enemy followed.

The Khakis only returned a few shots before their officers shouted at the top of their voices: 'Fix bayonets!' For the Boer sentries that was enough. When they heard the Khakis clamp their bayonets to the muzzles of their rifles, fear overcame them and they ran for their lives. The British promptly occupied the abandoned emplacement and damaged one of our Long Toms as well as a smaller gun with explosives. They then retreated, taking parts of the damaged guns with them.

In the meantime a strong British unit attacked one of our laagers in the north. However, the burghers were ready for them and repulsed them soon after daybreak with gun and rifle fire. In our opinion the Khakis suffered heavy casualties, even though we later heard that only three of them were killed and 21 wounded. On our side one burgher was killed and one wounded.

As for the Long Tom gun: its breech-block is missing and the front end of its muzzle is damaged. It has already been entrained and sent to Pretoria where the engineers at the railway workshop will attempt to repair it. It is a good thing that trains from the north can reach Modderspruit Station again, since it would otherwise have taken many days for the gun to be hauled back to Volksrust by oxen.

Boers haul Long Tom through a river on the way to Ladysmith

OUR MILITARY OFFICERS

General Louis Botha

Louis Botha is the ninth of 13 children of Louis Botha and his wife Salomina Adriana van Rooyen, who both participated in the Great Trek as children. The young Louis was born in Natal, where his parents were farming, in 1862. Subsequently the family moved to the Vrede district in the northern Free State, where Botha spent his youth. The only formal education he received was about two years at a farm school.

In 1884, when he was 21 years old, Botha moved back to Natal. He was one of the Boers who assisted Dinizulu, the son of the late King Cetshwayo, to regain the Zulu throne against claimants who were supported by the British. Dinizulu rewarded those Boers with land on which they established the New Republic. In 1886 Botha settled on the farm Waterval in the Republic and was elected field cornet in the same year. He was generally recognised as a successful farmer with strong leadership qualities.

After the New Republic was incorporated into the South African Republic as the Vryheid district in 1888, Botha became one of its most influential burghers.

In 1896 he was elected to the First Volksraad. He was one of the Volksraad members who most vehemently protested against British interference in the South African Republic.

With the outbreak of the war in October Botha held no military rank. He possesses only limited military experience and no formal military training. He joined the Vryheid Commando and participated in the Battle of Talana on 20 October as an ordinary burgher. Ten days later he was present at Modderspruit when the British forces attacked the Boer positions from Ladysmith. Since General Meyer was feeling ill, he appointed Botha as provisional general over the Boers under his command. Botha handled the battle so well that Commandant-General Joubert officially promoted him to the rank of general.

Louis Botha's rise from ordinary burgher to general in one month is probably an unequalled feat in world history. He is a popular figure with a strong personality. His wife Annie, whom he married in 1886, and their four children reside in Pretoria.

A Republican ambulance train

20

THE War Reporter
WEEKLY EDITION

Number 10   Pretoria, South African Republic   16 December 1899

BATTLE AT STORMBERG
Huge Boer victory – British suffer heavy casualties

Bloemfontein, 13 December – Last week we reported that Chief Commandant Olivier had arrived at the Stormberg Railway Junction and proceeded with preparations to repulse a possible British attack. On President Steyn's orders Chief Commandant Grobler left Stormberg three days later, on 9 December, with 400 men to go to the assistance of General Hendrik Schoeman at Colesberg. That left Olivier with about 1 000 burghers and two guns.

Olivier was not aware that a British force was approaching Stormberg. This force consisted of 3 000 men with 16 guns and five machine-guns and was commanded by General Gatacre. They reached the Boer position at about daybreak on 10 December. We subsequently heard that they were not aware that they had actually reached Stormberg and were not at all prepared for the warm reception that our burghers gave them.

The burghers, who had taken up position on Kissie Hill, only became aware of the British presence when the vanguard had almost reached the foot of the hill. It was the sentries in the southwest who first saw the long row of marching soldiers and fired on them; the other sentries then realised what was happening and also started firing. This warned the burghers in the main laager, most of whom were still asleep at that time, and soon they all participated in the battle.

For our men it seemed as if the British were also totally surprised. The soldiers who were captured confirmed this afterwards. Some of the soldiers began ascending Kissie Hill, but our men fired furiously at them. A group of soldiers stormed towards the north and occupied a deserted hillock. The British artillerymen took to their heels – probably to get out of reach of the burghers' Mausers. One gun, however, got stuck in a sandy ravine and the burghers shot its whole mule team down, whereupon the gunners deserted it.

The other British guns opened fire on us after a while, but made no real impression. Our gunner, Sergeant Muller, answered the British fire with his 75mm Krupp gun. Some of the British foot soldiers braved our sharpshooters' fire and almost reached the top of the hill, but were confronted by a vertical rocky ridge of about three metres. That obstacle turned out to be a major advantage to us. In the final instance, however, it was our determined, accurate rifle fire that assured our victory.

The British contributed to their own defeat. The soldiers furthest to the south began fleeing while those in the north were still busy attacking. The British gunners did us a huge favour by firing on the summit of the hill at the very time that their infantry soldiers reached it. A number of British officers and numerous soldiers were put out of action by the exploding shells. No wonder then that the British in the north soon afterwards began fleeing downhill. The burghers followed them, keeping up a heavy fire, until confronted by the British artillery and lancers.

Chief Commandant Grobler and his burghers who left Stormberg the previous day were still within hearing distance when the first shots rang out that morning. They immediately turned back and soon began firing on the Khakis from the west, thus contributing to the hasty British retreat. The Boer artillery furthermore drove back a British armoured train that came steaming up from the direction of Molteno. The British retreat was in full swing by six o'clock in the morning.

British casualties amounted to at least 25 soldiers killed, about 100 wounded and more than 600 captured. The burghers furthermore captured three of their guns as well as 17 000 rounds of ammunition, hundreds of rifles with bayonets, a supply wagon and a number of mules. On the Republican side five men were killed and 16 wounded.

Our correspondent feels that by not pursuing the enemy our officers missed an ideal opportunity to capture the whole British force. Once again they were too cautious.

Boers with a British Armstrong gun captured at Stormberg

Stormberg: a gathering of Boers give thanks after their victory

LATE NEWS: TELEGRAM FROM GENERAL BOTHA
Boer victory at Colenso – British guns captured

Pretoria, 15 December – At a quarter past eight this evening President Kruger received the following telegram from General Botha. It was made available to us an hour later. We publish it in the form we received it:

'The God of our fathers has today granted us a magnificent victory. We repulsed the enemy on all sides when they attacked in three directions. While they were heavily bombarding our positions we allowed them to bring 12 guns right up to the river, and immediately after their horses were unhooked, we opened fire with our Mausers, killing most of the crews and driving them back. They only managed to rescue two guns. We captured the other 10 beautiful huge guns, with 13 fully loaded ammunition wagons. We also made prisoner about 150 of their best men, including numerous officers, who had repeatedly attempted very courageously to rescue the guns. The loss of the enemy is probably terrible. Their dead are scattered all over the battlefield and I think number about 2 000 men. On our side approximately 30 are killed or wounded. I will report in detail as soon as possible.

'I can now with a thankful heart congratulate you and the Afrikaner people on this spectacular victory. I am forced to request you to let the British government know that the placing of guns under protection of Red Cross flags as they have done during this battle on three occasions, will not be allowed. We have already brought the captured guns over the Tugela River, and I request the government to proclaim a general day of thanksgiving to bring the thanks to Him who really deserves the praise for presenting us with this victory.'

At this stage we know nothing more, except a telegram from Bloemfontein confirming the receipt of a similar message from Botha to the Free State government. We have no doubt that this news is dependable and that we have been blessed with a massive victory.

DERELICTION OF DUTY AT LADYSMITH
Smuts ready to punish the guilty

Modderspruit, 14 December – Last week we reported on the damage done to a Long Tom by a courageous patrol of Khakis at Ladysmith. State Attorney Jan Smuts is in our main laager at the moment to investigate this shameful incident. Both Smuts and Commandant-General Joubert, who is still being treated in the hospital in Volksrust, as well as the government in Pretoria, ascribe the British success to the gross carelessness and dereliction of duty on the part of the officers who were supposed to be guarding the hill and the guns. Smuts is of the opinion that Commandant Weilbach of the Heidelberg Commando and the other officers who were responsible for this debacle should be demoted and even punished. We have been informed that the government and the Commandant-General share this opinion.

The lack of wakefulness on the Boer side was again revealed on the evening of 9 December when a British unit managed to damage a culvert on the railway line between Glencoe and Wasbank. For General Daniël Erasmus this was a huge shock, but he subsequently did virtually nothing to render his guards more effective. Consequently they were not ready for the next British attack on a gun position that took place on the evening of 10 December.

This time the British target was our gun emplacement on Vaalkop, northwest of the town. Our men did not notice the enemy before they reached the summit. Consequently the soldiers again managed to occupy the emplacement. The majority of the burghers who were supposed to be guarding the position woke up with a start and scampered away in the dark. A few of our artillerymen and sentries were too slow and were put out of action by the soldiers with their bayonets.

The Khakis were probably surprised to find that there was no gun in the emplacement. Our artillerymen had moved it some distance away earlier that afternoon and camouflaged it with canvas. However after a while the soldiers found the gun and damaged it with explosives.

The British then fell back. By that time all the Boers were awake and attempted to cut them off from Ladysmith. A number of heavy skirmishes followed and continued until the soldiers found their way back to Ladysmith by daybreak. In the end the British suffered heavy casualties, namely about 17 dead, 40 wounded and six captured. On the Republican side four burghers were killed, five wounded and three captured.

The positive result of these episodes is that the wakefulness of the Boers has now markedly improved. Provisional Commandant-General Schalk Burger has issued orders to construct more fortifications and trenches at the gun emplacements, and meticulously ensures that his orders are carried out.

State Attorney Jan Smuts

BRITISH REPULSED AT MAGERSFONTEIN

Remarkable Boer victory over Methuen

Jacobsdal, 14 December – When General Piet Cronjé ordered the Republican forces to retreat on 28 November, immediately after the battle at Modder River, few of us doubted that our next position would be on the low hills around Scholtz Nek and Spytfontein. However, that did not happen. On 4 December General Koos de la Rey convinced the war council meeting of the senior officers on the western front that the low hills at Magersfontein must be converted into their main defensive position. In addition he convinced the war council that the burghers should not take up position on the top or against the slopes of the hills, but rather dig trenches at the foot of the hills. President Steyn strongly supported these proposals.

The Boers took up position over a wide front. The southeastern end of their position was at Moss Drift on the Modder River, some 10 kilometres west of the railway line. The northwestern end was at Langeberg, some 15 kilometres north of Modder River and to the west of the railway line. The total length of the Boer line was about 15 kilometres.

The centre of the Boer position was at Magersfontein Kop, which rises some 60 metres above the valley, to the east of the railway line and about 10 kilometres northeast of the British camp at the Modder River. From this low hill one had an excellent view of the whole valley right up to the British camp and over a long stretch of the railway line.

Since De la Rey believed that the British commander would expect the Boers to prepare their defensive positions on the low hills as they did at Belmont and Graspan, he expected that the British gunners would concentrate their bombardment on the hills. That was why he suggested that the burghers should avoid the hills and dig their trenches at the foot of the hills. They actually did build a few fortifications in the hills, but this was to persuade the British that the whole Republican force was taking up position there again.

Following De la Rey's orders, the Boers took great care with the preparation of their defences at Magersfontein. They dug trenches about one metre deep and one metre wide, with walls going straight down, so that a defender could stand upright in them while firing at the enemy. The ground walls in front of the trenches were carefully covered with branches and grass in order to make them as invisible as possible. These ground walls also provided some cover. Another suggestion of De la Rey's was that the burghers who did not own horses should take up position in the centre, while those with horses were stationed on the flanks. The General argued that those without horses would fight more courageously since it would not be easy for them to retreat. On the other hand, the burghers with horses on the flanks could be used to outflank the enemy if they could be pinned down in the centre. There is a resemblance between this tactic and the British tactic of placing their mounted men on the flanks.

BRITISH COMMUNICATIONS DISRUPTED

One of the most important decisions taken at the war council of 4 December was that Commandant Prinsloo should proceed southwards with a strong patrol to destroy the British railway link and cut the telegraph line between Modder River and the Orange River. Prinsloo left on 5 December with 1 000 mounted burghers, two guns and a number of scouts. In the meantime, groups of burghers sporadically harassed the British patrols on the Modder River, thus drawing attention away from Prinsloo's expedition.

Prinsloo and his burghers reached the area of Graspan Station by 6 December – probably without being seen. They took up position in the same low hills where the battle took place on 25 November. Before daybreak the next morning they destroyed a culvert some five kilometres from Enslin Station with dynamite. Then they started breaking up the railway line.

While the burghers were busy with this hard work, the gunners began firing on the British garrison at Enslin Station immediately after daybreak. Major Albrecht and his artillery managed to shoot down all the buildings at the station, but the Khakis defended their position courageously. After a few hours a large British force including lancers and artillery arrived from the direction of the Modder River and immediately attacked the burghers. Prinsloo considered that it would be futile to attempt a defence, and since he had already accomplished his main task, he decided to retreat. His casualties amounted to six wounded, two of whom were left behind and were probably captured by the British. We have no idea what the British casualties were.

Unfortunately one can only regard Prinsloo's expedition as a failure. It became known later that he had failed to order somebody to cut the telegraph line between Enslin and the Modder River. That was probably why so many British soldiers arrived so soon to relieve the garrison at Enslin. Our scouts furthermore reported that the British had managed to repair the railway line before sunset that same day.

Both the Free State authorities and General Cronjé are of the opinion that Prinsloo acted incompetently and indecisively. As a result he was demoted without ceremony. In the opinion of the burghers, the British would have suffered heavily had De la Rey rather than Prinsloo been in command of the expedition. Unfortunately this valiant warrior from Lichtenburg is still suffering from the wound that was inflicted upon him at Modder River. The sooner he recovers, the better it will be for the Republican cause.

PRELUDE TO THE BATTLE AT MAGERSFONTEIN

On 8 December Cronjé's scouts reported that thousands more British soldiers with about ten guns had arrived at their headquarters at Modder River. Our officers had no doubt that the British would attack again at any moment. In spite of their setbacks in the three previous battles on this front, our men were full of confidence that they would be able to repulse the enemy this time. General Cronjé was determined to remain steadfast. As a precaution he ensured that burghers manned our fortifications day and night.

On Saturday 9 and Sunday 10 December the British bombarded the low hills around Magersfontein intermittently. On Saturday afternoon the British bombardment was particularly heavy. Shells fired by one unidentified gun tore huge holes in the earth where they exploded. Our burghers felt as though hell was breaking loose behind them – since fortunately the total British bombardment was aimed at the hills and the shells flew harmlessly over their heads before exploding. The Boers were safe in their trenches in front of the hills, and their total casualties were only three wounded. The bombardment was nevertheless frightening, and our men were relieved when it finally ended at six o'clock that evening.

Cronjé's scouts reported that by 10 December there were altogether 15 000 Khakis in General Methuen's force, as well as 33 guns and 16 machine guns. In our 15 kilometres of trenches there were approximately 8 000 burghers with five Krupp guns and five rapid-fire guns. Our commander in the battle the next day was General Cronjé. Even though De la Rey did all the planning, he was not present, since he had to go to the field hospital north of Kimberley to have his shoulder wound treated.

General Methuen

THE BATTLE OF MAGERSFONTEIN

By the evening of 10 December the Boers were convinced that the British attack was imminent. Cronjé had earlier received a telegram from Commandant-General Piet Joubert that included a message of encouragement to the commandos, urging them to fight bravely. Cronjé read the message to the burghers and then addressed them in his own words, urging them not to lose faith.

The Boers were correct – the attack took place the next day. As they did at Belmont, the British began approaching our positions long before daybreak on 11 December. Fortunately they did not know where our burghers were waiting for them. This became clear when the soldiers marched in closed formation straight towards the trenches. The burghers knew that they were coming long before they could see the first Khakis, since they could hear the soldiers' boots crunching on the rocks.

When the first soldiers were close enough the Boers opened a heavy fire. Their target was a packed mass of Scottish soldiers wearing their uniform kilts. Their fate was a bitter one, since those who were not killed outright, dived to the ground and were forced to stay right where they were for the rest of the day under the threat of the Boer rifle fire.

Some soldiers retreated and were attacked by the Scandinavian Corps which fought on the Republican side as volunteers. These men were overconfident and had moved out of their trenches earlier. They were soon surrounded by a huge number of Khakis, but the Scandinavians kept on fighting like wildcats until all of them had been killed or wounded. In the process they inflicted heavy casualties on the British.

The British gunners had resumed their bombardment that morning, but fortunately again aimed at the hills. After about an hour the British sent up their balloon to inspect our positions from the air. Later on some of the gunners were told or observed on their own that our trenches were at the foot of the hills and began bombing our men there. As a result the burghers were forced to take cover and could not openly carry on eliminating the soldiers in front of them. The British gunners could not force the burghers to retreat, however, and the British cavalry with their lances were equally incapable of forcing a breakthrough, since the burghers fought bravely against them.

By one o'clock that afternoon our men on the left flank began forcing the British back. This soon led to a general retreat of Khakis. On the right flank the burghers also managed to force the British back. In the centre, directly in front of Magersfontein Kop, the battle remained static. One of the burghers said afterwards that the worst aspect of the battle was the sight of the bodies of the British soldiers who were killed and were out there in the sun directly in front of our trenches the whole day long. The agony of wounded soldiers calling for help was equally tormenting to many burghers.

By four o'clock the British retreat over the whole length of the battlefield became disorderly. This presented an excellent opportunity for the Boers to follow up their victory and inflict a heavy defeat on the British force. However, the burghers were so exhausted after going without sleep through the previous night while waiting in a tense state for the enemy and subsequently defending their position the whole day long in the hot sun that they simply had no energy left for a pursuit. In addition, they were so relieved at finally gaining a victory that they were not prepared to risk losing their advantage by a reckless pursuit.

END AND AFTERMATH OF THE BATTLE

The last shots of the battle were fired by late afternoon and at about six o'clock there were only dead and wounded left on the battlefield. The Boers then climbed out of their trenches and began helping with the treatment of the survivors. Many instances were witnessed of burghers carrying water to wounded British soldiers.

We have been informed that the British losses in this battle totalled at least 288 dead, 700 wounded and 100 lost. On the Republican side 71 were killed, including Captain Flygare and 42 members of the Scandinavian Corps, and 184 wounded.

One cannot but regard the battle of Magersfontein as a huge defeat for the British. They were forced to abandon the battlefield and fall back all the way to their camp at the Modder River. On the other hand, our officers did not follow up their victory or attempt to annihilate the British force. De la Rey is angry about this. He believes that our men would have destroyed General Methuen's whole army corps had they acted more decisively. The Republican forces are now busy strengthening their trenches and position here at Magersfontein.

Boers firing from their trenches during the battle of Magersfontein, as photographed by a Boer doctor

FROM THE EDITOR

A week of spectacular successes for our forces! At last our determination, our courage and our faith have been crowned with wonderful victories! Their names – Stormberg, Magersfontein, Colenso – will become part of our people's history, comparable to Blood River and Majuba. We rejoice with the heroes of our struggle for freedom. We heard of our victory at Colenso only a few hours ago. We will report on that in detail in our next issue. Today our pages are filled with reports on the victories at Stormberg and Magersfontein.

Unfortunately, we have to report on reverses, ineptness and cowardice too. The British again managed to occupy one of our gun emplacements at Ladysmith. This, as well as our incapacity to break the British communication lines at Graspan, on which we report in this issue, is inexcusable. We trust that our military authorities will ensure that this never happens again.

What direction the war will take now is impossible to predict. We believe it will take the enemy a long time to recover from their setbacks. They suffered severe reverses on all fronts. They may either decide that they have had enough or they may want to revenge the humiliating defeats they suffered. The Republics certainly have not yet won the war. We expect a number of quiet weeks now – which is as it should be around Christmas time.

The Republican authorities have just announced that the victories of our burghers on the battlefield are to be commemorated this Sunday as a Day of Thanksgiving. We hereby call upon our readers to carry out our authorities' wishes in the proper way.

OUR MILITARY OFFICERS

General Hendrik Olivier

Jan Hendrik Olivier was born in 1848. His parents lived in the Burgersdorp district in the Cape Colony, but later moved to Zastron in the Orange Free State. Olivier joined the Free State border police when he was 15 years old and later became a field cornet. With his participation in the war between the Free State and the Basuto of King Moshweshwe he not only gained valuable military experience, but was also rewarded with the farm Olifantsbeen, where he became a wealthy farmer.

In 1883 Olivier was elected as member of the Volksraad of the Orange Free State for the Caledon River ward. With the outbreak of this war two months ago he was appointed as commandant of the Rouxville-Zastron Commando. He and his burghers took up position all along the Orange River to keep the British out of the Republic. Last month he was in command of the occupation of Aliwal North, Burgersdorp and other towns in the districts of the Cape Colony bordering the Free State, and eventually of the railway junction at Stormberg.

Olivier is a tall man of athletic build. He has a strong face, large black beard and jovial expression. He had been a relatively unknown figure in Pretoria until his glorious victory over the British on 10 December, but now everyone refers to him as the Hero of Stormberg.

General J.H. Olivier

THE
War Reporter
WEEKLY EDITION

Number 11 | Pretoria, South African Republic | 23 December 1899

THE BATTLE OF COLENSO
MAJOR VICTORY FOR LOUIS BOTHA

Pretoria, 22 December – Last week we published the message telegraphed by General Louis Botha from the Natal front in which he announced the victory of the Republican forces over the British at the Tugela River on 15 December. Our correspondent on the front has compiled the following detailed report on the battle. It is clear that our highest expectations have been surpassed and that the Republican forces have indeed scored one of their most brilliant victories ever in this war. The total British loss in this battle was 143 men killed in action, 756 wounded, 240 missing and 38 made prisoner of war. We lost seven men killed in action, 30 wounded and one drowned. The general who deserves the most praise for the victory is Botha himself, who carried the mantle of our indisposed Commandant-General Piet Joubert with great distinction.

BOER DEFENSIVE PREPARATIONS

We reported last week that the war council on the Natal front had decided to use the northern bank of the Tugela River both east and west of the demolished railway bridge at Colenso as a defensive line. Botha had no doubt that General Buller, the British commander, would attempt to break through to Ladysmith somewhere close to the railway line, since he depended on trains for supplies and could not venture far away with his huge force. Our young general took his officers with him to the front and discussed with each one exactly where and how his burghers should prepare defensive positions. This included digging trenches as well as building fortifications of stones and sandbags.

The defensive line was about 10 kilometres in length. On the eve of the British attack Botha had about 4 500 burghers available to man this front. In the end about 3 000 burghers actually took part in the battle. In addition he had five guns of varying calibres under the command of Captain Lood Pretorius at his disposal. These were positioned in emplacements a little distance north of the Tugela. The burghers carefully camouflaged the trenches, fortifications and emplacements. In addition they built mock emplacements in which they placed fake guns made of sheet metal.

The burghers guarded their positions night and day. Sentries on night duty were not allowed to smoke or to use any lights. Botha himself often visited the positions and talked to the burghers to boost their morale. One of the Reuters correspondents with the Boers, Jimmy Roos, reported as follows on Botha's activities:

'General Louis Botha's tent at Colenso is an ordinary bell type captured at Dundee. Inside there is a convertible stretcher and a chair on which he sits when he is in the laager. A packing case serves as his table. Botha has particular reverence for age and always rises when an elderly, white-bearded burgher enters his tent. Burghers drop into the tent all day long to bring reports or to hear the news. Botha has no private life. He eats, drinks and sleeps before a coming and going procession. Reports are received and dispatches dictated in the presence of a dozen chance visitors.'

The success of Botha's defensive strategy depended on surprise. Therefore he issued strict orders that nobody should open fire before he himself gave the sign to fire by firing one shot with the biggest field gun. He added that he would not do that before the British attack, but would wait until the attackers were within easy rifle range of the Boer trenches.

The weak link in Botha's defensive position was Hlangwane Hill to the south of the Tugela – in other words on the British side of the river, which means that it would be difficult to defend against a determined British attack. The Boers who occupy it would feel exposed. Fortunately Field Cornet A.J. Dercksen of the Boksburg Ward of the Heidelberg Commando volunteered to occupy the hill with 400 burghers. Botha promised to protect him with covering fire from the guns stationed in the heights north of the Tugela. Even President Kruger sent Dercksen a telegram from Pretoria to thank him and his burghers for their willingness to defend such an exposed position. Two days before the Battle of Colenso Botha sent Acting Commandant A.Z.A. Briel of Soutpansberg with 250 burghers to Hlangwane as reinforcements for Dercksen.

In spite of the fact that his scouts reported that General Buller had about 20 000 soldiers with 44 guns and 18 machine guns at their disposal, Botha was full of confidence. Three days before the battle he telegraphed President Kruger that the officers and burghers were in high spirits and ready for the battle. Even though the enemy was much more numerous than his forces and had many more guns, they would, Botha declared, with the help of the Almighty, do their best to inflict a defeat on the British if and when they attacked.

Our men had an excellent view of the flat terrain south of the Tugela from the unbroken ridge of low hills on the north bank of the river. From 12 December they noted heightened activity in the British camp, including a movement of troops to the north. The general Boer opinion was that an attack was imminent.

From about seven o'clock on the morning of 13 December the British opened a heavy bombardment in the general direction of the Boers. The naval guns made a deafening noise and the exploding grenades kicked up great dust clouds, but invariably landed way behind the Boer positions and caused no damage.

CRISIS ON HLANGWANE HILL

Late on the afternoon of 13 December General Botha was suddenly confronted by a major crisis. Acting Commandant Briel and his 250 Soutpansberg burghers as well as a number of Dercksen's Boksburgers abandoned their position at Hlangwane and bluntly stated that it was untenable. Botha immediately convened a war council meeting. In spite of orders from both President Kruger in Pretoria and Acting Commandant General Schalk Burger at Ladysmith, the council decided to recall Dercksen and abandon Hlangwane. Thus Botha lost an extremely valuable tactical position at a time when an enemy attack seemed imminent.

It seems as if Botha never slept on the night of 13–14 December. He inspected the front the whole night and addressed the burghers in the various positions with words of encouragement. Early the next morning another war council was held. A little while before the meeting began Botha received a telegram from President Kruger in Pretoria. We later heard that Captain Danie Theron had telegraphed Kruger early that morning and informed the President that the whole Boer front could collapse. Kruger telegraphed the following:

'My friends, I received a report that you are abandoning your positions. If you give up your positions we might as well hand the whole country to the enemy. Remain steadfast in your positions and fight till you drop dead. The hills south of the river cannot be abandoned. Fear God, not the enemy. I believe it is not the burghers who are abandoning their positions but the officers. Please answer by telling me what the situation is.'

From nine o'clock that morning, 14 December, the British resumed their bombardment. Under those circumstances the war council met again. Botha read Kruger's telegram as well as other messages to the officers. He managed to convince them to reoccupy Hlangwane and to remain in their positions. They decided by lot who would have to occupy Hlangwane. Commandant Jozua Joubert of Wakkerstroom and J.A. Muller of Standerton were selected. They had about 800 burghers for the task.

The British bombardment ended after about two hours without the Boers suffering any casualties. The Boers did not fire back a single shot.

THE NIGHT PRECEDING THE BATTLE

On the evening of 14 December the Boer commandos were spread from east to west in the following order: On Hlangwane south of the Tugela River there were 800 burghers under Commandant Joubert. Next came the Krugersdorp Commando under Acting Commandant Sarel Oosthuizen supported by a number of smaller units. The Heidelberg Commando under Commandant S.B. Buys was positioned near the road bridge at Colenso, and then came the Swaziland Police under Commandant Chris Botha, the Soutpansberg Commando under Commandant Van Rensburg and the Ermelo Commando under Commandant J.N.H. (Hans) Grobler. Further to the west a Free State commando under General Andries Cronjé, the Johannesburg burghers of Commandant Ben Viljoen and the Middelburgers of Commandant Piet Trichardt formed the extreme right flank opposite Potgietersdrift.

General Botha (seated in the centre) with his burghers

On the night of 14–15 December Botha slept on sandbags in a gun emplacement above the Tugela. At about one o'clock he heard a Boer gunner inquire from his comrade if he could see all the lights at Chievely. Botha immediately rose. There were indeed numerous lights in the British camp. It was clear that they were preparing to attack. The word spread quickly all over the Boer lines and everyone finalised their preparations in the dark.

At last the day broke. In the half-light of dawn the Boers could see a huge cloud of dust above Chievely. The British were approaching in long, broad, brown moving lines. Botha and Captain Lood Pretorius watched the spectacle from the gun emplacement. Botha was satisfied to note that the British approached exactly those sectors where he had placed most of his defenders.

THE BRITISH ATTACK

From 20 minutes past five on the morning of 15 December the British resumed their bombardment. However, the Boers did not fire back. Virtually all the shells flew high over the heads of the Boers or into the mock gun emplacements on the heights. In the meantime the soldiers marched onwards towards the trenches of the concealed Boers, who made no move to reveal their presence.

To Botha's surprise the British vanguard in the centre consisted of gunners with 12 15-pounder Armstrong field guns. They moved far ahead of the Khaki infantry to within rifle range of the concealed burghers. The gunners unhooked the guns in neat rows right in the open and by six o'clock prepared to begin firing. Botha could wait no longer and ordered Pretorius to fire the signal shot.

The burghers in the trenches were by that time extremely excited and immediately responded to Botha's signal by opening fire on the guns in front of them. The Boer artillery soon joined the attack. The Khaki gunners returned this fire, but apparently did not know where the Boer fire came from, since they fired wildly and aimlessly.

Botha told our reporter after the battle that the Krugersdorp burghers of Commandant Oosthuizen and the Heidelbergers of Buys fired so accurately and were so well supported by our artillery that the British gunners who were not killed were soon forced to abandon their guns. Indeed, when our men captured these guns later that day they found that six of them were loaded, but never fired. Their prize included 12 ammunition wagons with 1 300 artillery shells in addition to the guns.

On the Republican right flank the Khakis similarly advanced within easy rifle range of the Boer defenders. At about six o'clock they entered a 'bog' in the river, blissfully unaware that Boers were in position on both sides of them now. When the Boers suddenly opened fire with guns and Mausers, the crossfire soon caused panic in the British ranks. One of the burghers, Tobias Smuts of Ermelo, gave us the following account of events:

'It is almost impossible to describe the scene that took place in front of us. Soldiers were falling everywhere. They had nowhere to hide. Those who fell down to search for cover, were chased up again by the exploding shells of our French guns. Those who ran towards the river were mowed down by the burghers with their rifles. But the enemy is courageous. Again and again they charged towards us. It is strange how people allow themselves to be killed for a wrong cause. In the end our fire was too fierce even for their bravest men. Only a few ever saw the beautiful stream of the river.'

Continued overleaf

FROM THE EDITOR

A quiet week on the fronts: the British forces are probably licking their wounds, which should keep them busy for a long time. However, our burghers should guard against nurturing the illusion that they have done enough to win the war. We all hope that the British will now agree to negotiate, but first reports from British newspapers indicate that their losses in what they call 'Black Week' could lead to the conviction that it is essential for 'Anglo-Saxon pride' to avenge those defeats.

We heartily agree with the sentiments expressed this week by the Rev H.S. Bosman at a funeral in Pretoria. May the Almighty soon open the hearts of the British people to the realisation that they have embarked on an unjust war. We have no designs to take anything from the British people – all we are fighting for is to defend our own freedom.

Commandant Jozua Joubert

continued

THE ENEMY REPULSED

By about 10 o'clock the enemy was falling back in a chaotic retreat. At one stage it looked to us as if their gunners fired on their own men by accident, probably mistaking them for Boers. They left hundreds of dead and wounded soldiers behind. Some of the soldiers who were captured by us said that they never saw one Boer during the whole engagement.

Unfortunately the Boer commandos on the right flank, who were supposed to cross the river and outflank the British, never entered the battle. It seems as if the newly appointed Fighting General Christiaan Fourie misunderstood his orders. As a result, the British managed to retreat safely, whereas they could easily have been overwhelmed.

In the meanwhile the British attempted to save their abandoned guns in the centre of the battlefield. A number of enemy soldiers displayed magnificent courage and indeed managed to retrieve two of the guns under a hail of Mauser bullets.

On the left flank a mounted British unit rode out towards Hlangwane. They dismounted near the hill and approached the invisible Boer positions on foot. In the end those Khakis too were rudely surprised when the burghers suddenly opened fire, pinning them down in the open. They suffered heavy casualties, especially when by about noon they stood up again to retreat. Commandant Jozua Joubert was wounded during the battle, after he had acted very courageously the whole day long, moving between the burghers and encouraging them to keep firing.

The last engagement of the battle took place at about two o'clock that afternoon when the British attempted to prevent a group of Boer volunteers who had crossed the river from capturing the abandoned guns. In the end the Boers had to physically overwhelm Colonel Bullock, the British commander in this area, with blows of their fists to force him to surrender. They then took about 150 Khakis prisoner and hauled the 10 Armstrong guns through the river. Thus the Battle of Colenso ended.

Republican artillerymen in their gun emplacement at Colenso

Boers loading the British guns captured at Colenso on a train

SIEGE OF LADYSMITH

Modderspruit, 22 December – The Boer siege of the British garrison in this northern Natal town is still continuing. It is becoming clear that the Khakis will not be forced into surrendering by sporadic bombardments alone. Our Long Tom guns are even firing a few shells at night, and the British naval guns usually answer these from Ladysmith with lyddite grenades. Most of the burghers have pieces of canvas with which they build shelters for themselves while on sentry duty. They all sleep fully dressed, with their arms and water bottles right next to them. Each must have 200 rounds of ammunition with them when they go on sentry duty.

The burghers who manned the Boer fortifications here at Ladysmith a week ago at the time of the battle of Colenso, could clearly hear the roar of the guns from the battlefield and were aware that a full-scale fight was in progress. They were, of course, highly anxious about the eventual outcome since they knew that General Botha was fighting against a huge force of well-trained soldiers. Their relief was immense that evening when they heard the news of the massive Boer victory.

The next day, 16 December, was thus again, as it was for the Voortrekkers in 1838, a day of joy and thankfulness. At the main laager the Reverend P.S. Snyman held a sermon in which he reminded the burghers that 16 December is a blessed date and that they have now more reason than ever to commemorate it as a Sabbath. The burghers then built a cairn of stone as a memorial.

BRITISH REVERSES IN 'BLACK WEEK' PREDICTED

Pretoria, 20 December – A friend of the Boer cause in England – or shall we rather say an outspoken British critic of his government's evil policies in South Africa – sent us the text of a speech made by W.T. Stead, a well-known British liberal journalist, at Westminster Chapel in London immediately after the outbreak of the war. In this speech he predicted that his government's actions would be disastrous for Britain. The lie he refers to is the story that is being told to the British public that the Boer Republics are the aggressors in this confrontation. We quote the following extract from Stead's speech, which certainly sounds like a prediction come true:

'The real root question which underlies everything, and of which this present trouble in the Transvaal is but a symptom, is the question whether or not to believe that there is a God who judgeth in the earth, who loves righteousness, and who abhors a lie. The whole of our trouble in the Transvaal springs out of the deliberate conviction, frankly expressed and unhesitatingly acted upon, that this is not true, and that it is sometimes good policy to tell a lie and stick to it. Knowing that we are going forth to battle with a lie in our right hand, I tremble as to the result …

'I know that in this matter I am as a voice crying in the wilderness. I know that in the present moment of passion and fury, when passion is excited, and the streets ring with the cheers for the soldiers going to fight in this unholy quarrel, my voice will hardly be heard. But mark my words; if I am right we shall not have long to wait before we shall find that God is not dead, neither is He asleep; and if, as I believe, He loves this England of His, and this people of His, although but a small remnant are still faithful to Him, then, as upon Israel of old when they sinned and went in opposition to the Divine will, will descend disaster after disaster, until we turn from lying, and all these evil ways, into the paths of justice and truth.'

We applaud this statement.

A FUNERAL IN PRETORIA
Sampie van Zijl laid to rest

Pretoria, 15 December – Amongst those Boers who were killed during the British surprise attack on Vaalkop northwest of Ladysmith on 10 December was the 31-year-old Egbert Leander van Zijl, who was a popular figure under the nickname Sampie. During his solemn funeral service here in Pretoria the Reverend H.S. Bosman of the Dutch Reformed Church said: 'God has indicated for each a place here on earth, and for our people He has reserved the south of this huge African continent. This war, for us, is one for justice and the light will go up since thousands of noble hearts in England will sooner or later realise that they have been misled by people who arrived here very poor but became extremely rich and now want to take our country from us. But we will fight to the end and God will build the core of the freedom of our people on the unity of all Afrikaners.'

ESCAPE FROM STAATS MODEL SCHOOL
Warrant issued for journalist Churchill

Pretoria, 15 December – Most of our readers will be aware that British officers who are made prisoners of war are detained at the Staats Model School in Pretoria. On Tuesday 12 December the only escape up to now from the schoolyard took place. The prisoner who got away is the journalist Winston Churchill. Last month we reported that he had been captured in Natal when the Boers overpowered a British armoured train at Chievely. Journalists are usually immediately released, but since Churchill actively participated in the fight that followed and had a revolver with him, he was made prisoner.

After his escape was noted early on Wednesday morning, the authorities issued a warrant for his arrest.

Winston Churchill (right) as a captive of the Transvaal forces

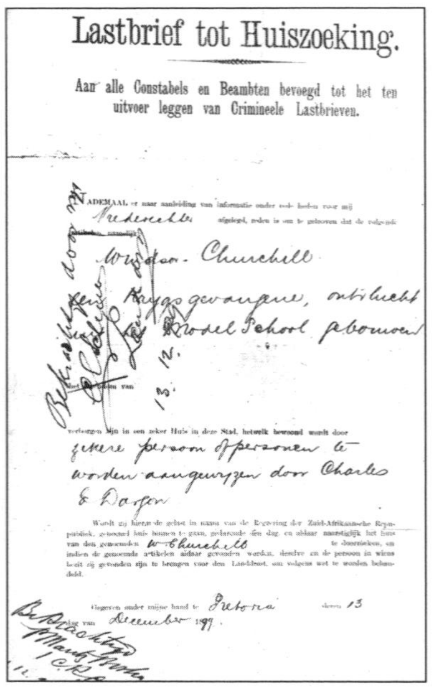

The warrant for Churchill's arrest

OUR MILITARY OFFICERS

Captain Lood Pretorius

Johannes Lodewicus Pretorius, the Boer gunner who fired the first shot from our side in the Battle of Colenso, was born in 1871 on the farm Welgegund in the Pretoria district. His father was a well-known public figure and former commander of the State Artillery, Henning Pretorius. His mother was Cornelia Magdalena Bouwer.

As a young man Lood Pretorius was employed as an official in the office of the Commandant General in Pretoria. In 1896 he joined the State Artillery as a second lieutenant and in 1898 participated in the campaign against the Bavenda of Chief Mphephu. Immediately after the outbreak of this war ten weeks ago he proceeded to the Natal front as commander of the Third Battery of the State Artillery. On 20 October he participated in the Battle of Talana, hitting the British camp with the very first shot from his gun. Ten days later he also took part in the Battle of Modderspruit.

The State Historian, Nicolaas Hofmeyr, writes of Pretorius that he is regarded as the most accurate gunner amongst our artillery officers. Whatever he aims at, he hits. He is a tall, slender man with delicate features and looks quite aristocratic with his pointed beard. He is known as a congenial man of few words, a man of deeds rather than words, who usually remains in the background but steps forward when needed. His strong personality, his courage and his undoubted talents quickly earned him the respect of the burghers and especially of General Louis Botha, who said in an interview after the Battle of Colenso: 'I would like to give the highest praise to Captain Pretorius. The courage he displayed is almost past belief. He rode in the most fearless fashion up and down our lines, from one gun to another, exposed every minute to death, and the inspiring effect he had on his men was something to remember. Such courage I have never seen equalled.'

Captain J.L. Pretorius

THE War Reporter

WEEKLY EDITION

Number 12   Pretoria, South African Republic   30 December 1899

CHRISTMAS DAY AT THE FRONT

Pretoria, 29 December – Mrs Alida Badenhorst sent us sections of letters that her husband, Frikkie, who is a farmer in the Western Transvaal, wrote to her from the battlefront at Modder River. From this our readers should gain a glimpse of how our brave burghers react to the trauma of this terrible war. On Christmas Day Badenhorst wrote:

'This evening as I walked along the trenches I heard someone praying. I went close to the place where I heard the prayer. There I saw some 20 men on their knees; in other places there was singing. I thought to myself – now I know why the war has come; the Lord wills that the people shall learn to pray. Many a man who never knelt has now learnt to pray, and those who never thought of God now speak of the Almighty power. So has the Lord always a purpose in what He sends us, even in this cruel war.'

From the Boer laagers at Ladysmith, Wilhelm Mangold of the Heidelberg Commando sent us a report that reflects a much more celebratory mood in this festive season: 'On 23 December the postmaster of Heidelberg, Frans Broers, arrived with a whole wagon full of Christmas presents for us. This included trunks full of cake, fruit, wine, beer, all sorts of liquors, plenty of tobacco, white enamel mugs and diaries. On Christmas Day itself we had a huge Christmas dinner. The best cooks in the laager began preparing the dishes from early that morning. When all the pots were on the fire, the black servants could hardly keep up with the demand for firewood.

'At 12 o'clock the signal was given to join the dinner, and burghers converged from all sides. Each had to bring his own cutlery. We used trunks as tables and huge stones as chairs. Our guest of honour was General Schalk Burger, who was formally welcomed. After the Reverend had said grace, we started eating all the wonderful dishes. These included soup, meat, vegetables, fruit and cake. So much was left over that not even the servants could finish it off.

'Postmaster Broers held a brief festive address in which he conveyed us all the good wishes from our friends at home. Then he handed over our presents, which for the most part consisted of corked bottles. Broers was somewhat worried that we would not be able to open the bottles. Fortunately he misjudged our preparedness, since what is a soldier without a corkscrew? From all over the place one could hear: "Here's one," and soon all our mugs were filled. In addition, the Ladies' Committee from Pretoria sent us 12 huge Christmas puddings.

'Later that afternoon the time arrived to hand out presents. The Heidelberg Commando is highly satisfied with the regimental flag that we received. It was made by the women of Heidelberg and contains the combined colours of the Transvaal and Free State flags.'

For the Irish Brigade Christmas Day in their camp outside Ladysmith was also a joyous occasion. Colonel John Blake, their commander, told our correspondent that it was more than just joyous: 'It was a day of jubilee without a queen, a day for brave and patriotic hearts to assemble, a day for a liberty-loving and God-fearing people to rejoice and be merry. When Christmas Day approached we decided to have horse races, athletic sports and some kind of a banquet. The Irish boys went to the different commandos, invited all who had fast horses to come and try their luck, and all who felt that they could run, jump, throw heavy weights, etc. A half-mile track was prepared, plenty of food was cooked, and all was in readiness when Christmas Day came.

'Boers with fast horses were there; athletes representing all commandos; there were generals, commandants and field cornets. Young ladies and old ones too, from Pretoria, Johannesburg, Dundee and other towns, were entertained by the Irish boys. All gazed in admiration at the colours that waved to and fro with the breeze, for they saw the *Vierkleur*, the Green Flag with the Harp, the Stars and Stripes, the Tricolor of France, and the German and Dutch flags that floated over the Irish camp.

'Since the Irish boys earlier acquired a good racehorse in Pretoria, they easily won all the races, while the Boers captured nearly all the prizes in athletics. The sports having come to an end, all went to the camp and enjoyed the meats, cakes, pies, etc., but it was a painfully dry banquet. Several cases of liquid refreshments had been ordered, but some thirsty party had appropriated them at Modderspruit Station, so we had to use coffee as a substitute.

'Having feasted, all joined and sang first, "God save Ireland", then the anthem of the Transvaal and of the Orange Free State, and then all, happy and satisfied, dispersed and returned to their respective camps to attend evening services.'

From the eastern Free State is it reported that the women here prepared for Christmas time with a will, since it provided them with the joyful opportunity to liven up the lives of the burghers on the front. They baked cakes and other delicacies on a huge scale and sent them to the commandos on the borders. Some women collected the ingredients from the shop owners and other friends, while others did the baking. The general willingness to contribute was wonderful to note. So many delicacies were packed into trunks and sent to the borders that there would certainly be enough for the New Year celebrations as well. And to round off everything the women decorated the trunks with paper in the colours of the Republic.

Christmas Day in a burgher camp at Ladysmith

THE BRITISH 'BLACK WEEK'
Buller branded as the scapegoat

Pretoria, 28 December – Since last week's issue, we have received quantities of news from overseas, making it clear that the three British defeats in the period 10–15 December, namely at Stormberg, Magersfontein and Colenso, sent shock waves through our enemy's vast empire. The British press refers to this period as the Black Week. And predictably, the English soon identified a scapegoat to blame for their military incapacity against the Boers. The man thus branded is General Redvers Buller, and the saviour, according to British predictions, will be Field Marshal Lord Frederick Roberts, whose son Freddie was killed in battle at Colenso.

Roberts has been appointed to replace Buller as British commander-in-chief in South Africa. We understand that in spite of his small stature and advanced age, Roberts has a reputation for dogged determination. He departed from Britain by ship on 23 December and will reach Cape Town early next month. General Lord Horatio Kitchener, who is in Khartoum at present, will serve as Roberts's second-in-command and chief of staff.

THE NORTHERN FRONT
Tension between white and black continues

Pretoria, 29 December – After the attack by Chief Linchwe's Bakgatla on the Transvaal border town of Derdepoort on 25 November, the tension between white and black in that area has continued to simmer. After consulting a number of witnesses on the events at Derdepoort and the abduction of the women and children that followed, including the sworn affidavits of the abducted women themselves, our conclusion is that most of the initial reports were somewhat exaggerated. The women were certainly not molested. The attack upon them and their subsequent abduction nevertheless constitutes a dastardly act.

The panic that followed the attack generated widespread emotional outbursts. Most newspaper articles on the incident were extremely partial and fuelled the emotion and confusion. The British queen was severely criticised: it was her soldiers who instigated the Bakgatla to attack the whites. Even the foreign envoys in the South African Republic became involved in the issue. On 28 November State Secretary F.W. Reitz informed these dignitaries about the events at Derdepoort during a gathering in Pretoria. The result of this was that the British government and people were deluged with criticism for their presumed arming and instigating of black communities against the Boers. In one of the biggest Dutch dailies, the *Nieuwe Rotterdaamsche Courant*, there was a full-page protest by the Dutch people about the events at Derdepoort.

High Commissioner Milner made a feeble attempt at denial by claiming that it was not the British policy to arm blacks against the Boers. His excuse for the events was that the Boers were themselves responsible, due to their warlike actions against the black people. As far as we are concerned his standpoint is nothing but pure hypocrisy. We are only prepared to concede to Milner that he certainly has much more intimate knowledge than we do of warlike actions against other communities, since the English are virtually continuously involved in such actions.

While the British were justly being castigated in the newspapers for their role in the events at Derdepoort, some sections of the public were calling for revenge and retribution. We were not surprised to hear that a revenge attack followed on 22 December. A Boer commando led by Fighting General Willem C. Janse van Rensburg attacked the main Bakgatla settlement, and in the battle that followed three burghers as well as about 150 Bakgatla were killed.

SIEGE OF MAFEKING

Pretoria, 29 December – The siege continues, with a minimum of effort on both sides. One cannot but regard the Boer commander, General Kootjie Snyman, as incapable and unsuited for his commission. He is satisfied to remain passive and merely bombard the town sporadically. Our correspondent at Mafeking has no doubt that Snyman has no empathy with the vast majority of burghers and that they have no respect for him. As for the British within the town, they are equally passive and merely answer our sporadic shelling with counter-bombardments.

On 2 December one of our patrols captured a British woman who introduced herself as Lady Sarah Wilson and claimed that she was a journalist for the British newspaper *Daily Mail*. Earlier on she had written a letter to General Snyman to request permission to visit Mafeking, but had been refused. She nevertheless arrived on a mule wagon and simply attempted to drive straight into the besieged town. She was captured and detained at the military hospital, where she was questioned and her luggage examined. The burghers generally agree that Snyman was probably not the correct person to interrogate her. As Abraham Stafleu dryly remarked to us: 'She probably learnt more from General Snyman than he learnt from her.'

Colonel Baden-Powell, the British commander in Mafeking, somehow became aware that we were detaining Lady Sarah. He immediately sent a messenger to propose her exchange for a Mrs Delport who wanted to leave Mafeking. Snyman refused. Eventually Lady Sarah was exchanged on 7 December for Petrus Viljoen, a grandson of the celebrated big game hunter, Commandant Jan Viljoen, who died a few years ago. Petrus was in Rhodesia when the war broke out, was captured there and brought to Mafeking where he was charged with horse theft. His brother Jan, who is a burgher in the laager, is delighted about his release.

Petrus Viljoen naturally brought us a lot of information on circumstances within the besieged town. He says that there is a big shortage of supplies and that conditions are extremely grim for the townspeople – not so much as a result of our bombardments but rather due to shrinking food sources. The black inhabitants are finding it especially hard to cope. He says our bombs do not cause much damage, since Baden-Powell has dug underground bomb shelters that serve as hiding places.

Continued overleaf

Before the exchange: Lady Sarah Wilson at the Boer hospital outside Mafeking

Petrus Viljoen, blindfolded, before leaving Mafeking for the exchange

continued
There is a permanent guard on duty who gives a sign when he sees smoke at our Long Tom and then everybody seeks shelter. However, Viljoen can now indicate to our gunners where they should aim.

Burghers and Khakis together during the ceasefire on 26 December

SKIRMISH AT PLATBOOMFORT

On the day after Christmas the enemy did launch an attack on our position at Platboomfort, north of the town. The English call it Game Tree Hill. This onslaught began with a bombardment, followed by an attack of foot soldiers supported by an armoured train. The Boers repulsed the attackers with ease. Altogether 25 British were killed, 23 wounded and three made prisoner of war. On the Boer side two burghers were killed and seven wounded.

FATE OF BOER PRISONERS OF WAR
Exclusive report by one of them from Cape Town

Pretoria, 29 December – From time to time, we have reported on burghers being captured in engagements with the enemy and made prisoners of war. Virtually all these prisoners are taken to Cape Town. Today we received an exclusive report on the condition of these prisoners of war written by one of them, namely Leendert Ruijssenaers, who was a member of the Hollander Corps captured after the disastrous Battle of Elandslaagte in October. Here is his report on the adventures he and his unfortunate comrades have experienced:

'On the day after the battle I was ordered to assist with the treatment of the wounded and the burying of the dead. That evening we were taken to Elandslaagte Station where we loaded the wounded onto an ambulance train. The Boer captives were loaded onto open trucks where an English officer and a few soldiers guarded us.

'When we arrived in Ladysmith at ten o'clock that night we were immediately marched to the prison and locked up behind high walls. We were left in the courtyard with no roof between us and the open sky. It was bitterly cold and we were hungry. Many could not sleep since they were shivering throughout the night that followed.

'The next morning we were each given a piece of bread and a rusty tin cup filled with brown liquid they called tea. That evening we were told to be ready to leave again. At about ten o'clock, after 24 hours in Ladysmith, we were marched back to the station. We were crammed into third-class wagons and were soon on our way to Pietermaritzburg, where we arrived the next morning.

'In the Natal capital we were again taken to prison. We were locked up like ordinary criminals – 13 or 14 men to a cell with insufficient light and only a small, barred window high on one wall. The food was insufficient and we were only allowed to leave our cells and exercise in the courtyard for three hours per day. Fortunately we spent only two days there before leaving by train for Durban.

'On 26 October we boarded the steamship *Putiala*, which had been used to transport troops and horses, in Durban harbour. The ship anchored some distance from the quay in the harbour and we were allowed to write letters. We knew these would be censored before being mailed. After two days a warship arrived and under its escort we departed for Simonstown.

'Since the *Putiala* rolled quite vigorously almost all of us were seasick. For many Boers who had never been at sea this was a severe punishment. It went on for five days. The sea was rough and the ship rolled so badly that one captive broke his leg and another his arm. We were not given proper food, there were no facilities to wash on board and we were still dressed in the same clothes that we had been wearing when we were captured at Elandslaagte.

'On Thursday 2 November the *Putiala* dropped anchor in Simonstown Bay. We were then transferred to the prison boat, the *Penelope*. We were welcomed in a particularly friendly spirit by Captain Robert Bruce, who introduced himself as the chief of prisoners of war. He has subsequently treated us sympathetically. There is even a dining room with tables and benches on the *Penelope* and the food is better than anything we had previously received.

'We were given hammocks to sleep in and clean blankets, and had an opportunity to wash our dirty clothes. Soon we were allowed to receive visitors. Some friendly people from Cape Town sent us books, fruit, delicacies and other things that made life bearable. We remain on deck till nine o'clock each evening, when a gun fires on the *Doris* as signal that we have to hang out our hammocks and sleep. Although we are prisoners and have no freedom, we have few complaints.'

A PRISONER ESCAPES

'On 19 December the escape of Keppel de Meillon took place. That night he hung onto a thick rope and was lowered to the level of the ocean through one of the portholes of the *Penelope*. Since the ship was attached to a buoy only about 300 metres from the shore, it was possible for a good swimmer – and De Meillon is one – to cover that distance. One of us kept the sailor who was on guard on the ship's bridge occupied. Since it was a clear, moonlight night we soon saw the arranged signal by which De Meillon indicated that he had safely reached the shore.

'The next morning we heard the whistle and we had to answer and the guards then established that one man was missing. Their faces darkened considerably. They counted again. De Meillon was nowhere to be seen. The foreman of his table, Smith, now joined the officers in searching everywhere in corners and holes, and even in the old cannons – but no trace of the missing man was found. We found it hard not to give all away by sniggering, since Smith pulled all sorts of faces behind the backs of the officers while acting as if he was seriously taking part in the search.

'Smith then ventured the opinion that the missing man probably drowned; he had been very depressed lately and often sat on his own. Two other prisoners stated they heard cries for help at eleven o'clock the previous evening. They jumped from their hammocks and investigated, but since they found nothing wrong concluded that a prisoner had shouted out in his sleep. Several prisoners declared that they were aware that De Meillon could not swim.

'Soon the British officers were convinced that the missing man had drowned. One of them rowed to the admiral's ship, the *Doris*, and soon returned with a diver with all sorts of equipment. All of us looked over the railing with concerned faces. Smith put up such a show that an English officer was heard to say: 'The poor man, I hope we find him!' But the diver only found old shoes and other oddities on the bottom of the sea, and no De Meillon, since by then he was probably in Cape Town.

'After six hours the diver gave up. The officers probably realised that we had taken them for a ride, since that same evening they began placing thick bars in front of all the portholes. Sleeping on deck was henceforth prohibited, the number of guards doubled and all talking after nine o'clock in the evening was forbidden. In addition they took down descriptions of all of us, since we had told them that De Meillon is about 40 years old with a black beard. In actual fact he is 20 and blond.

'The De Meillon incident certainly has helped to break the monotony of our existence in cramped quarters on the deck of the ship. Virtually our only other diversions are the regular visits by ministers who preach to us and, from about the middle of November, sporadic visits from people in Cape Town.'

Boers captured at Elandslaagte marched off by the Khakis

FROM THE EDITOR

The end of a year is usually a time for reflection. Twelve weeks ago many of us believed that peace would have been restored by now. Those expectations have been dashed. We can but hope that the war will be a nightmare of the past a year from now.

Not much has happened on the military front in the past week. The British will probably refrain from rash actions while awaiting the arrival of Lord Roberts, the newly appointed commander-in-chief. It is possible, of course, that General Buller will attempt to restore his bruised reputation by relieving Ladysmith before Roberts arrives. In 1881, in the Transvaal War of Independence, General Colley attempted to restore his reputation after his reverses at Laingsnek and Schuinshoogte by occupying Majuba. That action led to his final defeat and death. Buller knows his history, and will probably be more cautious. But the Republican commanders should nevertheless remain wide awake, since an attack on an unsuspecting enemy is always a good tactic.

OUR MILITARY OFFICERS

Commandant Adriaan Diederichs

In spite of their joy over their great victory over the Khakis at Magersfontein on 11 December, many Free State burghers are mourning the death of the highly respected and beloved Commandant Diederichs, who was killed in the battle.

Adriaan Petrus Johannes Diederichs was born in 1841 in the southern Free State in the present Smithfield district while the Great Trek was still in progress. His parents were Jacob Hendrik Diederichs and his wife Cornelia Aletha van Wijk. As a young man Diederichs settled in the present district of Ladybrand. He participated in the wars between the Free State Republic and the Basuto of King Moshweshwe in the 1860s. Immediately after the wars he was elected Field Cornet of the district in 1868. In the 1870s he played a leading role in the establishment of the town Ladybrand.

In the 1880s Diederichs briefly joined the founders of the Republic Land Goosen on the Transvaal western border, but when that venture failed, he returned to Ladybrand where he continued playing a prominent role. With the outbreak of this war exactly two months before his death, he was elected Commandant of his district. He was not destined to ever enjoy the fruits of victory. His burghers made a decisive contribution to halt the British on the battlefield at Magersfontein but he never saw the end result.

Commandant Diederichs is survived by his wife Martha Maria Magdalena Wolmarans, five sons and four daughters.

Commandant A.P.J. Diederichs

THE War Reporter
WEEKLY EDITION

Number 13 — Pretoria, South African Republic — 6 January 1900

BRITISH OCCUPY DOUGLAS
Debacle on New Year's Day

Magersfontein, 4 January – On 15 November last year, a Boer force under Commandant J.J. Jordaan, assisted by Judge J.B.M. Hertzog, occupied Douglas, a small town on the Vaal River southwest of Kimberley. They also occupied Barkly West and Griquatown, reading out proclamations by Chief Commandant C.J. Wessels in terms of which the whole of Griqualand West was declared an occupied territory, subject to Free State martial law. In addition they hoisted the Free State flag, took over government offices, appointed a magistrate and gave jurisdiction over the whole Griqualand West to that official.

The defence of Douglas and the maintenance of law and order were the responsibility of a small commando of Free Staters at first, but in due course the task was transferred to a group of Cape Afrikaners under Commandant J. Scholtz, whose laager was between trees at the foot of a hill right next to the town. These Cape Afrikaners are strictly speaking rebels, since they have joined enemy forces that occupy a British colony and are actively supporting a foreign government.

On New Year's morning there were only about 60 people in the rebel laager when they were unexpectedly attacked by a British force of some 500 men with a few guns and machine guns. At that time more than half of the rebels were visiting their families at home to celebrate the arrival of the New Year after attending the church services held in town the day before. The men in the laager itself had celebrated the coming of the new century with abandon the previous evening, and had no sentries out. As a result they got a massive surprise when a British bomb suddenly exploded in their camp.

Commandant Scholtz was some distance from the laager when the attack commenced, and realising that the camp was in danger of being overrun he galloped for Magersfontein to get help. In the meantime the other rebels in the laager defended themselves courageously. However, by four o'clock that afternoon, after 14 of them had been killed, the remainder – 38 men, seven of them wounded – surrendered. Two British soldiers were killed and two wounded.

The British, commanded by Colonel Pilcher, occupied the town, to the joy of the pro-British inhabitants. According to our reporter the soldiers subsequently plundered the shops and got drunk on looted alcohol. That evening they amused themselves by forcing their prisoners of war to throw the ammunition from their laager into a huge fire, where it exploded to the delight of the soldiers.

The British celebrations were of short duration, since on 3 January they heard a rumour that General Cronjé was on his way with 800 burghers, with the intention of capturing them. Pilcher's reaction was to abandon Douglas and flee to Belmont Station, south of the Modder River. Many of the pro-British inhabitants followed him, since they were afraid of revenge at the hands of the rebels who had not been captured by the British. Our men promptly reoccupied the town.

THE MAGERSFONTEIN FRONT

Pretoria, 5 January – At Magersfontein the Boers are still busy extending and improving their system of trenches and fortifications. The burghers are full of confidence that they will be able to resist any British onslaught. A renewed frontal assault by the Khakis on our trenches at Magersfontein would probably be doomed to failure – but will our men be able to prevent the British outflanking the trenches?

An increasing number of women and children are arriving at the laagers at Magersfontein and making themselves at home there. Some Boer officers believe this will break down the weak discipline in the laagers even further; others argue that it is a good thing, since the burghers whose families are now in the laagers will no longer whine for leave to go and visit their homes.

In the meantime, enemy patrols have committed acts that infuriate the Republican authorities. They conduct looting raids into the Free State, capturing livestock and even torching farmhouses, including the house of Commandant D.S. Lubbe. We believe their objective is to intimidate the burghers to such an extent that they would rather return to their farms to defend their possessions than wait on the front for another day.

One of the Free State burghers on this front, Schalk Burger, is a diligent diarist. He sent us the following account of life on the front at Magersfontein:

'From 13 December everything was silent, except the guns have regularly exchanged shots. It is an unpleasant and gloomy existence in these forts that consist of trenches where we have now been forced to stay for almost a month. At night we must diligently carry out sentry duties, and in the day we hide in the trenches in wind and weather and the hot sun in order not to be mown down by the bombs, since the enemy are always shelling us and let no opportunity go by.

'Thus it happened that the enemy fired on our fort one afternoon, while two brothers Wolfaard of the Potchefstroom district were walking past. We were warning them to come and take cover in our trench until the bombardment was over, when a bomb exploded right next to them and seriously wounded them both. Fortunately they recovered.

'In a rocky area next to our forts, some 40 yards from the foot of the hill, there is a thorn tree where we often sit in the shade when the sun is very hot. It has become a habit and we felt comfortable since the enemy never shoots in the middle of the day.

'One day there were about 40 of us under the tree, at ease, when our Commandant Ignatius du Preez called on me from the trench to fetch the newspaper and read it out to the men. I immediately stood up with a few friends and walked towards the Commandant. Suddenly one of us noted that the enemy was opening fire, which was quite uncommon at that time of the day. The agreed warning, upon which everyone would dive for cover, was a shout: "There it is!" When the shout came all the burghers under the tree ran for the trench. The last man had barely dived in when a lyddite shell exploded right next to the trunk of the tree with such force that pieces of shrapnel, of rock and of tree landed within the trench. It was a blessing that the Commandant had called me, since we would otherwise not have noticed that the enemy was firing and would not have been able to prevent a blood-bath.

'On another day the British advanced with two guns towards Sergeant Tuynsma's gun emplacement and fired a total of 48 lyddite shells on our gun, destroying one of its wheels. One bomb landed directly under the gun carriage and unfortunately the bombs and gunpowder ignited

Boers in their laager at Magersfontein

Republican officers at Magersfontein

BRITISH PRISONERS OF WAR IN TRANSVAAL
Transferred from Pretoria to Waterval

Pretoria, 3 January – The care of the numerous prisoners of war being brought from the front to Pretoria, since they cannot be held captive in the veld, is becoming a huge problem. There are already 2 500 British prisoners of war, including 80 officers, here in our capital. At first the racetrack west of the city centre was properly fenced in and used to accommodate the prisoners of war. Since there are now too many of them to accommodate at the racetrack, the authorities decided to transfer all of them to Waterval.

The new camp is right next to the railway line to Pietersburg, approximately 20 kilometres north of the city. It will probably be a more secure place of custody and the detention of the prisoners will be less of a headache for the government there. The camp is surrounded by barbed wire and guarded by numerous armed Boers.

Die Volksstem, a Pretoria newspaper with little sympathy for the enemy, describes the transfer of the prisoners of war in the following humorous way: 'As a result of the increasing summer heat, the directors of the excellent Hotel Racetrack politely requested the guests who were dallying there if the time was not ripe to escape from the city of Pretoria to the well-positioned summer retreat, "Waterval".

The main attraction of the healthy, unbounded rural life is so overwhelming that the guests are at present leaving in groups of about 300 at a time for the journey to that destination. The remainder will leave tomorrow, accompanied by some 600 tourists who recently arrived from the Cape Colony. The silence and fresh air of Waterval will have a calming influence on these gentlemen, who became quite heated in the recent past and discussed leaving us without paying their account. They will now probably return to their previously untroubled way of life.'

The Waterval prisoner-of-war camp, with Republican guards in the foreground, above, and Khaki prisoners below

27

FROM THE EDITOR

No major confrontation occurred in the past week. Far from indicating that the war is nearing its end, however, there are clear indications that the British are determined to fight on indefinitely, with new soldiers arriving virtually daily from all over the world, including Canada, Australia and New Zealand.

Sieges of the British garrisons in Ladysmith, Mafeking and Kimberley continue, though with hardly any determination by our burghers. Perhaps it is high time to abandon the last two: those two towns have no strategic value and the burghers who are stationed there would be better employed providing a defence against the expected British onslaught over the Orange and Tugela Rivers.

News from the fronts underlines one very disturbing phenomenon. Many burghers are becoming tired of the war. They find the sitting and waiting in the laagers, the never-ending sentry duty and the absence of action extremely boring. Boredom, rather than the Khakis, is becoming the biggest threat to the burghers' morale. In addition the Republican authorities will have to end the in-fighting between our officers, since a house divided against itself cannot stand.

CLASHES IN THE STORMBERG

Stormberg, 4 January – Since the Republican victory at Stormberg on 10 December last year, the British force on that front has been considerably reinforced. Shortly before Christmas our scouts reported that the British commander, General Gatacre, had more than 6 500 men with 32 guns at his disposal. On the other hand, Chief Commandant J.H. Olivier's force consisted of 1 100 men with four guns, two of them Armstrong guns captured by the Boers from the British in the battle of Stormberg.

On 23 December a British force attacked Dordrecht with two armoured trains and a large number of foot soldiers, including Cape Colonial units. About 200 Cape Rebels had been guarding the town, with a Free State magistrate, P.J. de Wet, wielding authority. The British repulsed the rebel force and drove out the magistrate, even assaulting women in their eagerness to establish control over Dordrecht, according to De Wet.

Chief Commandant Olivier was furious when he was informed of this development. He immediately dispatched a force of 300 burghers with a gun to re-establish Republican authority in the town. These burghers encountered a strong British patrol of more than 500 men with four guns at Labuschagne's Nek outside Dordrecht at about noon on 30 December. After a fierce battle, which went on through the night into the next day, they defeated the Khakis and drove them off. The burghers captured eight soldiers, including an Afrikaner, and found the bodies of some members of the British patrol. The extent of the British casualties is not known. On the Republican side, Field Cornet Gert Barnard was killed and eight men wounded.

The Boers reoccupied Dordrecht on 3 January. They were furious when they noted that the British had broken open the houses of Afrikaners and looted and damaged them. One can only hope that damaging the houses of civilians will never become an official part of British military tactics in South Africa.

Olivier moved towards the south from Stormberg on the same day, 3 January, with 1 000 men and two guns, to test the resolve of Gatacre's force. The British soon noticed this move and sent out an armoured train to counter it the same day. The Boer gunners opened fire on this train and repulsed it after two shots. Boers and Khakis exchanged rifle fire over a long distance, but apparently nobody was hit. Olivier subsequently decided that he could not repulse Gatacre without taking the risk of heavy casualties, and abandoned his plans.

BRITISH PROPAGANDA POEMS

The thin line between satire and insult

Pretoria, 5 January – The line between satire and insult is often extremely fine. In the last few weeks a number of British propaganda poems have emerged here in the Transvaal capital. Even though we would hate to be called a vehicle of enemy propaganda, we feel that the following two poems are excellent examples of a poem telling more about the poet than about the subject he or she is describing.

By reading the first poem our readers will gain a deep insight into the arrogant mentality of the ruthless enemy that confronts us in this war. The poem claims to be about President Kruger and the poet is the imperialist word-magician Rudyard Kipling. It was written about two weeks before the outbreak of the war:

Sloven, sullen, savage, secret,
uncontrolled,
Laying on a new land evil of the old;
He shall take his tribute, toll of all our
ware,
He shall change our gold for arms –
arms we may not bear.

This is not satire. It is meant to be insulting, as indicated by the choice of words such as 'sloven', 'savage' and 'evil', and of course 'tribute' instead of 'tax', which the civilised English would prefer. We are used to English insults, and accept them as a legacy of the superiority complex that shapes the domineering mentality of their race. What remains mind-boggling is the arrogance reflected in Kipling's choice of words in the last two lines: 'our ware', 'our gold'. We have no idea where the poet gets the notion that he and his people have any more legitimate claim to the gold of the Transvaal than a cab driver in Calcutta, a cowboy in Colorado or a fisherman in Finland.

The next poem is true satire. We do not know the identity of the poet, but the poem was published in the *Ladysmith Bombshell*. The contents reveal that it was written after the outbreak of war by somebody inside Ladysmith who daily experienced the Boer bombardment of the besieged town. It is aimed at Commandant-General Piet Joubert. He is not insulted, but referred to as 'slim', a word reserved in South African English for somebody who has outwitted you. He is called 'Jew', which refers to his extensive business ventures. He is challenged to attack the British garrison in broad daylight. He is clearly informed that the besieged in Ladysmith do not regard him as brave and that the shells he showers on Ladysmith hit churches, hospitals and civilian targets instead of only the military. Whoever reads this poem smiles and even feels some sympathy for the poor folks who find themselves under British protection in the town where it was written. Here it is:

To General Slim Piet

Hail mighty Oom: Jew Boer
Proud leader of a dirty crew
Who shell at night instead of fight
as savage Bourbon Tartars do.

Your deeds of valour at the sound
the nations well may quake
The sick and wounded down you strike
The Church and Town Hall break.

The nature folk you blandly strip
of cattle clothes and money
and thus you prove you're closely bred
To sow and wolf or monkey.

Oh slippery one at last you've hit
The biggest marks in town
Days twenty four you've done your best
To shell the Red Cross down.

But still it waves and up its back
Stands honour, brave and true
Our warrior lads but wait the word
to meet and share and square with you.

WAR OF WORDS IN COLESBERG

Republican commanders differ on tactics

Bloemfontein, 5 January – A development that may in the long run have major advantages for the enemy is the disagreement between the Republican officers in the vicinity of Colesberg. This is an important front, since a main railway line to the Free State runs through Colesberg. Consequently, we trust that the issues will soon be resolved to everybody's satisfaction.

Until the outbreak of this internal war of words, the Republican forces had some success in repulsing the enemy. On 16 December last year, Commandant Haveman and Field Cornet Piet de Wet, the brother of Fighting General Christiaan de Wet, drove a huge British patrol that had occupied Vaalkop, 20 kilometres south of Colesberg, back all the way to Arundel station, 10 kilometres further to the south. Since then, however, our forces have allowed the initiative to slip to General French, the British commander.

The core of the problem here at Colesberg seems to be that the commander of the Republican forces on this front, General Hendrik Schoeman, refuses to take any risks. He believes that his forces should at all times be fully prepared to counter a sudden British attack that could cut them off from the Free State. Schoeman proposed to his war council on 27 December that the most southerly units of the burgher forces should be recalled to Colesberg itself, since they would have better defensive positions available around the town. The war council actually approved his proposal, but both Presidents Kruger and Steyn objected, since a retreat would favour the enemy. Schoeman nevertheless proceeded with the retreat, convinced that it was in the best interest of the Republican forces.

The retreat of Schoeman and his burghers to Colesberg on 29 December was immediately followed by the occupation of the abandoned Boer fortifications by French's soldiers, who then began harassing the new Boer positions around Colesberg. This news was greeted with concern by the Republican authorities here in Bloemfontein as well as in Pretoria. Both the Republican presidents, as well as some of the more decisive officers, believe that General Schoeman and his Free State colleague, Esaias Grobler, who was in the vicinity of Colesberg at that time, should have attacked and driven the Khakis back.

Those two generals, however, did not believe themselves to be strong enough for such a venture. President Kruger consequently dispatched 650 men of the Transvaal Mounted Police under the command of Commandant Van Dam to the southern Free State. In addition, 350 burghers from the northern Transvaal were ordered a few days later to proceed to the southern Free State as soon as possible. General F.A. (Big Freek) Grobler would be in overall command of these burghers, numbering 1 000.

Before daybreak on 1 January, French and his Khaki forces attacked Colesberg itself. Their attack on the main Boer position was repulsed, but they presented a serious threat to the Boers' northern communication links. When the battle came to an end that evening, the British were still in possession of some of the low hills outside Colesberg. Nevertheless, Schoeman believed that his burghers had defeated the enemy and reported thus to President Kruger.

The fighting around Colesberg resumed on 2 and 3 January without either of the two opposing forces being able to gain the upper hand. The majority of the burghers chose to concentrate their attention on plundering a British supply train that had derailed at Plewman Halt just south of the town. No noteworthy casualties were suffered by either side.

On 3 January Piet de Wet succeeded Esaias Grobler, who is in poor health, as provisional Free State head commandant. The next day De Wet attempted with great determination to drive the British from their positions, but was driven back with a loss of about five burghers killed, 10 wounded and 15 taken prisoner. The British also suffered casualties in this encounter.

After these setbacks for the burghers at Colesberg, serious differences of opinion erupted between their commanders. De Wet accused Schoeman of leaving him in the lurch by not supporting his attack on the enemy. It is true that there is a general feeling among the burghers at Colesberg that Schoeman is an incapable military leader and does not possess the necessary drive to be in command of a whole front. It is equally clear that the Republican authorities will have to intervene to prevent a real catastrophe.

Colesberg, with Coles Kop in the background

Commandant van Dam's policemen parade through Johannesburg before leaving for Colesberg

OUR MILITARY OFFICERS

General Schalk Burger

Schalk Burger was born in 1852 in the Lydenburg district. His father was a member of the Transvaal Volksraad and both his grandfathers were well-known public figures. On his father's side there was the Voortrekker Kootjie Burger, who was a member of the Volksraad in both Natal and Transvaal, and on his mother's side Commandant-General W.F. Joubert of Lydenburg.

Burger was schooled at home when he was a child but also received some education from the Voortrekker teacher J.G. Bantjes. As a young man he served as a clerk of the field cornet of Lydenburg. In 1876 he participated in the South African Republic's campaign against the Bapedi of Sekhukhune, and in 1880–81 he was a provisional field cornet in the Transvaal War of Independence. After this war he participated in some of the campaigns of the Republic against rebellious black communities.

In 1885 Burger was elected commandant of Lydenburg and a year later became a member of the Volksraad for Lydenburg. Since his advice is always highly regarded, he serves on numerous commissions and in 1895 was elected chairman of the First Volksraad. A year later he became a member of the Executive Council, on which he served with well-known leaders such as Generals Piet Joubert, Piet Cronjé and the late Jan Kock.

Burger is known as a supporter of Joubert and a progressive. He did all he could to hinder the outbreak of the war. Shortly before the outbreak he was appointed general and commander of the Lydenburg commandos in the war. His pre-war criticism of President Kruger is now forgotten, and he has proved himself a loyal officer. He is at present the commander of the Boers who are besieging Ladysmith.

General Schalk Burger

THE
War Reporter
WEEKLY EDITION

Number 14 **Pretoria, South African Republic** **13 January 1900**

BLOODY BATTLE AT PLATRAND

BOER ATTACK ON LADYSMITH REPULSED

Moddersspruit, 10 January – On 6 January the Boer besiegers of Ladysmith finally launched a determined attack on the British defenders. Their target was a hill known as Platrand, on the southern side of town, where the British had erected extensive fortifications. Commandant General Joubert regarded Platrand as the key to Ladysmith. If the Boers could establish themselves on that low hill, they would be able to make life in the besieged town impossible for the defenders. Joubert had the support of both President Kruger and the Transvaal State Attorney, Jannie Smuts, while the celebrated French volunteer, Count De Villebois-Maureuil, presented him with a plan of action.

The proposal that the Boers should attempt to occupy Platrand was discussed at length last Wednesday at a joint war council meeting of the Transvaal and Free State officers who are participating in the siege of Ladysmith. Commandant General Joubert, who is back on the front even though he has not yet recovered sufficiently to be able to ride a horse, was the chairman. The council decided that the attack should take place on 6 January. Chief Commandant Marthinus Prinsloo would lead the Free State burghers against the western part of Platrand and General Schalk Burger would lead the Transvaal attack on the eastern part. All the other officers and burghers, as well as the Boer guns, would concentrate on making life for the British defenders in and around Ladysmith as difficult as possible so that General White would not be able to send reinforcements to the defenders of Platrand.

The Boer commanders knew very little about the British positions on Platrand, since Khakis had occupied the hill continuously ever since the beginning of the siege. Our scouts had inspected the long, narrow hilltop through their binoculars and telescopes, and noticed that it was covered with numerous bulwarks and fortifications over a distance of about four kilometres from east to west. Information gained from black people in the vicinity and from refugees from Ladysmith indicated that the British called the western part of the hilltop Wagon Hill and the eastern part Caesar's Camp, and that about 1 000 soldiers were stationed on it. The distance from the centre of Platrand to Ladysmith was only about four kilometres, which meant that reinforcements could easily be sent from the town.

THE NOCTURNAL ATTACK

The burghers of the Winburg, Kroonstad, Harrismith and Heilbron Commandos started their march on Wagon Hill at ten o'clock on Friday evening and arrived at the foot of Platrand soon after midnight. Their commander, Commandant Cornelis de Villiers of the Harrismith Commando, had participated in the assault on Colley's force on Majuba Hill as a volunteer when he was a young man. Now this courageous veteran was the commander in a battle that was unfortunately destined to end in disappointment for the burghers.

The Free State burghers had hoped to keep their presence on the slope of Platrand a secret as long as possible, but this was impossible. As the well-known Reverend J.D. Kestell afterwards remarked, the noise of shoes marching over loose rocks sounded like the hooves of a herd of horses in the silence of the night. The British could not help hearing the Boers ascending the hillside. Nevertheless it was already three o'clock in the morning when the first rather awkward shout of a British sentry broke the silence of the night. 'Halt, who goes there?' All the burghers froze, but nobody answered. Moments later the British sentries started shooting wildly into the darkness. Thus began the battle of Platrand.

The Free State burghers immediately charged to the summit, but failed to overrun the British defensive positions. After daybreak they did manage to pin the Khakis down with accurate rifle fire, but the battle soon became static, with the British regularly sending new soldiers into the battle. The Free Staters could not be dislodged, however – on the contrary, at one stage they drove the Khakis some distance back.

THE BATTLE FOR THE SUMMIT

Like their Free State compatriots, the Transvaal burghers who were to attack Caesar's camp left their laagers the previous evening. Their main force consisted of two full commandos, namely Utrecht and Vryheid, as well as field cornet wards of the Heidelberg and Wakkerstroom commandos. The latter reached the eastern rim of Platrand by four o'clock that morning without being noticed and even managed to overrun the most easterly British fortifications. Soon afterwards the other burghers also reached the summit. A fierce shooting battle went on for hours, but unfortunately the Heidelberg burghers could not hold the fort that they had occupied, since the British repulsed them in a heavy assault. The problem was that no new burghers arrived to reinforce or replace those who carried out the initial attack.

As the day went on, it became very hot. The burghers became increasingly tired, especially since they had been on the move since the previous evening, and in many cases had no water left. Salvation only came in the late afternoon in the form of a heavy thunderstorm. Since the Transvaalers would have to cross a stream if forced to retreat, they became afraid that they would be cut off from the laager by rising water. In addition they began running out of ammunition. As darkness fell, therefore, they disengaged from the battle and began retreating, wading through waist-high water when they crossed the stream.

Republican artillerymen firing on British positions on Platrand

While the coming of the rain signalled the end of the battle for the Transvaal burghers, the Free Staters had no plans to fall back. Even though the relief from heaven seemed to have inspired the British to fight even harder, they held on to their positions on Wagon Hill for another two hours. It was only when they noticed after darkness had descended that the Transvaalers had retreated, that they realised that their efforts were in vain. The totally exhausted Free State burghers retreated to their laagers disappointed but in an orderly fashion.

If all had gone according to plan the other Boer commandos would have threatened Ladysmith from all sides while the attack on Platrand was being launched. The British would then not have been in a position to send reinforcements to Platrand. Some Boer units did co-operate – the Long Tom on Bulwana fired 111 shots that day, which the Boer gunners had considered impossible, their previous record being 90 shots per day. The other diversionary attacks never materialised, however. The burghers ascribed this to General Schalk Burger's lack of military skills.

The Boer ambulances were very busy after the fight, since the casualties were high. A total of about 65 burghers were killed or died of wounds, and more than 120 others were wounded. The doctors, Carl Menning, Anton Brullbeck, Johan Heese and Theodor Dönges, worked throughout the night treating all the wounded. Those who had died were buried next morning, Sunday 7 January. The British commander in Ladysmith, General White, allowed the Boers to retrieve their fallen comrades from the battlefield for that purpose. On the British side the casualties amounted, as far as we could establish, to 140 men dead and 275 wounded.

We have often heard the accusation that our burghers are cowardly and would not be able to storm a British fortification determinedly. Here at Platrand the Boers have now shown that they can attack courageously. Their lack of success is the result of the inability of the Boer commanders to act decisively, and the cowardice of those burghers who failed to assist those fighting in the front line. The vast majority of the burghers are prepared to charge the enemy in battle. They realise that such an attack could result in heavy casualties, but declare unanimously that they would prefer one hard, bloody battle to months of boredom, of having to do guard duty, of anxiety and uncertainty and a never-ending siege.

FROM THE EDITOR

This week our attention will be focused on events on the Natal front, and the failure of the Republican attempt to capture Platrand, the British-held key to Ladysmith. The Free State burghers led by Commandant C.J. de Villiers distinguished themselves in battle, but there appears to have been a lack of co-ordination between them and their comrades from Transvaal. Our military authorities will have to ensure proper co-ordination, since victories depend on thorough planning and meticulous execution of plans as much as courage.

With the arrival of Lord Roberts, a new element has entered the war. Nobody can tell what the new British commander-in-chief's campaign plans are. He is now in Cape Town. Time will tell if he will, like Buller, attempt to break the Boer resistance on the Natal front, or concentrate on the wide expanses of the Free State southern and western borders. So far, the British commanders in South Africa have not revealed themselves as creative strategists, and Roberts will probably rely on massive numbers in his quest for glory. However, the Republican military authorities would be wise to take all precautions against a surprise movement on the side of the enemy.

In the meantime, in England, and indeed across the whole British Empire, the government of Lord Salisbury is still proclaiming that Britain is fighting in self-defence. According to its claim, the Boer republics were the aggressors, since they not only issued the ultimatum, but also immediately invaded British colonies (Natal and the Cape Colony). Those claims leave one speechless with anger and frustration, since they are based on a total misrepresentation of the truth. If ever people acted in self-defence, it was our governments. The British were surrounding them with drawn daggers like a band of murderers would surround an unfortunate person with the intent to kill and rob him of his belongings. Our governments took preventative action in self-defence and have no aggressive aims against Britain or any of her colonies.

ROBERTS IN SOUTH AFRICA

Cape Town, 10 January – Field Marshal Lord Frederick Roberts arrived in Cape Town today to take up the post of commander-in-chief of British forces in South Africa. The local English language newspapers are publishing lengthy reports on the career of the slightly built warrior who has the responsibility to salvage British honour in our country. For the benefit of our readers, we repeat the most important particulars.

Roberts was born in 1832 in India and spent altogether 39 of his 68 years in that part of the world. He was 19 when he became an officer and 25 when he was awarded the Victoria Cross for bravery during the British suppression of the Indian Mutiny of 1857. In 1880 he made a name for himself with his march from Kabul to Kandahar. Early the next year he was supposed to succeed the late General Colley as British commander in South Africa after the latter was killed on the summit of Majuba Hill, but the Transvaal War of Independence ended before Roberts actually arrived here in April 1881.

In 1885 Roberts became the commander-in-chief of the British forces in India, and in 1895 commander-in-chief in Ireland. In latter years he was promoted to the rank of field marshal – the highest rank in the British army. We hear that he repeatedly asked to be given the command in South Africa should a war break out between Boer and Brit, but the British Prime Minister, Lord Salisbury, considered him too old for the job.

According to British newspapers it was the setbacks that the British army suffered in Black Week that led to the Cabinet's decision to replace Sir Redvers Buller with Roberts. And now he has arrived to subdue the Republics. Exactly how he and his chief-of-staff, General Lord Kitchener, hope to carry out their duty we do not know. Time will tell if Lord Roberts of Kandahar, as he is officially called, will be able to achieve what Buller has failed to accomplish.

The new Commander-in-Chief, Field Marshall Lord Frederick Roberts

Number 14   13 January 1900

PLATRAND: KESTELL'S REPORT

Modderspruit, 11 January – The Reverend J.D. Kestell, who accompanied the Free State burghers when they attacked the Khakis on Platrand on 6 January, compiled the following eyewitness report of the battle for our correspondent:

'How terrible the firing was! It never ceased for a moment, for if the burghers did not rush out, from time to time, to assail the forts, the English charged us. It was during these attacks that the pick of our men fell. Whenever a sangar was attacked a destructive fire was directed on our men, and then some gallant fellows would always remain behind struck down. In this manner Field Cornet Cilliers of Heilbron, and of the Harrismith Commando: Kootjie Odendaal, Marthinus Potgieter, Gert Wessels, Zacharias de Jager, Jacob de Villiers and Piet Minny, were killed; and Hermanus Wessels and others were mortally wounded. They were mostly hit in the head, for the English as well as the Boers were on the watch, and whenever anyone put out his head from behind a stone or a fort, he was immediately fired at.

'It was a fearful day – a day that no one who was there will ever forget. The heat too was unbearable. The sun shot down his pitiless rays upon us, and the higher he rose the hotter it became. It was terrible to see the dead lying uncovered in the scorching rays; and our poor wounded suffered indescribable tortures from thirst.

'How glad I was that I could do something for the wounded. I bandaged those within reach. I also rendered the first help to the British wounded; one Tommy said to me, after I had bandaged him: "I feel easier now." And a sergeant of the Imperial Light Horse, who had discovered that I was a minister, remarked: "You are preaching a good sermon today."

'How slowly too the time dragged! "What o'clock is it?" someone asked. It was then only ten o'clock, and it seemed as if we had been fighting more than a day, for up to that moment the firing had continued unabated. Twelve o'clock passed, one o'clock, two o'clock – and still the fire was kept up; and still the burning rays of the sun were scorching us.

'Clouds! But they threw no shadow over us. Everywhere small patches of shade chequered the hills and valleys; but they seemed to avoid us.

'But a black mass of cloud is rising in the west, and we know now that everything will soon be wrapped in shadow. Nearer and nearer to the zenith the clouds are rising. What is that deep rumbling in the distance? Thunder! Nearer and nearer it sounds, and presently we hear it overhead above the din of the musketry and the boom of the cannon. How insignificant the crash of the cannon sounds now. It is as the crackle of fireworks when compared with the mighty voice of God!

'At five o'clock great drops splashed on the rocks. Presently the rain fell in torrents, and I could wash the blood of the wounded from my hands in it.

'It was now, just when the rain was descending in sheets of water and the thunder-claps were shaking the hill, that the enemy redoubled their efforts to drive us off the ledge, and our men had to do their utmost to repel the determined onslaught. Had they been driven down to the plain below, every burgher fleeing for his life would have formed a target for the enemy. The fight was now fiercer than at any time during the day. It was fearful to hear the roar of the thunder up above, and the crash of the rifles below.

'But the enemy did not succeed in driving us off. We remained there two and a half hours longer. Meanwhile we had been able to quench our thirst. We had made folds in our mackintoshes in which we caught the rain, and then sucked it up. Streams of water too dashed down through the rocks. These streams of water came from the forts a few yards above us, and were red in colour. Was it red earth, or was it the blood of friend and foe that coloured the water?

'We had been on the hill for 16 hours under a most severe fire. When it became dark Commandant De Villiers realised that no reinforcements would come. Now we retired. Commandant De Villiers waited till the last man had gone, then fired some shots in the air to make the English think that we were still in our positions. We then tramped through the water, till we reached our horses, and then rode to the laager, depressed in spirits, for we had left very dear ones behind us.'

The Reverend J.D. Kestell

THE SIEGE OF LADYSMITH

Modderspruit, 11 January – The siege of Ladysmith is still proceeding, but carried out with diminishing vigour by the Boer forces. In the report on the Battle of Platrand elsewhere in this issue, mention is made of a heavy bombardment by our artillery on the British garrison in the town. We recently managed to obtain the latest edition of the newspaper titled the *Ladysmith Bombshell*, which is being published by civilians who are besieged by the Khakis. It contains the following poem, reflecting an undisguised respect on the side of the British for our Long Tom guns with their six-inch diameter barrels.

THE SIX-INCH GUN

There is a famous hill looks down
Five miles away on Ladysmith town
With a long flat ridge that meets the sky
Almost a thousand feet on high
   And on the ridge there is mounted one
   Long-range terrible six-inch gun.

And down in the street a bugle is blown
When the cloud of smoke on the sky is thrown
For it's sixty seconds before the roar
Reverberates o'er, and a second more
   Till the shell comes down with a whiz and stun
   From that long-range terrible six-inch gun.

And men and women walk up and down
The long hot streets of Ladysmith town
And the housewives work in the usual round
And the children play till the warning sound
   Then into their holes they scurry and run
   From the whistling sound of the six-inch gun.

For the shells they weigh a hundred pound
Bursting wherever they strike the ground
While the strong concussion shakes the air
And shatters the window-panes everywhere
   And we may laugh – but there's little fun
   In the bursting shell from the six-inch gun.

Oh! 'twas whistle and jest with the carbineers gay
As they cleaned their steeds at break of day
But like a thunderclap there fell
In the midst of the horses and men a shell
   And the sight we saw was a fearful one
   After the shell from the six-inch gun.

Though the foe may beset us on every side
We'll find some cheer in the Christmas tide
We will laugh and be gay, but a tear will be shed
And a thought be given to the gallant dead
   Cut off in the midst of their life and fun
   By the long-range terrible six-inch gun.

Commandant-General Piet Joubert leads a war council meeting near Tugela

OUR MILITARY OFFICERS

General Andries Cronjé

Andries Petrus Cronjé, the oldest general in the forces of the Orange Free State, was born near Riversdal in the Cape Colony in 1833. His parents are Johannes Daniël Cronjé and Dina Judith Gertruida Woudrina Rahl, who have been married for over 70 years and are both in their nineties.

Cronjé moved to the north of the Orange River with his parents in 1839. When he was 15 years old, he participated in the Battle of Boomplaats against the British forces of Governor Sir Harry Smith in 1848. He also gained military experience in the wars between the Republic of the Orange Free State and the Basuto in the 1850s and 1860s, and achieved the rank of field cornet.

Cronjé became a well-known and respected figure in the central Free State community. In 1879 he was elected to the Volksraad, of which he remained a member almost continually until last year. In 1895 he was elected commandant of Winburg.

On the eve of this war last October Cronjé led his commando to the Natal front. President Steyn, of whom he is a confidant, appointed him as fighting general. He led the Free State forces in their first major encounter of the war, namely at Rietfontein in October last year, 51 years after his last battle with British forces. This time he was on the winning side. Since December last year he has been stationed at the Tugela River as commander of the Free State forces on that part of the front.

General Andries Cronjé

A Republican laager in Natal

BRITISH POPULATION MISLED BY A BLATANT LIE

Pretoria, 10 January – Our readers will find it hard to believe, but the story is actually being spread in Britain and over the whole British Empire by publications such as the *Standard* that Queen Victoria's government is making war on the Republics in self-defence, since the Republics sent out the ultimatum! Unfortunately some people in England believe that deliberate lie. However, there are prominent journalists like W.T. Stead who do their utmost to state the truth, namely that the Republics were forced into the war by Britain. We have just received the text of a report that Stead published on 9 January in the *Review of Reviews* in which he forcefully exposes the corruptive power of falsehood:

'Are we in the right in this war? It is a question worth considering. It is not settled by waving the Union Jack – not even by chanting "Rule Britannia". The attempt to silence its consideration by brutal violence and rowdy clamour is well calculated to give pause to all reflecting men. The Jewish mob which cried out "Crucify Him! Crucify Him!" imagined that they had effectually carried their point. They gained their immediate end no doubt. Not even the pleading voice of the Roman judge could be heard above the din. They got their way and secured the Crucifixion. But it brought them an immorality and infamy, and afforded us the supreme example of the murderous results which are apt to follow when the stormy clamour of an excited mob is allowed to silence the still small voice of reason and justice.'

THE War Reporter
WEEKLY EDITION

Number 15   Pretoria, South African Republic   20 January 1900

TENSION RISING ON THE NATAL FRONT
Buller threatens Boers on upper Tugela

Modderspruit, 19 January – The large-scale movement of British soldiers, guns and supplies from Frere to the upper Tugela make it seem certain that General Buller plans to break through our defence lines in that area. From 10 January there has been a steady stream of Khakis moving westwards. From afar they look like a colony of ants on the move. In addition to the thousands of soldiers participating in the movement, there are also a few hundred wagons in the British convoy. From the heights north of the Tugela, we have a good view of the enemy's movements through our binoculars. It is clear that their movement is accompanied by massive difficulties. The steam tractors that they use to haul their huge guns immediately got stuck in the mud, of which there is enough due to the continuous rain. The same is happening to their wagons. The British force is progressing with difficulty.

There were not many Boers south of the Tugela when the British began their onslaught – only a commando of Free State burghers under General Andries Cronjé who had entrenched themselves on the hills south of Potgietersdrif. When they noted the British advance, they crossed the strong-flowing river in good time to ensure that they would not be cut off from the rest of our forces. Thus the British found the drift unoccupied. On 11 January a number of them started crossing the river at the drift. The day after that virtually the whole British force had occupied the low hills that Cronjé's burghers had abandoned. They appear to be placing their headquarters at that spot.

Generals Louis Botha, Schalk Burger and Lukas Meyer have been implementing measures to defend the upper Tugela against a possible British attack since the beginning of January. When the British march to the upper Tugela began, Botha moved Boer commandos in the same direction on the northern side of the river. The burghers are outnumbered by the British, but they are much more mobile, and should be able to defend a specific area if their commanders note that the British intend attacking at that direction. The morale of the burghers is tremendously high. On 16 January Fighting General Tobias Smuts of Ermelo assured our correspondent: 'We are full of confidence for the struggle that lies ahead, trusting in our God, in what is right and in the help that we will get from above. The struggle will be difficult but we will survive.'

On 17 January the British began crossing the Tugela River at Trichardsdrif some eight kilometres west of Potgietersdrif. They launched a heavy bombardment on the low hills north of the river, but the burghers did not fire back. The British at Potgietersdrif in the meantime began crossing the river in even greater numbers, and launched a half-hearted attack on our positions in the hills, but it was clear to our officers that these were diversionary attacks and that the actual target was the area north of Trichardsdrif, the Tabanyama hills west of Spioenkop, a high hill that offers a view over the whole surrounding area. General Burger immediately began moving most of his force to that area. The burghers had begun arriving there two days ago and immediately started digging trenches and building entrenchments. According to General Botha, who seems to be exhausted and overworked, there are at present about 1 500 burghers on the upper Tugela.

The only notable action in this area took place yesterday on the hills west of Tabanyama. This was the first serious skirmish between units of Buller's Natal Field Force and the Boers north of the Tugela River. A British patrol became involved in a fight with a unit of some 200 burghers from Pretoria and Heilbron commanded respectively by Field Cornets Opperman and Mentz. The burghers were in due course forced to fall back, but 35 of them were surrounded and after 11 men, including Mentz, had been killed and seven wounded, the rest surrendered.

When our reporter left that part of the front with the first light this morning to proceed here, it was clear that both sides were preparing for a great battle.

REPORT BY WILHELM MANGOLD

Modderspruit, 19 January – Our correspondent has sent us the following report on developments in Natal, compiled by Wilhelm Mangold of the Heidelberg town commando:

'On 16 January 70 men of the Heidelberg town commando left their positions around Ladysmith to go to the battlefront on the upper Tugela. Their orders were to help in stopping the British force of General Buller. They would, after seven days, be relieved and would take enough provisions with them for this period. Their commander is General Schalk Burger. After ten hours on horseback they reached Potgietersdrif that evening and immediately took up position above the Tugela River. Even though they were dead tired after the whole day in the saddle, they were immediately ordered to build entrenchments and dig trenches. That they did as well as they could, even though in the darkness of the night in an unknown place it was not an easy task. Afterwards they covered the raw ground with grass to camouflage their position as much as possible. They also built bush and grass shelters through which they could see well but which made them invisible to the enemy.

'The British began bombarding the Boer positions along the Tugela at sunrise on 17 January. Their target was the neat fortifications of sandbags built by the Boer artillerymen. The Boer guns were not in those emplacements, however, but set up some distance away in well-camouflaged positions. Consequently the British bombardment was totally ineffective. For the burghers their biggest travail that day was their never-ending hunger and thirst that they could only relieve that evening when they were allowed to leave their trenches. Opportunity to rest was just not available. After they had made coffee and tended to their horses, which were cared for by a few men behind the low hills, they had to build trenches again. This kept them busy right up to the early morning hours.

'One of the Boer fortifications with a trench right in front of it is situated on a hillock not far from the Tugela River. On the afternoon of 18 January a large number of British foot soldiers charged that position and fired on it over a long distance with their guns and rifles. There were no Boers in either the trench or the fortification at that time, since the burghers found shelter in the shade of trees. In order not to reveal their position, they did not fire back on the enemy. Our gunners counted that the British fired more than 400 shots. It was so intense that the hillock on which the fortification was built became invisible as a result of the smoke and dust clouds. You as a reader can hardly imagine what a rumble of roaring guns and exploding shells this brought about. The British sent up an air balloon to reconnoiter our positions. We expected an attack after dark and prepared for it, but nothing further happened. Our total losses only amounted to a few men wounded.'

The burghers here on the upper Tugela are positive and full of courage. Indeed, they look forward to an attack by the British infantry, since they believe that they will beat them off even more effectively than Botha thrashed Buller's soldiers at Colenso last month. It is an open question if they will attack again at all. It seems as if they are still hesitant, which indicates that they learnt a thorough lesson at Colenso.

CIVILIANS GO ON THEIR WAY

Pretoria, 11 January – It is often amazing to see how some civilians manage to carry on with their usual daily practices in the midst of destruction and the drama of war. Nicolaas Hofmeyr reports from the Natal front that he was visiting the widely dispersed Boer laagers on the morning after the battle of Platrand earlier this month when he came across a small community of black farmers who were calmly ploughing the soil. Thus they were busy with fruitful labour in the midst of useless destruction.

A Boer sentry post near Spioenkop in Natal

A Boer camp near Colenso

FROM THE EDITOR

An unhealthy situation has emerged on all fronts: we seem to be conceding the initiative to the enemy. Nowhere do the Boer forces still have freedom of movement, or dictate the order of events, as they did during the first few weeks of the war. Now we are tending to react to the enemy's movements – a particularly unhealthy situation, since no state can win a war if it cannot force its will on the opponent.

In addition to this lack of initiative, the most worrying news of the past week is the fact that our officers are not working as a team on all fronts. Too many follow their own heads, disregarding the orders of their superiors. As a result, our supreme commanders are finding it increasingly difficult to plan in advance. In addition, there are simply too many burghers who are not prepared to give their very best in the struggle. The British far outnumber our forces and all the Republican officers will have to co-operate to resist them. Our Republic's motto is, after all, *Unity is strength*.

NEWS FROM THE QUIETER FRONTS

THE NORTHERN FRONT

Pretoria, 19 January – Our scouts report from the far north that the British force commanded by General Plumer abandoned Fort Tuli on 27 December and started moving to the southwest. It seems certain that his intention is to restore British authority in Bechuanaland west of Mafeking. From what we hear, his force is making slow progress and nothing is to be feared from it.

THE WESTERN FRONT

Magersfontein, 18 January – Since the battle at Magersfontein on 11 December, there has been no direct clash between the British at the Modder River and the Republican forces here on this front. The only hostilities are the sporadic bombardment of Boer positions by the British. The Boer artillerymen have only answered on two occasions, since General Cronjé prefers not to waste ammunition.

We have heard from reliable sources that Cronjé has received explicit orders from both President Kruger and Commandant-General Joubert to attack the British communication lines south of the Modder River. However, Cronjé is not prepared to comply, since he believes that the risk is too great and the chances of success too small. He is still totally convinced that the British are too dependent on the railway line to move away from it at all. That is why he is not taking any measures to defend the long Free State borderline between the Modder River and the Orange River. He concedes that the British could cross the borderline quite easily, but argues that their dependence on the railway line will force them back very quickly.

KURUMAN AT LAST OCCUPIED

Vryburg, 8 January – On 24 November last year we reported on events at Kuruman, where the British authorities had decided to resist occupation by Republican forces. Field Cornet Visser was preparing to besiege the town when General Cronjé recalled him to Vryburg.

Early in December Visser, now promoted to the rank of commandant, returned to Kuruman with a force of 500 burghers. Since the British garrison still refused to surrender, the burghers laid siege to the town on 5 December. The defenders had in the meantime erected a number of small fortresses at strategic places around the town. On 16 December the burghers launched an attack on those fortresses, but occupied only one.

The siege finally ended on New Year's Day, when the burghers bombarded the town with a recently acquired seven-pounder muzzle-loader gun. It was impossible to shoot accurately, but after about 100 shots, the British raised the white flag.

A total of 132 men, 70 of them black members of the Cape police, became our prisoners of war. The enemy informed us that three of their number had been killed during the siege. On the Boer side one man was wounded. Commandant Visser is elated that the siege ended in victory, since the enemy defended stoutly.

THE COLESBERG FRONT

Springfontein, 16 January – Even though there has not yet been a major battle on this front, the British under command of General French are keeping our burghers busy. Good news is that the clash between the Republican officers has subsided and there are many burghers on their way here to help stem the British onslaught.

President Kruger reacted to the rumours of General Schoeman's alleged incapability and decided in co-operation with President Steyn to send a commission of inquiry to Colesberg, consisting of A.D.W. Wolmarans, member of the Transvaal Executive Committee, A. Fischer, the Free State government secretary and Generals Koos de la Rey and Manie Lemmer. They arrived in Colesberg on 8 January and found there were no grounds for the complaints against Schoeman. The commission furthermore expressed the opinion that the British threat to the safety of the southern Free State was so great that General De la Rey should remain in Colesberg for the time being. He was offered the post of commander-in-chief of the Transvaal burghers at Colesberg, but declined the appointment since, as he stated, 'I do not want to steal this honour from other officers.'

On the night of 5–6 January, while the commissioners of inquiry were still on their way to Colesberg, the British attempted to occupy Graskop, a hillock some four kilometres to the north of the town. This onslaught was repulsed by about 100 Heilbron burghers under the command of Commandant Rooi Frans van Vuuren, assisted by 15 Johannesburg policemen under command of Lieutenant D. Marais. The large numbers of casualties on both sides confirm that it was a heavy battle. Of the British 37 were killed and about 100 taken prisoner, 30 of them wounded. We have been told that another 23 wounded Khakis escaped. The Boer loss was seven men, including Marais, and 15 wounded.

On 9 January the British took up position at Slingerfontein, some 20 kilometres southeast of Colesberg. The Boers could not prevent this, since their attention was taken up the whole day by British troop movements and a bombardment west of the town. It seems possible that these were diversionary tactics. General Schoeman subsequently decided to place General de la Rey in control of the area east of Colesberg.

De la Rey began putting pressure on the British position at Slingerfontein from 10 January. The scale at Colesberg swung heavily in favour of the British on 12 January when they managed to haul a gun all the way to the top of Cole's Kop. The Boers were most unpleasantly surprised early the next morning when the British artillery began bombarding them from the summit of that hill. First the buildings in the town, including the Wesleyan church building, were targeted. Next came the Boer camp, including the ambulance wagon with a huge Red Cross on it, forcing the burghers to shift their camp.

On 14 January, while the British were still busy bombarding Colesberg, they almost managed to outwit our forces with a surprise attack on the Colesberg wagon bridge across the Orange River. Fortunately General Freek Grobler's burghers noticed this and managed to drive the Khakis back. Yesterday (the 15th) the burghers of General De la Rey were again involved in heavy skirmishes with the enemy at Slingerfontein.

So far, the Republican forces have managed to hold their own around Colesberg. However, Boer scouts report that many hundreds of British soldiers supported by artillery are proceeding in this direction. It is clear that the Khakis are determined to effect a breakthrough on this front.

THE STORMBERG FRONT

Bloemfontein, 18 January – On this front there was no notable fighting in the past week. The main Republican force is still in possession of Stormberg, while the British are digging in at Molteno some 15 kilometres southeast of that important railway junction.

The Republican garrison that guards over Dordrecht won a skirmish with a British unit on 7–8 January. Two soldiers were killed and six, including a black man, taken prisoner of war. From then onwards everything was quiet on that front.

FATE OF BOER PRISONERS OF WAR

Cape Town, 18 January – An English language newspaper published in the Mother City this week published a short report on the fate of about 430 Boer prisoners of war. At first they were held on board the ship *Penelope* in Simon's Town harbour. Then they were detained in the dock hospital in Cape Town before being transferred to the ship *Manilla*. After a number of burghers attempted to escape by plunging overboard, the prisoners of war were taken back to Simonstown and transferred to the troop ship *Catalonia*, which is anchored some distance from the coast to minimise the possibility of attempts to escape.

The author of the report writes that he was received with curiosity by the vast majority of Boers on board the *Catalonia*. They were only too happy that something was breaking the terrible boredom of an unlimited detention. He recognised numerous prisoners of war whom he had met previously in Bloemfontein, Johannesburg, Pretoria or in the Boer camp at Sandspruit. One of the prisoners reminded him of his promise to come and hunt springbok with him, to which the journalist answered that this would now have to wait since the burgher had gambled on shooting Khakis.

There were prisoners to be seen all over the deck. Some of them were reading, while some were playing draughts and others attempted to fish. Most of them seemed terribly bored, but others were involved in serious discussion. Many kept themselves busy by taunting the guards, especially over British setbacks in the war.

The journalist enjoyed dinner with the prisoners in the late afternoon. The meal consisted of cooked meat, potatoes, onions, bread and coffee and there was enough for everybody. The journalist also visited their sleeping quarters, which seemed rather crowded and unpleasant and the prisoners complained endlessly about them. The ship's captain, however, laughed this away by claiming that he had brought 1 200 British soldiers on board this same ship to South Africa and they had never complained. According to the journalist this is but a weak excuse, since the conditions really seem bad. Hopefully their detention on board this ship will only be a temporary measure.

The prisoners do not have extensive duties. They are expected to keep their quarters clean. On certain specific days they may receive visitors on board and they may receive luxuries such as deck chairs, food, clothes and tobacco from their visitors, but neither money nor alcohol.

The journalist's report ends with the observation that it is good that the Boer prisoners are well treated. We quote his words in this regard as follows: 'The men against whom we fight today are the brothers and cousins of many of our compatriots, and will after the war become our compatriots themselves. We have to bring this war to a successful conclusion, but have continually to keep a post-war settlement in mind. Each gesture of goodwill towards the prisoners of war who are in our hands, will make the settlement after war easier and will make the feeling of bitterness which will necessarily follow, less. It would serve no purpose to treat the prisoners of war harshly. It would be much better to end the war as quickly as possible and to keep ourselves from any acts which would stimulate a feeling of racial hatred.'

CHILDREN'S SONGS

Pretoria, 19 January – A reader from the eastern Free State sent us the words of a few songs she heard her children sing at school to taunt the English-speaking children. The first is about messages sent by heliograph between General Buller at the Tugela River and General White, the British commander in Ladysmith:

Hold the fort for I am coming
Says Buller by helio
Quick as light flashes the answer of
 White:
Aren't you coming slow?

The second one describes the appetising dinnertime menu at Mafeking:

A sausage made of horse
Four-and-twenty locusts
Served with weevil sauce
When the dish was opened
The locusts took to wing.
Wasn't that a lovely way
To dine in Mafeking?

OUR MILITARY OFFICERS

General Hendrik Schoeman

Hendrik Jacobus Schoeman is the son of one of the best-known and most controversial pioneers of the South African Republic, Commandant-General Stephanus Schoeman. His mother was Gertina Johanna Schutte. Schoeman was born in 1840 in Pietermaritzburg, but soon afterwards moved with his parents and most of the Natal Voortrekkers to the area north of the Vaal River. He received very little formal education.

Like most of his contemporaries, Schoeman became a farmer. From 1868 his most important farm was Schoemansrust on the Crocodile River at Hartebeespoort, some 20 kilometres west of Pretoria. His participation in public issues began in 1879 when he was elected as a member of the People's Committee of the Transvaal Boers who resisted the British annexation of their Republic. In the Transvaal War of Independence of 1880–81 he was appointed by the Triumvirate as General and was involved in the siege of the British garrison in Pretoria.

From 1881 Schoeman served in numerous Transvaal government commissions and filled numerous posts. In 1885 he was elected a member of the Volksraad and soon afterwards a member of the Executive Council. In the same year, however, he resigned and subsequently kept himself busy with personal affairs.

With the outbreak of this war last October, Schoeman went to the Natal front as an ordinary burgher. Even though he is plagued by rheumatism and cannot mount a horse unaided, he was later that month appointed commander of the Transvaal forces who went to the Free State southern border to protect that Republic against a British invasion. Schoeman soon revealed that he was a particularly careful commander whose main concern is the safety of his burghers.

General Hendrik Schoeman

Republican prisoners of war on board a British troop ship

THE War Reporter

WEEKLY EDITION

Number 16   Pretoria, South African Republic   27 January 1900

'MAGNIFICENT VICTORY' ON SPIOENKOP
BOTHA'S FIRST TELEGRAM TO PRESIDENT KRUGER

Pretoria, 25 January – The first report on the Boer victory over the British forces in the battle of Spioenkop reached Pretoria today in a telegram from General Louis Botha to President Kruger: 'Battle over and by the grace of God a magnificent victory for us. The enemy driven out of their positions and their losses are great … The battlefield therefore is ours … It breaks my heart to say that so many of our gallant heroes have also been killed or wounded … It is incredible that such a small handful of men, with the help of the Most High, could fight and withstand the mighty Britain.'

FROM THE EDITOR

An excellent week for the Republican forces! Our burghers halted the British offensive on the Natal front at both Tabanyama Hill and Spioenkop, inflicting heavy losses on the Khakis especially at Spioenkop. It will take at least a month before the British authorities can form a serious threat for our forces on the Natal front again.

The siege of the British garrisons in Ladysmith, Kimberley and Mafeking proceeds unabated, although there has lately been little action on these fronts. We report on disturbing events at Mafeking, including particulars of the inhuman treatment of black would-be escapees from the siege. We trust that our authorities will intervene to end this scandalous behaviour forthwith.

On the other fronts not much that is newsworthy has happened, but we hear rumours that the British are building up their forces. We may sooner or later have to confront a major offensive on the southern and western fronts.

Spioenkop, with burghers in the foreground

BLOODY CLASHES ON NATAL FRONT
Four-day battle at Tabanyama

Natal front, 23 January – General Buller's British forces launched a determined four-day offensive against the Republican forces on the upper Tugela River. The Boers' capacity to defend their position was stretched to the limit, but fortunately they held out and this morning the Khakis began falling back.

On 19 January a number of the commandos who had recently begun digging themselves in on the slopes overlooking the upper Tugela were ordered to move even further westwards past Spioenkop to the foothills of the Drakensberg. Since General Louis Botha expected a British attempt to break through there, the burghers took up position on the broad and flat summit of Tabanyama Hill, from where they had a breathtaking view of the mountains and the Tugela valley – though they had very little time to enjoy the scenery, since they had to dig trenches and build fortifications.

On 20 January the burghers on Tabanyama Hill were sporadically involved in long-distance skirmishes with the Khakis. The British artillery continually moved closer, starting a four-hour bombardment of the Boer positions at seven o'clock that morning. The effect of this bombardment was minimal, as the burghers had erected two emplacements for each of their guns, and moved between them continuously in order to baffle the enemy. At first the Boer gunners were silent, but at about one o'clock that afternoon they suddenly opened fire, forcing the Khakis to stop their bombardment.

The British infantry were by that time preparing to attack. The burghers were in a magnificent position for defence, since the Khakis would, once they reached the summit and became visible to the Boer gunners, have to cross a flat, open plain more than a kilometre across before they reached the Boer positions. Even more advantageous for the Boer riflemen was that their fortifications would be invisible to the British artillery, which was forced to fire blindly and seldom hit any target.

The British infantry began advancing on the southeastern flank of the Boer line, but the burghers waited until they were within striking distance before they all began firing simultaneously. This instantly halted the British advance.

A VALIANT THREESOME

Among the burghers on the battlefield, three men stood out in terms of bravery. Henri Slegtkamp, Jack Hindon and H. de Roos faced the advancing Khakis alone from a hillock on the British left flank, and fired so heavily on the soldiers that the latter hesitated. Even the Boer commander on Tabanyama, General Louis Botha, was surprised by this, since he had been under the impression that all the burghers had fallen back. What made the undertaking of these three courageous burghers even more noteworthy was that they hoisted a defiant five-coloured flag on the hillock – the red, white, blue and green Transvaal flag (the *Vierkleur* or four-colour) with an orange line across it (orange and white are the major colours of the Orange Free State flag). This unexpected attack on their left flank deterred the Khakis from attacking the Boer position that day, and they fell back by late afternoon.

PRESIDENT STEYN ON THE BATTLEFIELD

For many burghers the highlight of the day was President Steyn's visit to the front. He went from group to group to encourage the burghers. At one stage he was targeted by the enemy when he moved to the Free State burghers in the front line to give them moral support. His presence was a tremendous boost to the enthusiasm of the burghers.

On Sunday morning, 21 January, the fighting resumed. The British now had big guns in position and fired on the Boer position the whole day long. In some areas they drove the burghers back short distances, but in the process suffered heavy casualties themselves. At first, the Boer artillerymen experienced a shortage of ammunition and could not effectively reply to the British bombardment, but when they received additional ammunition, they resumed their bombardment of the enemy with vigour. Some burghers who were close enough even fired on the British artillery with their Mausers. Eventually the Khakis were forced to take cover and ended their bombardment.

It is a godsend for the Boers that the British did not launch another full-scale attack on 21 January. According to our reporter, the burghers' morale was at rock-bottom by that evening for various reasons, despite President Steyn's efforts. They were totally exhausted, since they had been in the front line for almost a week fighting by day and building fortifications or digging trenches by night. To make it worse, their supplies were running low. The front line was now a long way from the commissary depot at Modderspruit Station and there were not enough ox-wagons to transport sufficient food and ammunition to the fighting men, who were forced to live on meat, rusks and water. Then there were not enough doctors and field ambulances. Burghers who became ill or were wounded were treated by their comrades right there in the veld. The continuous bombardment was wrecking the nerves of some, who simply abandoned their positions. In addition, many burghers had been promised that they would be relieved after seven days, but after 10 days they were still on the front and beginning to feel impatient.

Early on the morning of 22 January the British resumed their bombardment of the Boer positions with new vigour. This stretched the nerves of the burghers even further and the tension threatened to reach breaking point. In many cases burghers abandoned their badly damaged fortifications and fell back. General Botha himself was totally exhausted after all his attempts to soothe the burghers and convince them to stay in their positions. He began to fear the worst. In addition he had a narrow personal escape when his horse was wounded under him while he was moving between the positions. Fortunately that incident failed to break his resolve and he remained a valuable source of inspiration for the burghers.

Botha was not the only pillar of strength in the Boer ranks that day. President Steyn kept moving tirelessly between the burghers, encouraging them to remain steadfast. Most of the burghers did stay in position and in due course even those who had abandoned their positions returned to the front.

This morning the British artillery is still shelling our positions but the crisis has passed and the burghers are determined to maintain the front line. Our impression is that the British are falling back and have abandoned their attempt to break through at Tabanyama.

On the Boer side the total casualties from 20 January to this morning are fewer than 100, at least 12 of them killed. The total British casualties in dead and wounded are, according to reliable sources, approximately 600, including at least 50 killed.

De Roos and Slegtkamp at Tabanyama

33

Number 16   27 January 1900

GLORIOUS BOER VICTORY ON SPIOENKOP
General Botha forces Khakis back once again

Natal front, 26 January – From 20 January onwards the British had been pressurising the Boer positions on Spioenkop, a high hill overlooking the Tugela River on the eastern side of Tabanyama. On the 24th this resulted in a full-scale battle – the bloodiest of the war thus far. There were only about 200 of our burghers on the summit of Spioenkop that day when they were attacked before dawn by a force of at least 1 700 Khakis who had ascended the southern slope of the hill under cover of darkness.

The burghers were surprised at daybreak when they suddenly noted the British advance. The first to spot the British were a guard post of 15 burghers of the Vryheid Commando. They fired on the enemy, but fled when charged and gave the alarm so that soon all the Boers in the vicinity knew what was going on.

The British soldiers, in the meantime, entrenched themselves on the hard, rocky surface of the summit. They dug a trench at least 300 metres long, although not very deep. The middle section of the trench tends to the north but its two flanks point backwards towards the Tugela River on both the west and the east. Our burghers could not do anything to hinder the British, since the whole summit of Spioenkop was at that time covered in thick mist.

General Schalk Burger, who is responsible for the defence of this part of the front, was shocked when he heard that the British were on the hill. He immediately ordered Commandant Hendrik Prinsloo of the Carolina Commando to dislodge the enemy. Prinsloo in turn ordered 25 of his burghers to climb up to the summit while he himself hastened on horseback to General Botha's headquarters on a low hill near Spioenkop to ask for advice.

Botha reacted by immediately issuing orders that all the burghers should as quickly as possible take up position on the heights around Spioenkop and that the artillerymen should set up their guns. As a result seven Boer guns were quickly brought into position on hills in a half-moon formation around Spioenkop.

THE FIRST PHASE OF THE BATTLE

The 25 burghers of the Carolina Commando began firing on the Khakis on the summit of Spioenkop soon after seven o'clock that morning when the mist began lifting. The soldiers drove them back. Fortunately at this stage a few hundred men commanded by Commandant Prinsloo and Commandant 'Red Daniël' Opperman of the Pretoria district began climbing towards the summit. Their climb can be compared to that of the Boers who ascended Majuba 19 years ago to confront General Colley's redcoats in the Transvaal War of Independence. The main difference was that covering fire was supplied by guns stationed on neighbouring hills, while the Boers had no artillery at Majuba, but numerous Boer sharpshooters who were stationed on the foothills of Majuba itself. In both cases the covering fire had the crucial effect of pinning the soldiers down on the summit of the hill and allowing the attackers to reach the crest unhindered.

The soldiers on the summit of Spioenkop could find nowhere to hide and suffered heavy casualties, not only from the Republican guns, but also from sharpshooters. The burghers who reached Aloe Hill, north-northeast of Spioenkop and less than 400 metres from its summit, had a clear view of the enemy and could fire with great accuracy on their opponents. The Boer artillerymen similarly had a good view of the enemy from their positions. The result was a devastating rain of shells and bullets that caused huge casualties among the British.

One of the first burghers who reached the summit of Spioenkop after climbing up the northern slope was the heliographer Louis Bothma. He subsequently had a determining effect on the course of events since he took up position with his heliograph on the northeastern end of the summit and from there signalled to the various Boer guns where they should aim to achieve the best results. The Khakis could not withstand this type of fire. Their commander, General Woodgate, suffered a fate similar to that of Colley on Majuba when he was mortally wounded.

THE BATTLE FOR THE SUMMIT

The soldiers on the eastern side of Spioenkop's summit were the first to yield. They had suffered severely under fire from the east and northeast, especially from Aloe Hill, as well as from the north after Prinsloo's burghers reached the summit of Spioenkop itself. Those trapped in the trench suffered terribly.

By midday all the Khakis on Spioenkop's summit had been forced to seek cover in the trench. The burghers were now full of confidence. They knew they were exerting tremendous pressure on the enemy. Many hurried to Spioenkop from Tabanyama Hill. Fortunately the enemy did not attack Tabanyama on that same day, since the burghers would not have been able to defend both positions simultaneously. Now, however, they believed they could gain the upper hand.

By one o'clock victory seemed imminent when dozens of Khakis surrendered. Soon afterwards large numbers of fresh British troops arrived on the crest of the hill. Suddenly our men were again at the receiving end of severe pressure. A bayonet charge drove the burghers back a little distance, but they held the summit. Fierce rifle battles raged between the two sides. At this time the Boers suffered their worst casualties.

Our correspondent talked to numerous people who were on the summit of Spioenkop while the battle raged. Two American volunteers fighting on the Republican side, Alan Hiley and John Hassell, described the death of Field Cornet Badenhorst of Vryheid in gruesome detail. They say that he was standing behind a large rock shooting at the enemy. Suddenly he swung around and sank with a groan to a sitting position, with his back against the rock. He was hit between the eyes, but was still alive:

'Hour after hour he sat with wide-open eyes. His death certain, no one moved him … Men with spare ammunition hurrying past would give this well known man a glance of pity … The noise of the battle and the passing men had no apparent effect on the deadened brain or staring gaze, but sitting erect until noon, suddenly, with a guttural she-e-e-et a stream of blood poured from the hole in his fore-

Burghers of the Carolina Commando at Spioenkop just before the battle

Boers on Spioenkop

Spioenkop, with two burghers in the foreground

Boers building fortifications on Spioenkop

A British entrenchment made on Spioenkop, the night before the battle

Spioenkop after the battle

British soldiers killed in action on Spioenkop

head and the bravest man we ever knew sank dead and limp to the earth.'

REITZ'S EYE-WITNESS ACCOUNT OF THE BATTLE

One of the Pretoria burghers who participated in the battle was Deneys Reitz, the 18-year-old son of the Transvaal State Secretary. Young Reitz describes the ascent of the hill:

'Dead and dying men lay all along the way, and there was proof that the Pretoria men had gone by for I soon came upon the body of John Malherbe, our Corporal's brother, with a bullet between his eyes; a few paces further lay two more dead men of our commando. Further on I found my tent-mate, poor Robert Reinecke, shot through the head, and not far off L. de Villiers of our corporalship lay dead. Yet higher up was Krige … with a bullet through both lungs, still alive, and beyond him Walter de Vos of my tent shot through the chest, but smiling cheerfully as we passed. Apart from the Pretoria men there were many other dead and wounded, mostly Carolina burghers from the eastern Transvaal …

'Halfway across lay the huddled body of a dead man and now that I had time to look more carefully at him I recognised Charles Jeppe, the last of my tent-mates. His death affected me keenly, for we had been particularly good friends …

'The English troops lay so near that one could have tossed a biscuit among them, and whilst the losses which they were causing us were only too evident, we on our side did not know that we were inflicting even greater damage upon them. Our casualties lay hideously among us, but theirs were screened from view behind the breastwork, so that the comfort of knowing that we were giving worse than we received was denied us.'

As the day wore on the tribulations on both sides increased. Reitz continues:

'The sun became hotter and hotter, and we had neither food nor water. Around us lay scores of dead and wounded men, a depressing sight, and by midday a feeling of discouragement had gained ground that was only kept in check by Commandant Opperman's forceful personality and vigorous language to any man who seemed wavering. Had it not been for him the majority would have gone far sooner than they did, for the belief spread that we were being left in the lurch …

'As the hours dragged on a trickle of men slipped down the hill, and in spite of his watchful eye this gradual wastage so depleted our strength that long before nightfall we were holding the blood-spattered ledge with a mere handful of rifles. I wanted to go too, but the thought of Isaac and my other friends saved me from deserting …

'The hours went by; we kept watch, peering over and firing whenever a helmet showed itself, and in reply the soldiers volleyed unremittingly. We were hungry, thirsty and tired; around us were the dead men covered with swarms of flies attracted by the smell of blood. We did not know the cruel losses that the English were suffering, and we believed that they were easily holding their own, so discouragement spread as the shadows lengthened.

'Batches of men left the line, openly defying Red Daniel who was impotent in the face of this wholesale defection, and when at last the sun set I do not think there were 60 men left on the ledge.'

DARKNESS ENDS THE BATTLE

Throughout this whole period the Boer artillery kept firing away at the enemy. By late afternoon the Khakis gained a major tactical advantage when they forced the Boers to remove two of their guns from Twin Peaks, two hills east of Spioenkop. The Khakis actually began occupying these hills, from where they would have had a commanding position, but darkness came at this time and soon afterwards the British soldiers withdrew again to the south.

Mercifully the daylight now faded and with that the fighting ended. The burghers on the summit of Spioenkop itself were so tired by dark that the majority of them retired to the valley north of it to get some rest. Reitz told our correspondent:

'Darkness fell swiftly the firing died away, and there was silence, save for a rare shot and the moans of the wounded. For a long time I remained at my post, staring into the night to where the enemy lay, so close that I could hear the cries of their wounded and the murmur of voices from behind their breastwork.

'Afterwards my nerves began to go and I thought I saw figures with bayonets stealing forward. When I tried to find the men who earlier in the evening had been beside me, they were gone. Almost in a panic I left my place and hastened along the fringe of rocks in search of company, and to my immense relief heard a gruff 'werda'. It was Commandant Opperman still in his place with about two dozen men. He told me to stay beside him, and we remained here until after ten o'clock, listening to the enemy who were talking and stumbling about in the darkness beyond.'

Opperman and his men left the summit then. Their idea was to resume the battle at first light. Only a small number of Boksburg and Krugersdorp men remained behind. Many of the other burghers and even some senior officers believed that they had lost the battle and that it would be better to retreat. General Botha had his hands full to restore their morale.

THE MOST PLEASANT SURPRISE

It was altogether a miserable bunch of burghers who ascended the summit of Spioenkop early on the morning of the 25th. To their great surprise and relief, however, they found when they reached the summit that the British were gone, presumably even less prepared for another hard battle.

The total Boer casualties in the battle of Spioenkop were heavy. Altogether 58 burghers were killed and 140 wounded. On the British side the devastation was much greater. It was a terrible sight to behold. In the trenches there were places where the British bodies lay three deep. It is clear that the Republican artillery wreaked havoc. From a reliable source we have heard that approximately 225 soldiers were killed and 550 wounded. In addition the burghers took 300 prisoners of war.

While both sides tended their wounded and buried their dead, all the British soldiers fell back across the Tugela River. There is no danger of an imminent British breakthrough on this front.

A grave for the brave – Spioenkop, 26 January 1900

Number 16   27 January 1900

OUR MILITARY OFFICERS

THE HEROES OF SPIOENKOP

Commandant Hendrik Prinsloo

Hendrik Frederik Prinsloo, one of the heroes of this week's Battle of Spioenkop, is a descendant of one of the rebels of Slagtersnek who was executed in 1816 for participating in that Rebellion. He was born in 1861 near Kroonstad in the Orange Free State and named after his father. As a child he moved with his parents to the Lydenburg district in the Transvaal.

Prinsloo's military career began in the Transvaal War of Independence, in which he participated as a young burgher. Two years later he earned widespread respect in the so-called Mapog War when he carried a wounded burgher to safety from a very dangerous position. In 1896 he became a field cornet in the Carolina Commando. Two years later he participated in the South African Republic's successful campaign against the Venda of Chief Mphephu. He was known as a very able officer and in June last year became commandant of his commando.

At the outbreak of this war last October, his commando was sent to the Swaziland border. In December they were transferred to the Natal front where they participated in the battles against Buller's forces. It was at Spioenkop that he proved his value as an officer, however. In discussions of the battle one often hears the remark that had it not been for the bravery of Prinsloo and his burghers in the initial phases of the battle, the Boers would have found it difficult to regain the summit of the hill. His courage was an inspiration to all the burghers.

Commandant H.F. Prinsloo

Field Cornet Daniël Opperman

Daniël Jacobus Elardus Opperman is a big, attractive man with flaming red hair. Not surprisingly, his nickname is Red (Rooi) Daniël. He was born in 1861 on the farm Doornkloof, immediately south of Pretoria, and has lived there ever since. His parents were Daniël Jacobus Opperman and Petronella Erendina Opperman.

We have virtually no information on Opperman's youth. He took part in numerous campaigns that the South African Republic undertook against black communities and gained a reputation for exceptional bravery. By 1893 he was the assistant field cornet of the Witwatersrand ward of the Pretoria Commando. Two years later he was elected field cornet. He is married to Louisa Catharina Erasmus and they have five children.

When the war broke out last October Opperman and his burghers were sent into Natal. He participated in the siege of Ladysmith but remained in the background. Last week he and his men were transferred to the Tugela front. They fought with distinction in the Battle of Tabanyama. However it was Opperman's heroic leadership on the summit of Spioenkop that won acclaim for this charismatic officer.

War Reporter has no photograph of this able officer.

MESSAGE FROM PRESIDENT KRUGER TO BURGHERS

Pretoria, 20 January – Our venerable State President issued the following message of encouragement to all the commanders a few days ago with the clear order that it had to be read to all the burghers. It reflects his deeply anchored belief in God as well as the biblical grounding of his principles. We publish it here in shortened and translated form:

'Through the blessing of God, we find ourselves at present in a position where we can, with great effort, bring our undertaking to a successful conclusion. It is, however, essential that we will employ our whole force, that all burghers that can in any way do their duty, should go to the war front and that those who are at home on leave should not linger long but should return as quickly as possible, each to the front where his officer is waiting for him.

'Brothers, I request you urgently to keep your eyes on the Almighty, who has often assisted our people with miracles in their endeavours in South Africa. Read and sing Psalm 33 from verse 7 to the end. God tempers his children as gold is tempered with fire. Think of this: the enemy are destroying our farms, in the Cape Colony they are, according to reports, seizing the property of Afrikaners and selling or damaging it. Even in the Orange Free State they are destroying farms.

'I do not have to inform you of all the damage done by the enemy, since you are aware of it, but I want to point out the onslaught of the enemy. Read Psalm 83. It is the onslaught of the devil against Christ and his church. It is an onslaught from olden times, but God will not allow the extermination of his church. You know that our cause is just and cannot be doubted. I read through the whole Bible, but found no other way than to do what we are doing, namely to fight in the name of the Almighty.'

Above: Boer artillerymen shelling the enemy
Top left: Burghers on sentry duty on the Natal front
Bottom left: Members of the Bicycle Scout Corps in a Republican laager in Natal

SIEGE OF MAFEKING
Inhuman treatment of blacks upsets Kruger

Klein Marico laager near Mafeking, 26 January – Since the beginning of this month the burghers besieging the British garrison at Mafeking have had increasing problems with black people fleeing the town or rustling livestock. The war council of General Snyman has an uncompromising policy: those who are caught for livestock theft are summarily executed. Those who attempt to leave the town are summarily forced back.

Not all the burghers agree with this policy. On Sunday 7 January, for example, a large group of black women pleaded to be allowed to leave Mafeking. Some of these poor creatures were so debilitated and hungry they could hardly walk. One of the burghers inquired from General Snyman what they should do. We are told that the General answered: 'Chase them back, and shoot them if they come out again.'

This order is unacceptable to many of the burghers. They believe that the black women and children should be allowed to leave Mafeking, firstly since the Boers are not fighting against women and children, and secondly since such a gesture would probably convince many other blacks to choose Boer humanity above British 'protection'.

That Snyman is serious with his order that blacks should not be allowed to leave Mafeking has been confirmed a number of times during the month. On 16 January, for example, two burghers of the ward Molopo who arrested two black fugitives instead of chasing them back into Mafeking were sentenced to 'saddle carrying' – that is, a specified period of carrying their saddles on their shoulders. That same day, six sentries received the same sentence for allowing a horseman from Mafeking to steal about 20 cattle.

The reason why the commanders of the Boers at Mafeking are so determined that nobody should leave the town is of course that they hope the whole garrison will sooner or later be forced by a shortage of food to surrender. The argument is simple: the larger the number of people who have to eat, the sooner they will have to surrender. Naturally the Boers look forward eagerly to that day.

President Kruger was horrified when he was informed of the shooting of black thieves at Mafeking. He was so upset that he immediately wrote a letter to Snyman in which he stated clearly that cattle-thieves must not be shot except if they attempt to flee. They must be brought before the war council and be sentenced to either corporal punishment or forced labour, but nothing worse. That Snyman had exceeded his powers cannot be doubted.

Snyman oversteps the bounds of the war customs of the Boer Republics in other respects as well. On 19 January he ordered about 180 Rolong men, subjects of Chief Makgobi Motsewakhumo, to come to his laager and armed them, with orders to ensure that no black person left or entered Mafeking. Colonel Baden-Powell heard of this and wrote to Snyman complaining that this was against the usages of civilised warfare. Snyman's reply, however, was that his armed Rolong were not used against the British in Mafeking, but merely against black people who were ignoring orders.

In the meantime the besieged and the besiegers continue to exchange fire. A number of Boers have been killed in the last month, and according to particulars we have received from Mafeking, there have been casualties in the town. Both sides accuse each other of misusing the white flag. In addition, Baden-Powell busily disseminates false information to make his people more positive and to upset us. We procured a copy of the newssheet *Mafeking Mail* in which he alleges that British soldiers have relieved the besieged garrisons in both Ladysmith and Kimberley. That is of course not true.

36

THE War Reporter
WEEKLY EDITION

Number 17   Pretoria, South African Republic   3 February 1900

PLAN TO END SIEGE OF LADYSMITH
Dam wall of sandbags in Klip River

Modderspruit, 2 February – On 29 January a team of about 500 black workers arrived at the main laager outside Ladysmith to undertake a special assignment. Commandant-General Joubert has decided to implement the proposal of a Free State burgher, Krause, to attempt the flooding of the besieged town. Krause proposes the damming up of the Klip River, which winds its way through the town and then through a narrow gorge past Bulwana Hill just below the town. This will result in the formation of a huge lake that will flood the hollow in which the town is situated. The water line will be above the British camp and their underground ammunition magazines will be flooded. It is estimated that approximately 20 000 sandbags will be sufficient, if placed in position, to build a wall 10 metres in height.

Krause presented his plan to Chief Commandant Marthinus Prinsloo, who was so excited about it that he forwarded it to both President Steyn and Commandant-General Joubert on 13 January. They too thought that it was a brilliant idea. Surveyors and engineers were asked for their opinions and measurements were taken on the terrain. It is estimated that 500 workers working full-time will take about eight days to pack the wall of sandbags, after which it will take only about two days for the dam to fill up, since the Klip River is flowing strongly after all the rain that fell this summer.

Time alone will tell if this plan will work. The labourers are already busy and a huge number of bags are being stacked in a row over the whole width of the river. Many officers and burghers are sceptical and doubt that the wall will be strong enough to hold back enough water to flood the whole Ladysmith basin.

CONDITIONS IN LADYSMITH CRITICAL

It is becoming clearer every day that there is a huge shortage of essentials in Ladysmith. An Indian man who fled the town but was captured by the Boers, says that his entire rations for eight days consisted of only 1,1 kilogram of maize meal. That is why he as well as many other Indians, including stretcher-bearers doing duty in the British army, are forced by hunger to leave the town. We often study the town through binoculars from our fortifications and have no doubt that an increasing number of funerals are being held every day.

The number of burghers involved in the siege is now so small that the Republicans can no longer consider undertaking any form of aggressive action. The majority of burghers have been transferred to the Tugela River front, to Magersfontein or to the southern Free State front. There are only 16 guns left on the hills around the town and they bombard the garrison only sporadically, firing one or two shots per day to remind the Khakis that the siege is still on.

The journalists who cover this siege agree that the burghers are extremely bored. Some burghers loyally write letters to their friends and family, even though they have very little to report on. The majority prefer to swim in the rivers or compete in athletics or other traditional games. Virtually all the burghers complain that they are getting tired of just sitting here and of the war in general. This is a very unhealthy and even dangerous state of affairs. The initial Republican enthusiasm to do battle against the enemy has completely evaporated on this front.

Construction of the dam in the Klip River

CLASHES IN AND AROUND COLESBERG
British forces becoming a serious threat

Colesberg, 1 February – In our previous report on developments on the southern front, we mentioned that the British were increasing their pressure on the Boer forces in the vicinity of Colesberg. Generals Hendrik Schoeman, Freek Grobler and Koos de la Rey of the Transvaal and Chief Commandant Piet de Wet of the Free State are finding it extremely difficult to prevent a British breakthrough.

In the past two weeks several hundred British soldiers and dozens of artillery units have joined those already present on this front. These new arrivals are being stationed on the flanks of the British line. In that way General French is continually extending the front to the west and the east. The Republican commanders are forced to spread their burghers out over a similar extended line in order to oppose a possible British attack. As a result of this the Republican forces are so thinly spread over the total front of about 60 kilometres from Bastersnek to Ratelpoort, that they cannot go on the offensive anywhere.

KHAKIS HARASS PRO-REPUBLICANS IN CAPE COLONY

The British have recently adopted a new tactic that frustrates the Boers tremendously. They send out patrols that damage the property of Cape Afrikaners suspected of supporting the Republics. General de la Rey feels so furious about this that he has considered establishing highly mobile punitive commandos to pursue the British plunder patrols. This is more easily said than done, however, since the horses of the Boers are simply too weak to keep up with those of the British and there are too few burghers available to defend the front sufficiently.

The major advantage to the Boers on this front is that the British themselves are extremely cautious and seldom launch direct attacks on Boer positions. On 16 January there was a skirmish between Lieutenant De Hart's policemen and a British plunder patrol in which our men gained the upper hand and captured a number of excellent horses. On 17 January the British artillery bombarded the Boer positions in Colesberg itself. On the same day the British left flank advanced to within effective range of the Colesberg wagon bridge over the Orange River and bombarded it. All the shots missed, which was fortunate, since the Boers had placed dynamite under the spans of the bridge a few days previously with the aim of destroying the bridge should they themselves be forced to fall back across the river. On 18 and 19 January there were skirmishes again on both flanks of the front, but nobody could gain any advantage.

BRITISH ATTACKS NIPPED IN THE BUD

A few days later the Khakis launched a determined effort to outflank the Boer positions on the western side of Colesberg. Just before dark on 24 January a force estimated by our scouts to consist of 1 000 soldiers with at least 12 guns occupied Bastersnek, about 20 kilometres northwest of Colesberg. Early the next morning those units advanced eastwards in the direction of Plessispoort, where the wagon road from Colesberg to the Orange River winds through low hills.

In an attempt to draw the attention of the burghers on other parts of the front away from this advance, the British troops who were stationed directly opposite and to the east of Colesberg launched mock attacks and bombarded the Boer positions. These were so successful that General de la Rey spent the whole day rallying his burghers and only heard about events in the northwest late that afternoon.

Fortunately their tactics did not win the day for the British. General Groot Freek Grobler and his burghers were too alert to allow that. Grobler's burghers, who had good horses, harassed one section of the Khakis with their Mausers and their guns. Grobler's other burghers, who were defending Plessispoort, led the second section of Khakis into an ambush and fired so heavily on them that they were forced to retreat by four o'clock that afternoon.

The casualties in this skirmish were not high. Five burghers were wounded, one of whom subsequently died. We have no idea of the numbers of British casualties. What we do know is that the British superiority in numbers here in the Colesberg area threatens to overwhelm our defences. We have learned that both Grobler and De la Rey have been pleading with the authorities to send more burghers to this front. The usual answer is that there are simply none available and that they must trust in God.

For the Republican officers here on the southern front that advice is not of much comfort. They feel that it would be better to abandon Colesberg and fall back to the Orange River, since the front will then be less extended and it will only be necessary to defend the Colesberg wagon bridge and the Norvalspont train bridge. President Kruger would not allow this. We also heard that General Cronjé believes that the enemy is busy with a mock offensive here in the Colesberg area. He still believes that their main assault will be on the southwestern front at the Modder River, in other words opposite his own positions at Magersfontein.

In the past week a few hundred burghers from other fronts have arrived here to strengthen the Republican defence line, but General Schoeman and Chief Commandant Piet de Wet, the joint commanders of the Boers on this front, are still not satisfied. Their complaint now is that all the new arrivals either join De la Rey's men on the eastern flank or Grobler on the western flank and that nobody has remained in the centre at Colesberg itself.

At present the Boers here number 4 680 men with eight guns. It is a huge force and we trust that they will be able to halt any British offensive in this barren area, where water and fodder are scarce and any advance difficult.

Boer gunners with a rapid-fire gun, Ladysmith

FROM THE EDITOR

The siege of the British garrison in Ladysmith has entered its fifth month and at last the end may be in sight. In this issue we report on the construction of a wall of sandbags to dam up the Klip River with the purpose of flooding the British camp in the besieged town. Reports from Ladysmith indicate that there is famine in the town and that the inhabitants are in poor condition.

With the besiegers of Ladysmith, namely the Republican forces who have not yet been transferred to the other fronts, things are not going very well either. The most disturbing aspect is moral degradation. In a few Dutch newspapers of which copies have reached us, all the burghers are portrayed as heroes. How wonderful if that were true! Unfortunately there are amongst our people many unscrupulous opportunists whose main objective seems to be to enrich themselves instead of wholeheartedly supporting the struggle against the enemy.

The military officer introduced to our readers this week is a young man on whom we report with the highest praise. If all our burghers were made of the same metal as Major J.F. Welmarans, the British would not have been able to stand up to us at all. This 26-year-old officer deserves the recognition and support of all who associate themselves with our fight for freedom.

HOFMEYR WRITES ON THE LADYSMITH SIEGE

Pretoria, 2 February – The historian Nicolaas Hofmeyr sent us the following report on his observations of conditions around Ladysmith. The picture he sketches is not a very positive one: perhaps our military authorities made a mistake besieging the British garrison there. Here is his report:

'Things are becoming extremely boring here at Ladysmith. Our most prominent enemy is a small Natal fly that is more headstrong than anything else in the world. The heat is becoming unbearable as well. We have visited a number of laagers and found that the most general complaint is tedium. The burghers with intellect and energy are driven to insanity by the fact that they have nothing to do and feel depressed and downhearted when they contemplate the future.

'The vast majority of the burghers are farmers and fathers of families. They dream up all sorts of excuses to obtain a leave letter. Only the "poor whites" find this a paradise. For them the vicinity of Ladysmith is a "land of milk and honey". There is an abundance of fresh meat and bread, coffee and tea, infinite stocks of tobacco, as much as one wants, and everything is free. This is an absolute fool's paradise – at least that is what it seems to be. All the poor whites are dressed in brand-new outfits from head to toe. There is a war to be waged! "What an agreeable situation!" The longer it lasts, the better. For the first time in their lives they are at a place where there is enough of everything.

'At each laager some burghers operate a "General clothes and shoe shop" in a tent or a room. The needy burghers proceed there to state their wishes. Nobody gets anything without signing a receipt on which he acknowledges receiving a suit of clothing or a pair of boots with the name of his commando and ward written on it. It is easy to supply any name whatsoever since nobody checks its correctness. Constant streams of clothes and shoes flow by train from Pretoria to the laagers. But at the destinations there is never enough, since the demand for clothing is impossible to satisfy. All the rivers flow into the sea of burghers but that sea is never filled. Now some observant people have established where the leakage is: many burghers possess a rather flexible conscience. When they go home on leave they take suitcases filled to capacity with new clothes. It is a mere coincidence that those suitcases are empty when their owners return to the front. It is no wonder that the dam cannot fill up: there are too many holes in the wall!'

CONDITIONS ON THE WESTERN FRONT

In the trenches at Magersfontein

Pretoria, 2 February – Mrs Alida Badenhorst sent us the following report from the Western Transvaal. It consists of quotations from letters that her husband, Frikkie, sent her from the front at Magersfontein. In one letter he describes the laager itself:

'Our laager is three-sided, each side being four hundred metres long, and each outside line is made of two rows of tent-wagons one beside the other. Inside the laager is filled with tents, Red Cross wagons, ammunition and provisions – also a telegraph office. It looks like a big town. The laager is close to the river so we have plenty of water. The river is always full of burghers swimming about; they are not allowed to swim above our camp, for we get our drinking water there.'

On the daily tasks such as the slaughtering of sheep for food supply he writes: 'I was ordered to do the slaughtering today. We slaughtered 12 sheep. It is the meat for the men of the ward who are in this camp. The others are in the trenches and slaughtering is done for them there. In the laager there are seven field cornet wards, and you can imagine how many sheep must be slaughtered for both camp and trenches each day. I asked the corporal how many animals are slaughtered each month: more than 4 000 sheep and 100 oxen, he replied, only for the Transvaalers, and more for the Free State burghers.'

On the availability and supply of other food Badenhorst writes: 'The wagons often arrive with maize, biscuits, coffee and sugar, clothes and shoes. Bread we have in abundance as well as meat. Other food is scarce. Rice was available only once, beans also only once, potatoes a few times.'

We even gain some insight into the general appearance of the burghers from his letters:

'I can tell you a change has come among our people. All of them are humble; this is shown even in their clothing. Some of the clerks who were always much over-dressed, now go simply clad and look like old Boers. Some burghers' clothes are already in tatters, but those whose clothes are very badly torn, get new clothes from the government. Huge supplies of clothes are sent here, but there are more people than clothes.'

In numerous letters he writes about the British bombardment of their entrenchments:

'The English fire on us every day, but on Christmas Day they kept quiet and not a single shot was heard. On Sundays they fire as usual. They also fire with poisoned shells, but thank God these have done no harm here. The grass turns yellow where they burst and green smoke rises. When they fall near a man he gets sleepy, even in battle, and those round him have to shake him to keep him awake. Where shells from the big guns burst, they make a hole in the ground large enough for a man to creep into. But God's protection is wonderful. Only a few men have been wounded so far.

'Watching a bombardment from a distance one would not think any man could come out alive, for the entire line of the trenches is a billowing cloud of smoke and earth blown up by the shells, so that nothing can be seen. Brother Jan and I stood watching it together one day: "I wish my wife could see this," he said.

Badenhorst does not approve of the presence of women in the Boer laager: 'There are a few women here who have come to visit their husbands, old Aunt Sarie Lemmer is here and little Maans Lemmer's wife. For my part I wish I could be with you, not you here; this laager is no place for women.'

Finally he writes about the conditions on sentry duty: 'Last night I slept on the bank of the river. The river is in flood and I had to sleep there to give warning if the water level rose to dangerous levels. We slept at the ferry; the other guard was on the other side – the dispatch riders cross the river on the ferry. My blanket was so full of burweed seed that it could never become clean again; the burweed grows thick all along the river. There are also stinging nettles near the river. On guard duty one never sleeps peacefully. We are often startled; one hears cattle and then perhaps horses; then it is the train and at night sometimes the music of the English. The drum makes such a noise that one never knows if the English army is approaching or not.'

Boer shelters at Magersfontein

'HE DID FIGHT'

Free State laager near Ladysmith, 2 February – The Reverend J.D. Kestell, the well-known Free State field preacher, recently related the following humorous incident to our correspondent:

'Last month, shortly before the battle of Spioenkop, I was in conversation with Commandant C.J. de Villiers on the upper Tugela. Amongst the burghers who arrived as reinforcements on that part of the front, there was a young man of 15 or 16 years old. He was riding a little brown horse and looked somewhat destitute.

'"Commandant," he asked De Villiers, "I hear they say it's a fight out there."

'"Yes," the commandant agrees. "And you, where are you going now?"

'"I am going to fight," answered the youngster and proceeded on his little pony.

'A day or so later we again met the young man. He looked quite different. In the place of his rather modest hat, he had a soldier's bonnet on his head. His little brown pony was fully laden with all sorts of supplies originating from at least one or two soldiers. He had three Lee-Metford rifles and a number of water canisters hanging from his shoulders. A few bayonets that made clicking noises against his horse's flanks as well as a shovel of the type that the soldiers use to dig trenches hung from his saddle. At least three bandoliers full of ammunition were tied around his middle.

'Commandant De Villiers made a brief comment: "He did fight!"

SLANDEROUS STATEMENTS BY BULLER

Modderspruit, 2 February – In the pocket book of one of the British officers taken prisoner of war at Spioenkop, the men of our secret service came upon a transcription of a message that Buller issued to his soldiers on 12 January. This message contains shocking and completely unfounded allegations regarding the morality of the Republican burghers. Commandant-General Joubert gave us permission to publish it in its entirety. Here it is in Buller's own words:

'We shall be shortly opposed by a clever, unscrupulous enemy; let no man allow himself to be deceived by them. If a white flag is displayed, it means nothing unless the Force displaying it halt, throw down their arms, and throw up their hands at the same time. If they get a chance the enemy will try and mislead us by false words of command and false bugle sounds; everyone must guard against being deceived by such conduct. Above all, if any are ever surprised by a sudden volley at close quarters, let there be no hesitation; do not turn from it, but rush at it. That is the road to victory and safety. A retreat is fatal; the one thing the enemy cannot stand is our being at close quarters with them. We are fighting for the health and safety of our comrades; we are fighting in defence of our flag against an enemy, who has forced war upon us for the worst and lowest motives by treachery, conspiracy and deceit. Let us bear ourselves as our cause deserves.'

Our readers will not blame us if we state bluntly that General Buller has allowed himself to be mastered by the power of the lie. To state – in addition to his distorted portrayal of our burghers – that we forced the war upon them is as ridiculous as blaming the Aborigines in Australia for the fall of the Roman Empire. Up to now we have had some respect for the integrity of this most senior British officer. However, that era has come to an end. We will have to accept that we have to do with a shameless, merciless enemy.

OUR MILITARY OFFICERS

Major J.F. Wolmarans

Jan Francois Wolmarans was born in 1873 in the Potchefstroom district. His father, J.M.A. Wolmarans, was formerly a member of the Executive Council and his mother is Jacoba Catharina Schutte. Wolmarans was only 15 years old when he and two other youngsters from the Transvaal went to the Netherlands to undergo artillery training. After two years of intensive training he returned in 1892 and initially worked in the State Artillery.

Wolmarans's career in the Transvaal State Artillery officially began in 1894 when he was appointed a second lieutenant after successfully writing the qualifying examination. In the course of the next few years he participated in numerous campaigns against black communities. Early in 1896 he was involved in the rounding-up of the Jameson invaders. Soon afterwards, when he was 22 years old, he was promoted to the rank of captain and appointed as commander of the First Battery of the Mounted Artillery of the South African Republic. In 1898 he participated in the campaign against the Bavenda of Chief Mphephu. Early in 1899 he was promoted to the rank of major.

Wolmarans and his battery entered Natal immediately after the outbreak of this war last October. He participated in the battles of Dundee and Modderspruit and has since then been active in the siege of Ladysmith. The Long Tom on Bulwana Hill functions under his command. Last month his battery was transferred to the Upper Tugela where it participated in the battles of Tabanyama and Spioenkop.

The State historian Nicolaas Hofmeyr describes Wolmarans as one of our best and most able artillery officers. He is young and strong and does not mind sleeping flat on the ground with his tent comrades. His sunny and friendly disposition makes him a popular figure. Since he remains calm and extremely courageous even under the heaviest fire, he is respected and trusted by all his officers and men. He is sober in conduct, moderate in his use of language, a master of his discipline, clean and neat – indeed an officer his corps can be proud of.

Major J.F. Wolmarans

THE War Reporter
WEEKLY EDITION

Number 18 — Pretoria, South African Republic — 10 February 1900

NATAL: MAJOR BATTLE AT VAALKRANS
BULLER'S KHAKI FORCE AGAIN REPULSED BY THE BOERS

Natal front, 8 February – The total Republican force on the Natal front consists at present of only about 3 600 burghers with 10 guns and two pom-poms, spread over a distance of about 30 kilometres. Opposing them is a massive and well-armed force of at least 25 000. Our men are constantly expecting a British attack and are prepared for it – indeed, on 5 February the British attempted to break through at Vaalkrans, between Spioenkop and Colenso.

General Louis Botha was not at the front at that time, but in Pretoria. After the battle of Spioenkop, he had been under the impression that it would take the British at least two weeks to resume their advance. For that reason he took leave to go to the capital to attend to some personal matters, leaving General Schalk Burger in command. Many other officers and burghers followed Botha's example, which explains the small numbers available to resist the British attack.

BOER DEFENCE PREPARATIONS

For the commanders of the burghers who are guarding the Tugela River front in the vicinity of Vaalkrans, namely Fighting General Tobias Smuts of Ermelo and Commandant Ben Viljoen of Johannesburg, it was clear from the beginning of this month that the British were making intensive preparations in that sector. They sent an urgent message to Burger to send reinforcements to their positions, but in vain – 750 men had recently been sent to the Free State southern front on orders of the Presidents, and Burger did not wish to weaken his defence line at Spioenkop any further, since he was convinced that the British would attack there again.

On the orders of Commandant-General Joubert, who was visiting the front in spite of his poor health and the fact that he could no longer ride on horseback, the burghers began building fortifications and digging trenches on the threatened part of the front. In addition a few guns, including at the very last moment a Long Tom siege gun, were set up in emplacements on the low hills. Botha was urgently requested to return to the front, and answered that he would come as soon as possible. Fortunately the British did not attack immediately, but kept themselves busy with thorough preparations for the onslaught.

THE BRITISH ATTACK

The British infantry began crossing a pontoon bridge over the Tugela River under cover of an artillery bombardment from about six o'clock on the morning of 5 February. They immediately charged the Boer positions on the Brakfontein heights west of Vaalkrans. Later in the morning the Boer commanders realised that this was a mock attack, since the Khakis retreated when the Republican artillery started bombarding them. In the meantime the British built a pontoon bridge over the Tugela directly south of Vaalkrans and soon large numbers of soldiers began crossing.

From shortly after nine o'clock the British gunners began a massive bombardment of the Boer positions on Vaalkrans. Viljoen and Smuts sent urgent messages requesting support from Burger as well as other Boer officers, but in vain. Viljoen's men held on to their positions and repulsed the first British attack, but a large number of them, including Viljoen himself, were killed or wounded. The general was hit by a flying piece of shrapnel and badly shaken. His burghers were forced to fall back a short distance, taking their pom-pom gun with them, and dug in behind Groenkop to continue their defence. The summit of Vaalkrans was left deserted and the Khakis occupied it late in the afternoon, but were not able to follow up their breakthrough in order to make a significant advance.

All the Boer officers expected that the British would resume their attack that night or early the next morning. They made preparations under cover of darkness, transferring approximately 1 000 burghers to that part of the front. In addition the Boer artillerymen set up a number of guns in emplacements in a half circle around Vaalkrans. By daybreak they were ready to bombard the British attackers, cheered by the knowledge that General Louis Botha had arrived to resume command.

THE REPULSE

The Long Tom gun began activities on 6 February by bombarding the summit of Vaalkrans. The other Boer guns soon followed its example. To the Boer onlookers this bombardment seemed to cause consternation amongst the Khakis and probably brought an end to their plans to resume the offensive. Indeed, even though the battle went on until the evening, it became stationary. In the meantime the burghers strengthened their positions and prepared to repulse the enemy from Vaalkrans the next day.

The fighting remained stationary yesterday (7 February) with an artillery duel between the gunners on the opposing sides. The Boers expected that the British would at some stage launch a full-scale attack with their infantry, but this never happened. However last night all the Khakis returned to the south of the Tugela, removing their pontoon bridge from the river. It was a massive relief for the exhausted burghers, whose nerves had been stretched to breaking point by the continuous explosion of British lyddite bombs, when they noted by daybreak that the enemy was gone. They had successfully repulsed the British attack!

The general feeling here on the front is that it was the perseverance of the Johannesburg Commando led by Commandant Ben Viljoen and of the Boer artillerymen that assured our victory. The price for this success was high. Total casualties on the Republican side were 38 men killed and 45 wounded; the British loss was only 25 men killed but 350 wounded.

Our scouts report that the total British force is falling back to Frere Station. Perhaps Buller has had enough! It is possible that the British are merely trying to deceive us, since none of us believe that Buller will rest before he has relieved Ladysmith. We are certainly not prepared to allow him that success without a major confrontation.

A lyddite shell bursts in front of a Boer gun emplacement at Vaalkrans

FROM THE EDITOR

Another good week for the Republican forces, with the failure of General Buller's umpteenth attempt to relieve the British garrison in Ladysmith. Though the British superiority in numbers is increasing every day, it seems as if the fight has gone out of the Khakis, at least in Natal.

On the Stormberg and Colesberg fronts the British forces are quiet and the Republican forces are easily holding their own. The only notable clash outside Natal this week was on the western front, where General Christiaan de Wet, who is building up a terrific reputation for himself, managed to counter a British flank movement at Koedoesberg. Several Boer officers, including General Piet Cronjé, claim that he achieved a huge victory. Others argue that this was a British mock attack aimed at leading Boer attention away from the place where the British probably intend launching their major offensive on this front.

That there will be a major offensive cannot be doubted. We receive numerous reports of the gathering of a vast British force on the Free State southwestern border. Apparently the British commander himself, Field Marshal Roberts, is on his way there. We trust that our forces will be able to defend the Republican borders successfully.

In the meantime the siege of the British garrisons in Kimberley, Mafeking and Ladysmith continues, as does construction of the wall of sandbags in the Klip River, in an attempt to dam up enough water to flood Ladysmith.

A Boer pom-pom gun

THE FIGHT AT VAALKRANS

Account by a Boer commander

Natal front, 9 February – Commandant Ben Viljoen of the Johannesburg Commando, one of the heroes of the Boer success at Vaalkrans, compiled the following report on his experiences of the battle:

'For some days it had been clear to me what the enemy intended to do, but I wired in vain to the commander-in-chief to send me reinforcements. I was left to defend a front two and a half kilometres in length with only about 400 men. The Commandant-General was only prepared to send me one of the huge siege guns – a Long Tom. It was placed at the rear of our position to defend Vaalkrans.

'Early on the morning of 5 February my position was heavily bombarded. By sunrise four of my burghers had already been put out of action. I happened to be on the right flank with 95 burghers and a pom-pom. Assistant Commandant Japie du Preez commanded the left flank. The enemy threw two pontoon bridges over the Tugela River. From ten o'clock troops poured across. We fired on the soldiers, but they charged time and again. The number of my fighting men was rapidly diminishing.

'To me it seemed as if the entire firepower of the enemy guns were now concentrated on my position. I may say this was the heaviest bombardment I witnessed during the whole of the campaign. Their big lyddite guns sent over huge shells that mowed down all the trees on the hill, while about 50 field guns were incessantly barking away from a shorter range.

'In vain I implored the nearest general for reinforcements and requested our artillery to aim at the enemy's guns. At last, however, the Long Tom commenced operations, but the artillerymen in charge had omitted to put the powder in a safe place and it was soon struck by a lyddite shell that set the whole of it on fire. This compelled us to send to the main laager near Ladysmith for a fresh supply of powder.

'On looking about me to see how my burghers were getting on I found that many around me had been killed and others were wounded. The clothes of the latter were burnt and they cried out for help in great agony.

'Our pom-pom had long since been silenced by the enemy. At least 30 of my burghers had been put out of the fight. The enemy's infantry was advancing nearer and nearer. I knelt down behind a rocky outcrop, along with some of the men, and we kept firing away at 400 paces, but although we sent a good many to eternal rest, the fire of the few burghers who were left was too weak to stem the onslaught of overwhelming numbers.

'Suddenly a lyddite shell burst over our heads. Four burghers beside me were blown to pieces. My rifle was smashed. It seemed to me as if a huge cauldron of boiling fat had burst over me and for some minutes I must have lost consciousness. A mouthful of brandy and water (which I always carried with me) was given me and restored me somewhat, and when I opened my eyes I saw the enemy climbing the hill on three sides of us, some of them only 100 metres away. I ordered my men to fall back and took charge of the pom-pom. We retired under heavy rifle and gunfire. Of the 95 burghers with me, 20 had been killed and 24 wounded.

'We had taken up another position at 1 700 paces and fired our pom-pom at the enemy who had now occupied our position of a few minutes previously. Fortunately Japie du Preez held his position throughout, and his loss was only four wounded.

'Next morning the fight was renewed, but I was temporarily done for and was taken to the ambulance.'

Vaalkrans: Boers firing on the enemy

FROM LADYSMITH TO COLESBERG

Bloemfontein, 9 February – On 2 February the war council of the Republican forces in Natal received an urgent telegraphic request from Presidents Kruger and Steyn to send a large number of burghers to the southern front in order to contain the British threat in the vicinity of Colesberg. The request was approved and some 800 burghers of different wards of the Heidelberg Commando left by train for the southern Free State on 4 February. One of those burghers was Wilhelm Mangold, who described their transfer to the southern front:

We were informed on the evening of 2 February that we would be transferred. Early the next morning we gathered our belongings, loaded our wagons and by ten o'clock were on our way to Elandslaagte railway station. By the evening we reached our destination. It took us the whole night to load our ox-wagons onto the train. The next morning it was the turn of our horses and oxen. Everybody helped eagerly, since we were promised that we would be allowed to spend a few days in Heidelberg to visit our loved ones.

'The train journey from Elandslaagte to Heidelberg took an unbelievable 33 hours. We were overjoyed when we finally arrived. The whole station was packed with people who welcomed us. The two days of freedom that we were granted in Heidelberg were passed with eating and drinking. Now again, as five months before, we packed our commando trunks. This time I did not take as much biltong and rusks, but cookies and all sorts of delicacies.

'Yesterday afternoon we again left Heidelberg by train, ready for new adventures. Initially all the burghers were silent, but after a while the atmosphere improved since we were happy to go to Colesberg. We were tired of whiling away the time at Ladysmith. We wanted to fight. The youngsters among us were the most boisterous. They told all the young ladies in Heidelberg how courageous they were. Even the fiercest mother-in-laws were so impressed that they lowered the flag and made no attempt to dissuade talk of marriages after the war.

'At Viljoen's Drift an approaching train that was taking 30 Khakis as prisoners of war to Pretoria waited for us. One of the Khakis was wounded. I gave him a few cigarettes and he told me that he had only been married for three weeks when he had to leave for South Africa. He added that fearful stories regarding the Boers were told to him in Britain, including that they treated prisoners of war harshly. His personal experience is that no word of that is true and he has been enjoying excellent treatment.

'The whole night we heard people laughing and singing in a neighbouring coupé. This morning we established what the cause of that festive mood was. The old chaps in that coupé boasted amongst themselves about the stomach medicine that their wives had packed for them, and they all tasted it round after round. Each wonderful liquid contained unique ingredients. There was peach juice, gin, rum, brandy, whisky and numerous other medicines, each prepared according to a recipe. For stomach upsets, vermouth with extracts of bitter leaves is added. A very strong substance added by some is called *boegoe*. As a result of all the liquids gobbled up so joyously by these men, a number of them got rather tipsy, or as they say in this area, ended up high in the branches.

'Among the Heidelberg burghers one always finds good-natured mocking. Field Cornet George Meyer's men are known as the "laager of the cowards" since they did not guard the Long Tom gun well enough on the night of 7–8 December last year. Field Cornet Dolf Spruyt's men are known as the "laager of the frightened", since they often sounded false alarms outside Ladysmith. The Heidelberg town ward is known as the "laager of the wet ones", not because we camped in the rain, but since we possess huge quantities of liquor. I have no doubt that names such as these contribute to a sense of camaraderie.

'The fact that we were welcomed in such a friendly way here in Bloemfontein with coffee and sandwiches contributed to building up the burghers' morale. Our horses were also provided with water and fodder. Hence the men from Heidelberg cannot wait to test their valour against the enemy.'

OUR MILITARY OFFICERS

Commandant Ben Viljoen

Benjamin Johannes Viljoen was born in 1868 in the Wodehouse district of the Cape Colony. He is the eldest son of Wynand Johannes Viljoen and his wife Susanna Magdalena Storm. As a young boy he lived with his parents on a farm near Umtata in the Transkei, where his mother educated him. To a large extent he grew up in the veld, where he learned the skills of horse riding and field-craft.

Viljoen married Helena Beatrix Els in 1889. They moved to Johannesburg the next year. He joined the police force and became an officer in the Mounted Section. Later on he settled in Krugersdorp. His interest in military affairs led him to fight in campaigns against rebellious black communities. At the end of 1895 he participated in the suppression of the Jameson raid. Afterwards he founded the Krugersdorp Volunteer Corps.

In addition to his military interest, Viljoen is an enthusiastic journalist. In 1898 he was elected to the Second Volksraad as member for Krugersdorp. He was an outspoken supporter of an agreement with the Uitlanders to prevent war, but when the war became unavoidable he was appointed Commandant of the Johannesburg Commando last year.

With the war finally a reality, Viljoen and his commando invaded Natal as part of the forces of the late General Jan Kock. He was involved in the battles of Elandslaagte, Colenso and Spioenkop, and in the siege of the British garrison in Ladysmith. The past week he and his commando found themselves at the receiving end of the British assault on Vaalkrans. They behaved with great courage and distinction. Viljoen himself was wounded, but kept on leading his men throughout the most critical period of the battle. We wish him a speedy recovery.

Commandant Ben Viljoen

DE WET HALTS KHAKIS ON WESTERN FRONT

BOERS BATTLE VALIANTLY IN CLASH AT KOEDOESBERG

Magersfontein, 9 February – On 3 February General Cronjé's scouts reported that a few hundred British soldiers, including Scottish soldiers and artillery, had departed from General Methuen's camp on the Modder River and were advancing in a westerly direction.

As our scouts observed them from a safe distance, the soldiers moved slowly across the veld. By evening they had reached Fraserdrift, some 10 kilometres from Methuen's camp. The mounted soldiers crossed the river and approached Koedoesberg on the northern side of it. A Boer guard post of 15 men who were stationed on that low, flat hill immediately retreated. The Khakis then occupied the southern part of the wide expanse of the summit unopposed and began building fortifications. On 4 February the British soldiers even began building a fort on a hillock close to Fraserdrift on the northern side of the river, about one kilometre south of Koedoesberg.

The Boer scouts arrived at Magersfontein that same afternoon with this news. At the time General Christiaan de Wet, who had been transferred from Natal to the western front in mid-December, was in the laager. On receiving the message, he immediately ordered Acting Commandant Du Plooy to go with 100 men and investigate. In addition he requested permission from General Cronjé, the Republican commander on the western front, to attack that British force. Cronjé was unwilling to provide burghers for such a venture. He expressed the opinion that the British were simply attempting to draw the Boer attention away from Magersfontein so that they could overrun our fortifications. For that reason he was only prepared to place 350 men at De Wet's disposal.

De Wet eventually proceeded to Koedoesberg with 300 men and reached his destination late in the afternoon of 5 February. On arrival he established that Du Plooy had been involved in a lively battle with the British the whole day long. De Wet and his men, who were mostly Cape rebels under the command of Commandants Stoffel Froneman and J.H. Visser and Field Cornet Geyser, immediately rushed to Du Plooy's assistance. The British repulsed them with accurate rifle fire and the Boers could not accomplish anything that afternoon.

After dark the whole Boer force retired to eat and rest, but before daybreak they were back in position. When it was light enough to see clearly the battle flared up again. On this day, 6 February, the Boers advanced on the British fortifications with great care, and by evening they were only 350 metres or so from the enemy. That same afternoon 200 men and a Krupp gun, commanded by Commandant Andries Cronjé, arrived at Koedoesberg as reinforcements.

On 7 February, once again the burghers were in position early and fired on the enemy with their Mausers. Under cover of this fire Major Albrecht of the Orange Free State artillery set up the Krupp gun and from ten o'clock began bombarding the British fortifications. The third shot was right on target and destroyed part of a retaining wall. The British artillery answered Albrecht's fire but the Boer gunners forced the British guns to disengage and to seek shelter.

By the afternoon of 7 February the British position on the southern part of the summit of Koedoesberg was becoming untenable. Even though there were, according to our scouts, about 2 000 Khakis and only 600 burghers, De Wet led his men with great inspiration and they were in awe of his courage. At four o'clock, however, the situation suddenly changed when hundreds of mounted British troops with 12 guns arrived at Koedoesberg from the direction of their camp at the Modder River. De Wet and his men now had to fight back desperately to counter a British attempt to encircle them.

By evening the danger had been averted, and De Wet and his officers discussed their position. Some of the burghers had been fighting for three successive days and were so tired that they fell asleep during the battle. Moreover, Koedoesberg was of no direct military significance. For that reason De Wet's impromptu war council decided to retreat a short distance and to take up defensive positions in a ridge of low hills north of Koedoesberg. In this retreat in the night the burghers' water cart was left behind. It eventually fell into the hands of the enemy.

Yesterday morning (8 February) the burghers looked on from a distance as the Khakis carefully approached the crest of Koedoesberg. They were clearly not aware that De Wet and his force had retreated. Later that day the British soldiers attempted to advance northwards but were halted at the new Boer defensive positions. These positions were strengthened during the day with the arrival of a few hundred burghers who now formed an uninterrupted line all the way from Koedoesberg to Magersfontein.

In the four days of fighting in and around Koedoesberg, the Boers suffered a total loss of three men killed and 14 wounded. We do not know the numbers of the British casualties, but our scouts did not note any unusual activity such as a large movement of stretcher-bearers, to indicate that it had been heavy.

THE War Reporter
WEEKLY EDITION

Number 19   Pretoria, South African Republic   17 February 1900

CRISIS ON FREE STATE WESTERN BORDER
BRITISH OUTFLANK MAGERSFONTEIN, THREATEN CRONJÉ'S FLANK

Petrusburg, 16 February – The British on the western front have been busy building up their forces over the last few weeks, and they suddenly resumed their offensive on 11 February. This was exactly two months after the Boer forces halted General Methuen's offensive at Magersfontein and four months after the outbreak of the war. The British supreme commander in South Africa, Field Marshal Roberts, personally led the renewed offensive. According to reliable sources he had a force of approximately 50 000 soldiers with more than 100 guns at his disposal.

The total force at General Piet Cronjé's disposal was hardly 4 000 burghers. Nevertheless Cronjé was full of confidence that he would be able to halt the British, since he had erected powerful entrenchments at Magersfontein and believed that the British were so dependent on the railway lines that they would not dare to move any distance away from them. His misjudgement of the British resolve appears to have left him in a difficult position.

Roberts followed a strange route and in the process completely confused the Boer commanders. He sent his forces southwards from Modder River to the Enslin Station, from there eastwards across Ramdam to Watervals Drift and Diekels Drift on the Riet River and subsequently northwards to Rondawels Drift and Klip Drift on the Modder River. On 11 February Cronjé heard that Khakis in large numbers were invading the Free State north of Ramdam. His immediate reaction was to send General Christiaan de Wet with 500 men and two guns to confront the enemy. He did not want to send all his forces, since he suspected that the invaders were busy with a mock attack and still planned to attack the Boer entrenchments near the railway line at Magersfontein.

The British mounted brigades invading the Free State across Ramdam are led by General French, who earlier fought against the Republican forces at Colesberg. They evaded De Wet's burghers at Watervals Drift on 12 February, proceeded northwards and crossed the Riet River east of Jacobsdal.

KHAKI SUPPLY CONVOY CAPTURED

De Wet yesterday attacked a British supply convoy camping near Bloubank. The General himself gave our correspondent the following account of events:

'The 300–400 troops who were guarding the column offered a stout resistance. After fighting for two hours the English received reinforcements with guns. As I knew that it would be a serious blow to Roberts to lose the provisions he was expecting, I was firmly resolved to capture the convoy. The battle raged on until it became dark. We remained that night in our positions. To our great surprise we saw the following morning that the English had gone. The enemy's camp was entirely deserted. Our booty was gigantic.'

Indeed, De Wet captured more than 180 fully loaded wagons, about 2 800 cattle, a number of horses and about 100 Lee Metford rifles. He took 58 Khakis prisoner of war. The wagons were loaded with an enormous supply of food, including biscuits, tinned meat, tea and rice as well as fodder, liquor and ammunition. De Wet immediately ordered Commandant Piet Fourie to take the captured convoy to Bloemfontein via Koffiefontein and Edenburg. A guard of 250 men with the weakest horses acted as escort. They had no easy task, since virtually all the black wagon drivers had earlier fled. To inspan 180 wagons is a huge job. Fortunately virtually all Fourie's burghers are farmers with extensive experience with trek oxen. They got the convoy moving within a reasonably short time.

BRITISH BREAKTHROUGH TO KIMBERLEY

While De Wet was capturing the British convoy, two huge British units crossed the Riet River from the south. One section occupied Jacobsdal on 15 February. Another, consisting of about 600 mounted soldiers, crossed the Riet River at Diekels Drift on the 13th. They proceeded northwards, crossed the Modder River at Klip Drift and Rondawels Drift and then set course for Kimberley. Cronjé ordered Commandants Stoffel Froneman of the Ladybrand Commando, Tollie de Beer of the Bloemhof Commando and M.J. Wolmarans of the Potchefstroom Commando with 800 men to halt the enemy. Major Albrecht accompanied them with a Krupp gun. They did manage to halt the British infantry at the Modder River, but the mounted Khakis evaded them at Rondawels Drift.

Led by General French, the mounted Khakis advanced northwards from Rondawels Drift to Kimberley. Froneman's burghers attacked them on 14 February and a number of skirmishes took place, but the Khakis could not be halted. Subsequently there was no strong force between French and Kimberley, since the commandos of Chief Commandant I.S. Ferreira and Commandant W.J. Kolbe, who were supposed to guard the entrance to Kimberley at Alexanderfontein, had abandoned their positions and retreated the previous day. General S.P. du Toit attempted to stem the British approach with 200 burghers at Alexanderfontein, but failed in his endeavours. As a result French entered the besieged Kimberley at about six o'clock on the evening of 16 February with his 600 mounted Khakis, relieving the city after a siege of almost four months.

It was now clear to General Cronjé that the British were outflanking him and that his entrenchments at Magersfontein had become obsolete. Therefore he ordered Commandant J.J.C. Greyling of Hoopstad and the Transvaal burghers who were still at Magersfontein yesterday evening to fall back towards Bloemfontein with all their supplies and wagons. The retreat had begun but they only made very slow progress, since there were 400 wagons as well as a huge number of women and children in the laager. The burghers trekked throughout the night. Soon after sunrise the Khakis attacked the rearguard of the laager. Cronjé sent mounted burghers to repulse this attack. When our correspondent left the scene to telegraph the news of the retreat to us, the laager had reached the farm Klipkraaldrif and was still being threatened by the British.

GOOD NEWS FROM THE SOUTHERN FRONT
British forced to retreat from the vicinity of Colesberg

Colesberg, 15 February – Our burghers have driven the British under General Clements back 30 kilometres south of Colesberg. What made this possible is that the British authorities have weakened their forces on this front.

In January this year the Republican forces at Colesberg were continuously under threat by huge British forces under General French, making it necessary to send many burghers from other fronts to Colesberg. From the last week in January the pressure from the British side declined drastically, though the Boer commanders did not realise immediately that French himself had been transferred to the western front and that many soldiers had gone there with him. Information received in the meantime from British prisoners of war and informants indicates that the Boer forces at Colesberg numbered about the same as the British forces in this area by the first week of February.

When the Boers realised that the British had depleted their forces they wasted no time. General Koos de la Rey immediately pressurised the enemy east of Colesberg and forced them to retreat to the south. Generals Schoeman and Grobler and Chief Commandant Piet de Wet similarly entered the fray with new confidence, not only forcing the Khakis back but also taking many prisoners and capturing huge supplies.

Our correspondent reports that De la Rey may have missed an opportunity to encircle the whole British force and force them to surrender. On Saturday 10 February he approached the British camp in the low hills at Slingerfontein and prepared to attack on Monday. (De la Rey does not believe in fighting on a Sunday except when forced to do so.) This delay gave the British the opportunity to retreat from Slingerfontein as well as from their positions close to and west of Colesberg all the way to Rensburg Station on the Sunday. Not all the British abandoned Slingerfontein, however. On Monday 12 February the Boers were involved in a furious battle with the Khakis there. Neither side could gain the upper hand.

The British suffered heavy casualties in these encounters. Our estimation is that at least 200 were killed or wounded. De la Rey believed that he was in a good position to force the whole British force to surrender, and the Khakis seemed to realise this, since on the night of 12–13 February they abandoned their last positions in the vicinity of Colesberg and retreated southwards in haste. Consequently there is no bothersome British gun left on Cole's Kop.

The burghers at Slingerfontein, including Commandant van Dam's policemen, who fought with great valour against the Khakis the previous day, only realised after sunrise that the British had retreated – apparently in a hurry, since they left about 70 tents standing in their camp. In addition they abandoned supplies such as water carts, rifles and ammunition, bayonets, food, fodder, clothing and blankets. The Boers took everything.

The British fell back to Rensburg Station on 13 February, and when Boers appeared there they retreated even further to Arundel Station yesterday, suffering a further 150 casualties. The total Boer loss was light and the victory significant.

The mystery solved. The Boers often speculated on how the Khakis got their guns to the top of Cole's Kop. This photograph shows the winch they used.

General Koos de la Rey

FROM THE EDITOR

That the British would sooner or later launch a full-scale offensive was to be expected. Where and when that would occur was less clear – and how it would be done was totally uncertain. But this week it happened, leaving our military officers totally baffled. Even General Piet Cronjé, who had warned throughout that the offensive would come on the western front, since the biggest British military build-up was taking place there, did not expect that the British would attempt to outflank his positions on the left flank.

That we are now confronted by an absolute crisis is not to be doubted by anyone. Confusing reports on the situation in the western Free State make it impossible for us to say with any precision what is actually happening. What we are certain about is the following: Cronjé has abandoned his position at Magersfontein without a battle, since he is threatened with encirclement. The British have relieved Kimberley without any major clash, since the Republican forces were caught unawares. It sounds almost impossible: there were no major battles – but our defensive line is in tatters.

It would be easy to search for a scapegoat, but that would serve no purpose. What is essential is that calm thought should prevail. Our military leaders must act quickly and decisively to organise a new front. The burghers who suffer from 'leave sickness' must return to the front immediately. Together all of us must sustain the same power of faith that carried our forefathers through the battles of Blood River and Majuba – or else the present crisis will turn into a catastrophe.

Not all the news from the fronts is negative. On the southern front and specifically in the vicinity of Colesberg Generals De la Rey and Schoeman are busy forcing the British onto the defensive. The burghers at Mafeking are pursuing the siege with vigour. Some of them are busy with a campaign against the British forces in Bechuanaland. In Natal General Buller's huge Khaki force makes no headway yet against our depleted forces. The crisis is on the western front, where the Republicans will have their hands full with the British for the next few weeks.

MIXED FEELINGS ABOUT LIFE ON COMMANDO
Jan F.E. Celliers reports on conditions at Colesberg

Colesberg, 12 February – One of the burghers in the Boer laager here at Colesberg is Jan F.E. Celliers of the Pretoria commando. He was the city librarian before the war and is a son of the late Jan Celliers, who was a well-known journalist. At the request of our local correspondent, he compiled the following report on his experiences of life on commando:

'Though not very comfortable, life on commando presents advantages and comforts that one misses in ordinary life. To mention but one virtue: it is a huge relief to be released from all the cares associated with money and the control of finances for three or four months! Those feelings of guilt, that measuring and fitting to meet the claims of creditors, that processing and calculating – away, away! What a relief not to have to spend most of your powers and best hours of the day on insignificant issues, and not to be worried by it through the night. In one month we do not have to spend a shilling here. It is as if we have returned to the years of our childhood, with the difference that the longing to possess and to spend is totally absent. Life has made us tired of money and all its cares. As far as I am concerned, I would rejoice in the day when the government would be able to care for all the people in a continuous, peaceful commando family life.

'The loafing every day without participating in any actual struggle does have its negative influences on our people. Requests to take leave multiply by the day. Burghers develop imagined as well as actual maladies on a massive scale. An amazing number of men have wives or children at home who are ill. Everything is used as an excuse to request leave. Others on the other hand want to attack the enemy without informing or receiving permission from the general. It is becoming more difficult every day to control the whole bunch. Under these circumstances I find truth in the Chinese proverb: "The dog in the cage is bothered by his fleas; the dog on the hunt is not aware of his fleas."

'Yesterday afternoon the Reverend Meiring of Johannesburg held a religious service for us. When I saw the men sitting on or kneeling between the rocks I thought back on how our forefathers in France more than 200 years ago, when the Huguenots were persecuted for their Calvinist religion, also gathered in the wilderness to hold religious services, surrounded by an enemy but guarded against surprise attacks by sentries placed around them. And here their descendants are gathered in the same way under the open heaven, surrounded by a huge enemy force, but nevertheless calm and not afraid, protected by the same God and singing the same hymns as their forefathers centuries ago. Will God allow that such a rock of the ages that has resisted so many storms should be crushed by bloodthirsty attacks of treason, hypocrisy and love of money?'

NATAL FRONT STABLE
BOERS STILL HOLD THEIR POSITIONS

Tugela River, 16 February – Here on the Natal front the Republican forces are still holding out against the enemy. Certain factors are making it increasingly difficult, however. According to reports, more and more British units are joining Buller's forces, while the Boer forces are being scaled down, since hundreds of Free State burghers are being withdrawn to protect their Republic against the British threat from the southwest. That includes the whole Winburg Commando of 850 men who are returning to the Free State at the request of President Steyn.

Action over the past week indicates that the British will in future concentrate their offensive on the Boer positions east of Colenso. On that part of the front the burghers occupy a number of hills south of the Tugela River, including Hlangwane Hill some three kilometres northeast of Colenso; an isolated hill called Hussar Hill just north of the Bloukrans River some five kilometres southeast of Colenso; and the hills called Groenkop, Cingolo and Monte Christo east and northeast of Hlangwane. The Boers have dug trenches and built fortifications on all these positions.

On 12 February a huge British force launched a surprise attack on the Boer fortifications on Hussar Hill. The sentries occupying the fortifications fired a few shots and then retreated a little distance, whereupon the British occupied the hill. The burghers – a number of Boksburgers commanded by Field Cornet A.J. Dercksen, members of the Middelburg Commando and a few burghers from Bethal – kept firing on the Khakis from a distance and made life uncomfortable for them. By one o'clock that afternoon the soldiers abandoned the hill again. This filled the burghers with new courage and they launched a full-scale attack. In the skirmish that followed the burghers courageously pursued the retreating British, only ending their pursuit when British forces began bombarding them from the direction of the railway line with heavy guns. Only five burghers were wounded in this battle.

On 13 February there was no sign of Khakis east of Colenso, but early the next morning scouts noted a huge British troop movement. Their target seemed to be Hussar Hill once again. The Boer artillery soon greeted the Khakis with a bombardment. The British artillery answered with such a massive counter-bombardment that they soon silenced the Boer guns. The huge British force easily managed to drive the Boer sentries off Hussar Hill and were in occupation by half past eight that morning. The retreating Boers, supported by many of their comrades who rushed to their support from their positions in the north, again fired heavily on the British with their rifles but this time could not manage to dislodge them. After a while they ended their attempt since they were ordered not to waste ammunition.

General Lukas Meyer, the commander of the Boers on this part of the front, was convinced that the Khakis would now attempt to occupy the strategically situated Hlangwane Hill. He signalled his conviction to General Louis Botha and then proceeded to Hlangwane to inspect the situation. Commandant-General Joubert was so upset when he heard of this new British threat that he ordered that new reinforcements should immediately be sent to Meyer. A large number of burghers as well as a number of guns, including a Long Tom, are being transferred to that part of the front as we go to press.

In the meantime it has become clear to us that the British target is not Hlangwane. To Meyer's shock thousands moved even further east, with the obvious intention of outflanking the Boer left flank. Meyer's reaction was to form a commando from various burgher units to put pressure on the British, forcing them to halt and defend themselves. To Meyer's huge relief they fell back to the south late in the afternoon of the 14th and began preparing defensive positions. Meyer's initial conclusion was that he had scored a victory over the British, but during the night they sporadically bombarded the Boer positions and after sunrise this morning it was clear from the summit of Hlangwane that they had not given up at all. Meyer now believes that the British will resume their advance soon, and informed President Kruger of this in a message. Consequently the burghers have spent the whole day building fortifications and gun emplacements and digging more trenches on Hlangwane.

Boer laager at Platkop on the Tugela River

Boer artillerymen in a gun emplacement

OUR MILITARY OFFICERS

General Christiaan de Wet

Christiaan Rudolph de Wet was born in 1854 on the farm Leeuwkop in the Smithfield district. His parents were Jacobus Ignatius De Wet and Aletta Susanna Margaretha Strydom. As a child he was a typical farm boy, first on Leeuwkop, then on Kalkfontein, where the present town of Reddersburg is situated, and lastly on Nuwejaarsfontein close to the present Dewetsdorp, which was named after his father.

De Wet enjoyed only a few months of formal education, since he had to assist with farm activities from a young age. In the process he learnt to know the veld in the Free State where he is at present fighting the British with some success. He never learned to speak English. When he was 19 he married the 17-year-old Cornelia Margaretha Kruger. They have eight sons and eight daughters.

After the discovery of diamonds in the western Free State, De Wet briefly became a transport rider to Kimberley. Subsequently he moved to the northern Free State and in 1880 to the Heidelberg district in the Transvaal. He joined the protest movement of the Transvaal Afrikaners against the British annexation of their Republic in 1877 and in December 1880 he attended the people's meeting at Paardekraal. Subsequently he participated in the battles at Laingsnek, Schuinshoogte and Majuba.

After the war and the re-establishment of Transvaal's independence, De Wet became the field cornet of the ward Rooikoppies in Heidelberg. He moved to Lydenburg and was in 1885 elected as the Volksraad member for that area. After attending only one Transvaal Volksraad session, however, he moved back to the Orange Free State. In 1889 he was elected to the Free State Volksraad. He remained a member until 1898 and participated in numerous debates.

When De Wet heard of the Jameson invasion at the end of 1895, he took his rifle and hurried to Pretoria to assist in repulsing the invaders. When he arrived, however, Jameson had already been captured. Early the next year he was a major supporter of M.T. Steyn in the presidential election in the Free State. He supported the movement for closer unification between the Republics and became known as an outspoken critic of the leading British figures in South Africa such as Cecil John Rhodes and Sir Alfred Milner.

By the second half of last year De Wet no longer doubted that war would come. More than a month before the outbreak of the war he sent his son Kotie to buy him a good horse. When the latter returned with a snow-white horse that would be visible over a long distance, De Wet reportedly commented: 'Do you want me dead?' De Wet and this loyal horse, Fleur, have in the meantime become inseparable.

With the outbreak of the war De Wet joined the Heilbron Commando as an ordinary burgher and was commandeered to the Natal border. Three of his sons, Kotie, Isak and Christiaan, accompanied him. All three of them are members of his personal staff and often act as his scouts. Within the first month he was elected acting commandant when his commandant became ill. He made a name for himself for the first time on 30 October last year in the battle of Nicholson's Nek outside Ladysmith. In December he was appointed as fighting general on the western border of the Free State.

The Republican historian, Nicolaas Hofmeyr, describes de Wet as a short but forceful figure. 'He is not a person who immediately impresses you. But if you look at him carefully, you note a strong chin that reflects decisiveness and firmness. He lisps when he speaks, but is eloquent and known for his witticisms. At the corners of his mouth there is often a smile but he has a very short temper. When he removes his hat one immediately notices a broad forehead cut by deep frown marks. His whole bearing reflects a calm self-confidence. Once he has made a decision, he stands by it. When he walks away from you, you note that he is made of steel: strongly built but elastic, fast and fiery. It is as if he possesses the powers of concentration and the bodily flexibility of a gladiator from Roman times. This modest child of the veld possesses unlimited military talent.'

General C.R. de Wet

THE War Reporter
WEEKLY EDITION

Number 20 — Pretoria, South African Republic — 24 February 1900

SITUATION IN WESTERN FREE STATE CRITICAL
Cronjé's burghers battle to survive at Paardeberg

Bloemfontein, 23 February – The war has entered a critical phase for the Republican forces in the Free State. Last week we reported that General Piet Cronjé and his laager of about 4 000 men with 400 wagons had abandoned their entrenchments at Magersfontein. They then moved up the northern bank of the Modder River in an easterly direction, with the object of rushing to the defence of Bloemfontein. They repulsed an enemy attack on 16 February at Klipkraaldrif. That same evening Cronjé and his laager moved further eastwards, aiming to cross the Modder River at Koedoes Drift and join forces with Chief Commandant Christiaan de Wet.

Virtually nothing came of Cronjé's plans. De Wet claims that on 17 February he was not even aware that Cronjé had abandoned Magersfontein. As a result he did not rush to the laager's assistance. In the meantime about 200 of Cronjé's wagons crossed the Modder River at Perdebergs Drift that morning and proceeded to Bloemfontein. The rest moved further upstream and outspanned at Wolwekraal at about eight o'clock. There they enjoyed breakfast in peace.

Wolwekraal and the neighbouring Vendusie Drift are vulnerable but also easily defendable. They are vulnerable to artillery because of their position in a depression right next to the river, surrounded by low hills that provide a view of the entire depression. The deep banks of the river, on the other hand, give an advantage in defence against foot soldiers.

Cronjé did not aim to linger there, however. He ordered his convoy to cross the river at Vendusiedrif. Soon afterwards he received a report that a British force was approaching from the north. It was the cavalry of General French, who had a number of guns with them. Soon after eleven o'clock the British began bombarding the convoy.

The first bombs that exploded in the midst of the wagons caused panic. The black drivers and leaders ran for their lives, and the oxen that were not yet inspanned stampeded in the direction of the enemy. Most of the burghers scurried for cover next to the river. Only the artillery commanded by the courageous Major Albrecht and the burghers of Commandants Froneman and De Beer had the presence of mind to attack the Khakis, but did not have enough firing power to repulse them.

Cronjé had too few trek oxen left to move his laager to a better defensive position that night. Refusing to leave it behind to be captured by the British forces, he decided that his burghers should dig themselves in along the river and defend themselves against possible attacks until Boer forces from the outside could drive the enemy off.

THE BATTLE OF PAARDEBERG

As Cronjé expected, the British resumed their attack on the Boer positions at Vendusie Drift near Paardeberg early on Sunday morning, 18 February. As usual, the attack began with a heavy bombardment, apparently targeting the wagon laager. Numerous wagons were hit and some took fire, exploding the ammunition that had not been off-loaded. Albrecht's guns were hopelessly outnumbered and could not possibly answer the British artillery.

At seven o'clock the British infantry attacked. They had to approach the Boer entrenchments over the open ground and became defenceless targets for the well-camouflaged burghers. By nine o'clock they were checked and pinned down in the sun for the rest of the day, forced to remain motionless so as not to draw fire. Numerous attacks by the infantry later that day suffered the same fate. The burghers defended themselves with virtually superhuman courage and inflicted terrible carnage.

The only advantage gained by the enemy was that they managed to encircle Cronjé's laager completely that day. Later on they lost this advantage again when other Boer forces arrived at the battle site. De Wet, who by that time had been informed of Cronjé's dilemma, approached Paardeberg from the south. His burghers occupied Oskoppies – two low hills about four kilometres directly south of Vendusie Drift – and dislodged the Khakis from that part of the front.

It would be misleading to claim that the Boers scored a victory in this battle, since the British maintained their positions on virtually the whole battlefield. The price they had to pay for this advantage was terribly high, however. Our scouts have heard that the total British loss on Sunday 18 February alone was at least 300 soldiers killed and 900 wounded, in addition to 60 captured by the burghers. That represents the biggest British loss on any single day thus far in this war. On the Boer side the total loss was about 70 men.

De Wet received news directly from Cronjé's laager for the first time when Commandant Paul Schutte reached Oskoppies. He had escaped from the laager earlier that evening under the cover of darkness. Schutte brought bad news, namely that the situation in the laager was critical. The oxen had fallen into the hands of the Khakis and all the wagons had been blasted to pieces.

THE SIEGE OF CRONJÉ'S LAAGER

Early on the morning of 19 February Cronjé sent a message to Lord Roberts requesting an armistice of 24 hours to allow him to attend to his wounded and bury his dead. Roberts replied that he would only be satisfied with unconditional surrender. Cronjé answered with the following message: 'Since you are so unmerciful as not to accord me the time asked for, nothing remains for me to do but as you wish.' Obviously the British inferred that Cronjé intended to surrender, and sent an intermediary to the laager. However what Cronjé meant was that since Roberts obviously did not want an armistice, the Boers would fulfil his wish and keep on fighting. The intermediary returned with the following message from Cronjé to Roberts: 'There appears to be a great mistake in your lordship's mind. What I really said was – Since you are so unmerciful as not to accord me the time asked for, nothing remains for me to do. Do as you wish. During my life-time I shall never surrender. If you wish to bombard, fire away. I have spoken!' The British then resumed their uncompromising bombardment of the Boer laager.

By the third day of the siege, Tuesday 20 February, all Albrecht's guns except one pom-pom were damaged beyond repair. From then onwards the Boers had to confront more than 70 British guns with only their rifles. By this time the Modder River was flooding its banks and making Cronjé's position even more precarious. At the narrowest place it was at least 30 metres broad and so deep that nobody could get through.

The outlook for the Boers in the laager was dismal: Cronjé decided that all those who still had horses should attempt to escape and join forces on the outside. All the available Boer forces should then attempt to break through the British lines from the outside and relieve the laager.

At dusk two commandants, namely Stoffel Froneman and F.J Potgieter of Wolmaransstad galloped out with 50 burghers. Only 20 men reached De Wet's laager: the others were either shot or captured. Those who got through brought news of Cronjé's critical situation with them.

On 21 February Roberts sent Cronjé a message offering to allow the women and children to leave the laager and to make British doctors and medicine available to the Boers. Cronjé rejected the offer. Apparently the women refused to leave the laager, preferring to be with their men in this hour of crisis. As for medical assistance, Cronjé was afraid that the doctors would merely come to the laager to gain information on his position.

In the meantime, the British proceeded with their bombardment of the laager at Paardeberg. Some bombs exploded in the Boer trenches, causing loss of life. Almost as terrible was the continuing rain, which made everybody's life a misery. How Cronjé and his people manage to survive is unimaginable for anybody looking on from the outside.

Yesterday the British sent up an air balloon to inspect the Boer positions from above. The general commentary of the Boers on this was that our authorities should have invested in balloons before the war rather than in the fortresses around Pretoria, and gained an invaluable military advantage by looking down on the enemy and their fortifications like a bird does from high up in the sky.

BRITISH PROPAGANDA

Soon after the last group of British officers left Cronjé's laager after delivering the message from Roberts, Boer officers reported a disturbing development. These visitors had distributed a notice that contained a proclamation addressed to the citizens of the Orange Free State. It was pure propaganda, in which Roberts attempted to convince our burghers to stop

Continued overleaf

Boers in their laager at Paardeberg

Cronjé's laager on its way to Paardeberg

FROM THE EDITOR

The future seems gloomy to the Republican forces. Both in the western Free State and on the Natal front the Khakis threaten to gain the upper hand. At times the enemy's numerical advantage seems simply too massive for the Boers to handle. However, we trust that our talented officers and valiant burghers led by General Louis Botha and Chief Commandant Christiaan de Wet will manage to stem the tide long enough.

Long enough? Yes, since our hope is still alive that pressure from European heads of state on Britain to end the war will eventually be successful. According to reliable sources the French and the Dutch in particular are continually pressurising the British Prime Minister, Lord Salisbury. He is also under pressure from the leader of the opposition in the British Parliament, Sir Henry Campbell-Bannerman, since the war is costing infinitely more than the British taxpayers were led to expect. All we can do is to keep fighting, since sooner or later the British will no longer be able to continue with the war.

This week we only report on developments in Natal and the Free State, since these are at present by far the most important fronts. There are activities on the other fronts as well, but we will report on those in future issues. The war is entering a critical phase, and we call on all our readers to remain true to the Republican cause.

Chief Commandant Ignatius Ferreira

continued

fighting and made vague promises to them.

Roberts asserted in this proclamation that had the Free State Republic remained neutral, Britain would have respected its independence. We can assure him that Sir Alfred Milner has never heard the word respect, but that is another story. Roberts then accused the Free State authorities of unnecessary aggression by invading British colonies. Next a jewel of a statement follows, one of those sickening expressions of the everlasting British compulsion to protect other people against themselves. Roberts alleged that the British would be delighted to protect the inhabitants of the Free State from the evils brought upon them by the wrongful actions of their government. He then warned the burghers to desist from any further hostility. And following this warning, he made the sweet promise that all burghers 'who were found staying in their homes and quietly pursuing their ordinary occupations, would not be made to suffer in their person or property on account of their having taken up arms in obedience to the order of their Government'.

This proclamation reminds one of the English nursery rhyme in which the spider invites the fly with sweet words to enter her parlour. Does Roberts sincerely believe that our burghers are so stupid as to believe that the British would leave them in peace? Our people learnt as children to pray: 'Father, protect us against the "goodwill" of the British.'

CHRISTIAAN DE WET SUCCEEDS FERREIRA

While the siege of Cronjé's laager is continuing in all its intensity, the Republican forces on the outside are frantically working out plans to save the laager. The officer in charge of these attempts is Chief Commandant Christiaan de Wet, who was promoted to this rank after a very unfortunate incident when Chief Commandant I.S. Ferreira was accidentally shot by one of his own sentries earlier this week. De Wet is now for all practical purposes the commander of all the Free State burghers on the western front.

On Wednesday the British cavalry almost managed to encircle those of De Wet's burghers who were stationed closest to Paardeberg. They had to fight the whole day long and then give up their positions in order to escape. In the chaos of the flight Commandant C. Spruyt of the Heidelberg Commando as well as at least 40 other burghers fell into the hands of the enemy. As a result nothing came of the plans to attempt to relieve Cronjé's laager.

When our correspondent left the field of battle yesterday, the British were mercilessly bombarding Cronjé's laager with about 100 guns. This does not cause a major loss of life, since the burghers are well entrenched and keep a low profile, but it certainly destroys their morale.

Chief Commandant Christiaan de Wet

BOERS UNDER PRESSURE ON NATAL FRONT

British occupy Cingolo; burghers fight back valiantly

Tugela front, 18 February – The total Boer force on the Tugela River front consists at present of barely 3 000 men with two guns and two pom-poms, while the British field an estimated 25 000 soldiers with 70 guns. One of the burghers' major advantages is their high level of mobility. The Boer scouts continuously keep the British under observation, and the commandos move up and down the front to occupy whatever position is threatened by the Khakis.

The British began bombarding the Boer positions on 15 February and kept that up the next day. Most of the bombs exploded harmlessly, but one was a direct hit, bursting in a trench occupied by a number of burghers from Swaziland and Middelburg. Altogether seven burghers were killed and seven wounded. Commandant Chris Botha of the Swaziland Commando and his adjutant, Field Cornet Koot Opperman, subsequently suffered from bomb shock and were out of action for a few days. In the meantime the Boer gunners on the front fired back at the British with their few guns and made life difficult for the enemy.

On 16 February the Boers occupied the strategically situated Cingolo Hill on their far left flank in reaction to a British troop movement. When the attack came, British infantry soldiers began approaching Cingolo from their new positions in the south. A section of mounted troops rushed forward and reached the foot of the hill. When some soldiers began ascending the hill, our burghers fired on them from a thicket and they retreated again. The same happened when the infantry approached later on.

On 17 February the British artillery fired away from early morning. Their bombardment was as heavy, if not heavier than all three previous days combined. The only part of the Boer positions not fired upon was Cingolo – probably to persuade our officers that they were not interested in that hill. The Boer artillery soon joined the battle. One of the Boer guns was put out of action when a British shell exploded immediately above it and either killed or wounded its whole crew.

In the meantime, on the summit of Cingolo Commandant Van Rensburg of the Soutpansberg Commando realised that he would be attacked and urgently requested reinforcements from General Christiaan Fourie, General Lukas Meyer's fighting general on this part of the front. Fourie had not visited the hill to study the situation at first hand, and was blissfully certain that there were 1 300 burghers there: in fact there were fewer than 300 – not nearly enough to halt a British attack. Van Rensburg moved his burghers down from the summit to the foot of the hill, and soon after nine o'clock they became involved in a shooting battle with the British foot soldiers. In the meantime mounted British soldiers approached Cingolo from the east and traded shots with the burghers in that area.

There were simply too few burghers to confront the British on all sides. By 12 o'clock the first Khakis had reached the summit. With that the battle was won, since all the burghers had to retreat to escape encirclement and captivity. By two o'clock the first British infantry had reached the summit, and the burghers were falling back in a northerly and northwesterly direction.

Cingolo was now finally in British hands. According to reliable sources four Khakis were killed and 30 wounded in the battle. On the Boer side one man was killed and eight wounded. It was Buller's first significant success against the Republican forces.

Transvaal State Artillery with Krupp gun

BRITISH OCCUPY MONTE CRISTO, GROENKOP AND HLANGWANE

Tugela front, 21 February – After occupying Cingolo the enemy continued their bombardment and slowly wore down the Boer resolve on all parts of the front. Two other problems the Boers had to deal with were that their ammunition supply was seriously depleted and that the officers who were guarding the Tugela west of Colenso were unwilling to release their burghers for the defence of the positions east of the railway line. As a result there were not enough defenders available to confront the massive British onslaught in the east.

When the British infantry attacked the Boer positions on Monte Cristo on 18 February, the burghers put up a brave defence, but the Khaki numbers were so overwhelming that they could not keep them back forever. By 10 o'clock, when encirclement seemed imminent, the burghers abandoned their positions at the foot of Monte Cristo. In spite of their small numbers, some burghers who did not fall back all the way, supported by artillery from Groenkop, pinned the British down on the summit of Monte Cristo and inflicted heavy casualties on them.

When they noted this, other British troops stormed the Boer positions at Groenkop. This assured victory for the enemy, since the burghers on Groenkop had to retreat hastily to avoid being encircled. Now the burghers who were still on Monte Cristo found themselves in an extremely vulnerable position, and they too had to fall back in a hurry. The British were then in complete control, even occupying the Boer camp in the depression north of Groenkop, which was a heavy blow for the already demoralised burghers.

Virtually all the burghers south of the Tugela River on Hlangwane Hill and its vicinity started to worry that the British would capture them. Many of them simply began to flee back to the Tugela in the north. It is fortunate that the British could not pursue them, since if they had they would probably have opened up a breach in the Republican defensive line that day.

By the evening of 18 February the Boer positions south of the Tugela were restricted to Hlangwane Hill and a few smaller hillocks on the southern bank of the river north and east of Hlangwane. Generals Botha and Meyer decided that they should do all in their power to keep those positions. Botha himself went to Hlangwane that evening and called on the burghers to remain courageous. He also made arrangements to send more burghers to that part of the front.

The British resumed their offensive on Hlangwane early the next morning. While they bombarded the Boer positions from several sides, mounted and foot soldiers moved closer. Most of the burghers fell back, firing on the enemy from the northern bank of the Tugela. By eleven o'clock the British had occupied virtually the whole of Hlangwane, except for an entrenchment that was stubbornly defended by the burghers of the Bethal Commando. On the summit of Hlangwane the British occupied the abandoned Boer laager and captured wagon-loads of ammunition.

In the course of the afternoon the situation of the Boers south of the Tugela became critical. General Botha was not there himself at that time, since he was carrying out an investigation to the east following a rumour (which proved to be false) that the British were crossing the Tugela. In his absence the war council decided that all the burghers stationed south of the river should return to the northern bank. This decision was carried out immediately.

Botha was furious when he was informed of this on his return and attempted in vain to convince the officers to reconsider their decision. They argued their decision was tactically correct. The retreat of the burghers that same evening and early the next morning meant that for the first time since the beginning of November there were no burghers stationed south of the Tugela.

In all these battles south of the river we have heard that a total of 25 British were killed, 276 wounded and four are missing. The Boer loss is 15 men killed and 71 wounded.

OUR MILITARY OFFICERS

Major F.W.R. Albrecht

Friedrich Wilhelm Richard Albrecht was born in 1848 in Potsdam, Prussia. On leaving school he joined the Prussian field artillery in Berlin as a non-commissioned officer. His first war experience followed soon afterwards, when he participated in numerous battles in the Franco-Prussian War of 1870–71.

In 1880 Albrecht immigrated to the Orange Free State, where he was appointed commander of the Artillery Corps with the rank of captain. He not only reorganised the Corps on the Prussian military model, but extended it and ensured that artillery barracks were added to the fort in Bloemfontein. In 1889 he became commander of the Free State Mounted Service Force, which carries out police duties.

From 1891 the Free State government began buying new guns for the Artillery Corps. Albrecht was sent to Germany for that purpose in 1892. He continuously improved the Corps and kept it ready for war, adding a field telegraph section in 1897.

When war broke out last year, the members of the Corps became celebrated for their good discipline, hardiness and military skills – characteristics that made them battle-ready and for which Albrecht deserves the credit. He has served with distinction on the western front, especially in the battles around Kimberley, at Modder River and at Magersfontein. During the past few days he has continued to conduct himself with dignity – but now he is challenged by the greatest test in his career.

Major F.W.R. Albrecht

THE War Reporter
WEEKLY EDITION

Number 21   Pretoria, South African Republic   3 March 1900

CRISIS IN THE WESTERN FREE STATE
Attempts to relieve Cronjé at Paardeberg fail

Bloemfontein, 26 February – Last week we reported on the failure of Chief Commandant Christiaan de Wet's attempts to break the British encirclement of General Cronjé's laager on the northern bank of the Modder River and to allow the besieged burghers to escape. The position of Cronjé and his burghers became more hopeless by the day. They had sufficient ammunition but not enough food to hold out indefinitely. Major Albrecht's last serviceable cannon was destroyed on 20 February.

When the sun came out on 23 February, for the first time in days, Cronjé communicated the following message to De Wet via heliograph. We quote directly from the message: 'Here with me things are still the same. The enemy bombards our positions and laager. Have enough food for perhaps a day or two, and some ammunition. Some burghers conduct themselves poorly, but I'll attempt to inspire them with courage …'

De Wet's burghers made another attempt that same morning to break through the ring of British troops around Cronjé. General Philip Botha began a frontal assault, which failed to make progress. Even though their supply of artillery ammunition was running out the burghers fired on the enemy with three guns – two of them rather ancient – but were silenced by the British artillery and had to fall back in haste. Not everybody managed to get away: Commandant H. Theunissen of Winburg was taken prisoner with some 80 burghers.

In spite of this setback, there were six officers with a few thousand burghers ready under De Wet's command in the western Free State on 23 February. General Andries P.J. Cronjé, a brother of General Piet Cronjé, led the Transvaal burghers. The generals in command of the Free State burghers were Philip Botha, Stoffel Froneman, A.P. Cronjé, C.J. Wessels and W.J. Kolbe. These officers and their burghers felt that another attempt to break through the British siege of the Boers at Paardeberg would serve no purpose.

In the meantime the British were busy closing the ring around the Paardeberg laager tighter every moment. From their aerial balloon they could probably see exactly where the Boer trenches were and indicate to their artillery where they should aim. The lyddite gas obviously had a negative effect on the burghers, causing severe headaches amongst other things. The lack of room and shortage of fresh food, coupled with excessive mud as a result of all the rain, contributed to the unpleasantness. In addition there was a terrible stench: there were no sanitary facilities and the carcasses of numerous dead horses and trek animals were spread all around them.

THERON'S EPIC RECONNAISSANCE

This was the state of affairs when Captain Danie Theron of the Transvaal Scout Corps made his way to Cronjé's laager on 25 February. On his return he described the situation as horrendous. There was hardly any food and what there was had been rendered inedible by pollution. The burghers in the laager were powerless in the face of the enemy.

The valiant Theron made his way to the laager at the request of De Wet's council of war, crawling on his hands and knees through the British line. He carried a message requesting Cronjé to assemble his burghers on the banks of the Modder River and attack the British troops south-east of his laager. De Wet would simultaneously attack that position from the outside and provide cover while Cronjé and his burghers attempted to break through.

Theron's daring feat seemed to have been in vain. Cronjé pleaded with his officers to accept De Wet's proposals, but the council of war – physically and emotionally drained, hungry and tired of the war in general – was not prepared to implement the plan, insisting that the strong-flowing Modder River was uncrossable.

Theron left Cronjé's laager again on the evening of Sunday the 25th. At that stage some burghers were preparing to build a chain bridge that would allow them to cross the river. On his return to De Wet, Theron did not seem to hold any hope that it would be possible to rescue Cronjé and his burghers. It seemed as if Cronjé's war council was turning against him, seeing no sense in prolonging their defence.

BOER LAAGER AT PAARDEBERG SURRENDERS
WAR COUNCIL TURNS AGAINST THE BRAVE PIET CRONJÉ

Bloemfontein, 2 March – The news of General Piet Cronjé's surrender to Lord Roberts's forces has now been confirmed from numerous quarters. A Dutch doctor who was in Cronjé's laager turned up in De Wet's laager this morning. According to him, Cronjé held a war council meeting on Monday morning (the 26th) to attempt to convince his officers that they had to break through the British lines. Some officers, however, felt that such an attempt would only lead to further loss of life and that it would be better to surrender. To make matters worse, the British bombardment was even heavier that day and Cronjé's chain bridge was completely wrecked. Commandant M.J. Wolmarans of Potchefstroom spoke for those burghers who wanted to surrender, and even drew up a petition. That evening Cronjé again called all his officers to a war council and encouraged them to keep fighting – but in vain, since with the sole exception of Commandant Brits, they unanimously decided to surrender.

De Wet and his burghers were ready to support an attempt by Cronjé to escape between Sunday evening and daybreak on Monday. On Monday evening they were ready again, but again there was no sign that Cronjé was attempting to break out. And when in the night some shooting was heard from the direction of Cronjé's laager, nobody attempted to go out and establish what it was. On Tuesday morning, however, they prepared to go and help, unaware that Cronjé had by then surrendered. Of course, nothing further happened.

Cronjé and his burghers were, we are informed, involved in a fierce rifle battle with the British on the southwestern side of the laager early on Tuesday morning (the 27th, Majuba Day). After about 15 minutes, reportedly, some burghers raised the white flag. Soon this became a general practice and at six o'clock Cronjé sent messengers to Lord Roberts to inform him that they would surrender. Soon afterwards the general, dressed in an old green coat, was taken to Roberts' headquarters with his sjambok in his hand.

Approximately 4 000 burghers thus fell into British hands as prisoners of war. The burghers outside the laager, from De Wet downwards, were devastated by this news, which became known yesterday. Some were angry that Cronjé had surrendered specifically on Majuba Day and had not held out one day longer; others regarded it as a miracle that he had held out that long at all. More important is the fact that many burghers, wondering if there is any sense in proceeding with the war, are returning to their farms without leave.

Cronjé meets Roberts after his surrender

PRESIDENTS CALL FOR FAITH AND HOPE
British breakthrough a devastating setback

Pretoria, 2 March – For President Kruger the events of the past few days, and especially Cronjé's surrender, were bitter blows. He did his utmost up to the very end to organise assistance for Cronjé. In addition, he called on all the ministers and all congregations of Afrikaans churches last Sunday to make that night a night of prayer and to beg God to save General Cronjé. A nightly vigil had to be held for three nights.

President Steyn issued a similar call in the Orange Free State. Prayer meetings were held throughout the Republics. On 26 February Steyn, accompanied by Abraham Fischer and A.D.W. Wolmarans, visited the Paardeberg area at the request of Chief Commandant De Wet to encourage the burghers. On Majuba Day Steyn visited a number of commandos and addressed the burghers. At that stage he was not aware that Cronjé had already surrendered.

After the British breakthrough on the Natal front, the burghers retreated to the Biggarsberg in such a disorderly hurry that Commandant-General Joubert called in the assistance of President Kruger to re-establish order. Kruger left for the Natal front on Wednesday evening (the 28th) in a special train from Pretoria, even though he suffered from an eye infection. One of the Boers who was present, Philip Pienaar of the Transvaal Telegraphic Service, gave our correspondent the following account of the President's visit to the front:

'President Kruger arrived at Glencoe in the morning. The burghers were called together, and the President, leaning out of the window of his railway carriage, asked them to join him in singing a psalm. He then offered up a fervent prayer for guidance after which he addressed the burghers, reproaching them for their want of confidence in an all-powerful Providence, and exhorting them to take courage afresh and continue the struggle for the sake of their posterity, which one day would judge their acts.

'"Whither would you flee?" he asked us. "The enemy will pursue you, and tear you from the arms of your wives. The man who surrenders takes the first step into exile. Brothers! Stand firm, and you will not be forsaken!'

'As the father of his people spoke, the doubts and fears that had filled the breasts of the multitude disappeared. Forgotten were the days and weeks of hunger, heat, and thirst; forgotten the ghastly shrapnel showers, the soul-crushing crash of the awful lyddite shell, the unnerving possibility of sudden death that for months had grimly loomed across their lives, and every man felt glorious fires of patriotism rekindle in his bosom.

'It was wonderful to see the change in the spirit of the burghers. Where but a moment before had been disheartened mutterings and sulky looks were now smiling faces and cheerful conversation.'

After addressing the burghers, Kruger called for volunteers to accompany him since he wanted to fire on the enemy himself. That made a deep impression on the burghers and nobody thought of any danger afterwards.

Later that day, after long discussions with Commandant-General Joubert, Kruger wandered through the laager and talked to the burghers. He looked healthy and in good spirits – and his influence over the burghers was undeniable. This morning he returned to Pretoria. We have been informed that he will soon go to the Free State to talk to the burghers there.

FROM THE EDITOR

Despite our constant awareness of the inexorable British military build-up, nobody anticipated the catastrophe that the Republican forces suffered on Majuba Day. The double British breakthrough means that our worst nightmares have been realised. The loss of more than 4 000 burghers in the western Free State – in one day is a devastating setback, while the loss of the Tugela front, which had served as an incomparably safe natural fortress for four months against a growing mass of enemy soldiers, leaves us without protection in Natal.

It is a truism that character is revealed when confronted by a crisis. Is the Boer character strong enough for our Republics to survive this crisis? Two issues are involved here. First, are the reasons for the Republics' decision last year to use war as a political weapon still valid? Second, is there any sense in going on with the war? Our answer to both questions is: Yes! To surrender now would mean the subjugation of us all under the British yoke. Our forefathers trekked from the Cape Colony in the 1830s to escape the British yoke. In 1880–81 they fought the Transvaal War of Independence to rid themselves of unwelcome British rule. The re-establishment of British supremacy would lead to the end of the Boer nation. We refused to accept that last year, and we still reject it now.

As regards the sense in going on with this war, we remind our readers that there is increasing pressure on the British government to put its South African affairs in order as quickly as possible. If the British cannot subdue us militarily in a short time, they will have to come to an agreement with us. The cost of war will eventually become so high that they will have to negotiate. That is our salvation.

OUR MILITARY OFFICERS

Captain Danie Theron

Daniël Johannes Stephanus Theron was born in 1872 at Tulbagh in the Cape Colony. After matriculating in Cape Town he qualified in 1889 as a teacher and taught at a school in the Orange Free State until 1891. He then moved to the Soutpansberg district in the Transvaal where he farmed for two years. He subsequently qualified as an attorney and in 1897 established a law practice in Krugersdorp.

Theron suddenly became a well-known figure last year when he assaulted the editor of the *Star* newspaper, W.F. Moneypenny, after the latter insulted the Boers in an editorial and refused to retract his slanderous allegations. Theron afterwards gave numerous speeches and wrote letters to the press supporting President Kruger in his conflict with the Uitlanders and with Britain. That made him a popular figure amongst patriotic burghers, who began talking of him as a future leader.

Shortly before the outbreak of the war, Theron established the Bicycle Scout Corps, of which he became the commander with the rank of captain. During the first phase of the war, until the end of January, he was active in Natal. From the beginning of last month he visited numerous commandos before joining De Wet's laager on 22 February. Theron's courageous exploits in carrying messages to Cronjé's laager at Paardeberg by crawling through the enemy lines during the night earned him wide respect. Our best wishes accompany this brave and brilliant officer in his further exploits during this war.

Captain Danie Theron

BOERS HOLD THEIR OWN ON THE TUGELA FRONT

British attack on Hedge Hill repulsed

Modderspruit, 23 February – Over the past three days our burghers have had to withstand a heavy enemy onslaught, but they passed this test with flying colours. On 20 February the British had already crossed the Tugela River directly north of Colenso and occupied General Botha's former entrenchments on the red hills. The disheartened burghers now had to prepare new entrenchments. Fortunately many black workers who had worked on the dam in the Klip River – the project had failed – were still in the vicinity and were now used to prepare the entrenchments.

Having constructed a pontoon bridge over the Tugela River west of Hlangwane on the 20th, the British resumed their attack on the Boer positions in the hills north of the river. On 21 February they failed to occupy the Boer position at Rooikop, being forced to retreat from the battlefield after dark, after our burghers had pinned them down all afternoon. Our loss was only one burgher killed and seven wounded, while the British, according to a reliable source, lost 111 men dead or wounded. The burghers were extremely relieved by the result of this battle and it filled them with new courage and faith.

According to our scouts, there were more than 20 000 British soldiers with 40 guns north of the river yesterday morning. In the afternoon they launched a full-scale attack on our entrenchments on two adjoining heights, namely Hedge Hill and Horseshoe Hill. The bombardment that preceded these attacks was more devastating than anything we have thus far experienced on the Natal front. Our burghers withstood both the bombardment and the attack, however, and drove the enemy back with accurate rifle fire. The battle is still raging today but the British are failing to make any headway. We have no doubt that their casualties are heavy, but we have no official or reliable information on either their or our losses.

BATTLES ON HEDGE HILL AND TERRACE HILL STILL RAGING

Modderspruit, 26 February – The British attack on Hedge Hill on 22 and 23 February was undertaken by a brigade under the command of General Wynne. Late on the afternoon of 23 February, after a heavy bombardment, the fighting spread to the Boer position on Terrace Hill. Generals Lucas Meyer and Louis Botha expected that sooner or later the British would attack Terrace Hill, and entrenched it thoroughly. Several commandos occupied it and were placed under the command of Field Cornet Sarel Oosthuizen of Krugersdorp, who was appointed as fighting general by Meyer. The Boers repulsed one British attack after the other, but the Khakis kept coming. Their attacks proceeded throughout the day on Saturday 24 February, but the Boers manfully defended their positions and by late afternoon the British had fallen back in disarray. Some Boer officers wanted the burghers to take the offensive and wipe out the retreating enemy, but Meyer and Botha realised that their men were desperately tired and decided to give them the opportunity to rest.

Yesterday morning everything was silent. It was Sunday, and the Boers wanted to spend it as a Sabbath. Oosthuizen was prepared to allow a truce until the evening, during which time the wounded were treated and the dead were buried. Our correspondent believes that the British exploited the opportunity to observe our positions.

Both sides, but especially the British, suffered heavy casualties in these engagements. At least 196 Khakis were killed, 912 were wounded and 74 taken prisoner, while on the Boer side at least 22 burghers were killed and 80 wounded. Even though the British could take neither Hedge nor Terrace Hill, we hear that they now call the first Wynne's Hill and the second Hart's Hill after the Generals (Wynne and Hart) who respectively led the British attack on those positions.

Flare grenades used by Khakis on the Tugela front

BRITISH BREAKTHROUGH AT PIETER'S HILL

Boers abandon their positions, retreat in disorder

Elandslaagte, 2 March – While both the British and the Boers were busy treating their wounded and burying their dead on Hedge Hill and Terrace Hill last Sunday, thousands of British soldiers retreated southwards across the Tugela River by their pontoon bridge. The burghers noted this and did not interfere, speculating that General Buller was falling back all the way to his camps again. They were tired of fighting and looked forward to an opportunity to rest.

Next morning the Boer scouts noticed that the British had disassembled and removed their pontoon bridge in the night. The fact that the British did not keep up their usual heavy bombardment contributed to the Boer belief that the British were falling back. The Boer artillery did not fire heavily on the Khakis either, since ammunition was running out.

On the 26th the Boers heard that the British were invading the Vryheid district through Zululand. Consequently a number of burghers from Vryheid, Utrecht, Piet Retief and even Wakkerstroom left the front and hastened to the vicinity of Vryheid to repulse the invasion. Other burghers were on their way to the Free State to fight the British in that republic. Consequently there were not many more than 1 000 burghers on the Tugela front facing Buller's forces by Tuesday 27 February. They could only guess where the next British onslaught would be, and did not know where to entrench themselves. Everything was quiet at daybreak that morning. There had been a request from both Republican governments that Majuba Day should be commemorated as a day of compassion, and most of the burghers hoped for a peaceful day.

A rude surprise was in store for them. The British resumed their bombardment of the Boer positions early that morning. At the same time, they were busy constructing a new pontoon bridge over the Tugela downstream from Terrace Hill and some distance south of Pieter's Hill. The burghers were not aware of this, or of the fact that thousands of soldiers were crossing the river by late morning, and only noted the approaching enemy early that afternoon, when the British infantry launched a full-scale attack on the Boer entrenchments.

The burghers in the vicinity of Pieter's Hill initially put up a stiff resistance, as did the burghers on Hart's Hill far in the southeast. However, the British pressure was exerted on such a wide front that the hopelessly outnumbered burghers could not keep them back over the whole line. In addition, they began running out of ammunition – especially artillery shells. By late afternoon the Khakis forced the burghers to abandon Railway Hill, north of Terrace Hill. Soon afterwards they occupied Hart's Hill. With the coming of darkness, all the Boers were in retreat. The British breakthrough on the Tugela front was a reality. Buller's vast army had prevailed.

Lieutenant Colonel Trichard of the Transvaal State Artillery removed his guns from the emplacements by half past eight in the evening and General Meyer telegraphed to Commandant General Joubert that all was lost. Joubert telegraphed back that they must keep on fighting. Meyer and Botha thereupon convened a war council meeting. This council decided that it was impossible to carry out Joubert's order and that the wise thing would be to fall back in an orderly fashion to avoid being encircled by the enemy.

The battles on the Tugela front on 27 February resulted in heavy casualties. On the British side at least 87 men were killed and more than 400 wounded. On the Boer side at least 34 men were killed and 115 wounded. In addition more than 80 burghers, including a number of wounded, were made prisoners of war by the British.

SIEGE OF LADYSMITH ENDS

One of the immediate results of the British breakthrough at the Tugela was that the Boers ended their siege of Ladysmith, after 118 days. When the burghers elsewhere on the Natal front heard that the British had broken through, they realised that they were all in danger of being encircled. It was a downhearted group of Boer officers who had to order the abandonment of their fortifications around Ladysmith on the evening of 27 February. The burghers were told to fall back in the direction of the Biggarsberg mountain range, since the victorious British were approaching fast. The Khakis officially relieved Ladysmith on 28 February.

THE War Reporter
WEEKLY EDITION

Number 22 — Pretoria, South African Republic — 10 March 1900

DE WET REPULSED FROM POPLAR GROVE
BOERS ALMOST SURROUNDED

Bloemfontein, 9 March – After Cronjé's surrender at Paardeberg last week, the British in the western Free State were inactive for a number of days. We surmise that there was not enough food for the soldiers and fodder for the horses and they had to await the arrival of their supply convoys. This absence of action led many Boers, including Chief Commandant Christiaan de Wet, to believe that Lord Roberts did not intend to occupy Bloemfontein. De Wet stated that opinion in telegrams up to four days ago. In his opinion the British were preparing to invade the Transvaal via Veertien Strome (a village north of Kimberley) and to proceed from there straight to Johannesburg and Pretoria.

President Steyn holds a different opinion. He has no doubt that the British target is the Free State capital. That is why De Wet, despite his convictions, was stationed with the greater part of the Boer forces, namely about 5 000 burghers with seven guns, on both sides of the Modder River Poort between Roberts's main force and Bloemfontein. De Wet planned to attack the British positions west of him at an opportune moment.

Even though there was sporadic firing between De Wet's burghers and British patrols that ventured close to the Boer positions, including a skirmish on 5 March when 10 burghers were lightly wounded, the Boers only realised the next day that the British were not retreating at all, but were indeed busy outflanking their left flank. Colonel de Villabois Mareuil, who undertook a long reconnaissance trip with two other French officers, confirmed these reports, but De Wet was only informed on the night of 6–7 March. His surprise was therefore great early on the morning of the 7th when the British unexpectedly attacked his positions; all the more so because President Kruger, whom he himself had told there was no danger, was on his way to visit the laager at Poplar Grove.

Fortunately, General Philip Botha, at the southern tip of the Boer position, at Seven Hills, was ready for the British outflanking manoeuvre. During the night he ordered as many burghers as possible to form a line in an easterly direction. From about seven o'clock the British cavalry repeatedly clashed with this line and were eventually pinned down in the valley. The British sent more units of cavalry into the battle, but the Boer sharpshooters halted those newcomers in their tracks. This prompt action by Botha and his men probably saved De Wet's total force from being surrounded.

PANIC IN THE MAIN POSITIONS

In the main Boer entrenchments between Seven Hills and the Modder River the situation developed less favourably. The British bombardment of the Boer positions with heavy guns was a psychological ordeal. Until that morning the burghers had believed that the British would not attack, since they had heard from Chief Commandant De Wet himself that the Khakis were on their way to Veertien Strome. Suddenly they were involved in a life-and-death struggle, and plagued in addition by a massive swarm of locusts that was driven on by the Khakis and descended on the Boer positions in its own desperate flight.

When heavy rifle fire erupted on their left – where General Philip Botha's burghers were mercifully managing to halt the outflanking movement – panic seized the burghers in the main position. Fearing that they would, like Cronjé's burghers, be surrounded and be forced by a cruel bombardment into surrendering, numerous burghers began fleeing. De Wet was not aware of this. Neither was President Kruger who, dressed in a black suit and wearing a top hat, arrived in a horse carriage in De Wet's laager at Poplar Grove at 10 o'clock.

Kruger had been in the laager scarcely 10 minutes and was still busy talking with De Wet when the latter was informed of the critical situation in the main position. He immediately requested Kruger to leave, since there was a great risk that the President would be surrounded with De Wet's burghers. Then he gave his attention to the defence of his positions.

At that stage De Wet could do nothing to halt the British attack. His main position was already crumbling. Burghers everywhere were fleeing wildly. Many left all their belongings behind. The Chief Commandant kept his cool. He ordered all the burghers who were not panicking, to fall back a few kilometres and then form a new line from Sagkraal in the north to Boskop in the south, a distance of about 12 kilometres. There they managed shortly before dusk to form a relatively orderly line and subsequently fell back further east towards Abrahamskraal.

If one considers the long duration of the fighting in the vicinity of Poplar Grove, the casualties on both sides were relatively light. On the Boer side at least one burgher was killed and one wounded, while the British losses, according to reliable sources, amounted to eight men killed and 49 wounded. The British captured one Boer gun, a Krupp that was left behind on Loogkop where the burghers fled in panic.

It would be easy to put the blame for this defeat squarely on the shoulders of the burghers who abandoned the main position. Certainly many of them exhibited a lack of courage. The officers, including De Wet, must bear their part of the blame, however. They totally misjudged the enemy's plans and misled the burghers by telling them that everything was under control. After what happened to Cronjé's laager last week, one cannot really blame the burghers for allowing their fear of being surrounded to take the upper hand. The fact that De Wet managed to stem their flight and halt the British advance towards dusk gives some cause for hope.

Chief Commandant Christiaan De Wet

NEWS FROM THE SOUTHERN FRONT
Boer forces considerably reduced

Pretoria, 9 March – In our previous report on the situation on the southern front, we reported on how the Boer forces had managed to drive the British back from Colesberg to Arundel. That was in the middle of February. General Hendrik Schoeman and Chief Commandant Piet de Wet were in command, with Generals Koos de la Rey and Freek Grobler leading the burghers in the actual fighting. After the British took up position at Arundel, the burghers dug themselves in and for the time being refrained from offensive action.

On 18 February the Republican officers held a war council to discuss the possibility of launching an attack on the important railway junction at Noupoort, south of Arundel. Schoeman rejected the idea, arguing that it was too dangerous and the horses too emaciated for such an endeavour. De la Rey nevertheless attacked the British position at Rietfontein, close to Arundel station, on 20 February. What he did not know, however, was that Chief Commandant De Wet had left the front with a large number of Free State burghers the previous evening at the request of President Steyn to go to the aid of Cronjé at Paardeberg. Schoeman and Grobler's forces were now so reduced that they could not render any assistance to De la Rey.

De la Rey's burghers kept the British under pressure for a considerable time during the morning, but by the afternoon the scale had swung against them. Schoeman and Grobler fired on the Khakis with their guns but could contribute little more. With the coming of dark De la Rey retreated.

Early next morning a dejected De la Rey received a telegram that immediately filled him with new vigour. It was from President Steyn and announced his appointment as provisional chief commandant of the Free State forces on the southern front. Two days later, however, his burghers were again driven back by the British, who seem to have received considerable reinforcements with the arrival of new units from the south. Next morning, 24 February, the Khakis again attacked in full force. This time Grobler and his burghers halted them in their tracks through determined defence.

This was the situation when De la Rey received an order to proceed to Bloemfontein as quickly as possible with at least 1 000 burghers in order to assist with the defence of the capital. He appointed General H.R. Lemmer as provisional chief commandant, and left the following day.

After De la Rey and about 1 500 burghers left the southern front, the Transvaal authorities decided to transfer General Hendrik Schoeman to Bloemfontein as well. His new duties will be to assist Executive Council member A.D.W. Wolmarans in sending deserters back to the Transvaal front. Lemmer and General Grobler are to fall back in an orderly fashion from Colesberg northwards to the Orange River, ensuring that none of the train bridges across that river fall into British hands.

Executive Council member Wolmarans addressing the burghers at Norvalspont

SHAMELESS RUMOUR-MONGERING AMONG THE OFFICERS

The latest news from the southern front is that Schoeman is not prepared to accept Lemmer's appointment as commander in his place. He believes that he deserves that position and that he has been demoted as General. He is now spreading negative rumours about Chief Commandant Lemmer and his activities and thus undermining the confidence of the burghers in their new commander – highly improper conduct for an officer.

Lemmer, in the meantime, is carrying out his duties meticulously. From 23 February the burghers began falling back from the south. By 26 February Grobler's burghers were back in Colesberg. Two days later a number of officers who were considered to be confidants of Schoeman, including Commandant Preller (Schoeman's brother-in-law), decided without having been attacked and without Lemmer's permission to fall back even further, thus placing the whole Boer line in jeopardy. In addition they began stirring

Continued overleaf

continued

up feelings against Lemmer amongst their burghers.

When the Transvaal military authorities heard these reports they immediately dispatched General De la Rey and Executive Council member Wolmarans to Norvalspont to re-establish order. On their arrival De la Rey and Wolmarans called the burghers together. They immediately established that Preller was the instigator, discharged him and sent him back to Pretoria. Soon afterwards Schoeman too left for Pretoria, since he refused to carry out his duties with regard to the deserters.

BRIDGES OVER THE ORANGE RIVER WRECKED

By the beginning of this month, the Republican forces under Lemmer's command were digging themselves in immediately south of the Orange River. They kept a close watch on British forces south of their positions, and sporadically became involved in skirmishes. In the meantime they took all their supplies back over the river to the Free State. On 2 March General Grobler fell back across the river with his burghers, followed by Lemmer himself and his burghers, who crossed the railway bridge on the night of 5–6 March. After they had all crossed, an engineer of the Dutch South African Railway Company destroyed the 600 metre bridge with dynamite at exactly half past two in the morning. One of the pillars of the bridge as well as three of the 12 spans were wrecked, which means that the British would not be able to use the bridge against the Republican forces.

Yesterday evening the burghers also destroyed the wagon bridge over the Orange River with dynamite. With that the Boer presence in the Cape Colony in the vicinity of Colesberg came to an end after many months.

Norvalspont railway bridge, destroyed by the Boers

FROM THE EDITOR

The crisis in the Free State continues to escalate. The Republics are faced by the biggest challenge in their existence – that goes without saying. What is needed now is calm consideration of steps that are necessary to find a solution, rather than impulsive, emotional accusations as to who is responsible for the crisis. The negotiations between the Presidents, on which we report this week, will hopefully prevent a total catastrophe.

It is not for us to criticise the tactics of the Republican forces. We do wonder, however, if there is any sense in continuing with our relatively limited and extremely demoralised and war-weary force of burghers to confront the overwhelming might of the enemy forces. Their morale is high after their successive victories of the last few weeks, and to halt them would be extremely difficult. Perhaps we should target their major weakness, namely their dependence on supply trains for food and fodder, without which their tens of thousand of soldiers and horses cannot survive. According to Georges de Villabois-Mareuil, an experienced French colonel who has joined the Boer forces, this is our only hope. We have not seen any sign that our military authorities contemplate using this tactic, however.

The establishment of Theron's Reconnaissance Corps deserves high praise. We hope it will solve a problem that has often crippled our forces, namely unsatisfactory scouting work. Our best wishes accompany the creative commander of the Corps, Captain Danie Theron.

KRUGER IN THE FREE STATE
ENCOURAGES BURGHERS TO PERSEVERE

Bloemfontein, 7 March – President Kruger is determined to keep encouraging the Republican forces to stand firm. Last week he was on the Natal front; on Monday (the 5th) he arrived by train here in Bloemfontein to be greeted by an excited crowd whom he exhorted to remain united and unflinching in their faith.

From the station Kruger accompanied President Steyn to the Presidency. We have been informed that they discussed how to end the war. One of their decisions is to address a letter to the British Prime Minister, Lord Salisbury, regarding a possible settlement, but with the Republics remaining independent. Second, they decided to issue a joint call to all states, especially the United States of America, Germany, Austria, Belgium, France, Holland, Italy, Russia and Switzerland, to intervene in order to broker a settlement that would be acceptable to both sides. And third, they decided to send a deputation overseas to attempt to bring about intervention on behalf of the Republics. The members of the delegation would be Abraham Fischer, C.H. Wessels and A.D.W. Wolmarans.

From Bloemfontein Kruger went to the front at Poplar Grove, where he almost fell into the hands of the Khakis (see report elsewhere in this number). Our correspondent reports that the President, in the short while that he was on the battlefield, reproached the burghers a few times for their lack of resolution. When one of the British shells exploded close to his carriage, it is reported that he jokingly commented that it was a pill from the Queen. Everybody who was present agreed that Oom Paul certainly deserved the reputation that he gained as a young man of not being afraid of anything.

DEVELOPMENTS IN NATAL

Glencoe, 8 March – The British breakthrough on the Tugela front and their relief of the besieged garrison in Ladysmith does not mean that all military activities in Natal have now ended. It is still of major importance for the Republican forces to protect the Orange Free State and Transvaal borders from being crossed by the British from Natal. With this in mind, the Free State commandos in Natal took up position in the Drakensberg Mountains and the Transvaal commandos in the Biggarsberg Mountains within Natal.

On 5 March, while the Transvaal commandos took up their new positions, Commandant-General Piet Joubert appointed General Louis Botha as the commander of all the Transvaal generals in Natal. His new positions stretch over a distance of at least 200 kilometres or 20 hours on horseback. We do not know the total strength in numbers of the 16 commandos in the Biggarsberg Mountains.

The Free State forces in the Drakensberg Mountains comprise about 3 000 burghers under Chief Commandant Marthinus Prinsloo. Numerous Free Staters have been transferred to Bloemfontein in the past week to assist in the defence of the capital.

Why the British did not immediately follow up their victory at the Tugela River, we cannot explain. The Boer forces were mentally in a state of collapse and had retreated in disorder. Fortunately Buller did not realise this, and elected to take up defensive positions around Ladysmith. This allowed the Boer officers a few days' grace to re-establish order. President Kruger's visit to the front, on which we reported last week, certainly helped to restore a positive frame of mind.

This lasted only a few days, unfortunately. Our correspondent reports that the bad news from the Free State immediately broke down the improvement in the Boers' spirits. In addition, some of them are receiving letters from home almost daily in which their loved ones beg them to return. Not surprisingly, desertion amongst the burghers is taking on epidemic proportions. No official leave is allowed and the railways may not transport any burgher without a leave document. Nevertheless many burghers disappear from the front every day, recklessly betraying their national duty.

A railway bridge in the Biggarsberg blown up by Boers

NEW RECONNAISSANCE UNIT FORMED

Bloemfontein, 7 March – Last Sunday, the well-known Transvaal Scout, Captain Danie Theron, formed the first military unit that officially consists of burghers of both Republics. It is called Theron's Reconnaissance Corps. Theron himself is the commander. Both Presidents support the founding of this unit.

The Corps will comprise a maximum of 100 scouts, to be selected by Theron himself. Each commando has been requested to provide the best possible scouts for the unit, each of them with two horses so as to be able to cover long distances with ease.

Some of the British officers held as prisoners of war in the Staats Model School in Pretoria were recently transferred to Waterval north of the city

---

OUR MILITARY OFFICERS

General Philip Botha

Philip Rudolph Botha was born in 1851 in the Greytown district of Natal. His parents were Louis Botha and his wife Salomina Adriana von Rooyen. He is the eldest brother of the commander of the Transvaal forces in Natal, General Louis Botha. He was 18 years old when he trekked from Natal with his parents in 1869. They settled near Vrede in the Free State, where Botha has farmed ever since.

With the outbreak of the war Botha joined the Free State forces as a common burgher. In January he was appointed assistant fighting general, a rank he still holds. Last month he participated with distinction in the attempts to break the encirclement of Cronjé's laager at Paardeberg. In the past few days he has made a big impression with his military talent at Poplar Grove, as we report in this number. This officer is certainly of the same metal as his brother Louis.

General Philip Botha is married to Maria Magdalena Wessels. They have 11 children.

General Philip Botha

THE War Reporter
WEEKLY EDITION

Number 23   Pretoria, South African Republic   17 March 1900

BLOEMFONTEIN OCCUPIED
Boer forces powerless in the Free State

Kroonstad, 16 March – When it became clear that the British forces could not be checked the Free State government was hurriedly moved to Kroonstad. On 10 March General Koos de la Rey and Chief Commandant Christiaan de Wet made a last desperate effort to halt the British offensive at Abrahamskraal. (See report on next page.) On the same day a deputation of the Bloemfontein City Council met with President Steyn and requested him not to defend the city since this could lead to its bombardment. Steyn answered that there was no danger of that since the front was not close to the city. The deputation was not satisfied with his answer, demanding nothing less than to be handed full control of the city. This the President was not prepared to grant, since it would not only be unconstitutional, but it was also clear that deputation member J.G. Fraser, a wily old opponent of Republican freedom, planned to make common cause with the Khakis. Many burghers feel that his actions bordered on treason and that he should have been arrested.

The Military Commission of the Orange Free State, of which Steyn and De Wet are members, had already decided on 8 March to defend Bloemfontein. That was before the battle at Abrahamskraal. When the news reached the capital on 11 March that the British had broken through at Abrahamskraal as well, the Free State government decided to introduce emergency measures. That included moving the seat of the government temporarily to Kroonstad in the north.

On Monday 12 March a number of prominent Boer officers and members of the Free State government held a day-long war council meeting immediately outside Bloemfontein. We subsequently heard that the council could not reach unanimity on the issue of the defence of the Free State capital. Some officers were under the impression that a decision was actually taken to defend the city as long as possible. Others reckon that no final decision was taken. It is therefore no surprise that nothing came of the possible defence. The burghers are simply too demoralised to put up effective resistance. In addition there are too many influential people, including the mayor, B.O. Kellner, who feel that there is no point in continuing with the war.

The only burghers who were ready to defend Bloemfontein were De la Rey's men to the west and De Wet's men to the southwest of the city. Commandant Weilbach's Heidelbergers were requested by De Wet to defend the city in the north. Not knowing the area, they were led directly into the approaching British force by unknown guides who seem to have been traitors. They were forced to defend themselves and by dusk had retreated to a low hill east of the city. De Wet was furious with the Heidelbergers, but the fact is that the defence was never properly coordinated.

Under these circumstances the Free State government finally decided not to defend Bloemfontein. There was too much of a risk that the enemy would destroy the city. The British are, after all, notorious for devastating the capitals of their opponents. In 1814, for example, they deliberately demolished all the most important buildings in Washington, the capital of the United States of America, including the Congress building and the White House.

President Steyn and his personal staff left Bloemfontein on Monday evening in a horse-drawn carriage. They could not leave by train, since a group of pro-British Bloemfontein citizens had damaged the railway line at the Bloemfontein Station to such an extent that no trains could leave. The damaging of the railway was a very unpleasant surprise for the Free State authorities since it meant that 25 locomotives, 10 passenger wagons and 124 goods wagons would fall into British hands. It is an inexcusable error that this rolling material was not removed to the north in time.

The British vanguard reached the outskirts of Bloemfontein at midnight on 12–13 March. They too destroyed the railway line, both south and north of the capital, in the course of the night. In some cases they became involved in skirmishes with Boers, but the latter did not make any serious attempt to halt them. Soon after daybreak it was clear to De la Rey and De Wet that their position was hopeless, and they decided to retreat to the north. The British forces advanced towards the city and at 11 o'clock began entering Bloemfontein from the south.

An inhabitant from the capital managed to smuggle a report on that morning's events to us. According to him Mayor Kellner, Fraser and Magistrate Papenfus waited on the British in the Bloemfontein Club. In the course of the morning they decided to ride out to welcome Lord Roberts and hand the keys of the government offices to him. In addition they hoisted a huge white flag as signal of surrender.

Afterwards a deadly silence prevailed in the city. From the south a mass of British troops approached. Amongst them was Roberts in his carriage. It was only when he entered the city that a cheer rose from the pro-British inhabitants, thus breaking the silence. Suddenly one could see British flags and rosettes everywhere. It was shocking to observe the huge enthusiasm with which the British yoke was welcomed by many of the inhabitants of Bloemfontein.

The British soldiers did not look like conquerors. They seemed tired and dirty. Some were so exhausted that they could barely walk. Their horses seemed battered. Nevertheless the pro-British Bloemfontein citizens held dazzling feasts that evening. Roberts himself occupied the Presidency and his soldiers pitched camps west and southwest of the city.

Our correspondent reports that Chief Commandant Christiaan de Wet gave all the Free State burghers leave to return temporarily to their farms. Those who wished to go on with the war were told to report at the Sand River Railway Bridge on 25 March. De Wet himself, his brother Chief Commandant Piet de Wet and Fighting Generals J.B. Wessels, A.P. Cronjé, Stoffel Froneman, W.J. Kolbe and Philip Botha proceeded to the new capital via Brandfort.

At Brandfort De Wet met Commandant-General Piet Joubert, who had hurried to this front to salvage whatever he could. Joubert confronted De Wet about the fact that he had granted leave to all his burghers. De Wet answered that he had acted correctly, since you cannot hunt hares with unwilling dogs. A good opportunity to rest would probably fill the burghers with new courage and enthusiasm. The Transvaal commandos were not included in this leave arrangement and were retreating towards the Sand River.

The last Republican council of war before British occupation of Bloemfontein

British forces enter Bloemfontein

REPUBLICAN FORCES WITHDRAW FROM NORTHEASTERN CAPE

Pretoria, 16 March – It is not only on the western and southern fronts that the Republican forces are retreating. We have just heard from Smithfield that General J.H. Olivier's burghers have withdrawn from the northeastern Cape. These burghers had held their front with ease since the beginning of the year, but had not been able to inflict any damage on the enemy.

By the beginning of March Olivier's burghers were retreating. Commandant Gideon de Wet's commando of 400 Cape Rebels covered their retirement. These rebels were involved in an extended skirmish with a huge Khaki force at Labuschagne's Nek north of Dordrecht on 3–5 March. By the third morning they were so tired, hungry and thirsty that they had no option but to retreat. Their heroic defence cost them 25 casualties (eight men killed and 17 wounded). They claim that the enemy's casualties amounted to 14 men killed and 29 wounded.

The British pursued the Boers vigorously and on 9 March occupied Jamestown. Olivier's burghers in the meantime crossed the Orange River at Aliwal North with their full convoy. The next day the British caught up with them and attacked them on the northern bank of the river. The Boers managed to repulse the attackers but the latter gained possession of the wagon bridge and thus prevented the Boers from implementing their plans to blow it up. Fortunately they did manage to destroy the railway bridge over the Orange River at Bethulie with dynamite.

Earlier this week President Steyn ordered Olivier's forces to fall back to the north immediately and join the rest of the Republican forces in the northern Free State. On 13 March they united with the burghers of Chief Commandant Lemmer and General Grobler, who are falling back from Norvalspont, at Kommissie Drift. Their combined convoy is very big, consisting of about 750 ox-wagons with supplies, 10 guns, about 1 000 servants and even a few women and children – altogether about 6 000 souls. It takes four hours on horseback to ride past the whole convoy. They have enough food, but to find firewood for so many people is difficult in this treeless area.

49

FIERCE BATTLE AT ABRAHAMSKRAAL

BRITISH REPULSE REPUBLICAN FORCES ONCE AGAIN

Kroonstad, 15 March – The last battle before the occupation of Bloemfontein took place on and around the farm Abrahamskraal, about 66 kilometres west of Bloemfontein. Most Boers had retreated all the way to Abrahamskraal on the night after the battle at Poplar Grove on 7 March.

It is sad to have to mention that not nearly all the burghers dug in at Abrahamskraal. Despite President Kruger's pleas and then threats, many of the retreating burghers fled right past him all the way back to their farms. Fortunately a good number remained loyal to their cause and took up position at Abrahamskraal. They could enjoy two days of rest, but last Saturday (10 March) the British were upon them again.

The Republican commanders in the battle that followed were Generals Koos de la Rey and Christiaan de Wet. The total Boer force at Abrahamskraal consisted of only about 3 000 men with 12 guns and pom-poms. Of those only about 1 500 burghers actually took part in the battle. These burghers were spread over a front that covered more than 20 kilometres from north to south. We do not know exactly how strong the British force was, but reliable sources indicate that Roberts himself was in command with more than 30 000 soldiers and 30 guns at his disposal.

After a sporadic firing dual between the Boers at Abrahamskraal and British patrols on 9 March, the full-scale British attack followed on the 10th. The first British target was the Boer position on the low hills of Abrahamskraal directly south of the Modder River. Mounted British soldiers approached soon after sunrise and were halted by rifle fire. While the British and Boer artillery exchanged fire from about 10 o'clock that morning, British cavalry units were also checked by the rifle fire of the burghers at Damvlei.

De la Rey and De Wet expected that the British would, if they were checked in the north, attempt to make a breakthrough in the south. De la Rey himself was at Driefontein, southwest of Damvlei, from where he observed the British through his binoculars from a low hill. His burghers had taken up position early that morning on the Driefontein hills. The leisurely way in which the British approached these hills indicated that they did not expect to find any Boers there. When they came close, however, the burghers greeted them enthusiastically with pompom and rifle fire. The Khakis hurriedly retreated for at least a kilometre.

As expected, the British then began bombarding the Driefontein hills and in due course made a cavalry charge. At noon a mass of British infantry charged into heavy rifle and artillery fire. The soldiers attacked courageously and their numbers were so overwhelming that the burghers were eventually driven back a short distance. The Boers however fought valiantly from behind the shelter provided by rocks and bushes and made life unpleasant for the British. All along the front the burghers halted the Khakis in their tracks.

At noon the British initiated an attempt to outflank the Boer positions in the south. De Wet had expected such a move and positioned the Heidelbergers under Commandant Weilbach in the valley southeast of his position to counter the enemy. The burghers had a field gun and pom-pom with them and soon forced the Khakis back.

The burghers managed to stem the British advance until about three o'clock. Unfortunately the situation was bound to change, since many started running out of ammunition. At one stage the British made a bayonet charge, but Lieutenant De Hart's policemen checked them. The Khakis certainly suffered heavy casualties and according to the burghers one soldier hoisted a white flag. When a number of burghers stood up from their shelters, other soldiers fired on them and Commandant J.J. de Beer was wounded. Subsequently the battle resumed in full force.

The Boer resistance finally broke when they ran out of ammunition. They had fought so valiantly that the Khakis only gained the upper hand by dusk, however. The Boers now had no option but to retreat. In an attempt to confuse the pursuing Khakis, they lighted a number of fires, fired a few shots in the air, and retired at about half past six. Thus they ensured that the whole Boer force could fall back in an orderly fashion without leaving any guns or supplies behind and without a significant number of burghers being taken prisoner of war.

The casualties in this battle at Abrahamskraal were high. On the Republican side at least 30 men were killed, 47 wounded and 20 captured. We have heard that at least 60 Khakis were killed and 360 wounded.

The Heidelberg commando retreated throughout the night in an attempt to find safety. At dawn the next morning, Sunday 11 March, they could see British soldiers in the distance marching towards Bloemfontein. Soon afterwards they were ordered to join the other commandos at Bainsvlei, west of the Free State capital. The Heidelbergers resumed their retreat and by midday reached their destination, where they were given an hour to rest before taking to the road again – this time to take up position south of Bloemfontein. It was only by the evening that they could, after two tough days, finally lay their exhausted bodies down.

BOERS FALL BACK FROM SOUTHERN FREE STATE

RETREAT A BITTER EXPERIENCE FOR THE BURGHERS

Smithfield, 16 March – Our correspondent with the Boer forces in the southern Free State reports that the Republican forces are falling back to the north. One of the burghers of the Pretoria commando, Jan Celliers, provided us with a written report on the retreat. According to him the preparations for this huge trek to the north were rather disorderly. Last Monday (5 March) they were at Norvalspont busy preparing to take all their goods and supplies to Donkerpoort Station in the Free State.

Celliers writes: 'The confusion is accompanied by a strange attraction. There are wagons everywhere, some loaded, some half-loaded. Heaps of goods, saddles, bags, foodstuff, on the wagons, under the wagons, in heaps against the walls, indoors and outdoors. Oxen and horses are loaded on the train trucks and then unloaded again. Shouting and screaming and confused scurrying accompanies this.

'We had a good breakfast this morning. It consisted of a cup of coffee that we begged here and a few biscuits that we stole there. We do not know where we are going to have lunch, or where we will find shelter tonight. But we are not hungry and we do not care if the train leaves today or only tomorrow.'

They did get away that afternoon, and soon after dark they were at Donkerpoort. The next day new trains arrived continuously from Norvalspont. The biggest frustration for most burghers was that they did not know what was going on. Celliers's report continues:

'The situation is to us totally incomprehensible. All of us are still full of hope, in spite of the setback with Cronjé, of which we only received confirmation today. Nobody feels depressed about it. If we are ordered to go forward, we will all go forward without hesitation. Now the command is retreat. This seems to have to do with an attempt to achieve peace. It is said that European powers want to intervene, but cannot bring this about since we have forces on British territory. That is the reason why our people have been called back from the Cape into Republican territory, so that there could be peace. Exactly how we do not know. We will have to wait and see.'

In the course of the next few days the burghers' illusion that peace was about to be concluded was repeatedly shattered. The enemy fired on them with heavy guns from the southern bank of the Orange River and the Boers fired back. Celliers's section was sent to the riverfront and participated in the firing. Fortunately they suffered no significant casualties.

On Monday 12 March they received orders to begin falling back to the northern Free State. To them this was another incomprehensible order, since, as Celliers writes, they were in good positions on the banks of the Orange River and could resist a huge enemy force there. However, soon after sundown they began packing their wagons and left. It was already one o'clock that night when they outspanned to get some rest.

On Tuesday they trekked again the whole day long. Celliers describes their progress in a singularly humorous way: 'Early in the morning we went forward again; or should I rather say backward? As far as we can see in front of us and behind us there is a long line of wagons, horsemen and livestock – all trekking on the dusty road. No news has reached us and we do not know what is happening on the war front.'

Yesterday they reached Springfontein. Celliers writes that total chaos reigned there: 'What an indescribable confusion at the station. The whole commissariat was left there. Everyone could take whatever he wanted, everyone scratched in the heaps of supplies to see what they could loot. We are told that the railway line between here and Bloemfontein has been damaged and that we have to leave again as soon as possible. For the first time I detect an anxiety in my heart that I may perhaps be taken prisoner. In the never-ending line we continue our trek. We walk for long distances to make the load less heavy for our animals. This goes on until after nightfall, when we finally outspan.'

Before dawn this morning they rose again to resume the trek. All were soaking wet from the dew. Only then did they hear that the Free State capital had been occupied by the British two days previously. Celliers's reaction to this is: 'We are told that Bloemfontein has been occupied by the enemy without any battle. I cannot believe this, since the cowardly disposition of a section of our burghers is incomprehensible to me. I emphasise the word section, since such a disposition is not be found in our ranks at all.'

We have just heard that the British began crossing the Orange River at Norvalspont yesterday.

Scene at Norvalspont Station when the Boer retreat began

Pretoria burghers at Norvalspont

FROM THE EDITOR

When the war broke out, the last thing that any Boer expected was that the Free State capital would be in British hands before the next winter – but it has happened. Thousands of burghers have completely lost hope, and the Republican forces seem to be disintegrating in some areas. Do we really have any grounds for hope that we will reach our war objectives?

The heroic defence that our burghers put up at Abrahamskraal reminds us that the British forces are not invincible. We must guard against being blinded by their huge numbers, since such forces are often very vulnerable – a lesson even the mighty Napoleon Bonaparte learned to his dismay when he invaded Russia with his *Grande Armée* in 1812. If we can cut Roberts and his invaders off from sufficient water sources for all their soldiers and their horses, and disrupt their lines of supply, and divide their forces so that they can no longer act in unison, it will soon become clear that they are a giant with feet of clay.

The best news of the past week is that the British are exhausted after the campaign of the last month, and will be unable to resume the offensive soon. Our military authorities now have an opportunity to stem the panic that has taken hold of our burghers here and there. We have been informed of an important war council meeting at Kroonstad today to discuss future tactics. Our best wishes accompany our leaders. May they come up with creative solutions!

OUR MILITARY OFFICERS

Commandant J.D. Weilbach

Johan Daniel Weilbach was born in 1839 in the Uitenhage district of the Cape Colony. He is the son of Johan Frederick Weilbach and his wife Maria Aletta Fredrika Landman. In the 1860s he moved to the Orange Free State and participated in the wars between the Free State Republic and the Basotho of King Moshweshwe. Subsequently he moved to the vicinity of Heidelberg in the Transvaal where he became the commandant of the district.

In 1880–81 Weilbach participated in the Transvaal War of Independence. He initially participated in the siege of the British garrison in Potchefstroom, but from the end of January participated on the Natal front in the battles of Laingsnek, Schuinshoogte and Majuba. With C.N.J. du Plessis he wrote a highly readable book on the war. It was published in 1882 under the title *Geschiedenis van de Emigrante-Boeren en van den Vrijheids-Oorlog* and is the best book on that war written from the Boer perspective.

While Weilbach was farming on Faraosfontein, he led the Heidelberg commando in numerous campaigns against rebellious black communities, including the Bavenda in 1898. With the outbreak of this war last October he accompanied his commando to the Natal front. His headstrong nature has at times made him unpopular with his co-officers and at one stage it was rumoured that he would be discharged. In December last year he was indeed temporarily dismissed since he was accused of being responsible for the fact that the British managed to capture a Boer gun emplacement at Ladysmith on 8 December. It was however never ascertained beyond reasonable doubt that he had acted culpably.

From early this month Weilbach is back in the saddle as commander of the Heidelbergers. The highlight of his military activities until now in this war is without doubt the valiant way in which he and his burghers defended their positions in last week's battle at Abrahamskraal. Their bravery and military prowess contributed significantly to the fact that the Boers could manage to retreat in an orderly fashion from the battlefield and thus rob the massive British forces of a huge victory. We certainly hope that the earlier problems with regard to Weilbach's actions are something of the past and will now disappear forever.

Commandant J.D. Weilbach

THE War Reporter
WEEKLY EDITION

Number 24 — Pretoria, South African Republic — 24 March 1900

KRUGER TO KROONSTAD
President seen off by huge crowd

Pretoria, 17 March – President Paul Kruger, accompanied by a number of officials of the Transvaal government, left Pretoria on a special train at eight o'clock yesterday evening for Kroonstad, where talks will be held with the Free State government and Republican military authorities. A large crowd flocked to the station to see the elderly President off. He briefly addressed the crowd and as usual called on them to stay faithful to God and His word, since then they would achieve victory.

The President added that many people regard the Republic's prospects as hopeless. The massive numbers of the British forces and the presence of enemies in our midst tend to make one lose faith. However, if the small crowd of Boers trust in God, He will fill them with new hope. They will then be able to form a human wall against oppression.

In conclusion the President pointed out to the crowd that the fate of the Boers is in the hands of God the Father, without whose will no hair falls from our heads. God is placing his people under pressure to humiliate them in the face of their sins. The Afrikaner people are at present subjected to a struggle. Liberation will follow, even if it takes a long while before He finally brings an end to their travails.

After his speech Kruger made himself at home in his compartment and the train steamed from the station, to loud cheers from the crowd.

ANOTHER PAPER BOMB
Roberts threatens Free State burghers

Kroonstad, 20 March – On 15 March Lord Roberts, the British Commander in Chief, issued another proclamation in which he attempted to entice the Free Staters into surrendering their weapons. In this proclamation he offered all the burghers participating in the war the following conditions:

'All burghers who have not taken a prominent part in the policy which has led to the war between Her Majesty and the Orange Free State, or commanded any forces of the Republic, or commandeered or used violence to any British subjects, and who are willing to lay down their arms at once, and to bind themselves by an oath to abstain from further participation in the war, will be given passes to allow them to return to their homes and will not be made prisoners of war, nor will their property be taken from them.'

The Republican burghers, especially the Free Staters, must take careful note of what is printed above. They are not only expected to remain quietly on their farms and proceed with their daily tasks if they do not want to be molested by British troops, but they can only receive these privileges if they obtain a written notification in the form of a pass. Each one has to bind himself with an oath to the Khakis to refrain from taking up arms again. And each one must hand his weapons that he needs for self-defence and for hunting to the Khakis. If they refuse they will be sent away as prisoners of war and their property will be confiscated.

That is not all. Even burghers who are prepared to accept these conditions risk being accused of having taken a prominent role in the 'policy which has led to the war' or that they have treated British subjects harshly. Such a burgher would no longer qualify for clemency but would be taken away as a prisoner of war and his property would be confiscated.

IMPORTANT WAR COUNCIL MEETING IN KROONSTAD
Kruger and Steyn fill Boers with new fortitude

Kroonstad, 17 March – Here in Kroonstad a very important war council meeting took place today, attended by President Kruger of the Transvaal and President Steyn of the Orange Free State. At Kruger's arrival at the station this morning Steyn and a huge number of burghers gave him an enthusiastic welcome. Even though it was raining quite heavily, Kruger addressed the burghers, encouraging them to keep fighting and to believe that since their cause is just they will eventually achieve victory.

Steyn also addressed the burghers. He pointed out that Lord Salisbury's rejection of the Boer peace proposals (see report elsewhere in this issue) left the Republics with no option but to keep fighting courageously. In addition the British High Commissioner in the Cape, Sir Alfred Milner, had openly declared that it was his aim to extinguish Afrikanerdom. For that reason the struggle will have to continue to the bitter end: nobody may give up. If there is anybody who does not agree with this, the President challenged the crowd, that person is free to go. Nobody left the gathering.

Commandant-General Piet Joubert also called on the burghers to confront the enemy like men and to fight them with complete faith in God. Lastly Chief Commandant Christiaan de Wet said some words on the battle at Abrahamskraal and the surrender of Bloemfontein.

DECISIONS OF THE WAR COUNCIL

This meeting began soon after the abovementioned public gathering. In addition to the two presidents, 23 military officers of both republics were present. The most important task of this meeting was to decide on the military tactics that the Boers would follow forthwith. The meeting decided, inter alia, that instead of attempting to confront the enemy from defensive positions, the burghers should concentrate on destroying the enemy's lines of communications. They also decided to divide the Boer armies into small units and to do away with all wagon laagers. Only light vehicles for the transportation of ammunition and provisions would be allowed. The commandos should consist only of burghers with a horse and rifle. Within each field cornetcy corporals would each be in command of 25 men. Mechanisms to enforce military discipline, such as the imposition of fines and arrangements in connection with the expulsion of officers, were introduced. And last, the war council decided that all the mines, including the coal mines in northern Natal, should be destroyed to ensure that the British could not use them for military purposes.

Assembly at Kroonstad

FROM BLOEMFONTEIN TO SAND RIVER
MANGOLD DESCRIBES THE RETREAT OF THE HEIDELBERGERS

Kroonstad, 22 March – On Tuesday 13 March our commando was on a low hill some five kilometres east of Bloemfontein when we were informed that the British had occupied the city. That was at about nine o'clock in the morning. Since we wanted to ensure at all costs that we would not be taken prisoner of war, we immediately abandoned our sheltering hill and fell back in the direction of Winburg. Initially we trekked on our own over the abandoned country and we saw no sign of any other commando. At the Vet River we came upon other wagons all loaded with provisions. In due course a large transport convoy developed. We escorted it by forming a vanguard and flank guard.

Two days later, on the 15th, we reached Winburg. There we were informed that the British were advancing along the railway line towards Winburg. We therefore proceeded in the direction of the Sand River, where there is a high railway bridge across the river. We were heartily welcomed at all farm dwellings in this vicinity and treated on milk and coffee by the bucket. On Saturday the 17th we reached our destination. At last we could peacefully roast our mutton and veal on the fire and enjoy our bread, liquor and cigarettes, of which we had enough. Furthermore we could now wash and bath to our hearts' delight.

The seriousness of the war was with us, however, and we were on guard all the time. Sentries were continuously placed out and in the evenings we knee-haltered our horses and bound them together with a long rope. We were informed that the Khakis were still in Bloemfontein and that Captain Theron was in Brandfort with his Scout Corps to keep an eye on them. Subsequently our guard was considerably weakened.

On 20 March Commandant-General Piet Joubert, accompanied by President Steyn and the foreign attachés, arrived by train at Sand River. In a forceful speech Joubert reminded the burghers that the British and the Boers had signed the Sand River Convention in this area in 1852. For that reason we have to defend the Sand River to the best of our ability. His words were something like the following: 'If the English gain the upper hand and we are subjugated, I assure you that you will never be able to defend yourselves again. We have to keep fighting until our independence is absolutely assured.' Before he left he shook the hands of each of us. Even though he is almost 70 years old, he has an upright bearing and a steady tread, but it is clear that the high demands of the past few months have tired out our Commandant-General.

During the course of the 20th numerous commandos from Natal joined us, as well as a train with eight guns and their crews under the command of Lieutenant Colonel Fanie Trichard. This addition brings our total strength to approximately 8 000 burghers.

FROM THE EDITOR

The most important event of the past week was the meeting of the Republican military authorities in Kroonstad. The decisions that the extended war council took there reflect in our opinion a total change in the military approach of the Boers. What is now planned is what the Spanish call guerrilla war, where small groups of soldiers carry out raids on the enemy – enabling small units to harass a huge conventional force.

The contents of the peace letter written by the Republican presidents to the British government, as well as the enemy's answer, were made public this week. The British Prime Minister, Lord Salisbury, not only rejects the peace initiative, but in addition alleges that the Republics are responsible for the war. Thus he perpetuates the old lie of calling the Republics the aggressors. The British call those who do not bow to their greed and who defend themselves against British supremacy, aggressors. Salisbury furthermore bluntly states in his answer that the British are waging the war to destroy the future existence of the Republics. Their explicit objective is to turn all our burghers into British subjects. The Imperial yoke will be ours and our descendants' burden to carry if we do not fend them off.

Also newsworthy in the past week is the proclamation issued by Lord Roberts to the burghers of the Orange Free State. Only the most simple-minded Boer would subject himself to Roberts under the conditions spelled out in that proclamation. We have bad news for the Khaki commander. Our burghers are not idiots. They would never trust a Brit, since on all the previous occasions when they were trusting enough to let themselves be tempted, they were rewarded with a stab in the back. Think of all the agreements the enemy concluded with our governments and subsequently failed to honour, including the Sand River Convention of 1852 and London Convention of 1884. The word of a Brit is not worth the paper it is written on. All our burghers, but especially Boer officers, understand – now better than ever – that if they want to remain in possession of their property, and if they do not want to be sent away as prisoners of war, they have no choice but to keep fighting against the invader for all they are worth.

PRESIDENT STEYN ISSUES PROCLAMATION

Forceful call on burghers to keep fighting

Pretoria, 21 March – The government printer here in Pretoria has just finished printing 10 000 copies of a proclamation that will be distributed in the Orange Free State. In this proclamation, President Steyn urgently appeals to the burghers to keep on fighting. Here we publish a few extracts:

'Burghers, brothers! The enemy is invading our country and now attempts to divide us in order to subjugate us with ease. Divide and rule has always been their policy in South Africa and from Roberts's latest proclamation it is clear that it is also his policy. We can assure the enemy that it will not be easy to cause division among the burghers of the Free State.

'As a temptation to divide us, Roberts promises to leave all burghers who abandon the struggle in peace. It seems as if he wants to reward the burghers for disloyalty and cowardice.

'Can you insult anybody more blatantly than by offering to bribe him to abandon his holy duty and to become disloyal to himself, his people and his descendants? Brothers, you have a noble duty to fulfil. You should with God's help keep the pledge that your forefathers entrusted to you. Your children and their descendants will demand a report on your guardianship from you.

'Do not let yourself be misled by the wiliness of the enemy. Anybody who attempts to encourage others to be disloyal cannot himself be trustworthy. The enemy will only remain true to his promises until he has his foot on the neck of the Afrikaner people. How can the Brit, who has already broken all his holy conventions with our people, now be trusted to remain true to his wily promises?

'Brothers, even though our capital is occupied by the enemy, the struggle has not been lost. Indeed, this gives us all the more reason to keep fighting. Our forces are not dependent on a city. Keep up your valour and stay true to your faith. God will not abandon his plans with our people. Keep on fighting. When the night is at its darkest, daylight is the closest.'

In a second proclamation that was issued with the above, President Steyn declares officially that the Republic of the Orange Free State is still in existence and that Roberts's proclamation has no judicial force; that the Free State burghers are still subject to martial law, and that burghers who support the enemy are committing treason and exposing themselves to severe punishment.

PEACE INITIATIVE IN VAIN

Britain rejects Republican proposals

Pretoria, 19 March – The Transvaal government has just released the contents of the telegram that the Republican presidents sent to the British government earlier this month, as well as the answer of the British Prime Minster, Lord Salisbury. The Presidents wrote on 5 March:

'The blood and tears of thousands who have suffered in this war and the prospect of moral and material ruin that now threaten South Africa, compel both belligerents to reflect calmly and as if they were in the presence of the Holy Trinity why they are fighting and whether these reasons can justify the terrible suffering and destruction. Under these circumstances and in the light of statements by various British statesmen that we entered the war in order to undermine Her Majesty's authority in South Africa and to implement authorities independent of Her Majesty across the whole South Africa, we regard it as our duty to declare solemnly that we entered the war solely as a measure to defend and safeguard the independence of the South African Republic, which was in our opinion threatened. We are moreover pursuing the war solely to guarantee the indisputable independence of both republics as sovereign independent states and to obtain the assurance that Her Majesty's subjects who supported the Republics in this war will not be made to suffer in their persons or their property. Under these conditions, these conditions only, we now desire to see peace restored in South Africa and an end to the evil which now reigns. If, however, Her Majesty's government is resolved to destroy the independence of the Republics, we will have no option but to keep fighting until the bitter end.'

Salisbury summarily rejected this peace offer. In a telegram dated 11 March he alleged that 'the British Empire has been compelled to confront an invasion which has entailed a costly war, and the loss of thousands of precious lives. This great calamity has been the penalty which Great Britain has suffered for having in recent years acquiesced in the existence of the two republics'. Under these circumstances 'Her Majesty's government can only answer Your Honours' telegram that we are not prepared to assent to the independence either of the South African Republic or of the Orange Free State.'

Lord Salisbury

RETREAT OF BOER FORCES FROM SOUTHERN FREE STATE

Khakis begin occupying Free State towns

Kroonstad, 23 March – Last week we reported on the abandonment by the Boer forces of the southern Free State. That process was successfully completed this week. Last Saturday the commandos were still in the veld in the vicinity of Wepener in the southern Free State. With incomparable determination they trekked northwards virtually day and night, with General Freek Grobler and his burghers in the vanguard, General Lemmer in the middle and Chief Commandant Olivier in the rearguard.

On Monday the 19th some 200 burghers of Wepener joined Grobler's commandos at Jammersbergsdrif. Two days later some 300 burghers from the Ladybrand district attached themselves to Olivier's laager. A number of burghers are still too afraid that their properties will be confiscated by the British and are currently refusing to rejoin their commando.

Both Commandant-General Joubert and President Steyn were continuously kept informed on the progress of this Republican force. Captain Danie Theron's Reconnaissance Corps gathered information on a daily basis and was not only well informed on the movements of the Khaki forces, but also identified and arrested burghers who made common cause with the enemy – for example by distributing proclamations on their behalf.

MODDER RIVER RAILWAY BRIDGE DESTROYED

On the night of 18–19 March the Theron Reconnaissance Corps destroyed the railway bridge across the Modder River at Glen with dynamite in order to make it unserviceable for the British. An American engineer, Turner, placed the explosive devices in position. He first blew up the two pillars, which caused the three spans to collapse into the river, and then destroyed the spans by exploding dynamite approximately in the centre of each. The next day a strong British unit arrived at Glen – too late to prevent the destruction of the bridge.

Theron himself then left for the area east of Bloemfontein, where he reported on Tuesday the 20th that General French had occupied Thaba Nchu with a force of between 2 000 and 6 000 mounted soldiers.

The occupation was not opposed. Indeed, both the magistrate and a number of the inhabitants received the British in a particularly friendly fashion. This news upset both Steyn and Joubert, but fortunately it became clear yesterday that French has fewer soldiers than originally reported – only 1 700. Patrols of this force are busy doing reconnaissance in the direction of Dewetsdorp and Ladybrand. As far as Theron could ascertain, the Khakis have occupied virtually all the towns in the southern Free State.

THE TREK FROM THE SOUTHERN FREE STATE

CELLIERS'S LATEST EYEWITNESS REPORT

Pretoria, 23 March – On Monday 10 March the burghers who are trekking back from the southern Free State passed Jammersbergsdrif. Jan F.E. Celliers, one of the burghers who participated in this trek, sent us a report on their progress today in which he writes that both the burghers and their animals are becoming increasingly exhausted. He says he is filled with pity for the poor oxen that haul the wagons since they never get sufficient time to recover. They keep loyally pulling forward with bowed backs and scraping hoofs when they have to draw a wagon up a steep incline.

On Tuesday evening they encountered a heavy rainstorm. Everybody desperately looked for shelter. Celliers says he was fortunate enough to find a relatively dry spot under a wagon. Once he had stretched himself out, he could not move, since he was hemmed in on all sides by the other 'guests' in that 'boardinghouse'. He stuffed his clothes, shoes and hat in between the irons above his head. Fortunately there was a watertight piece of canvas on the side from which the rain came that protected them against the wetness.

After the rain of the night, the road became extremely muddy. This made the trek even more difficult. For the poor animals that had to haul the wagons, it became virtually impossible. Against an incline on the other side of a deep drift the mud became almost knee-deep. One hears shouting, the balking of the oxen, drivers and oxen fall down in the mud and struggle desperately to get to their feet again, but the command remains: Forward. The burghers had no choice but to help in pushing the wagons up the steep inclines.

In spite of all the troubles, the men remain cheerful. For the poor animals it is different. Many cannot proceed any further. They are then merely outspanned and abandoned next to the road. And there they stand, Celliers relates, motionless with their eyes half-closed and not even capable of munching a single mouthful of grass. But they are silent, silent as always.

Every now and then the burghers trekked past fields full of watermelons. That was to them a true blessing. All of them stormed into the field and returned to the wagons loaded with booty, on which they feasted while trekking onwards.

This morning they reached Modderpoort, the Anglican Mission station northwest of Ladybrand. Celliers and one of the other burghers quickly visited the town on horseback, using the opportunity to telegraph this information via Ficksburg to us here in Pretoria.

Jan F.E. Celliers

OUR MILITARY OFFICERS

General Freek Grobler

Frederik Albertus (Big Freek) Grobler has an impressive appearance. We know very little about his early history. He was born in about 1850 in the Waterberg district of the South African Republic and grew up there. He participated in the Transvaal War of Independence of 1880–81, when he took part in the siege of the British garrison at Marabastad in the far northern Transvaal. In 1891 he became field cornet of the ward Zwagershoek in the Waterberg district. In the course of the next few years he participated in the campaigns of the South African Republic against a number of black communities.

When this war seemed inevitable last year, the Transvaal military authorities appointed Grobler as Assistant General of all the commandos in the districts Waterberg and Soutpansberg, as well as a part of Rustenburg. His task was to guard the northern and northwestern borders of the Transvaal against enemy invasions. In addition he had to break up the railway line between Gaborone and Bulawayo and repulse the British garrisons from that area.

Grobler found it impossible to carry out these orders properly, largely since he could not gain the co-operation of his officers. The only British post against which they actually campaigned was, as we reported at the time, that of Colonel Plumer at Fort Tuli. Since it became clear that the British were no real threat in the north, the Transvaal military authorities decided to transfer Grobler with the majority of his burghers to the front at Colesberg. There the northern Transvaalers acted with great valour and Grobler himself with distinction.

Freek Grobler and his commando form part of the Boer forces who were recalled from the south late last month and are now on their way to join the Republican forces in the northern Free State. He participated in this major trek with urgency and tenacity and proves to be a capable leader under the most difficult circumstances imaginable.

General Freek Grobler

THE War Reporter
WEEKLY EDITION

Number 25   Pretoria, South African Republic   31 March 1900

PIET JOUBERT DIES

Pretoria, 30 March – There is deep sadness in the Transvaal capital over the death of our beloved Commandant-General Piet Joubert, who died on Tuesday evening. Last week he was in the Orange Free State, where he addressed the burghers at the Sand River Railway Bridge and encouraged them to render loyal military service. Back in Pretoria he worked in his office on Saturday morning and later that day attended the farewell function of the honourable Leon of the French Creusot arms factory.

General Joubert's health had not been satisfactory for some time. He had never fully recovered from the injuries he sustained last November when he fell from his horse in Natal. In addition he contracted a bad cold in the Free State. On Saturday evening his condition suddenly deteriorated, and a doctor diagnosed heavy inflammation of his stomach lining. By Sunday his condition became critical. His close family gathered at his house in Visagie Street to say their farewells. By Tuesday afternoon all hope that he would recover was abandoned and at 11 o'clock that evening he died. We have been told that Joubert accepted the fact that he was nearing the end with resignation, as one would expect from a Christian. He often murmured Christian hymns on his deathbed.

The news of his death spread from the capital over the whole Republic and to all the war fronts as from Wednesday morning. It was received with shock and sorrow. For many burghers it is an irreparable loss. Numerous expressions of sympathy reached his wife and children by messenger, letter or telegram. President Steyn wrote the following: 'Accept my deepest sympathy in the great and unrecoverable loss that you and your children suffered with the death of your husband, my friend Commandant P.J. Joubert. But let it be of comfort to you, Mrs Joubert, that in everything he did, he always revealed a strong loyalty to duty and a deep love for his fatherland. Thus he set a worthy example to his children and to the Afrikaner nation that will shine in the history of our people. God will comfort you and your children in this hour of pain.'

Even Lord Roberts expressed his sympathy in the following telegram to President Kruger: 'I have just received the news of General Joubert's death and I desire at once to offer my sincere condolences to your Honour and the Burghers of the S. African Republic on this sad event. I would ask you to convey to General Joubert's family the expression of my most respectful sympathy in their bereavements and to assure them also from me that all ranks of Her Majesty's forces, now serving in South Africa, share my feeling of deep regret at the sudden and untimely end of so distinguished a General who devoted his life to the service of his country and whose personal gallantry was only surpassed by his humane conduct and chivalrous bearing under all circumstances.'

Since it was the wish of the Commandant-General to be buried on his farm Rustfontein in the Wakkerstroom district, where he had lived for many years, only a memorial service was held in Pretoria. This took place on Thursday afternoon in the church building of the Dutch Reformed Church. After the service the funeral procession moved slowly to the station. People stood along the streets to pay their last respects to General Joubert.

At the station a deeply moved President Kruger paid homage to his lifelong comrade in front of a silent crowd. 'I have lost somebody who stood at my side from the time when we were both young men, many years ago,' he said. 'It seems to me as if I am now the only survivor of all the men who struggled for our fatherland and our people in those early years.' After paying tribute to Joubert's role in the war, he announced that the Commandant-General's wish that the young Louis Botha should succeed him in that office would be honoured.

A special train with Joubert's mortal remains then left for Volksrust, where the funeral will take place today.

Commandant-General Piet Joubert's coffin in his house in Pretoria

KHAKIS REPULSED FROM LADYBRAND
Boer forces in strong position in eastern Free State

Kroonstad, 30 March – Last week we reported that General French had occupied Thaba Nchu with a mounted force of about 1 700 Khakis and sent out patrols in the direction of Dewetsdorp and Ladybrand. One of the British patrols entrenched themselves at Newberry's Mill on the Leeu River, about halfway between Thaba Nchu and Ladybrand. The British forced all the Free State burghers whom they could round up to surrender and threatened them with Roberts's proclamation. On 26 March the British commander at Newberry's Mill, Colonel Pilcher, began preparations to occupy Ladybrand. A group of Captain Danie Theron's scouts attempted to repulse the 250 Khakis in Pilcher's force with rifle fire, but failed. Pilcher moved unopposed into the town. At the post office he found that Theron had already destroyed the telegraph machine to make it unusable for the British.

Pilcher had barely had the opportunity to arrest the field cornet, Tom Smith, the magistrate and magistrate's clerk when a British scout charged into town on horseback with the report that a huge Boer commando was approaching from the northeast. The Khaki colonel reacted in panic. He immediately ordered that the retreat should be blown and his men hurriedly abandoned the town. Many townspeople fired on them to encourage them to leave even faster. At least one soldier was wounded.

There was indeed a Boer commando approaching, and they occupied Ladybrand within an hour after Pilcher's Khakis had left. It was the burghers of the Ladybrand and Ficksburg Commandos under the leadership of Commandant Jan Crowther. Since the period of leave granted by Chief Commandant Christiaan de Wet to all Free State burghers whom was now coming to an end, Crowther's burghers were preparing to join the forces of Chief Commandant Olivier at Modderpoort (some 20 kilometres north of Ladybrand). President Steyn had earlier called on them to occupy Ladybrand and Theron kept them informed on British movements. Crowther and his burghers left Modderpoort on the morning of the 26th and experienced no opposition when they occupied the town after Pilcher's flight.

While Crowther arrested the traitors in Ladybrand who had co-operated with Pilcher, and sent them for safe custody to Kroonstad, Theron and his scouts proceeded with their reconnaissance work. President Steyn was himself in the eastern Free State on Tuesday the 27th, welcoming the burghers of Generals Grobler and Lemmer and Chief Commandant Olivier after their long northward trek from Stormberg and Colesberg in the south. He treated them to a long and emotional speech encouraging them to keep fighting for all they were worth. His repeated entreaty was that they should not now, after a few defeats, surrender to the enemy. He assured them that he was extremely thankful that they had completed their trek and that their huge endeavour would never be forgotten. According to him it was one of the most important and most successful manoeuvres of the whole war.

Yesterday Steyn was back in Kroonstad. He reported that the burghers who had taken part in the long trek were still full of fighting spirit but that they were experiencing a critical shortage of horses. Many were already forced to walk.

General Jan Crowther

FROM THE EDITOR

The sudden death of our respected Commandant-General, Petrus Jacobus Joubert, has dominated the news over the past week. Next to President Kruger, he was without doubt the major figure in the South African Republic, playing a prominent role in virtually every important event for 30 years. We described his life history in our first issue, when he became the first officer in our weekly series on Republican military leaders. All that remains for us now is to express our deepest sympathy to Mrs Joubert and her children.

Good news this past week came when Generals Grobler and Lemmer and Chief Commandant Olivier and their burghers successfully completed their heroic retreat from the Cape Colony. Commandant Jan Crowther and his burghers' reoccupation of Ladybrand was another encouraging event. In the meantime the burghers of Captain Danie Theron's Scout Corps are making life all but easy for adventurous British soldiers. It is good that the Khakis are left in no doubt that the burghers are far from surrendering in this war.

OUR MILITARY OFFICERS

General Tobias Smuts

Tobias Smuts was born in 1861 in the Lydenburg district in Transvaal. His father was Adriaan Smuts and his mother Rachel Margaretha Joubert. Not much is known about his early career. He did receive some education in Stellenbosch in the Cape Colony. After working in the civil service of the South African Republic for some time, *inter alia* as magistrate's clerk in Ermelo, he began farming in that district.

As for his military experience, he participated in a number of the campaigns of the South African Republic against rebellious black communities. By 1898 he was already the Commandant of the Ermelo Commando in the campaign against the Bavenda of Chief Mphephu. In addition to his high military position he was elected as a member of the First Volksraad last year.

With the outbreak of this war last October Smuts proceeded to the Natal front with the Ermelo Commando as assistant commandant. He participated in numerous battles, including Modderspruit, Colenso, Spioenkop and Vaalkrans. In January he was promoted to the rank of fighting general. Earlier this month, when he was placed in command of the Transvaal burghers who were transferred to the Orange Free State, he was made assistant commandant-general.

Smuts is an endearing person who enjoys the highest respect of his burghers due to his personal bravery. He is deeply religious. His outspoken belief is that the power of the Republics does not lie in huge numbers but in faith in God. He is married to Johanna Jacoba Buhrmann. They have three children.

General Tobias Smuts

ACTIVITIES NORTH OF BLOEMFONTEIN

Burghers prepare to check Khakis

Kroonstad, 30 March – The Republican forces in the northern Free State have been considerably strengthened in the past two weeks by the arrival of several commandos transferred from the Natal front. The commander of the Transvaal forces in the Free State is General Koos de la Rey, and his burghers were concentrated more or less at the Sand River Railway Bridge at the start of this week. The Free State forces are gathered at the Smaldeel Station west of Winburg. Huge numbers of burghers had taken advantage of Chief Commandant De Wet's permission to take leave, but have now returned at the conclusion of their period of holiday at the end of last week. They have rested well and are full of resolve. Some of them pitched camp at Brandfort, a small village about halfway between Bloemfontein and Winburg.

President Steyn addresses the Free State burghers at Smaldeel

Theron's Scout Corps are meticulously proceeding with their task of keeping an eye on the British. Last Friday afternoon (the 23rd) a section stationed in the vicinity of Glen under Lieutenant Banie Enslin noticed four British officers and a soldier crossing the Modder River and patrolling to the north. They followed the British for about 20 kilometres and engaged them in a shooting battle. One officer was killed and the other four were wounded. Enslin and his men took them to a farmyard from where a farm labourer was sent to Glen to fetch a British ambulance. The Scouts seized the saddled horses as well as the soldiers' pocket books and documents, which will be handed over to our military authorities.

Last Sunday (the 25th) the scouts noted a strong unit of mounted British soldiers riding from Glen along the railway line in the direction of Brandfort. They immediately sent an emergency message to the Free State commandos who were camping just north of Brandfort – too late however, since the British reached the town by one o'clock that afternoon, before the burghers were ready for them. Fortunately there were eight burghers in the town and they courageously charged the British. A fierce rifle battle followed in which four British were wounded and four taken prisoner. The British retreated to Glen before the burghers from the camp could enter the fray.

From Monday virtually all the Transvaal commandos were transferred to Brandfort. General Tobias Smuts is the temporary commander, since De la Rey is not well. On Tuesday the 27th, soon after the arrival of Smuts's commandos at Brandfort, he, De Wet and their officers held a war council meeting during which they discussed future co-operation. Their decisions were not made public.

SKIRMISH AT KAREE STATION

Soon after dark on the evening of 28 March, De Wet left the laager at Brandfort with a force of about 1 500 Free State burghers. They moved off in an easterly direction with the object of preventing General French's forces at Thaba Nchu from occupying any other Free State town. The other Free State burghers at Brandfort had earlier taken up position on the low hills east of the railway line, just north of Glen, under command of Generals Philip Botha and W.J. Kolbe. Their aim was to prevent the British from repairing the railway bridge across the Modder River.

Smuts's Transvaal burghers were supposed to occupy the low hills west of the railway line that evening. Even though they were ready, they could not leave immediately, since they did not know the area and the guides who had to accompany them did not appear. It was only shortly before daybreak that the guides finally arrived and they began moving – too late, since the British soldiers from the south had already begun occupying the low hills north of the Modder River.

The burghers nevertheless occupied the low hills near Karee Station and then became involved in a full-scale battle. The enemy bombarded the Boers and at the same time made a fruitless attempt to outflank the Republican positions with mounted units. After a while British infantry soldiers also entered the battle, but the burghers of Utrecht and Wakkerstroom checked them with accurate rifle fire. Since there was a real danger that the Boer positions might eventually be outflanked by the British, Smuts ordered a retreat to Brandfort after about six hours. Lieutenant Colonel Trichard covered the retreat so effectively with his guns that the British could not interfere at all. By that evening all the burghers, including the Free State men who were stationed east of the railway line, were safely back in their entrenchments at Brandfort.

Yesterday's skirmish at Karee ended in a tactical victory for the enemy. It was an expensive victory, however. Their total casualties, according to reliable sources, were more than 200 men of whom 22, including two officers, were killed, some 180 wounded and five taken prisoner. The Boer casualties were three men dead and 18 wounded. We have been informed that a report on the battle was sent to Chief Commandant Christiaan de Wet by means of the heliograph

General Kolbe (standing far left) and his officers in the veld

MOCK WARFARE ON BECHUANALAND BORDER

Useless expedition against British at Ramotswa

Pretoria, 23 March – One of the members of the Boer ambulance personnel at Mafeking, Abraham Stafleu, sent us the following report some time ago. It contains the story of the total failure of an expedition to drive Colonel Plumer's Khakis from the Transvaal western border. Stafleu, whose reports we have published before, is quite outspoken on the lack of professionalism in the Republican military services, but is a sharp observer and a fiery patriot. His report provides insight into a number of the weaknesses that often cripple the Republican forces:

'General Snyman and his war council decided on 1 February that 200 men had to proceed from Mafeking to the area of Crocodile Pools in the north. Their task would be to attack the British unit stationed at the railway line between Mafeking and Bulawayo. The expedition consisted of 100 burghers from the Marico Commando under Field Cornet Hansie Snyman as well as 100 Rustenburgers. I had to accompany them to tend to the sick and wounded.

'On Sunday 4 February we enjoyed the piano music in Salinger's Marico Hotel until late in the evening. Early the next morning we struck out to the north. Our route took us to the beautifully situated Dinokana village with its large number of grass huts as well as buildings constructed with bricks, a beautiful church and well-tended fruit tress and gardens. Subheadman Michael Moilwa of the Bahurutshe himself welcomed the commando and indicated to us where we could outspan and water our oxen, mules and horses.

'On Tuesday the 6th we passed through the narrow gorge of the Ngotwane River. It is a virtually impassible road and a wonder that no wagon broke down with all the bumping over huge rocks and tree roots and through all the holes. It was a terrific din with all the wagons creaking, the whips cracking and the drivers and leaders shouting at each other and the oxen. I was very thankful when we finally made it through the pass and reached a sandy road again.

'It was almost dark on Wednesday 7 February when we reached the laager of the Bushveld Commando. Field Cornet Beukes of Groot Marico received us and told us that malaria fever was bad. His laager seemed well entrenched, surrounded by strong walls with loopholes and deep trenches. They had one gun at their disposal. Immediately to the west of the laager they had built forts on two low hills. These were manned day and night.

'Both the Marico burghers and Rustenburg burghers of Field Cornet Malan pitched camp next to the Bushveld burghers. Commandant Botha called all the burghers together on the 8th and welcomed them on the campaign. He mentioned plans to break up the railway line north of the British position at Ramotswa, in order to cut them off from the north. That evening an elderly burgher, Piet Lemmer, led us in worship. His simple but serious and well-intended words made a good impression on all of us while his sincere prayer to God strengthened and encouraged us.

'On Friday 9 February the Khakis of Colonel Plumer bombarded our most northerly fort with their guns. Fortunately nobody was injured. The next day they fired a further five bombs at our northern fort. One of these exploded in the fort, but without hurting our comrades. What was strange to me was that black women from the area were allowed to enter our laager to sell fruit and milk. It was possible for them to report all that occurred in our camp to the British.

'Some time before daybreak on Monday 12 February we heard heavy firing with rifles as well the dull sound of exploding dynamite mines from the direction of the most northerly fort. Later on we heard that the British had launched an attack on the laager on foot. The Boers fired back desperately to ward off the attack. Numerous witnesses reported afterwards that Captain von Dalwig encouraged the burghers with the order: "Shoot lower, my children, so that they may die slowly." It was he who exploded the dynamite mines. Altogether five Khakis died in the onslaught and 24 were wounded.

'On Tuesday 13 February General Willem C. Janse van Rensburg arrived from Derdepoort with 150 men to assist us. The next day he and all the officers held a war council meeting. It was a strange sight to watch all the members of the council, a total of 43 of them, walking with their camp stools on their backs or in their hands like a little commando into the dense bushes. The burghers could not but joke at this huge talk assembly. What they talked about, we do not know.

'The next day they held another war council and then took a decision that the burghers awaited with great expectations: the enemy would be attacked. That evening at 11 o'clock mounted burghers would advance on the enemy. The burghers who had no horses would remain at the laagers to defend it.

'At half past 10 that evening the adjutant woke up Field Cornet Hansie Snyman. Moments later everybody was up and busy saddling their horses. It was a silent turmoil of snorting horses, tinkling stirrups, rubbing clothes and whispering voices. As a sign of recognition in the dark each burgher wore a broad white ribbon around his hat. With the greeting "God be with you and good luck," at least 500 burghers with three guns left the laager in the moonlight.

'At sunrise we followed the tracks of the guns with the ambulance wagon to go to the support of any possible wounded. We had not even reached the first slope, when we stumbled upon a man with a white ribbon around his hat who shouted: "You may turn around, the whole commando is returning." We refused to believe him and went further. Then other men appeared. It almost looked like a flight, but we had not heard a single shot. At that we also turned around.

'Soon afterwards we heard the whole history. The burghers were only about 400 or 500 metres from the enemy position when the General, instead of ordering the attack, convened a war council. The vast majority of the officers then decided not to attack. The burghers had to turn around. The excuse was that they did not have water to cool the rapid-fire guns.

'Many of the burghers, as well as the officers who wanted to attack, feel bitter about these events. Field Cornet Pieter Swart is crying with anger and regret. To return to the laager like this is a shame. Some officers wanted to attack anyway, but the General's order was strict: "Return!" There and then the officers lost their control over the burghers. The men listened to neither general nor field cornet. In disorder they rushed back. In the chaos our ammunition wagon almost fell into the hands of the enemy.

'The mood amongst the burghers at that time differed totally from the previous one. They swore where they had previously prayed. Field Cornet Snyman's face was like a piece of ironstone but he remains silent. The burghers were grumpy and dissatisfied and were saying less kind things about the General and the other officers. A number of burghers immediately drew up a request to be discharged. They said they would go and fight in Natal and would no longer serve there.

'On Monday 19 February all the Rustenburgers left like one man when a report reached us that the Bakgatla of Chief Linchwe were threatening Boer farms in that district. In addition our scouts had noted that the British had disappeared. The road to Mafeking on their side of the border was trampled into dust by their wagons, horses and oxen. Thus they had slipped away.

'The next morning our burghers also decided to leave. General Van Rensburg wanted to hold them back, but the general feeling was: "Let us go, let us get away from this wretched place." In a moment everything was loaded and we were on the road. Some burghers wanted to visit their homes first. Both the Commandant and the Field Cornet expressly prohibited this, but the burghers did whatever they wished. It was not even remotely all of us who eventually came back all the way to Mafeking.'

THE War Reporter
WEEKLY EDITION

Number 26 — Pretoria, South African Republic — 7 April 1900

DE WET TRIUMPHS AT SANNASPOS
ACHIEVES THREE OBJECTIVES SIMULTANEOUSLY

Kroonstad, 2 April – Last week we reported that De Wet had left the Boer laager at Brandfort on the evening of 28 March with a force of some 1 500 Free State burghers, with the stated objective of preventing the further occupation of towns in the eastern Free State by the British forces. What his burghers did not know was that he actually had other plans. De Wet himself told our correspondent that his true purpose was to attack the British garrison stationed at Sannaspos, some 28 kilometres east of Bloemfontein. Sannaspos is a station on the railway line that is at present being constructed between Bloemfontein and Ladybrand. It is some three kilometres west of the retaining wall in the Modder River and the pump station from where water is pumped to Bloemfontein. This is the Free State capital's most important source of water: by occupying it, we could place the British forces in Bloemfontein in an untenable position.

While De Wet and his men proceeded first in an easterly and later in a southerly direction, scouts kept the Chief Commandant continuously informed on the British forces' strength and position. They reported that Chief Commandant J.H. Olivier was driving a unit of Khakis back from the direction of Ladybrand towards Thaba Nchu, which is situated east of Sannaspos. In addition, De Wet learned that the British garrison at Sannaspos consisted of barely 200 men. When, on 30 March, he heard that a huge British supply convoy was approaching Sannaspos, he decided to occupy the waterworks immediately and to capture both the garrison and the convoy.

At about four o'clock that afternoon he confidentially informed his four fighting generals, namely Andries Cronjé, Jan Wessels, Stoffel Froneman and Piet de Wet, about his plans. The four of them were ordered to take up position with 1 150 burghers and four guns northeast of Sannaspos and to bombard the garrison at first light. They also had to ensure that the British force at Thaba Nchu would not be able to rush to the aid of the garrison at Sannaspos. De Wet himself, with the remaining 350 burghers under the command of Commandants Piet Fourie and Coen Nel, would take up position some five kilometres west of Sannaspos, where the main wagon road between Bloemfontein and Thaba Nchu crosses the Koornspruit at a drift. The idea was that De Wet and his men would take up position in the valley of the spruit itself, on both sides of the drift. They believed that the British would flee in a westerly direction along the road from Sannaspos as soon as they were bombarded from the northeast. It would then be possible to capture both the Khakis and the large convoy.

The American journalist Howard Hillegas gave our correspondent the following description of the burghers' nocturnal trek to Sannaspos:

'When darkness came on, a halt was made so that the burghers might prepare a meal, and that the general might hear from the scouts. As the moon rose over the dark peak of Thaba Nchu mountain, the burghers lighted their pipes and sang psalms and hymns until the peaceful valley resounded with their voices. When the order "*Opzaal*" (saddle up) was shouted out, the mule train came into motion and the burghers mounted their horses. A chill night air arose, and shivering burghers wrapped blankets around their shoulders. There was no sound to mark the nocturnal passage of the army but the clatter of horses' hoofs and the wagons rumbling over the stones. Lights appeared at farmhouse windows, and at their gates were women and children with bread and bowls of milk and prayers for the burghers. Native huts with their inhabitants standing like spectres before the doors appeared like monstrous ant-heaps – all these were passed, but the drooping eyes of the burghers saw nothing.

'At midnight another halt was made, horses were off-saddled and men lay down on the veld to sleep. The generals and officers met in council of war and plans were formed before the sleeping burghers were aroused and the trek was resumed. The burghers were not informed of the imminence of a battle; but they required no such announcement from their generals. After another four hours of trekking over veld, hillock, sluit and donga another halt was made. The burghers again dismounted and lay down on the earth beside their horses to get some rest. The officers in the meantime met to finalise their battle plans and to hear news about enemy movements from the scouts. The first dim rays of the day came over the tops of the eastern hills when the burghers were aroused for the last time and proceeded to the positions chosen by their leaders.'

De Wet, who never slept that night, related that he was not at that stage aware that the British force at Thaba Nchu, commanded by General Broadwood, was also trekking towards Sannaspos that night. However, De Wet and his men reached their objective unnoticed and took up position in the Koornspruit before daybreak. It was only then that De Wet realised that he would have many more Khakis to deal with than had originally been anticipated. He nevertheless prepared for the enemy, since he was in an excellent position. De Wet ordered that nobody should fire: they should attempt to capture the British with as little show as possible, in order to keep their presence secret as long as possible.

Soon after it became light, the Boer guns began firing from the northeast. The exploding shells had the desired effect on the British, since they fled wildly down the road. Right at the front were a number of scotch carts with civilians, including women and children. The burghers allowed them to go through and ordered them to move on to a farmhouse close by without giving any signal that there was any danger, or face being shot.

After the carts came the wagons of the convoy, escorted by British soldiers. Some of these Khakis were so alarmed when they suddenly saw the Boers at the drift that they surrendered without even being asked to do so. The British at the back at first noted nothing out of the ordinary. The burghers captured about 200 soldiers within a short while. Soon however there was such a congestion of wagons and people at the drift that a British officer arrived to investigate the cause of the delay. He soon saw what was happening and ordered the soldiers to retreat.

De Wet now realised that the easy part of the operation was over and ordered his burghers to fire on the retreating Khakis. The latter fired back, but without inflicting much damage on the burghers; nor could they salvage the five guns that had already been hauled right up to the drift. A long-drawn-out rifle battle over a long distance followed. This went fairly evenly until the burghers of Cronjé and the other generals, who had crossed the Modder River from the east, entered the battle at Sannaspos. Broadwood then realised that his position was untenable and ordered his soldiers to flee to the south and the north-northwest.

De Wet's burghers once again captured a number of soldiers, but could not check the British flight. Nevertheless they could claim a great victory. They had captured five guns, 18 carts and almost 100 wagons almost fully loaded with supplies, in addition to numerous horses and other animals. On the British side at least 18 men were killed and 130 wounded, and our men took 426 Khakis prisoner of war. On the Boer side six men were killed and 11 wounded.

De Wet, accompanied by three men, left the battlefield at Sannaspos soon after the battle. Before his departure he made arrangements for the occupation of the waterworks by the Boers and for the removal of the prisoners of war and the captured supplies. He temporarily transferred the command over his burghers to Generals Piet de Wet and Andries Cronjé.

American journalist Howard Hillegas

Burghers receive orders after the battle

Boers hauling captured British wagon through Koornspruit drift

FROM THE EDITOR

Last month we were all in sackcloth and ashes. March 1900 commenced with the shattering news that Cronjé had surrendered on Majuba Day with 3 000 burghers. At the same time we heard that the British had broken through on the Natal front and relieved Ladysmith. Soon afterwards we heard that our burghers had failed in their endeavour to halt the enemy, first at Poplar Grove and then at Abrahamskraal. Who will ever forget the grief when we were told in the middle of March that the British flag was waving over the Free State capital? And right at the end of the month our cup overflowed with sorrow when we heard of the death of our respected Commandant-General Piet Joubert.

For the first time in our lives, we – and, we believe, most of our readers – could understand something of how gloomy the Voortrekkers must have felt in Natal in October 1838 after suffering one shattering blow after another: the murder of Piet Retief and his men in the first half of February of that year; the loss of 500 lives in the Zulu attacks on the defenceless Voortrekker laagers at Weenen, Bloukrans and its vicinity 10 days later; the defeat against the Zulu at Italeni in April when Piet Uys and his valiant son Dirkie were killed; the death of Gerrit Martiz by the end of the winter.

Many of the old Voortrekkers subsequently recounted that they were so dejected that they wanted to return to the Cape, to submission to the British flag …

Fortunately they did not do that. True to their ideals and to the memory of their fallen comrades who had given their lives for freedom, the Voortrekkers did not lose hope. In December 1838 they humbled themselves before God by making a Vow and resumed the struggle with renewed faith. The victory at Blood River soon followed and the Trek was saved. That did not mean the end of their travails, and many clashes followed, especially with the British, but the Voortrekker legacy to us is our beloved Republics.

Are we now, in our struggle, going to display the faithful courage of our Voortrekker predecessors? Are we going to remain true to our ideals, as they did? April 1900 began with two resounding victories by the burghers of Chief Commandant Christiaan de Wet. Is he the man who is destined to fill the shoes of the most successful Voortrekker leader, Andries Pretorius? It is not for us to decide on things like this. Sannaspos is not Blood River. Like the Voortrekkers of the olden days, we will be confronted by numerous battles, and much suffering. They eventually managed to triumph over their dejection and despair to lay the foundations of our freedom. Our task today is to follow their example, to transform our dejection into positive action and to preserve our dearly bought freedom for our descendants.

Unfortunately we also have to report on a setback also this week. The courageous French Colonel, Georges de Villabois-Mareuil, was not one of our burghers by descent. However, we mourn his death as if he was one of us, since he was one of the most prominent of all the foreigners who came from all over the world to throw their weight behind our cause. Thus he earns a position of glory in the ranks of our national heroes. It is our duty to ensure that he and the other foreigners who paid the ultimate price did not spill their blood in vain for our freedom.

55

ANOTHER TRIUMPH FOR DE WET

Defeats British force at Mostertshoek

Kroonstad, 5 April – Chief Commandant De Wet has just achieved his second triumph over the British within a week. On 3 April he and his burghers attacked a British force at Mostertshoek east of Reddersburg and forced them to surrender after a lengthy battle.

De Wet himself told our reporter that after the battle at Sannaspos he rode on horseback towards Dewetsdorp to carry out reconnaissance work. On 1 April he heard that a British force had occupied Dewetsdorp. He immediately sent an order to Generals Jan Wessels, Stoffel Froneman and A.I. de Villiers to come to his aid with 1 500 burghers and three guns. In the meantime he ordered the commandeering of all the burghers in the area who had not yet rejoined the commandos after the lapse of their leave.

On 2 April De Wet heard that the British had left Dewetsdorp again and were on their way to Reddersburg. He pursued them with 110 burghers he had scraped together – even though the majority were not even armed. The next day General Froneman joined him with the vanguard of about 700 burghers. These men as well as their horses were totally exhausted, having trekked uninterruptedly through the night. At De Wet's request, however, they kept pursuing the Khakis.

Burghers with Khaki prisoners of war

Apparently the British were not yet aware of their pursuers when they reached the farm Mostertshoek, some seven kilometres east of Reddersburg, on the afternoon of 2 April. There De Wet and his burghers caught up with them. The Chief Commandant immediately sent a letter to the commanding officer of the Khakis requesting their surrender to prevent the spilling of blood. The British rejected this request and a fierce skirmish followed. Neither side could gain the upper hand that afternoon. The Boers kept a good guard throughout the night to ensure that the British would not slip away. In addition, their forces were strengthened in the course of the night by burghers who had not been able to keep up with the pursuit the previous day.

By dawn on 3 April De Wet had about 800 men with three Krupp guns at his disposal. At about half past five they began firing on the British and at half past 10 the latter raised the white flag. Unfortunately some soldiers kept on firing afterwards and in this period fatally wounded Field Cornet J. du Plessis of Kroonstad. The burghers were very angry about this and some began firing again. Even though the British now hoisted numerous white flags, it was some while before the battle finally ended.

The result of this battle was a resounding victory for the Boers. They captured all the weapons, remaining ammunition and supplies of the British. Altogether 10 Khakis had been killed and 35 wounded. The latter plus the other 546 Khakis, including their commander, Captain W.J. McWhinnie, were taken prisoner. The Boer loss seems to have been three men killed and three wounded. De Wet immediately arranged for the transfer of the British prisoners of war to Pretoria and then left on a further mission.

CATASTROPHIC BATTLE AT BOSHOF

Colonel De Villebois-Mareuil killed

Hoopstad, 6 April – The foreign legion that had recently been established by Fighting General Georges de Villebois-Mareuil was involved in a disastrous skirmish with a British unit at Boshof yesterday. Villebois-Mareuil himself, as well as six of his men, was killed and 11 wounded, mainly because they refused to surrender. The other 51 were made prisoners of war. It seems that a number of Khakis were also killed or wounded.

The town Boshof is about 50 kilometres northeast of Kimberley. The British occupied it on 11 March and a few hundred soldiers were stationed there. Soon afterwards they sporadically attempted to cross the Vaal River via the railway bridge at Warrenton. The burghers of General Sarel du Toit and Commandant F.J. Potgieter had managed to check them, but Villebois was alarmed at these clashes and at recurrent rumours that the British were building up their forces at Kimberley and planned a full-scale invasion of the Transvaal from there. Even though he had hardly begun organising his International Legion, and had not yet incorporated nearly all the foreign volunteer corps into it, he decided to act immediately to disrupt the British plans. He ordered his Chief of Staff, Colonel E.I. Maximov, to proceed with organising the legion, while he himself took off in a westerly direction at the head of a mounted section of fewer than 100 men on 24 March. His force consisted of about 50 Dutch volunteers under Commandant Smorenburg, 25 French volunteers under Lieutenant Pierre de Breda, and 11 Afrikaners under Field Cornet Walter Coleman. They took with them a mule wagon loaded with dynamite and manned by a few black drivers.

Even though Villebois was in a hurry, he and his men made slow progress towards Hoopstad, since the sun was very hot by day and some of their horses were in poor condition. They reached Hoopstad on 1 April, and resumed their journey in a southwesterly direction that same evening. Two days later they reached the farm Leeukop, some 30 kilometres north of Boshof. Field Cornet Daniels, whose scouts continually kept him informed on British troop movements, received them there. Villebois and Daniels there and then agreed on a joint campaign plan to overwhelm the British garrison in Boshof the following evening.

After Villebois had left to implement the campaign plan, Daniels heard on 4 April that a whole British division was on its way to Boshof and had virtually reached the town. He immediately sent a report on this to Villebois and added that they could not proceed with their plan of attack, since their force of barely 400 burghers would have to face at least 10 000 Khakis. Villebois's reaction was that it was a false report and merely an excuse advanced because Daniels and his burghers were not prepared to fight. He decided to go ahead with his attack, even though he did not have time to send out scouts to ascertain if Daniels was correct. It was a fatal blunder.

In the pitch-dark of the night that followed, things worked out quite differently from the way Villebois planned. Their guide either got lost, as he himself subsequently alleged, or took the wrong road deliberately, as Villebois seems to have suspected. The result was that they did not reach their attack position in time. Villebois then decided to move around Boshof with the objective of proceeding with his original plan, which was to destroy the railway line south of Kimberley. By nine o' clock the next morning, he and his men reached the farm Kareepan, some eight kilometres southeast of Boshof, where they off-saddled and planned to rest till the evening.

The British, who had reached Boshof by then, seem to have been aware of the presence of Villebois and his small force, and immediately sent out a whole army, consisting of foot soldiers, mounted soldiers and guns, against them. Since they had been on the move throughout the previous night, Villebois and his men were so exhausted that they never saw the British coming. Consequently they were surrounded. When they finally realised their predicament, a number of the Hollanders and all the Boers recommended to Villebois that they should jump on their horses and flee, since the alternative was either death or captivity. Apparently the French Colonel was too proud to flee. His decision was that they should hold out till the evening and then retreat under cover of the night. A few men, including J.H. Meyer and his son, nevertheless immediately fled and managed to escape.

What happened subsequently, we do not know. Apparently the British surrounded Villebois and his men and bombarded them from early in the afternoon. Pom-poms and rifles were also used against the handful of volunteers. The fight kept on till dusk, when the white flag was raised, probably immediately after Villebois himself was mown down by a British shell and killed on impact.

COMMANDANT-GENERAL JOUBERT'S FUNERAL

Volksrust, 2 April – The funeral of the late Commandant-General Piet Joubert took place on Friday 30 March on his farm Rustfontein. His mortal remains arrived early that morning from Pretoria on a special train. A huge crowd was gathered on the Volksrust station for the occasion. The Transvaal *Vierkleur* flag hung at half-mast from the building. From the station the coffin with Joubert's remains was taken on a gun carriage to Rustfontein, a distance of some 28 kilometres. A *Vierkleur* was draped on the coffin.

The general staff led the procession to the cemetery. Joubert's horse, with a black cloth draped over its back, walked in front of the gun carriage. At least 20 horse carriages, including President Kruger's coach, which was brought along in the special train so that Joubert's family could sit in it for the procession, as well as a whole carriage full of wreaths, followed the gun carriage. Numerous burghers formed a guard of honour along the road.

At Rustfontein the Reverend D.P. Ackerman led the funeral service, addressing the mourners from the huge veranda in front of the deceased's farmhouse. After the service the local magistrate and then General Louis Botha, Joubert's designated successor, paid tribute to the late Commandant-General. Botha praised the deceased and stated that it was clear that Joubert never would have bowed under the British yoke. His example should serve as an encouragement for everybody to remain determined and to keep fighting courageously for freedom, since their most valuable asset was their complete independence.

While the coffin was being lowered into the grave, a number of specially appointed burghers fired three rifle salvos into the air. For many of those present at the funeral it was noticeable how many black people of the district were present to convey their last respects to the deceased.

OUR MILITARY OFFICERS

General Georges de Villebois-Mareuil

Georges Henri Anne-Marie Victor de Villebois-Mareuil was a man with a glorious past. He was born in 1847 in Nantes, France, and was the eldest son of the 19th duke of the Chateau de Bois Corbeau. After completing his training at the St Cyr Military College he became an officer in the French Army in 1868. In the Franco-Prussian War of 1870–71 he was severely wounded, decorated on the battlefield, and promoted to Captain.

In the course of the next two decades, Villebois attended further staff training courses, and participated with distinction in colonial campaigns. He also wrote a number of books on military affairs. He became a member of the personal staff of the French Minister of War and served as a Corps commander. For a short while he was the youngest full colonel in the France Army. However, in 1895 he was so upset when an active command post was not awarded to him, that he resigned from the army.

After keeping himself busy with writing for the next four years and attempting to bring about a national revival in France, Villebois decided at the end of last year to join the Boer Republics in their struggle against Britain. At the recommendation of the South African Republic's Special Envoy in Europe, Dr W.J. Leyds, the late Commandant-General Piet Joubert appointed him as his military advisor soon after his arrival in Pretoria last November. Villebois consistently recommended that the Boers should act more offensively, but could convince neither Joubert nor General Piet Cronjé to do so. He was present in Natal at the Battle of Colenso in December last year and at Platrand a month later. Subsequently he went to the western front, where he witnessed the events at Paardeberg, but escaped in good time from British encirclement.

On 10 March Joubert appointed Villebois as Fighting General and ordered him to organise all foreign volunteers into an international legion under his command. On 17 March Villebois was in Kroonstad, where his appointment was confirmed by the Republican presidents and the military tactics he had recommended, namely that the Boer forces should divide into smaller units under responsible commanders who should then attack the enemy and cut off their communication lines, were approved. He was so glad about this that he was anxious to personally demonstrate the effectiveness of such tactics in warfare as soon as possible. The result was his over-hasty actions at Boshof, which led to his encirclement and death. Bravery was one of his strongest characteristics and contributed to his end.

The 'French Colonel', as Villebois was called by the burghers, was of medium height and strongly built, with a high forehead, light blue eyes and a prominent moustache. It is a tragedy that this noble European paid such a price for our freedom so soon after his appointment as general. We owe it to him to do the best we can to remain loyal to the ideals he shared with us.

Georges de Villebois-Mareuil

THE War Reporter

WEEKLY EDITION

Number 27 — Pretoria, South African Republic — 14 April 1900

DE WET BESIEGES KHAKIS NEAR WEPENER

Enemy under pressure from all sides

Ladybrand, 12 April – Chief Commandant Christiaan de Wet is continuously in the news these days. After his glorious victories over the Khakis at Sannaspos and Mostertshoek, the whole southern Free State east of the main railway line, with the exception of a garrison at Wepener, was liberated from British troops. Our courageous Chief Commandant's reaction was that the task should be completed. During the battle at Mostertshoek on 4 April he sent out scouts, and soon after the battle he left in the direction of Smithfield.

That evening De Wet divided his forces. General Stoffel Froneman and Commandant Johannes Swanepoel proceeded to Smithfield to attack a British garrison that, according to reports, was stationed there.

De Wet himself had been ordered by President Steyn to proceed to the west to sabotage the railway line south of Bloemfontein and thus cut off the British army's supplies. Since he did not have any dynamite at his disposal, he decided to proceed to Wepener and force the British garrison there into captivity while waiting for dynamite to be sent to him.

On 6 April De Wet and his men were at Daspoort, some 10 kilometres north of Jammerbergsdrift, which crosses the Caledon River. He was informed that Colonel Dagety was at the drift with about 1 900 men, armed with seven guns. The Cape Mounted Rifles and Brabant's Horse were part of his force. All the reports indicated that the garrison was well entrenched, but De Wet decided to attack.

The first attack took place early on the morning of 7 April, but the burghers could not pierce the entrenchments. On 9 April a second attack followed. It was continued from early morning till late that evening, and was accompanied by a heavy bombardment. The British defences could still not be broken. Seven burghers were wounded in this battle. The Boers noted through their binoculars that the British had suffered casualties, but no specific statistics are available. On the night of 10–11 April a third unsuccessful Boer attack took place. De Wet told our reporter that he sincerely believed that he would be able to overpower the entrenchments by an all-out charge, but he did not want to take the risk of suffering heavy casualties.

The siege of the British garrison at Jammerbergsdrift is still in progress. We have no doubt that the poor Khakis will soon surrender. Chief Commandant De Wet's men have totally surrounded them and have captured at least 800 of the garrison's oxen and 300 of the horses.

In addition the burghers are determined to force the members of the Cape Mounted Rifles and Brabant's Horse into surrendering, since they feel that it is wrong for South Africans to fight against their co-South Africans. They have no doubt that the members of those units, most of them inhabitants of the Cape Colony, are only fighting for the five shillings per day that they receive as payment from the British.

KHAKIS STILL BESIEGED IN MAFEKING

Boer laager outside Mafeking, 13 April – The siege of the British garrison in Mafeking is still in progress exactly six months after it started. Since the beginning of the year there has been little action on this front. Abraham Stafleu, who has on previous occasions reported for us on the siege, compiled the following report on events in Mafeking and surrounding areas:

'On 25 February we held a prayer meeting for General Cronjé and his men on the order of President Kruger. We were told that Cronjé's laager was surrounded by the enemy and in a desperate situation. The burghers here are unhappy since they are not fully informed on the turn of events. They believe that telegrams on conditions elsewhere in the country are only made public after General Snyman has revised them.

'It was clear to the burghers of the Klein Marico fort that the British were planning some form of action against them. Night after night they could hear people digging, but at daybreak there was no visible sign of any trenches. The conclusion was that the enemy were digging a tunnel in an attempt to undermine the fort and blow it into oblivion. No serious attempt was made to establish if the enemy were actually busy with a tunnel, and no counter-measures were taken. Later on we heard from a British officer who had been made prisoner of war that they actually attempted to build some sort of launch pad. Their aim was to send an unmanned vehicle filled with dynamite towards our fort in an attempt to blow it into the air. That has not yet happened.

'Majuba Day, 27 February, went by without a fuss. Of Cronjé's bitter fate we knew nothing. On the contrary: a telegram from the government that stated that we should not be concerned about Cronjé, since he had sufficient food supplies and ammunition, was read to us. Little did we know that he had surrendered that very day. Only a few shots were fired around Mafeking and it cost us two casualties. Behind the wall of the Groot Marico laager the burghers were grilling meat. Their precautions were so lax that they made their fire directly opposite a loophole. One shot fired by a Khaki went through the hole and hit two burghers at the same time. Louis Meintjies died in minutes and Gert van Staden was wounded in the stomach.

'At this stage our men carried out experiments with hand bombs. They wanted to use these to attack a trench that the enemy was busy digging towards the Klein Marico fort. However, the projectiles were of a bad quality and most of them did not explode. On the evening of 3 March six burghers nevertheless attempted to capture the enemy trenches by using the hand bombs. Armed with these devices they proceeded to the end of the trench. From there they threw the hand bombs in the direction of the enemy. The latter fired back and one of the six burghers was hit. Soon afterwards the attackers returned.

'We are busy shifting our forts ever closer to the besieged town. This does not produce any major advantage for us. Indeed, it rather means that the enemy finds it easier to fire at our burghers. The two sides are so close together that they often shout to each other while hiding behind their ground walls. Many wisecracks are aimed at each other but little of significance has happened so far. Most of the discussions are in the form of insults traded between Boer and Brit.

'The state of affairs at Mafeking has changed very little in the past few months. The lack of military leadership of the Boers has still not been corrected. Only futile attempts have been made to try to establish who the "traitor" is who informs the enemy about everything that happens in the laager or is discussed "in secret" at war council meetings. Some of the burghers accused Spencer Drake, General Snyman's adjutant, and even though there was no evidence against Drake, Snyman acceded to demands to fire him.

'That did not change the situation at all. Everybody still knows exactly what is discussed in the war council, since the meetings are held in Snyman's headquarters, of which the windows were virtually always wide open. Anyone can (and many do) listen from the verandah to what is discussed inside. The ordinary burghers in the forts then discuss the decisions. There are black servants everywhere and they overhear these discus-

Continued overleaf

Members of the Klein Marico Commando outside Mafeking

Boer artilleryman and burgher at Mafeking

FROM THE EDITOR

In spite of all the setbacks of the past six weeks, positive developments fill us with renewed hope for the future course of the war. Chief Commandant Christiaan de Wet's spectacular victory at Sannaspos markedly boosted the morale of the burghers – many who had earlier left for their homes in disappointment are now taking up arms again and rejoining the commandos.

In this issue we report on De Wet's siege of a British unit at Jammerbergsdrift near Wepener. Our courageous Chief Commandant believed that he would be able to capture the enemy positions, but the risk of suffering heavy casualties was unacceptably high. His decision against a charge reflects one of the biggest differences between Boer and Brit. As an elderly burgher remarked to one of our correspondents: 'The British fight to die, the Boers fight to live.'

De Wet and the other Boer officers realise all too well that we cannot afford heavy casualties. Our numbers are too small for that – but in any case, it is against our whole culture. We have been taught over many generations that we have to survive at all costs, every single one of us. In a patriarchal society such as ours, the death of a father is a catastrophe for his family. That is why our burghers cannot recklessly and ruthlessly storm into a battle. In a people's army such as ours, care is a virtue. Cowardice can in no way be excused. There are and have been cowards amongst our burghers, and even cowardly burgher officers. However, it would be a blatant generalisation to call all the burghers cowards. The valour of the vast majority against the Khaki hordes has undeniably been proved.

continued

sions. And they tell it to other blacks until the news spreads to within the besieged Mafeking. White people are thus personally responsible for the spreading of the "war council secrets".'

SUCCESSFUL PATROL TO LOBATSE

'One of the most important events in this area in the past few months was the patrol to Lobatse in Bechuanaland. On Saturday 10 March about 100 burghers of the Marico Commando under the command of General Snyman left the laager on horseback. Commandant Botha and Field Cornets Hansie Snyman, Arie Oberholzer and Manie Lemmer accompanied them. At Witpoortjie, Commandant Hans Eloff of Swartruggens with another 100 burghers on horseback joined them. They took along guns commanded by Sergeant Klein.

'The commando's objective was to capture the British unit of Colonel Plumer at Lobatse. At Pitsani, which is called "Jameson's Hillocks" by the burghers since Dr L.S. Jameson started his infamous invasion from there in December 1895, they stopped for a few days and thoroughly destroyed the railway line. On 14 March a British armoured train suddenly approached Pitsani from the north. The burghers were not quick enough to capture it and it hurriedly steamed away when the engine driver became aware of the Boers.

'Early the next morning a scout reported that he could see Khakis approaching. The order was immediately issued to saddle all the horses. Each burgher charged on his own towards the enemy as soon as he was ready. It was a British patrol and was put to flight by the burghers. Three Khakis, including an officer, were captured. Subsequently, the burghers proceeded with the patrol.

'By noon on 15 March there was another confrontation between the Boers and the British. This took place in a dense, hilly area and the thorn bushes were, at places, impenetrable. Here also, the Khakis were quickly put to flight and the Boers occupied their deserted camp. General Snyman was happy with this victory and with the booty, which included seven trunks of Lee Metford ammunition.

'Later that afternoon, when the Boers entered the outskirts of Lobatse, they were again involved in a skirmish with the Khakis. A British officer was killed early on in this encounter. The next day, the Boers bombarded the British camp at Lobatse with one of their guns. After a few shots, the Khakis retreated. However, the burghers only occupied Lobatse and the British camp on 17 March. When they had entered the fort, General Snyman led them in prayer to thank God that the British had fled.

'Soon afterwards, Captain Von Dalwig noticed that the British armoured train was once again approaching. He immediately set up his gun. After a few shots, he hit the train. It immediately began steaming back to the north, but had to wait for a second train to pull it away. After occupying Lobatse, and damaging the railway line, the burghers returned to Mafeking.'

PLUMER'S KHAKIS DRIVEN OFF

'On 31 March, the Boers at Mafeking were startled by the news that Colonel Plumer had reached Ramatlabama from the north with a huge British force and was on his way to Mafeking itself with 300 mounted men. However, he was confronted by the burghers of Field Cornet Fourie of Rustenburg. The latter called on all the burghers to rush to his aid. Soon a general fight was in full swing. However, only a handful of burghers took part in this battle. Nevertheless, they drove Plumer's soldiers back all the way to Ramatlabama, when the arrival of night ended the fight.

'For the Boers this skirmish ended in a notable victory. A total of nine Khakis, including two officers, were killed and four officers and 26 men wounded. Thirteen Khakis were made prisoner of war, one of whom died the next day. All the bodies as well as the wounded, with the exception of one officer, were handed over to Colonel Baden-Powell in Mafeking. On the Boer side one man was killed and two wounded.'

CLASHES WITH BLACKS OUTSIDE MAFEKING

'On 5 April the burghers received a report in the course of the night that a large group of blacks had escaped from Mafeking. Patrols were immediately sent out to search for the blacks and pursue them. It was not until the next afternoon that they were found in a patch of thorn bushes near Rooigrond. The burghers would probably never have spotted them if they had not fired first. Their target was the elderly Willem Ludick who rode on horseback through the bushes a little distance from the other burghers. The bullet hit Ludick in the chest. He only had enough strength left to wave with his hat to draw the attention of the other burghers before tumbling dead from his horse.

'The other burghers were furious about this incident. They immediately surrounded the patch of thorn bushes where the blacks were hiding and sent a messenger back to the laager to request assistance. A large number of mounted Boers and artillerymen with a gun came to their aid. The blacks defended themselves courageously but had no chance. The gun was aimed at them and literally shot them to pieces. The burghers kept on firing until nothing in the bush moved. At least 24 blacks were killed. We have heard that only one survived the massacre by hiding in an aardvark hole until dark. That night he made his way back to Mafeking where, we are informed, he related what had happened.

'Since that very unsavoury incident, nothing of any note has happened here at Mafeking.'

Boer laager outside Mafeking

NATAL: A LULL IN MILITARY ACTIVITY
BOERS STILL HOLD THEIR OWN

Glencoe, 30 March – Here in Natal little that is newsworthy has happened since our last report three weeks ago. Neither side has attempted any offensive action. The line of defence that the burghers occupied at the beginning of the month has remained more or less static. The only change of major proportions is that a large number of Boers, and probably a large percentage of the Khakis as well, have been transferred to the front in the Orange Free State.

It is difficult for the Republican commandos on the Natal front to predict Khaki plans and decide on preventative measures. Opportunities for offensive action often occur but the Boers are not taking them. Their most important task is to prevent a new British breakthrough. For that reason the burghers spend all their energy on making their positions impenetrable.

On 13 March, a British patrol on the far left flank of the Boers crossed the defensive line, destroyed the home of Field Cornet Van den Berg of Vryheid and captured his livestock. The small number of burghers on that part of the front were powerless to confront the Khakis. On 16 March two valiant burghers of General Sarel Oosthuizen's Krugersdorp commando crawled to the British camp at Elandslaagte soon after dark, took two Natal policemen prisoner and captured 22 head of cattle. Subsequently there was talk on the Boer trenches of a full-scale attack on the British camp, but this never took place.

It had been clear to the Transvaal military authorities for some time that the greatest military threat was not from Natal, but from the southern Free State. On 13 March the late Commandant-General Joubert had ordered General Louis Botha to send 2 000 burghers from Natal to the northern Free State, and Botha had dispatched General Tobias Smuts with 1 200 men of the Wakkerstroom and Ermelo Commandos as well as three guns.

Botha subsequently began wondering if it would not be in the best interests of the Boers in Natal to fall back all the way to the Drakensberg at Laing's Nek. The railway line tunnels the mountain there. A tunnel can easily be destroyed. It would be much more difficult for the enemy to restore the railway communications through a sabotaged tunnel than to replace a damaged railway bridge across a river.

Laing's Nek, with the historic Majuba mountain right next to it, was the front that the Boers easily held during the Transvaal War of Independence of 1880–81. All indications are that it would still be easy to defend the Nek against even a massive British force. According to reports Botha actually proposed a retreat to that line. We have heard that the late Commandant-General Joubert seriously considered the proposal but eventually decided against it, since he did not want to abandon such a huge part of Natal without being forced to do it.

On 18 March the Republican military officers here at Glencoe held a general war council meeting. They decided unanimously that since the military situation in the Free State was no longer critical, the Boers would hold their positions in the Biggarsberg as long as possible.

FREE STATE COMMANDOS IN THE DRAKENSBERG

Free State burghers have made entrenchments in the Drakensberg mountain range from Oliviershoek Pass in the west to the De Beers Pass in the east. Since Chief Commandant Prinsloo has left for the eastern Free State, their commander is Commandant Hattingh of Senekal. Our correspondent visited the entrenchments a few days ago and met the well-known Reverend J.D. Kestell. The latter informed him that the burghers find it extremely boring to sit week upon week in their entrenchments without having any contact with the enemy, since the enemy are not moving closer at all. They spend their leisure hours building shelters for their horses, playing *jukskei*, cricket and football, carving walking sticks or swimming. It seems like a waste of time while the burghers in other parts of the Orange Free State are locked in a life-and-death struggle. However the burghers are not complaining, since by occupying the Drakensberg they are guarding the border districts in which they themselves live.

Kestell furthermore relates that the Free State women are not allowing their men to be discouraged. The burghers who receive leave to go home find that their women are just as courageous now as at the beginning of the war.

Moreover they find that while the men are at the front, their women are proceeding with farming activities. It is the women that ensure that the farm workers plough and sow and that there will be a big harvest this season. It is wonderful to see how the Boer woman personifies the love for freedom. She stands unrelenting at the side of her husband in the battle for freedom. She refuses to allow her husband to leave the front without good reason. May it be that the Boer women will never have to suffer any punishment for their patriotism.

Railway culvert in Biggarsberg mountains damaged by the Boers

OUR MILITARY OFFICERS

General Stoffel Froneman

Christoffel Cornelis Froneman was born in 1846 near Winburg in what was then called Transorangia. We have no information whatsoever on his origins or his early career, apart from reports that as a young man he conducted himself with distinction in the wars between the Orange Free State and the Basotho of King Moshweshwe. With the outbreak of this war in October last year, he was the commandant of the Ladybrand Commando.

Early in February this year Froneman participated with Chief Commandant Christiaan de Wet in the battle at Koedoesberg west of the Boer positions at Magersfontein. Shortly afterwards he and his commando participated in the battle of Paardeberg, but managed to escape before General Piet Cronjé's surrender. Subsequently the Free State military authorities promoted him to the rank of general.

Two weeks ago Froneman participated in the illustrious Boer victory at Sannaspos and since then he has been active in the campaigns against the British in the southeast Free State. He works closely and with great success with Chief Commandant de Wet in their strategy to confuse the British military authorities. In this process Froneman has made a name for himself as a courageous and enterprising officer.

General Stoffel Froneman on horseback

THE War Reporter
WEEKLY EDITION

Number 28   Pretoria, South African Republic   21 April 1900

FREE STATE VOLKSRAAD MEETS AT KROONSTAD
OPENING SPEECH BY PRESIDENT STEYN

Kroonstad, 18 April – Since Bloemfontein is occupied by the British, the annual Free State Volksraad meeting is taking place here in Kroonstad, the temporary capital. The meeting place is a big hall in Herman's Hotel. President Steyn delivered the opening address on Monday 2 April. Here are some extracts from his inspiring speech:

'Even though the enemy has occupied Bloemfontein, and I have been forced to move the seat of the government temporarily to Kroonstad, it is with a feeling of confidence in the future that I heartily welcome you here for the normal scheduled annual session.

'Notwithstanding your attempts as well as those of the government to preserve the peace, war was forced on the South African Republic and the Orange Free State by the British government. When the war broke out we rushed to the aid of our sister Republic.

'The Republics have entered this struggle with no objective other than to defend their independence, which has cost our forefathers so much blood and which is so highly esteemed by us. Even though the capture of General Cronjé and his valiant burghers and the occupation of Bloemfontein were heavy blows to us, it is a joyous privilege for me to announce that our burghers are still filled with courage and determined to fight and if necessary to die for the protection of our hard-won independence, as indeed many of our dear, courageous and never to be forgotten heroes have done.

'In this war against two small Republics the enemy did not hesitate to make use of wily proclamations in an attempt to sow discord amongst our population. I often made the people aware of the danger of those proclamations by counter-proclamations, and I am happy to communicate to you that as far as I know very few of our people have acted so weakly or with such cowardice as to subject themselves freely to the enemy.

'In an attempt to restrict the spilling of blood and to reassure the civilised world once more that we have no wish to occupy neighbouring colonies, and have no other purpose than to fight for freedom and justice, the State President of the South African Republic and I wrote a letter to the Prime Minister of Great Britain to restore the peace. Instead of coming to our assistance in our attempts, we received an answer which will be tabled to you from which you will clearly see that the British have started this war with no other purpose than to destroy the two Republics.

'The Executive Council and I have already done all we could to preserve the peace and we will leave nothing undone to restore peace.

'The government of the South African Republic as well as our government have found it expedient to send a joint commission consisting of Abraham Fischer, C.H. Wessels and A.D.W. Wolmarans to Europe and the United States of America in an attempt to convince the civilised powers to intervene in order to bring an end to the spilling of blood. Each of us should pray that their endeavour will be blessed.

'I end with the sincere prayer that we will receive the power to carry this holy struggle for freedom and justice that we have entered in all seriousness in the name of the Holy Trinity on to a successful conclusion, since God will ensure that we do not simply abandon our independence which we bought with blood.'

From the right: President M.T. Steyn, his wife and a Russian doctor at Kroonstad

President Steyn with his wife among friends in Kroonstad

KHAKIS REPULSED AT HOUWATER
Boer mission to De Aar cancelled due to false reports

Pretoria, 19 April – We have just received the first reports of a battle in the northwestern Cape at Houwater that took place more than a month ago. This battle was the outcome of an expedition that we knew about but did not report on since the Republican authorities wanted to keep it secret. It was undertaken on the initiative of Lieutenant Koos Jooste, previously a vice-captain of Commandant Danie Theron's Bicycle Scout Corps. His proposal was a dual one, namely first to recruit Afrikaners in the northwestern Cape who supported the Republican cause and second to destroy the railway line on which Roberts and his Khakis are so dependent somewhere near De Aar.

When the expedition finally left Magersfontein at the end of January in the direction of Prieska, it was a much bigger venture than had been proposed by Jooste a month earlier. General P.J. Liebenberg of Potchefstroom was the commander and Commandant Lucas Steenkamp, a Cape Rebel from the eastern Cape and one of the earliest proponents of a Republican invasion of the northwestern Cape, also took part in it. The expedition consisted of about 200 men with a field gun and a Maxim gun. The British initially sent a strong patrol to intercept them, but the Boers were aware of this patrol and managed to evade them.

Liebenberg's expedition crossed the Orange River at Swemkuil on 12 February and reached Prieska four days later. Unfortunately there was no unanimity among the commanders on the main purpose of the expedition. For Liebenberg and Steenkamp, who often differed on numerous issues with each other, the main purpose was to recruit Cape Rebels. Jooste and Andries de Wet preferred, as their orders specified, to concentrate on the destruction of the railway line between Kimberley and Beaufort West.

The Liebenberg expedition occupied Prieska on 16 February without being resisted. The General proclaimed the district as an area occupied by the Free State and hoisted the flags of the Republics. The police and the magistrate were relieved of their duties, and a *landdrost*, Frans Smeer, and *heemraad* were appointed. Loyalists were given one week to leave the newly declared Republican area. Furthermore they immediately began recruiting volunteers to join the Republican forces as Cape rebels.

The burghers did not linger in this area. Already on 17 February, the day after the occupation of Prieska, Commandant B.J. Schutte occupied Omdraaivlei, a farm on the Ongers River about halfway between Prieska and Britstown and only about 100 kilometres northwest of De Aar. He also took over the local post office. In the meantime other members of the expedition proceeded in a westerly direction to occupy other towns, as is described in a separate report in this issue. Liebenberg himself went to Griquatown, where he managed to recruit 200 new recruits in Griqualand West. In Prieska and its vicinity at least 350 men were recruited. These successes contributed to Liebenberg's decision that the time was ripe to attempt to destroy the railway line.

On 28 February Liebenberg advanced in a southerly direction with his artillery and 200 men. By 4 March he had reached Omdraaivlei, where Commandant Steenkamp arrived on the same day with a number of burghers and Cape rebels. Steenkamp immediately left again, indicating that he had to go to the Kenhardt district. It is possible that he left since he and Liebenberg found it impossible to co-operate.

Liebenberg had heard that a huge British force was approaching from the direction of Britstown and decided to confront it. On 5 March he and his men, burghers as well as rebels, were on the farm Houwater. The rebels under the leadership of Field Cornet Jan van der Westhuizen took up good defensive positions while Liebenberg's men were still out in the open at daybreak on 6 March.

That was the situation when the rebels opened fire early that morning on the approaching British force. The enemy set up their six guns and fired back. The rebels, who had never before been the target of a bombardment, were initially so shocked that they almost took flight. Liebenberg saved the day for the Boers when he charged forward over the open plain with his own guns and commenced an accurate bombardment on the British guns. This filled the rebels with new courage and, led by the brave Van der Westhuizen, they joined the attack. This was too much for the British, and they hurriedly retreated. The Boers pursued the Khakis till dark but could not manage to encircle them.

The burghers were ready to resume the battle early the next morning, but the British had retreated in the course of the night. This means that Liebenberg scored a significant victory. We have heard that a total of three Khakis were killed, 14

Continued overleaf

continued

wounded and six made prisoner of war. On the Boer side two men were killed and three wounded. Liebenberg decided to stay at Houwater for the time being in the hope that more rebels would join his forces. However, he did not have enough ammunition to go on the offensive.

This was the situation when Liebenberg heard that the British had broken through at Magersfontein and had forced Cronjé to surrender. The report came from Chief Commandant Christiaan de Wet and included a request that Liebenberg should return to assist with the defence of the Free State. Liebenberg decided to remain where he was, however, since President Kruger had personally promised to dispatch him 64 trunks of ammunition.

LIEBENBERG MISLED, ABANDONS PRIESKA

On 15 March General Liebenberg received a false report from General J.J.M. Breytenbach in Griqualand West from which he could draw no other conclusion than that President Kruger was ordering him to return immediately. Liebenberg was deeply disappointed since he felt that he was leaving the Cape rebels in the lurch. After his return to Griquatown, he told our correspondent that the rebels had pleaded with him to remain with them to protect them from the British. He could not, he answered, but would leave 25 of his best men as well as rifles and ammunition behind. That did not help. Immediately after his departure the rebels threw their rifles down in disgust and returned to their houses in despair.

The British reoccupied Prieska on 19 March and captured a huge supply of the Boer ammunition. By that time Liebenberg was in Griquatown. There too the rebels pleaded with him to help them, but his impression was that he had to return to the Transvaal on the orders of President Kruger to help with its defence. A few days later Liebenberg received the bitter news that the British in the Prieska area were capturing all the rebels.

Liebenberg realised that he had been misled. While he was in Griquatown he met Field Cornet Cronjé, who was on his way to him with the 64 trunks of ammunition, and who informed him that he had not been supposed to retreat. Liebenberg was furious but could do nothing to save the situation. In addition he found Griqualand West in total disorder and in despair, since the same General Breytenbach who had misled him had advised the rebels in that area to lay down their arms. The British flag was even waving over the town – something which he immediately put an end to. In addition he immediately called upon the rebels of Griqualand West to keep fighting. And now, after almost being recalled from Griqualand West all due to a misunderstanding, Liebenberg still finds himself in that area and acts as general over all the rebels in the vicinity of Griquatown and Postmasburg.

UPRISING IN THE NORTHWESTERN CAPE FAILS

British re-establish control over the lower Orange River

Pretoria, 20 April – Soon after the occupation of Prieska (see this issue), 16 men led by Lieutenants Koos Jooste and Andries de Wet and Field Cornet Borrius left with 300 rifles and 20 000 rounds of ammunition to occupy Kenhardt. On the way, four men, namely Field Cornet Borrius, Walters, Elias Nel and Herman Judelewitz, accompanied by a few rebels, turned off to Kakamas. They reached that town on Sunday 25 February while the Reverend Schröder was busy leading a sermon. The armed Boers listened to the sermon through the door and the open windows.

After the service Schröder came outside and told one of the men: 'Today is the day of the Lord and not one for war.' There was great excitement in the town, however. The visitors proceeded to Jan Redelinghuys's house for a cup of coffee and from there to the police camp, where they hoisted the Free State flag and ordered Andries Louw, the police sergeant, from his house. Louw and his three constables immediately joined the Boer forces. Three days later Borrius and his group went to the police post at Skuitdrif. The policemen there also joined the Boer forces.

At Kakamas the recruitment of rebels soon produced significant results. By the time Borrius returned to the town, altogether 54 men were ready to join. They were told to gather with the other rebels from the district at Kenhardt on 13 March.

Jooste, accompanied by 15 men, had in the meantime occupied Kenhardt on Wednesday 28 February. This was accomplished without loss of life but they did encounter some resistance. On the evening of 27 February the magistrate of Kenhardt, F.C. Garstin, was informed that the Boers were approaching. Garstin was a British loyalist and had earlier organised a group of Coloureds into a town guard for the defence of the town. They waited for the Boer commando some two and a half kilometres outside of the town.

The Boers were unsuspectingly approaching Kenhardt when the town guard suddenly ordered them to halt. Their reaction was to fire on the defenders. The latter fired back from their entrenchments. The Boers then retreated and formulated a plan to force the town into surrendering. De Kock, who had previously worked in a shop in Kenhardt, approached the town guard under a white flag. Granted permission to interview Garstin, he demanded the surrender of the town within an hour, or the Boers would bombard it.

These tactics worked perfectly. Garstin believed that the Boers had a gun and conceded. He accompanied De Kock back to the town guard and ordered them to go home. The Boers disarmed them and thus the town guard of Kenhardt came to an end. Jooste and his men moved into the town. When Garstin enquired where their gun was, Jooste answered: 'The closest one is about 150 kilometres from here.' The outwitted magistrate and his officials were then locked into the prison.

Jooste appropriated the cash that he found in the offices of the divisional council and government offices. After about a week in jail all the officials were told to leave town. A war council was elected at Kenhardt and John Loxton was appointed *landdrost*. A number of field cornets were appointed. Of the five policemen of Kenhardt, four joined the Boer forces while the fifth went down to the south. About 200 recruits for the Boer forces gathered at Kenhardt on 1 March and were addressed by Commandant Lucas Steenkamp, who made a brief appearance in the town. The new recruits were then given some training.

Jooste issued a proclamation on 4 March in which he declared that the Kenhardt district was incorporated into the Orange Free State and gave his field cornets the power to commandeer horses, mules and supplies. He also declared that all adult men were liable for military service. In terms of the proclamations, the field cornets could order the rebels to assemble at Kenhardt on 13 March with a horse, food for eight days, a rifle and ammunition. The recruits from Kakamas joined this rebel force on 13 March, after which three rebels were sent back to Kakamas to continue with the recruitment of men in the town and in the district. Jan de Wet of Upington was sent to Frierdale for that purpose.

In the meantime, Lieutenants Jooste and De Wet went from Kenhardt to Upington, where they joined Commandant Steenkamp. The Free State flag was hoisted, and a war council was elected on Saturday 10 March. On this occasion about 200 rebels were in the town. After some hesitation the Reverend Schröder – a leading figure in the area, who was elected as member of the Cape Parliament by the Prieska constituency last year – accepted the position of chairman of the war council

All pro-British people and officials from Upington and the Gordonia district were ordered by Jooste to leave the district. The mayor, the secretary and most of the members of the municipal council supported the Boer cause. Jooste and his party next began recruiting rebels to join the Republican forces. These rebels were told to gather at Upington on 21 March.

The uprising at Upington lasted for only 10 or 11 days. The Republican officers had too little time to organise a systematic rebellion, and left before some of the men who had been commandeered from the district reached the town. Jooste also visited Keimoes but it seems that he did not occupy that town.

In the meantime British forces were on their way to the lower Orange River valley with the obvious intention of suppressing the pro-Republican uprising in that area. Colonel Adye with 550 men was advancing on Prieska and Colonel Parsons with 450 men approached Kenhardt. Without being aware of the approaching enemy, the Republican commando split into two groups on its own account. One group of about 120 men went to Prieska to join General Liebenberg. The other group of about 130 under Field Cornet Borrius remained at Kenhardt, but when they were told that a British force was approaching from the direction of Vanwyksvlei, they entrenched themselves at Rietfontein, some two kilometres south of Kenhardt.

Before a battle took place, however, Borrius heard of Cronjé's surrender at Paardeberg and that Liebenberg was returning to the Free State. Commandant Steenkamp was in Upington when he heard the same news, and was informed that he had to return to the Free State to assist in defending it against British occupation. This order had never been issued by the Republican military authorities, but Steenkamp was not in a position to verify it. For the Colonial rebels this news was a disaster. They now had to decide whether to go with the Boer officers back to the Republics or to surrender to the British and take the consequences of their action.

Early on the morning of 20 March Commandant Steenkamp held a war council in Upington. This council decided to disband the rebel force. Steenkamp was so disgusted that he left in a northwesterly direction, stating that he would go to German South West Africa. Borrius and his commando left Rietfontein, and Borrius advised the rebels to disappear. The majority of the rebel commando at Kenhardt decided to surrender. Some went quietly back home, buried their weapons and ammunition and made as if nothing had happened. Others surrendered their weapons at Kenhardt and were allowed by the British, who had by this time arrived, to return home after being given a 'rebel pass'. Borrius himself, Judelewitz and a few of the rebels left in the direction of Upington. By the end of March the six-week uprising of the Cape Afrikaners of Gordonia, Kakamas and Kenhardt had ended.

The general collapse of the uprising in the northwestern Cape left many people in that area believing that they were left in the lurch by the Transvaalers and Free Staters. On 18 March the British reoccupied Prieska, on 31 March Kenhardt and on 3 April Upington. They stationed small garrisons in each of these centres.

Commandant Lucas Steenkamp's Cape Rebel laager

FROM THE EDITOR

There have been no significant military developments within the Boer republics in the past week. The lull in fighting allows us to inform our readers on war-related developments that occurred elsewhere, as well as on other events that are of major importance to the future of the republics.

The course of events in the northwestern districts of the Cape Colony can only be described as an embarrassment to the Republican military authorities. Early in February an expedition whose aims were not quite clear was launched under the command of officers who were not prepared to co-operate. They were nevertheless exceptionally successful in withstanding British attempts to disrupt their activities and in their recruitment of Cape Rebels to join the Republican war effort. However, the in-fighting between the officers, the lack of well-coordinated communication links with the Republican authorities in Pretoria, the spreading of false information and the success of the British offensive since the middle of February together ultimately led to the total failure of the expedition.

The consequences of this failure are tragic, namely that a large number of pro-Boer Cape Rebels have been left in the lurch. Those men who so enthusiastically rallied to our course, as well as their wives and families, have now probably lost their confidence in the trustworthiness of the Republican Boers for all time. It is a pity. A wonderful opportunity to spread the war front and thus thin out the British force over an ever-widening area has probably been permanently wasted.

OUR MILITARY OFFICERS

Lieutenant Koos Jooste

Jacobus Petrus Jooste was born in 1868 in Worcester in the Cape Colony. He is the son of Jacobus Petrus Jooste and Maria Elizabeth Christina Swanevelder. He went to school in Worcester and afterwards farmed for some time in Griqualand West. In 1892 he and his parents settled on the diamond fields with the objective of establishing a wagon factory.

A year later Jooste moved to Pretoria where he worked for a business enterprise and in 1897 became the manager of a coal business.

Jooste achieved fame as a sportsman, being the first person to travel from Pretoria to Cape Town by bicycle, covering the distance in 133 hours (overnight time excluded), despite the bad quality of the roads. In 1898 he again travelled by bicycle to Cape Town. With his return to Pretoria, State Secretary F.W. Reitz handed him a commemorative medal. Jooste is convinced that a bicycle is the most suitable vehicle in South Africa.

Soon before the outbreak of the war last year, Jooste joined Danie Theron in founding the Bicycle Scout Corps to carry out military scouting work. He became the second-in-command of the Corps, with the rank of lieutenant. On the eve of the war he undertook an extensive inquiry into the safety of the country's borders against possible invasions from Bechuanaland, Rhodesia and Swaziland. His report made him well known even in the highest government circles.

With the outbreak of war Jooste was placed in charge of the bicycle unit of the Scout Corps. He served on the Natal front before playing a leading role in activities in the northwestern Cape, as reported in this issue. He is a bachelor.

Koos Jooste

THE War Reporter
WEEKLY EDITION

Number 29   Pretoria, South African Republic   28 April 1900

SPECIAL DEPUTATION TO EUROPE
Fischer, Wessels and Wolmarans arrive in Milan

Pretoria, 25 April – In *The War Reporter* of 10 March 1900 we reported that the two Republican State Presidents had decided to send a mission abroad to seek intervention or support from foreign powers on behalf of the Republics. The three members of the deputation are Abraham Fischer, Cornelius Wessels and A.D.W. Wolmarans, accompanied by J.M. de Bruijn, a telegraphist from Pretoria who can speak a number of European languages. The deputation left Pretoria on a special train for Lourenço Marques, the only harbour in Southern Africa with which the Republics have contact that is not under British occupation, on 11 March.

On their arrival at Lourenço Marques the next day they were met by the Portuguese Consul, and on 13 March they boarded a German ship, the *Kaizer*, and sailed up the east coast of Africa. They sent a progress report on 5 April from Port Said in Egypt, where they made contact with W.J. Leyds, the former state secretary and at present special envoy of the South African Republic in Europe, as well as with H.P.N. Muller, the Consul General of the Orange Free State in The Netherlands.

From Port Said they crossed the eastern Mediterranean and arrived in Naples in Italy on 10 April. There Muller and other Republican officials who are at present in Europe received them. The deputation proceeded by train to Milan, where they arrived on the 12th. From there they reported by telegraph on their progress, indicating that Leyds had received them there. After intensive discussions with Leyds and Muller the deputation decided to go to The Netherlands first. Fischer believes that this is the best place to start their mission, since the ties of kinship between our Republics and our country of origin are particularly strong at the moment. Leyds believes that it would be better to visit Berlin as soon as possible, since the outspoken support of the German Emperor Wilhelm II is crucial for the success of the mission. However, Muller believes the Emperor would not be prepared to receive the deputation and visiting Berlin would be a waste of time. We believe our deputation will have a blessed visit.

Dr W.J. Leyds

Republican deputation members A.D.W. Wolmarans, C.H. Wessels and A. Fischer, and their secretary, J.M. de Bruin

FUTILE SIEGE AT JAMMERBERGSDRIF
DE WET FORCED TO RETIRE AFTER SIXTEEN DAYS

Kroonstad, 26 April – Two weeks ago we reported that Chief Commandant Christiaan de Wet was besieging a British garrison at Jammerbergsdrif, some five kilometres northwest of Wepener. His efforts were in vain, since yesterday he had to abandon the siege when reinforcements arrived for the British garrison. During the siege of 16 days altogether 34 British were killed and 146 wounded, as far as we could ascertain. On the Boer side 11 burghers were killed and 25 wounded.

De Wet's force at Jammerbergsdrif consisted of about 6 000 burghers at its maximum, including several men who had taken up arms again after enjoying a few weeks' leave. De Wet feels that we must thank Lord Roberts for the fact that so many burghers are rejoining our forces. In the proclamations he issued earlier on, he guaranteed the property and personal freedom of burghers who surrendered, but many burghers who quietly returned to their farms have in fact been captured and locked up by the Khakis. In addition the British have plundered numerous Boer farms. By contravening his own proclamations, Roberts is irreparably damaging his credibility. The burghers now realise, as President Steyn warned them, that a British officer cannot be trusted. In one of his reports De Wet sarcastically remarked that Roberts is by far the best recruiting officer that the Boers have ever had.

De Wet was initially under the impression that the British garrison consisted of only 1 000 men. It has now become known that there are 1 900 Khakis at Jammerbergsdrif. They were in communication with the outside world by means of a heliograph and could request assistance from Bloemfontein. De Wet himself was in almost daily heliographic communication with President Steyn. While busy with the siege, he heard that strong British units were approaching from Bethany railway halt (south of Bloemfontein) and from Aliwal North. The column from Bethany consisted of about 12 000 Khakis. Since General Piet de Wet's commando could not check them, Chief Commandant De Wet sent a part of his force under Commandant Piet Fourie, and later on reinforcements under Commandant J.H.B. Wessels to help. By 20 April, General Piet de Wet had 2 000 burghers available. That same day the British attacked them on the farm Constantia, a little distance south of Dewetsdorp, but the burghers repulsed the enemy.

BRITISH ONSLAUGHT FROM THE SOUTH

In the meantime, General Froneman proceeded to Smithfield on the orders of Chief Commandant de Wet to halt the British column approaching from Aliwal North. The British retreated again before the burghers arrived. Froneman and his commando pursued them but could not overtake them before they reached their base in Aliwal North. However he did not return with empty hands, since some 500 burghers who had earlier returned to their farms once again joined his commando.

Froneman was hardly back at Jammerbergsdrif when Chief Commandant de Wet sent him on yet another expedition – this time to repulse a British column of about 4 000 men that was approaching Wepener from Aliwal North. The enemy clashed with Froneman's force of 600 men at Boesmankop, some 30 kilometres south of Wepener, on 21 April. Froneman thought that the British could outflank his position, and reported thus to Chief Commandant de Wet, who immediately sent General J.H. Olivier with 300 men of the commandos of Smithfield and Wepener. This Boer force was still not big enough to check the British completely, but retarded their offensive to such an extent that they could not accomplish anything against De Wet. By the 24th Froneman and Oliver held the front a good 20 kilometres south of Wepener.

THE THREAT FROM BLOEMFONTEIN

These were not the only forces in the south that forced Chief Commandant De Wet to abandon his siege of the British garrison at Jammerbergsdrif. The British had in the meantime sent a third large column out against him: this time directly from the Free State capital. On 22 April this column reached Leeukop, some 30 kilometres southeast of Bloemfontein. General Manie Lemmer was stationed there with about 400 burghers. The British attacked them and attempted to outflank them, but through wise application of his forces in the hilly area, Lemmer outwitted the enemy. During the battle four burghers were wounded and two Khakis were taken prisoner of war. From a reliable source we have heard that two British soldiers were killed and 19 wounded.

That night Lemmer and his burghers retreated and joined the forces of General Piet de Wet at Dewetsdorp. At Lemmer's request Commandant Fourie was sent with 800 Free State burghers from Brandfort to assist them. They joined him early on the morning of 24 April. Later that day the British attacked them at Roodekop. The burghers gave a good account of themselves but had to fall back. Their loss was three men dead, eight wounded and one missing. What the British loss was we do not know, but the burghers believe that it was considerable.

The biggest problem now was that the British could easily encircle General Piet de Wet and then Chief Commandant Christiaan de Wet as well. Consequently General Piet de Wet, who was aware of this possibility, decided to fall back to the north immediately to escape the British net. He sent a message on this critical situation to his brother and prepared for an orderly retreat.

THE BOER RETREAT

Chief Commandant de Wet made a last desperate attempt to capture the British column at Jammerbergsdrif on 24 April, but failed. That same morning he received his brother's message that the British were gaining the upper hand at Dewetsdorp, only 30 kilometres northwest of Jammerbergsdrif. Realising that if that happened the Khakis would be able to cut him and the other Boers in the southern Free State off from the Republican forces in the north, he decided to abandon the siege of the garrison, and sent a message to Generals Froneman and Olivier to retreat to the north to escape encirclement. To ensure that the British would hardly notice their movements, the burghers left their positions after dark that evening, but they were not out of danger yet. Piet de Wet's burghers barely managed to keep the enemy at bay with masterly rearguard actions.

The Boer destination was the hilly area around Thaba Nchu. Unfortunately, a British column was hurrying there from Bloemfontein. These Khakis attacked and repulsed the 200 Transvaal burghers who were guarding the water works at Sannaspos on 22 April. The burghers wanted to destroy the water works before leaving but President Steyn prohibited this since it would be very expensive to repair the pumps after the war. They merely removed some of the machinery of the pumps in order to hide it. Without spare parts, which the British would not be able to acquire or manufacture locally, the pumps could not work at all. The British did occupy the water works but were repulsed by the burghers of General Freek Grobler when they attempted to cross the Modder River.

The next day, the British did cross the river with hundreds of reinforcements but the burghers, strengthened by the arrival of General Philip Botha and his men, made life difficult for them. Yesterday there was a full-scale battle between Boer and Brit at Ysternek, some 10 kilometres west of Thaba Nchu. Even though the British eventually repulsed the Boers, it took them virtually the whole day and they suffered heavy losses in comparison with the relatively light casualties on the side of the Boers. This morning the British finally managed to occupy Thaba Nchu.

By their courageous defence Generals Grobler and Botha accomplished a valuable task. They not only gave Chief Commandant de Wet and all the Republican forces in the south an opportunity to evade the British, but also allowed them to fall back in an orderly fashion and thus ensure that their supplies, including ammunition wagons, would not fall into British hands.

FROM THE EDITOR

The past fortnight has been a relatively calm period on the war front, with no major battles taking place. Lord Roberts's main force is still in Bloemfontein. The Transvaal forces are divided between units on the Natal front, the northern Free State and the burghers besieging Mafeking. On that there is nothing to report.

The Free State forces under Chief Commandant Christiaan de Wet have been active in the area southeast of Bloemfontein. De Wet himself made an attempt to force the British column at Jammerbergsdrif to surrender, but failed. From our present perspective it is clear that his attempt was a senseless waste of time and of manpower. It would have been of much greater advantage to the Boer cause if De Wet had demolished the wagon bridge across the Orange River at Norvalspont, since Roberts would then have found it more difficult to provide his huge army with supplies. Indeed the Boers have inflicted little damage on the British in recent times.

There are positive signs however, notably the fact that many Free State burghers are again taking up arms. And the mission of influential leaders to Europe to recruit support for the Republican cause cannot do us any harm. After last month's rather dismal prospects, the silver lining around the dark cloud that hangs across our freedom is becoming more visible every day.

ROBERTS STILL IN BLOEMFONTEIN

Kroonstad, 27 April – It is almost six weeks since the Khakis occupied the Free State capital and Lord Roberts is still not making any visible preparations to resume his offensive. We have heard from reliable sources in Bloemfontein that several thousand British soldiers have contracted stomach fever after drinking polluted water from the Modder River. A few hundred have already died. Since Roberts must give his soldiers time to recover, he has postponed his offensive. That he will resume it sooner or later is certain, since he is continually building up his forces in Bloemfontein. In the meantime British units are mercilessly hunting Boer commandos in the southern Free State.

It may sound inhuman to make the following statement, since so many British soldiers are dying of disease, but it certainly is true that Chief Commandant de Wet deserves the credit for this British setback since he captured the Bloemfontein water works at Sannaspos last month. The result of that success was that the British experienced a shortage of fresh water and were forced to use dubious water sources.

CELLIERS REPORTS ON LIFE ON COMMANDO

Kroonstad, 26 April – Jan F.E. Celliers, the former city librarian of Pretoria and member of the Pretoria Commando, tonight visited the temporary Free State capital. At the request of our correspondent he compiled the following brief report on his experiences of life on commando during the past month:

'At the beginning of this month we were still busy with our major trek from the Orange River to Kroonstad. Since we had to proceed as quickly as possible, there was not much time to prepare food. Our rusks were finished by then, but we did have flour and often baked *stormjaers*. These consist of a mixture of flour and a little bit of baking powder. The dough is dipped with a spoon into a pot of cooking water that contains a few cups of melted fat. Each spoonful rises to make a round brown loaf that has quite a decent taste. I quickly learned to put a few of these in my pockets to be ready for the hunger that stalks one later on.

'One of our biggest problems on the treeless plains of the Free State is to find enough fuel. We usually make use of dry cow dung, but this is not easy to find. Sometimes we negotiate with the local black people to give us dry dung in exchange for the head, feet and skin of sheep that we have slaughtered.

'On the evening of 1 April we reached a beautiful campsite full of trees next to the Vals River at Kroonstad. Water, shade and wood were suddenly no longer a rarity. At last we could bath again. The biggest joy for me was that I was given a leave-letter the next day to visit my wife and children. That same evening we left Kroonstad on a packed train and at 10 o'clock on the morning of 3 April we were in Pretoria, where I spent a week.

'On Wednesday 11 April we were back in Kroonstad. At the station the train carrying 470 British soldiers captured by Chief Commandant de Wet at Mostertshoek passed us on the way to the prisoner-of-war camp near Pretoria. The Khakis sang 'Rule Britannia' and 'God save the Queen' with abandon.

'It was only on the evening of 11 April that my comrade and I again reached our laager. Apart from two black servants, there was not a soul in sight. We had barely had the opportunity to boil water for our coffee and roast our meat when rain started falling. As we usually do when it rains, we pulled a canvas over the wagon and arranged a spot to sleep, but that evening nature seemed determined to make our return as unpleasant as possible. The raindrops ran down the canvas, quickly found small holes in it, and sent forth streams of water onto our blankets and onto us. What a change from the previous week's peaceful and warm room at home! But I'm definitely not unhappy or in sackcloth. I feel satisfied and proud to participate in this gigantic encounter that will forever influence the fate of our Afrikaans mothers and children.

'The next week was an easy time for us. I visited Kroonstad on more than one occasion. Mostly we would just stay with the wagons, or if it rained, under the wagons, conversing or reading. This Monday (the 23rd) we were ordered to pack up and move on. The owner of the farm where our laager was situated only had to accept our presence for 20 days and that time had now expired. We found it difficult to inspan the oxen and the mules, since these animals did not feel that it was a good time to move on. And when we were at last ready to go, the news came that plans had been changed and we could stay where we were.

'Today we did trek to a new laager position a few kilometres upstream. It is a beautiful spot, but we are now 20 kilometres from Kroonstad. There are masses of man-made iron tools in this area. This morning I took a walk along the river to search for a few examples, and when I returned I found that my comrades had in the meantime been called up to the front. I had to stay behind to look after the wagons. Unfortunately news from the front seems to indicate that our easy life will soon end.'

BOER PRISONERS OF WAR IN THE CAPE

Pretoria, 27 April – Some time ago we published a report on conditions under which Boer prisoners of war are held captive. Mrs Alida Badenhorst of the Potchefstroom district, who sent us particulars on conditions on the western front in February, has now sent us first-hand reports on the prisoners of war. These are in the form of extracts from letters that her husband, Frikkie Badenhorst, had written to her from the Cape. He is one of the burghers who were in General Cronjé's laager when they surrendered on Majuba Day. On 5 March he wrote to her that they were being held in the Simonstown harbour on board the troop ship *Manilla*:

'On 27 February we left the Modder River and on 4 March arrived in Cape Town. Next day we came on to Simon's Bay. Now we are on the sea. Some of us were a bit seasick. How many of us are on this ship I know not. We are from 14 to 16 men in bunks, and tables down the centre. Breakfast consists of tea and bread; at noon we have beef and potatoes; for supper, bread and tea again. We do not complain about the food. Nature is very beautiful here; before us the mountains and behind us the sea.'

According to Badenhorst many burghers became ill and died on board the *Manilla*. As a result the burghers were put on land again. On 14 April he wrote to his wife about his new circumstances: 'In the camp there is not much more room than on the ship. Here we have tents. Each tent contains 13 men. Every tent has a foreman and every section a corporal. There are 2 000 prisoners of war here, so you can imagine what a bustle there is. Our tent is quiet; it stands on one side in a corner. Our foreman is a quiet, religious man. Our camp lies on the sea-shore at the foot of a mountain.'

On 21 April he wrote again, saying that they were temporarily shifted to a camp at Green Point, but then back to Simonstown again. On the weather he writes that sometimes it rains for days on end, but 'then again the sun shines brightly and warm and we can go and bathe in the sea. We are allowed to bathe twice a week. We sometimes see great fish swimming about – huge animals.'

Our readers should not get the impression that the prisoners of war are leading an easy life. They are powerless prisoners and their anxiety and their longing for their loved ones dominate their lives. Virtually daily Badenhorst writes of bad news they have received: 'Hans Kruger, the foreman of our tent, is sad; he got a letter to say that his youngest son is dead; another man had word from home that his wife had died. Koos Badenhorst heard that two of his children were lost.'

It is not only the bad news from home that makes them unhappy. Death often occurs in the camp itself. Badenhorst tells of the conditions under which his son-in-law Gys Joubert died of the fever, and of his funeral. Something else that fills the prisoners with anxiety is the possibility that they will be sent to St Helena, some 2 000 kilometres from Cape Town in the Atlantic Ocean. That is the island where the famous French Emperor Napoleon Bonaparte was detained after his defeat at Waterloo and where he actually died. A number of captured Boers have already been shipped there, including General Piet Cronjé who arrived at St Helena on 11 April.

Boer prisoners of war at the beach directly beneath their camp in Simonstown

OUR MILITARY OFFICERS

General P.D. de Wet

Pieter Daniël de Wet was born in 1861 on the farm Nuwejaarsfontein near Dewetsdorp in the Orange Free State. He is a younger brother of Chief Commandant Christiaan de Wet, whose career we have already reported on. The younger De Wet was only seven years old when his mother died. We do not know if he received any form of formal education. His school was the farm, where he assisted his father with farming activities. In the process he gained incomparable knowledge of the veld, especially in the southeastern Free State where he is at present involved in numerous confrontations with the enemy.

De Wet was 18 years old when he accompanied his brother Christiaan to the Transvaal. They settled near Heidelberg as farmers. De Wet was present at the People's Assembly at Paardekraal in December 1880 when the Transvaal Afrikaners re-established their independence. He participated in the Transvaal War of Independence on the Natal front and fought in the Boer victory over the British in the famous battle of Majuba on 27 February 1881. The next year he gained further military experience in the so-called Mapoch War.

In 1883 De Wet once again moved to the Free State and began farming near Lindley. From 1893 to 1897 he was a member of the Free State Volksraad. In 1898 he settled in Pretoria and became a confidant of President Kruger. Last year, just before the outbreak of war, he returned to Lindley where he became field cornet of the local commando. He is known as a capable and affluent farmer and is an influential and popular member of his community.

With the outbreak of the war last October De Wet proceeded to the Natal front as field cornet at the head of about 200 Lindley burghers. He participated in numerous battles, exhibiting a natural military talent and impressing everybody with his calm courage and his ability to sum up a situation. No wonder then that he was promoted to the rank of general before the end of the year. That was when he succeeded Chief Commandant Esaias Grobler as Chief Commandant of the Free State commandos south of the Orange River.

De Wet's headquarters were now at Colesberg, where he came under the influence of General Koos de la Rey, who taught him the value of offensive action. He served with distinction and thus fulfilled the promise he had shown from early on as a military leader. With the beginning of the British offensive in the western Free State in February, he was recalled from Colesberg to the Bloemfontein area to help defend the capital.

In the past month De Wet has fought with his brother Christiaan in the eastern Free State. He played a prominent role in the famous Boer victory at Sannaspos and has since continued to play a major role in the Dewetsdorp area.

Piet de Wet is a strongly built man with blond hair who immediately makes a positive impression on people who meet him. He is a serious, deeply religious man. It is clear that he thinks carefully about situations before making an assessment and is not afraid to take up unpopular standpoints when he is convinced that his convictions are justified.

De Wet and his wife Susanna Margaretha de Wet have eleven children.

General Piet de Wet

The War Reporter
Weekly Edition

Number 30   Pretoria, South African Republic   5 May 1900

AMMUNITION FACTORY EXPLODES IN JOHANNESBURG
TWELVE PEOPLE DIE; POLICE SUSPECT SABOTAGE

Pretoria, 30 April – The news on everyone's lips is the huge explosion that shook Johannesburg on 24 April, partially destroying the Begbie ammunition factory. According to the police 12 people died in the explosion, some of the bodies mutilated beyond recognition, and 32 were injured, including the director of the factory, Grunberg. A huge supply of ammunition was destroyed but the machinery and the implements of the factory were not badly damaged.

This explosion was certainly the work of saboteurs. The clearest indication that this dastardly deed was done by malicious people was found by the police soon after the explosion – a tunnel that leads from the scene of destruction to a hotel next door. They do not know yet who the saboteurs were, but there is no doubt that a large proportion of Johannesburg's present population are English-speaking people who do not attempt to hide their contempt for the Boers from the public eye. Perhaps a small number of English conspirators imitated the act of Guy Fawkes and his cronies, who attempted to damage the cause of their enemy through an explosion 300 years ago.

No person who did not witness the explosion or view the damage can imagine how frightening the results were. By coincidence, one of the correspondents of the daily newspaper *De Volksstem* was in the area when the catastrophe occurred. He agreed to report on the disaster for us:

'I was about two minutes' walking distance from the Begbie factory at half past five that afternoon. It is a less affluent part of Johannesburg, between the city and Jeppestown. Most of the businesses had been closed and the streets were deserted. I was lost in thought as I walked down the street, when I was suddenly swept from my feet by a massive explosion that temporarily affected my hearing. Lying on the ground somewhat dazed, I saw a huge column of flames with above it a mountain of smoke and dust from which pieces of corrugated iron, burning beams and numerous other objects rained down. My guess is that the column of smoke and fire must have been at least 100 metres high and equally broad. It took a few minutes before it began to dissolve.

'After I had recovered from my first shock, I became aware of a mass of screaming women and children who were running up and down the streets that had been deserted moments previously. Taken up by the human stream I rushed to the scene of the explosion, where a scene of destruction awaited me. On the left hand side of the street one could see only flames and smoke. The buildings were gone. In their place there was a moving sea of flame and it flashed back tints of red, yellow and brown against the wall of the main building of the Begbie factory, which was still standing. Injured survivors covered in blood, with handkerchiefs over the mauled parts of their bodies, came crawling from the wreckage. Here and there bombs and grenades were still exploding. The ever-growing number of spectators stood in deadly silence, with their mouths agape, staring at the scene in front of them as though hypnotised by the fire.

'The crowd grew every minute – a mixed bunch of men and women, white and black, who arrived on foot, on bicycle, on horseback or by cart. The fire brigade soon arrived on the scene and doused the fire. It was subsequently pitch dark, since all the electrical lights in the area had been put out of action by the shock of the explosion. While the fire brigade men were supporting the wounded and attempting to control the crowd, people with lamps arrived on the scene. The injured were taken on stretchers to the wagons of the Red Cross that made their welcome arrival soon after dark. Doctors treated them there. The only people who did not help at all were the hundreds of Johannesburg English-speaking inhabitants, who stood some distance away with cigarettes or pipes in their mouths and their hands in their pockets, criticising all that was being done.'

The Johannesburg Fire Brigade at the Begbie explosion

Damage caused by the Begbie explosion

Destruction caused by the Begbie explosion

FROM THE EDITOR

Bad news from the front north of Bloemfontein: all indications are that the British are resuming their offensive. What is needed now is for our military officers to remain calm and confront the enemy with the greatest degree of solidarity that is humanly possible. That seems to be our only hope, since there is no natural obstacle between Bloemfontein and Pretoria such as a mountain range to serve as a defensive position.

In the light of the absolute necessity for co-operation, the British breakthrough at Houtnek north of Thaba Nchu is even more of a tragedy. Elsewhere in this issue we report on the incapacity of the Boer forces to assist one another in the face of threats from the enemy. Ultimately, the defence of the most important position, namely Toba Mountain, was left in the hands of foreign volunteers. The latter conducted themselves extremely valiantly but received a minimum of assistance from the Boers. That is nothing less than a humiliation for our name.

Lack of co-operation is not the only weakness crippling the Boers. There are without doubt a few thousand burghers who simply evade their duty and take 'leave' without permission. They seem to feel: let the other men do the dirty work; I will merely save my own skin. The pursuit of selfish interests is the surest way to defeat. Return to the front, burghers – the enemy threatens to overwhelm us. Be loyal to our motto: *Unity is Strength*!

SKIRMISHES IN THE NORTHWEST FREE STATE
BOERS HALT ENCIRCLING ACTION

Hoopstad, 3 May – Since the death of General De Villabois-Mareuil and the destruction of his commando by the British on 5 April, the Republican forces in the northwest Free State and along the Vaal River have been all too aware of the dangers threatening them from the direction of Kimberley. Rumours did the rounds that the Khakis were preparing to cross the Vaal River with gigantic armies. Despite the near panic this sometimes caused, up to now the Republican forces have been able to defend their positions.

The Boer forces in this area comprise five main groups: a number of commandos under General Sarel du Toit at Veertien Strome, the forces under General Andries Cronjé at Christiania, Commandant Theunissen's burghers at Bloemhof, and the burghers of Field Cornet Daniels near Boshof and Commandant Diedericks here at Hoopstad.

On 8 April Cronjé received numerous reports that the British were on their way from Boshof to Hoopstad, and immediately prepared to confront them with some 400 burghers. By 10 April he was on the farm Gannapan, about halfway between Hoopstad and Boshof, when he heard that the enemy were still at their camp at Boshof – the alarm was merely the enemy's reconnaissance patrols which sporadically visited that area. Five days later, on 15 April, Cronjé moved his commando closer to Boshof. They pitched camp at Plessisdam and made plans to attack the Khakis camped at Swartkoppiesfontein, north of Boshof.

In the meantime, on 13 April Commandant Diedericks received reports that the British were moving from Boshof directly eastwards in order to attack the Boer forces at Brandfort, north of Bloemfontein. According to Captain Danie Theron's scouts, there were 1 200 British foot soldiers and 700 mounted soldiers as well as a battery of artillery in this column. Diedericks and his 400 burghers confronted the enemy on 14 April on the farm Boesmansfontein and pursued them all the way back to Boshof. We have been told that the British loss was 13 men, while the burghers suffered no casualties.

Early on the morning of 20 April Cronjé's burghers became aware of a huge British column moving in their direction. Cronjé sent a mounted commando that repulsed the Khakis and pursued the fleeing soldiers with enthusiasm, even managing to overrun their camp at Swartkoppiesfontein. With the Boers on their heels the Khakis retreated all the way to Boshof, where nightfall ended the

continued overleaf

continued

fight. In this battle one burgher was mortally and one lightly wounded. The British loss, according to reliable sources, was 12 men dead, six wounded and eight made prisoners of war.

Cronjé decided to return to his defensive positions north of the Vaal River. He left Commandant Diedericks, whose commando had grown to about 600 men, behind to halt any possible enemy movements in the direction of Brandfort or Hoopstad. President Kruger approved these steps, since messages received from General du Toit at Veertien Strome indicated that the British onslaught would be from the southwest. On 27 April Cronjé was back at Christiana, ready to assist Du Toit in an emergency.

GENERAL DU TOIT UNDER PRESSURE AT VEERTIEN STROME

At Veertien Strome, on the northern bank of the Vaal River, Du Toit has about 2 000 burghers at his disposal. The British are camping near Warrenton, south of the river. In the first few days of April nothing of military significance happened, but on the 6th the Khakis unexpectedly launched a heavy bombardment and kept it up the whole day, inflicting serious damage on the Boer camp, but no injuries. That night Du Toit set up his guns to face the enemy, and the next day there was a short-lived artillery duel, again without injury.

These British attacks were easily repulsed but nevertheless posed a source of anxiety to the Transvaal military authorities. Commandant-General Louis Botha believes that this confirms that the danger is no longer threatening from the Natal front. The British will approach Pretoria either through the northern Free State or the southwestern Transvaal or from both directions simultaneously. For that reason he transferred another two commandos, namely the Krugersdorp Commando and the Irish Brigade, from Natal on 14 April to serve on these fronts. The Irish were sent to Brandfort and the Krugersdorp men by train to Klerksdorp, where the railway line ends, with orders to hasten on horseback from there to Du Toit at Veertien Strome.

The Krugersdorp burghers were still in Pretoria on 22 April when the British once again attacked the Boer position at Veertien Strome. The enemy directed rifle fire on the laager of the Wolmaranstad Commando all day without causing any injuries, though numerous tents were damaged. The Boers fired back, nobody knows with what effect. On 23 April things were quiet. The next day, however, the British bombarded the Boer entrenchments with a number of guns. The burghers fired back enthusiastically, but two of their three guns broke down in the course of the day. The casualties on the Boer side that day amounted to two men dead and eight wounded. The British casualties are unknown. On the 25th everything was quiet again, except for the occasional rifle shot from either side.

For the next few days things remained quiet, but Du Toit felt increasingly powerless as he received reports of a huge enemy military build-up south of the Vaal River opposite his positions at Veertien Strome. He was not prepared to attack the enemy, but realised that he himself was in a vulnerable position. In addition he could do nothing about the aerial balloon that went up every day south of the river and from which the British spied on his positions. On 28 April the balloon was in position while the British were heavily bombarding the Boer entrenchments. By this time they probably knew exactly what Du Toit's fortifications looked like and how strong his force was.

Even though the Republican forces on the western front have weathered the storm so far, the future looks dismal. An easy solution for this critical situation does not exist.

OUR MILITARY OFFICERS

Colonel E.I. Maximov

Evgeni Iakovlevich Maximov was born in 1849 in Pushkin, Russia. After his school education in St. Petersburg he studied at the Technological Institute and then the Law Faculty of the University of St. Petersburg. In 1869, however, he decided on a military career and joined the Mounted Grenadiers as a volunteer. He soon became an officer and took part in many wars and field battles. In the course of time he achieved the rank of Lieutenant Colonel.

In 1899 Maximov came to South Africa as a freelance journalist. He reached Pretoria about two months ago via Delagoa Bay. From there he went to the Free State, where he impressed the Boers with his shooting and horse-breaking ability. After the occupation of Bloemfontein by the British, Maximov joined the Republican forces as an ordinary burgher. At Kroonstad General De Villabois-Mareuil convinced him to become the second-in-command of his recently established International Legion. After De Villabois-Mareuil was killed last month, Maximov took a few Dutch and Russian Volunteers under his command.

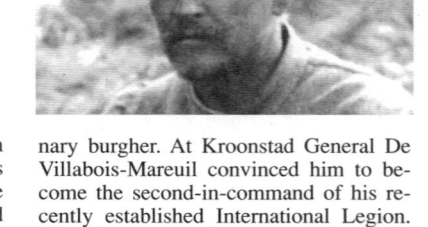

The Russian colonel's real test as a Republican soldier followed in the past week, and he passed with flying colours. All the reports indicate that he led the Foreigners with great valour in the battle of Toba Mountain, even after being wounded twice. It was not his fault that his men were forced to retreat. Maximov is at present in the hospital in Kroonstad for treatment. We wish him a speedy recovery, since it is clear that his services will be of great value to the Republics in future.

BRITISH BREAKTHROUGH AT HOUTNEK

Heavy battles around Thaba Nchu

Kroonstad, 3 May – After Chief Commandant Christiaan de Wet's retreat from the southeastern Free State (see last week's report), he and his burghers occupied Swartlapberg Mountain southeast of Thaba Nchu. At the same time, some Republican burghers occupied the low hills north and northwest of Swartlapberg. All these mountains form a continuous chain, rendered virtually impenetrable by ravines in many places. As a result the burghers felt safe in that area.

The first clash at Thaba Nchu occurred at dusk on 27 April. A British patrol that left that town late in the afternoon and occupied Schuinshoogte was attacked and driven back by the burghers. According to a reliable source at least 12 Khakis were killed or wounded, while the Boers suffered no casualties.

The next morning the British attacked the Boers on Swartlapberg with a huge force and attempted to encircle them. The attempt failed when General J.B. Wessels's burghers pinned the British flank down at Sprinkaansnek. A British unit that arrived on the scene to repulse Wessels's burghers was itself surprised by the arrival of assistant Chief Commandant J.H. Olivier's burghers. The British suffered heavy casualties, including at least one man killed and 10 taken prisoner, before the remainder fled.

On 29 April the Khakis renewed their attempts to drive the burghers off Swartlapberg, but again failed. Indeed, the burghers repulsed the enemy from the mountain, after which Chief Commandant de Wet ordered them to attack the British camp directly south of Thaba Nchu. This caused consternation amongst the Khakis, even though they had such a huge force that the burghers stood no realistic chance. The burghers managed to capture one British water cart, one supply wagon, 178 oxen and 15 horses.

By 30 April, after these skirmishes following directly on the exhausting retreat from Jammersbergsdrif, Chief Commandant de Wet's burghers were completely worn out. Moreover, from the top of the mountain they could see a huge cloud of dust on the wagon road between Bloemfontein and Thaba Nchu, an indication that hundreds of fresh British troops were on their way.

Suddenly the exhausted burghers, fearing that they would be encircled, began to panic. Burghers from numerous commandos simply packed their belongings and began retreating in the direction of Korannaberg Mountain. De Wet had his hands full restoring order and in one or two cases even used his sjambok to discipline unruly burghers. Eventually all of them remained behind and stuck to their positions.

TITANIC BATTLE ON TOBA MOUNTAIN

De Wet's commando was not the only Boer force in the vicinity of Thaba Nchu. Since the Republican military authorities were aware that the British might attempt to break through to the north from Thaba Nchu, they placed General Philip Botha, assisted by Generals W.J. Kolbe and Freek Grobler, in this area to defend all the wagon roads from the vicinity of Thaba Nchu to Winburg. The most important position was that on Toba Mountain (which some burghers called Tubaberg or Thababerg), a high, flat hillock west of the wagon road between the two towns. Toba Mountain is connected by a ridge known as Houtnek to heights in the east.

Even before daybreak on 30 April the burghers on both Toba Mountain and in the positions on the heights in the east, became aware of the approach of a strong British force from the south. By half past nine that morning the Khakis were already so close that the Boers started firing on them with both guns and rifles. The British fired back in an orderly fashion and moved ever closer. It became clear to the burghers that the British plan was to attack Toba Mountain.

Defence of the positions on Toba Mountain was the responsibility of General Kolbe. His forces included the remains of the late General De Villabois-Mareuil's International Legion. Colonel Evgeni Maximov, Villebois's announced successor, was the commander of these Foreigners, as they are called, comprising about 40 Dutchmen and a few Russians. The Free State German Corps as well as a number of American volunteers were also under Kolbe's command on Toba Mountain.

Kolbe's Foreigners could not prevent the British vanguard from reaching the summit, but pinned them down there. After the Boer artillery had subjected the British main force and rearguard to an accurate bombardment, some of the Khakis in the front line lost hope. It was hardly nine o'clock when five soldiers, including a captain, surrendered to the German Corps. Soon afterwards the Foreigners executed a gallant charge on the Khakis. The most valiant of the foreigners was Colonel Maximov, who was wounded twice but kept on charging. Eventually the two forces were hardly 200 metres apart, still firing determinedly on each other. The British charged the Foreigners twice but were repulsed each time. Eventually the arrival of the night ended the fight.

The Foreigners on Toba Mountain were all set to resume battle the next morning, when they received a message from General Philip Botha at midnight to return to the laager for dinner. When they returned to the summit just before daybreak, they found to their dismay that the British had in the meantime begun outflanking their positions to the west. Maximov and Commandant Lorenz of the German Corps did their utmost to repulse the Khakis, but simply did not have enough manpower. When they realised by the afternoon that they would be encircled, they retreated in an orderly fashion from the mountain.

The battle on Toba Mountain cost the British more than 100 casualties and the Republican forces fewer than 50, of whom six were killed and about 28, including Maximov, were wounded. In addition to Toba Mountain, the Khakis yesterday (1 May) also managed to occupy Houtnek. According to General Grobler that position was thinly occupied by a force of only 26 men led by Acting Commandant Smit of Waterberg. They were attacked by a huge Khaki force, and retreated after two hours of fierce defence. Smit was made a prisoner of war since he remained behind with his son Johannes, who was killed in the battle. Three burghers were wounded. After these setbacks the Republican forces fell back to the north.

It is not clear why there were so few burghers involved in the defence of Toba Mountain and Houtnek. There are rumours afloat that the burghers of Generals Kolbe and Philip Botha attempted at that critical stage to capture a British supply column. It is not known where General Grobler's burghers were at the time of the battle. It is clear that there was no co-operation between these Boer generals – a tragic mistake which may cost the Republican forces dearly.

BRITISH FORCES OVERRUN BRANDFORT

De la Rey powerless against huge Khaki numbers

Kroonstad, 4 May – It is too early to state that Lord Roberts, who according to reliable sources commands a force of 25 000 soldiers with 80 guns and 49 machine guns, has begun his long-expected offensive against the Republican forces, but some developments indicate that he has. The most important of these indicators is the large-scale British attack on Boer defensive lines in the vicinity of Brandfort that began yesterday. It was not an unexpected attack. General De la Rey, the Boer commander at Brandfort, had awaited it for a week. The question was not *if* the British would attack, but rather with how many soldiers, and where.

All last month De la Rey had worried about the presence and activities of the British column at Boshof, some distance east of the Kimberley–Mafeking railway line. Numerous rumours and reports that those troops were on their way to Hoopstad made him wonder if the British would not attempt to break through along the Vet River to the rear of the main Republican force at Brandfort. On 8 April, in an attempt to get clarity on this, he sent a reconnaissance patrol commanded by Ernst Freiherr von Rangel out in a westerly direction. The information these scouts brought back reassured him that the British were not planning an attack.

On 21 April De la Rey sent word from Brandfort that the British troops might attack any day. Another nine days went by before De la Rey's scouts reported early on the morning of 30 April that mounted British troops were advancing. The Khakis drove off General Tobias Smuts's sentries from the farm Roodeheuvel southeast of Brandfort, but the burghers launched a counter-attack and pushed the Khakis back again. That same afternoon De la Rey sent out 250 burghers against a British column that was moving towards Winburg about 30 kilometres east of Brandfort. These burghers caught up with the British soon before dark and forced them back.

At the beginning of this week, De la Rey's total force in the vicinity of Brandfort consisted of only between 1 500 and 1 800 burghers. There should be many more, but huge numbers take 'leave' without permission and return to their homes or farms. De la Rey's burghers belong to the Heidelberg, Ermelo and Wakkerstroom Commandos. In addition 120 men of Colonel Blake's Irish Brigade arrived at Brandfort from the Natal front two days ago.

Yesterday morning at seven o'clock De la Rey received a message from his scouts that a huge British force was approaching. By nine o'clock it was clear that a massive British offensive over a wide front on both sides of the railway line was developing. Strong mounted units made up the flanks of this approaching mass of troops. For the Boer scouts it was clear that these mounted Khakis would be able to outflank and encircle any Boer force that attempted to halt the offensive.

In spite of the massive size of the British force (at least 8 000, by Boer calculations), the Heidelbergers and the Irish Brigade, together only about 450 men without any artillery, kept the Khaki left flank in check from three low hills southeast of Brandfort for a few hours up to one o'clock that afternoon, after which they had to retreat to escape encirclement.

On the Boer left flank, east of the railway line, the burghers also managed to stem the British offensive for many hours. This success was achieved by Fighting General Adriaan de la Rey, the brother of General Koos de la Rey, who surprised the British by charging at them with the Ermelo Commando. Unfortunately he himself was wounded early in the battle, but Commandant J.N.H. Grobler displayed particular military talent by keeping the British back at Keeromsberg southeast of Brandfort until dusk.

Since there was an unacceptably high risk that the British would eventually manage to encircle his whole force, De la Rey last night ordered his men to abandon their positions at Brandfort and to fall back to the north. The total Boer losses yesterday were one man dead and 17 wounded. We do not know what the British losses were. The Boer scouts claim that they saw the British ambulance personnel treating a large number of Khakis. Numerous civilians attached themselves to the retreating burghers. The last action of the burghers before abandoning Brandfort was to destroy the railway bridge across the Keeromspruit.

Colonel Blake

THE War Reporter
WEEKLY EDITION

Number 31   Pretoria, South African Republic   12 May 1900

FIGHTING AT THE VET RIVER
Huge railway bridge demolished

Kroonstad, 6 May – After the Republican forces retreated from Brandfort last week, they decided to take up position at the Vet River about 30 kilometres north of Brandfort. General Koos de Rey's forces were depleted by desertion, but he received reinforcements on 4 May when Commandant Abraham Malan's Afrikaander Cavalry Corps (ACC) of about 100 men joined him. The ACC took part in their first skirmish the same day that the Khakis attacked the retreating burghers. Determined defence fortunately assured that the burghers could cross the river safely, with only one man wounded. It is not clear if the British suffered casualties.

De la Rey decided in the light of the seemingly unstoppable onslaught of the British from the south, to order the destruction of the huge railway bridge across the Vet River that same day. The task was carried out by members of the Irish Brigade. The first attempt failed, whereupon a train truck fully loaded with dynamite was pushed back towards the bridge and the last pillars were blown up.

De la Rey's force consisted of only about 1 200 burghers at the Vet River on the morning of 5 May. They were spread out over a broad front, some 20 kilometres from west to east. The British attacked them on that morning in a manner well known to the Boers by now. The infantry, supported by the artillery, moved up the centre, while the cavalry attempted to outflank the Boer positions on the sides. The burghers gave a good account of themselves – especially the six guns that were stationed directly behind De la Rey's main position next to the railway line. The experienced and shrewd Lieutenant Colonel Fanie Trichard, the commander of the Transvaal State Artillery, set his guns up so craftily that the British never discovered their emplacements, even though they fired on the Boers the whole day long.

The Boers defended their position for the best part of the day. It was only late in the afternoon that the British finally managed to cross the Vet River on the furthest eastern flank of the Republican positions. This meant that they would be able to outflank the Boer positions in the west. De la Rey was furious when he heard of the breakthrough. Soon afterwards he was also informed that the British had crossed the Vet River on his western flank south of Winburg and had occupied the town, further increasing the likelihood that the Boer commandos could be surrounded. As a result De la Rey ordered his forces to fall back to Smaldeel Station that same evening.

According to De la Rey some 10 burghers were wounded. The British took a number of prisoner of war, but since so many Boers are deserting, it is impossible to guess exactly how many. British casualties are not known.

Blowing up the Vet River railway bridge

BRITISH OCCUPY WINBURG

Sand River, 9 May – In addition to their advance all along the railway line from Bloemfontein towards the Republican position on the Vet River, the Khakis are also advancing directly to the north with a huge force from Thaba Nchu. We reported last week on the British breakthrough at Houtnek on this front. In the meantime we have heard with regret that one of the bravest Free State officers, Commandant D.S. Lubbe, was shot through the leg in this battle and made a prisoner of war.

Chief Commandant Christiaan de Wet has just told our reporter that the British breakthrough forced him to abandon his positions in the Swartlapberg Mountain southeast of Thaba Nchu and hasten to the Sand River to help check the main British advance. Before he left he ordered General A.I. de Villiers to stay behind with Commandants P.H. de Villiers (Ficksburg), Jan Crowther (Ladybrand), Paul Roux (Senekal) and J.F. Potgieter (Smithfield) in an attempt to ensure that the eastern Free State, the granary of the Republic, does not fall into the hands of the enemy. There is an exceptionally good harvest this year, for which we are thankful to the farmers' wives. In the absence of their husbands on war duty, the women tend the fields with the help of their daughters, young sons and farm workers. This grain will be of great value to the Boer forces in the months ahead.

After the British breakthrough at Houtnek they resumed their northward advance. General Philip Botha and the fighting generals under his command, namely W. Kolbe, A.P. Cronjé, Freek Grobler and Manie Lemmer, fell back towards Winburg. At Baviaansberg Mountain, some 30 kilometres south of Winburg, they halted and held a war council. Even though their forces had been depleted by deserters, they decided to attempt to check the British. Generals Kolbe and Grobler and Commandant Pieterse would occupy Tabaksberg Mountain on the eastern side of the wagon road early on the morning of 4 May with 350 burghers, while General Cronjé and his burghers would take up position on Baviaansberg.

Things did not develop the way the war council expected. The British were too quick. When Grobler and Kolbe began ascending the eastern side of Tabaksberg at half past seven that morning, they were welcomed by enemy fire from the summit. This caused some confusion amongst the burghers and many of them spontaneously fell back. Since Grobler did not know this area at all and could not find shelter for his burghers, he decided on an orderly retreat rather than risk the capture of his guns.

On Baviaansberg things were rather hopeless as well. At half past two that afternoon a huge British force charged the mountain under cover of gunfire. The burghers only put up a weak resistance and the Khakis soon occupied the summit. Thus the fight ended. Altogether six burghers remained behind on the battlefield and were probably taken prisoner of war. British casualties are unknown.

The only advantage that the Boers gained from this fight was that they held the Khakis long enough for General Philip Botha's convoy to negotiate the virtually impassable drifts over the Vet River some 10 kilometres north of Baviaansberg. The British reached the drifts only by that evening, by which time the whole Republican force in this area had slipped through.

The Boers considered attempting to check the British the next day along the bank of the Little Vet River, but abandoned that idea when assistant Chief Commandant J.H. Olivier arrived early that morning with a message from Chief Commandant Christiaan de Wet ordering all the commandos to fall back to the Sand River north of Winburg. De Wet also indicated that he would join them as soon as possible and attempt to check the British onslaught. The burghers consequently fell back to the north and Winburg was occupied unopposed by the British that day. The force that occupied Winburg consists, according to reliable sources, of more than 10 000 Khakis commanded by General Ian Hamilton.

General W.J. Kolbe

Number 31 12 May 1900

REPUBLICAN FORCES CRUMBLE

Boer authorities struggle to maintain order

Kroonstad, 10 May – One of the most damaging results of the victorious British advance north of Bloemfontein is that numerous burghers have decided to abandon the struggle. These burghers state bluntly that there is no sense in going on with the war: Lord Roberts will spare no cost to occupy Pretoria. Resistance would be as futile as attempting to douse a veld fire with barbed wire – and if it were to be attempted, a lot of Boer blood would be spilled for a cause already lost.

By 4 May tens of dozens of Transvaal and Free State burghers had already fled past Smaldeel Station on the main line between Bloemfontein and Kroonstad west of Winburg. When President Kruger was informed of this, he sent a request from Pretoria to President Steyn to do anything possible to stem the flight. The Transvaal burghers had to be informed that it was a criminal offence to evade military service (in other words, to desert) and that deserters would be fined or imprisoned. This did not help. Not even the respected General Koos de la Rey could convince the burghers to do their duty. The Transvaal government consequently began implementing steps against deserters.

On 5 May, when the Boer officers on De la Rey's left flank decided to retire to the Sand River, the last burghers to leave Winburg were not even prepared to load the masses of war supplies in that town onto the last train. Consequently that train arrived practically empty at Smaldeel and from there proceeded to Kroonstad. All the supplies subsequently fell into the hands of the enemy. Cornelis Plokhooy, a foreign volunteer, told our correspondent that he was furious and disappointed in the lack of patriotism exhibited by numerous burghers:

'What I saw in Winburg I will never forget. We rode on horseback down the main street past the church and there groups of young men, burghers of the Orange Free State, were waiting unarmed for the British. They are surrendering, the rogues! They are no longer fighting for the land of their birth, but bow under the yoke of the hated Englishman. This leaves a poor impression on any foreigner who witnesses this. We asked ourselves: If the burghers of this country feel so little for their freedom, is there any sense in a foreigner risking his life for them?

'A little distance further on we came upon a group of men and women, Afrikaners and English, who were donned in festive clothing and awaiting the British as saviours. How pathetic! How angry we are! We began insulting them as traitors as we rode by. That was the only way we had of venting our feelings.'

In addition to the shocking disloyalty displayed by some burghers, there are many factors outside the control of patriotic commando members that contribute to the crumbling of their power. This includes their lack of good horses. There already are many hundreds of foot soldiers in the Republican forces at the front. These burghers often are the first to retreat. Since they have no horses, they cannot fall back quickly. And since they are always afraid of being surrounded and becoming prisoners of war, they retreat at the first signs of a possible Khaki success or outflanking movement.

It is a major problem that there are no surplus horses available. Earlier this month President Kruger gave orders that as many horses and saddles as possible should be sent to the front in double quick time. President Steyn also realised that drastic action was necessary to procure horses. Many officers argue that the people on the farms might as well give their horses to the Boers, since the British will, if they are not checked, take those horses anyway when they occupy the farms. Today the Free State President ordered Chief Commandant de Wet to empower 10 people he can trust to go out and gather as many horses as possible, with the exception of pregnant mares, for the use of burghers who have no horses.

BOERS REPULSED FROM SAND RIVER

EVEN LOUIS BOTHA FALTERS AFTER INITIAL SUCCESS

Kroonstad, 11 May – After the resumption of the British offensive and the Boer retreat from Brandfort, it became evident to the Republican authorities that drastic measures had to be taken. On 3 May President Kruger ordered Acting Commandant-General Louis Botha from Natal to the Free State front. Botha brought the Standerton and Bethal Commandos with him. Their combined strength should be about 2 000 burghers, but there is hardly one half of that number. Other commandos were also ordered to this front, including the Mounted Police under Commandant G.M.J. van Dam, and the Rustenburg Commando.

While these units were on their way here, General de la Rey decided to place the burghers who were falling back from the Vet River in a defensive position along the Doorn River, some 20 kilometres to the north. Since most of his officers preferred to fall back all the way to the Sand River, De la Rey remained behind with only a few men to demolish the railway bridge across the Doorn River. A total of 15 cases of dynamite were used for this purpose. The result was the total demolition of the bridge on 6 May.

When De la Rey arrived at Sand River by train that evening, he was bitterly disappointed to learn that some burghers had already begun retreating to Kroonstad. He immediately issued orders that they had to be sent back. Soon afterwards, that same evening, he heard good news as well. That was that General Piet de Wet was only about 30 kilometres to the east with 6 000 burghers and that Chief Commandant Christiaan de Wet was rushing up from the direction of Thaba Nchu. And the next day Louis Botha arrived at Sand River from Natal to take over the command of the Transvaal burghers on the front.

At the time of Botha's arrival the burghers in the vicinity of the Sand River railway bridge were commanded by Commandant Malan. De la Rey was visiting Piet de Wet. A number of burghers, including the Irish Volunteers commanded by Colonel Blake, were busy demolishing the railway line between Sand River and Doorn Spruit as thoroughly as possible with dynamite. The units were all aware of the approaching British columns – a long distance rifle battle was already in progress when Botha arrived, and Blake's men had begun placing dynamite in the railway bridge across the Sand River in order to demolish it.

The Acting Commandant-General immediately took control of the situation and ordered his gunners to bombard the approaching Khakis. The latter fired back, but ineffectively. When counter-attacked they retreated in disorder, and the burghers pursued them until halted by darkness. Shortly before the end of this skirmish, the train bridge was exploded. All the stone pillars of this bridge, which was 152 metres in length and 25 metres high, were destroyed and three spans collapsed.

On 8 May there was no sign of the enemy but by the next day it was clear that the British were preparing to attack. Botha meticulously prepared to face them. With the inclusion of the Free State burghers in the east he had more than 6 000 burghers and 12 guns at his disposal. This force was spread over a front of about 30 kilometres in width to prevent the British outflanking Boer positions.

The British attack began on 10 May at first light. They easily crossed the river in the west, but by late morning the burghers had managed to halt their outflanking manoeuvres in the northwest. A simultaneous attempt to outflank Boer positions in the east was also checked for most of the morning. The Boers were forced to give so much attention to developments on their flanks, however, that Roberts's main force in the centre easily crossed the Sand River, pushed the Boer resistance out of their way and marched virtually unopposed to the Ventersburg Railway Station. Botha, whose presence had inspired the burghers tremendously, was totally incapable of checking the Khaki masses.

British casualties in the battles since 7 May are not known. Most of the Boer officers claim they were high, but they have no evidence on this issue. The burghers captured 13 Khakis as prisoners of war and they allege that their casualties were indeed high. Even the extent of Boer casualties is difficult to establish. It seems as though approximately 10 burghers were killed, the same number wounded and some 70 taken prisoner. A number of the latter may just as well have deserted and may even be on their farms already.

The results of this British victory may be devastating. There is no natural defensive position between the Sand River and Kroonstad. The occupation of the temporary Boer capital by the enemy is imminent. North of Kroonstad there are only wide plains and no natural defensive positions. The victorious British forces seem to be unstoppable. It will take a supernatural effort to keep them out of the Transvaal.

REPUBLICAN DEPUTATION TO THE NETHERLANDS

Friendly reception by Prime Minister and Queen

Rotterdam, 3 May – We can report with satisfaction that the Republican deputation consisting of Abraham Fischer, C. H. Wessels and A.D.W. Wolmarans received a hearty welcome in The Netherlands. They arrived in mid-April in the Dutch capital, and on the 16th they had a private interview with Prime Minister Pierson in company with Dr Leyds, the special envoy of the South African Republic. No statement was released afterwards and we do not know what they discussed.

On 18 April Fischer and Leyds visited the Minister of Foreign Affairs, De Beaufort, but it was only on 26 April that the deputation had an official interview with the Minister. Even though Fischer and his colleagues had realised by that time that they should not expect much, they were bitterly disappointed when De Beaufort explained that the Dutch could do nothing for the Boers – at least that was how they interpreted his explanation. The deputation members answered that if they could get no support in Europe and specifically in the Netherlands, they would advise the Republican authorities to abandon the war. De Beaufort indicated that any intervention on the Dutch side, no matter how superficial, would contribute to a hardening of public opinion in Britain and would rather work against the Boer cause. Fischer, nevertheless, requested that the Dutch should attempt, since 'one can never predict how the dice will roll'.

On 19 April the deputation was received by Queen Wilhelmina and subsequently even by the Queen mother. It is not known what the two royals told them: the mere fact that they were received enhances their stature enormously. Fischer, Wessels and Wolmarans subsequently negotiated with the representatives of the Dutch Women's League for International Disarmament. Fischer informed them in a passionate speech that their objectives and those of the Republics were the same. The Republics did not want to arm, but were forced to do so; they did not want war, but were forced into it. What the Republics want is peace and harmony, not war and deathblows.

It is clear that the Dutch government will not intervene – unless France, Russia, Germany and the United States of America jointly intervene and thus put pressure on Britain. On the other hand, the Dutch people, Queen and government unanimously support the Republic's war effort and will help where they can.

The deputation's next objective is a visit to America in an attempt to convince President McKinley's administration to intervene on the Boer side. On 28 April they had discussions with numerous foreign societies that support the Boer cause, in preparation for this visit. Yesterday they arrived here in Rotterdam to prepare for their journey to America. A crowd of thousands of singing and rejoicing people welcomed them in this busiest harbour city in Europe. This morning they went to the harbour accompanied by song and music. An abundance of wreaths, albums, valuable medals and other gifts were handed to them by the crowd of well wishers. It took them literally hours to reach the quay from where they boarded the *Maasdam*.

At five o'clock this afternoon the huge passenger liner finally left. Dozens of small steamboats and myriad other ocean-going boats of various kinds, all packed with people, accompanied the *Maasdam* out of the harbour. It was an amazing sight and mirrors the huge enthusiasm for the Republican cause that has taken hold of this cradle of the Afrikaner nation.

FROM THE EDITOR

Last week was not an easy one for the Republican forces, with a series of setbacks and only a few positive developments. The prevalence of desertion from the Boer forces is worrying, as well as the incapacity of their military authorities to do anything about it. We doubt if it possible to force the burghers back to the front. As Chief Commandant Christiaan de Wet remarked shortly after the British occupation of Bloemfontein: 'You cannot hunt hares with unwilling dogs.' It is equally difficult to confront a victorious military force with demoralised warriors.

On the diplomatic front, the Republican deputation in Europe receives massive moral support, but is given an unmistakable cold shoulder when actual intervention is mentioned. It is to be doubted if any meaningful support will be forthcoming from the United States of America either. The Americans simply do not have sufficient interests in South Africa to be prepared to protect them at the cost of good relations with Britain. The fact is that we are on our own. The future of the Republics will be determined firstly by the way in which the burghers defend their freedom.

OUR MILITARY OFFICERS

Colonel John Blake

John Y.F. Blake is the American commander of the Irish Brigade in the Republican forces. He was born in 1856 in the American State of Missouri and raised on a cattle farm in Texas. In 1871 he enrolled at the Arkansas State University. Subsequently he entered the military academy in West Point, graduating in 1880. In the decade that followed he fought against the Apache Indians in the southwest of the USA, then resigned from the American armed forces.

In 1895 Blake visited Southern Africa and decided to settle here at least temporarily. The next year he participated in the suppression of the Matebele uprising in Rhodesia. Subsequently he moved to the Witwatersrand. With the outbreak of the war last October he immediately offered his services to the Transvaal military authorities. He was appointed as a Colonel and established the Irish Brigade, made up mostly of Irish Americans who were working on the gold fields.

Blake is a courageous fighter and his brigade has an excellent reputation. They initially served on the Natal front but this month participated in the attempts to halt the British offensive through the Orange Free State. He and his men are often in the forefront of the battles. Unfortunately one of his hands was badly hurt in the Battle of Modderspruit in Natal last October. Of all the foreign officers, he is probably the one with the most military talent – perhaps as a result of his experiences in the wars against the American Indians.

Colonel John Blake

THE War Reporter
WEEKLY EDITION

Number 32 — Pretoria, South African Republic — 19 May 1900

KROONSTAD OCCUPIED BY THE KHAKIS
BOER FORCES RETREAT TO THE RENOSTER RIVER

Renoster River, 18 May – The massive British force of Field Marshal Roberts occupied Kroonstad last Saturday. The fate of the temporary Free State capital was sealed on 10 May, with the negative result of the clash at Sand River. The burghers defending Kroonstad occupied positions on the Bosrand, a few kilometres south of the town. This was not a good defensive position and could easily be outflanked. Nevertheless Commandant-General Louis Botha ordered the Transvaal and Free State burghers to occupy it on 11 May. He had a few guns at his disposal. The British approached the Bosrand from the south by late morning. The Boers opened fire on them and the Khakis fired back but neither could gain the upper hand.

By this time the burghers were anything but confident of their ability to halt the Khakis. The same situation as last week, when a large number of Transvaal burghers simply deserted from the front, now threatened to occur amongst the Free State burghers. Fortunately President Steyn's courage did wonders for morale when he arrived on the Bosrand with a bandolier instead of the usual presidential sash around his shoulders and a Mauser rifle in his hands.

While the battle at Bosrand was raging, Chief Commandant Christiaan de Wet and General Philip Botha, who were just outside Kroonstad at that time, decided that there would be no sense in attempting to defend the town, especially since a number of scouts reported that the British cavalry was already outflanking the town. Consequently the burghers took as many supplies as possible to the station, including almost all their guns, loaded them on trains and sent them away to the north. At five o'clock that afternoon President Steyn left the town on horseback. Just outside of Kroonstad he climbed into a carriage and proceeded to Heilbron, which will now serve as capital.

Botha retreated from the Bosrand soon before dark when it became clear to him that the British would attempt to encircle the Boer forces. He ensured that Colonel Blake and his Irish Brigade destroyed a shed packed with war supplies in Kroonstad and blew up the bridge across the Vals River.

The last Republican forces had retreated from the town by 11 o'clock that evening under his leadership. By that time a British patrol had destroyed the culvert on the railway line directly north of the town, but the last train had fortunately already departed.

It seems that the British only realised after dawn on the 12th that the Boers had abandoned Kroonstad. By two o'clock that afternoon the first Khakis entered the dusty streets of the town with great ceremony. In the meantime the Boers had retreated to the north and taken up position here at the Renoster River. They destroyed all the railway culverts and bridges from Kroonstad to Roodewal Station with dynamite to slow down the British advance.

Last week, just before the British breakthrough at the Sand River, the war council of the Boer forces took two important decisions. The first was to burn the veld in front of the advancing British troops to eliminate the advantage that their Khaki coloured uniforms allowed them. The second was to bring the Creusot siege guns, or Long Toms as they are called by the burghers, to the front as a counter to the huge British naval guns. In an attempt to increase the mobility of the Long Toms, the war council proposed that experiments should be carried out to mount one of the guns on an open railway truck.

Reports from elsewhere in the Orange Free State indicate one setback after another for the Republican forces. British columns have occupied Lindley, Ladybrand, Clocolan and Hoopstad – and Roberts and his forces will sooner or later resume their advance from Kroonstad.

De Wet (third from left) and Botha (third from right) discussing strategy at Kroonstad

Boers trucking guns at Kroonstad

BOER ATTACK ON MAFEKING FAILS
Commandant Sarel Eloff made prisoner of war

Boer laager outside Mafeking, 13 May – After the Boers successfully withstood Colonel Plumer's attempt to relieve the British garrison from Bechuanaland on 31 March, nothing of military importance occurred around Mafeking. The Khakis in the town were simply too well entrenched in underground tunnels and behind bulwarks. The Long Tom gun that was used to bombard the British was later on returned to Pretoria since it could accomplish nothing against the enemy.

The besiegers never seriously considered attacking the town. They kept themselves occupied by ensuring that no food could reach Mafeking, believing that sooner or later the garrison would be forced by starvation to surrender. Early last month President Kruger suggested to General J.P. Snyman, the commander of the Boer forces at Mafeking, that he should recruit volunteers to storm the town. Each volunteer would be paid five pounds in cash and promised a part of the booty. Snyman was not prepared to do that, since he was afraid that the attack would end in failure.

The only Boer officer who was in favour of storming Mafeking was Commandant Sarel Eloff, the grandson of the President. He claimed that 400 volunteers would be sufficient to carry out the task, and the authorities in Pretoria accepted his offer to lead a charge. Failing to recruit enough volunteers amongst the burghers around Mafeking, Eloff spread his recruitment campaign to Johannesburg and Pretoria with advertisements in newspapers. In this way he gathered a force of only about 100 volunteers, including groups of French, German and Swiss men, who arrived here at the laagers last week.

After consultations with General Snyman on the way in which the remaining burghers would support the charge with diversionary attacks and supportive actions, Eloff and his total force of 260 volunteers completed their preparations for the charge on the evening of 11 May. Soon after midnight yesterday morning they made their way to the dry bed of the Molopo River west of the town with the aim of attacking from there. As far as they could ascertain, the British were not prepared for what would happen at all.

At four o'clock yesterday morning Eloff began his attack. Initially everything progressed according to plan. The burghers reached the Barolong town some two kilometres southwest of the centre of Mafeking without encountering much resistance. Here they torched a few huts as a signal for Snyman to launch diversionary attacks on other parts of Mafeking. The sound of exploding bombs and of gunfire from all around spurred Eloff and his men on. Soon they arrived at the old fort of the British South African Police between the Barolong town and the main town. The British garrison there were totally surprised by their unexpected visitors and were easily forced to surrender. A total of 32 Khakis, including Colonel Baden-Powell's second-in-command, Colonel Hoare, were taken prisoner and detained in a storage room. However, Eloff and his volunteers, of whom only about 100 had reached the fort, could not make any further progress on their own.

As for Snyman, he simply did not honour his part of the arrangement. His failure to attack the town with any determination gave Baden-Powell the opportunity to regain the initiative. He encircled Eloff and his men in the fort with the assistance of armed Barolong men and fired heavily on them. The battle went on for the whole day, and by seven o'clock that evening it was clear that all was lost. Eloff and his officers agreed that a number of the volunteers would attempt to flee in the dark while the rest would remain behind.

The volunteers who had to flee ran as quickly as possible from the fort, taking the same route by which they had entered the town that morning. They made use of walls and houses to find shelter, since the Khakis fired wildly on them. Eventually they reached the safety of the dry bed of the Molopo River, where they found a group of the volunteers whom they had left behind early that morning when they stormed the town. These volunteers had fought the whole day to ensure that the Boers in the fort would not be made prisoners of war and were delighted to meet their comrades. All of them now retreated together. A British force attempted to confront them but they got away and eventually reached the safety of the Boer laager. Six of them were wounded during their flight.

As for Eloff and the other volunteers, we heard today via a British messenger that they surrendered soon after their comrades had fled. The messenger even brought a photograph of Eloff that was taken this morning as evidence that he was in their hands. Thus the attack on Mafeking ended in a total disaster for the Boers. Altogether 98 burghers were made prisoners of war while 10 men were killed. British losses, according to this messenger, were a total of four Khakis and eight Barolong warriors killed and about 20 wounded.

The British South African Police fort in Mafeking, briefly occupied by Commandant Eloff

FROM THE EDITOR

The prospects for the Boer Republics – especially the Orange Free State – are still anything but rosy. Indeed, the total failure of the Republican forces to avert the British occupation of Kroonstad is cause for concern. From the far southwestern districts of the Transvaal we have received unconfirmed reports that Christiana has been occupied by the Khakis – the first town in the ZAR to suffer that fate. And from Natal the news is that the Transvaal forces have retreated to Laing's Nek.

In addition to the fall of Kroonstad, the saddest news of the week is that fact that the British have managed to relieve the besieged garrison of Mafeking. This siege was a catastrophe for the Republican cause, from beginning to end. The implications are much greater than simply that a small town has been relieved. Mafeking has become a symbol of British determination and Boer incompetence, and the opportunity to turn this perception around has now finally disappeared.

Positive developments that we report on this week include the steadfastness displayed by the Boer women. We trust that their determination not to falter in their stand against the enemy will become the measure for all the actions of the Republicans.

MAFEKING RELIEVED BY THE BRITISH

De la Rey fails to hold back the Khakis

In the veld near Mafeking, 17 May – The British garrison in Mafeking was relieved today. General J.P. Snyman, the commander of the Boer forces during the siege, had already heard on 6 May that a large British column was approaching the town. On 9 May he received an order from Commandant-General Louis Botha to send burghers in a southerly direction to attempt to check the British column near Kraaipan. He immediately gathered a force for that purpose.

General P.J. Liebenberg, commanding a joint force of Western Transvaal burghers and Cape rebels from Griqualand West, also received an order to hold back that British column. Liebenberg and his men joined a commando of about 200 burghers from Mafeking under Commandant Daantjie Botha on 12 May. Their combined strength amounted to approximately 450 men with four guns. They took up position at Koedoesrand, about 60 kilometres from here, and were determined to confront the Khakis. On Sunday 13 May, however, they heard that a British column of about 1 300 men was bypassing them in the west. Liebenberg immediately ordered his men to charge the enemy even though it was almost dusk. A brief skirmish followed in which men on both sides were killed or wounded.

General Koos de la Rey joined Liebenberg's forces a day or so later at Rietfontein. He had been at the Sand River last week when he heard that the British had resumed their offensive on the Transvaal western border. That was alarming news for him, since many burghers who came from that area might simply abandon their commandos and go home to protect their farms. In an attempt to arrange an orderly turn of events, De la Rey requested a transfer to the western border on 9 May. Both President Kruger and Commandant-General Botha approved of his request.

On Tuesday 15 May Boer scouts reported that the British column from the south, commanded by Colonel Mahon, had united with the forces of Colonel Plumer, against whom the Boers had previously fought north of Mafeking. The combined Khaki force, consisting of about 2 000 men with 14 guns, was at that time at Jan Massibi's village about 30 kilometres west of the besieged town.

The last battle before the British relief of the siege took place yesterday on Israel's Farm. Generals De la Rey and Liebenberg positioned their burghers on both sides of the Molopo River along the route they expected the British would use to approach Mafeking. As De la Rey expected, the British moved into the ambush, but the burghers failed to use the opportunity to destroy the enemy force. When the Khakis realised that they were virtually surrounded, they charged wildly at the burghers. The inexperienced Rustenburg Commando fought off two British attacks but them suddenly fled for no apparent reason. That gave the Khakis an opportunity to escape.

Liebenberg's commando south of the river was still in position when darkness set in that evening. Unaware that the Rustenburg burghers had fled, De la Rey went to the north to investigate the situation. That almost resulted in his own capture. De la Rey told our correspondent today:

'At eight o'clock yesterday evening I walked with my two sons to the white house next to the Molopo River where I had left the Marico Commando. We passed between mounted men when somebody called out: "Halt, who goes there?" Only then did I realise that the commandos had gone and that we were in the midst of the enemy. I did not answer: my sons and I merely turned around and walked away. The 10 mules of our ammunition wagon were all killed, but our artillerymen managed to haul the guns away. One of our men was wounded and the horses of a few others killed.'

The Boer loss in this battle was one man killed and eight wounded, while the British losses, according to a reliable source, were 40 killed and wounded.

Yesterday evening a section of nine British soldiers of Mahon and Plumer's joint column entered Mafeking unhindered. Early this morning, at about half past three, a huge British force entered the town, again unhindered, and their commander, Colonel Mahon, officially announced the relief of the town. Thus the siege ended after 216 days.

Snyman heard of the British entry into Mafeking before daybreak, and immediately ordered all his laagers to retreat. The Rustenburg laager got away unhindered, but at sunrise Snyman's main laager was still static. The British artillery used the opportunity to bombard the laager with the 12-pounder guns that had arrived with Mahon's column. These guns are much more potent than any previous British artillery used in this area. As a result most of the burghers fled for their lives. A treasure of property and supplies, including numerous wagons, tents, a small gun and even the field hospital, was abandoned and fell into British hands. Thus a useless siege that brought no glory at all to the Boers ended in a total humiliation for Snyman and his burghers.

BRITISH OFFENSIVE IN NATAL

BOERS RETREAT TO LAING'S NEK

Volksrust, 17 May – After the departure of Commandant-General Botha with a number of Boer commandos to the main front in the Orange Free State, some 4 000 Transvaal burghers remained behind in Natal under the command of General Lukas Meyer. Commandant Chris Botha was acting commander between Meyer's departure for the Volksraad session in Pretoria and his return on 11 May.

The Transvaal burghers have been rather passive in the past month, concentrating on defence. The single exception was when Captain Ricchiardi carried out a raid on the coal mine at Elandslaagte with 20 men of the Italian Corps on 7 May. Two Italians were wounded in a fierce exchange of fire, but they managed to capture the mine manager. We do not know what the British losses were.

Next day, General Buller's forces launched a full-scale offensive from Ladysmith. Three days later, Buller and his vanguard reached the drift of the Sundays River. The burghers had taken up excellent positions in the Biggarsberg mountain range to confront the Khakis, but on Monday 14 May, tragically, it seems as if a misunderstanding occurred when Meyer misinterpreted a message from Commandant-General Botha and ordered a general retreat to the north. The British used the opportunity to occupy both Glencoe and Dundee.

On 16 May the retreating Boer forces reached the Laing's Nek area, where the Boers in 1881 had successfully checked General Colley's forces and achieved the glorious victory on Majuba Hill. Meyer's plan was to repeat that achievement. He ordered his burghers to prepare defensive positions and at his command the railway tunnel at Laing's Nek was dynamited so that it would not be of use to the British in the future. During their retreat the Boers had destroyed literally every bridge, culvert and pump station between Ladysmith and Laing's Nek. They are now determined to stick to their positions and to retreat not an inch further than the Drakensberg.

While the burghers are digging themselves in, the Khakis occupied Newcastle today.

The railway tunnel at Laing's Nek destroyed by Boer forces

General Lukas Meyer

THE BOER WOMEN AND THE WAR

Are the Khakis doomed to face female commandos?

Pretoria, 18 May – One often hears older people relate that the success of the Great Trek, 60 years ago, was due to the Voortrekker women. When the spirits of the Voortrekker men in Natal ran out by the winter of 1838, after the death of Piet Retief, Piet Uys and Gerrit Maritz, and after Hendrik Potgieter had left for the Transvaal, it was the women who encouraged them to keep going. A few years later, the elderly people point out, when the British annexed Natal and many of the men believed that further resistance would be futile, it was the women who said: 'We would rather walk with bare feet back across the Drakensberg to our freedom than remain under the British yoke.'

Events in the past month indicate that the Afrikaner women of today are every bit as determined as their predecessors of 60 years ago not to accept British rule. For the men who return to their houses with leave and who are then unwilling to return to the front, they have a clear message: women have much more respect for those men who fight for the fatherland than for those that remain at home. For cowards and weaklings they have no time whatsoever.

The *Standard & Diggers' News* of 23 April contains the text of a memorial from 18 women of the Carolina district in which they request Commandant Hendrik Prinsloo to commandeer all the men in their ward who are not doing military duty.

These men, the women claim, are healthy burghers with no disabilities and it is known that in peacetime they aspire with loud mouths to become candidates for public positions. Now they are sitting at home protecting their own interests. This is totally unacceptable.

It is clear that the loyal and proud Boer women especially detest deserters. Every day we hear of cases where women have notified the Republican military authorities of the presence of deserters on their own or neighbouring farms. Some deserters' wives threaten them that they will take up their rifles and take their places to serve in the commandos. Some women are deadly serious about the possibility of forming women's commandos. In the *Standard & Digger's News* of 5 May Maria Nel poses the question: 'Is it not time that the men who are too weak or too wretched to fight should return to their homes to look after the children so that the women can replace them at the front?' Another woman claims in the same newspaper that the men who are staying at home are nothing but accomplices in the murder and in the destruction of the fatherland. The women should go and fight instead, since one valiant woman is worth more than 100 cowardly men. Her proposal? Women should hold meetings in each town and ward and seriously consider the establishment of women's commandos.

Last week about 350 women of Maraisburg and Florida on the Witwatersrand gathered in the Irene Hall to consider ways of supporting the burghers on the front. Some of the more fiery speakers proposed that they should establish a Women's Corps. In the end resolutions were accepted in terms of which clerks and other non-fighting men who are fulfilling essential duties should be replaced by women, so that those men can proceed to the front to relieve the courageous burghers who had uninterruptedly been serving throughout the war up to now.

It is clear that the Boer women have had enough of weak-spirited burghers. But it is not only the women who feel unhappy about deserters and who are pleading for the establishment of a women's corps. There are many widows in the Republics who believe that their husbands did not die in vain, and who feel compelled to take their place and defend the fatherland against the merciless invader.

It is unlikely that the Khakis have taken the determination of the Boer women into account. If not, we have news for them. The speedy surrender of the Boer Republics is not even a possibility at the moment, since the women of the Republics will definitely not allow it!

OUR MILITARY OFFICERS

Commandant Sarel Eloff

Sarel Johannes Eloff is the oldest son of Frederik Christoffel Eloff of Pretoria and his wife Elsje Fransina Kruger, a daughter of State President Paul Kruger. He was born in 1870 in Rustenburg. After completing school he joined the South African Republic Police in Pretoria. His affable nature and his ability to work very hard made a good impression on everybody. In 1894 he was promoted to lieutenant and commander of the Krugersdorp police.

At the time of the Jameson Raid at the end of 1895 Eloff undertook a daring reconnaissance expedition that had a determining effect on the successful actions of the Republican forces against the invaders. Jameson's freebooters actually captured him during their advance on Johannesburg, but later on released him, after which he rode on horseback to spread the news from Rustenburg to Krugersdorp that the invaders were on their way. Thus the burgher forces were warned in time to take the necessary precautions against the invasion. After the capture of the freebooters, Eloff escorted Jameson and his officers from Krugersdorp to Pretoria.

Eloff's promotion to captain followed last year when he was appointed as the first commander of the recently completed Johannesburg fort. Soon after the outbreak of the war in October he was sent to the northern front. His first military experience was gained when he took command of the artillery during the fight between the Boers and the British in the Tuli area. After the events at Derdepoort on the Bechuanaland border in November, when the Bakgatla attacked the settlement and murdered a few white civilians, Eloff was sent to that area to contain the black communities.

His task on the Bechuanaland border did not provide enough challenges for Eloff. He requested to be transferred to a more active front. Last month he was given the rank of commandant and sent to Mafeking to support General Snyman in the siege of the British garrison. His plan to storm the town on 11 May (as is related elsewhere in this issue) failed due to reasons outside his control and he was made a prisoner of war.

Commandant Sarel Eloff

THE War Reporter
WEEKLY EDITION

Number 33 — Pretoria, South African Republic — 26 May 1900

BRITISH OCCUPY NORTHERN FREE STATE
Khaki vanguard crosses the Vaal

In the veld south of Johannesburg, 25 May – The British overran the Boer positions on the Renoster River in this week and advanced to the Vaal River. It will take a huge effort from our burghers to prevent the occupation of Johannesburg. In the meantime the Khakis are consolidating their hold on the northern Free State.

Since the British were clearly in a very strong position after occupying Kroonstad last week, the Free State government decided on Saturday to shift their seat from Heilbron in the northern Free State to Vrede far in the northeast. At that stage there were about 4 000 burghers stationed at the Renoster River north of Kroonstad. Their morale seemed to be high. However, only one day later, things went terribly wrong. The British moved to cross the Renoster, seemingly on their way to occupy Heilbron, and the left flank of the Boers bore the brunt of the attack. Even though the burghers fought courageously at first, they subsequently retreated with the excuse that they were afraid of being outflanked. That gave the Khakis the opportunity to cross the river and pitch camp on the north bank. The enemy casualties in this battle were very high, according to reliable sources: 62 Khakis killed and wounded and 20 taken prisoner of war. On the Boer side one man was killed and seven wounded.

The British breakthrough on the Renoster River was accomplished so easily that the Republican authorities were almost taken by surprise. President Steyn, assisted by Chief Commandant Christiaan de Wet, barely managed to escape in time from Heilbron, fleeing under bombardment in the direction of Frankfort.

Meanwhile the railway wagons with the Free State government documents were sent to the north, as was the Long Tom gun that had previously been mounted on a low-bed railway wagon. Some burghers feel that this Long Tom should have been used against the Khakis instead of being towed away. By the 22nd the Boers had fallen back to the Vaal River south of Vereeniging and the British had occupied Heilbron.

The British vanguard did not halt after its successes in the northern Free State. In spite of the attempts by the Republican forces to stop them a British unit crossed the Vaal River at the Old Viljoensdrift near Parys. Today British units also crossed the river at Lindequesdrift and from there proceeded in an easterly direction.

Boers crossing the Vaal River

REPUBLICAN FORCES STAND STRONG IN NATAL
GENERAL CHRISTIAAN BOTHA SUCCEEDS MEYER AS COMMANDER-IN-CHIEF

Volksrust, 25 May – Here on the Natal front, the Republican forces held their positions easily this week. In addition the burghers scored a decisive victory over a British patrol on 20 May at Scheepersnek, about 10 kilometres southwest of Vryheid.

Boer scouts noticed late that morning that a British patrol of 400 men with three guns was approaching Vryheid from the direction of Nqutu. This patrol seemed to be oblivious to the fact that there could be danger lurking, since the mounted Khakis were advancing far ahead of the infantry. Commandant Blignaut of the Swaziland Commando realised that an ideal opportunity was presenting itself to teach the British a lesson. His 80 men quickly took up sheltered positions in Scheepersnek. The inattentive Khaki horsemen rode straight into the trap before the burghers opened a murderous fire on them at short range. The Khakis fought back desperately and managed to fall back to Nqutu.

The Boer losses are one man killed, one wounded and one captured. This is minimal compared to the British loss of 27 dead, 25 wounded, 11 taken prisoner of war and 29 horses killed. In addition the burghers captured one machine gun and 26 horses. They are now filled with confidence for the future.

One of the most talked-about developments in the last week on this front is the appointment of General Christiaan Botha as the new commander-in-chief. We have heard that President Kruger himself has recalled General Lukas Meyer to Pretoria. The reason seems to be that Meyer refused to have a Long Tom gun stationed on the summit of Mol's Kop, from where the gunners would have had an excellent view of Laing's Nek pass, since he believed it would be too difficult to retrieve the gun from the hill if the Boers were forced to retire in a hurry.

In the meantime the British advance units in Natal have reached the Ingogo River immediately south of Laing's Nek. This is in the vicinity of Schuinshoogte, where the Transvaal burghers of General Nicolaas Smit convincingly defeated General Colley's redcoats during the Transvaal War of Independence on 8 February 1881. Last week there was a skirmish between a British patrol and burghers commanded by General D.J.E. Erasmus on O'Neill's Farm, on the slopes of Majuba Hill.

Railway bridge at Wasbank destroyed by Boers

FOREIGN MISSION IN AMERICA
HERO'S WELCOME BUT NO PROMISES OF SUPPORT

Pretoria, 25 May – The members of the foreign mission of the Boer Republics have been received as heroes in the United States of America. However, they have not yet managed to gain any significant support for the Boer cause. All indications are that the Republics will for the foreseeable future stand alone against the mighty British Empire.

The Boer deputation, consisting of Abraham Fischer and C.H. Wessels of the Orange Free State and A.D.W. Wolmarans of the Transvaal, left Rotterdam on 3 May on board the ship *Maasdam*. On their departure the deputation issued a statement that they were going to America to seek help to restore peace in South Africa. More than a century ago, the American people faced the same challenge as that confronting the Afrikaner people today; they too had to fight to defend their rights and freedom. The British press and government enjoy issuing all sorts of slanderous untruths about the Republics, and the deputation will enjoy having the opportunity to state their cause personally to the American people and government. Fischer stated it quite plainly: 'We pray for nothing but peace and the possession of something as dear to us as to the American people: our independence, without taking away any rights of any other people.'

According to telegraphic reports that reached us via the Atlantic Ocean, the news that the deputation was on its way generated tremendous enthusiasm among the Americans. The ship arrived in New York harbour on 15 May. A huge crowd welcomed them, including a committee of the inhabitants of New York City that was especially formed for this purpose. Since then numerous committees and societies have received them and dozens of addresses have been handed to them. In these they are repeatedly assured of the admiration of the Americans for the Boers' patriotism and heroic spirit, and of condolences for the difficult position in which they find themselves in the uneven struggle. The most important American newspapers, including the *New York Times* and the *Washington Post*, report prominently on the mission.

On 17 May the deputation was given a major honour when the freedom of the city of New York was granted to them. Subsequently they journeyed to the American capital, Washington DC. Here again they were enthusiastically welcomed. On 21 May their first official appointment followed when they were received by the American Secretary of State, John Hay. The latter was courteous, and perhaps even friendly, but he disappointed the deputation. He read a written, official statement in which the American President expressed the wish that the war in South Africa would soon come to an end. The President furthermore promised to do all in his power and to utilise any opportunity to mediate between Britain and the Republics. However, Hay added that the President would follow a policy of strict neutrality since it would be in everybody's best interest.

On 22 May President McKinley himself received the deputation members. He was particularly friendly, but did not change his point of view. Indeed, the general trend of all discussions between the deputation members and prominent Americans, as well as the editorials of the best known American newspapers, implies that the United States will do nothing to endanger its good relations with Britain. Nobody believes that direct American assistance to the Boer Republics will follow, even though at least 90 per cent of Americans are sympathetic towards the Boers.

Naturally, the members of the deputation are disappointed with this state of affairs. Fischer issued a statement saying that he appreciated the honesty of the American authorities. He added that the deputation would from now on put its emphasis on the collection of funds for widows and orphans in South Africa. The implication is that the deputation will, for the time being, remain in the United States.

69

FROM THE EDITOR

Our worst fears have been realised: the Khakis are in the Transvaal. It was simply not possible for the Republican military authorities and for the courageous burghers to check the enemy. There are numerous reasons for this, including the huge British numerical advantage, the many burghers who evade their duty, the lack of military talent of numerous Republican officers, and the unwillingness of foreign powers to put pressure on the British Empire to halt its military activities in South Africa.

What are we to do now? Some Republicans feel that the time has come for us to accept that our freedom is lost. They ask: will it necessarily be that terrible under British rule? Would it not be in our best interests to join the victor? The huge majority of Republicans, ourselves included, reject the option of throwing in the towel. The honour of our descendants demands from us to fulfil our duty to carry on with the struggle.

The occupation of Pretoria in the near future seems unavoidable. This will have a direct influence on the future of this newspaper, since our offices and printing press are in the capital. We are preparing to make use of a mobile printing press, and we face an uncertain future – but we promise to do our utmost to publish as usual.

NEWS FROM THE BRITISH CAPITAL

Ecstasy over relief of Mafeking

Pretoria, 25 May – It is reported from London that the British Minister of Colonies, Joseph Chamberlain, revealed the true British intentions as regards the Republics at a public meeting in Birmingham about two weeks ago. He announced that the British government plans to annex the Republics. We suspected all along that the driving force behind British policy in South Africa was naked imperialism. Now Chamberlain has confirmed our suspicions.

Other news from London is that the relief of Mafeking was greeted with excessive joy in the British capital. Traffic came to a standstill on the evening of 17 May when people started dancing in the streets.

The festivities went on for the best part of three nights and two days. According to the *Daily Telegraph*, it was an unequalled exhibition of enthusiasm in British history:

'Never have the scenes of irrepressible and irresistible enthusiasm ... been equalled in the memory of man or the records of the Empire. Never can they be forgotten by the generation which they have thrilled to the marrow and swept beyond all ordinary limits of nature by the splendid and passionate impulse of national enthusiasm flashed round the world, and making one vast electric circuit of the entire British race.'

THE CAPE GOVERNMENT AND THE WAR

Cape Town, 20 May – The Cape political scene is at present totally dominated by the war issue. The Cape Cabinet of Prime Minister W.P. Schreiner last month proposed to the British government that amnesty should be granted to all Cape rebels, excluding the leading figures. The British Minister of Colonies, Joseph Chamberlain, rejected this proposal since it would, he argues, be unjust to the 'loyalists'. According to Chamberlain, all the rebels must be punished. His answer divided the Cape Cabinet. Richard Solomon supports Chamberlain, while Dr. T.N.G. te Water rejects Chamberlain's opinion, since it ignores the Cape's constitutional right to self-government.

DEVELOPMENTS IN THE LOWER VAAL RIVER AREA

First Khakis enter Transvaal territory

Bloemhof, 20 May – The first British soldiers crossed the lower Vaal River near Windsorton on 4 May. General Sarel du Toit, who commanded a force of 700 burghers and Cape rebels with one field gun, confronted those Khakis at Rooidam, southwest of Warrenton, the next day. They managed to check all the British advances, and in the meantime sent urgent messages to General A.P.J. Cronjé to assist them. When the field gun became defunct and no help arrived, they retreated to the north. How great the British casualties were, we do not know. On the Boer side it was rather heavy: 11 men dead, 17 wounded and three taken prisoner of war.

On 6 May the British bombarded General du Toit's camp at Veertien Strome. The burghers initially offered stiff resistance, but retreated westwards when they realised that their position was becoming untenable. The British then occupied Veertien Strome village, and General Cronjé retreated with his burghers to Christiana.

Despite their success at Veertien Strome, the first British troops only entered the Transvaal on 15 May, crossing the Republican border west of Christiana. A day later those troops, led by General Hunter, occupied Christiana, making it the first Transvaal town to fall into British hands.

NEWS OF THE PRISONERS OF WAR

Dismal conditions in Green Point camp

Cape Town, 15 April – A Free State burgher, Schalk Burger, who was made a prisoner of war at Paardeberg, managed to send us the following report on conditions in the prisoner-of-war camp at Green Point in Cape Town:

'We left the Modder River on 3 March by train for Cape Town – 25 men in a cattle truck, so bunched up that we could hardly sit, much less sleep. We were amazed at the empty, rocky landscape between Victoria West Station and Laingsburg – with neither grass nor water, but only a few bushes. There is no place anywhere where one can plough the earth. When the sun rose on 5 March we were in Worcester, a large, picturesque town, with fruit and other trees. There seems to be enough water here and the whole area looks much better.

'At Wellington a young girl attempted to hand us a basket filled with fruit, but the guards chased her off. That was such a shock to her that she fainted. Soon we were in Cape Town with its bustle of railway lines, electrical trams, bicycles, horse cabbies and at least 150 ships in the bay. We had to get off the train and walk through the streets with our bundles. Three times we were halted for cameramen to take our pictures.

'While we were thus walking, some bystanders mocked us and others expressed sympathy. To me it felt as it must have felt to our Saviour when he had to carry his cross to Calvary – the one cried, the other mocked. Thus for example a brown man asked one of our elderly comrades: 'Hey, you *backvelder*, where is your pass? Where is Paul?' – probably meaning President Paul Kruger.

'In the harbour we boarded the ship *Orient* – a huge ship with six levels. There were altogether 1 800 of us on the ship, in addition to the crew. From the deck we had a beautiful view of the city at the foot of Table Mountain with Lion's Head and Devil's Peak on both sides, and at our back Robben Island.

'By dusk our journey to Simonstown began. Soon after breakfast the next morning we reached our destination. Simonstown is not an attractive village – it looks rather monotonous in the midst of barren, rocky mountains. There were 10 or more ships in the bay. Some of the others also had prisoners of war on deck.

'On our ships there were millions of lice. The hammocks and the blankets that were used by the troops and then by us, were overrun with lice. We were involved in a never-ending battle with those insects. That conflict went on for the 17 days that we were on the ocean. The rest of the time we spent washing our clothes, stitching, having religious meetings, reading and staring at the ocean with longing in our hearts.

'On 17 March the British fired a salute from the two warships in the bay and from the forts on the shore and hoisted numerous flags. On some ships there were no less than 50 flags. We were then informed that Bloemfontein had been occupied. The Khakis cheered and drank themselves into a stupor, while we prayed and cried since our capital was in the power of the enemy.

'A few days later we sailed back to Cape Town. We were offloaded again and had to walk with our bundles to the Green Point sports grounds. There we were divided into groups of 12 and placed in tents. I am the corporal in our tent. Each morning and each afternoon we are counted and then the British carry out tent inspection. Each Saturday we take down the tents so that everything can be disinfected with lime and carbolic acid.

'The camp is about 300 metres in length and 80 metres broad, and surrounded by a strong grid about two metres high. There are about 200 tents and approximately 2 000 prisoners of war in the camp. Armed guards surround it day and night. There are some 200 toilets and 16 bathhouses. On the one side there is a large pavilion. In addition there are cookhouses and washing rooms as well as a shop in one of the huge tents where those of us who have money can buy anything that they need.

'On Sundays the Reverend Alheit holds services for us on the pavilion. He has provided Bibles and hymn books for those of us who have none. In addition he has appointed teachers to educate the youngsters and provide reading matter. A lady from Stellenbosch sent us a harmonium.

'Within a week after our arrival measles and fever spread through the camp. After a few days 200 men were ill. Only then did we realise there was no hospital. Men died daily – up to seven on one day. We were frightened. We could not flee. Our condition was poor. Altogether 120 of us have so far died of diseases.

'In a camp like this there are many types of people. There are the religious ones and the atheists. There are the honourable ones and the mean ones, the thieves, those who seek glory and those who insult God. While some hold religious meetings or mourn over dead or dying relatives, others play cards or dance to the music of violins and concertinas.

'One evening at dusk an awful thing happened. A group of youngsters were busy singing hymns in the light of the electric lamp near the fence, when a guard suddenly fired on them and killed Philip Cronjé. There were immediately a thousand men present to see what had happened. The colonel and the doctor took away the dying Cronjé for treatment, but he succumbed within hours. It was heart-rending that our compatriot was thus killed without having done anything wrong. There would have been a sporting competition in our camp the next day, but we cancelled it out of sympathy with our friend.'

Boer prisoners of war being escorted through Cape Town

BOERS RETREAT TO THE VAAL RIVER

Mangold reports from the front line

Vereeniging, 24 May – Wilhelm Mangold of the Heidelberg Commando has just handed our correspondent the following report on the retreat to the Vaal River, during which he found himself in the front line most of the time.

'After we were forced to retreat from Kroonstad on 12 May, all the commandos took up defensive positions along the Renoster River. We burnt down the grass on the southern bank of the river and dug ourselves in carefully. Colonel Blake and the Irish Corps destroyed the railway line in several places, as a result of which the iron rails stood like huge horns in the air. We were deployed next to the railway line. About 800 metres behind us the authorities kept a train ready behind a hillock to pick up the burghers who had no horses as well as our supplies if we were forced to fall back quickly.

'The Boers without horses are not foot soldiers in the real sense of the word. Many have only themselves to blame for the fact that they are now on foot. Some did not look after their horses properly. Others lost their horses on purpose since they hoped to be relieved from active war service and from participation in battles on the grounds that they had no horses. Each Boer on foot has to carry his own blanket and other necessities on his back. As a result they look like a team of labourers looking for work. The mounted Boers often mock them mercilessly with questions such as: 'Looking for work, boy? What do you want per month? Where is your pass?'

'We spent eight days at the Renoster River. Unfortunately we no longer have tents, since ours were sent off somewhere from Brandfort and we have no idea what happened to them. On 20 May our commandant, J.D. Weilbach, was ordered to proceed with our whole commando to Heilbron to defend it against the enemy. We travelled non-stop for almost two days and two nights. After some time we heard gunfire, but were not allowed to investigate what was going on.

'On one occasion we came upon a poor Boer woman. She treated us to milk, coffee and bread and gave us eggs to take with us on the road when we left. In answer to a question about what we owed her, she refused to take any payment: "No, what are you thinking? I am a Boer woman. My husband is also in the veld. He told me it is wonderful if you are received in a friendly fashion when you are on the road. Our women would rather die than accept the yoke of the enemy on our necks. Don't even think of us, but think of the freedom of our country and keep fighting to the death for it."

'We failed to accomplish our task at Heilbron, and left again empty-handed in this direction. In the bitterly cold nights we had to stay in the veld without any shelter. Back at the railway line we came across a huge maize field. Since the commandos were on the retreat and the owners of the fields were gone, we burnt down the maize along with the grass next to the railway line. In an attempt to slow down the enemy's approach, we kept destroying all bridges and culverts.

'Yesterday evening we crossed the Vaal River. Many burghers surmise that we are going to take up strong defensive positions all along this river. Today is Queen Victoria's birthday. Many of us, including myself, unexpectedly got leave, since our military authorities do not expect a British attack. Even though this would be for 24 hours only, I am leaving for home now. Home is Heidelberg, five hours on horseback from here. It's going to be lovely to see the family again, even though it will only be for a few hours. Tomorrow we have to be back early. Everybody says we are going to resist the Khakis with all our force.'

OUR MILITARY OFFICERS

General Christiaan Botha

Christiaan Botha is a younger brother of Commandant General Louis Botha. He was born at Greytown in Natal in 1864. His parents were Louis Botha and his wife Salomina. Botha was one of the first inhabitants of the New Republic of which Vryheid was the capital. In 1887, when the New Republic was incorporated into the South African Republic as the Vryheid district, he automatically became a citizen of the ZAR.

Botha became the commandant of the Police in Swaziland in 1898. Last year, with the outbreak of this war, he and his men went to the Natal front. He participated in numerous battles in this area, including the battle of Colenso in December last year. On 16 February this year he narrowly escaped death when a lyddite shell fired by the enemy exploded in a trench where he sheltered, killing seven burghers in his immediate vicinity on impact.

After the British relief of Ladysmith, Botha and his men fell back to the north towards Laing's Nek, where he was promoted to Commander-in-Chief this week. Most burghers regard the promotion as a fitting reward for this courageous and capable young general.

General Chris Botha

THE War Reporter

WEEKLY EDITION

Number 34   Pretoria, South African Republic   2 June 1900

KRUGER LEAVES PRETORIA
CAPITAL WILL NOT BE DEFENDED

Pretoria, 30 May – Today it became known here in Pretoria that the government has left the city. President Kruger and a number of his advisors left by horse-drawn coach for Eerste Fabrieken, a railway station some distance east of Pretoria, yesterday evening. In order to ensure that panic would not spread amongst the inhabitants, the government made no announcement about this move and issued no public statement. The maintenance of law, order and peace in the city has been made the responsibility of the honourable Louis de Souza, the Secretary of the War Department, and P.J. Potgieter, the mayor. Militarily the city is under the command of General Lukas Meyer.

On the last full day that Kruger spent in Pretoria he was the centre of a very touching ceremony. His servants and officials were already busy packing his baggage when he received a young American schoolboy at his house. The visitor was Jimmy Smith, who handed Kruger an address that contains a message of sympathy with the President and the Boers in their independence struggle against the British Empire. The message was signed by 29 000 school boys of Philadelphia, Boston and New York in the United States. The Americans have themselves fought two wars to secure their own freedom from London. Smith also handed Kruger a Transvaal flag that was stitched in America.

It was no easy task for our elderly President to say farewell to his wife and to leave his house. Nobody knows how long it will be before his return. Early this morning he resumed his journey by train from Eerste Fabrieken on the eastern railway line to Machadodorp, which will serve as provisional capital.

This morning it became known here in Pretoria that General Lukas Meyer and Schalk Burger had given a letter to Mayor Potgieter authorising him to keep order in the town. As for the British prisoners of war, it has been decided that six or more of the highest ranking officers who are detained in the Staats Model School should be transferred to Waterval, some 25 kilometres north of the city, where approximately 3 000 British soldiers are being detained, to help maintain law and order there. About 300 burghers guard these prisoners, but the latter are becoming unruly. Potgieter must make it clear to them that violence will be answered with violence.

In the last place Potgieter was told that should it become impossible to check the British offensive, he should hand over the city to Lord Roberts or his representative, but that he would be responsible for law and order up to that moment. The city would not be defended. The government fear that the British will destroy all our beautiful buildings in a bombardment should we attempt to defend Pretoria. That was why they decided to abandon the city, as was done with Bloemfontein and Johannesburg. For some inhabitants of Pretoria this is a strange decision. In the past three years the government has spent thousands of pounds to build four forts – Schanskop, Klapperkop, Wonderboompoort and Daspoortrand – to defend the city. Now those forts are not even going to be used.

The news that President Kruger and the government have left led to the spreading of numerous alarmist and damaging rumours that have been greedily swallowed by some of the Pretorians. One such a rumour is that the President has made a secret deal with Roberts to hand the city over to him in exchange for a huge financial reward. This is a malignant lie. The second rumour is that the President took all the gold of the National Bank with him and is leaving his countrymen in a hopeless position. This rumour is not totally groundless. The government did indeed remove all the gold bars from the strong rooms of the bank and that gold is certainly worth a fortune. It has been transferred to an unknown but safe destination. The gold was certainly not with the President when he left on the train.

These rumours led to financial panic in Pretoria. Hundreds of clients of the commercial bank stormed to that institution and demanded their deposits. The money was of course not all available – a situation that created a panicky atmosphere in the city.

SCANDALOUS PLUNDERING OF STATE WAREHOUSE
Black day of lawlessness in central Pretoria

Pretoria, 31 May – While each true Republican in Pretoria is worried about the virtual certainty that the British will occupy the city, tonight many law-abiding and order-loving citizens are also filled with disgust at the scandalous activities of several dozens of Pretorians who are enriching themselves in a criminal way. Yesterday evening plunderers broke into the government magazines on the corner of Market and Visagie Streets, opposite the home of the late Commandant-General Piet Joubert, and carried away loot throughout the night. The severely depleted police force was helpless to prevent this. Indeed, it seems as if some members of the special police force participated in the plundering.

This morning the plundering continued in clear daylight. Many burghers merely indicated that they wanted fodder for their horses. Others explained to our correspondents that they were not actually doing anything wrong, since the supplies would fall into the hands of the British anyway and they wanted to prevent that.

While the plundering was still in progress, General Louis Botha suddenly arrived in the city on horseback. He addressed a crowd of well-wishers from the steps of the Government buildings, calling on everybody to preserve law and order. When a rumour subsequently spread that the British were on the point of occupying the city, the plunderers fled.

Pretorians looting state warehouses

ROBERTS 'ANNEXES' THE ORANGE FREE STATE
NEW NAME – ORANGE RIVER COLONY

Johannesburg, 28 May – Field Marshall Roberts and his British invaders reached the Vaal River on 27 May. The Khaki commander celebrated the event by formally annexing the Orange Free State as British territory. In the honour of Queen Victoria he post-dated the annexation to her birthday on 24 May. In the proclamation he declared that: 'The territories known as the Orange Free State are annexed to and form part of Her Majesty's dominions, and that provisionally and until Her Majesty's pleasure is fully declared, the said territories will be administered by me with such powers as aforesaid.'

Roberts in addition announced that the Free State will in future be known as the Orange River Colony. This proclamation and this name are of course not recognised by President Steyn and his government. Indeed, the annexation is a farce, since Roberts cannot in any way claim that he is effectively controlling the Free State territory. He only controls the big towns and the rural areas where British forces are stationed.

JOHANNESBURG OCCUPIED

Pretoria, 1 June – Johannesburg was occupied yesterday in terms of an agreement between Lord Roberts and Dr F.E.T. Krause, the special commandant of the Golden City. The day started on a positive note for the Khakis when they occupied Doornkop, the site west of the city where Jameson and his invaders had been forced to hoist the white flag four and a half years ago. Next they occupied Florida and Roodepoort on the West Rand. In Johannesburg itself Commandant Ben Viljoen commandeered a huge amount of supplies with which he and his men fell back to the north. Krause subsequently rode southwards out of the city and negotiated with the commanders of the British invading force. He convinced them to delay the occupation of the city for 24 hours, arguing that the overhasty occupation of the city while there were still burghers within it would lead to street fighting and the deaths of numerous women and children.

By yesterday morning all the burghers had left the Golden City and the Khakis occupied it unopposed.

RECONCILIATION CONGRESS IN GRAAFF-REINET
Discussion centres on Afrikaans businesses

Graaff-Reinet, 1 June – The huge People's Congress of the Reconciliation Movement yesterday took place here in Graaff-Reinet. It was attended by about 1 500 representatives from a large number of districts.

This movement of Cape Afrikaners and other sympathisers with the Republics is attempting to convince Britain by constitutional means to end the war with the Republics, which it still recognises as independent.

One result of this Congress was an assembly today of about 100 of the representatives to yesterday's meeting, who discussed the present state of Afrikaans businesses in the Cape Colony. Urged by some of the representatives, the meeting stated its sympathies and convictions in a resolution so that the representatives will have something concrete to take to their districts.

The message of this resolution is that Afrikaners should act in a self-supporting way on all business fronts. The resolution reads as follows:

'This meeting, representative of various districts in the Colony, believes that the time has arrived that the Afrikaans people should start acting independently on all business levels; that all Afrikaans businesses should be supported as well as possible; and that each of the representatives here present undertake to do all in his or her ability to support this principle in the interest of the Afrikaner people.'

FROM THE EDITOR

The Republican prospects in this war become more gloomy by the day. We are in the grip of a paralysing uncertainty about our future. President Kruger has left his capital. The enemy has occupied Johannesburg. Lord Roberts claims to have annexed the Orange Free State. The Transvaal government has decided not to defend Pretoria if it should come to that. It is clear that we will have to adapt to completely changed circumstances.

When we look at our sister Republic in the south, however, there seems to be some cause for hope. The notable victories scored this week by General Piet de Wet at Lindley and by General Abraham de Villiers at Biddulphsberg amply prove that the pursuit of the war will remain possible after the occupation of our capital. The Free State burghers have not all disappeared and we will not either. Our faith must not waver. It is not for us to know what the Almighty has destined for us, but we must always remember what President Kruger often reminds us to do: 'Those who trust in God, have nothing to fear.'

BRITISH ATTACK ON BIDDULPHSBERG REPULSED

Noteworthy victory for Free Staters against huge Khaki force

Bethlehem, 30 May – Yesterday a British force consisting of about 4 000 soldiers with 12 guns attacked a commando of about 400 burghers with three guns at Biddulphsberg west of Senekal. The commander of the Khakis was Lieutenant General Lesley Rundle. General Abraham de Villiers commanded the Boers.

The first skirmish took place on 25 May when burghers fired on scouts of the British force that occupied Senekal that day.

At least four Khakis were killed, four wounded and 13 taken prisoner of war. For the next two days everything was quiet, but on 28 May Rundle left Senekal with virtually his whole force and advanced directly on Biddulphsberg. By late afternoon they were only a few kilometres west of the mountain, where they pitched camp for the night. De Villiers's burghers fired with rifles and a field gun on the British but the latter did not fire back.

General De Villiers expected that the British would attack early yesterday morning and attempt to outflank his position. Consequently he strengthened his flanks and left only a small group of 38 burghers in the centre, in a donga at the foot of the hill. A small group of 46 burghers was stationed some distance behind the first group, from where they could rush to their assistance, and the guns were stationed higher up on the mountain.

De Villiers's expectations proved to be correct. The British did attack soon after daybreak and initially concentrated on the northern flank of the Boers. When the Boer artillery entered the battle with a pom-pom, the British gunners attempted to silence them. Even though the British bombardment was ineffective, after a while the Boer gunners stopped firing. The British foot soldiers probably thought that was the end of the Boer resistance and recklessly charged forward to capture the pom-pom.

That was exactly what De Villiers hoped that the Khakis would do, since they charged straight at the burghers in the donga, of whom they were obviously unaware. These burghers, led by Corporals Gert Delport and Petrus Rautenbach, waited until the Khakis were virtually on top of them before firing. The infantry came to a sudden halt, turned round and fled. Their officers managed to restore order and attacked a second and third time, but the burghers were ready for them.

A further shock was in store for the poor soldiers when the Boer artillery started firing again with their pom-pom. The shock turned into catastrophe when gunfire set fire to the tall, dry grass where the soldiers were hiding. This was a horrible experience for the Khakis. The uniforms of some of the soldiers caught fire, and while the unhurt Khakis fled in terror, the seriously wounded could not escape from the galloping flames.

General de Villiers realised that he had an excellent opportunity to score a major victory, and ordered his burghers to attack the fleeing enemy. He himself took the lead in this charge. Unfortunately he was severely wounded by shrapnel from a British gun that provided covering fire for the retreating soldiers.

The British casualties in this battle amounted to approximately 180 men, 47 of them killed, according to reliable sources. The Boer loss was one man killed and three wounded. De Villiers's wound is so severe that he needs medical attention urgently. Since there is no doctor in his commando, the burghers agreed with the British authorities in Senekal that the general would be left in their care for medical attention on condition that he would be released after his recovery. A more laudable example of humanity in the midst of a terrible war is hardly imaginable.

BRITISH FORCE AT LINDLEY OVERPOWERED

More than 400 Khakis made prisoners of war

Bethlehem, 1 June – A Boer commando yesterday managed to overrun the whole 13th Yeomanry battalion under the command of Colonel Spragge at Lindley. The Khakis have been active in the vicinity of this eastern Free State town since the end of last week. Last Friday, 25 May, a whole division of British soldiers under the command of General Colvile approached Lindley from Ventersburg. The Boer commandos in this vicinity made three attacks on this massive force but failed to halt its progress. Nevertheless they did, according to reliable sources, inflict a loss of 26 men, of whom six were killed and 20 wounded, on the British. Colvile's division reached Lindley only by the evening of 26 May, and stayed in the town for only one night, closely observed by General Piet de Wet's scouts. Early the next morning they left in a northerly direction.

This was not the end of the action. A few hours later, at about two o'clock on the afternoon of the 27th, Spragge's Yeomanry battalion, which consisted of mounted soldiers, approached the town from the west. De Wet's burghers fired on them from low hills in the area, whereupon Spragge occupied the town. The burghers immediately surrounded his force, and for the next two days fired continuously at a long distance on the Khakis, while systematically moving closer to the town and erecting fortifications as they progressed. By the 29th the burghers, whose numbers increased continuously throughout this period, since Commandant A.M. Prinsloo's men arrived in the vicinity, had progressed to the very edge of the town. Their rifle fire became increasingly heavy, but the Yeomanry managed to defend themselves.

Spragge stated after his surrender that he had faced two problems – insufficient supplies for his soldiers, and no fodder for the horses or oxen, which made him dependent on pasture. The Boers realised this and ensured that the Khakis had no place where their animals could graze in safety. With this they were relatively successful, since on 30 May they captured 16 Khakis after a skirmish over pastureland.

Spragge's second problem was that he would not be able to hold out should De Wet be reinforced with artillery. And that is what happened yesterday when four guns arrived in the Boer camp. Yesterday morning the Boer gunners began bombarding the British. Spragge realised that his position was hopeless and early in the afternoon surrendered with more than 500 men, including 21 officers. This number includes 55 wounded Khakis. In addition 25 Khakis had been killed. The Boer casualties were negligible.

MAJOR BATTLE AT KLIPRIVIERSBERG

Boers considerably slow down British offensive

Johannesburg, 30 May – The Republican forces have been involved in numerous determined attempts to halt the British northwards offensive in the last week. Unfortunately their efforts have all been in vain: the occupation of Johannesburg now seems unavoidable. The British began crossing the Vaal River at the end of last week. Last Saturday, General Hamilton's troops crossed the river at Wonderwaterdrift, an hour on horseback west of the railway bridge. They almost captured the 50 or so burghers who had been ordered to dynamite that bridge, but fortunately the burghers managed to complete their task before the Khakis arrived.

By Sunday morning (27 May) the Republican main force, stationed at Vereeniging, realised that the British could easily outflank them in the west and threaten Johannesburg. Consequently they fell back to the north towards the Klipriviersberg. The main British force crossed the Vaal River later that same day and occupied Vereeniging. In the meantime British cavalry proceeded in the direction of the West Rand, but the Boers were ready for them. Commandant Haveman and Major P.E. Erasmus of the State Artillery, who had a labour force of about 200 black men at their disposal, had been preparing fortifications of mining poles and barbed wire on the Klipriviersberg since 22 May. The burghers took up position in an extended line there, with General Lukas Meyer as acting commander.

At this stage, the Republican forces seemed to be in a chaotic state. Many burghers had simply deserted. Commandant Ben Viljoen, for example, had only about 70 burghers at his disposal, and hurried on to the Golden City to drive back the deserters. General De la Rey's burghers were slow to arrive from the west to take up position in the fortifications. On the positive side, there were many motivated and able men present on the front. One of them was Field Cornet Bam, who slowed down the enemy approach to Klipriviersberg quite appreciably with only 50 burghers until he himself was wounded and taken prisoner of war.

As the British vanguard approached Klipriviersberg on Sunday, Generals Lemmer and Grobler attacked them at Van Wyksrust and Vlakfontein. The burghers, armed only with rifles, nevertheless fought so effectively that the huge British force failed to make any progress. When the State Artillery arrived on the scene with three field guns and a pom-pom, the British retreated and left the Boers in control of the battlefield. During the night, however, the burghers fell back.

On the morning of the 28th, the British crossed the Klip River at Van Wyksrust and moved forward without scouting properly. Consequently they unknowingly moved to within firing range of seven Republican field guns that had been placed with great care on Klipriviersberg by Captain von Dalwig the previous evening. The Boer gunners zealously opened fire on the enemy. The British attacked with their cavalry, supported by field and rapid-fire guns as well as machine guns, but could not repulse the burghers. After a heavy battle the Khakis fell back to the south of the Klip River.

General Louis Botha revealed to us the contents of a telegraphic report on the battle that he sent to President Kruger. It reads as follows: 'After a hot, difficult day, it is with pleasure that I make known to you that our burghers, through the grace of the Almighty, could manage to hold their positions from the one to the other side of the front and will remain in their positions tonight. The enemy has been forced back at numerous places. On our side a number of burghers were wounded, but I do not know how many since the front is too wide. The enemy losses must have been considerable. The position occupied by us is on the western point of the Klipriviersberg where the fighting was at its heaviest. The enemy heavily bombarded us the whole day long. It seems as if the greatest part of the enemy force will come across Christiaan Neethling's farm. I ordered Assistant General Tobias Smuts to take up position on that part of the front.'

Yesterday morning the British again attacked with a large cavalry force, but could still not dislodge Captain von Dalwig's artillery. Generals Koos de la Rey, Sarel Oosthuizen and Gert Gravett repulsed the Khaki attack with rifle fire. By early afternoon, however, the scale swung in favour of the British when huge numbers of foot soldiers arrived on the scene. While these soldiers attacked the Republican gun positions, the cavalry began a major flanking movement towards the west.

The Boer scouts counted 32 British guns that were firing on the Republican positions by yesterday afternoon. The burghers simply could not hold out against the massive numbers of the enemy. By that time the British were attacking on a wide front, from Doornkop in the west to Klipriviersberg. It was already virtually dark when the first burgher unit – General Oosthuizen's commando on Doornkop – was compelled to retreat. The Khakis occupied the Boer positions without attempting to follow up their victory. According to reliable sources the total British casualties in this battle were about 250 men, of whom 47 were killed. We cannot even guess what the Boer casualties were.

While this battle was in progress, another British force was approaching Johannesburg from the south on a more easterly route, namely via the valley of the Natal Spruit. The Heidelberg Commando attempted to stop them near Elandsfontein, but fell back when three of their guns were put out of action. The Long Tom, mounted on a train truck, kept up a continuous fire on the Khakis, but also had to fall back when it seemed as if they would outflank the gunners and break up the railway line behind them. The main Khaki force subsequently occupied Germiston and Boksburg, where they captured seven locomotives and some 200 railway trucks.

General Louis Botha returning from Klipriviersberg

OUR MILITARY OFFICERS

General Abraham de Villiers

Hermanus Abraham Jacobus Bosman de Villiers was born in 1855. His birthplace was probably Hopetown in the Cape Colony, where his father was a farmer. He moved with his family to the area where Lichtenburg is now situated before he had reached his tenth year, and has lived in that area ever since. In 1886 he played a leading role in the district when he was elected to the first local school commission.

In the years that followed, De Villiers remained a leading citizen of Lichtenburg.

He served as member of the building commission of the large stone church building of the Dutch Reformed Church and in 1898 became the builder of the government school.

When the war broke out last year, he immediately joined the local commando, rapidly rising to the rank of general.

The head wound that he received this week in the fight at Biddulphsberg Mountain seems serious. His burghers surrendered him to the enemy for specialised medical treatment that they themselves cannot provide.

Our fervent prayers are that this courageous and talented general will soon recover.

General A. de Villiers

THE War Reporter
WEEKLY EDITION

Number 35   Machadodorp, South African Republic   9 June 1900

BRITISH OFFENSIVE REACHES PRETORIA
BOTHA POWERLESS AGAINST KHAKI HORDES

Machadodorp, 8 June – After the occupation by the British forces of Johannesburg on 31 May, Commandant-General Louis Botha was determined to slow down their march to the capital as long as possible. Immediately after his arrival in Pretoria last Saturday (2 June) he appointed a new, provisional city authority. In addition he released State Attorney Jan Smuts from his responsibilities and with the approval of the war council appointed him to join General De la Rey's commando.

The defence of Pretoria was of major importance for the Boers. In the first place many British leaders believed that the Republican resistance would crumble once Pretoria was occupied. Secondly there were numerous tasks that had to be carried out by the Transvaal authorities to ensure that the British occupation would not become an absolute catastrophe for the Republican cause. This included the transfer of the Republic's gold and money reserves to a place of safekeeping and the removal of all documents, ammunition reserves as well as apparatus such as a printing press to the provisional capital, Machadodorp.

Even though many burghers were under the impression that the Transvaal authorities would do everything in their power to defend Pretoria, Botha's determination to delay the Khakis did not mean that he had any inclination to attempt halting them at the city gates. Indeed, the Executive Council had earlier on concluded that the Boer forces would not be in a position to prevent the eventual occupation of the city by the British. Should they attempt to defend their capital, they would provide the enemy with an opportunity to bombard and destroy the city and also to inflict heavy casualties on the Boer forces. The best way forward would be to draw the Khakis into the rural areas and there pester their forces day and night by attacking them when least expected.

That defence would be futile was as clear as daylight. Commandant-General Botha had only 3 000 burghers at his disposal last weekend, while there were approximately 30 000 Khakis approaching. For that reason Botha did not attempt more than to delay the British advance as long as possible. He ordered his burghers to take up positions all along the Hennops River, from Irene in the east to Kwaggas Poort in the west.

On 4 June the British vanguard reached the Boer defensive line, and began attacking over its whole length. The burghers resisted courageously, even though they were aware that the capital itself would not be defended. The Boer guns under the command of Captains Lood Pretorius and Otto von Lossberg gave an excellent account of themselves against the mass of British guns. The Long Tom siege cannon mounted on its railway truck also fired from the railway line north of the Irene station; by three o'clock, however, it was withdrawn from the battlefield and towed in the direction of Bronkhorstspruit, since it was in real danger of being captured. A British column ordered to destroy the railway line somewhere east of Pretoria was halted by the Boers and failed to carry out the task. An attempt by the British artillery's heavy guns during the day to destroy the eastern railway line where it leaves Pretoria similarly failed.

Shortly before five o'clock in the afternoon, as the day began to fade, the British cavalry broke through on the Boer right flank. Soon afterwards they occupied a low hill west of the capital. General Botha received a message from Lord Roberts at dusk in which the latter demanded the surrender of the city. In answer Botha sent his secretary, Christoph Sandberg, to Roberts to request an armistice so that all the women, children and non-combatants could be removed from the city. Roberts was not prepared to accede but threatened that he would bombard the city should there be any further resistance. After receiving this message Botha realised that the moment of truth had arrived, took leave of his wife and left the city. In the dark the burghers began retreating to the east.

The total British loss during their march from Johannesburg to Pretoria was, according to reliable sources, about 50 men, of whom two were killed. What the Boer losses were we do not know.

Botha's success in slowing down the British onslaught up to 4 June did not prevent the eventual occupation of the city, but it did give State Attorney Jan Smuts and the other officials in Pretoria sufficient time to remove the most important supplies and other items from the city. State Secretary Reitz told our correspondent that they packed all the documents of the Secret Cabinet of the South African Republic into seven trunks and despatched these to Machadodorp by train. After emptying the strongroom of everything it contained and replacing it with 500 English copies of *A Century of Wrong* (a pamphlet that documents all the wrongs that the British have inflicted on the Boers ever since they occupied the Cape Colony about 100 years ago), Reitz locked the room and took the key with him when he himself departed. He says he hopes that Roberts will break open the strongroom, study the pamphlet and distribute it among his officers!

Commandant General Louis Botha

CONTINUATION OF WAR IN BALANCE
Steyn, De Wet convince Transvaalers to keep fighting

Machadodorp, 7 June – The Transvaal authorities were on the verge of surrendering without honour to the Khakis this week, but President Steyn of the Orange Free State brought them back to their senses with an almost threatening telegram. This was after President Kruger had informed Steyn by telegraph on 31 May that reports had reached him indicating that only a handful of burghers were still willing to continue the struggle, and that he was calling on Steyn to meet with him urgently for negotiations on future strategies. Soon after sending this message Kruger sent a follow-up report to Steyn that he had convened a war council meeting. He added that should the war council take a negative decision, he proposed that they should immediately negotiate with Lord Roberts so that the Republics could surrender their arms 'in protest'.

The war council meeting mentioned by President Kruger took place on 1 June. Among those who attended were Generals Botha and De la Rey and Commandant Ben Viljoen. The members were so disillusioned by the general feeling of dejection among both burghers and officers and the collapse of organised resistance against the British that they decided to propose to President Kruger that it was time to end the war. Kruger immediately telegraphed President Steyn to inform him of the decision.

Steyn reacted angrily to this decision. In a sharply worded telegram that same day he accused the Transvaal authorities of cowardice. He reminded his Transvaal brethren that they had involved the Free State in the war and brought calamity to the Cape Rebels. However, now that the war had entered their own territory they demanded a selfish and scandalous peace. To negotiate now, with the enemy at the pinnacle of their glory, would be senseless and would have disastrous results. The British would be satisfied with nothing less than the total suppression of the whole Afrikaner people. The Free Staters would fight to the bitter end, even if they had to fight alone, Steyn added.

Chief Commandant Christiaan de Wet was just as upset as Steyn was when the latter informed him that the Transvaalers considered surrendering. For him their despondency was comparable to the dejection of the Free State burghers when the Khakis occupied Bloemfontein. De Wet immediately telegraphed Commandant-General Botha and reminded him of that time, but added that the Free Staters were now full of confidence again, as their military successes of the past few weeks had indicated. De Wet furthermore reminded Botha that the Free State had given its all for the Transvaal's independence, and urged Botha to use all his influence to convince the Transvaalers to continue the struggle. Everything was not lost, he argued; even Pretoria's occupation was not sufficient reason to abandon the struggle. The Transvaalers could still, like the Free Staters, move in behind the enemy and make life so difficult for them that they would ultimately be forced to conclude a just agreement with the Republics.

The Transvaal war council discussed these telegrams from President Steyn and Chief Commandant De Wet last Saturday at a meeting in the council chamber of the Second Volksraad in Pretoria. Their influence on the dejected Transvaalers was incredible. According to State Attorney Jan Smuts, most of the officers were extremely ashamed when the admonishments from the Free State were read out to them. When Captain Danie Theron made a fiery speech in which he used the word traitor with reference to all who wanted to make peace, they reconsidered the whole issue. Commandant-General Botha and Smuts convinced the other officers that both their personal honour and the honour of their people were at stake: they would have to fight to the end. The war council consequently decided that they would retreat fighting to the east. They would not attempt to halt the British advance in a set-piece battle, since that would play into the hands of Lord Roberts. They would rather, as De Wet advised, make life difficult for the Khakis by harassing them day and night. The decision to continue with the war was unanimous.

President Kruger was delighted when he was informed by telegram of the change in the war council's spirit. In his telegraphic answer he encouraged the officers to remain loyal. He added that the enemy invaders were nothing but a gang of criminals who would, after having occupied the capital, spread in small columns all across the country and could then be attacked with ease, as was currently being done to the Khakis in the Free State.

FROM THE EDITOR

This is one of the darkest chapters in the history of our beloved Republic. On Tuesday a few of us were the unwilling eyewitnesses of a horrible display: a massive force removing the flag of our country from our government building in our capital and hoisting their hateful flag in its place to loud cheers from some of our own people. The wisdom of our motto, *Unity is strength*, as well as its opposite, namely that disunity destroys strength, was brought home painfully by these events.

The common people were not the only ones to be afflicted by disunity. Even our elderly President and some of our most respected officers wavered for a brief moment and the pursuance of the war was in the balance. Fortunately President Steyn and Chief Commandant De Wet heard that our leaders were vacillating. They called the Transvaal officers back to their senses and saved the honour of our people.

In history books one seldom reads of the cowards. The places of honour are taken by men and women who give their all for the self-respect, freedom and survival of their people. The same is true about nations. A nation that stands down when a huge challenge has to be faced has no future and does not deserve anybody's respect. The Afrikaner nation does not want to be known as such a nation. This week our fortunes are at their nadir, since our capital has been occupied. It is also a pinnacle, however, since despite severe setbacks our leaders have taken the honourable decision to keep on fighting against injustice, suppression and a future of servitude.

73

Number 35   9 June 1900

PRETORIA OCCUPIED UNOPPOSED
Union Jack waves above Transvaal Government Buildings

First British troops enter Pretoria

Kruger's house taken over by the British forces

Machadodorp, 7 June – The occupation of Pretoria by the British invaders occurred on 5 June without any violence. The first British soldiers marched into the town early that morning. Their first target was the two forts on the southern side of the city, namely Schanskop and Klapperkop. These were deserted when the soldiers reached them. Next they occupied the railway station in an attempt to prevent the transportation at that late stage of more supplies from the city, but all the trains had already left for Machadodorp or towards the north.

Since Lord Roberts had the previous evening threatened that he would bombard the city, and demanded the surrender of the capital before 10 o'clock that morning, Mayor P.J. Potgieter received him in the Fountains Valley to reach an agreement on the surrender. Early in the afternoon Roberts rode into the city on horseback at the head of 20 000 men. A large number of curious inhabitants stood along the streets to witness the occupation.

A crowd of a few hundred Pretorians awaited Roberts and the Khakis on Church Square. A guard of honour of British soldiers presented their rifles, a military band played the British national anthem and the elderly, slightly built Field Marshal saluted when the Union Jack, worked by Lady Roberts, was hoisted in front of the Government Building. The ceremony was accompanied by joyous applause by the soldiers as well as the English community of the city. For the Republican-minded Pretorians it was a tragedy in real life which they witnessed with pain in their hearts.

Telegraphic reports that reached Pretoria after the occupation indicate that the general international opinion is that the war will now end. A prominent Berlin newspaper's comment is: 'This is the last act of the drama.' A pro-Boer Belgian newspaper considers that further resistance by the Boers would be a waste of human life. The Italian Government even sent a congratulatory message to London. As could be expected there was patriotic rejoicing all over the British empire.

Above and right: British soldiers in Market Street on 5 June

British troops on Church Square on 5 June

Khaki parade on Church Square, 5 June 1900

Khakis on Church Square, 5 June 1900

Khakis on Church Square, 5 June 1900

Number 35 9 June 1900

BRITISH OCCUPATION OF PRETORIA

Accounts by Boer women who witnessed everything

Pretoria, 6 June – Our correspondent in the occupied capital approached two Boer women who witnessed the Khaki occupation yesterday and asked them how they experienced the traumatic event. The first, Jacoba Lorentz, says she is relieved that everything was conducted in an orderly manner, but bitter that things ended with this unjust outcome:

'Fortunately everything was conducted peacefully and orderly. The soldiers did not display their happiness in looks or gestures, but conducted themselves modestly and in a considerate way where they made contact with the public. That was what one expected from a civilised people, even though there had been numerous terrible stories in the newspaper of misconduct by soldiers, especially towards women, so that we awaited their arrival with trepidation and many women armed themselves to be able to defend themselves in the absence of their husbands against an excited and savage horde, as the soldiers had been portrayed.

'Fortunately everything went in an orderly fashion. They filled the streets and defiled on Church Square in a quiet and peaceful occupation. Lord Roberts's arrival was totally unnoticed, and no music or joyous exaltations that could be hurtful to us was heard or seen, and the English flag was only hoisted on the Government Building late in the day. It is a thorn in my eye, worse than I can express. The war is totally unjust and the English have simply stolen all that is ours: one cannot explain this annexation in any other way. And when one thinks about it, one feels rebellious over all this unjustness. How is it possible, we repeatedly cried out in the past months, that God allows injustice to be victorious? The actions of the English cry out to the heaven and demand revenge.'

The second woman interviewed by our correspondent was 22-year-old Johanna van Warmelo, whose late father was a respected pioneer minister of the Dutch Reformed Church in the Transvaal, and whose brothers are doing their duty as burghers in the field. She expressed her feelings as follows:

'It is only now that we are becoming aware of the reality of the war. It is only too true, the enemy marched into our beloved town in thousands this morning. On 30 May Mama and I heard the roar of cannon for the first time and yesterday the bombs began to burst in Sunnyside and we had to flee to Town for safety. Our forts were being bombarded and Harmony [the name of their house] was directly in the line of fire. The bursting of the great lyddite bombs on our hills caused terrific shocks and we fled leaving our dinner standing on the table. The shells went shrieking and whistling through the air over our heads and we were not out of danger one moment. Everywhere were great clouds of dust and smoke and the fragments of rock and shell fell like hail on the iron roofs. We have picked up fragments in our garden and behind the stable. We stayed with friends in town and came home when darkness fell … We are all prisoners and cut off from the whole world.

'I went to Town this morning to watch the troops marching in – my mother declined to go but I think such things will become of historical interest and everyone ought to see them, so I carefully put on my Transvaal colours and went to Town on my bicycle – met some friends with whom I stayed all the time while the marching and parading and shouting and band-playing went on. Sick at heart I watched all this – with boiling blood I noticed the jubilations of the half-breeds and blacks, the sporting of the red, white and blue by people who have been strictly "neutral" during the war and even by some who were red-hot Republicans not long ago (after Colenso, Magersfontein, Spioenkop). At first I shed some bitter tears but afterwards my pride came to my aid and I had the satisfaction of "cutting" the wearer of the red, white and blue right and left.

'I watched our own people a great deal more than the Tommies and I know all the loyal ones. The poor soldiers were really not worth looking at, covered with filth, footsore, weary. I can't say I admired them and yet one must admit that the discipline is perfect. At about three o'clock the Union Jack was hoisted on the Government Buildings, the bands played "God save the Queen", the soldiers cheered, and all the world seemed to go mad, only this poor child stood like a marble statue and soon afterwards she nearly fainted, what with heat, emotion and fatigue.

'My friends let me out of the crowd and I came home – it was more than flesh and blood could bear, but I shall never regret having seen what I saw today. There were some funny things, some pathetic things and many very touching things that helped to make this bitter day bearable. The greatest comfort to me was my Transvaal ribbon – everyone saw it, everyone knew my sentiments and in all that crowd of thousands I was one of the only women with enough courage to sport the *Vierkleur*. One of our people – a young man – stopped beside me and looking earnestly at me cried "Hurray for our *Vierkleur* – I have even more respect for it now" and he took off his hat almost reverently. I was quite touched and gave him a friendly "Good morning". If ever we shall require courage and patriotism and loyalty it is now and now I shall stick to my colours. I think there is a bitter time before us.

'Tonight we are surrounded by thousands of armed Tommies – they are camped out at our very gates and their fires are to be seen all along the roads and railway lines. We asked the men at the gate to see that no one came into Harmony and the officer was very respectful and promised that no one would molest us. My mother promptly sent them a basket of oranges by way of gratitude.'

Johanna van Warmelo

BRITISH PRISONERS OF WAR RELEASED

Churchill in Pretoria again

Machadodorp, 8 June – One of the most disheartening results of the Khaki invasion of Pretoria was that the latter managed to release the 129 British officers and 39 soldiers who were held prisoner of war in the building of the Staats Model School. The war council of Transvaal officers last month ordered specifically that the prisoners of war should not be released, but should be taken to a place of safe custody such as the terminus of the Selati Railway Line on the other side of Mariepskop. However, the speed of the British advance from the northern Free State to Pretoria surprised the Boers and they failed to bring about the transfer of the British officers who were prisoners of war. Winston Churchill, the British journalist who was captured while fighting for Buller's forces in Natal and was subsequently detained in the Staats Model School, but escaped last December, was one of the Khakis who was present at the release.

One of the Khakis had a Union Jack with him and hoisted it under loud applause in the place of the *Vierkleur* in front of the former school building. Our correspondent reports that it was a painful experience to see the broad smiles and hear the loud-mouthed bravado of the British officers when they walked out of the building, as if they had already won the war.

As for the other British prisoners of war – mostly ordinary soldiers and non-commissioned officers – who were detained at Waterval north of the city: the Boers took about 1 000 down the eastern railway line to a new place of detention. The invaders released the approximately 3 000 who were left behind on 6 June.

The journalist Winston Churchill

MILITARY ACTIVITIES ON THE NATAL FRONT

Volksrust, 8 June – On the Natal front the British have been exerting increased pressure on the Republican forces in the last two weeks. At the beginning of last week, on Monday 28 May, the burghers stationed at Laing's Nek noticed a British unit from the south crossing the Ingogo River. Lieutenant von Wichmann of the State Artillery immediately began firing on them with his Long Tom gun stationed on Mol's Kop. Even though it was a long distance – von Wichman guesses at least nine kilometres – this bombardment was so effective that the British retreated.

The next day, 29 May, General Christiaan Botha, the acting commander-in-chief on the Natal front, received one of those typically arrogant letters from British commanders to which our authorities are slowly becoming accustomed. It was adressed to Botha and General Daniël Erasmus by General Buller, and demanded that they should surrender since their position was hopeless. We do not know what Botha's answer was, but he certainly rejected the advice.

Last Tuesday, the enemy almost managed to occupy Utrecht. A British general accompanied by a large column of soldiers arrived at that Transvaal village on the Natal side of the Drakensberg in the course of the morning. The general negotiated with the local magistrate and they agreed that the latter would hand over the Transvaal flag as well as six rifles as a symbol of the town's surrender. The Boer warriors would leave the town and would not return. Soon after the burghers had retreated to the low hills in the vicinity, they noticed that the British themselves were marching from the town. The burghers returned, occupied the town again, repealed all British proclamations and arrested the magistrate.

Last Saturday General Christiaan Botha heard rumours that the Transvaal authorities considered surrendering to the British authorities. Since he was uncertain of exactly how he should handle the situation, he met General Buller at O'Neill's Farm at the foot of Laing's Nek Pass, the same place where the armistice was signed at the end of the Transvaal War of Independence. Buller and Botha agreed on an armistice of three days so that they could get clarity over the continuation of the war.

Botha's decision to conclude an armistice with Buller had disastrous, unforseen results. One of the burghers on this front, E.J. Weeber, told our correspondent that they were camping at Begin-der-Lyn at that time. They were confused about developments and had nothing to do. When they heard about the armistice, many burghers concluded that the war would soon be at an end. Large numbers of craven characters decided that it was time to return to their farms. Order broke down completely. Even officers lost interest in the Republican cause. The only activity in which many burghers participated was stealing the horses and other property of their comrades who had not abandoned the struggle. Thus Weeber himself lost his horse to a thief.

On 5 June Commandant-General Louis Botha sent a message to the Natal front that the Boers should not consider any peace overtures from the British. With that the armistice lapsed. Buller subsequently wasted no time. On 6 June he resumed his march northwards from Newcastle in full force. The British are making slow progress and up to this morning there has been no major confrontation.

PROCLAMATIONS BY LORD ROBERTS

Machadodorp, 8 June – We have learnt that immediately after his occupation of Johannesburg last Thursday the British commander-in-chief issued a proclamation specifically aimed at the burghers of the South African Republic. In this so-called Proclamation 1 of 1900, he promises that the British forces will as far as possible honour the personal rights and property of non-combatants. In addition he attempts to entice the burghers with vague promises to lay down their arms. Thus he declares that all burghers who did not take a prominent part in the policy that led to this war, and who had not used violence against British subjects or attempted to commandeer them, and who had not been guilty of activities contrary to customs of civilised warfare, and who are willing to lay down their arms immediately, and to commit themselves through a pledge not to take further part in this war, would receive passes which would allow them to return to their homes and not be made prisoners of war.

Fortunately our burghers are not fools. They know what happened in the Orange Free State to burghers who were misled by Roberts through similar promises. The British merely kept on acting against them as though they were combatants. For that reason our burghers would not be deluded by any proclamation.

On 6 June, the day after the occupation of Pretoria, Roberts issued Proclamation 2 of 1900, in terms of which all Transvaal farmers taking an oath of neutrality to Britain would be allowed to return unhindered to their farms and to retain their livestock. Passes would be issued to those farmers who intend trekking with their livestock to winter pastures in the bushveld. This sounds attractive – a real spoonful of honey in the mouth. If the promise had not been made by a British officer, one might have believed in its sincerity.

Roberts issued two further proclamations with regard to the Orange Free State this week. In the first he declares Martial Law in what he calls the Orange River Colony. The second is a paper bomb aimed at the burghers of the Orange Free State who are still fighting against the British. He threatens that all the burghers who are still involved in fighting on 15 June will be regarded as rebels and punished as such in person and property. More arrogance than this we can hardly imagine!

Number 35 9 June 1900

FIGHTING IN THE TRANSVAAL

Machadodorp, 8 June – In addition to the fighting in the immediate vicinity of Pretoria up to its occupation on 5 June, there were clashes between Boer and Brit at various other places within the boundaries of the Republic. Last Saturday a Boer force became involved in a skirmish with a mounted British column that seemed intent on sabotaging the eastern railway line near Bronkhorstspruit. Those Khakis were driven back with the loss of one man killed and at least 10 wounded without having achieved their objective.

OUR MILITARY OFFICERS

Commandant G.M.J. van Dam

Gerard Marie Johan van Dam was born in 1855 in Delftshaven, Netherlands. He is the son of George Charles Alexander van Dam and his wife Cornelia Dignia Kroep. Van Dam was 13 years old when his family immigrated to South Africa in 1868 and settled in Potchefstroom. Here he became a carpenter's apprentice and in due course started his own business. In 1877 he married Martha Magdalena Steyn. They have four sons and six daughters.

From 1877 Van Dam eagerly participated in the resistance of the Transvaal Afrikaners to the British annexation of their Republic. At the people's assembly at Paardekraal in 1880 he was appointed as a secretary of the Volksraad and after the occupation of Heidelberg he became a member of the re-established Boer government's financial commission.

In the War of Independence that followed he participated in the battles of Laing's Nek and Schuinshoogte. After peace was concluded, he acted as messenger of the Potchefstroom court and at times as magistrate or as public prosecutor.

In 1881 Van Dam joined the South African Mounted Police (ZARP) and was appointed commandant. In 1888 he became the chief of the ZARP in Klerksdorp and eight years later, in 1896, the Commandant of the ZARP in Johannesburg. In 1894 he published a police handbook at his own cost and in 1897 he was a member of a commission regarding police regulations.

With the outbreak of this war last October, Van Dam was the commander of some 400 policemen who initially guarded Johannesburg and then became a formidable fighting corps in numerous engagements. This included the battle at Nicholson's Nek last October.

At the end of 1899 he returned to Johannesburg and subsequently joined the forces of General H.J. Schoeman at Colesberg and afterwards that of General De la Rey at Slingerfontein. His men formed the rearguard during the trek back to the northern Free State. Last month he was recalled to Johannesburg and this week he participated with distinction in the fighting at the Hennop's River that delayed the British advance to Pretoria.

Commandant G.M.J. van Dam

HOW DO THE BURGHERS FEEL ABOUT THE OCCUPATION?
WILHELM MANGOLD ILLUMINATES AN IMPORTANT ISSUE

Middelburg, 7 June – One of the most important factors that will decide the course of the war in the immediate future is the spirit of the common Transvaal burghers. Will they be prepared to continue the struggle after the occupation of their capital, or will they just disappear from the battlefield or put the authorities in a position where they will be forced to surrender? The well-known Heidelberg burgher, Wilhelm Mangold, who has previously contributed reports, sent us this account of how he and his comrades received the news of the occupation. Fortunately his spirit seems to be highly positive:

'In the past few weeks we have often been involved in discussions on what would happen if Pretoria were to be occupied by the enemy. It happened earlier than we expected. Our capital, where our flag had fluttered for so many years, where our President governed his country and his people, where the poorest burgher could state his case directly to the President, is now in the hands of the enemy, an enemy who has for the duration of a century attempted to destroy the Afrikaner people. It is bitter news for us. What now? Is this the end of the war?

'There are people among us whom we've known to be disloyal all along and who now declare "Everything is lost." We who are loyal, however, say: "Never in our lives. Come what may, we will not lay down our arms and bow before the English – that we will not." Field Cornet Spruyt asked for silence and then declared: "Men, brothers, a heavy blow has hit us. We do not know what happened in Pretoria, but I swear here before God that I will fight to the death. Those who feel like I do lift up your right hands."

'I do not know if everybody raised their hands. I only know that my two comrades, Theo Jooste and John Biccard and I did. And we gave each other a handshake. We then knelt down and prayed to God to give us the strength to remain loyal to our pledge. We all sang the Transvaal anthem and then our regimental song, the "Afrikaanse Taal".

'In our group of about 50 men Afrikaners from Table Bay to the Limpopo River are actually joined together. Our threesome is the embodiment of the words of that song. Biccard was born in Cape Town, Jooste in Transvaal and I in Natal and here we are fighting together for one and the same cause, a free Afrikaner people!'

The American schoolboy Jimmy Smith (centre) with State Secretary Reitz in front of President Kruger's house

PHOTOGRAPHIC REPORT ON EVENTS OF THE PAST TWO WEEKS

Boer War Council discussing defence of Johannesburg

British occupation of Johannesburg: Generals Kitchener (right) and Hamilton (left) in front on horseback

British artillery move through the streets of Johannesburg

President Kruger in his railway coach on the evening that he left Pretoria

THE
War Reporter
WEEKLY EDITION

Number 36 | **Machadodorp, South African Republic** | **16 June 1900**

BRILLIANT BOER VICTORIES IN FREE STATE

Spectacular 'fireworks display' at Roodewal Station

Bethlehem, 14 June – The Free State forces continued where they left off last month by scoring further convincing victories over the Khakis. On Friday 1 June a British force commanded by General Methuen failed in its attempt to relieve the Khakis who had been taken prisoner by the burghers at Lindley. Methuen's soldiers attacked the rearguard of the Boer columns for five hours but eventually were driven back and abandoned their attempt. We have learnt that the British casualties in this battle were 26 men.

On Monday 4 June Chief Commandant Christiaan de Wet pounced on a British supply column of 56 wagons escorted by 160 foot soldiers at Swawelkrans, some 22 kilometres northwest of Heilbron. He easily captured the whole column, since the Khakis surrendered without a shot being fired. De Wet sent General Philip Botha eastwards to the laager of President Steyn with the loot as well as the prisoners of war and continued to plan an attack on British units guarding the Kroonstad–Viljoen's Drift railway line.

On Tuesday 5 June President Steyn arrived here in Bethlehem and declared this eastern Free State town the temporary capital of the Orange Free State. Two days later Chief Commandant De Wet and his burghers launched three simultaneous attacks on the British garrisons guarding the Viljoen's Drift–Kroonstad railway line in the vicinity of the Renoster River, north of Kroonstad. Captain Gideon Scheepers and his scouts had earlier reported to De Wet that the British had unloaded massive stores of war supplies at the stations all along the railway line. This had been done because the Transvaal commandos, during their northwards retreat last month, had damaged the railway lines and especially the numerous bridges so effectively that the British forces could not transport all their supplies. According to Scheepers, the supplies included foodstuffs, ammunition and clothing intended for Lord Roberts's forces in Pretoria.

The first attack was carried out by Commandant Lucas Steenkamp of the Heilbron Commando with 300 burghers on a British guard post at Vredefort Road Station north of the Renoster River. They captured the 38 Khakis without firing a shot. When a train filled with British soldiers suddenly arrived from the north, the burghers fired on it and it immediately steamed away again.

Assistant Chief Commandant Stoffel Froneman carried out the second attack. With a force consisting of 300 burghers and two guns he and Commandants F.J. du Plooy and Coen Nel carried out a very successful three-hour assault on a British regiment stationed at the Renoster River Bridge. Altogether 36 Khakis were killed and 104 wounded before the total force of 486 officers and men surrendered. The burghers also captured a large store of war supplies that the British had off-loaded at the damaged bridge. In addition they again demolished the bridge, which had been partly repaired by the British.

The third attack was carried out by De Wet himself and was even more successful. He and Commandant Piet Fourie with 80 burghers attacked a British garrison of 172 men who were guarding a number of fully loaded train trucks as well as an enormous store of war supplies at Roodewal Station. This is about three kilometres south of the Renoster River. After cutting the telegraph wires on both sides of the station De Wet sent a messenger under a white flag to demand the surrender of the column. The commander of the Khakis wrote his reply on the back of De Wet's message: 'We will not surrender.' De Wet's burghers immediately attacked. The fierce battle lasted for about five hours and was clinched in favour of the Free State forces when General Froneman and a number of his burghers arrived with two field guns from the Renoster River. The Khakis immediately surrendered when the bombs began falling in their midst.

The British casualties in this battle were eight men killed and 24 wounded. In addition the Boers removed some 500 crates of ammunition from the battlefield. De Wet afterwards gave the burghers permission to take whatever supplies they wanted for themselves. The rest of the ammunition, including thousands of lyddite bombs, as well as two bags full of postal material and a massive supply of other goods as well as the train, was blown into the air at 10 o'clock that evening in what the burghers described as the biggest fireworks display ever in the Free State. We have heard that the explosion could be seen in Kroonstad. All that was left was a crater 30 metres long, 18 metres wide and six metres deep.

In these three operations the Free State burghers have destroyed 18 kilometres of railway lines and telegraph wires. It will take the British many weeks to repair all this damage. Unfortunately our burghers have paid a price for this triple success: eight burghers killed and 24 wounded. The total British losses amounted to 45 dead, 123 wounded and 672 made prisoner of war.

The major advantage that these victories have for the Republican forces as a whole is neither the destruction of the enemy's ammunition, nor their loss of supplies (worth at least £100 000 sterling, by Chief Commandant De Wet's calculations). No, more important is the fact that the booty includes many thousands of sets of warm clothing, jackets, blankets, shoes, gloves and underclothing. All of this was destroyed in the explosion of the ammunition. British soldiers are already complaining about the bitterly cold nights on the Highveld. Now they will be even more bitter: the number of their sick will rise sharply, and that while their hospitals are already overflowing with the patients.

On the day after the fireworks display De Wet heard that a small British patrol of 38 men was on its way from Roodewal to Kroonstad. He immediately sent a number of General Froneman's burghers to capture them. While Field Cornet P.W. de Vos moved off to the east with all the prisoners of war, De Wet buried most of the ammunition at a secret place for possible future use.

On Monday 11 June De Wet's scouts reported that a huge British force was on its way from the north. The Chief Commandant was on his own farm, Roodepoort, on the Renoster River, about five kilometres from Roodewal, and decided to greet the British visitors with artillery fire. After an artillery dual that went on for about an hour, De Wet noticed that there was a risk that his burghers might be outflanked and immediately ordered their retreat.

Seven of the burghers were inside the ruins of a typical round stone house built many generations ago by black inhabitants of that area. They did not hear the command to retreat and were taken prisoner of war.

Railway bridge across Renoster River destroyed by the Boers

BOERS PUSHED BACK FROM DONKERHOEK

TRANSVAAL FORCES FIGHT COURAGEOUSLY BUT IN VAIN

Bronkhorstspruit, 14 June – Earlier this week the British forces attacked the Boer positions east of Pretoria at Donkerhoek, which the Khakis call Diamond Hill, and occupied it after two days of heavy fighting. The origins of this battle can be traced back to the Transvaal war council's decision to attempt to prevent the British from entering the Transvaal Highveld. The key to this part of the Republic is the ridge of low hills at Donkerhoek, some 25 kilometres east of the occupied capital, on both sides of the eastern railway line.

The Transvaal war council met on the day of the British occupation of the capital, 5 June, in the offices of the firm Lewis and Marks at Eerste Fabrieken on the eastern railway line between Pretoria and Donkerhoek. It was here that the decision was taken to confront the Khakis at Donkerhoek.

On 7 June the Boer officers again held a war council, this time at Van der Merwe Station. On this occasion they planned their defence in great detail. It was during this council that Field Cornet C.F. Beyers of the Boksburg Commando proposed that all officers that did not do their duty should be suspended. His proposal was not accepted, but each commandant declared that he and his burghers would do their utmost to make up for their loss of heart before the occupation of Pretoria.

Commandant-General Louis Botha was personally in command of the total of 4 000 burghers with their 23 guns. He stationed them with care on both sides of the railway line. Their front stretched from Doornfontein in the north across Donkerhoek to Klein Zonderhout in the south – a total distance of 40 kilometres. In the light of the now well-known British outflanking tactics, Botha took special care to strengthen the flanks, which left the centre somewhat brittle.

The British vanguard had already begun moving out of Pretoria in an easterly direction last Thursday, 7 June. By Friday mounted British patrols were scouting over a wide front in an attempt to identify weaknesses in the Boer positions. Lieutenant Colonel Trichard of the State Artillery gave them something to think about when he fired on them with the Long Tom mounted on the railway truck.

Roberts attacked the Boer positions on 11 June with a force of at least 14 000 soldiers with 70 guns. (Some sources give the figures as 20 000 Khakis, 80 guns and nine pom-poms.) The British onslaught began before daybreak and developed exactly as Botha expected, with strong mounted attacks on the Boer flanks and an infantry attack on the centre.

In the north the burghers of Generals De la Rey and Snyman, supported by accurate fire from Captain von Dalwig's guns, easily repulsed the British mounted attack. The same happened in the south and in the centre. Here the State Artillery commanded by Trichard made a major contribution, with artillery commanders Captain von Lossberg in the south and Lieutenant Thuynsma in the north deserving special mention.

Even though the British failed on the first day to outflank the Boer positions or break through in the centre, their superiority in numbers and guns proved to be a major threat. On the second day, Tuesday 12 June, Roberts concentrated his huge numbers on the southern flank, where General Tobias Smuts was in command. The British numbers were so overwhelming that the burghers could not hold them back on the slopes of Donkerhoek, but at the crest a surprise was in store for them: the burghers suddenly opened a murderous fire on them from positions that the soldiers seemed to have been unaware of up to that time. Consequently the soldiers were pinned to the ground and the result of the battle was in the balance for a few hours. Shortly before dark, however, the British managed to haul a number of guns to the top of the ridge and blasted an opening into the Boer defensive line.

Elsewhere on the front the British failed to make noteworthy progress. Far in the south the determined burghers of Commandant Ben Viljoen and General Christiaan Fourie halted them. In the north the burghers of Generals De la Rey, C.M. Douthwaite and Freek Grobler accomplished the same. Indeed, the latter were preparing to launch a counter-attack when they were notified of the British breakthrough in the centre, which made the whole Boer line indefensible.

In order to ensure that the tactical setback would not become a fiasco, Botha ordered all the burghers to retreat in an orderly fashion under cover of night. As Captain Matthys de Jager of the State Artillery remarked to our correspondent (quoting an old proverb): 'He who fights and runs away, lives to fight another day!' During the night of 12–13 June the Boers left their positions and fell back to the east. Thus the battle ended. Fortunately the Khakis probably only realised the next morning that the Boers had fallen back, since they made no attempt that evening to follow up their victory.

We are not sure precisely what the Boer casualties are. At least 30 burghers were killed, wounded or taken prisoner. On the British side we are aware of at least 28 Khakis who were killed and 145 wounded.

After setbacks such as this retreat from Donkerhoek the Boers usually spend many hours discussing the reasons for their defeat. In the midst of all the serious reflection a young burgher of the Johannesburg Commando, Roland Schikkerling, told our correspondent this amusing tale:

'Ben Viljoen has with him a servant named Mooiroos (Pretty Rose) who always accompanies his master into battle, and therefore has many opportunities of watching a fight from an officer's point of view, and of knowing the orders issued during the operation. He rides with generals and commandants and listens to their conversations. This Mooiroos is observant and talkative, and, after each fight, would give us his views and the reasons for the victory or the defeat. After this battle he told us that defeat was due to disregard of his advice as to the manner of the defence, the neglect of opportunities that had presented themselves, and, lastly, to the cowardice of a few officers. There is often much truth in his observations, and I am sure he would not make a bad commander. He is a confirmed dagga smoker.'

SETBACKS ON THE NATAL FRONT

Botha's Pass, Volksrust occupied by British forces

Standerton, 14 June – Despite the courageous attempts by the Boer forces to halt the British advance, General Buller has managed to gain significant breakthroughs in the past few days. Last Friday, 8 June, the British unexpectedly turned to the northwest from Newcastle and advanced on Botha's Pass. Generals Chris Botha and Joachim Fourie were not prepared for this.

Buller's attackers approached the Drakensberg on a six kilometre wide front. Their target was a Boer guard post on Van Wykskop that dominated the whole terrain. At that stage only 25 burghers manned it. British artillery bombarded the whole front while the infantry moved in.

By three o'clock in the afternoon the Khakis reached the top of the pass and the burghers realised that further defence would be futile. They torched the veld and fell back under cover of the smoke. With this breakthrough the first of Buller's Khakis reached the Orange Free State.

Last Sunday, a bitterly cold day, the British attacked Botha's small force of about 120 burghers at Gansvlei Kop on the Free State side of the Drakensberg. Botha and his men defended themselves admirably throughout the afternoon, but soon after dark decided to fall back.

In the meantime General Fourie's burghers dug trenches at Allemans Nek on both sides of the wagon road that links Botha's Pass to Volksrust and prepared for a confrontation. On Monday morning, 11 June, the enemy attacked them there. The infantry attack on the burghers' left flank was supported by artillery, but failed when the Boer artillery drove them back with well-aimed shots. By the afternoon hundreds of soldiers had arrived at the battle scene, and the Khakis resumed their attack over a broader front. Even though the Boers had only four guns and one pom-pom, they held their own easily until late afternoon when an estimated force of 1 000 fresh Khakis arrived from Botha's Pass. These reinforcements swung the battle in favour of the British. It was almost dusk when the burghers torched the veld and retreated. Through innovative utilisation of the terrain under Fourie's leadership they managed to fall back in an orderly fashion.

According to reliable sources, the total British loss in this battle at Allemans Nek was 28 killed and 134 wounded. On the Boer side four men were killed, but the number of wounded is not known to us.

After the British victory of Allemans Nek they resumed their march the next day, 12 June, and occupied Volksrust. This meant that the Boer positions at Laing's Nek, on which they had worked so diligently in the last few weeks, had been outflanked. The Boers abandoned those positions and fell back to the northeast.

FROM THE EDITOR

The direction the Boers will have to follow if we are to gain ultimate victory is clearer every day. Chief Commandant De Wet indicated this brilliantly with successive victories in the Orange Free State, and it was confirmed when the Transvaal forces again failed in a set-piece battle against massive Khaki forces. The lesson to be learnt from these encounters is clear: avoid confronting the enemy on their own terms. Rather concentrate on unexpected offensive operations in which the Republican burghers take the initiative. The British authorities are controlling the course of the war at present, but we have to take the initiative.

Many of our readers will, after this week's continued setbacks north of the Vaal River, think that it is madness to even talk of an eventual Boer victory. We believe that it is not madness at all. It is not glorious success on the battlefield alone that ensures an eventual victory. It is rather the capacity to impose your will on your enemy. The British have certainly not imposed their will on us, as has convincingly been demonstrated by the burghers of the Free State.

BRITISH ADVANCE IN WESTERN TRANSVAAL

General A.P.J. Cronjé outwitted at Klerksdorp

Wolhuterskop, 14 June – It is not only in the vicinity of Pretoria and on the Natal front that things are looking bad for the Transvaal forces. In the western Transvaal the enemy has occupied one town after the other in the past month and forced hundreds of Boers to surrender. It seems as if the burghers are leaderless, without a plan: they exhibit no determination to slow down the Khaki advance.

The Khakis occupied General de la Rey's home town, Lichtenburg, on 7 June, and soon afterwards Ventersdorp and Hartbeesfontein as well. General A.P.J. Cronjé, who had been granted sick leave by General de la Rey, was in Klerksdorp that day. In the course of the afternoon he received a telegram from the British officer in Hartbeesfontein, Captain Lambart, requesting Cronjé's permission to interview him in Klerksdorp. Cronjé agreed and soon before dark Lambart and his party met the General in the Tivoli Hotel.

It seems as if Lambart totally outwitted poor Cronjé. Giving him the devastating news that Roberts had occupied Pretoria, he told the General that a force of 20 000 Khakis was ready to occupy Klerksdorp. That was untrue, but Cronjé was so shocked that he asked permission from Lambart to discuss these developments with his burghers the next morning. Lambart agreed.

Cronjé and his 500 dejected burghers discussed Lambart's communications the next morning and decided to lay down arms.

Lambart subsequently occupied Klerkssdorp with 33 Khakis. Only then did the burghers realise that they had been misled. They were so dumbfounded, however, that they allowed the Khakis to have their way.

On Monday 11 June the British occupied Potchefstroom without encountering any resistance. Today they also occupied Rustenburg. We have heard in the meantime that General Cronjé, who had been outwitted so easily in Klerksdorp, and who has not yet completely recovered from his illness, has decided to take the oath of neutrality.

PROCLAMATION BY PRESIDENT STEYN

Rejects British annexation of the Free State Republic

Reitz, 12 June – In answer to a proclamation by Lord Roberts on 27 May, in which he announced the annexation of the Orange Free State under the name Orange River Colony, President Steyn yesterday issued a counter-proclamation here in Reitz. The most important stipulations in this proclamation are:

Great Britain forced the people of the Orange Free State and the ZAR into a most unjust war in October 1899. These two small Republics have now been waging an unequal battle against the huge British Empire for more than eight months. Lord Roberts had alleged in a proclamation dated 18 May 1900 that he had conquered the Orange Free State and annexed it in the name of the British Empire, but in fact the military forces of the Orange Free State have neither been defeated nor forced out of the country. The Orange Free State has not been conquered. The proclamation is thus in violation of international law.

The proclamation ends with the statement: 'Since the independence of the Orange Free State is still recognised by most of the civilised powers, I, Marthinus Theunis Steyn, State President of the Orange Free State, proclaim in consultation with the Executive Council, and on behalf of the independent people of the Orange Free State, that the annexation is not recognised and is thus of no value whatsoever. The people of the Orange Free State are and remain an independent people and refuse to subject themselves to British authority.'

WHY KRUGER LEFT PRETORIA

PRESIDENT'S FRANK INTERVIEW WITH JOURNALIST

Machadodorp, 9 June – A journalist of the British newspaper the *Daily Express* had the good fortune of being granted an interview by President Kruger on Thursday. He subsequently compiled a report for his newspaper and was friendly enough to give us a copy. Our readers will be interested to read what Kruger says to a foreign correspondent:

'I arrived here this morning, and found Messrs Kruger and Reitz established in a private railway carriage, which Mr Kruger ordered to be constructed some time ago, in view of the contingencies which have now arrived. The car was shunted on to a siding at Machadodorp Station, and is of a comfortable but not luxurious character.

'The ex-President was, as usual, smoking a long pipe, and although obviously depressed and worried, exhibited a quiet, determined, and persistent manner. He did not make the slightest objection to being interviewed. His usual reticence, in fact, seemed to have deserted him; and although there was nothing very startling in what he said, from the point of view of the war – as indeed was only to be expected – I think he let out more of his real personal feelings than he has ever done before.

'"Yes," he said, after salutations, "It is quite true that the British forces have occupied Pretoria. That, however, does not mean the end of the war. The burghers are fully determined to fight to the last, and will never surrender as long as five hundred armed men remain in the country. I feel deeply encouraged by the fine work which Commandant De Wet and President Steyn have been doing in the Free State."

'"But surely," I insisted, "the war must be over now that your capital is taken!"

'"Capital!" he exclaimed, with great energy; "what is a capital? It does not consist of any particular collection of bricks and mortar. The Republican capital, the seat of Government, is here in this car. There is no magic about my special site. Our country is invaded, it is true, but it is not conquered, and the Government is still effective."

'"I presume that your reason for leaving Pretoria was that you might not fall into the hands of the British?"

'The ex-President smiled feebly, and said he was not so foolish as to be taken prisoner. "I provided this means of locomotion," he said, "precisely for the same purpose that our burghers supply themselves with horses when they take the field. It is necessary that I should be able to move quickly from place to place. That is all. By-and-bye this car will take me back to Pretoria. For the present it enables me to keep away from Pretoria, where I could be of no service, and where I should only play into the hands of the enemy."

'"They say, Mr. Kruger, that you have brought with you gold to the value of something like two millions. I am instructed by my journal that this is reported in England."

'"It is not true. Whatever monetary resources I may have with me are simply those that we require for State purposes. At the same time I am not going to tell you where our treasure is. Let Lord Roberts find it if he can."

'"They also say in England that you contemplate taking refuge on the Dutch man-o'-war lying off Lourenço Marques."

'"That again is a lie," said the ex-President vehemently. "I know of no Dutch war-vessel. I am not contemplating taking refuge anywhere. I shall not leave my country. There will be no need for me to do anything of the kind."

'"And then, sir," I went on, "there is much surprise at your having left Mrs Kruger behind."

'"But why? Mrs Kruger is quite safe in Pretoria. She would only be put to personal inconvenience here. All communication between us is stopped, of course, but she will await my return with calmness and courage. She is a brave woman. I am here awaiting further information. We are surrounded by faithful burghers, and are quite safe."

'Mr Reitz then remarked, "You may depend upon it, the war is not yet over. Guerrilla warfare will go on over an enormous area. We intend to fight to the bitter end, and shall probably retire upon Lydenburg, where we can hold out for many months."

'"Yes," observed Mr Kruger, "it is only now that the real struggle has begun. I fear that there will still be much bloodshed, but the fault is that of the British Government."

'Raising his voice to an almost passionate height, he exclaimed: "The time has passed for us to talk. We have done plenty of that, but it has done us no good. There is now nothing left for us to do but to keep on fighting – keep on fighting."'

President Kruger

OUR MILITARY OFFICERS

General Christiaan Fourie

Christiaan Ernst Fourie was born in 1858 in the Lydenburg district. We know virtually nothing of his descent and his youth. As an adult he participated in numerous campaigns of the South African Republic against rebellious black communities, including the Pedi in the 1870s, and the Nzundza Ndebele in the 1880s. He is also a veteran of the Transvaal War of Independence of 1880-81.

Fourie settled on the farm Blesbokfontein in the district of Middelburg in 1888. Two years later he went to Mashonaland as member of a commission to investigate the possible settlement of Boers in that area north of the Limpopo. In 1896 he was elected Field Cornet and soon afterwards Commandant of the Middelburg district. He also served as Native Commissioner in that area.

After the outbreak of the war last October he and his burghers proceeded to the Natal front where he took part in a number of battles. In December last year he was promoted to the rank of fighting general. After the British breakthrough at Pieter's Heights at the end of February, he and his commando were transferred to the Transvaal Highveld. Earlier this week he participated with distinction in the Battle of Donkerhoek. This able officer celebrates his 42nd birthday tomorrow.

General C.E. Fourie

THE War Reporter
WEEKLY EDITION

Number 37 — Machadodorp, South African Republic — 23 June 1900

CHRISTIAAN DE WET'S HOME TORCHED
Roberts declares war on civilian population

Machadodorp, 22 June – Shocking reports of a new method of waging war by the British reached us this week. If one reads this alongside similar reports that reached us from Griqualand West last month, one cannot but be extremely concerned about the direction in which British tactics are heading. The fact is: Chief Commandant De Wet's house on his farm Roodepoort, close to the Renoster River railway bridge in the northern Free State, was burnt down on 16 June on the orders of none other than Lord Roberts himself. In addition Roberts threatens that he will order the torching of the houses of numerous civilians in both Republics. The fate of the women and children who live in those houses obviously leaves him cold.

Roberts reportedly explained his actions against De Wet in the following way: 'He, like all Free Staters now fighting against us, is a rebel and must be treated as such.' In addition we have heard that De Wet wrote the following in a letter to the officer who was in command of the destruction of his house: '…my house cost me £700, but it will cost you £7 000 000 before I get through with you …'

The ashes of the ruins of De Wet's house were probably still smouldering when Roberts fired his next shell at civilian targets in the Republics last Saturday. In his so-called Proclamation 5 he declared as follows: 'Whereas small parties of raiders have recently been doing wanton damage to public property in the O.R.C. and S.A.R. by destroying railway bridges and culverts and cutting the telegraph wires, and whereas such damage cannot be done without the knowledge and connivance of the neighbouring inhabitants, and the principal civil residents in the districts concerned. Now therefore I, … warn the said inhabitants and principal civil residents that, whenever public property is destroyed or injured in the manner specified above, they will be held responsible for aiding and abetting the offenders. The houses in the vicinity of the place where the damage is done will be burnt, and the principal civil residents will be made prisoners of war.'

From this is should be clear to everybody that Roberts has declared war against the civilian inhabitants of both Republics, including women and children.

In the meantime we have gained information about the humiliating way in which the enemy treats burghers who lay down their arms and return to their houses. A telegram that an honourable person addressed to the military commission of the Orange Free State thus reads: '15 June: Reliable reports have been received of burghers who willingly laid down their arms and stayed at home to the effect that if it were possible, they would crawl on their knees to join the commandos again. Others would commit suicide if that would improve their fate. To gain an idea of the humiliation to which these burghers who remained behind on or returned to their farms are subjected, it can be mentioned that when groups of soldiers or police officials arrive on their farms, they order the owner, a burgher, or perhaps rather a former burgher with an English pass, to cool down, water and stable their horses. The former burghers have to carry out these orders while the soldiers or police officers walk into their houses, demand cake and coffee and enjoy this while the farm owners' wives are forced to serve them. The former burgher who had surrendered is sometimes chased on foot for some distance and then kicked on the behind and ordered back home with a pass in his pocket with the farewell greeting: "Go back home, you coward!"'

As for the women and children: according to all laws of warfare and of humanity, women and children may not be threatened or molested in any way by the enemy. Generally speaking the enemy is not doing this. Indeed, we hear that it is going well with most of the women who remain behind on the farms and that the Khakis treat them cordially. However, we are concerned that this will not remain the case for any length of time, since Lord Roberts seems to be dissatisfied that his offensive against the civilians is not thorough enough.

On Tuesday he issued Proclamation 6. In this he broadens his previous proclamation by declaring that the inhabitants of the area where railway or telegraph wires are destroyed will be held responsible collectively for the damage. In addition, prominent inhabitants will be forced to ride on the military trains as hostages to prevent the Boers from attacking those trains.

Chief Commandant Christiaan de Wet's farmhouse – after the Khakis burnt it down

TRANSVAALERS GATHER AT BALMORAL
NEW MILITARY TACTICS IMPLEMENTED

Balmoral, 18 June – After the major battle at Donkerhoek last week, the Transvaal forces retreated to Balmoral, a small village on the railway line east of Bronkhorstspruit. The Long Tom gun mounted on the railway truck covered the Boer rearguard. A number of well-placed shots were sufficient for this loyal armament to terminate any British attempt at pursuit.

The railway truck that serves as mobile gun carriage for the 7,2 metre Long Tom gun is a common goods wagon. A steel plate 2,5 centimetres thick has been attached round the wagon as outer armour and on the inside a neat square of sandbags is packed as fortification. The floor of the wagon consists of a platform of thick beams on which the original gun-carriage is mounted. The gun is so well balanced that you can push the muzzle up and down or sideways with your hand. The insides of the barrel shine like a mirror. The projectiles are 50 centimetres in length and 15,5 centimetres in diameter.

The Transvaal officers held a war council meeting here in Balmoral last Thursday and confirmed the acceptance of a totally new military tactic. The defensive or passive tactics employed earlier on, which left the initiative in the hands of the enemy, will be completely abandoned. In their stead the Boers will employ active tactics, attacking the enemy as often as possible and especially attempting to obstruct their communication routes. Small groups of burghers will act independently of each other, forcing the Khaki commanders to divide their own forces and make them more vulnerable.

In addition to the main Republican force along the eastern railway line, over which Commandant-General Louis Botha will himself be the supreme commander, at least four other commandos will be reorganised in order to implement the new military tactic. The Heidelberg Commando under the command of Commandant S.B. Buys will attempt to disrupt the communication lines of the British in southern and southeastern Transvaal; General Sarel Oosthuizen will reorganise the burghers in the Krugersdorp district; the Potchefstroom Commando will be reorganised by F.G.A. Wolmarans and Koos Malan, and the Rustenburg Commando by Commandant Casper du Plessis.

At the request of President Kruger, Botha furthermore decided to send Generals Koos de la Rey and Manie Lemmer to the western Transvaal to reorganise and lead an offensive behind the enemy. Lemmer immediately left for Rustenburg to attempt to prevent the British from achieving their goal of confiscating all the horses and cattle in that area. Botha was initially unwilling to release De la Rey, since he regarded him as indispensable to halting the British offensive. De la Rey himself was unwilling to go, since he had been informed that the British had already taken possession of all the horses in the western districts of Transvaal. According to him, Boers cannot wage war without horses and it would serve no purpose for him to return to the western Transvaal.

It is not yet clear to us if De la Rey will eventually go to the western Transvaal.

Over the past few weeks the large-scale desertion of Transvaal burghers has remained a problem that needs to be addressed. Numerous burghers have totally lost their confidence in the officers who could not halt the British advance, some feeling that these officers are incapable or cowardly, while others state that the British numbers are simply too great – that even if the Republican military authorities had been extremely capable and courageous, they would have been bound to fail. Many burghers cannot understand why the expensive forts around Pretoria were not armed and used to defend the capital. They regard the statement by Commandant-General Botha on this issue as a feeble excuse behind which officers hide their obvious weaknesses. What is even more frustrating to the burghers who are still fighting is that although measures against deserters have been announced, and even President Kruger has promised that deserters will be punished, no notable action has ever been taken against those cowards.

The Executive Council of the South African Republic has given leave to Commandant-General Botha to confiscate all livestock, including all animals that can be used to haul vehicles and all horses, to ensure that the latter will not fall into the hands of the enemy.

FROM THE EDITOR

No large-scale battles took place in the past week, nor any progress in the direction of an eventual settlement. Indeed, British proclamations of the past week indicate that they are not interested in peace at all: their only goal seems to be the eventual humiliation of the Republican forces and authorities.

On what grounds do we draw such dismal conclusions? From the fact that Lord Roberts not only ordered the destruction of Chief Commandant Christiaan de Wet's house, but also threatens to destroy many other homes. It is of no consequence to him what will happen to the women and children who live in those houses. One could argue that Roberts is endlessly frustrated by the inability of his forces to bring an end to Boer resistance. What is more probable is that this is a calculated tactic to persuade the Boers to stop fighting. Last week he dangled a carrot by attempting to bribe Botha and De la Rey to surrender. His attempt failed. This week he waves the stick: threaten the burghers that they will lose their property, their houses, their women and their children, if not their lives, if they do not stop fighting; they will then certainly surrender – at least that seems to be Roberts's belief. That is a dastardly tactic, more likely to fill the Boers with bitterness than convince them to be flexible.

A railway truck serves as gun carriage for this Long Tom gun

DEVELOPMENTS IN THE NORTHWESTERN CAPE

Rebel forces in Lower Orange River area collapse

Machadodorp, 18 June – A number of reports on military activities in the northwestern Cape Colony reached us in the past few days. In most of these cases the British emerged as the victors, even though the burghers and/or Cape Rebels who support the Republican cause did, generally speaking, give a good account of themselves.

In the first place the uprising in the northwestern Cape that reached its zenith in February but collapsed after the start of Lord Roberts's offensive, had a tragic aftermath. At the end of last month a final, bloody skirmish took place at Kheis, near Upington on the Orange River. About 400 Rebels had hidden themselves on an island in the Orange River since March. Early on the morning of 28 May they were unexpectedly bombarded from the south by the artillery of a British force consisting of 350 men under Colonel Adye. Before the British foot soldiers could surround the island, the Rebels fled. Fortunately for them the British artillery also fired on their own foot soldiers, thus compounding Colonel Adye's problems.

The rebel laager, including thousands of cattle, was reportedly captured by the British, and many Boers were killed, including the Rebel commander, 24-year-old Herman Judelewitz. On the British side 10 Khakis were killed and 18 wounded.

The hundreds of Cape Rebels who have participated in the uprising in this vicinity are now in dire straits. By April the jail in Upington was filled to overflowing. At Kenhardt too, numerous people – probably more than 100 – are detained in a camp outside town.

THE SKIRMISH AT FABERSPUT

Two days after this battle, General Petrus de Villiers with some 600 Rebels of Griqualand West led by Commandants Vorster and Venter carried out a surprise attack on General Charles Warren's camp at Fabersput.

It was a well-planned attack from three directions at first light, though in the ensuing chaos nobody could distinguish between opponent and friend. After a while the British numbers were sufficient to check the Boer attack. Reports that have reached us claim that altogether 23 Khakis were killed and 32 wounded, while the Rebels lost 14 killed (38 killed and 50 wounded according to pro-British Cape newspapers).

On 20 June the British in turn carried out a surprise attack on General de Villiers and his Rebels. The General himself and 30 of his men managed to escape but the rest of the commando was forced to surrender to General Warren. It is a huge setback: 220 burghers, 280 horses, 80 wagons and more than 100 000 rounds of ammunition fell into the hands of the enemy.

WAR REPORTS FROM THE FREE STATE

MORE SUCCESSFUL BOER ATTACKS ON MAIN RAILWAY LINE

Machadodorp, 22 June – Numerous reports on war-related issues have reached us from the Orange Free State. General Abraham de Villiers, who was severely wounded last month in the battle at Biddulphsberg, is still in a critical condition. As a result, on 13 June President Steyn appointed Commandant Paul Roux as fighting general in his place. The very next day Roux led 200 burghers in an attack on a British guard post at the Sand River railway bridge. His aim was to destroy the temporarily repaired bridge. However, the British force fended off the attack. Steyn also appointed Judge J.B.M. Hertzog as fighting general and placed him in command of the whole southwestern part of the Orange Free State.

Yesterday evening there were newspaper reports of renewed attacks on enemy communication lines by the Free Staters on 14 June. General Froneman led the attack on a repaired railway bridge at Leeuspruit. The enemy defended their position with heavy gunfire. The burghers damaged a locomotive as well as a number of trucks loaded with utensils, wood and building material for the repair of railway bridges. All the goods as well as the repaired railway bridge with its wooden supports were set alight.

Altogether 58 Khakis as well as 300 black workers were captured and taken to President Steyn's laager somewhere at a secret place in the northern Free State. Froneman reports that his burghers were courageously supported by a small Transvaal commando of 105 burghers led by Piet Viljoen, the mining commissioner of Heidelberg who formerly served as magistrate of Potchef-stroom and has been elected as general by his burghers.

On 17 June Chief Commandant Christiaan de Wet himself attacked a convoy of 60 British supply wagons on their way from Vredefort Road to Heilbron to resupply General Colvile's forces. The burghers pinned the Khakis down in the open veld with accurate fire and were on the point of forcing them to surrender when reinforcements arrived from the direction of Heilbron with a number of naval guns. Since the burghers were now literally between two fires, they had to fall back.

De Wet subsequently trekked to the south to Paardekraal.

BOTHA ADDRESSES THE HEIDELBERGERS

Gives strong indication of future military tactics

Balmoral, 14 June – A war council meeting was held here today, and immediately afterwards Commandant-General Louis Botha visited the laager of the Heidelberg Commando. The burghers were bitterly disappointed to receive orders to return to their home district and voiced their frustration quite audibly. They did not want to go and guard a town, but to confront the enemy's main force like men. Botha's aim was to convince them that there was a good reason why they had to return to Heidelberg as soon as possible. One of the burghers, Wilhelm Mangold, who has previously written reports for us, made the following notes on Botha's speech:

'The Commandant-General greeted us in his normal friendly fashion, and indicated that he wanted to address us. He took up position on an anthill so that everybody could see him. At first he explained why Pretoria was not defended. Then he brought us up to date on the activities of the two Presidents in Machadodorp and the northeast Free State. The most important part of his speech however was an exposition of the future Boer military tactics. It seems as if this will entail guerrilla warfare. The burghers, he declared, must attack the enemy from behind and on their flanks and must attempt to cut off their essential supplies. That would make it very difficult for the British military authorities to care sufficiently for all their soldiers.

'Botha declared that General de la Rey is already on his way to the western Transvaal with 1 200 men to implement this tactic. General Chris Botha will concentrate on the railway line between Dundee and Newcastle in northern Natal and make that unserviceable. We of Heidelberg should do the same in the vicinity of our hometown to cause as much damage as possible to the enemy. By capturing a whole trainload of supplies, we can cause more damage to Lord Roberts than by a victory on the battlefield. And if it becomes too hot for us in that territory, we can temporarily cross the border into the Free State or even Natal.

'"But we will," Botha added, "never hand our country over to the enemy. In America George Washington fought for seven years against the English. His army was small and their condition extremely difficult, but he achieved his goal and America was liberated. Freedom and justice triumphed. We still have a lot of suffering ahead before the end of this war. We will perhaps have to fight against our own brothers, and will have to shoot them as traitors. Whatever happens, we must remember our motto: Unity is strength. And if we do our duty, God will not forsake us."

'In conclusion Botha made the following promise in his clear strong voice: "I give you my word of honour that I'll keep fighting against England even if I have no more than 100 men behind me. For me there is only one objective, namely freedom or to fight until death."

'After he had made his speech, the burghers asked General Botha if a rumour that Lord Roberts had attempted to bribe him was true. The General answered that an intermediary of Roberts had made the proposal. The proposal reveals that Roberts is not sure that he has the forces to achieve his objective with weapons and has decided on trying to bribe Boer leaders. As for himself, Botha stated that he would always be prepared to negotiate on a just basis with our independence as a precondition for peace, but will never surrender.

'Botha then concluded by reminding us of our responsibility towards our brothers in the Free State who unconditionally support us, and to our brothers in the Cape Colony who came to our assistance and to all our comrades who have already given their lives on the battlefield for our freedom, or who find themselves in hospitals or elsewhere where they are recovering from their wounds. Were all their sacrifices in vain? Our reputation demands from us that we do our duty towards these brothers.

'"Comrades," he added, "may God be with you. Trust Him. I wish you all the best and hope that you will exhibit in coming battles the same courage that you exhibited at Moddersspruit, Colenso, Spioenkop and Paardeberg."

'The meeting ended with three hurrahs. Those of us who moved towards him, received a friendly handshake from the General. The Heidelberg burghers then sang their flag song and departed from Balmoral to their home district filled with new spirit.'

General Louis Botha

OUR MILITARY OFFICERS

General Petrus de Villiers

Petrus Johannes de Villiers was born in 1853 in the Hopetown district of the Cape Colony. He is a son of the late Abraham Izak de Villiers and his wife Petronella Isabella Frederika de Villiers and is the elder brother of General Abraham de Villiers, who was seriously wounded last month.

De Villiers moved with his parents to Douglas in the Cape Colony in 1868 but later on, when his parents moved once again, this time to the Transvaal, he remained behind.

Soon afterwards, when he was only 17 years old, he was elected field cornet for the ward Kalkrand in Hopetown.

He married Susanna Maria de Klerk in 1873. They have eight children.

Even though he is a citizen of the Cape Colony, De Villiers had a keen interest in political developments in the two Boer Republics and openly sympathised with them. When the war broke out in October last year he immediately joined the Orange Free State forces. He took part in numerous engagements and exhibited such outstanding leadership qualities that General De la Rey promoted him to the rank of general. He has been especially active on the western border of the Free State and in Griqualand West, where he organised Cape rebel units to support the Boer cause.

De Villiers has made a name for himself as a persistent fighter and uncompromising patriot. He has a friendly nature and treats all his burghers with unqualified respect.

War Reporter has no photograph of this able officer.

WAR REPORTS FROM THE TRANSVAAL

Machadodorp, 22 June – The military activities of the past week have spread ever further across the Transvaal, even to the rear of the Boer forces here in the east. Last Sunday a British patrol that came through Swaziland managed to destroy a culvert at Kaap Muiden on the railway line between Nelspruit and Komatipoort. One of our goods trains derailed there soon afterwards. The engine driver died in the accident, while the stoker, conductor and six other persons on the train were severely injured. Repair work to the bridge immediately commenced, but the railway line to Delagoa Bay is still unusable. We have been informed that the unit that carried out this sabotage is known as Steinaecker's Horse and consists of both white mercenaries and armed black warriors.

About 500 British prisoners of war, including 15 officers, arrived in Standerton from the Orange Free State, and were immediately dispatched to the prisoner-of-war camp at Nooitgedacht.

On Monday 18 June the British occupied Krugersdorp and on Tuesday General Buller entered Volksrust. This is the first town in Transvaal to fall into his hands. A British force that crossed Moolman's Heights soon afterwards occupied Wakkerstroom. Yesterday afternoon at 12 o'clock the Republican forces destroyed the railway bridge across the Vaal River at Standerton.

In Sekhukhuneland fighting between black communities broke out and measures were immediately introduced to bring an end to that unrest.

The 18 locomotives and 148 railway trucks that had been employed on the Volksrust–Heidelberg railway line up to last weekend, were all made unusable before they fell into the hands of General Buller when he occupied Standerton yesterday.

THE War Reporter
WEEKLY EDITION

Number 38   Machadodorp, South African Republic   30 June 1900

UPHEAVALS IN CAPE COLONY POLITICS
SCHREINER RESIGNS AS PREMIER – SPRIGG HIS SUCCESSOR

Machadodorp, 29 June – British military technicians repaired the telegraph communications between Bloemfontein and Pretoria at Roodewal on 15 June. With that the week-long break that Chief Commandant De Wet had engineered with his highly successful raid on the railway line on 7 June came to an end. The advantage for us is that we have now once again received news from the Cape Colony via our contacts in Pretoria.

The latest important news is without doubt that Prime Minister W.P. Schreiner of the Cape Colony has resigned. He had no real option, since it had become impossible for him to carry out his duties in an honourable way. Schreiner wanted to lead the Cape into a peaceful situation, but this was totally unacceptable to the warmongering Sir Alfred Milner, the British High Commissioner.

The political point of dispute that led directly to Schreiner's resignation was the issue of how the Cape authorities should treat the Cape Rebels. In Schreiner's cabinet there was no unanimity on this issue. The Prime Minister himself, J.X. Merriman and Thomas te Water were in favour of amnesty, while Richard Solomon agreed with Milner that the Rebels had to be persecuted.

The caucus of Schreiner's governing party, the South African Party, met on 8 and 9 June and on both occasions rejected a compromise proposal by Schreiner which in effect meant that the Cape Rebels would be stripped of their voting rights for five years. The most important argument against the proposal was that it would play directly into Milner's hands, since the Cape Afrikaners would in the process lose the votes of thousands of supporters. The rejection of his proposal was the last straw for Schreiner. He had failed in his attempts to keep the support of both Milner and the majority of his Party, and resigned on 13 June.

Schreiner's successor is the veteran Cape politician Sir Gordon Sprigg, an outspoken British imperialist who has appointed a cabinet consisting of imperialist-minded politicians. The situation seems rather strange to us, since the Afrikaner Bond has a majority in the Cape Parliament. The fact is that five Afrikaner members of Parliament were absent when Schreiner resigned: two were in jail, namely the Revd C.W.H. Schröder of Prieska, who had joined the Cape Rebels, and P.J. de Wet; two were out of the country, namely Jotham Joubert and I.J. van der Walt, and one was in the Transvaal, namely Dr Hoffman. That left 46 members of the Afrikaner Bond, while Sprigg's Progressives have 43 seats – but two of them, including Cecil John Rhodes, are also out of the country. It seems strange to us that Milner did not demand in the Cape – as he has done in the Transvaal – that the majority of the citizens in the country should be in control.

GATHERINGS OF PRO-REPUBLICANS IN GRAAFF-REINET

At the beginning of this month we reported on a mass meeting of Cape Afrikaners at Graaff-Reinet on 30 May. In the meantime we have learned that it was attended by between 1 500 and 1 700 people. The chairman of the meeting was Jacob de Villiers, the brother of the Cape Chief Justice. In addition numerous prominent Afrikaners and even a number of English-speaking colonists were present. One of the latter was Olive Schreiner, the sister of W.P. Schreiner (who was still the Premier at that time) and author of the world-renowned book *Story of an African Farm*. The other prominent English-speaking person present was Arthur Cartwright, the editor of *South African News*.

The Republican cause was discussed in strong language and a resolution was accepted in favour of the unlimited independence of the two Republics. The deputies stated their opinion that the Republican Afrikaners would never become willing subjects of the British empire and predicted that if their independence were destroyed, they would grab the first opportunity to restore their freedom – even with armed violence if there was no other option. Furthermore it was decided that the Cape Colony should have the right to choose its own government, including a governor. The Afrikaner Bond undertook that they would, with the help of the two Republics, defend South Africa in the case of conflict with other powers. That would mean that in future Britain would not have to station troops in South Africa.

A last decision of the representatives was to collect money to send a deputation to Britain to inform the public there of the true state of affairs in South Africa. The deputies to Europe are Charles Molteno, the Revd Morris, Rossouw and De Waal, secretary of the Afrikaner Bond. The pro-Republican deputation of the Bond's Congress at Graaff-Reinet left for Europe on 20 June.

Two weeks after the Afrikaner gathering at Graaff-Reinet, the Afrikaner Bond's annual congress started in Paarl on 15 June. In his opening speech T.P. Theron, the chairman of the Bond, rejected all malicious accusations that the Bond was involved in a conspiracy with the Republics against British supremacy in South Africa. The congress nevertheless expressed its deep disappointment with British policy in South Africa, since it had led to an unjust war and completely ignored the feelings of the majority of the Cape voters. The Congress furthermore expressed the wish that peace would soon be restored and added that it can only be achieved if the independence of the Republics is honoured.

People's Congress at Graaff-Reinet

MARTIAL LAW IN PRETORIA
Permits, restrictions the order of the day

Machadodorp, 29 June – Reports from Pretoria point to a totally new dispensation in the former capital. We have received an extensive description of the present state of affairs from an inhabitant of the city. Our reporter is Johanna van Warmelo, the same young lady whom we quoted earlier this month when we reported on the British occupation of Pretoria. Her views are more or less representative of the strong Republican sentiments harboured by the vast majority of Boer women, both old and young. Here is her report:

'Khakis, Khakis everywhere – in the streets, in the stores, in every open spot in Sunnyside. Lord Roberts is living in the British Agency where the British representative Sir Walter Conyngham Greene lived till the outbreak of the war, and where the Republican ultimatum was handed to him on 9 October last year. Lord Kitchener lives in Blumlein's house and the Duke of Westminster in the architect Sytze Wierda's house – both also in Sunnyside. The Khaki officer who administers everything here in Pretoria is Major General Maxwell.

'If you want to ride your bicycle on the street, you have to obtain a permit signed by the military commissioner of police. The same applies if you want to travel by horse, by horse-cart or by wagon in the city. To obtain a permit you have to queue at Government Building. There are also activities for which you have to have a permit, such as being out of your house between seven o'clock in the evening and half past six in the morning. No black people are allowed in the city if they are not permanent workers within the city boundaries. All jeweller's shops are closed. The same is true for liquor stores, bars and black eating-houses. Trade in any form of wine or other alcoholic beverages is strictly prohibited, except if you have a permit for it. And if you commit a crime, you are punishable under martial law – a very uninviting prospect.

'I have ever since the day of the British occupation walked in the streets with a ribbon in the colours of the *Vierkleur* round my hat. My objective is to make my views known to friend and foe. A few mornings back an officer rode up to me in the street and ordered me to take off my Transvaal colours. I said: "You must first conquer the Transvaal before you dictate to us." "Well, I have told you now and if you don't take them off I shall be obliged to send someone to do so." Soon afterwards two soldiers came to take my *Vierkleur* by force. Since I did not want to suffer the humiliation of being roughly handled by soldiers, I replaced the ribbon with a white one. England is making herself ridiculous by this small-mindedness. The mighty British Empire afraid of a bit of ribbon round a girl's hat!'

THE FIELD MARSHAL AND THE *VIERKLEUR* RIBBON

'In the past week the ribbon issue led to a strange incident which endlessly amused the pro-Republican inhabitants of Pretoria. Mrs van Alphen, the wife of the Postmaster-General of the South African Republic, told me this morning that she went to Lord Roberts, with the *Vierkleur* on, to ask if he had given these orders. She was stopped three times by the police on her way but she showed them her revolver and dared any of them to lay a finger on her. They allowed her to pass when she said she was on her way to Lord Roberts. One of them said, "Don't interfere with the madam." (Revolvers have a way of inspiring respect, especially in the bosom of a Tommy.)

'Lord Roberts received her courteously and she sat alone with him in a room with a small table between them. She told him everything and objected to the way young girls had been taken to the Charge Office and forcibly deprived of their colours, and he said he thought himself that it was an unnecessary proceeding but the Governor wished it and he thought she had better obey. In her house and on her property she could do as she pleased but in public she must not expose herself to insult. "You are under British protection and for the time being I think you had better not wear your colours." "Well," she said, "if you wish it I shall take them off" (here she unpinned her *Vierkleur* and laid it on the table, from where Lord Roberts took it up and sat playing with it), "but I have threatened to shoot the first soldier who lays a finger on me, and that reminds me …" (here she got up in her slow and stately manner and drew her revolver from her pocket).

'Lord Roberts started up and stood erect before her, with staring eyes and crimson face). "Madam, you know ladies are not permitted to walk about with firearms." "Yes, I know, and that is what I have come to see you about. Will you give me a permit for it?" She put it on the table and he sat down and examined it. When he saw that it was unloaded the colour slowly left his face until it was as white as death. Poor old gentleman! He thought his end had come and he had escaped all these months only to fall by the hand of this formidable woman. When he had regained his composure he told her where she could go for a permit. She went at once by cab and found someone waiting to receive her and was shown every attention. Lord Roberts had telephoned at once. I don't think he will ever forget her but what an awful fright she must have given him.'

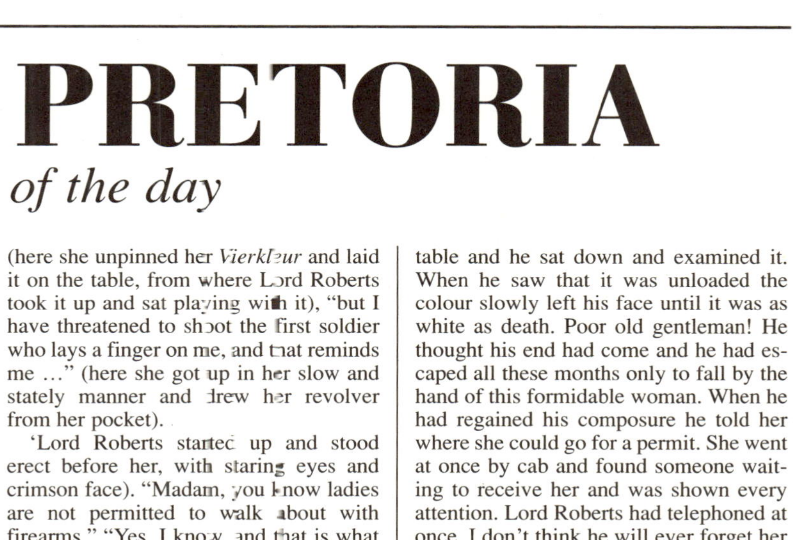

The British Agency, Pretoria

HEIDELBERG OCCUPIED BY BRITISH

Burghers destroy kilometres of railway lines

Greylingstad, 27 June - The Heidelberg Commando arrived in their home town from Balmoral on 19 June. Their main task is to disrupt the British supply routes as effectively as possible, and for that reason they made hardly any attempt to prevent the British occupation of Heidelberg last Saturday (23 June). At that time the Heidelberg burghers could not destroy the railway lines effectively at all since they were unable to obtain dynamite from any source.

Once again we have to thank Wilhelm Mangold of the Heidelberg commando for the following report on their experiences of the past five days or so: 'On the morning of 22 June our scouts reported that Khakis in huge numbers were marching from Elandsfontein in this direction. The Heidelberg commando immediately occupied the low hills north of the town. The first units of the enemy force became visible about an hour later. It immediately became clear to us that we would never be able to confront the massive number of Khakis. In addition the British artillery began bombarding our positions with shells and shrapnel soon afterwards. It did not bother us much, since Corporal John Spruyt could see the enemy guns and each time he saw a flash he called out 'Here the vulture comes!' We then ducked for shelter. One can clearly identify the somewhat harsh whistling sound of lyddite projectiles before they explode.

'Since the town of Heidelberg and its inhabitants would have suffered unnecessarily under a bombardment, we immediately abandoned our futile defensive manoeuvre. Our new commander, General Piet Viljoen, sent a message to the British General that we would retreat if the British would end their bombardment. The British agreed and by dusk we fell back.

'Of course we were as well prepared as one could be to survive the occupation of our beloved town. We had earlier taken all the provisions and ammunition that we could load on wagons from the town. Surplus supplies and even rifles had been set alight. Most of us who lived in town nevertheless felt sad to say farewell to our loving relatives, since there is no certainty as to when we will see them again. Our biggest concern is the fact that hundreds of black people have now suddenly left the services of their employers. These blacks conduct themselves with extreme arrogance against the Boer women. We assume that they will pilfer wherever they can. In my specific case my biggest blessing was that my wife did not attempt to convince me to surrender and to stay with her, but rather made it clear to me that she is proud to have a steadfast husband.

'Our commando left that night on horseback in the direction of Greylingstad. Early the next morning we found ourselves on a low hill from where we could, with the help of our binoculars, look on as the Khakis occupied our beautiful town. The cavalry arrived in large groups from the direction of Johannesburg, and the infantry marched in neat rows from the direction of Nigel. It was enough to make us sick. What we did not know at that time and only heard later, was that many of our town officials, including magistrate Wepener, received the Khakis with open arms, and willingly supplied all sorts of information to them. Some of the officials, who had earlier acted as though they were fiery Republicans, there and then entered the service of the enemy.

'Later that same morning the whole British occupation force advanced on our new positions. Their fighting pattern is by now well known to us: infantry on the left flank, artillery in the centre and cavalry on the right. We positioned ourselves in the low mountains southeast of Heidelberg. Unfortunately we had no guns to bombard the enemy from afar. The Khaki force consisted of several thousands of soldiers, while our commando had only 600 men. Since we had to spread out over a very wide front, we could not provide effective resistance. Consequently we fell back in an orderly fashion while fighting in the direction of De Villiersdorp (or Villiers, as some people call it). The fighting lasted until that evening. We suffered few casualties and have no idea of the number of enemy casualties.

'Our biggest problem at the moment is that there still are burghers who are deserting from commando. Some have even become "handsuppers" and joined the forces of the enemy. This is a bigger problem for us than the enemy's ammunition. Fortunately Commandant W.F. Pretorius joined us with 400 men from the Highveld, which means that our strength is again about 1 000 men. We thought of retreating all the way to the Free State, but have received orders to operate in the direction of Volksrust. We are attempting to destroy the railway line as effectively as possible, and to damage all the bridges and culverts whilst retreating from Heidelberg.'

FROM THE EDITOR

It is always dangerous to count your chickens before they are hatched, but there are definite signs of a renewed willingness of the Transvaal forces to fight after the depression that followed on the British occupation of Pretoria. Our readers will remember that a virtually total collapse of the Orange Free State Republic's armed forces took place within the first few weeks after the British occupation of Bloemfontein. A reawakening then took place. Now it seems as if a similar reawakening is taking place in our Republic.

There are numerous negative factors that we have to take into account. There are still burghers who are overcome by dejection, and we cannot wish that away. A further definite setback is that the Cape government of W.P. Schreiner has collapsed, and that he has been replaced as premier by an outspoken imperialist. These developments indicate that Milner and his henchmen have no regard for any law, not even the constitution of one of their own 'self-governing' colonies. They respect nothing that hinders the eventual attainment of their objective, namely undisputed British supremacy in South Africa.

MILITARY ACTIVITIES IN THE ORANGE FREE STATE

DE WET STILL DISRUPTING RAILWAY LINES TO THE NORTH

Reitz, 28 June – On 22 June Chief Commandant Christiaan de Wet again launched a three-pronged attack on the railway line north of Kroonstad. He himself burnt the first bridge at Serfontein Siding and broke up the railway line as well as the telegraph poles in that area. General Stoffel Froneman experienced strong resistance at the America Siding some 13 kilometres north of Kroonstad. When his burghers began destroying the railway line soon after sunrise, the British soldiers who were stationed at the siding fired so heavily on them that they were forced to retreat. One burgher was killed and four wounded, two of whom later died.

The simultaneous attack by General J.H. Olivier on the Heuningspruit Siding and the railway line at Katbosch was partly successful. Olivier sent a messenger to the commander of the 400-strong British garrison to demand its immediate surrender, but the Khakis rejected the demand. Olivier's burghers then began dynamiting both the railway and the telegraph line for substantial distances north as well as south of the station. The British garrison could not prevent this, but on the other hand Olivier and his burghers could not capture the garrison. General Froneman reached the battlefield at about nine o'clock with a Krupp gun and fired on the enemy, but without forcing them to surrender.

The fighting continued till late that afternoon, when help for the Khakis arrived from Kroonstad. Chief Commandant de Wet had by that time also reached the battlefield with his Krupp gun, but the British defenders still held out. When two strong Khaki columns arrived from Kroonstad, De Wet ordered the burghers to disengage and retreat to Paardekraal.

The total Boer casualties in these engagements were three burghers killed and three wounded. According to reliable sources seven soldiers were killed and 20 wounded on the British side.

There was also a lot of action in the area east of the railway line. General Paul Roux and his burghers attacked General Clements's Khakis in the area between Senekal and Winburg last Saturday, but Clements managed to retreat with his column and reached Winburg. Since he expected another attack from the Boers, two days later Clements ordered Colonel Grenfeld to attack the burghers from the rear. Instead, however, the burghers surprised the Khakis at Leliefontein near Senekal. A number of the Khakis fled all the way back to Ventersburg. What the British casualties in these skirmishes were, we do not know. The day before yesterday the Free Staters again became involved in a skirmish, this time at Lindley. We have not received any particulars, except a report that the Khakis suffered heavy casualties.

OUR MILITARY OFFICERS

General Paul Roux

Paul Hendrik Roux was born in 1862 in Hopetown in the northern Cape. He is the only son of Dirk Hendrik Dietz Roux and his wife Francina Johanna Wiid. He received his school education at the Paarl Gymnasium. Subsequently he studied at the Victoria College and the Theological Seminary at Stellenbosch. After qualifying and being admitted as a minister in 1889 he moved to the Transvaal, where he served the Dutch Reformed congregation of Braamfontein in Johannesburg. In the next year he became the minister of the Vredefort congregation in the Orange Free State. He served that congregation until 1897 when he moved to Senekal.

When the war broke out last October, the Reverend Roux joined the Senekal Commando as field minister. He soon revealed an exceptional talent for leadership. It was no surprise when he was elected Commandant of the Senekal commando in April. Earlier this month President Steyn promoted him to the rank of fighting general at the suggestion of Chief Commandant de Wet. De Wet feels that General Roux is an experienced man. He has served the commandos loyally as field minister and often found himself in the places where the heaviest fighting occurred, courageously tending to the wounded. In addition he gave the officers excellent advice regarding military issues, which indicates his exceptional military insight.

General Roux married Hester Helena Eksteen in 1891. They have three daughters.

General Paul Roux

MILITARY ACTIVITIES IN WESTERN TRANSVAAL

Massive dejection amongst the burghers

Machadodorp, 29 June – The biggest headache for the Republican military authorities in the western Transvaal is the burghers' spirit of dejection. Many have already surrendered their weapons or deserted their commandos. Earlier this month the Khakis occupied one town after the other in western Transvaal without experiencing any significant resistance. By the middle of June only small groups of burghers were attempting to combat the enemy here and there in the area west of Rustenburg. They made no impression on their adversary and scored no significant military successes.

Our correspondents have gained the impression that most of the burghers in the area closer to Pretoria have accepted the British occupation of their districts as an accomplished fact. It is only in the district of Krugersdorp that a strong resistance is notable. This is the area to which the war council at Balmoral sent General Sarel Oosthuizen on 15 June. The inhabitants of the Krugersdorp district have great respect for that officer, and things started to liven up immediately after his arrival in that area.

This reawakening of the burghers did not go unnoticed. The commander of the British occupation force in Krugersdorp, General Barton, has reportedly sent a written warning to Oosthuizen to end his commandeering of burghers and to surrender to the British, or face heavy punishment. The courageous General naturally did not heed the threat at all.

In addition to Oosthuizen, the strongly built General Manie Lemmer left Balmoral on 19 June. Only 25 men accompanied him to the Rustenburg district. Along the road he met Commandant Casper du Plessis, who was on his way to Commandant-General Botha with 150 men. Du Plessis and his burghers joined Lemmer's commando and began commandeering burghers in the Rustenburg area. We do not know how successful they have been.

ACTIVITIES ALONG THE EASTERN RAILWAY LINE

Machadodorp, 29 June – The position of the Boer forces along the eastern railway line was critical by the middle of last month. In the first place there is not enough food for the burghers, since the Transvaal commissary services are in a chaotic state. General de la Rey's commando, for example, only had the meat of their oxen to eat for days on end. They received no flour whatsoever to cook porridge and only received a few loaves of bread now and then. This was not nearly enough to supply the needs of all the burghers. This reflects very badly on our military authorities.

Commandant-General Louis Botha's problems are compounded by the absence of a good defensive position on the eastern Transvaal Highveld. Balmoral was not a suitable place for defensive positions. Botha, as a consequence, decided to send all the burghers who had no horses to the area of Machadodorp, where it would be easier to prepare defensive positions. He handed the duty to oversee the digging of trenches and the building of gun emplacements for inter alia the four Long Tom guns to Generals Joachim Fourie, Schalk Burger and Lukas Meyer.

Fortunately for the Boer forces the British have not yet resumed their expected eastward offensive from Donkerhoek. This lull in activity allows Botha to continue with measures to obtain horses for the burghers. He is accomplishing this through the use of powers granted to him at his request by the Executive Council to commandeer both slaughter and other livestock and to confiscate the horses of deserters.

Botha at one stage seriously considered taking up position at Donkerhoek again, but decided that it would not work when he realised that the burghers would not be prepared to carry out orders in that direction.

The arrival earlier this week at Balmoral of General Daniël Erasmus with approximately 1 200 burghers of the Pretoria and Middelburg commandos, who had formerly served on the Natal front, filled Botha with renewed confidence. He now feels ready to resume attacks on the enemy and to implement the decisions taken by the war council last week that the Boer forces should win back the initiative in this war.

THE War Reporter
WEEKLY EDITION

Number 39 — Machadodorp, South African Republic — 7 July 1900

THE MILITARY EVENTS IN TRANSVAAL
Developments along the eastern railway line

Machadodorp, 6 July – At the request of President Kruger his railway wagon has been moved permanently to the warmer climate of Waterval-Onder. This means that the government of the South African Republic and the officials who are stationed in Waterval Boven have to travel from Waterval Boven to Waterval Onder each day to conduct the affairs of the state.

Commandant-General Louis Botha left his laager at Balmoral last Wednesday and proceeded in a westerly direction with a strong commando. He plans to attack the British troops east of Pretoria.

DEVELOPMENTS IN SOUTHEASTERN TRANSVAAL

The burghers who defended Utrecht put up a courageous resistance against a British force that attacked them last Sunday, but eventually had to retreat after they had killed one soldier and taken three prisoners of war. The Khakis occupied Utrecht the next day. However, they abandoned the town again after they were told that Fighting General Hans Grobler was on his way there.

Last Friday (29 June) a Boer force halted a British unit that was on its way to Amersfoort. We do not know what the British losses in killed and wounded were, but three Khakis were taken prisoner of war. Two burghers were wounded. This Boer force destroyed the railway line and telegraph wires in numerous places between Sandspruit and Paardekop.

A Boer patrol was involved in a skirmish with a British patrol at Waterval in the Heidelberg district. Near the Val Station in the same area a small Boer patrol attacked a large British force that was on its way to Heidelberg. Unconfirmed reports give seven Khakis killed and two taken prisoner.

On 1 July the Transvaal forces reoccupied Wakkerstroom. Officials were appointed to officiate over the district. Two days later Boer commandos broke up about 350 metres of the railway line near Greylingstad and about one and a half kilometres of railway line at Vlaklaagte.

Yesterday a Boer patrol clashed with a British patrol at Standerton. The latter eventually fled. Two Khakis were made prisoner of war and three of their horses were killed.

DEVELOPMENTS IN WESTERN TRANSVAAL

General Koos de la Rey left Commandant-General Louis Botha's laager at Balmoral on Monday and moved off to the western part of the South African Republic. It is his intention to put pressure on the Khakis occupying the western districts. De la Rey has received extensive powers from President Kruger that will make it possible for him to establish virtually a separate government in western Transvaal.

In the meantime General Manie Lemmer reached the vicinity of Rustenburg. On Thursday (5 July) he sent an ultimatum to the British garrison of that town to surrender. Since the Khakis rejected the ultimatum, Lemmer and his burghers launched an attack, easily overpowering them, because their numbers had been severely reduced when Colonel Baden-Powell left the town on Tuesday. The burghers took possession of all the garrison's supplies and animals. A few hours later, however, a huge British force arrived, upon which Lemmer and his burghers left the town and occupied Olifants Nek in the Magaliesberg.

DEVELOPMENTS IN CENTRAL TRANSVAAL

Yesterday General Freek Grobler attacked a British guard post on a hill at Waterval, north of Pretoria.

Khaki casualties amounted to three men killed and nine taken prisoner; on the Boer side one man was killed and two wounded.

Waterval-Onder

MILITARY EVENTS IN THE FREE STATE
CHRISTIAAN DE WET ELECTED CHIEF COMMANDANT

Machadodorp, 6 July – Even though President Steyn had refused to allow an election for a Chief Commandant for the Free State forces, Chief Commandant Christiaan de Wet organised one in secret. His motivation was that he would not serve as appointed Chief Commandant without the certainty that the elected commandants of the Republic supported him. Most of the senior officers in the Free State were present, with the exception of Commandant Hattingh of Vrede and General Paul Roux. The result was: 26 votes for De Wet, three votes for Commandant J.H. Olivier, two votes for Chief Commandant Marthinus Prinsloo and one for Chief Commandant Piet de Wet. President Steyn was subsequently informed of the election and abides by it.

Our correspondent with the forces of Chief Commandant Christiaan de Wet reports that a large number of burghers have suddenly joined the laager. The reason for this is that British patrols are visiting farms and confiscating all the wagons and oxen. Since the burghers refuse to accept the confiscation of their property, they attempt to keep their wagons, horse-carts and other vehicles by bringing them to the commando.

For De Wet this poses an endless problem. He realises that the burghers want to protect their property, but a large wagon laager will increase his vulnerability. He does not, however, want to remove the wagons by force, since that would drive the burghers back into the hands of the enemy and would cause huge dents in the morale of his burghers.

On Tuesday 3 July, the enemy attacked a Free State commando on General Piet de Wet's farm, Elandsfontein, about 20 kilometres east of Lindley. It was mainly an artillery duel, though some shots were fired from the Boer rifles. The fighting died down by the evening, but was resumed by both sides on Wednesday morning.

At one stage the burghers prepared an ambush for an approaching British artillery battery, but their position was revealed when one of the Boer gunners fired too soon. The British artillery was consequently in a position to set up guns in time and to bombard the Boers. The Boer gunners fired back with great precision.

After a while the Khaki position became untenable when Commandant Michael Prinsloo charged them with about 100 burghers. In the chaos that resulted, the fleeing Khakis abandoned three or four of their guns in a wheat field. Chief Commandant Christiaan de Wet's artillery drove the British even further away. Prinsloo and his men reached the abandoned guns but could not move them away since they had no animals to use for this purpose.

De Wet immediately ordered that a number of his gun horses should be sent to haul the enemy guns away. Unfortunately both his own guns were malfunctioning at this critical stage. As a result he could not provide covering fire for Prinsloo and his men, and they were powerless to prevent the charging British reinforcements from repossessing the guns. All the burghers could do before falling back was to remove the breech-blocks of the British guns, which meant that the Khaki gunners could not immediately use their guns on the burghers.

The Free State forces are at present making their way towards Bethlehem with the objective of defending that town against an expected British attack.

BOER PRISONERS OF WAR ON ST HELENA
Eyewitness report by L.C. Ruijssenaers

Machadodorp, 3 July – An intermediary whose identity we are not in a position to divulge has handed us an extensive report with photographs on the arrival and conditions of the first Boers who were sent as prisoners of war to St Helena Island. The report is dated 31 May and was compiled by L.C. Ruijssenaers, the Hollander who sent us a report on the condition of Boer prisoners of war on board a prison ship in Simonstown harbour at the end of last year. He is now on St Helena – an island that is of course well known, since the famous French emperor, Napoleon Bonaparte, was detained and indeed died there about 80 years ago.

According to the information at our disposal, St Helena has a total land surface of 12 000 hectares. It is very mountainous and there is no natural harbour. Even though it is about 2 700 kilometres northwest of Cape Town, and not far south of the Equator, the temperature is mild. The approximately 3 000 permanent inhabitants of this British colony are very poor. The first Boer prisoners of war, including General Piet Cronjé, arrived on the island on 14 April. Ruijssenaers and the next group of prisoners arrived two weeks later. Here is his report on their experiences:

'On Monday 23 April we were informed that we would leave Simonstown that very day. We had to carry our own luggage to the railway station. It is a three-quarters of an hour walk and the heat was so exhausting that an elderly man died of exertion.

'We were loaded on cattle trucks and transported to Cape Town harbour under the guard of armed Tommies. There we boarded the steamer *Bavaria*. The ship was loaded to capacity – I have heard we were 1 500 prisoners of war on board. We received little food and our beds were hammocks – a device most of us had never seen. As a result we preferred to sit and sleep against the walls.

'On the evening of 25 April at six o'clock, the *Bavaria* weighed anchor and steamed off towards St Helena. Even though the sea was fairly calm, most of the Boers became seasick and "paid" in the usual fashion for this discomfort. Many Boers thought that they were dying from some sort of disease. One elderly burgher moaned pathetically: "Please help me, my old friend. Please ask the

Continued overleaf

continued

Englishman if he can't stop this ship. I will give him half my farm and my produce." Somewhat later the same man softly whispered: "Brother Hans, please tell the wife and the children how horrible my death was." Of course he did not die. All of us reached St. Helena in glowing health.

'Early on the morning of 1 May we noticed the island on the horizon. Two hours later we were staring at the naked, steep rocks of St Helena rising from the sea in front of us. This was no attractive or exciting sight, since we realised that we were now looking at the place in the middle of the ocean where we would be detained – for heaven only knew what length of time. But our disappointment became even bigger when we could not immediately leave the hateful ship. We had to wait for approximately three weeks on the crowded deck, since the water supply to our camp was, we were told, not yet ready.

'At last on 18 May a few small boats sailed to our ship and we were taken in them to the land. It was wonderful to feel solid ground under our feet again, even though we were now exiles on a lonely rock in the middle of a huge ocean. An escort of armed soldiers led us to our camp through the capital, Jamestown. The town looked old, decayed and dirty.

'The street that leads to our camp is known as Napoleon Street. It is a quiet mountain road. Many of the burghers who were not prepared to load their luggage on the wagons that were provided for that purpose were forced to put it down on the road after a while since they could not keep on carrying it.

'The further we proceeded up the hill, the more we accepted our fate, since with each footstep and around each corner of the road St Helena became more attractive. From the sea the island looked desolate and inhospitable, but the higher up we climbed, the greener it became, with livestock grazing on the slopes, palm trees, gardens and here and there even some farming activity. After three hours of climbing we reached a plateau and spotted our tents in the distance.

'Our camp is known as Deadwood Camp. It is thus called since strong trade winds are always blowing from the same direction, with the result that the trees and shrubs all bend over to one side. The trunks of all the trees are bent and the branches hang down to the ground as if the little life in them is being destroyed more every year. That explains the name Deadwood. Not far from our camp is the homestead Longwood, where Napoleon was detained and died.

General Piet Cronjé, his wife, staff and guards on St Helena

'When we finally reached our new prison we were totally exhausted after our long march, since we had during our lengthy sojourn on board the *Bavaria* become unaccustomed to any exercise. For many of us it was the 12th place where we had been detained. The British are treating us badly as prisoners of war. Even a dog is often better off than we are, but we cannot complain that there is no variation. Our general perception is that our life from now onwards will become rather boring.

'It was about three o'clock in the afternoon when we reached Deadwood Camp. Old friends who had arrived here as prisoners about a month before, including Captain Versélewel de Wit Hamer, came to look us up. They were anxious to hear the latest war news, but we knew nothing of the course of the war. We were too tired and hungry to enjoy lengthy discussions.

'There is one tent for every 12 men, and in each tent the British placed one kettle, 12 buckets, 12 spoons and 12 forks – everything neat and new – but no food, and that was what we longed for. Of what use is a new kettle and new cutlery when there is no food? Fortunately our friends who had been here for a few weeks could assist us with some of their supplies which they had collected and thus we could fill our empty stomachs with a sort of bread porridge.

'Soon after dark my tent mates and I prepared for bed. All of us lay with our feet to the centre in a circle and slept peacefully until about midnight, when we were rudely awakened when our little canvas house was virtually levelled by a heavy rain and a windstorm. This was not enjoyable at all, but through the combined use of all our power we managed to get the tent upright again and after about half an hour we were once again all sleeping peacefully on the wet ground as if nothing had happened.

'When we rose the next morning the whole camp had been turned into a pool of mud. Our friends told us that a rainstorm was nothing unusual, but a normal occurrence. Our reaction is that we would have to ask the British for gumboots since our shoes would not last in the wet climate.

'Soon after our arrival at Deadwood camp, we learnt that a young burgher of Schweizer-Renecke in the western Transvaal, Johannes Viljoen, was shot and killed by a British guard early one morning last month. The guard subsequently alleged that Viljoen attempted to crawl through the fence, but when his body was found moments after he was killed, it was safely within the enclosure. We believe it was a cowardly murder and that the excuse was laughable, but the military court of senior British officers found the guard not guilty. Viljoen was buried with full military honour.

'On 22 May there was boisterous jollification in the British camp barely 200 metres from our camp. They played music the whole afternoon and seemed overcome by joy. We asked a guard the reason for the festivities. "Oh," he answered, "a report reached us that Mafeking had been relieved and now we are celebrating." For us it felt like a defeat and the news did not make us happy at all. A huge number of Boers believed that it was a lie that Mafeking had been relieved and that the British merely said that to make us depressed. One group of Boers did not care about the news at all. Only a small number believe the news and witness the rowdy Khaki celebrations with hearts heavy with sorrow.

'Two days later there was a fresh celebration in the British camp. This time we were unaffected since it was their Queen's birthday. These events fortunately did provide some relief from monotony, since the ghost of boredom is already beginning to torment us.

'Here at Deadwood Camp we are about 600 metres above sea level, and sometimes covered in cloud the whole day long. Then it is dark and cold and often rainy, which means that everything becomes wet or at least damp. This takes all the fun out of our existence, which is further embittered by all sorts of bad news of war disasters.

'Yesterday we were told that the British were crossing the Vaal River and threatening Pretoria. Some of the Boers are singing hymns the whole day long and this makes me even more depressed. I prefer to go to bed early so that I can escape from the misery of our existence for as long as possible.'

FROM THE EDITOR

On the military front there have been no major battles or dramatic breakthroughs during the past week. There were a few skirmishes, with the Boer forces gaining the upper hand in some and the British in others. The Boers are still concentrating on the destruction of railway lines, with especial success in the southeastern Transvaal.

Of more important long-term significance is that the Republican deputation has still not managed to generate significant support for the cause of our independence. It is becoming clearer by the day that the public abroad supports us, but that no government, except perhaps Russia, is prepared to oppose the British government. Hopefully the foreign public will succeed in the course of time in forcing their governments to support us openly.

It is with great joy that we can, for the first time, publish a report on the fate of the Boer prisoners of war on St Helena Island. We believe that many of our readers have relatives who are held prisoner of war there. That our burghers are not having an enjoyable experience as prisoners of war is certain; however, we gain the impression that they are not being treated too badly.

THE REPUBLICAN DEPUTATION IN AMERICA

Still only moral support for Boer cause

Machadodorp, 3 July – The Republican deputation abroad, consisting of Abraham Fischer, C.H. Wessels and A.D.W. Wolmarans, ended their mission to the United States of America and set sail back to Europe on 28 June. In our previous report on their visit to America, we indicated that they could expect no official support. The members of the deputation consequently decided to attempt to influence the American government indirectly by spreading propaganda among the American people.

Soon after their visit to President McKinley, the members of the deputation visited the United States missions of Russia, Germany and France in quick succession. The Russian envoy was excited about their visit, but the French and German envoys were, diplomatically speaking, neutral. Wolmarans went so far as to propose to the French and Russian envoys that their governments should accept trusteeship over the Boer republics. We have heard that both envoys did telegraph that suggestion to their governments, that both their governments expressed great sympathy with the Republican cause, but both refused trusteeship.

After their negotiations with the American government and with foreign envoys in Washington, the deputation members visited a number of large American cities. They made speeches, issued statements, held press conferences and met various committees. In addition to visits to New York, Boston, Springfield, Buffalo, Chicago and Philadelphia, as well as numerous other cities, they also briefly visited Canada.

Shortly before their return to Europe, the deputation appointed a committee to act on their behalf and collect funds and spread information on the Republican cause. The members on this committee are Montague White, P.L. Wessels and Charles D. Pierce. It is clear to the members of the deputation that the American government will not intervene and that they would have to wait for the upcoming presidential election. A change of government in future may make a difference.

Before their return to Europe, Fischer made a last attempt to convince the Americans to come to the aid of the Republics. He declared that the Deputation 'do not want an alliance, and do not expect from America to commit an unfriendly deed against Britain. We merely beg from you to declare to the civilised world that the precedent which Britain plans to create by destroying the freedom and national existence of two independent states, is regarded with revulsion by the people of the United States of America.' This statement was published in most of the major American newspapers, but to date the Americans have made no official pro-Republican statement. We hope that their attitude will soon change.

TRANSVAAL GOVERNMENT PROCLAMATIONS

Machadodorp, 6 July – The government of the South African Republic has issued a number of proclamations and made a number of important decisions with regard to military issues in the past month.

In a proclamation of 28 June it was announced that action would be taken against shopkeepers who refuse to accept government notes as a means of payment. Government notes are issued in terms of Act 1 of 1900 and must be accepted as means of payment in the South African Republic. Refusal to accept government notes as a method of payment constitutes a refusal to recognise the legal status of the government. Consequently the President and Executive Council proclaim that any licensed shopkeeper who refuses to accept government notes as a means of payment for goods from his shop will immediately lose his licence and his shop will be closed.

On the same day the government published an Executive Council decision in terms of which the Commandant-General must order all commandants to appoint commissions of at least three persons to remove all horses as well as livestock, provisions and fodder and to place such items out of the reach of the enemy and at the disposal of commandos. The owners must be given receipts and the value of the items thus commissioned must be indicated. Even in the districts not threatened by the enemy at present, commissions must be appointed to procure horses for the commandos in a similar way.

On 29 June the government issued a proclamation in terms of which action must be taken against all officials who remain in a town occupied by the British without a legal excuse. Such action is not in accordance with their official oath and disregards their duty towards country and people. For that reason the government has decided that all officials who become disloyal in such a way, and who do not at the first possible opportunity join the Republican forces again, should immediately lose their positions and be regarded as discharged from public service, losing all claims to the payment of their salaries. Officials who in future act in such a way, must take note that they will receive no mercy.

The government requested that the contents of these proclamations should be made known as widely as possible. All our readers are requested to assist the government in this task.

OUR MILITARY OFFICERS

Commandant Michael Prinsloo

Antonie Michael Prinsloo was born in 1862 in Bloemfontein. He is the youngest son of Nicolaas Frans Prinsloo and his wife Isabella Rautenbach. Chief Commandant Marthinus Prinsloo is his elder brother. His father was farming in the district of Bloemfontein at the time of his birth, but soon afterwards the family moved to the farm Waterval in the Winburg district. In 1871 they moved again, this time to the farm Witbanksfontein in the Bethlehem district.

Prinsloo received scant formal education. His school was farm life and the veld. When he was 16 years old he took over the farm from his father. He is known as a diligent and hard-working farmer and at the outbreak of the war owned a herd of 200 cattle and 2 000 sheep. When the war began he joined the Bethlehem Commando as a burgher and went to the Natal front.

Prinsloo's first position of authority was that of Chief Corporal during the Siege of Ladysmith. Towards the end of last year he was transferred with a section of his commando to the Colesberg front, where he emerged as a leading figure. In January he was elected Field Cornet and in February Commandant of the Bethlehem Commando.

At the time of the retreat of the Boers across the Orange River, Prinsloo exhibited exceptional courage as a soldier. Even though he was wounded in the throat, he was one of the last men to leave the battlefield on 6 March.In May he participated in the Republican attempt to halt the British offensive towards the Vaal River. He played a prominent role in taking a British regiment prisoner of war at Lindley and subsequently he has been active in his own district.

Commandant A.M. Prinsloo

THE War Reporter
WEEKLY EDITION

Number 40 — Machadodorp, South African Republic — 14 July 1900

DE LA REY TRIUMPHS AT SILKAATSNEK
BRITISH GARRISON IN MAGALIESBERG TOTALLY OVERWHELMED

Magaliesberg, 12 July – General Koos de la Rey yesterday carried out an extremely daring but highly successful attack on a British garrison at Silkaatsnek in the Magaliesberg range northwest of Pretoria. The British casualties amounted to at least 23 men killed and 189, of whom 45 wounded, made prisoner of war. Their commander, Colonel H.R. Roberts, is one of the wounded captives. The Boer casualties were six men dead, including De la Rey's valiant adjutants Mussman and Röth, and eight wounded, of whom one, Assistant Field Cornet C.J. Lee, is in a critical condition.

De la Rey reached the Jericho Mission Station some 40 kilometres north of Silkaatsnek on 9 July. It was his plan to move from there to the south to cross the Magaliesberg. However, his scouts reported that the British had occupied all the crossings over the mountains. Consequently he decided to investigate the situation at Silkaatsnek personally, accompanied by a few of his staff officers.

It is at Silkaatsnek that the wagon road from Pretoria to Rustenburg crosses the Magaliesberg. This crossing is a few kilometres east of Hartbeespoort, where the Crocodile River bisects the mountain range. That *poort* is a few kilometres east of Kommandonek. Earlier this month British units occupied both Silkaatsnek and Kommandonek as well as the low hills at Rietfontein some distance south of Silkaatsnek, since that position commands the bridge over the Crocodile River.

The Khakis at Silkaatsnek dug in on a rocky outcrop in the middle of the Nek, where there is a good view of the valley to the north of the mountain range. They stated after the battle that they had heard rumours that the Boers were planning an attack, but had never expected that anybody could actually surprise them there.

De la Rey carefully inspected the British positions and noted that there were no sentries posted on the high ridges on both sides of Silkaatsnek. Convinced that he could easily overwhelm the whole position, he ordered 300 burghers from Jericho to join him. His plan of attack was simple. He would divide his force into three sections. He himself, with the burghers of Commandant H.C.W. Vermaas of Lichtenburg, would attack directly from the north across a rather bushy, flat area. The two other commandos would occupy the ridges east and west of Silkaatsnek and attack the enemy from there.

Late on the afternoon of 10 July one of De la Rey's field telegraphists brought him a challenging heliographic message. It was from the British telegraphist at Silkaatsnek and read: 'Why don't you come here and fight.' De la Rey's reaction was: 'Answer them we will come soon enough.'

De la Rey's men were in position long before dawn yesterday morning. The Bloemhof burghers under Commandant Tollie de Beer and the Cape Rebels under Commandant J.H. Visser occupied the ridge east of Silkaatsnek. Commandant Coetzee as well as a group of scouts commanded by Kirsten and Koos Boshoff occupied the ridge to the west. These two groups had to attack as soon as De la Rey's gunner, Captain Otto von Lossberg, began his bombardment of the British position on the Nek.

The closest burghers were hardly 250 metres from the British positions when the bombardment began at daybreak. From the east the attack was successful right from the start, repulsing the Khakis from the ridge on that side of the Nek. In the west the Boers encountered major difficulties since the mountainside was so steep that Kirsten's and Boshoff's men could not reach the top of the ridge. Consequently the Khakis could hold out on that side and slow down De la Rey's advance from the north. It took until the afternoon for the burghers on the west to drive the Khakis from that ridge, but at that point the British position became critical. They were surrounded, since De la Rey had earlier sent 80 burghers in a southerly direction round the Nek to prevent the escape of any soldiers. The Khakis had two guns at their disposal, but these were set up in such a way in their emplacements of rock and barbed wire that they could not fire at the easterly or westerly ridges. In addition they did not use their signal operators to request assistance.

At about sundown the British finally raised the white flag and surrendered. At that stage the closest burghers were less than 40 metres from the British gun emplacements and the Boer gun only about 600 metres away. No significant assistance arrived that day from Rietfontein for the Khakis. The British who were stationed there could not help but hear the roar of the guns. They did send out two field guns and a Maxim in the direction of Silkaatsnek, but were easily repulsed by the 80 burghers south of the Nek. We have heard that a large British force was dispatched from Pretoria, but arrived too late.

De la Rey's burghers can now boast a huge booty of two guns, both in excellent condition, numerous horses and mules, a large quantity of rifles and ammunition including shells for the guns. More and more burghers are by now using the British Lee-Metford rifles since they have run out of Mauser ammunition. Consequently this is a very welcome booty. In addition De la Rey's men have captured a number of wagons and carts.

The burghers hurriedly left the battlefield after the battle with their booty and took the prisoners of war with them, but left the wounded Khakis right there in the care of a British military doctor. De la Rey concluded his report on the battle with a word of congratulation to his burghers on their courageous fighting, but thanking God in the first place for the victory.

General Koos de la Rey on commando

BIG FIGHT AT DWARSVLEI
General Sarel Oosthuizen seriously wounded

Magaliesberg, 12 July – Yesterday there was heavy fighting between the Krugersdorp burghers and a British column at Dwarsvlei, some 16 kilometres northwest of Krugersdorp. Dwarsvlei farm belongs to the fiery Fighting General Sarel Oosthuizen, who is widely known as the Red Bull. Unfortunately Oosthuizen was seriously wounded towards the end of the fight and his burghers failed to capture the British column, even though they managed to drive them off.

Oosthuizen and his 150 burghers heard early yesterday morning from their scouts that a British column was approaching from Krugersdorp. Instead of retreating, Oosthuizen realised that he was being presented with an ideal opportunity to harass the enemy and thus implement the war council decisions taken at Balmoral last month. The British military authorities had earlier on sent a written warning to Oosthuizen that he should stop commandeering burghers, but he naturally ignored this. Indeed he regards the threat of severe punishment as a joke.

Oosthuizen's biggest problem was that he had only a small commando with him, while at least 1 500 Khakis, including infantry and mounted soldiers, were approaching. In addition not all the burghers had horses and they were armed with a variety of rifles, including even a few old Martini Henry muzzle-loaders. To make matters worse, their only gun, a hand Maxim, was unfit for use.

Oosthuizen thought that the British could be overwhelmed if he could create the illusion that there were many more burghers than he actually had. For that reason he ordered his men to take up position in a dispersed order on the low hills at Dwarsvlei and to move around as often as possible. When, at nine o'clock in the morning, the first Khakis approached the Boer positions, the burghers noted that they had three guns. Undaunted, they opened fire with their rifles as soon as the Khakis were close enough.

In the battle that followed and that went on till that evening, the burghers totally confused the huge British force. Some burghers especially concentrated on the British guns. According to our correspondent all the British guns together fired no more than 40 shots. The gun mules were soon put out of action, whereupon the Boer sharpshooters concentrated on the gunners themselves. Most of them were either killed or wounded. Other burghers attempted to capture the British supply wagons. In both cases the Khakis managed under great pressure to fend off the Boer attacks.

At dusk General Oosthuizen personally attempted to capture the guns. Accompanied by about 20 burghers, he advanced ever closer and was eventually only about 30 metres away. However, in the open area where the guns stood he and his men became easy targets. Koos van der Merwe was killed, while Isak Oosthuizen (the fighting general's brother) and Koos le Roux were lightly wounded. Oosthuizen persuaded the burghers to keep going. Suddenly he himself was wounded in the chest and right leg. Since the leg wound bled profusely, the burghers immediately carried him to his home, which was not far off.

With that the fight came to an end. It was already dark and the British forces promptly retreated in the moonlight. The Boers could not halt them. We have heard that in this engagement four Khakis were killed and 37 wounded. The Boer casualties are two dead and three wounded.

FROM THE EDITOR

The resounding Boer victory over a British garrison at Silkaatsnek, barely 30 kilometres west of the occupied Transvaal capital, will do wonders for the morale of all the burghers. They are now more willing than ever to carry on with the struggle and there are signs that increasing numbers of burghers are returning to the commandos.

Numerous reports from all over the Republics have reached us in the past week of battles and skirmishes in which large numbers of Khakis have been captured. It certainly seems as if the enemy is losing confidence. If they cannot confront us with a massive numerical advantage, they prefer to flee or merely surrender. The burghers on all fronts are fighting courageously and accomplishing much. During all these confrontations they have inflicted serious losses on the enemy, while their own casualties have been relatively small.

We have no doubt that the upturn in the morale of the Republican forces is the result of the decisions taken at Kroonstad in March and at Balmoral in June to confront the British with guerrilla tactics. In this way they are continually being harassed and their will to fight is likely to collapse.

SKIRMISH AT ONDERSTEPOORT

Magaliesberg, 12 July – While the battles at Silkaatsnek and Dwarsvlei were raging yesterday, there was also a skirmish at Onderstepoort immediately north of Pretoria. For a few days the Boer forces in that area, namely the Waterberg burghers commanded by General Freek Grobler, had been aware of the presence of a British garrison near Pyramid Station, about seven kilometres north of the Wonderboompoort through the Magaliesberg. Grobler and his men were busy planning an attack on these Khakis when the latter suddenly attacked them yesterday.

The British attack began soon after daybreak when they fired on a group of Boers at a farmhouse. The Boers immediately fired back. The British neatly moved in between two groups of Boers who then fired on the Khakis from both sides, stampeding their horses. The soldiers retreated in disorder. The burghers soon encircled them and when they ran out of ammunition and one of their officers was killed, 17 Khakis including two officers surrendered. The other Khakis had earlier fled to the south and left their comrades in the lurch.

This skirmish did wonders for the morale of the burghers. After their defeat at Donkerhoek last month they were somewhat depressed. Now they have something to be proud of again. In addition they have heard of De la Rey's success at Silkaatsnek. As a result they are again full of confidence and eager to go on with the war.

85

BRITISH FORCES OCCUPY BETHLEHEM

Boer attempts to repulse the enemy fail

Fouriesburg, 12 July – Last Saturday, 7 July, the British managed to occupy Bethlehem, the third temporary Free State capital after Kroonstad and Heilbron. President Steyn and his government had earlier on retreated from there. Fouriesburg at present serves as the capital, but the government is preparing to become totally mobile in future.

Chief Commandant Christiaan de Wet had planned to defend Bethlehem. He and his senior officers inspected the area around the town early on the morning of 6 July. Each officer and his men then took up position at the spot that they had to defend. De Wet placed the burghers who no longer had horses on Wolhuterskop, about four kilometres southwest of the town. The rest of the burghers were positioned in a half-moon formation north and northwest of the town. De Wet then sent a notice to the inhabitants of the town that he would defend it and advised the women and children to leave. Most of the inhabitants did indeed evacuate in a southerly direction.

The first units of the huge British force of between 7 000 and 8 000 soldiers with 18 guns approached Bethlehem that same afternoon. They were preceded by about 15 scouts, who soon reached a low hill north of the town, probably without seeing the Boer positions. The burghers waited till they were very close before firing, hitting nine and putting the rest to flight. Soon afterwards the battle was raging. The enemy attempted to outflank the Republican forces north of the town, but the burghers prevented this. When darkness came the tempo of fighting lessened.

On Saturday morning, 7 July, the British resumed their attack. This time they concentrated on the Boer left flank. Their bombardment of our positions was frightening. De Wet told our reporter that he himself witnessed the terrible effect of an exploding lyddite grenade. One of those landed on a rocky area about 200 metres from the position of Commandant Steenkamp's burghers and killed 25 horses.

The sharp edge of the British attack was aimed at the positions of Commandants Van Aardt and Piet Fourie. These officers and their men withstood the attack as long as possible, but they began to retreat at about noon, before De Wet could send burghers to their assistance.

The British victory was assured soon afterwards when they occupied the strategically positioned Wolhuterskop. The burghers who had been stationed there were forced to abandon a gun – one of the Armstrong guns captured last December by Olivier's men at Stormberg and which had been hauled to the top of Wolhuterskop with great exertion the previous evening – but they pushed the gun over the cliff before leaving and claim that it broke into pieces. Fortunately for the Boers the British did not pursue them with their mounted troops. According to reliable sources the British suffered casualties amounting to 107 dead and wounded. On the Boer side two men were killed and eight wounded.

While the British forces occupied Bethlehem, De Wet and his Free Staters retreated across Retief's Nek in the south into the Brandwater Basin. In this inhospitable area between Bethlehem and Fouriesburg the burghers feel safe. President Steyn waited at Retief's Nek for De Wet and his burghers.

A quiet moment in camp for burghers of the Orange Free State

CONFRONTATIONS EAST OF PRETORIA

In the veld east of Pretoria, 10 July – Last week we reported that Commandant-General Louis Botha was advancing in a westerly direction with his commandos to reoccupy his former positions at Donkerhoek. Last Friday this Boer force made contact with a huge British force of at least 3 000 men stationed near Tijgerpoort, southeast of Pretoria. On Saturday a group of burghers under Commandant Piet Trichardt and Field Cornet A.J. Dercksen attacked this force near Bapsfontein. The Khakis attempted an outflanking manoeuvre, but the burghers caught them unawares with a sudden counterattack. In the end the Khakis retreated to Tijgerpoort with the burghers in hot pursuit.

By early Sunday morning the burghers were ready to resume their attack. In the meantime, the Middelburg and Boksburg Commandos as well as a group of Johannesburg burghers under Lieutenant Oosthuizen with a Krupp gun and two machine guns had joined Commandant Trichardt's commando. This time they could not make any progress, since the Khakis seemed to have procured a number of guns the previous night. The result was a long-distance artillery duel that lasted the whole day, with neither side gaining the upper hand.

Yesterday morning the British attempted to resume the offensive over a front at least 20 kilometres wide. The burghers were forced to form small groups over a wide area to resist this onslaught. The burghers and the Khakis confronted each other with guns and rifles from early morning till late that afternoon. Again none of the opponents could gain the upper hand over the other.

In this three-day-long series of skirmishes 13 burghers were killed, including seven at the same moment when a lyddite grenade exploded close to them. A further 15 were wounded. We have heard that the British casualties amounted to at least 200 men. Commandant-General Botha declared after the battle that the burghers had fought with the courage of lions. When he received the above report, President Kruger sent a telegram of congratulations to the Commandant-General and his burghers, expressing the opinion that the burghers had regained their courage and his confidence that they would go on in this way.

Burghers ready for action

BRITISH PROCLAMATIONS

Machadodorp, 13 July – Field Marshal Roberts went on issuing proclamations this week in an attempt to intimidate the Boers. In one proclamation he warns all the inhabitants of the South African Republic to refrain from sheltering 'rebels'. In another proclamation issued in Krugersdorp on Monday it is declared that: 'If any of the men of the Krugersdorp district at present serving a commando do not surrender by 20 July and hand their arms to the imperial authorities, their properties will be confiscated and their families will become impoverished and homeless.'

GENERAL NEWS

Machadodorp, 13 July – State Secretary F.W. Reitz handed us a copy of a telegram that he had sent to the newspaper *Sun* in the United States of America. In this he clearly spells out the war objectives of the Boer Republics: 'President [Kruger] and his people have always and will always long for peace. Condition: Full independence and amnesty to the Colonials who fought with us. If not we fight to the bitter end.'

Reports from London indicate that British newspapers reacted with alarm to revelations of unsatisfactory treatment of sick soldiers in hospitals in South Africa. In Bloemfontein alone in the month of May 2 087 British soldiers had to be treated for stomach fever; 86 died. In Senekal in the Orange Free State all the houses are filled with sick soldiers, since the hospitals are filled to overflowing.

Numerous British newspapers report that Field Marshal Roberts will soon be returning to Britain. The continuous tension of the campaign has exhausted him to such an extent that he needs rest urgently.

According to the crew of a German postal boat that sailed into the harbour of Lourenço Marques on Monday, they could not get any coal in Durban. Apparently there are no railway trucks available to transport coal from the mines in the interior to the harbour.

Our correspondent in Fouriesburg in the eastern Free State reports that Chief Commandant Christiaan de Wet has sent a complaint to Roberts about the indiscriminate destruction of private property by British troops in the Orange Free State.

The first issue of the Free State government's new newspaper, *De Basuin*, was issued in Fouriesburg this week. News is printed on both sides of a single sheet.

Today the war council in Fouriesburg confirmed the sentence of five years of hard labour for treason earlier given to former Commandant S.G. Vilonel.

OUR MILITARY OFFICERS

Fighting General Sarel Oosthuizen

Sarel Francois Oosthuizen was born in 1862 on the family farm Sterkfontein in the Pretoria district, to the north of the present town of Krugersdorp. He is the son of Daniel Jacobus Oosthuizen and his wife Anna Susanna Oosthuizen. He grew up on Sterkfontein. His school was the farm and he began farming for himself at an early stage.

Oosthuizen's military career began in 1880–81 when he participated in the Transvaal War of Independence. He was a member of the Boer forces that successfully besieged the British garrison in Pretoria. Subsequently he participated in a number of campaigns against rebellious black communities in the South African Republic. Early in 1896 he was also involved in the capture of Jameson's freebooters.

Since Oosthuizen had become known as a capable warrior, the Krugersdorp burghers elected him as field cornet of his ward early last year. In October he proceeded to the Natal front in this capacity. Later that month he was lightly wounded at Talana, the first major battle of this war. In November he was present when the Boers derailed and captured the British armoured train at Chievely. It is indeed generally recognised that it was he who captured the well-known British war journalist, Winston Churchill, who actively participated in the fight that followed.

Oosthuizen, who impresses everybody with his fiery nature, his red hair and his huge beard, acted as temporary commander of the Krugersdorp Commando in the battle of Colenso last December. He and his men played a determining role in the capture of the 10 British guns in that battle. Early this year his reputation was enhanced by the prominent role he played in the Boer victory at Spioenkop. Subsequently he participated with great valour in the attempts to halt the British offensive along the Tugela River. In February he was promoted to the rank of fighting general. After the British breakthrough he helped with the establishment of the new front in the Biggarsberg range before being transferred with his commando to the southwestern Transvaal to assist in attempts to halt the British offensive there.

After the British forces had crossed the Vaal River, Oosthuizen assisted General de la Rey in temporarily halting the British advance at Doornkop on 29 May. Two weeks later he participated with distinction in the battle of Donkerhoek. In terms of the war council decision at Balmoral soon afterwards, he returned to his home district, where he had significant success in convincing dejected burghers to take up arms again. His first major battle afterwards was the clash at Dwarsvlei this week. The flamboyant Red Bull, as his burghers call him, was wounded in this battle. We trust that this loyal Republican, whom State Attorney Jan Smuts regards as one of the most courageous and able officers in the South African Republic, will soon be up and about again.

Oosthuizen is married to Susanna Cornelia Hendrika Johanna (Sannie) Alberts. They have three sons and six daughters, the youngest of whom is only three months old.

General Sarel Oosthuizen

THE War Reporter
WEEKLY EDITION

Number 41 — Machadodorp, South African Republic — 21 July 1900

KHAKIS TARGET BOER CIVILIANS
Roberts sends women and children to the front; more farm dwellings destroyed

Balmoral, 20 July – On Wednesday Lord Roberts sent a message to Commandant-General Louis Botha to inform him that the Pretoria families of burghers who were still fighting the British would be handed over to the commandos in the eastern Transvaal. The excuse for this inhumane action is, according to Roberts, the lack of supplies in Pretoria. The message reads as follows:

'Sir, I am directed by Lord Roberts to inform you that the British Government has notified a decision that it can no longer supply with food the wives and families of those in arms against it. It is therefore necessary to remove them from Pretoria without delay and I am to request you to be good enough to receive them to the number of about 1 000 at railhead at or near Pienaarspoort on Thursday morning next, the 19th instant. Lord Roberts desires me to add that he gives you this notice in order that suitable and timely arrangements for the reception of these families may be made.'

The British commander-in-chief had in earlier proclamations guaranteed the safety of civilians, but those promises are now being dishonoured. Botha immediately protested against Roberts's envisaged action. Nevertheless the British yesterday sent 412 women and children by train – loaded on open cattle trucks, even though it is midwinter – to Van der Merwe Station on the eastern railway line. The Transvaal government immediately took steps to provide accommodation in wagons for these homeless people. These arrangements are keeping Botha so busy that he finds it impossible to give attention to other military issues.

It is reported from Middelburg that a large number of women and children will be accommodated in the recently erected Town Hall building.

Assistant Commandant-General Chris Botha reports from the far southeastern Transvaal that the Khakis are maltreating Boer families on the farms in a scandalous and cowardly manner. His own house was destroyed with dynamite and set alight. The same happened to the dwellings of Field Cornet Badenhorst and the latter's son-in-law, Greyling. Another burgher, Cloete, had his house destroyed and his wife and children were abducted with violence. Hans Badenhorst, who had surrendered his arms and was living on his farm with his family, had earlier taken his livestock to a place of safety. The British had given him a permit to return his livestock to his farm, but the animals were hardly back when the Khakis took possession of everything, violently forced Badenhorst and his family from the farm and destroyed and burned down his dwelling. According to Botha, these are only a few of many similar cases.

A Boer farmhouse burned down by the Khakis

Women and children sent to the front by Roberts

DE WET LEAVES BRANDWATER BASIN
Free State burghers will confront Khakis over wide area

In the veld in the Free State, 20 July – President Steyn of the Orange Free State and his government, as well as Chief Commandant de Wet, have just moved out of the Brandwater Basin south of Bethlehem. Last Friday the Free State military officers who were in the basin held a huge joint war council meeting. De Wet explained to his co-officers that it was dangerous for them to gather all their forces together in the same area. An uninterrupted circle of hills surrounds the Brandwater Basin between Bethlehem in the north, Witsieshoek in the east and the Caledon River in the south. With the exception of a small number of mountain passes, there are long distances where it is impossible even for people on foot to cross the mountains. The passes are Retief's Nek, Slabbert's Nek, Witnek, Commando Nek and Noupoort Nek. The British will almost certainly attempt to occupy the passes, and thus cut off the Free State forces from the outside world and force them to surrender. For that reason De Wet proposed that they should divide into small groups and leave the basin in different directions.

The war council accepted De Wet's sound advice and decided to form three columns. We cannot of course divulge which direction each column will take, but De Wet allows us to report that he will lead one column, General Paul Roux the second one and General Jan Crowther the third.

President Steyn and the Free State government joined De Wet's column. Last Saturday Steyn took leave of his wife and children in Fouriesburg. He announced that he and the government would in future not be bound to a fixed capital. This means they will operate in the veld. The exact location of the government may not be divulged by anybody.

Last Sunday Steyn, De Wet and the Free State government moved out of the Brandwater Basin via Slabbert's Nek. A huge column of about 2 000 men, 400 wagons and carts and five field guns accompany them. The Khakis probably planned to corner De Wet within the basin, but he and his column slipped from the net. However, the enemy were soon on his heels. On Monday a huge Khaki force confronted De Wet's column at Witklip, north of the Bethlehem–Senekal wagon road, some distance west of Bethlehem. The Boer gunners managed to check the Khaki advance with an accurate bombardment. One burgher was killed in this skirmish and two were wounded. According to reliable reports, the British loss was one man dead and nine wounded.

It is reported that General Roux held a religious service in the Brandwater Basin on Sunday. On Tuesday he indicated to our correspondent that he was waiting for General Crowther, who was still in the Basin, to make contact with Commandants F.J.W.J. Hattingh and C.J. de Villiers, who are in command of the Vrede and Harrismith Commandos, respectively. It seems as if they are unwilling to leave their home districts.

Yesterday a huge British force of about 4 000 men commanded by General Broadwood attacked De Wet's scouts, under the command of Captain Danie Theron, near the village Petrus Steyn. The skirmish spread out over a wide area. At least eight burghers were killed. On the British side at least five Khakis were killed and 15 wounded.

At the same time another British column attacked De Wet's main column at Paardeplaats, near the wagon road between Lindley and Kroonstad. De Wet attempted to encircle a section of the enemy force to force it to surrender, but failed in this venture. The skirmish ended at dusk. The British casualties amounted to about 10 men and those of the Republicans five men.

FROM THE EDITOR

There was little action on the military front this past week. The only major confrontations took place southeast of Pretoria, and were inconclusive. Elsewhere in Transvaal the burghers resumed their attempts to disrupt railway and telegraph communications. From the Free State we have heard that the burgher commandos are moving out of the Brandwater Basin with the objective of implementing guerrilla tactics on as wide a front as possible. We still believe that that is the best way to confront the massive British force.

The most important but also most alarming development in the past week is the inhumane action of Lord Roberts against women and children. The Republican authorities find it hard to understand how the commander of the forces of the British people, who claim that they are highly civilised, can unscrupulously use the women and children of an opponent on a massive scale as pawns in a military confrontation. Perhaps Roberts is unaware of the fact that his government signed the Geneva Convention, which explicitly forbids such activities?

There are other actions that alarm us to the utmost and lead us to question the integrity of the highest-ranking British officers in our midst. In this issue there are reports on the destruction of farms and abduction of women and children from farms in the far southeastern Transvaal. This happens in spite of numerous promises that the British regularly make in their proclamations that they will leave civilians in peace – especially civilians who are not directly involved in the conflict. Our experience is that British promises are not worth the paper on which they are written.

A final very alarming development reported on in this issue is that the British forces are using armed blacks to harass our women, children and old people on the farms. It is clear that the British commanders do not hesitate to use questionable tactics. The worst is probably still in store for us.

MILITARY ACTIVITIES IN TRANSVAAL

RAILWAY LINES AND TELEGRAPH WIRES DESTROYED BY THE BURGHERS

Machadodorp, 20 July – During the night of 10–11 July the burghers wrecked a railway bridge at Witpoortdrif, between Greylingstad and Standerton. On 12 July Generals Chris Botha and Tobias Smuts attacked British positions at Paardekop Station and Sandspruit Station, respectively. Both were repulsed.

On 13 July British patrols moved out of Platrand and Paardekop Stations and bombarded the Boer gun emplacements, though without inflicting damage. The Boer gunfire easily repulsed the enemy's mounted forces.

In the vicinity of Doornhoek, near Greylingstad, a patrol of burghers was attacked by an enemy patrol on 14 July. Five Khakis were killed. The burghers suffered no casualties. The Khaki patrol returned to Standerton the next day.

Last Saturday (14 July) there was a skirmish between a mounted British reconnaissance unit and a Boer sentry post near Bronkhorstspruit.

On Monday 16 July the burghers destroyed a culvert on the railway line near Heidelberg.

The same day a British force occupied Rustenburg for the third time. Their commander this time is General Methuen, who has in the past found his match in the Republican forces – especially at Magersfontein.

On Tuesday the burghers launched an attack on a British guard post at Suikerbos. It failed.

On Wednesday a Boer patrol managed to repulse a British guard post on the railway line between Vlakfontein and Grey-lingstad.

Subsequently they destroyed the telegraph wires in that area, wrecked a railway culvert and damaged a few kilometres of the railway line, which had just been repaired after previous sabotage.

On Thursday the Boers destroyed a section of the railway line near Bank Station. That made it possible for them to capture a train when the locomotive derailed and to take the crew of the train prisoner.

HUGE BATTLE SOUTHEAST OF PRETORIA

Balmoral, 17 July – A huge battle raged between the Transvaal forces and the Khakis near Pretoria earlier this week. Neither side could gain the upper hand. On Sunday 15 July there was a war council meeting of all the Boer officers who were in the vicinity of Pretoria to discuss Commandant-General Louis Botha's request that they should launch a full-scale attack on the British forces east of the city to draw the attention of the enemy away from the Boer forces west of the city. The war council decided on simultaneous attacks on all the known British positions in that area.

Field Cornet Dercksen of Boksburg, assisted by the burghers of Middelburg, was to attack the most southerly enemy position. The rest of the burghers were to attack the British main force at Tijgerpoort in small groups led by Commandants Pienaar, Aucamp, Gravett, Kemp, Malan, Philip Oosthuizen and Blignaut. Commandant Ben Viljoen, who had just been promoted to the rank of fighting general by Botha, was placed in overall command of the attack.

The Boers launched their attack at dawn on Monday morning. The main British force consisted of at least 4 000 men with 20 guns and four or five machine guns. They were stationed from Tijgerpoort in the northeast across Rietvlei to Olifantsfontein in the south. General Viljoen's burghers had three field guns and two pom-poms available.

The burghers attacked with great valour on an open, flat terrain. A heavy battle with both guns and rifles went on until dark. Commandant-General Botha followed the course of the battle from a distance and afterwards declared that he had never witnessed such a gallant and determined Republican assault. In many places the burghers repulsed the British from their stone fortifications; sometimes the opponents were less than 100 metres apart. At one stage Commandant Pienaar's burghers were encircled by the Khakis and were so hard pressed that they attacked the enemy with the butts of their rifles. The strongest resistance against the Boers came from New Zealand and Irish units at Witpoort, on Viljoen's left flank.

Among the outstanding Boer commanders in this engagement were Commandant Aucamp and Field Cornet Christiaan Beyers, whose burghers approached to within 60 metres of a British field gun. They put the crew of the gun out of action and almost managed to capture it. Only the arrival of massive British reinforcements on this part of the battlefield forced the Boers to abandon their attack.

A British medical officer told one of our officers after the battle that their loss was seven killed and 30 wounded. The burghers hardly believe this: they estimate that the enemy lost at least 400 men. What is certain is that the burghers took 24 Khakis prisoner, including one captain and one lieutenant. The Boer losses are five men killed, 13 wounded (one by accident) and two captured. Field Cornet Greyling is one of the wounded. The Boers managed to capture 20 horses, a large supply of blankets, coats and boots (for which they are very thankful since they are suffering in the winter cold), and numerous trunks of Lee Metford ammunition.

THE WAR EXPERIENCE OF A BOER WOMEN

Report by Mrs Alida Badenhorst from the western Transvaal

We have previously published reports by Mrs Alida Badenhorst, whose husband has been a prisoner of war since Cronjé's surrender at Paardeberg. In the report that follows she recounts some of her war experiences. This report is dated Klerksdorp, 15 July:

'One evening towards the end of May I took my horse and rode down to our fields. All at once I saw towards the west a great crowd of horsemen and wagons moving slowly towards us. When they came nearer it turned out to be a Boer commando. The burghers told me that a large British camp was on the farm of General De la Rey and that massive forces of Khakis were on their way here. The commando slept on our yard without even asking permission! Between 500 and 600 men with wagons, carts and horses! One was begging wood, the other wanted milk and a third one bread. I kept making coffee all evening for the men. I was kind and friendly but must confess that I felt cross with the commandant. He is a good friend, but that night I felt upset. This was no place for a commando, a lonely woman's house – alone with five children in the midst of so many friendly men.

Alida Badenhorst

'That same evening someone knocked on the door. It was a Free Stater who said that the British were already in Hartbeesfontein and meant to advance at once. He informed us that three Khakis had arrived in that town with a white flag, took the Transvaal flag down at the telegraph office, and hoisted a British flag. One read a proclamation in terms of which women whose husbands are prisoners of war would not be molested at all and could keep their property.

'A few days later we heard that three Khakis had arrived in Klerksdorp. General Andries Cronjé gave the whole town over to them and promised that the burghers would lay down their arms. The commandant climbed on a wagon, and read a proclamation that each burgher must bring his rifle, his horse, his saddle and bridle and must sign something to indicate that he would stay neutral – and then they can return freely to their farms to resume their farming activities. I will never forget that day. It was a day of tears. I saw many a burgher weeping over the loss of his weapons.

'Now for the first time since the war began we were without news, as Klerksdorp is occupied by three Khakis who convinced our military officers that it would be futile to offer resistance, since about 60 000 Khakis with 60 guns are immediately outside the town. Consequently 600 burghers surrendered to three men. I thought about the Stadtholder of Leiden, Adriaan van der Werf. When the population shouted: "Let the Spaniards enter!" his courageous answer was: "Here I am, eat my body if you are hungry, but I have sworn an oath and would rather die than hand over and surrender my city to the enemy."

'But what did our leaders do? Surrender the town to three men. This is child's work, not the work of heroes.

'One night soon afterwards three or four burghers arrived at my house. They said that a great battle had occurred at Klipriviersberg. Subsequently they decided to surrender their arms. The British said that they should return to their farms and work them. They also said that the British had sent a message to General De la Rey that black people on the western border were killing Boer women and children. The British know that the burghers would want to return to their farms immediately to protect their families. This was a successful plan, since the whole Lichtenburg district surrendered their arms. The burghers now believe that there will soon be peace and that the prisoners of war will be back in two weeks. I thought to myself: I will abide by the will of God.

'One day about a month ago my brother-in-law went to town to take butter to the market. When he returned he brought the following news. Firstly that General De Wet had captured a train and took a massive booty, including a medal that had been sent to Lord Roberts as recognition of his occupation of Pretoria. Furthermore Generals De la Rey and Botha had fought a major battle at Donkerhoek where the British lost more troops than in any previous engagement in the war. Once more I felt a little hope. Our men were still fighting.

'The British are commandeering all the horses of the burghers. They themselves have to take the horses to Klerksdorp. We women also had to take our horses. It was bitter for us since each woman has her own favourite riding horse. It is becoming more difficult every day. We are directed to send in a list of all our possessions – how many cattle we have, how many horses, sheep and goats, mealies, grain – in one word ALL. We have to get a permit to keep anything.

'Each black servant must carry a pass. A black man and his wife must pay five shillings for a pass that is valid for only one month. This fell very hard on me, since I have many black servants on the farm and they all ask me for pass money. I must also have a permit for my house and one to enable me to travel. This is regulation upon regulation and rule upon rule.

'Early one morning last week I heard a bugle blow. I looked in the direction from which the sound came and saw a number of horses. It was a patrol of 50 or 100 men. They passed my house in the direction of Ventersdorp. For the first time I saw Khakis.

'Now patrols pass here every day. Also armed blacks, and where these arrive on a farm, they demand with rifle in hand everything they please. The poor women must give them whatever they want.

'Last week I wanted to slaughter a cow. I borrowed my sister's rifle for which she has a permit, shot the cow and gave the head to one of my farm workers. On Saturday afternoon just after lunch I saw through my window a buggy and three men on horseback approaching. It was a white man and three blacks. The white man said: "I have been told that you have a weapon in your house." I denied it. The man took out a pocketbook and began writing. One of the blacks then said: "Somewhere there is a weapon that can kill a cow." Then light came to me.

'I explained that I shot the cow with my sister's rifle for which she has a permit. The black man demanded: "I want the rifle with which the cow was killed and you must hand it over this moment." I explained again. The black man was still not satisfied and searched the house but could find nothing. Then he openly threatened: "Give up the rifle, that is all I want from you, but you can make ready for jail." I shouted at him: "I must go to jail since I shot a cow with a rifle for which there is a permit?" The white man answered: "Next week you will have to come to the court to make a statement with regard to the rifle." Then at last they departed and went to my sister to look at the rifle and the permit.

'Soon afterwards one of my black workers came to me and told me that the same white man and three armed blacks confronted them: "Where are the herd of livestock belonging to the government which you have hidden away?" They denied that they are hiding livestock. The four visitors then indicated that one of my other black workers had made that accusation. He told the lie that we were hiding livestock. My workers say that the British are paying each one who reveals where a rifle is hidden two pounds and also pay them for information about livestock.

'Now all is clear to me. And now I am even more furious with our burghers. It would have been better had they allowed themselves to be shot rather than hand their weapons to the Khakis. The result of their cowardice is that we have lost our freedom and are now under the command of black people. And I have to go to the court to explain my actions, which are perfectly legal. All that is left to us is to trust in God.'

OUR MILITARY OFFICERS

Commandant J.S.F. Blignaut

One of the commandants who this week led his burghers with distinction in the battle against the Khakis east of Pretoria is Commandant J.S.F. Blignaut. He is the eldest son of the late Pieter Blignaut, who was killed in the battle of Elandslaagte last October. Before the war Commandant Blignaut was a member of the State Artillery. Later on he joined the police service and served in Swaziland, first as sergeant and later as lieutenant.

With the outbreak of the war last year Blignaut served on the front as Commandant of the Swaziland Commando. At present he is a member of the Police Commando.

Commandant J. Blignaut

THE War Reporter WEEKLY EDITION

Number 42 | **Machadodorp, South African Republic** | **28 July 1900**

DE WET OUTWITS ENEMY AGAIN

CROSSES MAIN RAILWAY LINE; DESTROYS A MILITARY TRAIN

In the veld in the northern Free State, 26 July – Chief Commandant Christiaan de Wet is still quite easily outwitting the British forces that attempt to capture him. His biggest problem is the huge wagon laager that accompanies his forces, seriously hampering his freedom of movement.

Last Friday a very unfortunate incident took place as Chief Commandant de Wet and a few members of the Free State government ate breakfast on Cornelis Wessels's farm, Blesbokfontein, between Lindley and Heilbron. General Piet de Wet was also present, and he called his brother to one side. As they began walking away, hard words were exchanged between the two. After a short while the Chief Commandant shouted: "Are you mad?" He then turned around and went back to the house.

Chief Commandant De Wet later explained that he had lost his temper when his brother, in all seriousness, asked him if he thought that there was a future in continuing the war, and if he planned to keep on fighting. For the Chief Commandant this question was a terrible insult, since he has no intention of abandoning the fight for the freedom of his Republic. As for General Piet de Wet, he has now given up. Christiaan de Wet's sons say that Piet de Wet predicted that they would all be captured when they crossed the railway line. Today we heard the sad news that Piet de Wet had willingly surrendered himself to the British at Kroonstad.

Last Saturday night Christiaan de Wet faced a major challenge, namely to cross the main railway line north of Kroonstad near Serfontein Station. Captain Gideon Scheepers's scouts informed him that there were two British guard posts along the railway line, about five kilometres apart. These guard posts were not strong and on their own posed no danger to the burghers. However, they could sound the alarm, and bigger British units would then attack De Wet's commando. There was no time to be lost.

De Wet positioned his commando at Doornspruit in order to repulse a possible British attack. He himself told our reporter what happened next:

'As soon as night came I ordered the wagons to proceed in four rows, with an escort on each side, and with a rearguard and vanguard. Immediately behind the vanguard followed the President and myself. When we were about 20 minutes' march from the railway line, I ordered the two wings of my force, which were about three miles apart, to occupy the line to the right and left of Serfontein Siding.

'Before we had quite reached the railway, I ordered the vanguard to remain with the President, whilst I myself, with 15 men, rode on to cut the telegraph wire. Whilst we were engaged in this task, a train approached at full speed from the south. I had no dynamite with me, and I could neither blow it up nor derail it. I could only place stones on the line, but these were swept away by the cowcatcher, and so the train passed in safety.

'I had forbidden any shooting, for an engagement would have only produced the greatest confusion in my big laager.

'Just as the last wagon was crossing the line, I received a report that Captain Theron had captured a train to the south of us. Having ordered the wagons to proceed, I rode over to see what had happened. When I arrived at the scene of action I found that the train had come to a standstill owing to the breaking down of the engine, and that the English troops had at once opened fire on my men, but that it had not been long before the enemy surrendered. Four of the English, but only one of our burghers, had been wounded.

'It was very annoying that the laager was so far off, but it was impossible to carry off the valuable ammunition which we found on the train.

'I gave orders that the four wounded soldiers who were under the care of the conductor of the train should be taken from the hut in which I had found them, and placed in a van where they would be safe when I set fire to the train. After the burghers had helped themselves to sugar, coffee, and such things, I burned everything that was left. My 98 prisoners I took along with me.'

The scouts led by Theron joined Chief Commandant De Wet's commando again at Mahem Spruit. De Wet was so thrilled with the successful capture of the train that he immediately promoted Theron to the rank of Commandant. On Tuesday De Wet and his force reached Vredefort, where they loaded freshly milled wheat onto some of their wagons. The last five wagons had barely left the village when a patrol of about 600 Khaki soldiers arrived and seemed to be planning an attack. De Wet had only 400 men in his rearguard, but decided to resist the Khakis. He personally led a charge on the enemy and was followed by hundreds of burghers, while his gunners furthermore opened fire with their field guns. The British made for the horizon and the Boers pursued them until a large Khaki force came to the patrol's rescue.

The skirmish at Vredefort resulted in the death of five burghers and the wounding of at least 12 others, while the British suffered, according to reports, 39 casualties.

De Wet and his convoy proceeded in a northerly direction and tonight reached the farm Renosterspruit near the Vaal River. President Steyn and the Free State government are with them.

De Wet's commando crossing a drift

CRISIS IN THE BRANDWATER BASIN

Free State forces threatened with encirclement

In the veld near Bethlehem, 26 July – The situation of the Free State forces in the Brandwater Basin is not quite clear. Evidently there is no unanimity among the commanders over the best course to follow. Generals Jan Crowther and Paul Roux are both still in the basin with their burghers, in spite of last week's clear war council decisions and orders from Chief Commandant Christiaan de Wet. At the same time, the British forces are systematically occupying all the mountain passes. That limits the opportunities of the Free State burghers to escape by the hour.

Last Friday (20 July) a large British force of at least 1 300 men with six guns advanced from Bethlehem towards Spitskrans (called Spitskop by some burghers). A sentry post of about 50 Free Staters commanded by Field Cornet Gideon Blignaut guarded that position. At that stage Commandants F.J.W.J. Hattingh and C.J. de Villiers of the Vrede and Harrismith Commandos and their burghers found themselves on the farm Sebastopol northeast of Golden Gate. When De Villiers heard that the British were on their way to Spitskrans, he immediately rushed to the assistance of the Republican sentry post. His burghers reached Spitskrans on Saturday – just in time to support Blignaut and his men against the huge British force. The burghers fought courageously, but the Khakis reached the summit of the mountain east of them by early afternoon and by the evening were using their field guns to force the burghers to fall back. Thus the British managed to occupy Spitskrans. We have heard the enemy's total loss in this battle is three men dead and 27 wounded.

On Sunday the Boers attempted to recapture Spitskrans with a counter attack, but the enemy repulsed them. Monday was a day that the burghers, and presumably the Khakis as well, would like to forget. A fierce storm raged with heavy rain and snow on the high-lying areas. Towards the east of Spitskrans, where Commandant De Villiers and his burghers were seeking shelter, the snow was about five centimetres deep. The British nevertheless attacked the mountain pass at Retief's Nek. Chief Commandant Prinsloo's Free Staters managed in spite of the bitter cold to repulse one British attack after the other. At the same time another huge British force attacked Slabbert's Nek, but was repulsed by the burghers stationed there. By that evening Prinsloo and his men were relatively satisfied with their military performance in the cold.

Early on Tuesday morning it became clear that the British had exploited the relative complacency of the burghers after nightfall on Monday evening and had occupied strategically situated heights at both Retief's Nek and Slabbert's Nek. At Witnek, Nelspoort and Moolman's Nek the British were also not opposed when they dug themselves in. When day broke on Tuesday morning the Khakis could resume their offensive from relatively advantageous positions. Their gunners opened a murderous bombardment on Prinsloo's burghers with their field gun. By three o'clock that afternoon the latter's resistance crumbled and they retreated. The Khakis then occupied both Retief's Nek and Slabbert's Nek. As a result the position of the Free State burghers in the Brandwater Basin is now critical.

Yesterday a British unit commanded by General Rundle managed to occupy Commando Nek east of Ficksburg. This morning a huge British force of over 3 000 men with about 14 guns attacked the burghers of Commandants De Villiers and Haasbroek at Noupoort Nek. The Free State artillerymen – especially Sergeant Oosthuizen – gave the approaching troops a warm reception, but the British gunners launched a counter-bombardment that included lyddite shells. The burghers resisted courageously, but by two o'clock this afternoon they were threatened with encirclement. The order then came to retreat. Fortunately they did not flee blindly but fell back in an orderly fashion. It was difficult to get all the guns away quickly, since these had to be pulled through dongas and over hills. At times the burghers had to assist. Fortunately all went well. Indeed, we were pleasantly surprised when we established tonight that not one single burgher was even hurt in today's clashes – and that in spite of the heavy fighting earlier on. Only one gun had to be abandoned.

By sunset this evening the British had occupied Noupoort nek. Commandant De Villiers and his men are falling back in an easterly direction. The Khakis are now in command of all the most important entries into the Brandwater Basin. In addition, they have managed to occupy Fouriesburg.

FROM THE EDITOR

Though the struggle continues unabated, Republican forces are finding it increasingly difficult to remain standing against the huge British force. At the same time, the price that the British are paying to wage this war is becoming higher every day. What we have to contend with is in essence a war of attrition. The side that gives in first will lose. If the Boers can hold out long enough, the Republics will win. If the British can keep on affording the war, and their will to win remains alive until the Boers can no longer hold out against their overwhelming numbers, they will win. Time will tell.

In the meantime the war is still producing both positive and negative developments. One extremely negative development is that the war is causing unprecedented divisions within the Afrikaner community – divisions even within households, between brother and brother. In the past weeks the clash between Piet and Christiaan de Wet is indicative of this. Hard words are heard. Harsh statements are made. Divisions that lead to bitterness follow. How long will it take for the wounds caused by this division to heal? Is our fate going to be an Afrikaner community that is divided for ever?

A second extremely negative development is Lord Roberts's targeting of the civilian population of the Republics, on which we have reported before. Last week we informed our readers about his dumping of homeless women and children – who are homeless since the British army destroyed their farms – in the veld at Van der Merwe Station in the eastern Transvaal. This week we further report on the terrible fate of those desperate victims of British aggression.

On the positive side, suffering and challenges sometimes force the best in a person to the surface. The way in which our field telegraphists overcome the virtually impossible challenges that confront them is laudable. We have an old proverb: A Boer makes a plan. The plans that our men are making are simply fascinating. Their creativity gives one more hope for the future than all the empty promises of support from abroad.

Number 42 28 July 1900

DEVELOPMENTS EAST OF PRETORIA

In the veld east of Middelburg, 27 July – The main British force in Pretoria last Saturday began a full-scale advance from the former capital in an easterly direction. Commandant-General Louis Botha was at that time in no position to offer resistance, since his forces were still busy attending to the needs of the 400 women and children who had been dumped in the veld without any means of subsistence by Lord Roberts two days previously (see separate report). In addition the British offensive came on a wide front, more than 50 kilometres from north to south. In a desperate attempt to halt the enemy, Botha divided his force of 2 200 burghers into small groups with orders to slow down the progress of the Khakis as effectively as possible.

By Monday afternoon (23 July) the British vanguard was already approaching the valley of the Olifants River. Botha's burghers did not allow them to proceed unhindered. They fired on the Khakis from every vantage point and often forced the British artillery to be unhooked and set up for action, thus slowing down British progress significantly. According to some reports Roberts himself accompanied the advance up to Balmoral, but returned to Pretoria with his staff yesterday.

In the meantime, burghers and Khakis locked horns in a heavy battle on the eastern bank of the Olifants River, south of the railway line. However, General Botha had to retreat when those Khakis managed to outflank his forces. He explained in a telegram to President Kruger on Wednesday that they were simply powerless against the massive British numbers:

'It would be of no use to us to confront the enemy, since that would mean the end of the war. Each time we halt the enemy in the centre, they fall back in the direction of Pretoria and their flanks charge to the front. They would, if we failed to fall back, then outflank and encircle us as they did with General Cronjé. It is difficult to keep out of their reach. The British advance with a massive numerical advantage, and we have only 2 200 burghers to halt them, to offer battle, and to take our wagons to safe places.'

On Wednesday night a heavy thunderstorm erupted which made life for the men on both sides extremely uncomfortable, since it was followed by an icy wind. Many of the animals perished and even some of the men died of the cold.

Our burghers have, in the meantime, fallen back further towards the east. Today they were powerless to offer any resistance to the British occupation of Middelburg.

INNOVATIVE TELEGRAPHISTS

British messages often overheard

In the veld in the Free State, 25 July – One of the field telegraphists with Chief Commandant De Wet's forces in the northern Free State is Flippie Pienaar – a young man who was born in the Colesberg district of the Cape Colony but grew up in Johannesburg. That these men have an exciting life goes without saying, but it demands hard work, commitment and an innovative spirit. Pienaar recently explained to our correspondent how they go about their job, and his report illuminates another important facet of this destructive confrontation between Boer and Brit:

'One of a field telegraphist's most important instruments is his vibrator. That is an instrument that is so sensitive that it can send or receive a message over virtually any wire. With the British offensive in the Free State, the burghers did their utmost to destroy as many telegraph wires as possible to prevent the British from using those for military purposes. The destruction of telegraph wires is however not an insurmountable problem, since there are other ways also of sending a message by telegraph.

'In terms of the law in the Orange Free State, every farm has to be fenced. The farmers often use blocks of sandstone for fencing uprights. These usually are about 1,2 metres high and 25 centimetres square. These fencing uprights support an extensive network of fencing. Fence wires are not suitable for telephonic communication, but one can send telegraphic messages on such wires over long distances by using a vibrator. Certain conditions have to be met:

- The wire must be uninterrupted over the whole distance. That demands from the telegraphists to regularly inspect the whole length of the wire along which they intend sending messages.
- The wire must be isolated. That means that all cross wires that touch the top wire (the top fence wire is mostly used as telegraph wire) must be removed.
- At the entrance gates connection wires must be provided to connect the fence wires on both sides of the gate.

'Interruptions frequently occur. The Khakis have no respect for a fence wire and often clip it. Large animals sometimes break through the fences. Our own burghers who are not informed of the value of the wires also clip them at times – especially if they are retreating from Khaki forces. The connections are easy to repair, however. All that is necessary is a bit of extra wire and a wire spanner. By using fence wires for communication the officers remain in contact with each other quite easily – even when it is cloudy or in the middle of the night when it is impossible to use heliographs.'

The telegraphists also make use of the actual telegraph wires, but this is not safe, since anybody can listen in. Telegraphist Pienaar showed us how easy it is to tap a message. He took a piece of wire cable about 10 metres in length, cleaned about 30 centimetres of it in the middle, tied his wire spanner to the one end and threw the latter over the telegraph line. Both ends hung just above the ground. He attached the vibrator to the other end and could immediately hear a British telegraphist in Heilbron calling up the telegraph office in British-occupied Kroonstad. It was a message from General Ian Hamilton to Lord Roberts in which he announced his arrival in Heilbron, the details about the two battles fought during the march, the casualties and the state of his men: 'hungry but cheerful'.

After this message a real jewel followed, namely an order by the Chief of Staff to Hamilton on how he was to march from Heilbron; how Broadwood was to move from Ventersburg, the entire plan of the campaign for the next few weeks. This was news to gladden the heart of President Steyn after the few tough days and setbacks of the last few weeks!

Telegraphist Flippie Pienaar

PLIGHT OF CIVILIANS IN EASTERN TRANSVAAL

Machadodorp, 27 July – Last week we reported on the arrival by railroad at Van der Merwe Station east of Donkerhoek of hundreds of Boer women and children. They were dumped in the veld by the British army and left with nothing to subsist on in the middle of the winter. Since the Boers had already destroyed the railway bridges and culverts, they were forced to use wagons for the transportation of those women and children to places of safety. The British authorities chose this very time to resume their offensive. The Transvaal forces were inadequate to halt this offensive and a hasty general retreat began. Two American volunteers who are fighting with our burghers, Alan Hiley and John Hassell, gave our correspondent the following report of the retreat to the east:

'Hampered by a transport already overtaxed, the Republican retreat from Balmoral was most memorable. Hundreds of wagons and families and household goods, formed miles of an unbroken trek. At night, with the veldt fires to light the road and destroy the grass, this scene made a picture difficult to describe. The enormous, wide, clumsy wagons, lumbering along with their draught of 18, 20 and 22 oxen of all ages; the old grandfather and grandmother sitting in the fore of the hood; one grown son of perhaps 40, walking alongside, with his 10-foot bamboo whip-stock over his shoulder; the wives and children of the second and third generations gathered in the back of the wagon, exchanging queries with the passing horsemen, or peering anxiously to catch a glimpse of some of their men-folk coming to obtain food, from the incessant fighting in the rear; with grown girls riding their ponies astride, driving a few head of milch cows snatched from the wreck of a home; and indiscriminate bunches of sheep and goats being urged on by the black servants to keep pace; baskets of chickens and ducks, slung under the wagons; and the housedog running by the side mutely questioning the cause of such unusual things, and every wagon varying but slightly in general make-up, number of stock, and method of locomotion.

'Fatigued burghers relieved from duty protecting the rear against the extreme British advance, in their attempt to catch the commissary and satisfy hunger, would ride hour after hour past this apparently endless stream of wagons and stock. Every detail was vividly portrayed in the lurid glare of the burning grass, the flames licking around the dead and dying animals which had fallen by the roadside in their final trek.

'Mile by mile, winding in and out, this enormous trek followed the road, until they arrived in safety at Middelburg to-day, making only short halts at the watering places to rest their stock and cook their food.

'From that town the families began to separate, trekking in parties with their stock to the bushveldt in the north, where they hope to be free from immediate further annoyance or possibility of being followed, as it is a country bountifully covered with grass and protected by a thick undergrowth of bushes, which will make the operations of an invading force extremely hazardous, and easy to repulse by a few daring and active burghers. They have nothing further to fear except a famine in flour, as game is there abundant, and they can in relative safety await the course of events.'

OUR MILITARY OFFICERS

General P.J. Liebenberg

Petrus Johannes Liebenberg was born in 1857 near Hopetown in the Cape Colony. He is the son of Christiaan J. Liebenberg and his wife Catharina Petronella van der Westhuizen. Of his childhood years and education we know nothing. In 1874 he settled on the farm Witpoort in the Klerksdorp district. He participated in numerous campaigns against black communities and took part in the Transvaal War of Independence of 1880–81. In 1896 he became a member of the Second Volksraad of the South African Republic.

With the outbreak of this war in October 1899 Liebenberg went to the western border, where he took part in the first battle at Kraaipan on 12 October. He was involved in the siege of Mafeking for some time and subsequently took part in the battles at Modder River and at Magersfontein in December. At that stage he held the rank of commandant.

In January this year Liebenberg was promoted to the rank of fighting general and ordered to invade the Cape Colony to recruit rebels. He was particularly successful. On 15 February a Cape Rebel force under his command occupied Prieska and declared it a part of the Orange Free State. The number of Cape Afrikaners who joined his forces grew rapidly.

After the British occupation of Bloemfontein in March and the Boer retreat to the northern Free State, Liebenberg fell back to Griqualand West. With Rooidam as headquarters, he managed to hold out in that area until General Hunter forced his commando to retreat to the north in May. Liebenberg and General Koos de la Rey subsequently failed in their attempts to prevent the British relief of Mafeking.

Last month Liebenberg participated in the battle of Donkerhoek, after which he was appointed as the commander of the Potchefstroom Commando. This week he and his burghers reoccupied Klerksdorp after driving away the Khaki garrison of the town.

General P.J. Liebenberg

CLASHES IN SOUTH AND SOUTHEASTERN TRANSVAAL

In the veld near Heidelberg, 26 July – On this front the Transvaal burghers have been struggling to hold out for the past week or so. General Christiaan Botha could not prevent the British occupation of Graskop on the Natal–Johannesburg railway line last Sunday. General Tobias Smuts was supposed to defend Graskop with a combined force of 500 Ermelo burghers and 150 Carolina burghers. Smuts was not present though, since he was ill. The Ermelo burghers were not at their posts either. Neither was the commander of the Carolina burghers, but what his excuse was we do not know. Nevertheless, the Carolina burghers fought courageously under command of a field cornet. They fired sharply on the charging Khakis but were eventually forced to retreat to the Strydkraal Hills. The enemy's occupation of Graskop cost them severe casualties. The exact number is not known to us, but there were subsequently four ambulance wagons on the battlefield and they seemed to be quite active.

General Chris Botha aimed at attacking the occupiers of Graskop early on Monday morning, but in spite of his moving pleas, the burghers could not be convinced to charge the Khakis. The burghers felt it would serve no purpose to attack, since they would never be able to repulse the enemy. Botha reacted by suggesting that the burghers should attempt to ensure that the Khakis at Graskop received no food supplies whatsoever. However, even before they could implement those plans, the Khakis themselves attacked the burghers in the Strydkraal Hills on Monday morning. Another three days of heavy fighting followed, during which the burghers remained courageous in their resistance. The British eventually used their heavy naval guns in an attempt to repulse the Boers, but failed. The only reason why Botha's men eventually left the Strydkraal Hills yesterday was because the British threatened to encircle them.

In the meantime a British force commanded by General Howard overwhelmed a Boer sentry post and occupied the Rooikoppies at Amersfoort on Tuesday. On the same day a strong British force managed to dislodge a Boer commando, which had resisted them for three successive days, from Paardekop. Three burghers, including Captain Thomas of the Reconnaissance Corps, were killed and one was wounded. We do not know what the British casualties were, but they were probably severe.

THE War Reporter
WEEKLY EDITION

Number 43 — Machadodorp, South African Republic — 4 August 1900

DISASTER IN BRANDWATER BASIN
Prinsloo, Free State forces surrender to British

In the veld in the northern Free State, 3 August – Today was a bitter day for the burghers in Chief Commandant De Wet's laager in the northern Free State. The terrible news of former Chief Commandant Marthinus Prinsloo's surrender with all his commandos to the British in the Brandwater Basin has reached us. De Wet has just revealed that he had already received the news yesterday via his scouts who sent him a message from General Knox at Kroonstad, but had refused to believe it.

This morning De Wet received another message from Knox, saying that Prinsloo's secretary was in his camp with a report addressed to De Wet. Knox requested that this secretary – his name is Albert Grobler – should be allowed to deliver the message and would then provide further information. Knox probably thought that the secretary would also convince us to surrender.

De Wet answered by promising the secretary free passage. He himself, President Steyn and a few members of the Free State government met Grobler in the veld, since they did not wish to give him any opportunity to spy on their laager. The secretary then handed De Wet the following letter:

'Sir, I have been obliged, owing to the overwhelming forces of the enemy, to surrender unconditionally with all the Orange Free State laagers here. I have the honour to be, Sir, Your obedient servant, M. Prinsloo, Chief Commandant.'

De Wet was extremely angry when he read this letter. The fact that a large part of the Free State forces had surrendered in the Brandwater Basin was less of a shock to him than the fact that Marthinus Prinsloo still claimed for himself the title of Chief Commandant. Suddenly everything was clear to him. Prinsloo had resigned last month, claiming that it was for health reasons, but many believe that he actually resigned because Christiaan de Wet was elected Chief Commandant of the Free State forces in preference to him. Now Prinsloo has again taken up a leadership role, and has brought disaster to the Free State.

De Wet there and then wrote the following answer to Prinsloo: 'To Mr M. Prinsloo, Sir, I have the honour to acknowledge the receipt of your letter dated the 30th of last month. I am surprised to see that you call yourself Chief Commandant. By what right do you usurp that title? You have no right to act as Chief Commandant, I have the honour to be, C.R. de Wet, Chief Commandant.'

In the meantime we have heard from Prinsloo's envoy what happened in the Brandwater Basin. By the end of last week there seems to have been uncertainty among burghers and officers on who was the highest Free State commander in the Basin. General Paul Roux was in command of numerous commandos, but Prinsloo claimed that he was in command of all the commandos that had previously fallen under General Piet de Wet.

In order to get clarity on this very important issue in the absence of Chief Commandant Christiaan de Wet, the Free State officers held a war council meeting at Eerste Geluk in the Brandwater Basin. At this meeting the officers decided to elect a commander. Prinsloo was elected with a small majority. Soon after the election the war council received a report that all the commandos that were not directly represented at the war council were in favour of Roux. Prinsloo rejected those votes and the uncertainty continued.

By Friday afternoon most of the commandos in the Basin were moving towards Slaapkrans. On Saturday morning they were attacked there with cavalry and artillery by a huge British force that had in the meantime entered the Basin. The burghers fought back for all they were worth, but the British force was simply too big and the artillery in particular systematically broke down their resistance. By midnight it was clear that they had no hope of surviving.

Early on Sunday morning Prinsloo decided to play for time, and sent S.G. Vilonel in an attempt to convince the British commander, General Hunter, to agree to an armistice of four days. Vilonel had previously been a commandant, but Chief Commandant De Wet had demoted him in March. Later on he had been found guilty of treason by a military court under the chairmanship of Judge J.B.M. Hertzog, on a charge of having negotiated with the enemy. The Free State forces took him along as a prisoner when they entered the Brandwater Basin. And now, to our utter surprise, Prinsloo was using him as an envoy. The only plausible reason that Prinsloo can advance for this choice is that the British will probably accept Vilonel rather than any other Boer envoy.

When he returned, Vilonel reported that Hunter refused to accept an armistice but demanded unconditional surrender. One may wonder what role he played in Hunter's decision. Did Vilonel not perhaps tell Hunter that Prinsloo was merely playing for time? Can one trust someone who had earlier been found guilty of treason?

After receiving Hunter's demand Prinsloo decided to surrender, claiming to act on behalf of all the Free State commandos in the Brandwater Basin. Fortunately some officers, including Generals Froneman, Piet Fourie, Kolbe and Olivier, refused to accept his authority and fled over Golden Gate with about 1 500 burghers, eight field guns, a pom-pom and two machine guns. Generals Roux and Crowther are among the officers who surrendered with Prinsloo.

Former Chief Commandant Marthinus Prinsloo's surrender

MILITARY ACTIVITIES IN TRANSVAAL

Machadodorp, 3 August – Very little military activity took place north of the Vaal River in the past week. We have received a few brief reports from the western Transvaal. Last Sunday there was some fighting between a British unit and our forces at Frederikstad, a railway station about 20 kilometres northeast of Potchefstroom. Neither side could gain the upper hand. On Monday General Methuen entered Potchefstroom with a huge British force. Yesterday a British force of some 1 000 men with a few guns commanded by General Carrington occupied Zeerust, far in the western Transvaal.

In the eastern Transvaal a Boer force numbering a few hundred men commanded by General Joachim Fourie managed to repulse a British attack on Amersfoort. The burghers had to withstand a heavy bombardment, but stuck to their task. The British casualties amounted to at least 15 men killed, while the Boers suffered no casualties.

General Daniël Erasmus reports that his commando was involved in skirmishes in the area of the Elands River north of the eastern railway line. British casualties amounted to 25 soldiers dead and eight taken prisoner of war. The burghers captured 45 horses, a number of mules and oxen and a trolley loaded with supplies.

East of Middelburg, along the eastern railway line, there was a skirmish between a British patrol and a group of burghers on Monday. Four Khakis were killed and their officer mortally wounded.

In the vicinity of Pretoria, General Koos de la Rey took former General Hendrik Schoeman prisoner on Tuesday when the latter refused to carry out an order to escort a convoy of wagons. In the same area a British force of thousands of troops with guns occupied both Kommandonek and Silkaatsnek. It seems as if they intend to make the whole Magaliesberg range inaccessible to our burghers. The small garrison of burghers under the command of Field Cornet Coetzee, who was stationed at Silkaatsnek by General de la Rey, retreated when several hundred British soldiers charged them with bayonets. We have heard that the British paid a heavy price for this victory, namely 46 casualties.

FROM THE EDITOR

This was a black week for the Republican forces. Former Chief Commandant Marthinus Prinsloo has surrendered with a force of 4 300 Free State burghers, including three generals and nine commandants, in the Brandwater Basin. In the process three guns, a large supply of ammunition, cattle, sheep and more than 5 000 horses fell into British hands. The surrender has weakened the Orange Free State forces to such an extent that they will be unable to render any further meaningful resistance to the British army.

Many critics will renew their objections to carrying on with the war, as they did after the surrender of General Piet Cronjé in February. They will argue that the Republics might as well surrender, since they stand no realistic chance of eventually achieving a victory. To them our message, short and sweet, is: do not lose faith. The British cannot provision this massive war machine forever. The Boxer Rebellion in China is already claiming attention. At some stage they will realise that they cannot force the Boers to surrender unconditionally. They will then have to negotiate and our freedom will be assured.

A number of circumstances that have been forced on us by the present war conditions, including the scarcity of paper and the difficulty of relaying messages from the different fronts to our temporary printing press, compel us to turn the newspaper from a weekly into a monthly. In future it will, if circumstances allow, be issued on the first day of each month.

REPUBLICAN DEPUTATION ABROAD
Chinese uprising a mixed blessing

Machadodorp, 3 August – The Republican deputation that left for Europe in March in an attempt to gain the support of friendly powers is at present in France. Earlier this week we received extensive reports on their activities. The deputation members are received with overwhelming enthusiasm wherever they go, but have thus far had no success.

The deputation, consisting of Abraham Fischer, C.H. Wessels and A.D.W. Wolmarans, built up a huge support network in the United States of America when they visited that country in June. Unfortunately they could not convince the American government to put pressure on the British to abandon the war. On 28 June they left the USA for France, disappointed about their lack of success and hoping that they will do better in Europe.

The deputation arrived in the harbour Le Havre on 6 July. A huge and enthusiastic crowd was on the quay to welcome them. Dr W.J. Leyds, the South African Republic's special envoy in Europe, as well as Senator Pauliat, the vice-president of the French Senate, were there. Also present was a deputation of the recently formed French Committee for the Advancement of the Boer cause. Nevertheless the deputation is not under any illusions that assistance will easily be forthcoming from the French government itself. Britain and France are solid allies and have not since the fall of Emperor Napoleon I in 1815 been involved in any conflict with each other. The French would not want to endanger that alliance.

The deputation has arrived in France at a very awkward time. In the first place, an uprising against foreigners, known as the

Continued overleaf

continued

Boxer Rebellion, is taking place in China. The Chinese have murdered many Europeans, including Frenchmen, which of course is drawing public attention away from South Africa. The same is happening to the attention of the politicians, since the French government is seriously considering a punitive expedition to subdue the rebellious Chinese.

Even though the Boxer Rebellion is drawing attention from South Africa, it may in the long run have great advantages for the Boer Republics. The British are anxious about developments in China and have begun sending troops to that massive country. If they get involved in hostilities there on a large scale, they will no longer be able to give their full attention to the war against the Republics. It is even possible that the Chinese crisis will become so extensive that the British will be forced to end their war here.

A French cartoon on British brutality in South Africa

To return to the visit to France by the deputation – on 10 July they met the French Minister of Foreign Affairs in Paris. He was friendly and sympathetic but gave no specific assurances. The city council of Paris arranged an official reception for the deputation members that was accompanied by great ceremony but produced no concrete support. On 25 July the deputation members were guests of the President of the French Republic, who also restricted himself to expressions of sympathy.

The most promising event of the past week was the opening in Paris of the Congress of the Parliamentary Union of Arbitration. It was attended by representatives of parliaments of various nations whose most important objective is to attempt to implement a system whereby peace and justice would be protected by means of arbitration or friendly intervention between the civilised nations of the world.

At this Congress, Wessels, who is attending as a member of the Parliament of the Orange Free State, stated in a memorandum that the war was forced on the Boer Republics by Britain. Even though the Belgian and Russian representatives made strong pleas in favour of the Boers, the Congress eventually only accepted the following decision: 'The Congress deplores the fact that the powers involved in the present conflict between Britain and the South African Republics did not use all the means available for peaceful settlement of international disputes.'

It is clear that there is great sympathy for the Boer cause in France. This is revealed in the many publications in which Britain is branded as the destroyer of peace in this part of the world and in which the one-sided British interpretation of justice is ridiculed. Britain's obsession with its own glory and 'greatness' is often scoffed at by the sharp pens of journalists and cartoonists.

Since it is clear to the deputation that France will not place any pressure on the British government, they have informed President Kruger here in Machadodorp that they will soon proceed to Germany in an attempt to gain the support of the German government.

OUR MILITARY OFFICERS

General Daniël Erasmus

One of the best known officers in the Transvaal at the beginning of the war, and a military leader who still plays an active part, is General Daniël (Maroela) Erasmus of the Pretoria Commando. Daniël Jacobus Elardus Erasmus was born in 1845 on the farm Doringkloof some 10 kilometres south of the area where the city of Pretoria was founded in 1855. He is the eldest son of Daniël Elardus Erasmus and his wife Sarie Margaretha Jacobs. As a young man Erasmus was involved in the Transvaal Civil War as a supporter of Commandant-General Stephanus Schoeman (the father of General Hendrik Schoeman). In 1865 he was a member of the Transvaal commando that participated in the war between the Orange Free State and the Basuto. Soon afterwards he was elected as field cornet of the Hennops River ward in the Pretoria district.

In addition to his farming activities, Erasmus was an active hunter and trader in his young days. In 1880–81 he participated in the Transvaal War of Independence. He took part in the battle of Bronkhorstspruit on 20 December 1880. At that time he had the rank of field commandant. Subsequently he played a leading role in the siege of the British garrison in Pretoria. In the skirmish at Rooihuiskraal in February 1881 he was lightly wounded.

Erasmus's public career took off after the start of this war. In 1881 he became a member of the Volksraad for the Pretoria district. Subsequently he served on numerous government commissions. In 1884 he became commandant of the Pretoria district. Two years later he resigned from the Volksraad to give more attention to his farming interests. An active member of the Pretoria agriculture society, in 1895 he became the chairman of the commission that established a department of agriculture and stock-breeding for the South African Republic. He kept his rank of commandant throughout and served with distinction in numerous campaigns against black communities, including the Bapedi, the Hananwa and the Bavenda.

When the war clouds gathered at the beginning of October last year, Erasmus proceeded to the Natal front at the head of the Pretoria Commando. At Sandspruit the war council appointed him assistant commandant-general on 11 October, the day when the war began. The next day he and his burghers invaded Natal. At that time we often reported on his sometimes controversial role in events on that front, but in the recent past he has consistently acted with great vigour and done much to restore his reputation.

General Erasmus's first wife, Magdalena Margaretha Erasmus died in 1873. He later on married Sybella Margaretha Aletta Schabort.

General D.J.E. Erasmus

WAR CONDITIONS IN THE COLD OF WINTER

EYEWITNESS REPORT BY WILHELM MANGOLD OF HEIDELBERG

Highveld near Standerton, 25 July – It has been more than a month since our previous report on the activities of the Heidelberg commando. In the meantime these men have continued their pursuit of the war with their usual vigour. Here follows a report on their activities by Wilhelm Mangold, one of the distinguished members of the commando and a man who has often compiled reports for our paper. He writes as follows:

'After General Buller's occupation of Standerton at the end of last month, we initially searched for shelter in the mountains north of Greylingstad. It is now midwinter and the nights are bitterly cold. My top blanket is covered with frost every morning. In the evening I sleep within my homemade sleeping bag wearing both my winter coat and my raincoat with my waterproof canvas around me. Even then it is often so cold that I cannot sleep. Then I rise and seek warmth at a fire where there are always men sitting around drinking coffee, smoking their pipes and exchanging hunt and ghost stories. It is very sociable but extremely cold.

'On some evenings things become quite jolly. There are 11 German volunteers who joined us in the Heidelberg Commando. In the evening, when they are gathered around our fire of cow dung, they like to sing. They have good voices and we Afrikaners enjoy listening to them singing songs like 'Die Wacht am Rhein' and 'Morgenrot, Morgenrot'. The Boers sometimes try to sing with them and by now know some of the words. Sometimes the singing is accompanied by the baking of dough bread called vetkoeke. Some evenings we eat so many vetkoeke that we have only maize porridge and sheep's ribs left the next day.

'In the past month we have been continuously plagued by millions of ticks. They descend on any unfortunate victim without distinguishing between rank and position. Since they are hardly bigger than the heads of pins, one does not see them easily. There is no medicine for this plague.

'Some weeks ago we heard for the first time that the British had destroyed a house in our district. The unfortunate victim was Commandant S.B. Buys and his family. Buys heard on 1 July that his house and outbuildings had been destroyed. He immediately went there with 50 men to investigate. After his return he said that the Khakis had arrived at his home and given his wife 10 minutes to pack some food and clothes in trunks. Even before the 10 minutes had passed they torched the house. In addition they threw everything she attempted to save, including a photograph of her eldest son, into the flames. Commandant Buys's wife was forced to seek shelter with neighbours. We were endlessly angered when we heard about this, since we had not expected such actions from a civilised opponent.

'On 4 July we shifted position to Van Kolderskop near Kraal Station. Our objective was to sabotage the railway in that area. When we reached our destination the next day in thick mist, the Bethal burghers with their guns were already on the low hill. Captain von Dalwig of the State Artillery was with them. He had with him a pom-pom gun as well as one of the British Armstrong guns captured by our burghers at Colenso last December. Later that day Field Cornet Org Meyer joined us with another pom-pom as well as a Krupp gun.

'Soon after the mist cleared, we became involved in an inconclusive skirmish with about 60 British cavalrymen. Three of our youngsters had a confrontation with a patrol of five Khakis and put all of them out of action. The next day, 6 July, we were involved in an artillery duel with the enemy, but again the result was even.

'On the evening of 16 July a task force of 10 men was appointed to destroy the huge railway bridge across the Suikerbosrand River. I was one of the commanders instead of the Field Cornet who had become ill. By midnight we arrived there. We reconnoitred very carefully but could see no guard at the bridge. The explosives men, with two German authorities, immediately went into action. They placed the dynamite that they had brought all the way from Balmoral in position. Within half an hour the fuses were ignited and we retreated 300 metres. A few minutes later the dynamite exploded and the bridge was totally destroyed.

'After this successful action we often carried out nocturnal attacks, but often had to abandon our plans when we found the Khakis awaiting us. We suspect that handsuppers divulge our plans to them. Our suspicion was strengthened when one of our guard posts of six men surrendered to the British one night.

'On 12 July a huge force of perhaps 3 000 Khakis advanced on us. However, they did not attack, but pitched camp near us. That night we trekked to Mahemsfontein and the following day a full-scale battle took place. Our burghers managed to fend off the first British cavalry charge on our left flank with ease. The British however kept attacking and brought more guns from the direction of Greylingstad. The intensity of the British charge increased. Our men later on had to retire, but did that in an orderly fashion.

'On 14 July the enemy once again attacked, but we repulsed them. After this we rested for three days. In this period we heard that the British were building a wooden bridge to replace the Suikerbosrand railway bridge that we had previously destroyed. We decided to make an end to that. Last Thursday night (19 July) we went to the site on horseback. We took the necessary explosives, namely two trunks of dynamite, fuses and percussion caps with us. While I was placing the dynamite in position and somebody else was attaching the fuses, the other burghers broke up the railway line on both sides of the bridge. When everything was ready we ignited the fuses and immediately fell back 500 metres. We thought something went wrong since initially there was complete silence, when suddenly two gigantic flames shot into the air followed by a thunderous rattle. The structure flew in all directions. We quickly surveyed the damage. The bridge was once again totally demolished. It would take the British some time to make it serviceable.

'Soon after the second destruction of this bridge, we decided to attack the British camp at Vlakfontein not far from the destroyed bridge. Our plan was to attack with first light on 21 July so we approached our target on a bitterly cold evening. Corporal Bronkhorst and a few burghers went ahead and unexpectedly drew British small arms fire. The rest of us immediately charged the enemy. Our guns also entered the fray and we attempted to level a stone wall behind which the Khakis were hiding. This was soon successful and the Khakis retreated. We were ready to launch a full-scale attack when our guns suddenly became silent. Later on we heard that the Krupp ran out of ammunition and the pom-pom developed mechanical problems. That took the pressure off the Khakis. However, we kept on firing with our rifles.

'A huge setback occurred at this time when Corporal John Spruyt was fatally wounded. A bullet hit him in the head behind his eye. Some of the men helped me to remove his body to a safe place. The problem was that the battle was still raging and our ammunition was running low. Fortunately we managed to get the heavily wounded Spruyt to safety and to keep our position until the order came that we had to retreat.

'Corporal John Spruyt died yesterday afternoon (Sunday 22 July). On the same day we received orders to proceed to Carolina, which we did. However, 14 of us went to Spruyt's funeral today. Thus our futile attack on the camp of the Khakis ended in disaster and the loss of a personal friend. We will now follow the other men to Carolina.'

THE

War Reporter

MONTHLY EDITION

Number 44 | In die Veld, South African Republic | 1 September 1900

HUGE BATTLE AT BERGENDAL

Botha's forces fall back after courageous resistance

Nelspruit, 30 August – One of the biggest field battles in the war so far has just ended at Bergendal, between Belfast and Machadodorp. Commandant-General Louis Botha did all he could to halt the advance of the combined armies of Generals Roberts and Buller, who joined forces for the first time just before the battle. Eventually the burghers were forced to fall back. As a result, the Transvaal government has had to retreat to Nelspruit.

Botha expected that the British forces would use their proven attack formations when they advanced from the south and west on the temporary government seat at Machadodorp. That would have meant that infantry supported by artillery would attack the centre and large cavalry units would attempt to outflank the Boer positions. Botha prepared his forces to counter such an attack.

By Sunday, 19 August, Botha's approximately 5 000 burghers were in position in a straight line over a distance of about 80 kilometres, from Botha's Mountain in the north almost to Carolina in the south. Heliographs were set up to ensure communication over the whole length of the line, and plans were worked out to render assistance where it was needed most.

Since there was increased British activity north of the eastern railway line during the first 20 days of August, Botha had no doubt that the British would attempt to overrun the Boer positions in the north. As a result, he considerably strengthened the Boer forces on this flank – at the expense, of course, of the other flanks from which men were transferred. However, Botha could not weaken his southern flank, since after Buller's occupation of Amersfoort, Ermelo and Carolina earlier this month, British forces posed a considerable threat on that part of the front. He was thus forced to weaken his centre.

FIRST PHASE OF THE BATTLE

The battle of Bergendal began on 21 August with a skirmish between General Joachim Fourie's burghers and the British vanguard at Frischgewaagd on the Boer left flank. The burghers forced the Khakis to retreat. The next day, a group of Khakis again clashed with burghers in that area, and again were repulsed. On the 23rd, Buller concentrated on attacking Geluk in the south. Both the burghers with their rifles and Captain Alfred von Dalwig with his three guns participated in repulsing this attack. Unfortunately, Von Dalwig himself was severely wounded when shrapnel from a bursting shell hit him late that afternoon.

On the 24th the fighting came to a temporary standstill. Buller's forces at Geluk launched no further attacks and the Boers restricted their offensive activities to a long-distance artillery bombardment. In the centre of the Boer lines a British force managed to occupy Belfast. By that evening it was clear that, generally speaking, the Boer position was precarious. Botha had all four Long Toms at his disposal – the first time in the war that all these celebrated guns were together in one battle – and in addition, had 32 other guns of various types, but the ammunition supply for all of them was very low. And the British numerical advantage in men, guns and ammunition was overwhelming.

On Saturday, 25 August, the situation remained calm. The next day, however, the Boer scouts observed the enemy taking up positions in preparation for an attack. A huge British cavalry force, presumably commanded by General French, advanced northwards. In the south, a massive force, probably under Buller's command, approached Volstruispoort. The burghers fired on them for all they were worth and the British found it tough to reach Waaikraal, south of Dalmanutha. According to reliable sources, the Khakis suffered 48 casualties that day.

THE BRITISH BREAKTHROUGH

On Monday 27 August the battle reached its decisive phase. A huge British force attacked our forces at Bergendal, directly south of the railway line. To Botha, that specific position was of huge strategic value, and the burghers of the Krugersdorp Commando, as well as a section of the German Corps, were occupying it. A low hill on this part of the front, which is now called the Bergendal hillock by the burghers, was occupied by about 70 members of the South African Republic Police, or the ZARPs, as they are generally known. They were commanded by Commandant P.R. Oosthuizen, Commandant S van Lier and Lieutenant W.F. Pohlman, and had one pom-pom rapid-fire gun. It was on this position that the British attack was concentrated.

At 11 o'clock that morning the British launched a massive bombardment with shrapnel and lyddite shells directed especially at the Bergendal hillock. The Republican gunners fired back with their Long Toms and Krupp guns, but this did not silence the British. After three hours of uninterrupted bombardment, the British infantry approached the low hill. The ZARPs fired sharply on them, but the Khakis eventually reached the foot of the hill, even though they suffered heavy casualties. The British artillery then ended their bombardment, and the infantry fastened on their bayonets and charged up the hill. The valiant policemen slowed the charging Khakis down with accurate rifle fire, but gradually began running out of ammunition. As a result, they had to retreat. The brave Commandant Philip Oosthuizen, who was heavily wounded, was taken prisoner of war. By that time Lieutenant Pohlman and a considerable number of the ZARPs had been killed. Only 30 of the ZARPs came out unscathed. British casualties were probably much higher, but they could claim that they had broken through the Boer defensive line. Soon afterwards darkness descended and the battle activities came to a standstill.

Elsewhere along the line the Boers successfully defended their positions on Monday, but General Botha was forced to order his commandos to retreat to ensure that they would not be encircled. The burghers started falling back from Monday evening. That allowed the Khakis to occupy Machadodorp, Helvetia, Waterval-Boven and Waterval-Onder. A second significant result of the British breakthrough at Bergendal was that the Boers had to release 2 000 British prisoners of war from the camp at Nooitgedacht near Barberton.

The casualties in the battle of Bergendal were huge. From the beginning of the battle on 21 August up to the British breakthrough on the 27th they suffered, according to reliable sources, a loss of 300 men. On the 27th alone, the British loss was about 120 men, of whom 13 were killed. The total Boer loss was 78 men, of whom 39 were put out of action on Monday. Of those 14 were killed and 19 taken prisoner of war.

DE WET EVADES KHAKIS IN THE TRANSVAAL

CREAM OF BRITISH ARMY LEFT EMPTY-HANDED

Potchefstroom, 27 August – Chief Commandant Christiaan de Wet and the Free State government-in-the-veld have a busy month behind them. At the beginning of August De Wet and his commando, which at one stage consisted of about 2 500 men, were still hiding in the northern Free State in the vicinity of Reitzburg.

Commandant Danie Theron's scouts successfully derailed a British military train at Holfontein, south of Kroonstad, on 3 August. One of the passengers on the train was the American Consul-General in South Africa, Colonel Stowe who was accompanied by a British officer who was taking documents from Sir Alfred Milner to Lord Roberts. Chief Commandant De Wet was furious when he learned of this state of affairs. In a letter to Roberts he indignantly complained about the misuse of the immunity of foreign diplomats by the British authorities to convey military documents.

De Wet realised that he could not linger indefinitely in the northern Free State, since five or six generals, with between 40 000 and 50 000 troops, were gradually encircling him. He and his men began crossing the Vaal River at Schoemansdrift south of Potchefstroom on 6 August. Fortunately the British did not hinder this movement and the huge wagon laager could cross the river relatively easily. The water was low – not even reaching the axles of most wagons – and the crossing, though slow, went without a hitch.

The Venterskroon area where De Wet and his men entered the Transvaal is very hilly. The low hills are spaced in such a way that the Free Staters had to trek between two chains of hillocks for a distance of about 15 kilometres. That restricted their freedom of movement and made them extremely vulnerable to attack. As a result De Wet was anxious to keep moving. Only the vanguard of his force was across the river by dusk that evening and he had to wait for the rest.

THE CLASH AT TIJGERFONTEIN

Apparently the Khakis were aware of De Wet's movements, since on the morning of Tuesday 7 August they attacked the Free Staters, slowing down their progress. However, by three o'clock that afternoon the burghers had managed to drive the enemy off once again. With the Khakis retreating to Tijgerfontein, De Wet urged his men to advance as quickly as possible and to occupy the low hills

Olifants Nek

around Van Vuurer's Kloof on the northern side of the mountainous area.

De Wet's huge wagon laager was a millstone around his neck. On 8 August British forces launched an attack on the campsite of the Free Staters. De Wet ordered his men to take up a defensive position while the wagon drivers proceeded to the north with their wagons. The burghers held off the Khakis temporarily, and by the time they were forced to begin retreating the wagons were safe, trekking as hurriedly as possible across the hilly terrain towards the Gatsrand area. Thus the battle at Tijgerfontein came to an end. As for the casualties: they were not too severe. We have heard that on the British side seven men were killed and 24 wounded. On the Boer side four men were killed and only a few wounded.

FROM GATSRAND TO THE BUSHVELD

On Friday 10 August De Wet's commando, with thousands of British forces converging from all sides, crossed the Gatsrand. From there they proceeded to Frederikstad some 20 kilometres northeast of Potchefstroom, where they made contact with General Piet Liebenberg's Potchefstroom Commando. De Wet, Liebenberg and their men now proceeded northwards to the vicinity of Modderfontein, west of Ventersdorp. On 12 August a British force attacked them there. This British force was so massive that De Wet and his officers did not even consider trying to confront it. Their only option was to flee. Consequently they moved as quickly as possible to the north.

Continued overleaf

FROM THE EDITOR

British forces have held the upper hand in the war during the past month: indeed, their victory over Commandant-General Botha's main force at Bergendal (the British refer to the event as the battle of Dalmanutha) earlier this week means that the Republican forces are once again in crisis. On the other hand, Chief Commandant De Wet's masterly outmanoeuvring of a huge force that was pursuing him, as well as General De la Rey's repulsing of a British army from Swartruggens earlier this month, considerably strengthened the morale of the Republican forces.

The Boer cause is still far from lost. The British inability to destroy the Republican military forces has been proven over and over again in the past few months. They score one pyrrhic victory after the other, but in the meantime the Boers are regaining their moral ascendancy. De Wet's visit to Potchefstroom, where he encouraged the townspeople in a moving speech not to lose their confidence, is but one example of this, while Lord Roberts's umpteenth proclamation, in which he threatens the Boers with harsh measures, proves that the celebrated Field Marshal is becoming desperate.

Our message to our readers is: remain confident. Remember President Jan Brand's celebrated motto, 'Alles sal reg kom' (All will be well), and do your duty to ensure eventual success.

continued

At times they had to fight in order to slow down the British vanguard. Thus the laager was saved. The Khakis did manage to capture a few of De Wet's wagons as well as one of the Armstrong guns that had been captured by the Boers at Stormberg last December. De Wet was also forced to release his 80 prisoners of war.

On 14 August, De Wet and his commando crossed the Magaliesberg at Olifants Nek and set up a laager at the Hex River north of the mountain chain. On 16 August they moved further to the east in the direction of Pretoria and two days later reached the Crocodile River at Soutpan, northwest of Pretoria. From there President Steyn and a number of Free State government members departed eastwards for negotiations with the Transvaal government, escorted by Commandant Koos Boshoff with 30 men of the Pretoria Commando. Judge J.B.M. Hertzog is serving as Acting President of the Orange Free State in the meantime.

BACK ACROSS THE MAGALIESBERG

De Wet did not accompany Steyn on the remainder of his journey, but set off back to the Free State with 250 men. His aim was to draw the attention of the British away from the Free State government, but he was almost cornered against the northern slope of the Magaliesberg near Wolhuterskop. De Wet told our reporter that he and his men were on the farm Bokfontein on 21 August when they captured a British scout who told them that a huge British force was approaching from the direction of Pretoria. Indeed they soon noted other British forces in the area. They were metaphorically speaking between four fires!

De Wet had to find a quick solution. The only way out was to cross the Magaliesberg in a southerly direction. However, he did not know this area and he did not know if a crossing would be possible at all. Fortunately there was a way to be found, as De Wet related to our correspondent:

'Nearby we found a black man. I pointed to the Magalies Mountains and asked him: "Right before us, can a man cross there?"

'"No, Master, you cannot!" the black man answered.

'"Has a man never ridden across here?"

'"Yes, Master," replied the black man, "long ago."

'"Do baboons walk across?"

'"Yes, baboons do, but not a man."

'"Come on!" I said to my burghers. "There is our only way, and where a baboon can cross, we can cross."

'We climbed up unobserved to a bit of bush behind which we could hide from the Khakis. We then reached a ravine and ascended by it, still out of sight of the enemy, until we reached a point nearly halfway up the mountain. There we had to leave the ravine and continue our ascent in full view of the enemy.

'It was now so steep that we could not proceed any further on horseback. The burghers had to lead their horses, and had great difficulty in keeping their own footing. It frequently happened that a burgher fell and slipped backwards under his horse. The climb became increasingly difficult. When we had nearly reached the top of the mountain, there was a huge slab of granite as slippery as ice, and here men and horses stumbled still more, and were continually falling.

'We were, as I have said, in view of the enemy and were within range of their big guns! But nothing happened. The Khakis neither shot at us, nor did they pursue us. We reached the top of the mountain entirely exhausted. After having taken a little rest, we began to descend the mountain on the southern side.'

After a very difficult passage – one of the burghers stated afterwards that the descent was even more difficult than the ascent had been – they eventually reached the farm Remhoogte just before dusk. The enemy fortunately did not pursue them and they could finally relax.

By Friday 24 August De Wet and his commando were back in the Orange Free State, where he established his headquarters at Renosterpoort. Two days later he recrossed the Vaal River with 246 burghers and arrived in Potchefstroom, which had in the meantime been abandoned by the British. His main purpose was to get hold of dynamite to sabotage railway lines. During his visit a number of photographs were taken, of which the one below is published here.

Chief Commandant De Wet (third from right) and his staff in Potchefstroom

DE LA REY ACTIVE IN THE WESTERN TRANSVAAL

Besieges one British force, forces a second to flee

In the veld in the western Transvaal, 20 August – While Chief Commandant De Wet's Free Staters were finding it hard to avoid the Khakis at Venterskroon in the first half of August, General De la Rey was attacking a large British force at Brakfontein on the Elands River at Swartruggens. One of his objectives was to distract the attention of the British authorities, who obviously wanted to concentrate on the capture of De Wet. The Khakis had some weeks previously begun building fortifications at Brakfontein and a garrison was stationed there under Colonel Charles Hore, one of General Baden-Powell's officers during the Boer siege of Mafeking.

De la Rey was well aware of the activities of the British garrison at Brakfontein. The Khakis sent out patrols virtually every day, and masses of supplies were accumulated at Swartruggens, making it an inviting target for the Boers. De la Rey was also aware that the garrison consisted of about 500 men. Of those a big contingent were Australians who called themselves Bushmen. They had one fairly old field gun and two machine guns at their disposal. Their camp was situated on both sides of the Zeerust–Rustenburg wagon road.

De la Rey had a commando of about 500 burghers available. He himself commanded the Lichtenburg burghers, while General Manie Lemmer and Commandant Steenekamp commanded the Marico Commando and Krugersdorp burghers respectively. The Boers had four guns, a pom-pom and two machine guns. In the course of the night of 3–4 August they surrounded the British camp. The Khakis seemed to have been unaware of their presence, since they were holding a camp concert on the evening of 3 August.

On Saturday morning (4 August) the Boers fired on Khakis who were taking their horses to a watering hole at the river. The Khakis were so surprised that consternation erupted in their camp. While the burghers pinned them down with accurate rifle fire, the Boer artillerymen set up their guns on low hills in the vicinity. Soon a bombardment followed that caused a slaughter amongst the British horses and cattle. The Boers kept on attacking the whole day long and only stopped firing in the evening.

During the night that followed the burghers crept closer to the British camp and dug themselves in at places on the river bank. Early on the morning of Sunday 5 August they resumed their attack, but it quickly became clear that the Khakis too had strengthened their position during the night. 'Consequently the burghers could not make much progress.

De la Rey's scouts reported that day that a force of about 650 Khakis with four guns and four pom-poms were approaching the site of the battle at great speed from the direction of Zeerust. De la Rey could not afford to pull more than 75 burghers out of the attack on the British camp, but knew that he had to stop the Khakis who were advancing on Swartruggens.

Consequently he himself with 30 burghers, a gun and a pom-pom took up position south of the wagon road to Zeerust. Another 40 men of the Marico Commando under Lemmer were stationed in the hills north of the road. Five burghers – all members of De la Rey's personal staff – positioned themselves in low bushes directly next to the road. Their orders were not to shoot before the British were virtually on them.

By four o'clock that afternoon the British force was so close to De la Rey and Lemmer's positions that the burghers started shooting. The British kept coming on, however. Suddenly the five burghers next to the road opened a murderous fire on them from point blank range. The Khakis were so surprised that they immediately fell back. Both De la Rey's 30 and Lemmer's 40 men gained new courage from this and pursued the retreating Khakis. Their retreat quickly developed into a desperate flight.

To the burghers' surprise they subsequently heard that five days later the fleeing Khakis had fallen back all the way to Mafeking. In addition they had destroyed the military supplies at Groot Marico, Zeerust and Ottoshoop in their westward flight – probably to ensure that those supplies would not fall into Boer hands. We have heard that the frightened commander of those fleeing Khakis was General Sir Frederick Carrington, a veteran of numerous campaigns against black communities but with no experience of war against the Boers.

From Monday 6 August the Boer siege of the British camp at Brakfontein lost impetus. The Boer artillery kept firing but without causing much damage. At night both the Khakis and the burghers attempted attacks on each other's positions – but none with any success. De la Rey soon started questioning the sense of keeping on with the siege. On 16 August he was informed that he had succeeded in his objective of relieving the pressure on De Wet: the Chief Commandant had crossed the Magaliesberg unhindered at Olifants Nek two days earlier. He also heard that a huge British force was on its way to Brakfontein from the east. He therefore ordered his burghers to retreat and lifted the siege after 13 days. The burghers broke up their laager with as little fuss as possible and fell back.

De la Rey's siege of Brakfontein, which cost him four men, was of great value to the Boer cause despite being a failure. It gave De Wet the opportunity to break out of the British net around the Magaliesberg, while demonstrating that the western Transvaal burghers were still a force to be reckoned with. Many burghers who had previously surrendered are now rejoining the Boer forces. The war in this part of the country is not yet over.

From reliable sources we have heard that the total British losses during the siege amount to 80 men, of whom 22 were killed.

In the meantime we have received the sad news that Fighting General Sarel Oosthuizen died on 14 August from the wounds that he received in the Battle of Dwarsvlei a month earlier.

General De la Rey (left) and his burghers in the field

ANOTHER BRITISH PROCLAMATION

Burghers must now spy on their own people

Nelspruit, 30 August – Earlier this month Lord Roberts issued another proclamation in which the burghers are placed in a virtually impossible situation. Their personal freedom and protection against molestation will no longer be guaranteed, except if they have already surrendered. In terms of the proclamation all burghers who do not take the oath of neutrality will be regarded as prisoners of war and will be taken away or treated as the British please. All structures in which the enemy (in other words members of the Republican forces) is accommodated may be totally destroyed. Families on farms have to inform the British authorities about the presence of the enemy on their farms. If they fail to do this, it will be assumed that they are supporting the enemy. Burghers who break their oath of neutrality and rejoin the commandos of their own free will will be punished with a fine, prison sentence or even death. Furthermore all persons who surrendered their arms and took the oath of obedience will in future be treated as prisoners of war and may be deported.

By forcing the burghers who had returned to their farms to take the oath and to act as spies and informers on their own people, Roberts is actually forcing them to contravene their oath of neutrality. Only idiots and cowards would co-operate under these circumstances.

OUR MILITARY OFFICERS

This week we are honouring three officers who acted with great distinction and valour in the battle at Bergendal. All three are virtually unknown to us. We know that Philippus Rudolph Oosthuizen was born in 1867 and became a Commandant of the South African Republic Police in Johannesburg last year. S. van Lier was the Commandant of a volunteer corps and recently achieved his rank in the Johannesburg Police. Lieutenant W.F. Pohlmann is a member of the Johannesburg Police. The latter two gave their lives for the Republican cause at Bergendal, while Oosthuizen was made a prisoner of war.

Commandant Philip Oosthuizen (bottom centre) and the heroes of Bergendal

THE War Reporter

MONTHLY EDITION

Number 45 — In die Veld, South African Republic — 1 October 1900

ROBERTS 'ANNEXES' TRANSVAAL

British again target Boer civilians

Ohrigstad, 29 September – Earlier this month we received a report that the British commander-in-chief, Field Marshal Lord Roberts, had officially annexed the South African Republic on 1 September. In terms of Proclamation 14 of 1900, the Republic will henceforth be known as the Transvaal Colony. The proclamation furthermore states that all the burghers of the Orange Free State, except those who had remained on commando throughout, would henceforth be regarded as British citizens. Those who keep on fighting will be regarded as rebels.

On 3 September President Kruger issued a counter-proclamation in Nelspruit in which he declared Roberts's proclamation null and void. According to the President, the inhabitants of the South African Republic are still free and independent and refuse to subject themselves to British authority.

A few days later Commandant-General Louis Botha received a letter from Roberts in which the latter warns that all the burghers who are on commando in districts now occupied by the Khakis must prepare to accommodate their families in the veld. The expulsion of the families of the burghers from their homes will, according to Roberts, commence within a few days. The families from Pretoria will be the first to be taken to the front. Up to now this has not happened.

On 14 September Roberts again issued a noteworthy proclamation. In Proclamation 17 of that date he expressed the opinion that the war had degenerated into operations that were carried out in an irresponsible fashion by small or even meaningless groups of burghers. He felt that he would neglect his duty if he did not do all in his capacity to bring an end to this irregular war. He foresaw that his methods could be disastrous for the country and would entail endless suffering for the burghers and their families. The longer the struggle continued, the stricter he would have to be, he declared. He warned that no prisoner of war will be released as long as the Boers who are still fighting do not surrender unconditionally.

Elsewhere in the proclamation Roberts alleges that President Kruger and State Secretary Reitz have crossed the Portuguese border. That being the case, Kruger has officially resigned as president and has broken his ties with the South African Republic. According to Roberts the President's actions indicate that he regards the war as hopeless. The fact that he has turned his back on them should send a clear message to the Transvaal burghers that their prospects are hopeless. There can be only one result and that is a British victory. Roberts warns that he is forced to institute measures which will bring about untold misery for the burghers.

This proclamation draws conclusions based on factual errors. Kruger has neither resigned as president nor broken his ties with the South African Republic. He has been granted official leave by the Executive Council to go to Europe. Reitz is still within Transvaal and not in Portuguese East Africa. Intervention by foreign powers is not out of the question and the British have not necessarily won the war. Indeed, the burghers regard this proclamation as a despairing cry from the British commander-in-chief. It seems as if he is getting desperate and no longer believes in the possibility that he can indeed achieve success.

That the Khaki commanders are determined to target our civilians is as clear as can be. On 28 September they issued a notice in terms of which all burghers who surrendered on their own would not be sent out of South Africa. The livestock and property of burghers who continued fighting, or of burghers who had earlier made an oath of surrender but had now resumed fighting, would be confiscated and the homes of the leaders of the 'bands of sharpshooters' would be torched.

Last week the British committed a foul deed, one that one would not have expected from civilised people who signed the Hague Convention, which explicitly prohibits such actions. British soldiers have defaced the Paardekraal monument at Krugersdorp, by removing all the stones from the cairn underneath the monument. To ensure that the Boers would not be able to rebuild the cairn with the original stones, the Khakis loaded those stones on a train truck and dumped them in the Vaal River.

The cairn was built there in December 1880 by the burghers who attended the Paardekraal meeting on the eve of the Transvaal War of Independence. For those burghers the cairn served as a sign of their covenant that they would remain loyal and faithful in their struggle against British supremacy. One can conclude that the British felt extremely humiliated by their failure to conquer our burghers

According to absolutely reliable sources Lord Roberts himself has now ordered the destruction of the cairn. By destroying that symbol of our faith and determination he has allowed pettiness to get the better of him.

The Paardekraal Monument

KRUGER IN LOURENÇO MARQUES

Elderly President on his way to Europe

Lowveld, 13 September – On Monday 10 September the representatives of both the governments of the Republics consulted again at Nelspruit. On this occasion the Executive Council of the South African Republic decided to request President Kruger to go to Europe for a period of six months. In this way it could be assured that he would not fall into British hands and that he would get an opportunity to promote the Republican cause abroad. Kruger and his companions left for Portuguese East Africa that same day.

On 11 September they were at Hectorspruit, where State Secretary F.W. Reitz made the final arrangements for Kruger's departure. Most of the foreign attachés who had accompanied the Boer forces now decided to cross the border and return to their respective countries. The American volunteers Alan Hiley and John Hassell, who also left at this time, told our correspondent that after bidding farewell to everybody, Reitz, with bandoliers on his shoulders and rifle in hand, swung into his saddle and left on horseback to continue defending his country against the invaders.

Kruger and his party crossed the border soon afterwards and arrived in the harbour city of Lourenço Marques that same evening. They are now awaiting a ship from Holland to take them to Europe. Our correspondent in Lourenço Marques reports that Governor Machado has invited Kruger to stay as a guest of the Portuguese government in his residence.

The Executive Council appointed General Schalk Burger as provisional President. President Steyn and his party of 250 men left on their return journey to the Free State on 11 September. Since they have made good progress on their way back, we can announce that they initially moved to the north and then west to dodge the British.

Kruger in Laurenço Marques as guest of Governor Machado (seated on his left)

COMMANDANT DANIE THERON KILLED

Lonely hero's death for the bravest of the brave

In the veld in western Transvaal, 28 September – Earlier this month the Transvaal forces suffered a tragic loss with the death of the incomparable Commandant Danie Theron. On the last day of August, which was also the 20th birthday of Queen Wilhelmina of The Netherlands, Theron scored his last success against the British. He and his men captured a British military train at Klip River Station and took 30 soldiers prisoner of war. In the process they captured a large number of rifles and a huge supply of ammunition. The booty included a few bottles of liquor, in which the Dutchmen in his corps drank a toast to the health of their young Queen.

On Wednesday 5 September Theron was in the Gatsrand area. He and General Piet Liebenberg planned a joint attack on a British column. Theron was on his own doing reconnaissance when he came upon a patrol of seven Khakis. In his characteristic fearless way he immediately fired on the patrol. According to a reliable source he eventually killed three and wounded the other four Khakis. In the meantime a British column was closing in and started firing on Theron. He fired back sharply from a low hill and often changed his position – obviously in an attempt to impress the enemy that there was a large Boer force present. The British reaction was to set up their artillery and bombard Theron. After a while they had six field guns and a naval gun firing away on the Commandant, who kept firing back with his rifle. The end came when shrapnel from one of the many bursting shells hit and killed Theron.

Theron's death is widely mourned. Chief Commandant Christiaan de Wet's reaction was that this loyal and unforgettable Commandant's place could never be filled. There are few individuals in whom such a variety of values were united. He was not only incomparably brave, but revealed brilliant military talent. In addition his tenacity was legendary. If he received an order he carried it out. He fulfilled all the highest qualities of a soldier.

Theron's body was buried on the battlefield, but his scouts exhumed it again on 15 September and a few days later reburied him next to his fiancée, Hannie Neethling, on her father's farm Eikenhof near the Klip River. One of the late Commandant's cousins, Jan Theron, was appointed as his successor.

Number 45 1 October 1900

ON THE FRONT IN THE EASTERN TRANSVAAL

Eyewitness report by Wilhelm Mangold

Ohrigstad, 29 September – After the battle of Bergendal (on which we reported last month) the Boer commandos retreated to the south, east and northeast. Wilhelm Mangold of the Heidelberg Commando participated in the northeasterly retreat. He compiled the following eye-witness report on their experiences:

'Those of us of the ward Heidelberg Town proceeded with Commandant-General Louis Botha's forces northeast to Lydenburg. By eight o'clock on the morning of 28 August we off-saddled near Machadodorp. We were having breakfast when at least 500 mounted Khakis charged us. Even before we had resaddled, the bullets were flying around us. We had to find shelter immediately. Unfortunately our cart got stuck and we had to abandon it after distributing the ammunition among the men.

'Subsequently we retreated even further. On one farmyard there was a wagon heavily loaded with the furniture and provisions of fleeing women whose husbands were on commando. We had to cross a steep hill. Fortunately our artillery held the enemy back until we disappeared across the summit. At one stage we even used the Long Tom siege guns as field guns to slow down the enemy. This was highly successful and the Khakis actually retreated.

'About 20 kilometres south of Lydenburg we made a stand again. Gert Gravett, who was at that time appointed as fighting general, occupied a high hill east of us. Early on the morning of 2 September our artillery fired on the approaching enemy from that position with a Long Tom. The bombardment caused a fire and at least 100 tents and a number of Khaki wagons were consequently destroyed.

'The soldiers retreated and in the subsequent week only a few skirmishes took place.

'At this stage General Botha had about 2 000 men with three Long Tom guns, a few field guns and two pom-poms. General Ben Viljoen was retreating with about 1 800 men and one Long Tom all along the eastern railway line. The positions of Generals De Wet and De la Rey were unknown to the Heidelberg burghers. On 5 September we reached the vicinity of Lydenburg and camped there.

THE TREK ACROSS THE MOUNTAINS

'The next morning we were on the road again, since the British were approaching. That afternoon we crossed the mountain east of Lydenburg. The Khakis set up their guns in the middle of the town and fired on us. Fortunately they fired wildly and inaccurately. Our gunners fired back and fortunately did not do much damage to the town. Indeed, their fire was so effective that the enemy's bombardment was silenced. Our artillery also fired on the tent town of the Khakis and caused consternation there.

'On 8 September General Botha left for Nelspruit with the largest part of his forces. He left General Gravett behind as our commander. At the same time Christiaan Beyers, who had been appointed as assistant general by Botha a few days earlier, left for the north with one of the Long Tom guns. We were subsequently in a vulnerable position, since thick mist descended on us and allowed the Khakis to come close to our positions. Our gunners hauled the two Long Tom guns away with teams of oxen. At one stage the enemy soldiers were so close that the gunners considered destroying both Long Toms with dynamite. However, our soldiers used Martini Henry guns, which are much more effective at a short range than small-calibre rifles, to drive the Khakis back and thus saved the guns.

'On 9 September we were still struggling. We were forced to cross the high Mauch's Hill. The only route was the wagon road across the eastern slope of the hill. Commandant C. Spruyt covered the rearguard with 18 men. I was one of those. The Khakis continuously fired on us with shrapnel, but fortunately caused little damage. It was a miracle that we got out unscathed. Two of the burghers, Biccard and Jooste, were impudent enough to wave with their hats to the enemy and shout out: "Until next time, Khaki!"

'After a relatively peaceful night, the British resumed their attack on the morning of 10 September. We attempted to hold them back, but were forced to haul our guns out of reach of the Khakis. By the afternoon the enemy advanced close again and put severe pressure on our artillery. The guns' crew was too small to keep on shooting all the time. A few burghers had to assist in carrying the ammunition. Even though not one of our gunners was hit, the situation became so unbearable that they hauled the valuable gun away with a team of 20 oxen. At times up to 40 burghers had to assist with thongs to drag the gun up steep inclines or to break its momentum on steep descents.

'In the course of the next few days we trekked northwards to Pilgrim's Rest. There is a waterfall near the town and there we swam and relaxed while our horses regained their strength. At that time we temporarily lost contact with the outside world and had no idea what was happening on the other fronts.

PRESIDENT STEYN AT PILGRIM'S REST

'On 21 September President Steyn of the Orange Free State unexpectedly arrived in our midst. In a speech he announced President Kruger's departure for Europe to us. Steyn explained that it was no easy task to convince Kruger that such a step would be in the best interest of the South African Republic. When somebody asked if the war was ending, Steyn answered approximately as follows: "It is only just beginning! I will fight against Britain as long as I live or until all the Khakis leave our country. Even if only 300 men stay with me, I would not bow to our archenemy. If we carry out our duty, God will not abandon us."

'This was the first time that most of us had the opportunity to meet President Steyn. He made a very good impression on everyone. "He is a man, a real Afrikaner!" many burghers remarked. He swam with the burghers and invited everybody to fill their pipes from his presidential tobacco pouch – a privilege that can be compared to the award of a medal. His visit filled our men with new vigour.

'Commandant-General Louis Botha also briefly visited us at this time. Soon after he and Steyn left, the British attacked us again. We retreated northwards to Kaspersnek, where we arrived before dark. At an abandoned farmhouse we found 150 bags of maize. There was even a hand mill. That evening we cooked delicious maize porridge.

'After grinding as much maize meal as possible, and loading it on our horses, we resumed our journey, since our scouts reported that the British were approaching. This afternoon we finally arrived here in Ohrigstad. The latest reports indicate that the Khakis have retreated.'

FROM THE EDITOR

Almost a year has passed since the outbreak of war and the end is not yet in sight. There was no major field battle last month, and indeed little military activity. Nevertheless a number of significant developments have taken place: President Kruger has departed for Europe, Field Marshal Roberts has 'annexed' the South African Republic, and the Boer forces in the eastern Transvaal have been forced to destroy several of their guns to prevent their being captured by the British.

We reject Roberts's proclamation with the contempt that it deserves. In terms of international law, and the Hague Convention, it is not within his power to summarily end the independence of an internationally recognised state against which his country is officially waging a war. In addition the elderly Field Marshal's actions against civilians in the Republics often border on the cruellest form of inhumanity. In this edition, moreover, we report on his desecration of our greatest national monument. Our burghers, as well as our friends overseas, are beginning to question the British commander-in-chief's ability to act rationally. Does he not realise that his absolute obsession with victory and the application of barbaric methods to reach his goal is becoming an international embarrassment to his country rather than a source of pride? We hope that sooner or later he will realise that he is on the wrong track, since the possibility is increasing that the most important legacy of this war in the long run will be bitterness and suspicion between Boer and Brit in South Africa.

MILITARY ACTIVITIES ON VARIOUS FRONTS

DRASTIC REORGANISATION OF REPUBLICAN FORCES

Ohrigstad, 29 September – On 4 September the government of the South African Republic issued an *Extraordinary Government Gazette* in which Act no 5 of 1900 was published. The military forces of the Republics are in terms of this law drastically reorganised. Increased powers are bestowed on the Transvaal Commandant-General and on the Free State Chief Commandant. Since the manpower of numerous commandos has dwindled considerably, all the commandos are to be reorganised. A typical commando will consist of about 300 men under a commandant, with a field cornet in command of each 100 men. Either the Commandant-General or the Chief Commandant will be responsible for the appointment of commandants. Payment for all members of the commandos is envisaged.

WESTERN TRANSVAAL

In comparison with August, there was relatively little action on the front in the western Transvaal during the past month. On Friday 31 August General Koos de la Rey's burghers were involved in a skirmish on the farm Kwaggafontein south of Olifants Nek. Unfortunately De la Rey could not manage to capture the British convoy that he had targeted. In other battles the British also gained the upper hand. On 11 September, for example, a British force attacked and drove off Commandant Vermaas's laager at the eye of the Molopo River. Six days later a British force commanded by Lord Methuen repulsed a commando of about 400 burghers under Commandant Tollie de Beer and took 28 burghers prisoner of war.

NORTHERN TRANSVAAL

In northern Transvaal there was little action in the past month. On 1 September a Boer commando attacked a British patrol near Warmbaths. Most of the Khakis were wounded and one soldier made prisoner of war before the rest managed to get away. Five days later the whole British force stationed at Warmbaths retreated southwards to Pienaars River Station. This is now the most northerly British post on the railway line to Pietersburg.

EASTERN TRANSVAAL

Most of the military action in the past month took place in the eastern Transvaal. A separate report by Wilhelm Mangold covers the skirmishes in the vicinity of Lydenburg. South of the eastern railway line a British force unexpectedly reached Barberton in mid-September. Commandant Koot Opperman was powerless to halt them and barely managed to escape with 150 men of the Swaziland Commando.

Wednesday 12 September was a bitter day for the Transvaal State Artillery. Adjutant K. Roos had to blow up his Long Tom gun with dynamite near Hectorspruit. The wreckage was dumped into the Crocodile River. In the course of the next week the Transvaal State Artillery demolished a further 24 field guns for which they no longer had any ammunition left and similarly dumped the wrecked pieces into the Crocodile River. Commandant-General Louis Botha was himself a witness of this sad activity. On 17 September he and the government of the South African Republic left Hectorspruit, which is situated between Kaap Muiden and Komatipoort, and proceeded northwards. A week later they reached Pilgrim's Rest after traversing the Sabi Nature Reserve.

The British occupied Nelspruit on 18 September and Lord Roberts moved his headquarters there. Two days later the British vanguard reached Kaap Muiden, occupying it and Komatipoort on 24 September. Here they found a long row of burnt-out railway wagons that stood on the Selati Railway Line to the northeast, over a distance of 12 kilometres.

On the far eastern border a number of foreign volunteers who had fought on the Boer side crossed the border into Portuguese East Africa on 20 September. Five days later more than a thousand people, including more than 800 Transvaal burghers and some 200 women, boys and girls, crossed the border into Portuguese territory.

ORANGE FREE STATE

Activities have quietened down on the military front in the Orange Free State during the past month. The burghers of Commandant Gideon Scheepers carried out sabotage activities on railway lines on a number of occasions on the orders of Chief Commandant De Wet, but did not get involved in any confrontations. The only noteworthy clash took place at Ladybrand, where Commandant Piet Fourie made a futile attempt to force a British garrison of about 150 men to surrender.

A Boer Long Tom destroyed by its own crew

OUR MILITARY OFFICERS

General Gert Gravett

Gerhardus Hendrik Gravett was born at Alexandria in the Cape Colony in 1858. His grandfather was one of the British settlers who came to South Africa in 1820. His father, Richard Gravett, was born in Grahamstown and married an Afrikaans woman.

As a young man Gravett participated in numerous campaigns against black communities. From 1888 he has lived at Elandsfontein (Germiston). He became a transport rider and married Petronella Oosthuizen. They have two sons and three daughters. His business flourished and he became a wealthy man.

After the outbreak of the war last year Gravett joined the Transvaal forces as an ordinary burgher. He served with distinction on the Colesberg front, where he was elected field cornet.

Later, as commandant, Gravett made a name for himself with his masterful leadership during the Boer retreat from the Orange River through the Eastern Free State. He and his Germiston burghers took part in the battle of Donkerhoek in June 1900. His men were known as 'Gravett's Guinea Fowls', a title in which they took great pride. Subsequently Gravett was prominent in the Boer attempts to prevent the British capture of the eastern railway line. As commander of the Boer rearguard he served with distinction.

At the end of August Gravett participated in the Battle of Bergendal. Subsequently Commandant-General Louis Botha appointed him as fighting general. The fact that the Republican forces managed to haul two of the heavy Long Tom siege guns safely out of reach of the enemy across the mountains northeast of Lydenburg was largely due to Gravett's competence.

General Gert Gravett

THE War Reporter
MONTHLY EDITION

Number 46 — In die Veld, South African Republic — 1 November 1900

KRUGER LEAVES FOR EUROPE
DUTCH QUEEN PROVIDES SHIP TO TRANSPORT HIM

Lourenço Marques, 21 October – Since President Paul Kruger arrived here last month he has been accommodated against his will in the residence of the Portuguese governor, Antonio Machado. Kruger originally intended to stay with the Consul General of the South African Republic in Lourenço Marques, but was informed by the Governor on the day of his arrival that the Portuguese government had ordered him to take the President to his residence. The President was not allowed to receive any visitors and only his adjutant could accompany him. Kruger objected since it felt to him as if he was under house arrest. He believes it was due to British pressure that he has become an unwilling guest of Machado. Indeed, Kruger believes that the British Consul in Lourenço Marques controls that harbour and that Governor Machado is only nominally in charge.

It was under these unhappy circumstances that Kruger celebrated his 75th birthday in Machado's residence on 10 October. Not all was negative however, since it became known that the youthful Queen Wilhelmina of The Netherlands had specially sent a war ship to take Kruger to Europe. For the President this was excellent news and filled him with joy. We have heard from Europe that the Queen's decision was received with excitement everywhere but in Britain. Newspapers and pro-Boer organisations regard it as a deed of empathy and warm sympathy and believe that it will lead to a rise in support for the Republics.

Thus it came about that President Kruger and his party today boarded the ship *De Gelderland* and left as exiles for Europe. Kruger's aim is to generate as much support as possible for the Boer cause in Europe and elsewhere in the world and pressurise Britain to abandon the war. We support his mission fully and pray that it will be crowned with success. It is our wish that the elderly President should be granted the mercy to return to his fatherland some day soon.

The Dutch warship Gelderland

BATTLE AT FREDERIKSTAD
Heroic action by Boer volunteers ends in failure

In the veld in western Transvaal, 31 October – The only relatively big battle in this area in the past month took place last week at Frederikstad – a railway halt some 20 kilometres northeast of Potchefstroom. The Boers initiated the clash, but unfortunately they could not achieve a victory. Indeed, the battle ended in significant losses for the Republican forces – and had a nasty sequel.

The origins of the battle can be found in a request for assistance that General Liebenberg sent to Chief Commandant De Wet from the Potchefstroom area. De Wet crossed the Vaal River on 19 October and joined Liebenberg's men with his commando north of Potchefstroom the next day. The joint Republican forces now consisted of about 1 500 burghers with two Krupp guns and two pom-pom rapid-fire guns. They immediately took up position in a wide circle around General Barton's camp at Frederikstad. According to a reliable source Barton's forces consisted of more than 3 000 soldiers with seven guns, including a 120 mm naval gun as well as three rapid-fire guns. Liebenberg completely cut off the British communication links, leaving them only their heliograph by which to contact the outside world.

The first skirmish took place that same afternoon, when the burghers attacked a Khaki patrol that was returning to camp. The mounted Khakis rushed helter-skelter back to the camp, leaving the infantry in the lurch. However, even though the burghers attacked gallantly, they could not keep the foot soldiers from reaching the camp. The next day, Sunday 21 October, was peaceful and only the artillery on both sides fired on each other on Monday.

By Tuesday the 23rd De Wet believed that British forces were on their way to relieve Barton's men. He and Liebenberg consequently decided to force the British to surrender. The Khakis were dependent for drinking water on a small pond near the railway bridge. If they could be deprived of that water source, they would have to surrender. De Wet requested Generals Liebenberg and Froneman to mobilise 200 volunteers to take up position near the pond. The problem was that these volunteers could not be given covering fire from the main positions of the Boers. They would have to move to their position under the cover of night and would only be able to return safely under cover of the next night. In other words, they would be vulnerable to British counter-attacks for a whole day.

On Thursday 25 October the volunteers gathered long before daybreak. Even though only 100 men volunteered, they took the brave decision to proceed with the occupation of the position near the pond. They had to go there on foot but were in position and dug in before daybreak. Soon after daybreak black wagon drivers arrived from the British camp with mule wagons to get water. The Boers shouted at them to surrender but the drivers ran away and the burghers fired on them.

After this incident the British were aware of the Boer presence near the pond. A section of British soldiers arrived to attack the burghers, but were repulsed. The Khakis then launched a full-scale attack. De Wet was expecting this, and in an attempt to divert the attention of the Khakis, he launched an attack with the rest of the burghers on the other British positions. These attacks placed the British under huge pressure, but they were saved by the arrival of reinforcements of about 1 000 men from the north. De Wet only became aware of these reinforcements at a late stage, and did not have the opportunity to halt them.

In the meantime, the burghers at the pond were gallantly defending their position, but began experiencing a shortage of ammunition. Eventually they had to flee over the open veld. The British artillery opened fire on them and a number of burghers were hit. In the chaos that followed, some burghers hoisted a white flag while others continued firing. The result was catastrophic. About 80 burghers were killed, wounded or made prisoner of war. One of the wounded was Captain S.A. Cilliers of the Orange Free State Signal Corps, a grandson of the Voortrekker leader Sarel Cilliers. Neither De Wet nor Liebenberg could do anything to assist those burghers. Indeed, they themselves had to retreat to avoid being encircled by the Khakis. According to a reliable report the total British loss in this battle was 26 men dead and about 100 wounded.

The British were adamant that some burghers had misused white flags. As a retaliatory step they refused permission for the Republican doctor to visit the wounded. In addition three burghers were prosecuted in a military court. They were charged that they had begun shooting again after surrendering under a white flag, and had killed a British officer. The burghers were found guilty, sentenced to death and executed yesterday.

De Wet and his men found it difficult to cross the Vaal River back to the Free State after the battle at Frederikstad. The British halted them twice, exploding an ammunition wagon with a direct hit, before they finally crossed the river by moonlight at Rensburgsdrif near Parys last Saturday. De Wet suffered the loss of 24 burghers, two guns and eight wagons. By Monday he and his men were at the Renoster River, but today he was back north of the Vaal River at Ventersdorp, where he met President Steyn for the first time in six weeks. De Wet says that he and the President agreed on the importance of immediately launching an invasion of the Cape Colony.

MILITARY ACTIVITIES IN THE ORANGE FREE STATE

Renoster River, 31 October – In the past month a good deal of military activity has taken place in the Orange Free State. The Republican forces concentrated on the disruption of railway traffic and the occupation of small towns. On 1 October Chief Commandant Christiaan de Wet's burghers destroyed a British train at Wolwehoek. Exactly a week later about 100 burghers entered Ficksburg. The town police fled to Basutoland after offering weak resistance. On 18 October a Republican force of 60 burghers commanded by Commandant Gideon Scheepers attacked Philippolis. The defenders put up a stiff resistance and refused to surrender. After six days the Boers abandoned their siege when a large British force arrived at Philippolis.

The most active Free State force this month was General J.B.M. Hertzog's commando. On Tuesday 16 October they attacked Jagersfontein. Some 25 burghers stealthily entered the town and fired on the Khaki garrison.

After releasing all the prisoners from the prison and inflicting casualties on the Khakis, they moved off again. Three days later they attacked Fauresmith. However, the defenders repulsed them and by evening they retreated.

On Monday 22 October Hertzog and his men attacked Luckhoff and three days later 70 burghers of the commando attacked Jacobsdal, which was garrisoned by a small British force. The burghers stealthily entered the town at three o'clock in the morning and fired on the tents in the British camp on the Market Square. According to a reliable report they killed 14 and wounded 13 Khakis. The other Khakis held out until reinforcements arrived from the Modder River and the burghers had to flee.

On 26 October Hertzog himself attacked Koffiefontein, but his attack was repulsed.

Clearly, Hertzog was causing a headache for the British and some form of retaliation was to be expected. On Sunday 21 October the British authorities punished the civilian population of Jagersfontein, who had supported Hertzog on 16 October. Shortly before the Sunday church service was supposed to begin, the British detained 128 civilians, including 70 children. General Hertzog's wife, who was visiting her sister, and her son Albert were among the detained. They were only allowed a few moments to prepare for a long journey and were then taken by an armed convoy to Edenburg. Soon afterwards the British also made a group of women and children at Fauresmith prisoners of war. All these women and children are, we believe, being taken to Port Elizabeth, where they will be detained in corrugated iron houses on the racetrack.

The British love of destruction seems to know no bounds. On Tuesday 23 October Khaki forces commanded by General Hunter destroyed the northern Free State town of Bothaville. At least 48 houses were torched. Fortunately the church and a few public buildings were spared.

97

PRESIDENT STEYN CELEBRATES HIS BIRTHDAY IN TRANSVAAL

FESTIVITIES FOR THE BURGHERS AT ROOSSENEKAL

In the veld in eastern Transvaal, 14 October – In the light of all the setbacks that the Republican forces have suffered in the recent past, some of our readers might expect the atmosphere in the commandos to be sombre. That is by no means the case. In spite of their lack of necessities, and often of luxuries such as pipe tobacco and coffee, the burghers remain cheerful even under the most difficult circumstances. They declare without hesitation: 'Khaki can loot all our supplies, and burn down our farms, but our laugh he cannot take away!' The burghers are always looking for an excuse to have a festival. Gordon Fraser, a brother-in-law of President Steyn, recently sent our correspondent this report of such an event:

'On 2 October, President Steyn's birthday, we were at Roossenekal in the Steenkampsberg range northwest of Dullstroom. We decided to make something special of it.

'Very early that morning we fired a salute of 25 shots. The poor beggars who were still sleeping and unaware of what was going on, ran barefoot for their horses.

'Subsequently we held a grand parade through the streets. A hundred or so Transvaal burghers participated in this. We halted in front of the President and sang the old Free State anthem to him.

'President Steyn then addressed the burghers. We intended to stand in real military fashion in a straight line, but after he had spoken for a few minutes, we forgot about the line and swarmed about him like a swarm of bees around our king. I have heard Steyn hold forth in many speeches, but this was certainly his best. Not an eye remained dry. When he talked about his family, he had to remain silent himself for a few moments. This made a wonderful impression on everybody. We had two bottles of wine and one of peach brandy, and the most privileged of us had the opportunity to drink to the health of our President.'

President M.T. Steyn

FROM THE EDITOR

Another month has gone by without any military success for the Republican forces. In addition the artillery capacity of the Boers has been further diminished since for the second month in a row artillery pieces have had to be destroyed by the burghers themselves to ensure that the enemy could not capture them. Nevertheless the British did capture a few Boer guns. Even sadder news is that General Gert Gravett was mortally wounded in action and died on 26 October. The only positive development on the military front is that the morale of the fighting burghers is still high and that they are not misled by Lord Roberts's proclamations. This is confirmed in a lengthy report by Jan F.E. Celliers on conditions in a Boer laager.

As for the British war tactics, they are becoming more reprehensible by the day. The large-scale torching and destruction of farmhouses – at least 200 in the past month – as well as the destruction of the private property of fighting burghers indicates that Roberts is attempting to force the fighting burghers to lay down their arms by molesting the civilian population of the Republics.

A similar alarming development is the transfer of the families of burghers to refugee camps. Such camps have suddenly been erected all over South Africa. They are in effect nothing but prisoner-of-war camps for women and children. Our only hope is that the enemy will treat the civilians well, but the contents of the statements by Roberts and other Khaki leaders give no reassurance that these poor people can expect decent treatment.

The worst news of the past month is that the government of the British Prime Mister, Lord Salisbury, easily won the general election in that country. The result is not unexpected, but nevertheless disappointing, since a Liberal Party government would certainly have been more sympathetic towards the Boer Republics than the Conservatives are. All these developments indicate that an early peace is improbable. Our hope is now focused on President Kruger, who has just left for Europe. Perhaps he will convince friendly powers to pressurise Britain to pull out of the war in South Africa.

PROCLAMATIONS AND COUNTER-PROCLAMATIONS

In the veld in eastern Transvaal, 28 October – On 6 October Commandant-General Louis Botha issued a proclamation from Roossenekal in which he warned burghers against the distribution by the British authorities of false information regarding President Kruger's departure from the South African Republic. Botha points out that the government of the South African Republic is still in existence and pleads with the burghers to keep on fighting. He warns them against British promises and points out that burghers who do surrender, are taken as prisoners of war to St Helena or Ceylon. Botha warns prospective handsuppers that he will act against them. He has given Boer officers orders to do all in their power to keep burghers from surrendering. Botha believes that he will be forced to commandeer the movable property of handsuppers and to burn down their farms since these people do a lot of harm to the Republican cause.

Some two weeks later Botha protested in a letter to Lord Roberts against his military methods. He alleges that British soldiers are acting in barbaric ways by destroying the private dwellings of the families of fighting burghers and taking their food away from them. The worst is that this happens on the orders of Roberts himself. This reflects a feeling of revenge against burghers who are carrying out their loyal duties. Botha added that he intends pursuing this war in a humanitarian way but that Roberts's actions are forcing him likewise to take retaliatory action.

Lord Roberts reacted to this letter of Botha by stating that the Boers had, by taking up guerrilla warfare, forced him to use the strictest methods, as all civilised nations would do under such circumstances.

DEATH OF GENERAL GRAVETT

In the veld, 28 October – General Gert Gravett, whom Commandant-General Louis Botha recently appointed as Assistant Commandant-General for the North-Eastern Districts, died two days ago. He was accompanied by a small group of burghers when they became embroiled in a skirmish with the Khakis at Witpoort in the Mapochsgronden about a fortnight ago. Gravett was standing next to a Nordenfeldt Maxim gun when he was hit by shrapnel.

Deneys Reitz, the son of State Secretary F.W. Reitz, told our correspondent that he and his brother were present when the General died. Gravett's men had taken him into the bush after he was wounded to prevent his falling into the hands of the Khakis. Reitz reports that Gravett realised that his end was approaching, but that he bore his sufferings without complaint, and spoke of his coming death with resignation. The burghers buried him under a tree.

LIFE ON COMMANDO IN THE BUSHVELD

Report by Jan F.E. Celliers

In the veld north of the Magaliesberg, 31 October – Jan F.E. Celliers, the former city librarian of Pretoria, whose reports we have published in previous issues, sent us the following account of his experiences on commando. From this our readers will be able to understand how the burghers adapt to the demands and circumstances of war.

TRAPPED IN PRETORIA

'I arrived in Pretoria on 29 May. This was before the British occupation. I had been granted leave to remain at home until further orders. Those orders never reached me. On 4 June I participated in the last attempts to halt the British forces south of the town, but we had to retreat again. I considered leaving the town that night, but lingered too long and the next day the British occupied Pretoria. Since I did not plan to take the oath of neutrality or an oath of allegiance to the British queen, but rather to flee to take up my duty as burgher again, I decided to hide in my own yard.

'My self-inflicted house arrest was a bitterly unenjoyable experience. I had to keep myself out of sight and could only go outside after dark to get a little exercise. We left a trapdoor in the floor permanently open so that I could hide under the floor in case of emergency. I often found safety in there while a British soldier visited our dwelling. My wife cared for me with love, but my poor children could not understand what was going on. This was an untenable situation and I had to bring an end to it. To take an oath of neutrality was not a safe solution, since the British authorities send many "neutrals" away without providing reason, without a hearing as prisoners of war. My only option was to leave the city in secret and join the commandos again.'

ESCAPE FROM PRETORIA

'Since the method that our people use to escape from Pretoria must remain secret, I will merely indicate that I left Pretoria on Friday 24 August. That evening I slept on a friends' farm. They had earlier taken the oath of allegiance. Had Khakis discovered me there, my friends would probably have been taken away and their farmhouse would have been torched. For that reason I left again before daybreak. I walked the whole day but found no commando. That evening I found a safe place to sleep and the next day, Sunday 26 August, stayed with my protector to rest.

'On Monday morning I resumed my journey and by that evening reached the house of Piet Roos at Krokodilpoort.'

JOINING A COMMANDO

'I left Krokodilpoort on Thursday 13 September. This was soon after armed Boers visited the farm and indicated where I might perhaps find a commando. The next afternoon I joined Commandant C.P.S. Badenhorst's laager on the farm Waterval at Signal Hills, some 40 kilometres north of the Magaliesberg range. It was wonderful once again to be amongst free men with arms in their hands.

'On 17 September a black man with a white flag brought us a proclamation issued by Lord Roberts. In this it is alleged that President Kruger had resigned and broken all his official ties with the South African Republic. Roberts also threatens that he will not hesitate to use all the means at his disposal to subjugate the Boers.

'That Roberts is serious in his threat to use all possible means against the Republics, he has proven on numerous occasions. On 18 September we heard that the British had used dynamite to blow up the house of Piet Roos at Krokodilpoort where I had stayed a week before. Many burghers who are with us on commando have heard that their houses have been burned down. In addition the British soldiers damage dams, explode water furrows, break ploughs and chop down fruit trees. The women and children are loaded on wagons and taken to refugee camps.'

COMMANDO LIFE

'It is clear that embitterment against the Khakis is increasing by the day as a result of the torching and destruction of farm houses in the Magaliesberg area and the terrible treatment of the defenceless women. The men hardly talk about anything else. At the same time it is notable that the burghers do not complain about their lack of necessities. It seems to me as if the burghers who are here have agreed to remain satisfied with what they have – be it much or be it little. Many do not have enough clothing and the clothes they do have are patched in a multitude of ways. Threadbare soles of shoes are replaced by pieces of cattle skin fastened with thongs to the sides of the shoes.

'My own position is not particularly enviable. Nobody has a horse, a saddle or a stirrup for me. Nor a rifle. Now I am stuck with an ancient Westley Richards breech-loader of the type used before the Transvaal War of Independence. The one item that I do have which is in short supply is soap. One makes many friends in a laager if you are the fortunate owner of an item that the other burghers crave. Now I have numerous soap friends. When I wash either myself or my clothing, they arrive from all over and while eyeing my wealth, request politely if they can use it, since they find that 'soap is as scarce as medicine'. That is indeed the case, since our doctor has long since left. We have no ill or wounded burghers amongst us.

'Our food position is at times critical. Mostly we have only maize porridge and meat – that is, when we have meat, since often we have only maize porridge. In a few cases we had a little fat and used it to bake *vetkoeke* (dough cakes) – a welcome relief from the never-ending porridge, porridge, porridge. But even our maize flour is running low. Fortunately we got hold of a whole wagonload of sweet potatoes the other day. We have no coffee left either and the longing for that product is great. Therefore we made a plan, namely to burn rye grain to use as coffee. It is a difficult job to roast rye grain. You have to stir all the time. The sun burns from above and the fire from below, but you have to stir till all the little pellets are at last beginning to turn black. In addition to preparing food, I often have to do sentry duty at night, but up to now there have been no Khakis in our area.'

OUR MILITARY OFFICERS

General J.B.M. Hertzog

One of the new generation of Boer officers who has made a name for himself recently is James Barry Munnik Hertzog. He is better known as a lawyer – everybody calls him Judge – but he has developed into a very capable military commander.

Hertzog was born in the Cape Colony in 1866. His parents are the late Johannes Albertus Munnik Hertzog and his wife Susanna Maria Jacoba Hamman. He spent his early years on a farm, since his father farmed first in the Wellington district and later near Malmesbury. When he was six years old, his parents moved to the diamond fields at Kimberley and a few years later to Jagersfontein in the Orange Free State. When he was fifteen his father took him to Stellenbosch, where he received a sound school education. He spent eight years there and was awarded the BA degree by the Victoria College in 1889.

From Stellenbosch Hertzog went to The Netherlands, where in 1892 he gained a doctoral degree in law from the University of Amsterdam. After his return to South Africa he settled as an advocate in Pretoria. A year later he married Wilhelmina Jacoba (Mynie) Neethling. Hertzog was appointed as a judge in the Orange Free State in 1895. He moved to Bloemfontein where he built up a huge circle of friends that included President Steyn.

With the outbreak of this war last October, Hertzog became the legal advisor of the Chief Commandant of all the Free State forces. That gave him a seat on the war council. He often expressed himself in favour of a more offensive strategy. After the British occupation of Bloemfontein in March he became one of the major proponents of guerrilla warfare. In July President Steyn appointed him as fighting general with orders to mobilise the burghers in the southwestern Free State, an area that he knows well.

In September De Wet appointed Hertzog as Assistant Chief Commandant. He commands a force of approximately 1 200 burghers.

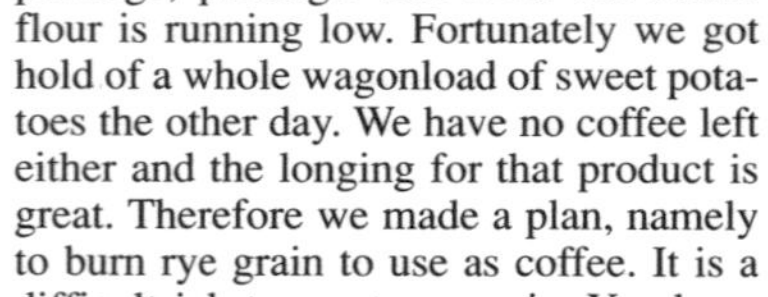

General Hertzog

THE War Reporter
MONTHLY EDITION

Number 47   In the Veld, South African Republic   1 December 1900

GENERAL WAR NEWS
Roberts hands over command to Kitchener

In the veld in eastern Transvaal, 30 November – Field Marshal Lord Roberts, the British commander-in-chief in South Africa, today officially handed over the command to his chief of staff, General Lord Kitchener. From what we hear, Roberts believes that the war has been won and that Kitchener will merely have to mop up what is left.

FARMS AND A TOWN DESTROYED BY THE KHAKIS

Numerous reports on the destruction of towns and the burning of farmhouses reached us in the past month. On 1 October a British force commanded by Major General Bruce Hamilton destroyed the village of Ventersburg in the northern Free State. Virtually all the houses and buildings in the town were demolished, including shops with their supplies. Soon afterwards Hamilton issued a statement in terms of which the British authorities would send no new supplies to Ventersburg. If the Boers do not want the inhabitants of the town to die of hunger, they will have to provide food for those people.

That the British plan to leave a trail of desolation was confirmed on Sunday 18 November by Field Marshal Roberts himself when he ordered in one of his proclamations (it is only the British who issue proclamations on a Sunday) that: 'all cattle and food supplies must be removed from all farms; and if that is not possible everything must be destroyed, even if the owner is not present'. This proclamation is of course a contravention of the Hague Convention, which we believe was signed by Britain.

SKIRMISH IN WESTERN TRANSVAAL

There were only a few military clashes in the western Transvaal in the last month. The only noteworthy fight was a skirmish on 10 November between the forces of General Methuen and the commando of General Manie Lemmer at Wonderfontein in the Klein Marico. The burghers were sheltering in the ravines for the night and were surprised by the Khakis at daybreak. The battle was a disaster for Lemmer's commando, since 40 men were killed, wounded or made prisoner. One of those who were killed was Piet Lemmer, the 65-year-old father of Commandant L.A.S. Lemmer.

Boer farmhouse ablaze near Dewetsdorp, Orange Free State

Ventersburg after its destruction by the British forces

P.J. Lemmer, who was killed in action, photographed earlier in the war with two other burghers, 15-year-old J.D.L. Botha and C. Pretorius

SKIRMISHES IN EASTERN TRANSVAAL

On Monday 19 November General Ben Viljoen and Commandant Chris Muller simultaneously attacked two railway stations on the eastern railway line, namely Balmoral and Wilge River. Viljoen's men occupied an outpost near Balmoral, but could not capture the station since it was too well fortified. Muller's men similarly captured a British bulwark on high ground some distance from the Wilge River Station and drove the British back to the station, but their success ended there.

The fighting went on for the whole day. Both sides had guns at their disposal. Muller said afterwards that one of the Boer shells exploded in the midst of the Khakis in a British entrenchment. A little later the British gunners hit the wheel of one of Muller's guns.

After dark the Boers once again retreated. They subsequently heard that 43 Khakis had died or been wounded that day.

TWO BRAVE OFFICERS KILLED

In the veld near Carolina, 7 November – General Joachim Fourie's commando is overwhelmed by sorrow tonight after a terrible setback struck them today. Fourie himself, as well as Commandant Hendrik Prinsloo, two of the bravest among the brave and heroes who had achieved everlasting fame at Spioenkop, were today both killed in action on the farm Witkloof. They planned to attack a British unit of about 1 400 men commanded by General Smith-Dorien, and to capture their six guns. The British retreated when Fourie and his burghers appeared and in the process their rearguard of about 100 men actually left the guns unprotected. The commando, with Fourie, Prinsloo and General Hans Grobler, charged the enemy on horseback and made good progress, but the Khakis fired back with their rifles and halted the burghers about 70 metres from the guns. It is here that both Fourie and Prinsloo were killed and Grobler wounded. We have heard that the Khakis, who in this case consisted mainly of Canadians, themselves suffered a loss of 31 men.

FROM THE EDITOR

In the past month the Republican forces have achieved variable success. Chief Commandant De Wet suffered his biggest setback at Bothaville, but soon afterwards restored his reputation with a good victory at Dewetsdorp. In the Transvaal General Ben Viljoen and Commandant Chris Muller gave a good account of themselves, but General Joachim Fourie's death is a tragic setback.

For Field Marshal Roberts the war is mercifully coming to an end. The news that he is returning to England was received with satisfaction by the commandos. The barbaric way in which Roberts conducted some aspects of the war quickly turned the respect that some burghers had for him up to about April into total disgust. Many burghers openly state that he has put to shame a British officer's uniform, and earnestly hope that his successor, Lord Kitchener, will be an improvement.

The news from Europe is not very encouraging. Germany will almost certainly not intervene on the side of the Republics – and as long as Germany remains passive, nobody else will place pressure on the British. Our hope now rests on President Kruger, who had just been received with unequalled enthusiasm in Europe. Hopefully his stature will convince the German and other governments that it is now high time to ensure that justice and right are re-established in the Republics.

HUGE BATTLE AT RENOSTERKOP

In the veld in the eastern Transvaal, 30 November – General Ben Viljoen was involved in a heavy battle with a British army at Renosterkop, some 24 kilometres north of Bronkhorstspruit, yesterday. Viljoen had earlier occupied the hill with about 1 000 burghers and ordered them to build entrenchments. Commandant Chris Muller heard on Tuesday that a huge British force was advancing on Renosterkop. He immediately went there with the Boksburg Commando and joined Viljoen.

Yesterday a force of at least 2 500 Khakis with at least nine guns attacked the Boers. The British commander was General Paget. The British attack began at dawn. It was an orthodox frontal assault with infantry that attacked the Boer entrenchments in the centre and mounted infantry that attempted to outflank the burghers on both sides. The battle front stretched over an area of five kilometres. The Boers managed to halt the British attack with gun and rifle fire.

After the burghers had held out the whole day long, Commandant Muller launched a counter-attack against one sector of the British line just before dark. It failed. Since Viljoen realised that the burghers did not have enough ammunition to fight for another full day, he ordered them to abandon the position in silence under cover of the night. The burghers managed to get away unnoticed through Poortjiesnek and retreated to the east.

As far as we could ascertain British casualties amount to 15 men dead and about 70 wounded.

Only two Boers were killed and 22 wounded.

99

FAILURE AND SUCCESS FOR DE WET

MAJOR DEFEAT AT BOTHAVILLE

In the veld in the Free State, 28 November – On 6 November General Christiaan de Wet and his commando suffered a huge setback at Doornkraal in the Bothaville district. De Wet himself, as well as President Steyn, who shortly before this tragedy joined De Wet's forces with the Free State government, barely managed to escape. At least nine burghers were killed and about 100, some of them wounded, were taken prisoner of war by the British. In addition the enemy captured all De Wet's guns. We have heard that on the British side 13 soldiers were killed and 33 wounded.

De Wet and his men were on their way from the Western Transvaal to the south of the Orange Free State when this catastrophe hit them. They arrived at Bothaville early on the morning of 5 November and met General Froneman with his burghers there. That same afternoon a strong British force appeared. A skirmish followed but the Khakis had fallen back to Bothaville by dusk. The burghers retreated in the opposite direction and pitched camp on the farm Doornkraal. By that evening the two opposing forces were at least 10 kilometres apart with the Vals River between them.

De Wet posted a sentry, whose corporal reported early next morning that they could only spot a few Khaki fires at Bothaville. He had barely left when a few shots were all of a sudden fired from close range. To De Wet's shock he noted that it was Khakis who were firing and that they were on a low hill barely 200 metres away from the area where the burghers were sleeping. Since it was just after sunrise, many burghers were at that stage still fast asleep under their blankets. Due to the poor work done by the sentries, the Khakis had totally surprised the burghers.

Chaos broke out in the Boer laager. Some of the burghers fired on the enemy, but most of them chose to saddle up their horses and flee as quickly as possible. De Wet had to saddle his own horse. Some of the burghers left their saddles behind and fled bareback. Dozens of burghers could not find their horses and ran away blindly. De Wet attempted to restore order: 'Do not flee, charge the enemy!' he shouted to the burghers. This did not help. And the irony is that those who did fight, suffered the most. De Wet jumped on his horse and attempted to convince the fleeing burghers to turn around, but in vain.

Only at one place did a number of burghers, including State Attorney Jacob de Villiers and Field Cornet Jan Viljoen, offer notable resistance. They found shelter behind a rock wall, and when the British artillery moved in too close to them, shot down all the artillery horses. All the other burghers fled blindly. The Boer gunners could not manage to save their guns, since in the chaos they could not find their artillery mules and horses to inspan.

Amongst those who were killed was Field Cornet Viljoen, and among the wounded was Jacob de Villiers, who was made prisoner of war. One of the wounded who managed to get away was General Froneman, who was only lightly wounded. The loss of the six guns, some of which had been captured at Colenso and some at Sannaspos, is a tragedy, but not a total disaster since their ammunition was virtually exhausted.

De Wet feels very dejected about the setback. He sincerely believes that the burghers would have been able to repulse the enemy had they stuck to their positions, since there were about 800 burghers and the enemy force was not much bigger. On the other hand, De Wet has great respect for the commander of the British attack, Colonel M.L. le Gallais, regarding him as one of the bravest Khaki commanders he has encountered. For that reason he was somewhat downhearted today when he was informed that le Gallais was one of the wounded Khakis who died of his wounds yesterday evening.

DE WET BREAKS THROUGH BLOCKHOUSE LINE

After their setback at Bothaville, De Wet and his commando proceeded to the south. On the way they broke through the British blockhouse line at Sprinkaansnek. They were forced to do this, since it was the Chief Commandant's objective to reach the southern Free State. In the first place he wants to confuse the British about his exact position and secondly he hopes to capture a British garrison somewhere in order to obtain horses, saddles and especially ammunition for his burghers. When they crossed the railway line north of Winburg, De Wet's men damaged the rails and destroyed some of the culverts with dynamite, sending a message to the British that their enthusiasm had not been dampened by the catastrophe at Bothaville.

The next obstacle in De Wet's way to the south was the row of small forts or blockhouses that the British had constructed from Bloemfontein across Thaba Nchu to Ladybrand. He decided to break through this line at Sprinkaansnek, where there are two forts approximately two kilometres apart, one south of the Nek and the other north of it.

De Wet's artillery comprised a Krupp gun and 16 shells – their total supply of artillery ammunition – with which to bombard the blockhouses. Virtually every shot was fully on target. Then the burghers charged through the opening between the two forts across the Nek. The British guards at the blockhouses fired sharply on them, but could not halt them. All the burghers got through and only one was lightly wounded. Subsequently the commando gathered again at the Modder River where they planned to spend the evening.

BRITISH GARRISON OF DEWETSDORP OVERWHELMED

After a siege lasting three days, on 23 November Chief Commandant Christiaan de Wet and his combined commandos managed to force the British garrison of Dewetsdorp to surrender. De Wet felt that it was important to achieve a victory over a British force in order to restore his burghers' pride after the defeat they had suffered earlier this month at Bothaville. Since he grew up in the Dewetsdorp area – indeed the town was named after his father by the Orange Free State Volksraad – he decided to attack the British garrison stationed here. His scouts reported that the garrison consisted of about 500 Khakis.

De Wet caught the garrison completely unawares. On 18 November he and his men were on a farm about nine kilometres north of the town. A patrol led by General Philip Botha rode around the town on horseback that day to spy on the British positions. The next day De Wet and his men openly advanced to the very edge of the town on horseback before suddenly scurrying away in a westerly direction. He hoped that the British garrison would conclude from that that the Boers were alarmed and would not attack the town. With that strategy they were successful. After their eventual occupation of the town they heard that the British reaction to the burgher 'flight' of 19 November was 'De Wet is too wise or too afraid to attack Dewetsdorp, where he certainly cannot succeed.'

On 20 November the burghers remained out of sight, but that evening they advanced on Dewetsdorp as quietly as possible. At daybreak on the 21st they charged the town from three directions. General Botha occupied the table hill on the southeastern side of the town. De Wet himself and Commandant Philip de Vos of the Kroonstad Commando occupied a low hill on the northern side of the town. Commandant Hendrik Lategan of Colesberg, who is a Cape Rebel leader, occupied the low hill on the western side. The burghers could clearly see that the Khakis had built strong entrenchments consisting of rock walls with sandbags and pigeonholes as well as trenches.

De Wet had 900 men at his disposal against the 500 Khakis, but he could not use all 900 in the attack. He had sent a strong patrol about 30 kilometres to the northwest on the wagon road from Bloemfontein to report if any British force should approach from that direction. Similar patrols were stationed on the roads to Thaba Nchu, Wepener and Reddersburg, and in addition some burghers had to stay as escort with President Steyn and the Free State government, who were accompanying the commando. As a result only 450 were available for the attack.

The burghers courageously attacked the British entrenchments, and made good progress especially in the southeast and in the north. They did not fall back that night, but on the 22nd resumed their attack at daybreak. Field Cornet Wessel Wessels acted with particular courage and was the first burgher to occupy a British entrenchment. By the evening they had occupied virtually all the British entrenchments on the southern side of the town.

On the northern side things did not go as well, since the British commanded a strong fortification and any attacker would have to charge over 200 metres of open country to reach it. De Wet advised Commandant de Vos to attack before daybreak the next morning, which De Vos did. The Khakis only became aware of the burghers when the latter had reached the entrenchment and fired sharply on them. Unfortunately two burghers were killed, but the other burghers jumped over the entrenchment and forced the British to surrender.

While this clash was taking place in the north, Field Cornet Wessels occupied the town from the south. The British garrison was subsequently only in possession of the entrenchment on the western side. They put up a stubborn resistance while the Free State artillery began bombarding them with their only remaining Krupp gun from the east. In the meantime a highly satisfied De Wet entered the town on horseback. Many old friends welcomed him with open arms and offered him one cup of coffee after the other. He had to continue with the fight, however, which only ended when the British hoisted the white flag at three o'clock that afternoon.

The Boers took 400 prisoners of war, including the commander of the garrison, Major Massey, and his seven officers. De Wet had no option but to let these men go again, since he had nowhere to house them. Of much more value than the prisoners of war were the supplies, including two Armstrong guns with 300 rounds of ammunition as well as a number of horses and mules and a huge store of Lee Metford rifles and ammunition.

The price for this victory was high: seven burghers were killed and 14 wounded. Though sad about this, the burghers feel positive again. All believe that this victory proves the British are not invincible.

REPUBLICAN DEPUTATION IN EUROPE

Visits to Germany and Russia fail

Marseilles, 23 October – We reported on the activities of the Republican deputation at the beginning of August, with information on the deputation's visit to the United States of America and to France. Those visits produced moral support for the Republics in their struggle against the British Empire, but nothing more. Unfortunately this is still the case, since no European power is willing to side openly with the Republics against Britain. We hope that President Kruger's arrival yesterday in Europe will turn the scale in our favour.

The visit of the deputation to Germany was a failure even before the arrival of the deputation members, namely A. Fischer and C.H. Wessels of the Orange Free State and A.D.W. Wolmarans of the Transvaal. The German Kaiser, Wilhelm II, had made it clear that he would not meet them. The deputation nevertheless went to Berlin, arriving on 7 August, but left for Russia immediately when the Kaiser repeated that he did not wish to meet them.

In the huge Tsarist Empire the prognosis was not positive either. The Russian Ambassador in Germany told them before they left that it would not be worth their while to visit his country. The deputation nevertheless left for Russia on 14 August, arriving in St. Petersburg, the capital, by train the next day. A huge crowd of interested Russians heartily and enthusiastically welcomed them, but that same evening the Russian police issued a prohibition on any rejoicing in the streets and the Russian newspapers were forbidden to publish anything about the deputation. It seemed as if the Russian government was afraid that its own repressed people would be carried away by the freedom message of the deputation.

Dr Leyds, the Transvaal Special Envoy in Europe who accompanies the deputation, had an interview with Tsar Nicholas II on 25 August, but this produced nothing. The Tsar merely expressed his sympathy with the Republics and promised to intervene if the situation became positive for intervention.

After the failure of their visit to both Russia and Germany, the deputation members returned to The Netherlands, where they will temporarily remain. Since all their attempts to convince friendly governments to intervene on their behalf have failed, they will in future concentrate on uniting European public opinion behind the Boer Republics.

PRESIDENT KRUGER ENTHUSIASTICALLY WELCOMED

The Republics' last hope for intervention on their behalf is the visit of President Kruger. He alone can possibly convince the German Kaiser to intervene on the side of the Republics or to put pressure on Britain to accept arbitration over its differences with the Republics. All commentators in Europe believe that if the Kaiser sides with the Republics, other heads of state will do the same.

President Kruger's visit is front-page news all over Europe. His arrival here in Marseilles today was an unprecedented spectacle. Hundreds of boats, including a large number of huge steamships, all of them loaded to capacity with joyous people, welcomed him in the harbour. At least 150 000 people were on the quay and on the streets of the city to welcome him. When the elderly President finally set foot on land at 11 o'clock in the morning, a thundering gun salute and a gigantic *Vierkleur* waving on a high flagpole with the Free State flag and the French *Tricolor* on either side welcomed him. He was officially welcomed by a French Senator and by the chairman of the local support group for the Republics. They immediately assured him of 'the great admiration of the whole world for him and the Boers'. Kruger answered in a short speech in which he stated his support for arbitration over the differences between Boer and Brit. His deep-set convictions and energy made a very good impression on the crowd.

From the harbour Kruger was taken on a coach through the masses lining the streets to the Hotel Noailles, where he is staying. On his arrival there he stood alone on the balcony waving to the people as the single, powerful symbol of the courageous Boer people in their heroic battle. It made an indelible impression on everybody who was privileged to witness the historic event.

OUR MILITARY OFFICERS

General Joachim Fourie

The military officer whom we highlight this month is the courageous General Joachim Fourie, whose death on the battlefield we reported in this issue.

Joachim Christoffel Fourie was born in Grahamstown in the Cape Colony in 1855. He was a son of Christiaan Ernst Fourie and his wife Catharina Espach. Fourie grew up in the Lydenburg district. His first military experience was during the Transvaal War of Independence of 1880–81. At that time he was a Field Cornet in the Lydenburg Commando. In the course of the next 18 years he gained further experience in clashes between the South African Republic and black communities. In 1893–94 he represented the Lydenburg district in the First Volksraad.

When this war between Boer and Brit broke out last October, Fourie made his way to the Natal front as an ordinary burgher and participated in numerous battles. In the battle of Spioenkop on 24 January he made a name for himself when he took part in the capture of Aloe Hill.

In March this year the burghers elected him Assistant General, even though he was still an ordinary burgher. Two months later Commandant-General Louis Botha promoted him to Assistant Commandant-General. Fourie was present at the failed attempts to halt General Buller's onslaught from Natal. Subsequently he was active in the Eastern Transvaal, commanding Boer forces in numerous battles. In addition to his commando members, who regard his death as a major setback, General Fourie's death is sorely felt by his wife Aletta Elizabeth de Clercq and their five children. We hereby express our condolences to them.

General Joachim Fourie

THE War Reporter
MONTHLY EDITION

Number 48 — In the Veld, South African Republic — 1 January 1901

MAJOR BATTLE AT NOOITGEDACHT
DE LA REY OUTWITS THE KHAKIS ONCE AGAIN

Magaliesberg, 13 December – The combined commandos of three Boer generals today scored a magnificent victory here over a huge British force. General Koos de la Rey had heard earlier this week that a sizeable British force was digging in on the farm Nooitgedacht on the southern slope of the Magaliesberg northwest of Hekpoort. Yesterday General Christiaan Beyers crossed the Magaliesberg at Boschfontein at the head of a strong commando from the northern Transvaal and joined De la Rey. Together with General Jan Smuts, who was formerly the State Attorney, De la Rey and Beyers inspected the British position from the top of the Magaliesberg. They spotted a few weaknesses in the entrenchments that had been constructed by General Clements and his approximately 2 000 soldiers with their 10 guns at Nooitgedacht. Since the three Boer generals together had about 2 500 burghers with five guns at their disposal, they decided to utilise the opportunity to attack the Khakis.

In terms of the Boer battle plan, Beyers had to attack the British positions on the summit of the mountain with about 1 000 burghers. These positions were situated on the two sides of a deep ravine. At the same time De la Rey and Smuts had to attack the main British position on the foothills with 700 burghers. The entrenchments there were spread out in a half-moon formation over a distance of about three kilometres, with fortifications all along the rim and a strong outpost at Vaalkop in the southeast.

De la Rey launched his attack at half past three this morning. Commandant C.J.J. Badenhorst's burghers bravely attacked the British main position from the southwest. The Khakis returned fire and halted Badenhorst's men. Beyers's burghers on the summit of the mountain entered the battle at about five o'clock. Commandants M.P. van Staden and Lodi Krause's men overwhelmed the Khakis west of the ravine and by seven o'clock this morning Commandants Jan Kemp and Marais's burghers had forced the Khakis east of the ravine to surrender. Those burghers then fired on the main British position from the summit. Most of the Khakis fled, whereupon the Boers in the foothills occupied their camp.

Even though De la Rey's men had achieved a magnificent victory, the success was not complete since they failed to prevent the escape of Clements and his main force. The fleeing Khakis barely managed to reach the safety of the fortification on Vaalkop, where they dug themselves in. On the positive side we must take into account that Clements left all his supplies behind. After hours of fighting, the burghers turned their interest to the prospects of booty and lost interest in the fighting. With that the battle ended.

The casualties on both sides were high. On the Boer side 32 burghers were killed and 46 wounded. As far as we could ascertain, 109 Khakis were killed and 186 wounded, while our men took at least 358 prisoner. The Boers captured 70 wagons loaded with supplies, 200 tents, 700 horses and mules, about 500 trek oxen and a huge supply of ammunition. As can be expected, the men are sad about the death of their comrades, but on the other hand are satisfied with having obtained sufficient supplies to resume the struggle for our freedom.

EYEWITNESS REPORT BY A BOER PARTICIPANT

Deneys Reitz, the son of State Secretary F.W. Reitz, who participated in the battle as one of Commandant Krause's burghers, gave our correspondent the following first-hand account of the fighting:

'We of the Africaander Cavalry Corps were on the extreme right at the edge of the cliff, with a drop of 180 metres below us. Beyers was with us, and to our left walked the Waterbergers, and beyond them the Zoutpansberg men. Before we had gone far, dawn lit the mountain-tops, and with it came a fierce rifle-fire from the enemy barricades some distance ahead.

'We had gone without sleep for two days and two nights, so that our spirits were low, and our advance came at once to a halt. Our line fell down behind rocks, and whatever shelter was to be had, leaving General Beyers walking alone, his revolver in one hand and a riding-switch in the other, imploring us to go on, but we hugged our cover against the hail of bullets lashing around us.

'From where I lay on the tops of the crags, I could look straight down into the English camp. I could almost have dropped a pebble upon the running soldiers and the white-tented streets and the long lines of picketed horses.

'As I looked down on the plain, from behind a jutting shoulder of the mountain came swinging into view a force of mounted men who galloped hard for the English camp. It was General de la Rey timing his attack to synchronise with our own. They closed in, and for a moment it seemed as if they would overwhelm the British, but then the soldiers rushed to their posts opening heavy fire. The plain became dotted with fallen men and horses, and the attack wavered and broke.

'The troops facing us on the mountain now made a mistake. Like ourselves, they were able to look down at the attack, and when they saw our men retire in confusion they set up loud shouts of triumph. Stung by their cries our whole force, on some sudden impulse, started to its feet and went pouring forward. There was no stopping us now, and we swept on shouting and yelling, men dropping freely as we went.

'Almost before we knew it, we were swarming over the walls, shooting and clubbing in hand-to-hand conflict. It was sharp work. I have confused recollection of fending bayonet thrusts and firing point-blank into men's faces; then of soldiers running to the rear or putting up their hands, and, as we stood panting and excited within the barricades, we could scarcely realise that the fight was won.

'We had now taken the main defences, but scattered rifle shots were coming from a nest of boulders to the rear, and General Beyers ordered Krause, our commandant, to clear the place. Krause took a dozen of us, and we worked our way forward in short rushes. But he grew impatient and told us to close in more quickly. The result was disastrous, for as we rose a salvo rung out which brought down four of our men. Having fired this parting volley, the soldiers, of whom there were only six, went running towards the mouth of the ravine which led down a cleft to their camp below.

'I hit one of them through the thigh, and Krause shot another dead, but the rest escaped. We walked back to see the extent of the damage, and it was bad enough. My old schoolfellow Jan Joubert, son of Piet Joubert the late Commandant-General, had a bad chest-wound, and the other three men were dead.

'I also went to see the soldier whom I had shot. He had a nasty wound, but he was bandaging it himself with the first-aid pad which they all carried, and he said he could manage. He was a typical Cockney, and bore me so little ill will that he brought out a portrait of his wife and children, and told me about them. I made him comfortable, and left him cheerfully smoking a cigarette.

'Krause asked me to take a water bottle from one of the dead soldiers, and go down into the ravine in search of water. I got a flask and went down the slope to the mouth of the gorge. Unknown to us there was a path to the English camp, along which reinforcements were climbing to dislodge us. I saw 20 or 30 soldiers already near the top, standing in a group not a stone's-throw from me, while many more were coming on behind in single file.

'I fired at once and dropped a man, the remainder disappearing amongst the trees. From here they opened fire on me, and I in turn had to take cover, dodging from rock to rock to get back to Krause. On hearing my news he took a number of men, and we ran down just in time to see the path crowded with soldiers. We lost no time in pouring close-range volleys into their midst. In less than a minute only dead and wounded were left; more than 20 men of the Imperial Yeomanry of London lying in the space of a few yards.

'This was a final clearing, and we now had the camp below at our mercy, for we were able to fire into it without opposition. Soon we could see the occupants retiring with their guns, and we descended the ravine and entered the camp.

'The camp was filled with supplies of all kinds, and such a smashing of cases, and ransacking of tents and wagons, had not been seen since we looted the Dundee camp long before. While we were at this, General Beyers came riding among us in a rage, and ordered us to follow the enemy, but we thought otherwise. We considered that the object of the attack was to capture supplies, and not soldiers, as soldiers would have to be liberated for want of somewhere to keep them and besides, if we went off, we might return to find the camp already looted during our absence. So we attended to the matter in hand, more especially as De la Rey's horsemen had recovered from their setback earlier in the morning, and could be seen stringing out across the veld towards where Clements and the balance of his troops were withdrawing down the valley in the direction of Pretoria. We told ourselves that we had done our part in the day's work, and that they could do the rest.'

Battlefield at Nooitgedacht: a – summit attacked by Beyers; b – position of Pretoria burghers; c – Clement's camp; d – height occupied by Kemp

Commandant Lodi Krause

General Jan Kemp

General Koos de la Rey

FROM THE EDITOR

December 1900 was the first month in a long time to see events developing more or less positively for the Boer Republics, with some notable successes against the British forces. With the beginning of the New Year, the confidence of the burghers is higher than at any time since February last year. In addition, the Boer forces have captured enough war supplies to continue with the struggle for an almost unlimited period.

A very important development that will make the waging of war impossible for Britain in the long run is the successful invasion into the Cape Colony by a number of Free State commandos. The British authorities will now have to send a huge number of military units to the Cape. This will be a big advantage to the Republics, since those units will be taken out of the Republics and thus deplete the British strength.

Numerous developments in the Cape Colony point to a rise in support for the Boers among the colonials. It is interesting to note that both Afrikaners and English-speaking colonists feel strongly that they have had enough of the British military authorities. British reaction to the pro-Republican statements of the Cape population indicates that the Boer Republics should never expect any sympathy from Governor Sir Alfred Milner, however.

'LADY ROBERTS' CAPTURED AT HELVETIA
Major victory for Ben Viljoen and Chris Muller

In the veld in the eastern Transvaal, 31 December – Two days ago Generals Ben Viljoen, Chris Muller and their burghers scored a magnificent victory over a British garrison at Helvetia here in the eastern Transvaal. The Khakis had previously erected a long line of fortified positions between Machadodorp and Lydenburg. At Helvetia, some 10 kilometres north of Machadodorp, Major Cotton was stationed with 350 men and a huge naval gun. Their trenches and stonewalls were spread over four low hills.

Viljoen and Muller inspected Helvetia soon after Christmas and decided on an attack. Very early on the morning of 29 December approximately 580 of Viljoen's burghers advanced on the British positions from two sides. Assistant General Chris Muller led the Boksburg Commando and the Johannesburg Police in an attack from the east, while Commandant Wynand Viljoen, assisted by Field Cornets Andries and Jack Pienaar, approached Helvetia with the Johannesburg Commando from the west. Fortunately for the burghers, the enemy did not expect an attack and had no sentries on duty. Since day had not yet broken when Muller's men reached the camp, most of the Khakis were sound asleep. According to one of the burghers, Frederik Rothman, our men could not aim properly in the dark and physically overpowered the dumbfounded soldiers, many of whom were still in their pyjamas.

The Khakis soon surrendered, allowing the Boers to capture their camp. Altogether eleven Khakis were killed and 29, including Major Cotton, were wounded. In addition 235 Khakis were captured and all their supplies, including the gigantic 4,7 inch (120 millimetre) naval gun with 'Lady Roberts' painted in white letters on the gun carriage, fell into Boer hands. On the Boer side three men were killed and five wounded.

Muller and his burghers were soon forced to retreat from the British camp, since they received a report that a huge British force was rushing towards Helvetia from the north. After setting fire to all the supplies that they had to leave behind, the burghers fell back to the south. Unfortunately they had to abandon the ammunition wagon of the 'Lady Roberts' when it became stuck in a donga.

State Secretary F.W. Reitz wrote the following poem about this event. In these satirical verses he not only ridicules the British commanders in South Africa, but jokes with the *trekboers* and the 'bushlancers' (Transvaal burghers who do not participate in the war but flee about with their livestock). He points out that Lord Roberts has returned to England leaving his Old Lady behind. While with the Boers, she will have to become accustomed to eating *mieliepap* (maize porridge).

State Secretary F.W. Reitz

THE 'LADY ROBERTS'

Here stands 'The Lady Roberts'
Yes! Ben Viljoen, well done!
And well done General Muller,
For you got us this gun.

The Trekboer and Bushlancer
Look at her as they pass,
And say 'My Goodness Gracious!'
Where got you this old lass?

Then we reply ''tis Ben Viljoen
'Has this old Lady sent
'And offered her as New Year's gift
'To our good President.'

The Trekboer then wakes up again
And drives his sheep along,
And even the poor Bushlancer
Begins to feel quite strong.

Lord Roberts 'E 'as ooked it 'Ome
He has scooted, poor old chap,
But he left th' old Lady here with us,
She's fond of 'mieliepap'.

Lord Roberts burns our houses down,
The women out he drives,
He cannot overcome the men,
So persecutes their wives.

But his old 'Lady Roberts'
Who lyddite spits for sport
He puts her at Helvetia,
For safety in a fort.

He thought there was no danger,
For that confounded Boer,
With his confounded Mauser
Would trouble her no more.

Hurra! for the Boksburgers,
Hurra! for the Police,
Let Kitchener gnash his teeth now
And ask 'If this be peace?'

They've got his ammunition
His lyddite gun to boot
And captured all his Tommies
Ere one of them could scoot.

Ere he could fire a cannon,
Or get his breeches on,
Boksburg had Tommy by the throat
And so the job was done.

'tis but 'Gorilla' warfare,
Says Mr Chamberlain,
But if this sort of thing goes on
The issue's pretty plain.

Lord Roberts of Kandahar,
Lord Kitchener of Khartoum,
Lord Buller of Colenso
Your mighty titles boom.

A British naval gun of the same type as 'Lady Roberts'

For what? Defenceless kaffirs
Armed but with spear and shield
You've slaughtered, oh, so merrily
On many a bloody field.

But now that you with White Men
And Mausers have to cope,
Kitchener lies at Pretoria
And the others had to 'slope'.

Yes, Roberts of Can 'there'
Is not Roberts of Can 'here',
And his little Picnic party
Is costing England dear.

Stand firm then Africanders
In Heaven put your Trust,
We shall not lose our Country
Because our Cause is *just*.

OTHER GLORIOUS BOER VICTORIES IN TRANSVAAL
KHAKIS FIND GOING TOUGH IN MAGALIESBERG

In the veld in the eastern Transvaal, 31 December – In addition to the major battle at Nooitgedacht and the defeat of the British garrison at Helvetia (see separate reports in this issue), this month has seen numerous confrontations, with a number of other Boer victories in the Transvaal. Generally speaking the Transvaal forces did very well: the British army could not, as was often the case in the previous six months, do as it wished. In addition the Transvaal forces captured huge supplies of stores of major military value.

On Monday 3 December General Koos de la Rey managed to capture a whole convoy of 138 wagons on its way from Pretoria to Rustenburg. De la Rey, General Jan Smuts and Commandant F.J. Boshoff had decided to attack the convoy when it passed through the Magaliesberg at Buffelspoort. They divided their burghers into three groups and planned to attack the convoy from three directions.

Not everything went precisely according to plan, since the convoy had already moved through the mountain pass during the night of 2–3 December. Smuts's burghers made contact with the convoy, accompanied by a strong escort of soldiers, at three o'clock that morning, when the wagons had already passed the place where De la Rey intended to attack them. The burghers nevertheless attacked. Since it was their main purpose to capture the convoy, they attempted to pin the escort down on the flanks with heavy fire and to overwhelm the rearguard. This tactic was successful. By one o'clock that afternoon the British rearguard had collapsed and the convoy fell into the hands of the burghers.

While Boshoff's men began hauling away the wagons, the rest of the burghers attempted to force the soldiers who were escorting the convoy to surrender. De la Rey soon abandoned those attempts, since the burghers were by late afternoon more interested in the booty than in total victory. They appropriated what supplies they could and burnt the rest, before moving off with the 1 800 trek oxen. The British loss was 18 men killed, 46 wounded and 54 made prisoner of war. De la Rey suffered the loss of two men killed and seven wounded.

Soon after the Republican success at Buffelspoort, General Manie Lemmer and his burghers attacked a second convoy at Vlakfontein, between Lichtenburg and Marico. Unfortunately this attempt ended in tragedy, since Lemmer himself was killed.

Less than a week after his memorable victory over General Clements at Nooitgedacht (see separate report) De la Rey almost managed once again to lead that beleaguered Khaki commander into an ambush. Once again it took place at Hekpoort – this time near Vaalkop. De la Rey ordered a number of his burghers to retreat before the Khakis, with the intention of attacking the flanks of the pursuers with his other burghers. However,

Boer scouts preparing an ambush at a railway line

Continued right

DE WET ACTIVE IN THE FREE STATE

In the veld in the Free State, 26 December – Chief Commandant Christiaan de Wet was not involved in any large-scale battle with the Khakis in the past month, but he and his men kept the enemy occupied. It was De Wet's plan to cross the border into the Cape Colony in order once again to mobilise the Republican-minded colonists, but due to heavy rain and the fact that the Orange River was in flood, he could not achieve his aim. Two other Free State commandos did press through to the Cape, as reported elsewhere in this issue.

At the beginning of December De Wet had about 2 500 men, with enough horses for everybody under his command. This number included the burghers of General Piet Fourie and Captain Gideon Scheepers. On Sunday 2 December De Wet's men were involved in a skirmish with the Khakis at Goede Hoop between Smithfield and Bethulie, but failed to gain the upper hand. Later that day General Hertzog's commando joined them at Karmel. Two days later they crossed the strong-flowing Caledon River in pouring rain at Kareefontein. Since the drift was almost impossible to negotiate, they left behind their Krupp gun, for which they had no ammunition.

From the Caledon River they proceeded directly south to the Orange River, which was flowing even stronger than the Caledon. De Wet believed that it would be unwise to attempt crossing the river with his commando. Consequently he ordered Hertzog, Commandant Pieter Kritzinger and Scheepers to undertake the crossing on their own with their commandos and to invade, respectively, the northwestern and eastern districts of the Cape Colony.

De Wet now faced the threat of being caught by the Khakis in the triangle between the Orange and Caledon Rivers, and realised that he would have to recross the Caledon as soon as possible. On Friday 7 December his commando was involved in a skirmish with Khakis at Kommissiebrug on the Caledon. De Wet bombarded the courageous British soldiers with the guns he had earlier captured at Dewetsdorp, but could not overwhelm them. Later that day the commando fortunately managed to cross the Caledon at another place. The river was so full that the guns were completely submerged when the burghers hauled them through.

After their escape De Wet and his commando proceeded to the north. By 10 December they had reached Helvetia between Smithfield and Dewetsdorp, where they rested. Soon afterwards they noted that huge columns of Khakis were pursuing them, but they easily shook them off. On Friday 14 December General Piet Fourie led a large commando through the British blockhouse line at Springkaansnek, some 24 kilometres east of Thaba Nchu. De Wet and President Steyn followed through safely. Altogether eight burghers were killed and 17 wounded in the process, and the British, who valiantly attempted to stop the burghers, captured 33 of our men. Commandant Sarel Haasbroek and his men were indeed cut off by the British, but broke through the line at Sannaspos a few days later and rejoined De Wet and his commando in the northern Free State.

On Christmas day they all assembled at Tafelkop. The burghers are in rags and tatters after all the campaigning, but listened with great respect to the immortal message: Peace on Earth and Goodwill toward Men.

De Wet's commando crosses the Orange River

FREE STATE FORCES INVADE CAPE COLONY

In the veld in the Free State, 31 December – Free State forces invaded the Cape Colony for the second time earlier this month. Their main purpose is firstly to spread the field of battle as wide as possible in order to relieve British pressure on the commandos in the Republics; and secondly to recruit as many Republican-minded Cape colonists as possible for active support. The British authorities reacted in a heated fashion to the invasion and on 20 December reintroduced martial law in the eastern districts of the Cape Colony. In addition General Kitchener personally went to Noupoort to oversee the attempts to repulse the invaders.

Two Free State commandos, led by Commandant Pieter Kritzinger and General Barry Hertzog, are involved in this invasion. Even before they crossed the Orange River, on Thursday 13 December, Kritzinger and his men captured a British column known as Brabant's Horse at Koesberg near Zastron. In the process 20 Khakis were killed or wounded and approximately 100 were taken prisoner of war.

Three days later Kritzinger, with Scheepers as his second-in-command, crossed the Orange River near Norvalspont with 200 men.

As for General Hertzog and his well-supplied force of about 1 200 burghers, they also crossed the Orange River on 16 December, at Sanddrift near Petrusville. The next day they occupied Philipstown and commandeered a number of horses. From there they proceeded in a south-westerly direction and crossed the main railway line from Cape Town to Kimberley on 18 December at Houtkraal, north of De Aar.

Four days later they occupied Britstown. The town guard, consisting of 15 soldiers and seven policemen, had earlier fled when Hertzog's advance guard, led by Commandant Niewoud, approached the town. Thus the burghers entered the town unhindered.

Hertzog himself arrived in Britstown on 23 December but left again the next day with his commando for Houwater, northwest of the town. On Christmas Day the British reoccupied Britstown. A day later they attacked Hertzog's forces at Houwater, but the burghers repulsed the attack. Hertzog subsequently retreated in the direction of Prieska. At this time the British acted in contravention of all the conventions of civilised warfare by capturing Hertzog's ambulance under the command of Doctor Ramsbottom and sending the medical personnel as prisoners of war to Bloemfontein. Hertzog and his Free State forces proceeded from there to Vosburg, which they occupied on 27 December after the town guard had summarily surrendered.

continued
when he heard a report that General French was approaching the battle scene with a huge mounted force, he ordered his burghers to retreat, since he did not want to lead them into a major battle in which they could suffer high casualties.

BRITISH SUPPLY TRAIN CAPTURED ON EASTERN RAILWAY LINE

The burghers in the eastern Transvaal scored a very welcome success against the Khakis on the eastern railway line on Monday 24 December. Lieutenant Colonel Fanie Trichard and his men captured a whole trainload of supplies, including Christmas presents meant for the Khakis, at Uitkyk Station, east of Middelburg. Field Cornet Piet Minnaar gave our correspondent the following report on this incident:

'By four o'clock that morning Jack de Wit and Lucas van As had placed the dynamite under the railway line. The proven method of using the firing mechanism of a rifle that would be triggered by the weight of the train was used. Twelve of us took up position in a culvert close by. It was a risky business, since we had no idea from which direction the train would approach. The remainder of our men hid on the edge of a pan. Three men remained behind with the horses. They had orders to charge in with all the horses if it became clear that we would have to flee.

'Fortunately the train came from Middelburg. It steamed slowly up the incline. We allowed the locomotive to go past, then we opened fire. The engine driver immediately increased speed. Moments later it crossed the dynamite, which exploded. The locomotive derailed and turned on its side. A brief shooting battle between us and the soldiers followed, but they soon surrendered. On our side one man was killed, but the Khakis suffered heavily.

'The whole train was loaded with supplies, including delicious dinners for the Khakis at Waterval Boven. We took as much as we could for ourselves, as well as the bags filled with letters and newspapers from which we gather news about the outside world. Our loot certainly ensured that we would enjoy a happy Christmas.'

Train derailed by the Boers

TREASON AND RUMOURS OF TREASON
Boer actions against traitors

In the veld in the eastern Transvaal, 31 December – One of the most disturbing developments for the Republican cause in this war is the activities of traitors. Treason in the time of war means the purposeful action of the burghers of one of the parties in the war to advance the cause of the enemy. Unfortunately there are numerous burghers of the Boer Republics, including well-known former officers, who are guilty of treason.

Former General Hendrik Schoeman is one of the prominent burghers standing accused of treason. Last month a war council heard his case in Nylstroom and found him not guilty. He was not released, however, and is at present held in the jail in Pietersburg.

Commandant-General Louis Botha is determined to identify and neutralise the traitors. Earlier this month he sent an order to all Transvaal officers and magistrates to compile a list of all the burghers in their areas who had surrendered and who had taken the British oath of neutrality. These burghers must be called up again and should they refuse, must be sent to the nearest jail immediately and punished according to law. All their movable property should be confiscated and a complete inventory of it should be drawn up. However, it should be ensured that their wives and children had sufficient means to stay alive. The burghers who took up arms against the enemy again should hand in all the passes and permits they received from the British. In addition these burghers should take an 'oath of neutrality contra-oath' declaring that they regarded their oath of neutrality as of no value whatsoever.

Traitors can expect no mercy if they are caught. Two days after Christmas General De la Rey's commando executed two burghers, namely J.A.B. de Beer and P.C. de Bruin, at Lapfontein near Klerksdorp in the western Transvaal, since they had been found guilty of treason. Another burgher, H.C. Boshoff, was pardoned because of his young age.

BRITISH ACTION AGAINST TRAITORS

The British also treat people whom they regard as traitors unmercifully. From the northeastern Cape it is reported that a black man, Alfred Malopi, was executed by a British firing squad in Aliwal North in early December after being found guilty of treason. In terms of the charge sheet against him, he was employed as a labourer by the British while at the same time divulging information on the British forces to the Republican forces.

From the southern Free State it is reported that Gideon de Wet, a well-known inhabitant of Rouxville, was sentenced to two years' imprisonment by a British military court. His 'crime' was that he took up a neutral stance after taking the oath of neutrality and refused to divulge information to the British.

Thirdly the Khakis hung a black man, Sekota, in Barberton in the eastern Transvaal, just before Christmas since a military court had found him guilty of collecting information on the British forces in a secret and treacherous way. In addition he allegedly stole some cattle.

Lastly it is reported from the western Cape that the editor of the newspaper, *Ons Land*, F.S. Malan, was sentenced to one year's imprisonment for criminal slander. Malan's very outspoken pro-Afrikaner paper published an article about an incident in the war that put the Khakis in a bad light. In this article, based on a letter received from Heidelberg in the Transvaal, it is alleged that General French bombarded a farmhouse. When he was informed that there were women and children in the house, French allegedly answered: 'I do not care a damn. Shoot the beggars. Afrikanerdom must be wiped out.' Five field guns were trained on the house and destroyed it. No assistance was given to the inhabitants.

THE TREASON OF THE 'JOINERS'

News from British-occupied Pretoria is that Meyer de Kock, a prominent burgher and local official in the Belfast area before the war, has openly joined the circle of traitors. De Kock and those who feel like him are not satisfied with mere neutrality, but have placed themselves at the disposal of the British to fight their own people. In the process they are nothing but joiners, since they have joined the enemy. On 21 December the joiners held a meeting in Pretoria under British protection to establish the so-called Burgher Peace Committee. The prominent joiners who attended this meeting included former generals Piet de Wet and A.P.J. Cronjé, as well as De Kock. They were all elected to leading positions in the Committee. Kitchener attended the meeting and informed the joiners about his military plans.

A few days after Christmas the Burgher Peace Committee accepted a proposal by De Kock to send 24 handsuppers with pamphlets to the Republican forces to indicate to the fighting burghers the 'hopelessness of their prospects' and convince them to surrender their arms.

General Hendrik Schoeman (standing far left) in the jail in Pietersburg

SUPPORT FOR REPUBLICS IN CAPE COLONY

In the veld in the eastern Transvaal, 30 December – In the six months that have passed since our previous report on pro-Republican activities in the Cape Colony, some very positive developments have taken place, even though not sufficient to bring about a change in the course of the war. The pro-Republicans in the Cape Colony have held numerous meetings during which they pleaded for the upholding of the independence of the Republics and sharply criticised the burning of farms in the Republics. A meeting of pro-Republican women was held at Somerset East in the Cape Colony on 12 October, during which a speech by the well-known Olive Schreiner, the sister of the former Cape Premier, was read. She sharply criticised the British who hold leadership positions in the colony, claiming that they are harming the British image irreparably so that nobody would in future hear the name England without attaching the word suppressor to it.

The most noteworthy recent meeting was the People's Congress that took place in Worcester on 6 December. Some of the Congress delegates travelled 300 kilometres by horse cart to reach a station from which they could take a train to Worcester.

Between nine and ten thousand people attended the congress. The British military authorities were so concerned about the massive attendance that they sent a section of Australian troops with guns to keep law and order.

The main speaker at the Congress was an English-speaking Cape Colonist, S.C. Cronwright-Schreiner, husband of the writer Olive Schreiner. He stated bluntly that the war was a crime and that capitalism forced Britain into it. He recommended that the Cape Afrikaners should make it clear to Britain that they would never accept the termination of the independence of the Republics. In addition they must demand unfettered control over their own internal affairs, and must make it clear that they do not want Sir Alfred Milner as governor. Milner has continuously insulted and slandered them in all possible ways and revealed himself as a small-minded political figure. Cronwright-Schreiner ended his speech to loud applause, with the words: 'Milner is not only a curse for South Africa, but disrupts the whole British Empire!'

The Congress took a few important decisions and elected a deputation to submit them to Milner. In the first place they demanded the termination of the war because of its unequalled destruction, the torching of farmhouses and the disruption of women and children. The danger was real that its legacy would be enduring hatred and bitterness. Secondly the Congress requested the upholding of the independence of the Republics, since that was the only way to assure peace in South Africa. Thirdly the Congress requested the recognition of the right of the inhabitants of the Cape Colony to manage their own affairs.

On 11 December a deputation of the Congress submitted these decisions to Milner with the request that he should forward them to the British government. Milner answered in his typically arrogant and high-handed fashion that he would send the decisions to Britain, but would add that he strongly disagreed. According to him the 'aggressive' trend of the decisions was unnecessary, since the war was 'one of the most humane wars that there has ever been in history'. In addition Milner said the decisions would merely serve to strengthen the resolve of the Republican burghers to carry on with their futile struggle.

Olive Schreiner

Burghers on commando with their excellent supply of biltong

OUR MILITARY OFFICERS

General Manie Lemmer

This month we report on the death of a beloved and brave officer, General Manie Lemmer. We have little information on his career. He was born in 1849 at Hartbeesfontein in the Potchefstroom district and became a stock farmer. In the early 1880s he fought on the side of Captain Moshette in the power struggle between the Rolong chiefs on the Transvaal western border. He was a field cornet of the volunteers who founded the Republic Land Goosen and was badly wounded in one of the engagements.

Before the outbreak of this war Lemmer represented his district in the Second Volksraad of the South African Republic. He was known as a level-headed and progressive member.

In October 1899 he participated as an ordinary burgher in the first engagement of the war at Kraaipan on the Transvaal western border. Soon afterwards he was appointed as fighting general. In that capacity he served with distinction in numerous battles on virtually all the fronts. In spite of many warnings by his burghers to be more careful, Lemmer often found himself at the centre of clashes. His burghers grieve his death, but it was no surprise to them when an enemy bullet hit him.

General Jan Smuts declared that Lemmer possessed both the meek character of a child and the courage of a lion. He was a soft-spoken, imperturbable man with excellent leadership qualities and a strong sense of responsibility. His death is a major blow for the Republican forces.

General Manie Lemmer

THE War Reporter
MONTHLY EDITION

Number 49   In the Veld, South African Republic   1 February 1901

QUEEN VICTORIA DIES

In the veld in the eastern Transvaal, 31 January – The whole British Empire is in mourning after the death of Queen Victoria, who passed away on 22 January after almost 64 years as British monarch. President Kruger, who is at present in Holland, sent a message of encouragement to her on the day before she died, but she was already unconscious and never took note of it. After a state funeral she will be buried in a mausoleum in Frogmore next to her husband, Prince Albert, who died 40 years ago.

Reports that Queen Victoria was very ill reached us earlier this month. It is also reported that Kaiser Wilhelm II of Germany, her grandson, visited her in London a few days before her death. One of her other grandsons was appointed as her successor, King Edward VII, two days after her death.

News from Cape Town is that the Boers in the prisoner-of-war camp at Green Point halted all their leisure activities until after the Queen's funeral. That was done as a sign of respect for their enemy's monarch.

In the meantime we continuously receive newspapers and newspaper cuttings with news of the war as published abroad. The contents of some of those reports are incredible. On 15 January a letter was published in the *Freeman's Journal* in Ireland in which General Kitchener is accused of serious misdeeds. The letter was allegedly written by a British officer in South Africa and states that Kitchener had ordered that the British soldiers should take no prisoners when they force the Boers to surrender, but should shoot all the burghers.

This letter was reprinted in a well-known London newspaper, *The Times*, a few days later.

A call was made on the British military authorities to repudiate the letter, but up to now they have ignored it.

Our correspondents in the field do not believe in the correctness of the statements. Kitchener does act harshly against the civilian population of the Republics, but we are not aware of any cases where British soldiers have summarily shot prisoners of war.

Queen Victoria

FROM THE EDITOR

The most newsworthy event last month was the death of Queen Victoria. In the light of her outspoken imperial sentiments, her lack of respect for her own government's conventions with the Republics, and her lack of empathy with the Boers' longing for freedom, it is difficult for any citizen of the Boer Republics to experience her passing away as a particular loss. Furthermore it is unlikely that her death and the coronation of the new British king, Edward VII, will have any influence on the course of the war here in South Africa.

On the military front the British were uncharacteristically silent for most of the month, then suddenly launched a massive assault on the Transvaal forces southeast of Pretoria. Reports stream in that they are making use of scorched earth tactics. Our hope is that these tactics will immediately be abandoned again, since vicious actions against their wives and children will certainly not be tolerated by the Boers and may lead to revenge.

In the meantime the Boer forces did well in numerous minor engagements with the Khakis. General Hertzog in particular is spreading panic amongst the British military authorities in the Cape Colony. The best indication of this is the British declaration of martial law in virtually every Cape district.

The ongoing establishment by the British authorities of refugee camps, which the fighting burghers regard as nothing other than prisoner-of-war camps where their families are detained under terrible conditions, is the most alarming development of the past month. However, even in this respect we note a small ray of hope. Emily Hobhouse, an Englishwoman who is widely known for her revelations of the mistreatment of women and children in the refugee camps, arrived in Bloemfontein this month. She visited the camp there as well as a few other camps and expressed her shock at the inhumane conditions in the camps. Her statements will certainly be publicised in Britain, so we trust and hope that things will soon improve considerably.

BRITISH FORCES USE SCORCHED EARTH TACTICS

In the veld, 31 January – The British army in Transvaal remained rather inactive for most of the month, but on Sunday 27 January suddenly launched a huge offensive. A gigantic British column had earlier gathered on a wide front from Mooiplaas east of Pretoria to Springs in the south. From this line they advanced relentlessly in an easterly direction. Our correspondent reports that more than 20 000 Khakis with more than 50 guns are involved in this drive. He believes that General French is in command. One of the burghers, Deneys Reitz of the Africaander Cavalry Corps, gave our correspondent the following eyewitness account:

'At Olifantsfontein General Botha came up with a small escort. He told us that Lord Roberts had decided to bring the Boers to their knees by a series of drives, in which vast numbers of troops were to sweep across the country like a drag-net.

'Two days after General Botha had ridden away, the storm broke upon us. As the sun rose, the skyline from west to east was dotted with English horsemen riding in a line that stretched as far as the eye could see, and behind this screen every road was black with columns, guns, and wagons, slowly moving forward.

'All that day we fell back, delaying the enemy horsemen by rifle-fire as far as possible, and breaking away when the gun-fire grew too hot. This went on till sunset without heavy losses on our side, despite the many batteries brought into play from every knoll and kopje.

'During the course of the next morning, pillars of smoke began to rise behind the English advance, and to our astonishment we saw that they were burning the farmhouses as they came. Towards noon word spread that, not only were they destroying all before them, but were actually capturing and sending away the women and children.

'At first we could hardly credit this, but when one wild-eyed woman after another galloped by, it was borne in on us that a more terrible chapter of the war was opening.

'The intention is to undermine the morale of the fighting men, but the effect is exactly the opposite, from what I see. Instead of weakening, they become only the more resolved to hold out.

'Towards dark the chase slowed down. It rained steadily all night, and we spent a miserable time lying in mud and water on the bare hillsides. At daybreak this morning we were all on the move again, but, owing to the rain and the heavy going, the English could only crawl in our wake, and we had little difficulty in keeping our distance.

'By now, the news has spread that the English are clearing the country, with the result that the entire civil population from the farms is moving.

'The plain is alive with wagons, carts, and vehicles of all descriptions, laden with women and children, while great numbers of horses, cattle, and sheep are being hurried onward by black herdboys, homes and ricks going up in flames behind them.'

A Boer farm house beeing blown up with dynamite

Boer farm houses destroyed by British troops

105

Number 49   1 Febuary 1901

HERTZOG IN THE CAPE COLONY
British military authorities caught unawares

Calvinia, 31 January – General Hertzog and his Free State burghers are still moving through the Cape Colony at a stunning pace. The vanguard of his commando, led by Commandant Charles Nieuwoudt, occupied Calvinia on 7 January. In the process they unfortunately became involved in a row with the local Coloured population, since a group of Coloureds pelted the commando with stones. On Nieuwoudt's orders the burghers detained Abraham Esau, who seems to have instigated the Coloured actions against the commando.

One of the clearest indications of the alarm that Hertzog's successes are generating in British military circles is the fact that on 17 January they declared martial law applicable to virtually the whole Cape Colony, except the harbours and the so-called native areas. In addition the British authorities are attempting to establish a Colonial Defence Force in the Cape. General Baden-Powell, the 'hero' of Mafeking, is currently organising the so-called South African Constabulary. It consists mainly of Cape colonial troops who are already serving in other British units.

Last month we reported that the white inhabitants of the Cape Colony have great enthusiasm for the Republican cause. It seems as if the Coloured population has a different standpoint. From Cape Town it is reported that Governor Sir Alfred Milner received a deputation claiming that it represents 100 000 Coloureds on 7 January. The deputation announced that they welcome the 'incorporation of the Boer Republics in the British Empire' (a step only recognised by Britain). They believe that justice, equality and freedom can only be guaranteed to them by the British and believe that the same is true for the Coloured communities in the 'former Republics'. Milner expressed his thanks to the deputation in vague terms.

General Hertzog (centre) and his staff in Vanrhynsdorp on 19 January. Klasie Havenga, his secretary, sits in front

FIRST NAVAL BATTLE OF THE WAR
HERTZOG'S BURGHERS FIRE ON BRITISH BATTLESHIP

Vanrhynsdorp, 26 January – General Hertzog's Free State burghers occupied Vanrhynsdorp on 19 January. He subsequently dispatched a number of his burghers to Lambertsbaai on the coast. On their arrival they saw a British battleship, the *HMS Sybille*, in the bay. After studying it carefully through their binoculars, some burghers fired on the ship with their rifles. The crew of the *Sybille* reacted with panic, but soon answered our burghers' fire with a few gunshots. It was a battle between a lion and a whale since neither could damage the other at all and the burghers soon returned here.

Hertzog was still in Vanrhynsdorp on 23 January when he heard of Queen Victoria's death. As a sign of respect he allowed the resident magistrate of the town to hoist the Union Jack at half-mast.

Commandant Nieuwoudt and his field cornets in Vanrhynsdorp, 19 January 1901

THE SO-CALLED REFUGEE CAMPS

In the veld in eastern Transvaal, 31 January – One of the most frightening developments in this ongoing war is the British establishment of 'refugee' camps. The name is misleading, since the vast majority of the inhabitants in those camps are women and children who are detained there against their will by the British. The conditions in these camps are anything but satisfactory for the detainees. Indeed, it is clear that the death rate amongst those inhabitants is abnormally high and the authorities find it impossible to provide in even the most basic needs of the detained people.

The first refugee camp of which we are aware was established in July last year at Mafeking. In August two more camps followed, namely at Bloemfontein and at Pietermaritzburg. Before the end of last year the British authorities had established camps at Kroonstad, Pretoria, Potchefstroom and Vereeniging. In the past month alone the number of camps have more than doubled with the establishment of such structures at ten places all over South Africa.

It seems as if the original idea was that only burghers and their families who willingly surrendered to the British would be accommodated in the camps. In October last year, however, the enemy began abducting the wives and children of burghers who are still fighting. We reported on a group of Free State women and children who were locked up in camps in Port Elizabeth. Strictly speaking those women and children are now British prisoners of war.

As far as we can establish, the British military authorities decided just before Christmas last year to establish refugee camps on a large scale. Lord Roberts's successor as British Commander-in-Chief, Lord Kitchener, seems to have decided that all men, women and children must be removed from the farms. According to Kitchener this would ensure that the burghers who are still fighting would not be able to procure necessities on the farms, which would considerably restrict their freedom of movement. For that reason Kitchener allegedly ordered his senior officers to establish refugee camps near the railway lines. We believe that the British even plan to force all the black people who live on Boer farms into such camps.

In the camps the British authorities differentiate between the Republicans who are detained there. The first category consists of true refugees, handsuppers and their families as well as other non-combatant civilians. The second category consists of the family members of burghers who are still on commando. The first category is privileged when it comes to the provision of accommodation and necessities.

The establishment of refugee camps is a contravention of all the customs of civilised warfare. In addition it is a contravention of the stipulations of both the Hague and the Geneva Conventions. Britain is a signatory to both. On 14 January President Steyn and Chief Commandant De Wet issued a proclamation in which they complained that the British forces are making war on women and children, capturing Boer ambulances and medical personnel, purposefully destroying private property, misusing white flags, arming blacks and spreading blasphemous propaganda against the Republics. In this proclamation Steyn and De Wet have announced that they would never degrade themselves to the level of making war on women and children. If the British do not end their destruction of the property of the burghers, the burghers would, when they invade the Cape Colony, in retaliation destroy the property of pro-British Cape subjects.

From Bloemfontein it is reported that an Englishwoman, Emily Hobhouse, one of the severest British critics of the system of refugee camps, visited the camp there. Hobhouse had established the South African Women and Children Distress Fund in London last year and has since collected a significant amount of money to provide assistance to victims in the refugee camps. She is extremely shocked by conditions in the camps and promises to put pressure on the British government to end the camp system or at least ensure better treatment for the detained.

The Bloemfontein refugee camp as Emily Hobhouse first saw it

Boer women in the midst of the remainder of their belongings

Miss Emily Hobhouse

Boer women arriving at a refugee camp

106

FIGHTING IN WESTERN TRANSVAAL

Gatsrand district, 31 January – On Wednesday 2 January there was a brief battle between the burghers of General De la Rey and a British column of about 2 000 men at Cyferfontein, about 40 kilometres southeast of Rustenburg, south of the Magaliesberg range. De la Rey hid the majority of his 700 burghers in tall grass in a valley, while a group of mounted burghers attacked the enemy. When the latter fired back, those burghers 'fled' through the centre of the ambush of hidden burghers. Unfortunately for the Khakis, their escort was foolish enough to follow the 'fleeing' burghers into the ambush. The fight was brief and bloody. We subsequently heard that 48 Khakis, including two officers, were killed or wounded and that they lost 70 horses. De la Rey retreated with his burghers without one of them being injured.

The second noteworthy clash took place on 23–24 January at Middelfontein, approximately 11 kilometres south of Olifants Nek. Commandant F.J. Potgieter of Wolmaransstad and his burghers attacked a British force there and virtually forced them to entrench themselves in an unfavourable position. The next day General De la Rey resumed the attack. Unfortunately the Boers could not capture the British camp, since a huge British force suddenly appeared from the direction of Ventersdorp. On the Boer side six men were killed and 19 wounded. We subsequently heard that the Khaki loss was at least 54 men killed or wounded.

The third clash in the western Transvaal this month began on the 29th at Modderfontein and ended today in a victory for the Boers. Modderfontein is of strategic importance, since the wagon road from Krugersdorp to Vereeniging crosses the wagon road from Potchefstroom to Johannesburg here. Last Saturday General Liebenberg and his burghers captured a water cart delivering water to the British garrison stationed at Modderfontein. On the 29th he and General Smuts established that the British garrison consisted of only about 100 men with two guns. While they were busy with their reconnaissance, a supply column accompanied by an armed escort of about 100 men arrived at Modderfontein. Smuts allowed the convoy to join the garrison unhindered, but soon after dark he and Liebenberg and their men positioned themselves with two guns with the objective of capturing the garrison and the convoy.

Early yesterday morning the Boers attacked. It was a tough battle, since the British defended their positions courageously. By late afternoon, however, the Boers had occupied all the British outposts. Before daybreak this morning the burghers resumed their attack. Nature provided valuable cover in the form of a heavy downpour. The British hardly fired back and by half past four this morning they had all surrendered. The huge number of empty whisky bottles and the general appearance of the soldiers, who seemed to have attempted to drown the trauma of their certain defeat earlier on, explained their weak resistance this morning.

With this victory the burghers captured a substantial supply of necessities, which is of both material and moral value. The casualties in this battle were small. A total of 26 Khakis were killed or wounded and the rest made prisoner of war. The casualties on the Boer side were also small. Smuts and Liebenberg have not yet decided what to do with their prisoners of war, but will probably just shake them out and let them go. They are first ascertaining if there are any traitors among the Khakis.

NEWS FROM THE FREE STATE

In the veld near Thaba Nchu, 31 January – Here in the Orange Free State a quiet month has ended with a spate of action in the last few days.

On 4 January General Philip Botha's commando attacked the bodyguard of the British commander-in-chief at Kromspruit near Lindley. A fierce fight ensued during which 13 Khakis were killed and 33 wounded. One of the Khakis who died was the commander of the bodyguard, Colonel Laing. The burghers made the other 154 members of the bodyguard prisoner of war.

On Friday 25 January an important meeting was held at Doringberg, north of Winburg. Virtually all the active Free State generals and commandants were present, as well as President Steyn and various members of the Free State government. Since Steyn's five-year term as president ends this month and it is impossible to hold a normal election, the meeting elected him as vice state president and swore him in in that capacity.

In addition to this formality, Chief Commandant De Wet announced a total reorganisation of the Free State military system. There will henceforth be seven regions. An assistant Chief Commandant will command each region. Each region will consist of between three and six districts, with a Commandant in command of each district. The seven assistant Chief Commandants are Hertzog and Badenhorst in the western Free State, and Hattingh and Michael Prinsloo, Wessels, Froneman and Piet Fourie in the eastern Free State.

On 27 January De Wet crossed the branch line between Smaldeel and Winburg in a southerly direction with a combined commando of more than 2 000 burghers. Two huge British forces immediately pursued him and on the 29th they joined battle at Tabaksberg Mountain. The burghers easily defended themselves and captured a British rapid-fire gun while putting many Khakis out of action. Yesterday De Wet and his men broke through the British blockhouse line west of Thaba Nchu. It is clear that the Khakis still have no answer to the tactics of the Free State Chief Commandant.

MILITARY ACTIVITIES IN SOUTHERN AND EASTERN TRANSVAAL

In the veld in the eastern Transvaal, 31 January – On Friday 5 January the Transvaal officers held a war council at Botha's Mountain near Belfast to discuss military plans. The result was a decision to launch an extensive attack on the British garrisons along the eastern railway line. At midnight that same evening the Boers attacked over a distance of 60 kilometres from Wonderfontein to Machadodorp. These attacks were resumed on Sunday 7 January. This whole area was at times blanketed by a fog bank that enabled the burghers to approach very close to the British fortifications.

The main attack, on 7 January, was that of Generals Ben Viljoen and Chris Muller. Their target was Belfast, where approximately 1 600 Khakis commanded by General Smith-Dorien were stationed. Muller soon overran the British fortifications north of Belfast. Unfortunately the Boers who attacked from the south were halted by the stiff Khaki defence. The result of the battle was in the balance for a long time. Since Viljoen was not prepared to risk high casualties, he cancelled the attack after dark that evening.

The Boer forces that attacked British garrisons at places like Pan, Wonderfontein, Nooitgedacht and Wildfontein that same day also failed, since the Boers avoided heavy casualties. We have been told that the total British loss in all these skirmishes was 24 men dead, 78 wounded and 70 made prisoner of war.

MERCILESS ACTION AGAINST TRAITORS

In the veld in the eastern Transvaal, 31 January – If there is one group of people who in all wars have to keep clear of their own authorities, it is traitors. It goes without saying that no fighting force has any mercy for individuals who earlier belonged to that force, but who during the struggle change sides and subsequently fight against their former comrades. Whatever such an individual's motives might be, a traitor is regarded as a back-stabber and worse than a stray dog, and as with stray dogs, traitors are summarily shot when caught.

This month, the Republican forces mercilessly clamped down on traitors and perhaps acted rather rashly in some cases. On 2 January, for example, General Philip Botha ordered that Lieutenant Cecil Boyle of the so-called Orange River Colony Police, who had earlier been found not guilty on charges of treason by a military court chaired by Chief Commandant De Wet, should be shot summarily. It was immediately done.

A few days later a military court in the Heilbron district discussed the fate of J.J. Morgendaal. This handsupper had acted as a 'voluntary peace emissary' to convince fighting burghers to abandon the struggle. Since the Free State government had officially declared war, Morgendaal's actions constituted treason. The Heilbron war council referred the case to De Wet. Morgendaal and his father-in-law, A. Wessels, who had also acted as 'peace emissary', were taken to De Wet's laager. On their arrival Morgendaal refused to carry out an order, upon which De Wet ordered that he should be shot. Unfortunately he was critically wounded and only died 10 days later of his wounds. In the meantime De Wet, who acted as chairman of the military court, found Wessels guilty of treason and sentenced him to death. However, he was given permission to plead to President Steyn for clemency.

In the Transvaal a number of traitors were prosecuted this month. On 16 January the military court of Commandant Vermaas of Lichtenburg found six prisoners of war guilty of treason and sentenced them to death. Three others were fined and banned to Bechuanaland. Six days later, on 22 January, General Ben Viljoen ordered the arrest of the notorious joiner Meyer de Kock, who had attempted to convince burghers in the Belfast area to surrender. De Kock was accused of treason and tried in a special military court under magistrate G. Joubert at Roossenekal. On 29 January he was found guilty and sentenced to death.

FIRING SQUAD DUTY

One of our correspondents, Naas Raubenheimer, reports that one of the most awful duties that any burgher can face is to be included in a firing squad. Raubenheimer recently witnessed the execution of four burghers who were sentenced to death by a Boer war council of General De la Rey's commando on charges of treason. A number of young Cape rebels were ordered to make up a firing squad to carry out the sentence. Each was given a Martini Henry rifle with which to undertake their gruesome task.

The members of the firing squad probably suffered almost as much anguish as the four condemned men, one of whom was a church elder whose long beard covered his chest. As the doomed prisoners were led to the place where they were to be executed, they began singing a burial hymn. This so disturbed the composure of the firing squad that when the command to fire was shouted out, some of them failed to shoot straight and one of the condemned traitors was only wounded. However the chief warder pulled out a revolver and brought a quick end to the wounded victim's agony.

THE CASE OF FORMER PRESIDENT PRETORIUS

One of the most unfortunate cases of a 'peace mission' was that of former president M.W. Pretorius. The 80-year-old founder of the South African Republic virtually became a 'joiner' when he attempted to convince Commandant-General Louis Botha to surrender at the request of General Kitchener. We have heard from Pretoria that he reported as follows on his return: 'Botha scolded me since I carry messages for the British. "If it had been somebody else I would have had him shot," he said.' Furthermore Botha sent the following message to Kitchener with Pretorius: 'Tell Kitchener that he must send his messages with soldiers under cover of a white flag. If he sends a Boer again we will shoot the messenger. In addition, we do not want peace, since we are fighting for our independence and will keep on fighting. Tell Kitchener that he controls the railway lines and we the rest of the country. We are not interested in peace.'

Kitchener's illusion that he can easily win the war by turning our Commandant-General into a traitor is now hopefully dead and buried.

M.W. Pretorius

OUR MILITARY OFFICERS

General Piet Fourie

Little is known in the Transvaal about Petrus Johannes (Piet) Fourie, one of Chief Commandant Christiaan de Wet's stalwarts in the Orange Free State. He was born in 1842 in the Cape Colony. His parents were Louis Jacobus Fourie and Maria Magdalena Pieterse. Fourie lived in the Free State from an early age and participated in the wars between that Republic and the legendary King Moshweshwe of the Basuto. Before the outbreak of this war he farmed near Bloemfontein and acted as justice of the peace in that district.

In October 1899 Fourie proceeded to the western front as Commandant of the Bloemfontein Commando. He participated in all the major battles on that front. After the British occupation of Bloemfontein, he again revealed his courage and determination in numerous encounters with the Khakis. He played a leading role in De Wet's noteworthy victories over the British forces at Sannaspos and Rooiwal.

Fourie's promotion to the rank of Assistant Chief Commandant for the districts of Bloemfontein, Smithfield, Rouxville and Wepener in August last year was a well-earned reward for this valiant warrior. In December last year he made his mark again when he blasted a way through the British blockhouse line at Sprinkaansnek.

Piet Fourie

PRISONERS OF WAR IN CEYLON
Impressions of one of the prisoners

In In the veld, 30 January – We have just received an eye-witness report on the Republican prisoners of war who have been sent to Ceylon. The author of this report is Jan Brink, General Crowther's adjutant.

'War, capture, banishment across the great ocean to the unknown East – all this makes such an indelible impression, that, for a time, it seems as if our senses are unable to receive any new impressions. And yet, here we are in the very midst of the island, in this dreary Diyatalawa, the 'Happy valley' for those who are not surrounded by three rows of barbed wire, each row seven wires, and are besides guarded by beings who consider that they have the right to shoot somebody inside the wire fence with a dum-dum bullet.

'Our journey to Ceylon on board the *Mongolian* started on Wednesday 15 August last year when we sailed out of Cape Town harbour. There were between 600 and 700 prisoners of war on board, mostly men from Senekal, Ladybrand and Ficksburg. Life on board was very monotonous indeed. Day after day we discussed the same subjects. How long would De Wet be able to hold out? How long would the war last? Would the great Christian Powers never interfere to put an end to this fearful war, which was carried on for no other purpose but for the possession of the gold-fields? What did the island of Ceylon look like? These were the questions of the day.

'At last, on 9 September, the coast of Ceylon came in sight. It was a great sight for us. We rejoiced at the prospect of being able once more to put our feet upon firm ground. We had had more than enough of our ever-rolling prison.

'The first impression one gets of Ceylon is that it must be a country where people starve and find it very hot. The moment one enters the harbour of Colombo, one sees people who are so slender and thin that they seem underfed. Their canoes, long-shaped vessels with one arm, are thin. Even the crows of the country are meagre. From the ship we stared in amazement on these meagre things. However we soon found that it is an island of great rainfall. The result is that very often articles in the houses are spoilt and covered with a woolly kind of substance. When the rain has ceased and the sun comes through, the heat is oppressive and unbearable.

'It took us a long time to go on shore. The last batch of prisoners only left the ship five days after our arrival, just one month after the day on which we had been put on that prison. We had nearly forgotten how to walk, and our heads seemed to reel at every step.

'Next we boarded a train that took us high into the mountains. After a journey of 10 and a half hours we passed through tunnel number 37, then reached a station, and ... here is Diyatalawa. The word was difficult to pronounce for us in the beginning, but now we are accustomed to it.

'At the moment that this is being written, there are about 4 785 prisoners of war in the camp at Diyatalawa, mostly Free Staters and Transvaalers by birth, but also some who had become so by the process of naturalisation; further some Cape Colonials, one black man, one Coloured and last, but not least, a number of 'foreign comrades', as we thankfully called the Uitlanders who fought on our side. They have been, for the greater part, removed to another camp at Ragama.

'The prisoners of war are living in huts of corrugated iron, with plank floors, each hut being 40 metres long by six metres wide. Formerly there were 64 men in such a hut, but this number has now been reduced to 56. The inhabitants of each hut are divided into table-companies of 14 each; each of these latter are under the supervision of a corporal, while a captain has the supervision of every hut. Three hut inspections are held each day.

'Our huts, which number 80, are divided into two villages, which are known among us as Krugersdorp and Steijnsburg. They are naturally not far distant from each other. Krugersdorp has a kind of a suburb, which bears the name of Measlesquare, because measles had broken out amongst a batch of prisoners camped there. At present a newly arrived batch of men are encamped there, but we are not aware of the reason why. There is no particular epidemic reigning, and those encamped in the square creep through the wires whenever they want.

'The majority of the officers, and also some of the clergymen, are staying in two huts specially built for them in Steijnsburg. They are permitted to walk outside the camp, within prescribed limits, on certain days and may, if provided with special passes, also visit Colombo and other places. Generals Roux and Olivier live in two small huts on a hillock between the two camps, and around their dwellings have been erected tents for their adjutants and some other officers mostly belonging to our artillery. Among the officers at Steijnsburg there are several who only discovered their rank on their way hither, while on the other hand, several officers were put among the burghers, and had a great deal of trouble to have their rank recognised, and to get permission to walk outside the camp.

'All the prisoners of war wear, as a protection against the sun, ugly hats or helmets of cork kindly provided by their hosts. The hats of the ordinary burghers have a ring of blue paint round them, those of the officers of red paint, and those of the hut captains of yellow.

'We pass our time by cooking our food and washing our clothes. We must fetch the necessary fuel from outside the camp, and also the rations; the latter in large baskets, and the wood in iron wagons, which are pushed along rails. We must keep our huts clean, and also air our bedding, whenever the state of the weather allows this.

'The prisoners pass their spare time in different ways. The majority perhaps do nothing else but walk about, sleep, eat, and talk about their experiences in the war. One of the huts, namely Number 1, has been put aside for school purposes and in this a number of teachers give instruction in elementary subjects, and also in modern languages, and this from morning to night. There are reading classes, and classes for writing and arithmetic which are attended by about 800 persons, while the classes for French and German naturally do not count so many pupils; further there are classes for more advanced pupils in Dutch, catechism classes and Bible classes. In the same hut the meetings of the Christian Endeavour Societies and Debating Societies are held. As a result the room is not empty during any part of the day.

'Between the two so-called villages, there stands a large house constructed of iron and plaited cadjan leaves, which is used in turns for religious services and entertainments. For the greater part of the day, it is used by those who wish to have a quiet place where they can sit and read or write a letter. The building is also intended for the holding of concerts, and has a platform with a curtain on which the battle of Magersfontein is depicted. In the officers' huts there are two reading rooms, which are well provided with books, religious as well as others, and for that reason reading is a favourite pastime with many. We are not altogether cut off from the outside world. The newspapers of Colombo are regularly received, having, however, to be paid for, and the news they contain about South Africa, scanty as it is, is eagerly read.

'Ceylon is a grand country. That, at all events, is the general idea of the Boer. He talks with great admiration about the country. But, for all that, his thoughts are always away in South Africa. Whatever is dear to him is there! There he wants to live, there to die, and there to be buried!'

The Diyatalawa camp in Ceylon

Boer prisoners of war at Sunday morning service in Dijatalawa Camp, Ceylon

Scene in Ragama Camp, Ceylon

THE War Reporter
MONTHLY EDITION

Number 50   In the Veld, South African Republic   1 March 1901

THE MIDDELBURG CONFERENCE
Peace negotiations between Kitchener and Botha

Middelburg, 28 February – Today Commandant-General Louis Botha and General Lord Kitchener held a five-hour long discussion in the eastern Transvaal town of Middelburg. The subject was the possible ending of the war. The two military commanders even discussed possible peace terms. However, since Kitchener insisted that the Republics be incorporated into the British Empire, it is out of the question for the Republican governments to accept the conditions. It is likewise clear that to continue the struggle is our only option.

As far as we could ascertain, Kitchener took the initiative to meet Botha for discussions. Mrs Annie Botha, the Commandant-General's wife, has since the British occupation of Pretoria last June been a virtual captive in the former capital. Earlier this month she had a meeting with Kitchener to complain about her treatment by British officials. Kitchener then acceded to her request to visit her husband on condition that she would attempt to convince him that it was fruitless to carry on with the war. This she absolutely refused to do. Kitchener then requested that she should tell her husband that he wanted to hold discussions with Botha. She agreed.

Mrs Botha travelled by train to Wakkerstroom. On her arrival the British placed a carriage and horses at her disposal, with which she resumed her journey to her husband. After receiving Kitchener's message from his wife, Botha held negotiations with the Transvaal government in the field. The government agreed that Botha could talk to Kitchener and even drew up a list of discussion points that he could mention in his talks. On her return to Pretoria, Mrs Botha took a letter from her husband with her. In this the British commander was informed that the Transvaal government had given Botha permission to negotiate.

Mrs Botha returned to Pretoria on 22 February and immediately handed the letter to Kitchener. We understand that he went to Middelburg the next day to meet General Botha. An invitation was sent to Botha to proceed there as soon as possible. Botha answered that he would be there today. He and a party of six men arrived exactly on time. They looked particularly neat and rode on well-kept horses.

The discussions took place from ten o'clock this morning till three o'clock this afternoon. A friendly spirit was notable throughout. Initially Botha and Kitchener talked alone, but at Botha's insistence his military secretary, N.J. de Wet and D. van Velden were later allowed to be present.

According to Botha, Kitchener immediately stated – and subsequently often repeated – that the Republics would have to give up their independence. This was of course unacceptable to Botha, but he nevertheless continued to discuss all the points that the Transvaal government requested him to table. Thus he officially complained to Kitchener about the British actions against Republican ambulances, upon which Kitchener promised to send medicine to our forces. Furthermore Botha complained about the detention of women and children like criminals in refugee camps. Kitchener answered that his action was justifiable on military grounds. Finally, Botha complained that the black people used by the British forces as soldiers were treating Boer women and children brutally. Kitchener dodged this accusation by claiming that no black people were dressed in British uniforms. At the end of the meeting Kitchener threatened that he would institute strict measures if the war did not end soon. Botha answered that the Boers were prepared to go on fighting indefinitely.

General Botha informed us immediately after the meeting that the war would continue. Since the British were not prepared to consider Boer demands for independence, he did not believe that it would serve any purpose to even talk about the conditions on which Kitchener was prepared to make peace.

Even though the meeting failed as a peace negotiation, Botha said that he was glad that he could meet Kitchener, since he now knew exactly what the demands of the British were.

No recognised Boer leader is in favour of peace if it entails incorporation into the British Empire. Even before the negotiations took place, Acting State President Schalk Burger wrote to Botha that he had after serious prayers and deep thought come to the conclusion that a conditional peace was out of the question. The Republics had to keep on fighting, even if it meant another tough winter with many sacrifices in the field.

Mrs Annie Botha

Botha (second from left) and Kitchener (third from left) at Middelburg

THE WAR IN EASTERN TRANSVAAL
MANGOLD WOUNDED – HIS PERSONAL REPORT

Ermelo, 11 February – The British forces continued the large-scale offensive that they launched last month against the Republican forces in the eastern Transvaal. In spite of the British army's huge numerical advantage, our burghers have thus far managed to hold their own. At Chrissiesmeer they even went on the offensive. Even though they could not gain the upper hand, the British can certainly have no doubt that our people are determined to continue fighting.

The clash at Chrissiesmeer occurred on 6 February. The previous day, a British unit had arrived at the little village of Bothwell nearby and pitched camp. Commandant-General Botha was aware of this and decided to attack them with the 2 000 burghers under his command. Shortly before three o'clock the next morning Botha's burghers opened heavy fire on the enemy camp. They soon occupied the British outposts but failed to capture their main camp. When the day dawned at about half past four, Botha realised that his men would become vulnerable and ordered them to retreat. Thick fog provided cover for the burghers as they fell back. With that the skirmish came to an end.

According to reliable sources the British loss was about 80 men of whom 23 were killed. In addition the British lost about 300 horses, many of them captured by the Boers. On the Boer side, nine men were killed and 21 wounded, one of them being Wilhelm Mangold of Heidelberg, who has previously written a number of reports for us. The British subsequently captured him and took him to their hospital in Ermelo. When the Khakis abandoned Ermelo on 11 February they left him behind. Our men reoccupied the town a few hours later and found Mangold in hospital. Since he is wounded in his face and cannot talk, he agreed to write us a report on the fight as well as on his experience of being wounded. Here it is:

'At sunset on 5 February General Louis Botha ordered that the British camp at Chrissiesmeer had to be attacked early the next morning. When it was dark we proceeded in that direction. One Rademeyer who lived in this vicinity acted as guide for the Heidelberg burghers and led us in the exact direction in spite of the fog.

'The Heidelberg Commando consisted of about 200 men. We rode through a huge marsh where our horses had to tread carefully to avoid being trapped in the deep mud. The moon came up and when the fog lifted for a moment, one could see our commando crawling like a gigantic snake over the veld. Such a nocturnal advance has a special attraction. The objective was to get as close as possible to the enemy and then to suddenly attack. We did not know exactly where the British camp was situated.

'Suddenly we halted and jumped from the saddle. We were still busy tying up our horses when fire was opened on us. We immediately charged forward on the order of Field Cornet Biccard and answered the enemy fire. Soon there was a heavy battle raging. As a result of the fogginess and the moonshine we could not see well. Our only indication of the enemy position was the flashes of their rifles when they themselves fired on us. As we charged we probably formed good targets for the enemy and it was not long before a few men were hit. We had no cover whatsoever. Such a nocturnal battle, in which you can only identify your enemy by the flashes of their rifles, is a frightful experience. You know that the moment you shoot you become a target for the enemy fire.

'The enemy was in a strong position, since instead of only one they had parallel rows of trenches. A full-scale charge would be necessary to dislodge them. Soon I heard the order: "Charge, Heidelberg, charge!" I kneeled to reload my rifle. The moment I rose a heavy blow struck my left cheek and I fell on my back. I immediately realised that I was wounded. I touched my face with my hands – they were covered in blood. I could feel the warm blood on my chest and then the terrible thought came to me: "and what about my dear wife?" And then I thought of my dear, elderly parents and I said to myself: "No, no, I cannot remain on my back here, even if I am dying."

'Suddenly Commandant Kunze was at my side. He helped me up. "Come with me, you are badly wounded," he said. I picked up my reliable old Mauser and my hat and walked with Kunze. I could feel my strength slipping. Kunze helped me on my horse and jumped in the saddle himself. We rode away from the scene of the battle. I felt as tired as if I had not slept at all for a whole night. I was thirsty and wanted something to drink. Only then did I realise that my bottom lip and left jaw had been totally shot away. I couldn't take in anything.

'Soon after dawn we reached Rademeyer's farm. His wife did her utmost to help us. Suddenly the bombs began bursting around us and we had to go on. I was still bleeding. The blood literally dripped all the way to my boots and my clothes were wet. Even my saddle and my horse were red with blood. After about two hours we finally reached an ambulance, but Doctor Bierens de Haan was still at the battlefront. He only arrived an hour later. By then the soldiers were on us and our comrades took leave of us. Thus we fell into the hands of the enemy, but they treated us well.

'After a night in which I slept peacefully thanks to a morphine injection, I felt somewhat stronger.

'Later that morning a huge number of Khakis arrived and these worked roughly with us. Even though some of us were badly wounded, they loaded us in a wagon and we were taken away. The Khakis totally wrecked our ambulance – something that Doctor de Haan seriously complained about. All the medicine, all the bandages, blankets, everything was destroyed or looted.

'After spending the night of 7 February in a tent in the British camp, we were loaded on an open wagon without any springs and taken to Ermelo the next day. It was a merciless journey in the rain and I experienced a lot of pain. That evening some soldiers pitied us and gave us not only a tent, but also some coffee. It is clear that there are some English soldiers who have some empathy for their fellow men.

'That day I heard that both the highly regarded and beloved Field Cornet Dolf Spruyt and Field Cornet John Biccard of Heidelberg had been killed. That news made me sad. Under those circumstances we continued on our journey to Ermelo the next morning. What a torment! A Boer girl gave me a little bit of milk and water with a teaspoon. That quenched my worst thirst, but I was very hungry and experienced severe pain. The wagon bumped unceasingly and my wound started bleeding again. I thought I was losing my faculties due to the pain. At last we reached Ermelo by three o'clock that afternoon where we were taken up in the Boer hospital. It was fantastic to rest in a clean bed after four days of suffering. The nurses gave me egg mixed with milk that I drank by means of a little pipe. I am feeling better now and believe that I will recover.'

DE WET, HERTZOG BACK IN THE FREE STATE

Burghers extremely tired after exhausting expedition

In the veld near Bothasdrif, 28 February – General Christiaan de Wet, accompanied by President Steyn and the Free State government, has been persevering in his attempts to spread the war into the Cape Colony. However, a combination of bad weather and the poor condition of the horses of the majority of the burghers slowed down progress to such an extent that they were forced to abandon their venture. Fortunately most the burghers managed to return to the Orange Free State unscathed.

At the end of last month, when he and Steyn decided on the invasion, De Wet was still in the northeastern Free State. It was a difficult undertaking from the start. Heavy rains had caused the Orange River to flow strongly, which made it difficult to cross. In addition, the Khakis thoroughly guarded all the river crossings. Consequently De Wet spread all sorts of false rumours in an attempt to confuse the enemy. Early in February General Stoffel Froneman and his burghers managed to capture a British supply train on the main railway line south of Bloemfontein near Jagersfontein by destroying the railway lines on both sides of it. Since the burghers were low on supplies, they helped themselves freely to saddles, blankets and ammunition before setting the train alight.

On Thursday 7 February De Wet and his commando crossed the railway line between Springfontein and Jagersfontein and proceeded to Philippolis. They moved as fast as possible, but the rain-soaked road meant that the mules struggled to haul the heavy guns and the oxen experienced similar difficulties with the wagons. Unfortunately three commandants, Michael Prinsloo, Andries van Tonder and P.W. de Vos, with 800 men, refused to leave the Free State. De Wet nevertheless pushed on. His commando now consisted of far less than 2 000 burghers.

CROSSING THE ORANGE RIVER TO THE SOUTH

De Wet sent the Theron Scout Corps ahead to ascertain if it would be possible to cross the Orange River at Sanddrift. One of the members of the Corps is a French volunteer of noble descent, the Marquis Robert de Kersauson de Pennendreff. He told our correspondent that when they reached the river at about ten o'clock on the morning of 9 February, it was flowing strongly. It would certainly have been impossible for wagons and carts to cross. They turned back to a clump of trees to rest and enjoy their lunch.

At about three o'clock that afternoon the Scout Corps returned to the river. To their delight the water level had receded considerably. By five o'clock they had decided that it was safe enough to attempt a crossing. Soon afterwards everybody had removed their clothing, rolled it into bundles with their blankets and tied it to their saddles. The crossing then began. Some took the stirrups in their hands and led their horses through. Others crossed while clinging to the tails of their horses. Eventually all of them were safely on the south bank of the Orange River.

Commandant Jan Theron, the commander of the Scout Corps, immediately sent out patrols in various directions to ascertain if there were Khakis in the vicinity. Sentries were posted and when night set in fires were made to dry their clothes. They were very excited to be in the Cape Colony at last. To express their feelings of joy they sang the anthems of the two Republics as well as numerous other commando songs. To their delight they heard singing from the northern bank soon afterwards, indicating that De Wet's commando had arrived. Indeed, those burghers crossed the river the next day, 10 February, with their guns, carts and wagons.

After resting for a day south of the river, the commando was on the move again. Since the Khakis were continually at their heels, they had to move forward without rest. On 12 February a British unit became involved in a skirmish with a group of burghers north of Hamelsfontein. A section of about 24 burghers under Commandant Wynand Malan and Corporal Manie Maritz were cut off from the rest of the commando and are now moving deep into the Cape Colony on their own. With the British at their heels De Wet and the rest of the burghers proceeded to the west. On 13 February they had to leave behind about 200 horses that were simply too weak to go on. There was not enough pasture since the locusts had eaten up everything. The burghers now had to walk, since there were no horses to commandeer in this vicinity.

TOUGH GOING THROUGH A MARSH AND ACROSS THE RAILWAY LINE

After it had rained endlessly throughout the night, the Khakis attacked the commando again on 14 February at Wolwekuil near Philipstown. The burghers inflicted heavy casualties on the reckless attackers, then continued on their way to the west. A major challenge lay ahead, since they had to cross a marsh after a heavy downpour. Even though the marsh was only about a kilometre wide, the water was knee-deep or more. This would not have been a problem if the bottom of the marsh had not been extremely muddy, but as it was, the horses sank to their knees into the mud and found it difficult to go on with the water reaching to their backs. And 1 400 mounted burghers had to go through. Many of the burghers dismounted or fell from their struggling horses and had to haul the poor animals through the marsh.

It was even more difficult to get the wagons and the guns through the marsh. The men had to inspan 50 oxen at the same time to haul one gun. The heavy ammunition wagons could not get through at all. De Wet decided to proceed with everybody who was through the marsh and left General Fourie behind to attempt to get the wagons through before daybreak. Fourie did his utmost, but could not get a single wagon to the other side. In the end he torched everything.

Soon after daybreak on 15 February, De Wet and his commando crossed the De Aar-Kimberley railway line unhindered. Even though he and his men had by then been trekking continuously in pouring rain for 24 hours, and had a night of physical exertion behind them, they proceeded for another two hours till they found sufficient grazing for their animals. Only then did they slaughter a few sheep and grill some meat before sleep got the better of them. After a very welcome and mercifully peaceful rest they moved off towards Strydenburg early the next morning. De Wet hoped to join Hertzog's commando there.

The enemy was still hot on their heels. On Sunday 17 February the Khakis caught up with De Wet's rearguard, which was commanded by Commandant Sarel Haasbroek. He and his burghers retreated to Gelukspoort. On the following day De Wet and his commando shook off their pursuers temporarily and rested at Vroupan. His position improved somewhat when the burghers managed to capture 200 horses, enabling many men to be mounted again.

DIFFICULT RETURN TO THE FREE STATE

On 19 February the enemy cornered De Wet's commando a short distance south of Prieska against the Brak River, which was in flood. Since it was impossible to cross the river, De Wet had only one option: he would have to return to the Free State. Under cover of the dark night he and his burghers retreated north up to the Orange River and then to the east. On 21 February they rested near Blaauwkop. The next day they found a boat next to the river. It was rather small but they decided to use it to cross the Orange. De Wet first ordered the men who had no horses to go, 10–12 at a time. By sundown about 250 men were on the other side but then the British were upon them and De Wet and the burghers who were still on the southern side had to proceed further to the east. Since they had no artillery ammunition left and the mules were exhausted, they abandoned a field gun and a rapid-fire gun. Unfortunately they had no dynamite to destroy those field pieces, and the Khakis would certainly capture them and use them against the Boers in future, but there was no other way out.

On Sunday 24 February De Wet and his burghers crossed the Kimberley–De Aar railway line about 12 kilometres south of the Orange River Station. They could not cross the flooded river itself, since all the drifts were unusable. In their search for a drift they proceeded further east with the Khakis at their heels.

As for General Hertzog and his burghers, they had been informed that De Wet planned to invade the Cape Colony at the beginning of this month and decided to join them. Consequently they left Vanrhynsdorp on 3 February and proceeded to the northeast. By Saturday 16 February Hertzog and his commando were approaching the village Britstown from the south when they were informed that a British force would attempt to cut them off.

Hertzog thereupon divided his commando into two groups. He himself proceeded with one group to Strydenburg, while Commandant Brand went to Britstown to gather supplies. The two groups rejoined forces again on 22 February at Zwingelpan, west of Strydenburg. The next day they entered that village and commandeered supplies. On 25 February they crossed the Kimberley–De Aar railway line at Poupan and destroyed part of the line with dynamite.

Early yesterday (27 February) Hertzog and his commando joined De Wet's commando on the southern side of the Orange River. Looking for a fordable drift, they proceeded further east and early this morning reached Bothasdrif, some 25 kilometres west of Norvalspont, after another night without rest. This was the 25th drift since they turned around at the Brak River, and at last the determination of the burghers paid off. The drift was fordable and the men crossed as quickly as possible. Cries of joy, hymns and other religious songs were on their lips as they trampled through the water back to the Free State. What a terrible expedition they had behind them!

And now, what about the future? De Wet and his Free Staters intend to rest for a short while. And then the Chief Commandant says they will resume the battle with renewed energy in the Orange Free State.

FROM THE EDITOR

There were no major battles last month. Early in February Commandant-General Louis Botha was involved in a skirmish at Chrissiesmeer, but could not gain the upper hand. To date, huge British forces have failed in their attempts to drive the Boers against their blockhouse lines.

Chief Commandant De Wet attempted once more to spread the battlefront to the Cape Colony. However, the weather was not in his favour and the burghers' horses were so weak that he was, as reported in this issue, forced to return to the Orange Free State after suffering untold hardships.

The clearest indication up to now that the British are becoming desperate to end the war is Lord Kitchener's attempt right at the end of last month to convince Commandant-General Botha to lay down arms. Our Commander-General made it clear to him that we will stop fighting only if our independence is guaranteed. On that condition our leaders are unanimous. The war will not end until the British abandon their obstinate demand that we lose our freedom.

OUR MILITARY OFFICERS

Chief Corporal Wilhelm Mangold

The military officer we highlight this month is Wilhelm Friedrich Christiaan Mangold of the Heidelberg Commando. He is well known not only for his frequent reports for us, but also for the courageous way in which he has used every opportunity to do his duty in this war for freedom and justice.

Mangold was born at Doornkop in Natal in 1872. His parents had immigrated a few years previously from Germany to South Africa. His father had been a soldier in Europe and participated *inter alia* in the Crimean War. In Natal he became a builder and a farmer. Mangold grew up on the farm where he was born. From his sixth year he attended the Mission School at Kirchdorf. When he was 16 he moved to Heidelberg in the Transvaal, where be became a builder, tombstone mason and a Transvaal burgher. Soon afterwards he married Louise Niesewand. She is 16 years older than he is and they have no children.

Mangold's own military career began in 1898 when he participated in the Republican campaign against the Bavenda. With the outbreak of this war he immediately joined the Republican forces, since he has completely wedded himself to the Boer cause. He has fought on numerous fronts and is one of the most loyal burghers. We trust that he will recover completely from his severe wounds and will soon be able to resume the battle against our arch-enemy.

Wilhelm Mangold

Boer farmhouse before Khakis blew it up and below the same house being blown up

THE War Reporter
MONTHLY EDITION

Number 51 — In the Veld, South African Republic — 1 April 1901

MILITARY DEVELOPMENTS
ORANGE FREE STATE: GENERAL PHILIP BOTHA KILLED

Eastern Free State, 31 March – On 7 March one of the most courageous and able Free State officers, General Philip Botha, was killed in a skirmish with the Khakis at Doornberg in the district of Ventersburg. He was the elder brother of Commandant-General Louis Botha. His death is a blow to the Republican forces in the northern Free State.

After Chief Commandant De Wet and his burghers returned to the Free State from the Cape at the end of last month, the commandos split into small groups. In De Wet's opinion, the time for huge set battles has passed and it will be better if the Boers form numerous groups, since the British will then also have to divide. For that reason he sent General Piet Fourie to the southeastern districts and General Hertzog to the southwestern districts of the Free State. President Steyn and the government have temporarily joined General Hertzog. De Wet himself, accompanied by a small bodyguard, moved northwards from Philippolis. By 11 March they had reached the Senekal district.

WESTERN TRANSVAAL

Magaliesberg, 31 March – A few inconclusive skirmishes took place between the Republican forces and the Khakis last month in the western Transvaal. Unfortunately the Republicans suffered a number of severe setbacks, including the death of well-known and capable officers and the loss of valuable equipment. On the other hand, the British forces were, in spite of their numerical advantage, in some cases badly bruised by our burghers.

On 2 February General Jan Kemp managed to outwit a huge British column at Dwarsvlei. From there he proceeded in the direction of Lichtenburg with his burghers to join forces with General Koos de la Rey. The latter, in the meantime, had conceived a plan to overrun the British garrison in Lichtenburg. This garrison consisted of approximately 750 men with two guns. They had thoroughly entrenched themselves behind fortifications and erected a barbed wire fence around the whole town. In addition they had constructed a fort with high earth walls in the middle of the town. These defensive works, combined with the presence of marshes east, south and west of the town, made Lichtenburg a difficult target. On the other hand, the town was a long distance away from any other British garrison, which meant that no units would be able to rush quickly to the rescue. For that reason De la Rey decided to attack.

On the day of Kemp's retreat from Dwarsvlei, 1 200 burghers under the command of Generals Liebenberg, Celliers and Smuts gathered at Zoetmelksvlei, about 10 kilometres west of Lichtenburg. De la Rey explained his plan of attack to the officers. Very early the next morning, Sunday 3 February, the Boers went into action. Unfortunately coordination was weak and General Liebenberg and his Potchefstroom burghers made contact with the enemy too early. A wild shooting match followed. After that it was impossible for the other burghers to surprise the enemy. The battle went on for the whole day. In the end only Commandant Hendrik Vermaas and his Lichtenburg burghers actually reached the main fortifications in the centre of the town. They could not force the Khakis to surrender, however, and eventually left the town again after sunset. That was when both sides agreed on an armistice of two hours to tend to their wounded.

After the fight De la Rey remarked: 'The enemy got a good hiding today and so did I.' Indeed, the Republican losses were higher than those of the Khakis. Both General Cilliers and Commandant L.A.S. Lemmer of Marico were wounded early in the battle and Field Cornet Blignaut of Marico was killed. In the end a total of 14 burghers were killed and 38 wounded, while the British losses amounted to 18 killed and 24 wounded.

On 22 March a British reconnaissance patrol suddenly appeared on the farm Geduld, north of Hartbeesfontein. The burghers saw them and surrounded them in a kraal. The British authorities immediately sent a force of 250 men to relieve the patrol. General De la Rey became aware of this and attacked the British task force. The Khakis barely managed to get away and reach their camp at Hartbeesfontein. In the skirmish at Geduld at least seven Khakis were killed and 13 wounded. The Boer loss was one man killed and one, namely General Jan Smuts, lightly wounded.

Two days after this incident a British mounted force launched a surprise attack on De la Rey and Kemp's convoy on the farms Wildfontein and Kafferskraal near Ventersdorp. The Khakis placed such severe pressure on the burghers that they were forced to abandon some of their guns, wagons and carts. Thus two of the Armstrong guns, captured by our burghers at Colenso in December 1899, are now back in the hands of the Khakis. In addition the latter took 140 burghers prisoner of war.

General Philip Botha and his staff on commando

CAPE REBELS

In the veld, 31 March – News from the Cape Colony is that the British authorities had four Cape Afrikaners shot last month on charges of actively supporting the Republican forces. The first was Hendrik van Heerden, a farmer of the farm Sewefontein near Cradock. A small group of Khakis arrested him after finding the tracks of a Boer commando on his farm. While Van Heerden and his escort were on their way to Cradock, the Boers attacked them and Van Heerden was wounded. The British left him with a woman who treated his wounds, but shortly afterwards returned and told him that he had been found guilty of treason since he had supported a Boer commando, and had been sentenced to death. Minutes later they took him away and a firing squad shot him on his own farm. His wife buried his remains. This happened on 2 March.

Exactly a week later, on 9 March, the British executed three Cape Afrikaners on charges that they were involved in the derailing by Commandant Wynand Malan's commando of a train at Taaibosch near De Aar. The executed men were Karel Nienaber, Petrus Nienaber and Jan Nieuwoudt.

Not all the news of the Cape Rebels is tragic. On Sunday 10 March a rebel commando occupied Aberdeen and released all the prisoners from the village's jail. Nine days later Commandant Gideon Scheepers and his commando were in the Jansenville district. A group of armed Coloureds fired on them from a farmhouse. Scheepers's men captured two of those Coloureds and executed them. In addition they released two Cape rebels and 10 Coloureds from prison.

Hendrik van Heerden  | **Petrus Nienaber**  | **Jan Nieuwoudt**

FROM THE EDITOR

Another month has gone, and it seems as if the British government is even less prepared than Lord Kitchener is to end the war. Commandant-General Louis Botha's opinion that the British government will not be satisfied with anything less than the complete eradication of the Afrikaner people seems entirely justified. In the meantime, they are destroying their own national pride and honour by waging war on women and children. From reports in this issue, however, our readers will note that neither the burghers in the veld, nor the prisoners of war, nor the women in the concentration camps are prepared to submit that easily. The pride of the Afrikaner people is much tougher than the Khakis had ever dreamed to find it.

THE TRAGEDY OF THE CONCENTRATION CAMPS
Emily Hobhouse reveals evil conditions

Cape Town, 26 March – The British establishment of so-called refugee camps in which the homeless civilians of the Republics – who are homeless since the British destroyed their houses – are locked up like animals in a pound, is increasingly becoming a tragedy. From the Cape we have heard that the camps are at present referred to as concentration camps. From the beginning of this month these camps will no longer be under military management, but directly under control of Governor Sir Alfred Milner. Hopefully the situation will now drastically improve, since if the mistreatment of women and children in the camps continues, the camps will soon be known as death camps.

Towards the middle of March the British authorities in the Orange Free State issued an order stating that they will remove all the civilians from the farms and destroy all surplus supplies on the farms, including all the grain and fodder. Furthermore they will remove all livestock and horses and break up all baking ovens and mills. Hundreds of farmhouses have been burnt down. One begins to wonder if there will eventually be anything left, or if the Republics will be turned into a desolate wasteland.

An interesting development this month was the visit of Miss Emily Hobhouse to numerous camps in the southern Free State and northern Cape. This English-

Continued overleaf

continued

woman has earned general recognition for her sharp and uncompromising criticism of the concentration camp system. Miss Hobhouse recently had a long talk with one of our correspondents. During

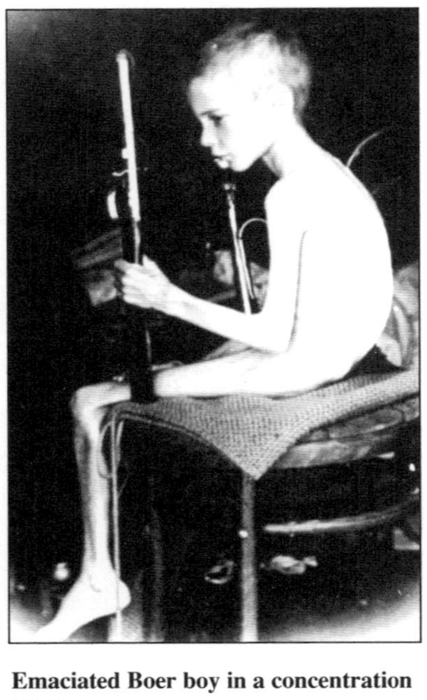

Emaciated Boer boy in a concentration camp

this conversation she provided valuable but at times shocking information. She says that she had a long interview with Milner in Cape Town in January, during which the latter conceded that the destruction of the farms was a mistake and that an improvement in the treatment of the women and children was absolutely essential. Unfortunately he did not indicate what improvement he had in mind.

Soon after her arrival in Bloemfontein towards the end of January Miss Hobhouse had a meeting with Major R.B. Cray, who is in command of all the camps in the Orange Free State. Cray complained to her that he was in a hopeless position, since there was simply no money to buy essentials such as warm clothing. In addition he lacks wagons and does not have the necessary rank to put issues in order. It frustrates him tremendously to note that things are wrong, but to see that nobody in any position of authority cares about that.

Miss Hobhouse says that she was speechless with shock about the conditions in the camps that she visited. The rows upon rows of tents are pitched in the open veld with no trees to provide shade. Inside the round bell tents it is stuffy and hot and there is usually no furniture – only British military blankets and perhaps an empty soap box to serve as table. When it rains, the inhabitants of the tents become wet since they all sleep on the

Concentration camp at Howick in Natal

ground and the water flows underneath the flaps. Many of the tent inhabitants, especially children, are lying sick on the ground in the tents. Miss Hobhouse says they look so emaciated and lifeless that they seem like withered flowers that have been thrown out from a vase. There is hardly any medicine and no soap, with the result that the children are not properly cleaned. The parents do not want their children to go to the hospital tent, since hardly any person returns alive. Most of the ill people are suffering from either measles or typhus fever.

Miss Hobhouse says that conditions in the concentration camp at Norvalspont are much better than in Bloemfontein, especially since there is sufficient fresh, clean water. But even there all the patients who have thus far been put in the hospital have died, since there are not enough trained medical personnel. The Camp Commandant, Captain du Plat Taylor, is sympathetic towards the people in the camp and he has seen to it that the soldiers built a tennis court, since he believes that the camp inhabitants should get some exercise. He plans to build two more courts soon. In addition he intends to establish a school for the children and to distribute clothing to those who have nothing.

The camp at Aliwal North is also in the eyes of Miss Hobhouse in an acceptable condition, since the commander, Major J.K. Apthorpe, concentrates on sympathetic and orderly administration.

The British authorities make a huge error if they believe that the camps will destroy the courage and faith of the Boer women in future. Miss Hobhouse says that the handsupper and former Boer general Piet de Wet visited the camp in Bloemfontein and attempted to convince the women to pressurise their husbands to surrender their arms. A huge number of women were present. At the end of his speech De Wet looked directly at a Mrs Botha and asked for her support. She looked deep into his eyes without saying a word, then shook her head, turned around and walked back to her tent in deathly silence, with all the other women following her. The poor pawn De Wet was left deserted on his platform.

NO EARLY PEACE AGREEMENT POSSIBLE

BRITISH EXTEND CONDITIONS; IMPOSSIBLE FOR REPUBLICS TO AGREE

In the veld in the eastern Transvaal, 30 March – Last month we reported on Commandant-General Louis Botha's negotiations with the British commander-in-chief, Lord Kitchener, in Middelburg, Transvaal. Hope rose in the hearts of many burghers that the war would soon be something of the past. In the meantime this hope has disappeared, since the British government seems to have extended the already far too strict conditions proposed by Kitchener. For the Boers it is totally impossible to comply with the British demands. The war goes on.

Since a number of false rumours had been spread amongst the burghers with regard to the Middelburg talks, Botha issued a statement on 16 March in which he explained the situation. After giving a review of his talks with Kitchener on 28 February, Botha mentioned the contents of a letter sent to him by Kitchener on 7 March. In this letter new conditions for an agreement were stated to the Republics. Botha immediately answered that he would forward the conditions to the Transvaal government, but added that Kitchener would obviously not be surprised, in the light of their talks in Middelburg, 'that I do not feel inclined to recommend to my government to seriously consider the terms proposed in the letter. I may add that my government and all my chief officers agree totally with my views.'

In addition to the above letter to Kitchener, Botha sent an open letter to all the burghers.

In this he stated right at the outset that the spirit of Kitchener's letter to him made it clear that the British government demanded nothing less than the demise of the Afrikaner people. The conditions were unacceptable. In the proposed political system, the voice of the people was not recognised at all. Our existence as a people was threatened. The war had already cost a lot of blood and tears, but it would be doubly difficult to let go of our country. Let us place our faith in God as Daniel did in the lion's den, Botha wrote, since He will show us the way out in His time and His way.

PRISONERS OF WAR ON ST HELENA ISLAND

In the veld in the eastern Transvaal, 2 March – One of the members of the Hollander Corps who was taken prisoner at Elandslaagte in October 1899, Leendert Ruijssenaers, has again managed to smuggle a report on conditions in the camp at St Helena Island to us through a sympathetic intermediary. Last year we published a report by this same author, but since then we have heard nothing further from the prisoners of war. For that reason this news, even though a bit dated, will be welcome to all our readers who have relatives on St Helena. Ruijssenaers writes:

'It is today the 1st of January 1901 and we have been here in Deadwood Camp for exactly eight months. In general things are going well with our men, since no major catastrophe such as a deadly epidemic has struck us. This does not mean that we are living in a paradise where everything is milk and honey. Not at all. We are prisoners and we have virtually no rights or privileges.

'At one stage the water pumps to our camp were blocked and we had to get along without water for a few days. We had only enough for one kettle of coffee per day. All of us looked and smelled like baboons, but fortunately there are no saloon mirrors here in which we can see ourselves. It was wonderful to be able to wash and shave and clean our clothes again after the pipes were repaired.

'We are now getting the opportunity to leave the camp every now and then. There is not much to see on St Helena, but we make the best of what there is. Thus we visit the grave site of the famous Emperor Napoleon. It is on one of the most beautiful spots in the island, deep down in the Geranium Valley, where the most beautiful wild flowers grow. There is a crystal clear stream where Napoleon preferred to drink water. It is said that he himself requested to be buried there. However, his remains are no longer there since he was interred in Paris.

'We also enjoy visiting Longwood, the house in which Napoleon lived here on the island. One day we even visited the Emperor's death room. There is no furniture in the room, but only a bronze bust of him with a laurel on his head in the corner where he breathed his last. After signing your name in the large visitor's book, you have seen the two most important sights on the island.

'Each 14 days or three weeks we have to dig a deep furrow at the camp for sanitary purposes. Each prisoner takes a turn to help. Some who are too highly bred or purely too lazy, refuse this work and receive five days' imprisonment. For that period they are locked up in a tent and guarded by an armed guard. They receive their normal ration of food but may not read or smoke and are doomed to five days of doing nothing.

'Each Sunday the English priest of the English church holds a church parade and service for the English soldiers. About 50 Boer prisoners who claim that they belong to the English church attend the ceremony on Sundays. They are traitors, these Boers, despicable traders of their land, who are not worth the value of the rope on which they should be hung. After the sermon the orchestra always plays the English anthem and all the soldiers join in singing 'God save the Queen'. Those 50 criminals are not ashamed to solemnly partake in the ceremony. When human beings receive the punishment they deserve, these criminals should not be overlooked.

'In July 1900 approximately 30 Boers signed a request to take the oath of allegiance to the British queen. The other Boers were extremely angry and held a large meeting to discuss taking action against the traitors. Commandant M.J. Wolmarans of Potchefstroom took the lead and declared that it was a shame to be wavering, while the blood of your brothers was flowing for your freedom and your fatherland. We had to talk to those traitors in a brotherly way, but if they persisted in their scheme we could not guarantee their life and safety, since nobody wanted to mingle with traitors. Subsequently we sang our anthem to the frustration of the English officers who were peering at us from behind our tents like naughty boys. The next day the holding of meetings in the camp was prohibited.

'One of the Afrikaners in Deadwood Camp who was given leave to work outside the camp is the blacksmith, Charles Smith, who in July 1900 married a local beauty. For most of the Boers it is shameful that one of their people has married a Coloured women and the whole camp was upset by this. It seems as if Smith and his wife are still happily married.

'In the course of time literally hundreds of houses or huts made of tin, old sacks and biscuit boxes arose in our camp. This little town is known as *Blikkiesdorp* (Tin Town). It is much easier to live in such a hut than with 12 men in a tent. At the same time a number of industries have emerged in our camp. Thus there are men who bake pancakes that they sell for two pennies per pancake with sugar and a cup of tea or coffee with sugar. Furthermore there are suitcase manufacturers who assemble the most beautiful suitcases from old biscuit boxes. Other prisoners of war make miniature ox-wagons and other types of carts and sell them to the English officers as souvenirs. There are also pipe makers, photographers, artists and even canteen keepers. Notwithstanding a strict prohibition on strong liquor in the camp, there are always flasks that find their way to these canteen keepers, and there are always buyers for liquor, since the Boers enjoy their drink now and then. In October last year the Camp Commandant heard that strong liquor enters our camp. The tell-tale pointed out the tin house in which the canteen keeper, Kootjie Doeleman, practised his business. A whole squad of soldiers pounced on the house, confiscated all the supplies and broke the place down. Doeleman was sentenced to 14 days in prison to give him time to think about all his sins.

'In November last year the imprisoned members of the former Hollander Corps built a large hall with the name *TOT NUT EN VERMAAK* (for use and leisure). The walls are of poles, old bags and pieces of flat iron and inside there are pews as well as long tables on which there are books and all types of periodicals. For a penny one can buy a cup of coffee or tea. On the opening evening the Dutchmen performed a drama titled "The beautiful Helena or the Virgin of Blikkiesdorp". The hall was especially decorated with green branches and flowers. All the actors were prisoners and the Boers laughed heartily.

'On the day before Christmas the Hollanders got permission to fell a huge tree in the government forest and erect it in the hall as Christmas tree. They decorated it and on Christmas Eve held a big festival during which all sorts of presents that had been received from Holland, especially cigars and tobacco, were distributed amongst the prisoners of war.

'A large number of us have been prisoners of war for this whole year. It was a long year, but now that it is past it seems to have been short. Are we going to be prisoners of war for another whole year? Unfortunately our fate is not within our control.'

OUR MILITARY OFFICERS

Commandant Hendrik Vermaas

Hendrik Cornelius Wilhelmus Vermaas was born in 1851. He became a farmer in the Ottosdal district. Before the war he was the assistant field cornet for Lichtenburg and when the war broke out 18 months ago, he was already Commandant of the Lichtenburg Commando. He is a respected inhabitant of the district and represented Lichtenburg on the Second Volksraad from 1891 to 1897.

In the first phase of the war Vermaas served on the western and southwestern fronts. The British occupation of the Republican capitals depressed him to such an extent that he considered giving up hope. In the course of time, however, he took up the struggle again. His heroic leadership of his burghers at Lichtenburg in the past month underlines his inborn leadership talents.

Commandant Hendrik Vermaas

THE War Reporter
MONTHLY EDITION

Number 52   In the Veld, South African Republic   1 May 1901

KRUGER AND THE REPUBLICAN DEPUTATION STILL ACTIVE IN EUROPE

Hilversum, 20 April – Even though there seems to be no realistic possibility now that foreign powers will intervene on the side of the Republics in their struggle for freedom, both President Kruger and the Republican deputation are still striving to turn the tide. Unfortunately it had become clear even before Kruger's arrival in Europe about six months ago that intervention was not on the agenda of any European power. This remains the case, although it seems as if the British people themselves may begin questioning the wisdom of going on with the war.

The deputation is doing all it can to enable justice to be victorious. Early in 1901 it approached the Permanent Court of Arbitration on the advice of the Dutch Minister of Foreign Affairs. This attempt failed, since only two countries that are members of the Court are prepared to take up the case, namely Switzerland and the United States of America.

Another failed attempt was Abraham Fischer's visit to the Vatican to convince the Pope to express himself in favour of justice for the Republics. On 20 January Fischer actually had an audience with Cardinal Rampolla, the State Secretary of Pope Leo XIII. The Cardinal informed him that the Pope would have liked to help, but that the British stance made any successful intervention from his side impossible.

President Kruger has been received by foremost politicians and heads of state in a number of European countries, but has failed to secure definite promises of intervention. In November last year he met President Loubert of France, while in Holland he has been the guest of Queen Wilhelmina on a number of occasions.

The failure of the deputation and of President Kruger's attempts to convince the European powers to intervene on the Republican side in the war is a great setback. The only glimmer of light is that public opinion in most countries remains enthusiastic in support of the Republican cause and loudly applauds every Boer victory. At each station where President Kruger arrives by train, huge crowds greet him and his party with loud acclamation. The representatives of the cities and the corporations and of various societies usually greet them with banners and addresses of welcome.

President Kruger waving to well-wishers from the balcony of the Hotel des Indes in The Hague

The President spent a few weeks in The Hague, Netherlands, where he received medical treatment for an eye infection. In addition he became very ill when a cold struck him and developed into influenza. Fortunately his condition, which was quite alarming, has now improved. He next went to Utrecht, where he stayed for 10 weeks and his eyes were successfully operated on.

On 6 April the President and his party arrived here in Hilversum, where they

Abraham Fischer

were welcomed by thousands of enthusiastic Hollanders. They are staying in Villa Casa Cara and plan to make it their base for the resumption of their campaign to recruit support for the Republics in Europe.

HARD TIMES IN THE VELD IN EASTERN TRANSVAAL
Blacks increasingly involved: Boer freedom of movement restricted

Eastern Transvaal, 30 April – With the winter approaching, conditions in the veld in eastern Transvaal have become critical in the past months. Women and children are locked in an intense battle to survive and to avoid being molested by Khakis or blacks. One of our burghers, Frederik Rothmann, sent us the following report of his experiences in the veld in that area:

'Dullstroom was in a sorry state even before the British occupied it again earlier this month. There had been 30 houses. With the exception of two and also the church, the rest were torched or blown up with dynamite by the Khakis. Women with small children lived within the ruins under sheets of corrugated iron until the British took them away. The district was densely populated, but the Khakis had burnt down all the houses. When a Khaki arrives at a house, he gives the wife 10 minutes to gather all the children and some supplies. If the occupants take too much, in the opinion of the Khakis, they throw everything back and set it alight. Sometimes while the housewife is busy gathering her last belongings, the Khakis tell blacks or Coloureds to take everything from her.

'Mrs Steenkamp, a widow of Skoonpoort, was treated very shamefully. Her daughter with her nine children lived with her. The daughter is also a widow, since her husband was killed in Natal early in the war. The women loaded all their belongings, including an old plough, on the wagon. A Coloured man told the officer of the burning party that the woman wanted to plough again to produce food and convinced him to destroy the plough. The whole wagon was immediately set alight and the women and nine children, all of them girls, saw all their property, including their linen and clothing, go up in flames. They have nothing left but the clothes on their bodies. Nevertheless the women are still facing up bravely where they are living under a fig tree. The mother of the children told me: "My only regret is that my daughters are not boys, since then they could kill the Khakis."

'At Belfast, the British dynamited the memorial commemorating the burghers killed in the Transvaal War of Independence.

'The Lydenburg Commando has virtually ceased to exist; the farmers either returned to their houses or trekked with a wagon and their families into the veld, rather than stay with the commando; the whole force of Commandant Schoeman consists of no more than 60 or 70 men. There is hardly any ammunition left for the few field guns we still have. No resistance could be expected from the Lydenburgers when the British went on the attack again by the middle of this month.

'Commandant Schoeman and his men decided to trek along the Dwars River to the Highveld with about 1 000 head of livestock, when they were unexpectedly attacked from behind by a commando of black warriors led by Khakis. Every man had to flee for his own life and virtually all the livestock fell into the hands of the blacks. We found shelter in the mountains and came upon about 30 families there. What would their fate be if the blacks were to discover them? I advised the families to return to the town and fall into the hands of the Khakis rather than be murdered by the blacks. Not that the Khakis leave the women in peace. Their mounted soldiers chase the women, capture them in the bushes and ravines and take them away as prisoners of war. Some are on wagons but others have to go on foot with a child on the one arm and another child by the hand. And then the British fire on the defenceless families with their fierce Maxim gun.

'In the Watervals River area conditions are even worse. Here a British commando of about 800 men with two batteries of artillery is active. They are accompanied by a black commando 'to clean into all the corners', as they state it. Where farms are some distance from the main road, the blacks look for the farmhouses and capture the men, women and children and take them to their employers. Along the whole Watervals River not more than 30 families were living and there was no Republican commando. But these families were not overlooked. A British officer took one woman from her house. She was allowed to take only one blanket and the clothes they were wearing for her and her child. The house with all its contents was then given over to the blacks to plunder. It is hard to imagine what the future now has in store for the poor woman.

'As for the burghers in the veld: they no longer think of battles – only of firing here on one or two, 10 or 20 Khakis. All the time we are on the lookout for the Khakis. If they annoy us on one mountain, we trek to the other one. The Khakis destroy our coffee mills if they find them – since they have heard that we are using them to grind our maize. When we have no coffee mills left, we will grind maize with round stones. It will be quite a task for the Khakis to destroy all the stones.'

Another burgher, Roland Schikkerling, told our correspondent of the Boers' flight in mid-April to escape from the British offensive north of Belfast: 'In wagons, in carts, on horseback and on foot came the men. Trekboers with their wagons, families, and cattle came, men, women, and children, many barefooted, driving oxen, cows, and sheep. All these trekboers had constantly fled before the enemy, but now realised that their independence had shrunk to this, and that for them the vast Transvaal had narrowed down to these few stony hills …

'Shall I ever forget the sight? The shouting and confusion of the excited people, each with his wagon, mule, or donkey, to which he desperately clung, loading and preparing to get away or meditating whether to remain and surrender. Oxen and mules were being inspanned and outspanned by women, many of whom were once wealthy but who, on account of their husbands being rebels, had fled their homes in Natal and the Cape Colony. Wandering about with the commandos with which they remained for safety, they had slowly shed the bulk of their fortunes. These unfortunate people were now to lose the last of their possessions. Many women sat in their wagons weeping, and even some men sobbed unrestrainedly. One girl of about 18, barefoot, and with hardly a dress to her body, was all alone catching and harnessing donkeys. No one cared to help her, all of them being too engaged in their own affairs.'

Blacks serving in the British Army

FROM THE EDITOR

On the battlefront the situation has not changed at all during the past month. Neither side is decisively gaining the upper hand. Within the Republics themselves the Republican forces are finding it increasingly difficult. Their hopes are at present focused on the commandos that are active in the Cape. Tens of thousands of British troops have been transferred to the Colony. This has two major advantages: the British can no longer give their full attention to the war within the Republics alone, and for the British taxpayer the cost of the war is escalating daily. From Europe, where President Kruger and the Republican Deputation are still attempting to recruit foreign support for our freedom struggle, we have heard that the pro-Boer movement is gaining significant support even in Britain itself.

A very alarming development for us is the increased use by the British army of black people in a fighting capacity against the Republics. No one can really blame any black who bows to the temptation of working for the Khakis for payment as the war is also making it very difficult for black people to survive. The Boers nevertheless feel bitter about black involvement. There is a very real danger that many Boers will in the long run build up a grudge against black people and retaliatory action in the future would under these circumstances come as no surprise.

ON THE BATTLE FRONT

KHAKI OFFENSIVES FAIL

In the veld, 30 April – Even though no major battle took place during the past month, the British forces were particularly active in their attempts to corner the Republican commandos –with a resounding lack of success. Our reporters from the different fronts provided the following information.

NORTHERN TRANSVAAL

British forces under General Plumer occupied the little town of Nylstroom on 1 April. For General Beyers, who was in Pietersburg at the time, it was clear that the British were advancing in his direction and that their force was so large that he would not be able to halt them. Consequently he decided to abandon the town with his 500 burghers.

The Boers left on 7 April. The next day Plumer's forces occupied Pietersburg. The only resistance they encountered came from a schoolmaster who attempted to halt the British with futile but misplaced valour. He hid himself in tall grass and shot two officers and a soldier before throwing his rifle on the ground and shouting that he was surrendering. The British summarily killed him with their bayonets. In Pietersburg they captured two locomotives, 36 wagons and all the supplies Beyers and his burghers had left behind. In addition they destroyed the *Zoutpansberg Wachter*'s printing press as well as four mills.

On 26 April 47 burghers surrendered to the enemy at Klipdam north of Pietersburg.

WESTERN TRANSVAAL

British forces were particularly active in the western Transvaal this month. On Sunday 14 April General Smuts's commando suffered a great setback in his absence when their camp at Goedvooruitzicht was overrun by the Khakis. Commandant Wolmarans, who was in command in Smuts's place and his approximately 500 burghers were caught totally by surprise when the British cavalry charged their camp. They attempted to offer resistance, but the British artillery drove them back and they had to flee for their lives. In addition to the camp the Khakis recaptured a 12-pounder gun that General De la Rey had captured from the British force at Silkaatsnek last July, as well as a pom-pom. Six burghers were killed, 10 wounded and 23 made prisoner of war. It is reported that on the British side only three men were wounded.

On 22 April a Boer commando attacked a British convoy that was escorted by 400 soldiers with two guns at Platberg near Klerksdorp. The Khakis offered stiff resistance and repulsed the attack. We have been told that the enemy suffered the loss of two men killed and three wounded, while on the Boer side one burgher was killed and one wounded. The Boers also took eight Khakis prisoner of war.

EASTERN TRANSVAAL

The eastern Transvaal saw a lot of action this month. The British forces continued with their futile attempts to corner the Boer commandos of Generals Louis and Chris Botha, Ben Viljoen and Chris Muller, as well as their commandants and the government in the veld, against blockhouse lines. In a few cases the burghers sabotaged railway lines and in one case destroyed a military train, namely at Witbank on 11 April. It was a good thing that this particular train fell into the hands of the Boers, since the loot included a number of postal bags that contained valuable information, including the plans and maps of a major attack planned by the enemy. According to the plans 40 000 soldiers were to advance from various directions – Pietersburg, Middelburg, Belfast, Machadodorp and Lydenburg – and hedge us in so that nobody could escape. We can now report, since the situation has totally changed, that the government was at Tautesberg, north of Middelburg, but has now moved as a result of this timely information in the captured postal bags.

At Tautesberg was the huge naval gun that our forces captured at Helvetia at the end of last year, namely the Lady Roberts. An artilleryman, Lieutenant Leopold, attempted to manufacture ammunition for it, but the first shell came out in pieces and it failed. Soon after the government left General Ben Viljoen received an order to destroy the Lady Roberts with dynamite so that it could not be of any future value to the British. Viljoen too had to flee to avoid encirclement by the Khakis, and destroyed his own guns and wagons.

On 16 April there was a skirmish between Boer and Brit near Dullstroom. Commandant Wynand Viljoen, General Muller and Commandant Taute attacked a British column that was approaching that town near Palmietfontein. Muller received a slight shoulder wound before the Boers once again retreated. The British subsequently occupied Dullstroom, Blinkwater, where they took about 100 Boksburg burghers prisoner of war, and also Roossenekal, where 60 burghers surrendered.

In the meantime Commandant Dawid Schoeman's Long Tom gun stood at Rooikrans but was practically useless, since the artillerymen had only 13 shots left. When the Khakis advanced in that direction, the crew hauled the gun to Klaas Prinsloo's farm, Rietfontein, in the valley of the Watervals River. Lieutenant A.S.D. Erasmus, the commander of this second-last of the original four Long Toms, placed the gun on a prominent hill close to Prinsloo's house from where he had a good view to the south. On 20 April, when the Khakis appeared in the south, Erasmus fired the 13 bombs on them. Subsequently the artillerymen destroyed the Long Tom by exploding about 20 kilograms of dynamite within its barrel.

On the day of the destruction of the Long Tom, Viljoen's men began to lose hope and he himself began wondering if they would ever be able to shake off the Khakis. At that stage Lieutenant Colonel Fanie Trichard of the State Artillery joined them. He told our reporter: 'I asked Viljoen what the plans were. The General answered that they were merely fleeing, since there was no possibility to fight. He indicated that he did not know how to get through the British line that had virtually encircled his forces. I knew that the enemy had occupied all the drifts, but that there was one drift across the Olifants River where I had to haul a gun through the river 17 years ago in the war against Nyabela. Perhaps we could go through there. Viljoen agreed that we would have to make an attempt.

'That evening all of us, about 600 men, trekked through valley and over hill to the west. At Maleoskop we passed within 1 000 metres of a British unit. I halted the column and went to Chief Ramapula's village. It was deep in the night. I woke him up and asked if there were British soldiers at his village. No, was his answer, but there are many in the area. The whole column then proceeded to the drift at Hoogebomen, where we went through the river in dead silence in single file. The river flowed strongly, but fortunately it was nowhere too deep. Luckily it was particularly bushy in the area, since day had broken by the time all of us were through. Later on I heard that there had been a British guard post only 300 metres from us next to the river, but we did not see them in the dense bush, and obviously they did not see us either.

'After crossing the river we proceeded in a northwesterly direction, but later on turned to the south to Pootjiesnek. At one stage we were uninterruptedly in the saddle for 19 hours. Many of the men, including our field preacher, the Reverend J.M. Louw, fell asleep while in the saddle, but most important of all was that we escaped from the British forces and are now safe again.'

The British attempt to capture the Transvaal government and General Viljoen thus failed, since all escaped from the net.

CAPE COLONY

A number of Republican officers and their burghers, assisted by Cape Afrikaners, continued to spread the battle front ever deeper into the Cape Colony last month. Prominent names that deserve mention in this regard are Commandants Kritzinger, Scheepers, Fouchee and Malan. Commandant Van Reenen returned to the Free State with about 300 burghers earlier this month, while Scheepers and his men captured 75 Khakis at Zeekoegat near Cradock on 6 April.

In the meantime, Commandant Malan was visited by three Cape Rebels of the Brandvlei area in the northern Cape who wanted to organise an uprising in that area. Malan immediately dispatched Corporal Salmon Maritz with 10 members of his corporalship to assist them. They include the French volunteer, Robert de Kersauson, and are accompanied by six Coloured servants.

They reached Brandvlei after two weeks of hard riding all the way from the Aberdeen district. It was worth their while, since they were heartily welcomed by about 60 Rebels. When they entered Brandvlei village, the women and children came out of the houses and applauded them. The Rebels explained to Maritz that they had initially been inclined to remain neutral in the war. However, when a British military unit visited their district, commandeered their horses and rifles and maltreated them, they decided to join the Republican cause. They drove off the small British garrison and now plan to remain in control of the district.

A day after their arrival in Brandvlei, Maritz and his men became involved in a skirmish with a British unit that had approached from the south. They easily overpowered the Khakis, although Maritz himself was wounded in the engagement. Fortunately it was not a serious wound. It seems as if there are numerous Rebels in that part of the Cape Colony and Maritz and his men are delighted about the pro-Republican sentiments that they encounter.

That the Republican military success in the Cape Colony is a major source of concern for the British was confirmed on 22 April when Lord Kitchener issued a notice in which he threatened all British subjects in the Cape Colony with strict action if military courts found that they were supporting the Republics in any way.

To rub salt into the wounds of the Cape authorities, Commandant Pieter Kritzinger's commando looted a British supply train near Molteno. He and his men returned to the Free State on 29 April after an expedition of more than four months in the Cape Colony, during which they moved along or by Venterstad, the Stormberg Mountains, Graaff-Reinet, Murraysburg, Aberdeen, Willowmore, Oudtshoorn, Mossel Bay, Cradock, Pearston and Tarkastad and often exchanged shots with British units.

FREE STATE

In the Orange Free State there has been action in numerous places during the past month, especially from the British side. In the southeast Free State the Republican forces near Dewetsdorp suffered a setback when the British captured Commandant Bresler with 83 burghers after a long pursuit. On 10 April three British columns began moving alongside each other from Kroonstad to the northwest. Their objective seems to have been to drive all the Boer commandos out of that area. After about 10 days they reached the Vaal River. They took all the inhabitants of the villages of Parys and Vredefort with them or drove them off. However, they made no contact with any Republican commando.

On 29 April a British column virtually destroyed the small town of Reitz in the eastern Free State. We have heard that only one house, namely that of the justice of the peace, is still standing.

LOATHSOME WAR DEEDS

In the veld, 30 April – The British inability to force the Republican commandos into submission on the battlefield has now led to increasingly loathsome war deeds by the enemy in an attempt to make it impossible for us to continue the war. In the past month our enemy has been particularly creative in this regard. Early in April Lord Kitchener, the British commander-in-chief, ordered that a so-called Cattle Ranger Corps be established. This Corps consists of former burghers who look after the livestock of the British military authorities in Pretoria and bring livestock from neighbouring districts to Pretoria. Reliable information indicates that the Corps also removes all livestock from the farms of the burghers, so that the British soldiers can focus their attention on more military affairs. Apparently members of the Corps receive as payment a percentage of the livestock that they seize. They each get a rifle and ammunition as well as a horse that is no longer deemed suitable for war duty by the Khakis. It seems as if it is a paying undertaking to steal on behalf of the Khakis, since there are already about 25 rangers.

From the southeastern Transvaal it is reported that the enemy are using Zulu warriors to loot cattle from Boers in that area. According to a reliable report a British officer, Colonel Bottomley, ordered King Dinizulu in a letter to arm warriors and cross the Transvaal border in order to steal cattle. A Zulu force of 6 000 warriors soon afterwards crossed the border and indeed began looting cattle from Boer farms. Armed burghers fired on the Zulus and killed at least two before the rest made off with a huge number of cattle.

Boer farmhouse looted and torched

OUR MILITARY OFFICERS

Lieutenant Colonel Fanie Trichard

Lieutenant Colonel Fanie Trichardt

Stephanus Petrus Erasmus Trichard comes from a very well-known Afrikaans family. His grandfather was the Voortrekker leader Louis Trichard and his father the adventurer and traveller Carolus Johannes Trichard. Trichard was born in 1849 in Ohrigstad and grew up in the Lydenburg district. As a young adult he farmed in the Middelburg district and he knows that area like the palm of his hand.

Trichard is a man with extensive military experience. He was barely 13 years old when he participated in a campaign against a black community for the first time. During the Transvaal War of Independence of 1880–81 he was present when the glorious victory at Majuba was achieved and in 1896 he assisted with the capture of the freebooter Jameson at Doornkop. In the meantime he had participated in campaigns against numerous rebellious black captains and communities including the Bapedi, the Hananwa and the Bavenda. In 1889 Trichard was elected Commandant of the Middelburg district. He remained in that post until he became commandant of the Transvaal State Artillery in 1897. His rank is that of lieutenant colonel. Soon before the outbreak of this war he proceeded to the Natal front at the head of a section of the State Artillery in September 1899. So far in the war he has participated in numerous battles on various fronts.

After the British capture of Pretoria in June last year, the State Artillery ended its existence as a separate unit. Even though the Transvaal government declared his post redundant, Trichard was allowed to keep his rank and was appointed as commandant of a burgher commando that consists mainly of former artillerymen. Since then he has been active against the Khakis in the district he knew so well as a child and a young man. In the past month his knowledge and his determination helped avoid certain disaster when he led Generals Ben Viljoen and Chris Muller and all their burghers out of the trap set for them by the Khakis.

THE War Reporter
MONTHLY EDITION

Number 53   In the Veld, South African Republic   1 June 1901

MISS EMILY HOBHOUSE ON CONCENTRATION CAMPS
Absence of care leads to untold tragedies

Cape Town, 7 May – Miss Emily Hobhouse, the Englishwoman who is waging a campaign to reveal the maltreatment of Republican women and children in the concentration camps, was very active last month. On 6 April she was in Kimberley and three days later she visited the camp in Mafeking. On 12 April she was in Warrenton, where she was a witness when the Khakis loaded women and children onto open coal trucks to transport them to a concentration camp. When those imprisoned women and children arrived in the camp in Kimberley the next day, there were only 25 tents available for the 240 of them.

From Kimberley she returned via De Aar to Bloemfontein. There she told our correspondent of her powerless fury when she arrived at the Springfontein Station. A train carrying about 600 Boers, mainly women and children in open trucks, stood on the station. 'It was bitterly cold. All night there had been a truly torrential downpour of rain and water was everywhere upon the ground. On the saturated ground they were trying to dry themselves and their goods. Some women were pushing their way to the platform to try to buy food for their children. The soldiers would not permit this. I expostulated. The men said that they were sorry for them, but they had to obey orders. So I took them all the food I had in the train with me. A woman said they had been travelling two days without any food supplies and the children were crying with hunger. I have just heard from a man who met the same train-load at Edenburg that four children died on the journey.'

On 21 April Miss Hobhouse arrived in Bloemfontein. Her plan was to proceed from there to the north to visit as many camps as possible. However, the British High Commissioner, Sir Alfred Milner, refused to give her a permit to proceed any further. It is clear that the British authorities plan to restrict her movements, since she is revealing to all and sundry how bad things really are in the camps.

Miss Hobhouse consequently decided to return by train to Cape Town and from there to London. On her way back she again visited the Springfontein Concentration Camp where, she related to our correspondent, a horrific scene of tragedy unfolded before her eyes: 'There, to my horror, still massed on the railway siding, I found the same unfortunate people whom I had seen when passing north 10 days previously. Their condition beggars description. The people massed there had no tents. Some crept under the railway trucks while some had begged bits of sailcloth from Tommies and sticking two or three sticks in the ground threw the canvas over, thus making a rude shelter in which, however, one could seldom stand upright.

'To such a shelter I was called to see a sick baby. The mother sat on her little trunk with the child across her knee. She had nothing to give it and the child was sinking fast. I thought a few drops of brandy might save it, but although I had money there was none to be had. We watched the child draw its last breath in reverent silence. The mother neither moved nor wept. It was her only child. Dry-eyed but deathly white, she sat there motionless looking not at the child but far, far away into depths of grief beyond all tears. A friend stood behind her who called upon Heaven to witness this tragedy and others crouching on the ground around her wept bitterly. The scene made an indelible impression on me.'

Miss Hobhouse left for Britain from Cape Town harbour today.

Boers being transported to concentration camps in open cattle trucks

The mortuary in the Kroonstad concentration camp

POSSIBLE PEACE NEGOTIATIONS
DISAGREEMENT BETWEEN TRANSVAAL AND ORANGE FREE STATE

In the veld in the eastern Free State, 30 May – Reports that have reached us during the past month indicate that the Free State authorities are not at all interested in peace negotiations that would lead to the loss of Republican independence. Chief Commandant Christiaan de Wet issued an open letter to his burghers on 1 April in which he declared that the majority of the burghers would never accept Kitchener's offers, even if the Republican governments did accept them, and that it was futile to even consider any offer, 'since the only reason why we fight is for the independence of our Republics'. Only the upholding of those aims can bring an end to the war.

It seems as if the Free State and the Transvaal authorities do not always speak from the same mouth, since there are Transvaalers who seem to be in favour of negotiations to bring an end to the war. On 10 May the most prominent Transvaal leaders actually held a council of war over the issue on the historic farm, De Emigratie, between Ermelo and Wakkerstroom. Commandant-General Louis Botha, Generals Ben Viljoen, Chris Botha and Jan Smuts, and members of the Transvaal government were present. In a spirit of pessimism they decided to open negotiations with the British authorities.

The main reason for this decision, Smuts subsequently explained to our correspondent, is the fear that the government may in future not be in any position of power to negotiate favourable conditions with the British. But no steps will be taken to execute any decision before reaching an agreement with the Free State government. If the Free State government was satisfied with the decisions, Smuts would act as intermediary in an attempt to send a telegram on the issue to President Kruger through the good offices of General Kitchener.

The Transvaal State Secretary, F.W. Reitz, wrote a letter to President Steyn on 15 May in which he informed him of the war council's decision. In the letter Reitz explained that the war council identified four extremely negative conditions, namely the decrease in the number of fighting burghers, the shortage of ammunition and supplies, the increasing inability of the government to provide strong leadership to the burghers under present war conditions and the loss of confidence since it had become clear that the Republican deputation had failed thus far to convince any foreign power to intervene on the side of the Boers. It was essential to approach Kitchener in this regard and a speedy answer from the Free State government was requested.

When he read Reitz's letter, President Steyn was filled with fury about his sister Republic's lack of confidence. He answered in a scolding tone that the Transvaalers were again threatening to leave the Free Staters and Cape Rebels in the lurch. The problems facing the Transvaalers also applied to the Free Staters. However, they remained unshakeable. What the Transvaalers should remember is that the Free Staters had placed their own future in the balance by entering the war on the side of their sister Republic. If the Transvaalers abandoned them now, it would mean the end of Afrikanerdom, since nobody would trust anybody again. Steyn believed that it would be suicide for the Afrikaner people to surrender at this stage. All the Republicans must remain steadfast and trust in God, since that was the basis of their power.

When General De la Rey heard of the war council decision he decided to go to the Free State for negotiations with Steyn and De Wet. On 27 May he met them near Reitz.

FROM THE EDITOR

Only a few battles were fought last month, with no noteworthy victory or defeat. The British forces are involved in two main activities, namely destruction of Boer farms and large-scale attempts to drive the Boer commandos into the blockhouse lines. With the first they are highly efficient, but their drives have so far produced virtually nothing. The only big battle took place towards the end of May at Vlakfontein in the western Transvaal. Its result was, like everything else this past month, not definitive at all.

Strictly speaking, the British can claim one success, namely that they have, through unrelenting pressure, forced the Boers to destroy their only remaining Long Tom gun, the legendary 'Jew'. On the other hand, the Boers can claim that they ensured that the British could not, in spite of their huge advantage in numbers and in armament, and continuous pressure, capture a single big Boer gun. The fact that the Boers are now left with virtually only their rifles to fight the British forces, means that there can no longer be any conventional battles. A Boer victory over the British forces is no longer a possibility either. What eventually determines the outcome of this war will depend on the following: how long will the British government be able to afford the massive, escalating expenses of this war? And how long will the Boers be prepared to hold out in the unequal battle against a brutal opponent?

Brutal, some readers might say, is too strong a word. Not if one reads the reports of Miss Hobhouse on various concentration camps. It is indeed shocking to read how inhumanely the Khakis treat the Boer women and children.

That the Boer leaders are unanimous in their resolve to carry on this war *ad infinitum* does not seem quite certain any more. Some members of the Transvaal government seem to be wavering. We agree with President Steyn of the Free State that it would be treasonous if the Transvaal were now to abandon the struggle. To surrender might be easy, but then our future would no longer be in our own hands. It is the duty of this generation to ensure that the fate of future generations of the Afrikaner people will not be in the hands of foreigners.

115

Number 53 1 June 1901

BOER PRISONERS OF WAR IN PORTUGAL

In the veld, 20 May – From Portugal we have received reports of the recent arrival of numerous Boer prisoners of war, including women and children who had been interned by the Portuguese after crossing the Transvaal border into Mozambique. The Portuguese, with their vast colonial empire, are powerless against British supremacy on the ocean. For that reason their government decided to do nothing that could provoke British retaliation. They recognise the British 'annexation' of the Boer Republics and accept that the Boers are no longer citizens of the Republics. For that reason they interned all the Boers in their colony of Mozambique and took them by ship to Portugal. By September last year there were already about 1 400 Boers in Mozambique who had surrendered their rifles, ammunition and horses to the Portuguese authorities. They were interned in the police barracks in Lourenço Marques. The men whose wives and children were there as well were detained in houses with their families. Foreigners who had fought on the side of the Boers were not interned, but were sent back to their countries of origin.

The conditions under which the interned Boers were detained were anything but pleasant.

The Portuguese found it difficult to supply them with sufficient food and medical services. By January this year malaria and stomach infection were very common. In addition the heat was unbearable and there was a continuous flea plague.

The first group of Boers to leave Mozambique consisted of about 700 men who were taken to Portugal on board the battleship *Benguella*. They left on 22 February. The second group followed on 8 March on board the *Zaire*. Both ships sailed around Cape Point and then up the African west coast. The *Benguella* reached Lisbon on 28 March and the *Zaire* on 2 April.

This ocean journey was for the vast majority of travellers a new experience. According to one of the women, Anna Kruger, the *Zaire* was dirty and there were fleas everywhere. According to Portuguese customs the food was prepared with excessive oil which made it inedible for many Boers. According to Flippie Pienaar, who journeyed on the *Benguella*, many Boers became seasick, especially at the beginning when the sea was stormy. Since the cabins were quite dark, the Boers elected to sleep on the deck where they had to face the elements. Four black men had elected to join the Boers into exile, and for them the cold was a terrible experience. Five Boers who had been ill when they left, died during the journey. Their bodies were dumped overboard. Three Boers on the *Zaire* suffered a similar fate.

When the *Benguella* arrived in Lisbon early on the morning of 28 March, the Boers received a hero's welcome. Thousands of Portuguese streamed to the harbour to gaze at the men who had for so many months fought in the veld like heroes for their freedom. The Boers were transported in trains to their places of internship. When the first train left, the Boers lifted their hats to the crowd. The latter cried out: 'Long live Transvaal! *Viva os Boers*!'

The Boers were also received like heroes at the places where they were interned.

Anna Kruger says that at the station where she is detained, Caldas da Rainha, thousands of curious Portuguese awaited them. They had heard that the Boers had long ears and long hair and now wanted to see what they looked like. They were surprised to see that the Boers were an attractive nation. The interned Boers had to walk a long distance through the town. They passed through rows of Portuguese people on both sides who threw rose leaves in front of them and called out: '*Viva os Boers.*' All the Boers certainly were made to feel very welcome in Portugal.

BIG BATTLE AT VLAKFONTEIN

KEMP ALMOST OVERWHELMS A BRITISH FORCE

Magaliesberg, 31 May – General Jan Kemp's burghers came within a hair's breath of a victory over a huge British force two days ago. Unfortunately some of the burghers fired on their compatriots in the confusion of the battle, which gave the fleeing Khakis an opportunity to regroup their forces. In the end, Kemp had to fall back and the British got away.

These events took place on the farm Vlakfontein north of the point where the wagon road between Ventersdorp and Rustenburg crosses the wagon road between Koster and Hekpoort. Kemp and his 400–500 burghers, with Commandants Van Deventer, Claassens and Oosthuizen among them, arrived on the farm Waterval in this area a few days before the battle. On 28 May General Dixon pitched camp at Vlakfontein with a force consisting of about 1 200 men with seven guns and a pom-pom. Kemp's scouts saw the Khakis and exchanged a few shots with Dixon's scouts. In the meantime Dixon's main force began destroying farmhouses and farms in the vicinity.

On 29 May Dixon's force proceeded westwards through a valley on Vlakfontein. To Kemp and his men, watching them from a low hill on the farm Spitskop in the north, it seemed as if the Khakis were preparing to attack them. Suddenly the Khakis halted, turned around and moved away in an easterly direction. Kemp subsequently told our reporter that he realised at that moment that the British soldiers were not aware of his presence. This was an opportunity second to none to utterly surprise them. He organised an attack, taking all possible precautions to stay out of sight. The burghers took up position behind a low hill. After about 90 minutes they were ready. As was his custom, Kemp and his men prayed before they went into action.

The first time that the Khakis saw them was probably when the burghers attacked their most northerly flank. This was a mock attack. The main attack caught the Khakis in the south totally unaware soon afterwards. They torched the veld and tried to find cover under the smoke. The same smoke provided the Boers with an ideal opportunity. Kemp personally rode out on his horse leading his force through the smoke screen in the charge on the Khakis. Some of the burghers fired on the Khakis from the saddle. Their target was two British guns on the battlefield. The British gunners resisted stoutly for a short while but then fled, and the Boers got hold of their two guns, which they then turned on the retreating Khakis.

At this stage of the battle – it was about two o'clock the afternoon – Kemp seemed poised for total victory. Then suddenly everything went wrong. Some of the burghers did not realise that it was their own men who were firing the guns, and fired on them, hitting two burghers. By the time the resulting confusion had been sorted out, the British had launched a counter-attack.

To escape encirclement, Kemp decided to retreat. There was no ammunition left for the guns, and since there were no horses to haul the guns away and no dynamite to destroy them, the burghers had to abandon them to be recaptured by the enemy.

At dusk both sides hoisted white flags to allow them to treat the wounded. Our correspondent heard from the British ambulance team that six officers and 51 other Khakis had been killed and about 130 wounded. If that is true, it is the biggest British loss in any single battle since the Battle of Nooitgedacht last December. Seven of Kemp's burghers were killed and two seriously wounded.

While the Boers were retreating, one of their *agterryers*, or black attendants, Windvoël, heroically came to the assistance of one of the burghers who found it difficult to mount his unwilling horse. Under heavy enemy fire he repeatedly helped the burgher and even fired on the enemy, thus ensuring that they both reached safety.

LAST REMAINING LONG TOM DESTROYED

Northern Transvaal, 1 May – The South African Republic's fourth and last Long Tom gun was destroyed by its crew yesterday, to ensure it would not fall into British hands. This was the gun that was damaged by the British outside Ladysmith in December 1899, as a result of which the front end of its muzzle had to be removed. Consequently the Boers from then onwards referred to it as 'Short Tom' or 'The Jew'.

The Jew did not depart without a fight. Early in April, when the British under General Plumer were advancing from Potgietersrus to Pietersburg, its crew set it up on the neck at Ysterberg. They fired vigorously at the enemy, but the Jew alone could not halt the huge force. Eventually they had to retreat, taking an easterly direction towards the Transvaal Drakensberg, where they hoped to evade the enemy. The trek was no joyful outing, since it rained continuously and the poor roads made the area almost impassable. The Jew was a heavy gun and often sank almost to its muzzle in the mud.

By the middle of April they were near Haenertsburg. There the going was even tougher, since that area is mountainous and the Jew often had to be hauled through drifts. Captain Heinrich du Toit, the gun's commander, realised that the British would be delighted to capture the Jew. He reckoned that the British would approach on the main road from Pietersburg. Consequently he set up the Jew on Berg Plaats. From there, there was a good view of both roads leading from Pietersburg, namely the one crossing Smitsdrif as well as the one via Houtboschdorp.

Boer scouts were sent out every day to observe the enemy's movements. On 27 April the Khakis arrived and managed to drive the Waterberg Commando from their position at Rhenosterpoort. It was clear that the British would use the northern route across Houtboschdorp. Du Toit now decided to move the gun further east across the farms Kromdraai and Goedvertrouwen to Feeskop on the farm Rondebult. The British forces reached Houtboschdorp on 29 April.

Yesterday morning (30 April) the Khakis advanced towards Feeskop, but it seemed as if they did not know where the Jew was. By early yesterday afternoon they were about seven kilometres from Feeskop when the Boer gunners fired on the enemy with the Jew. This fire was totally ineffective and inaccurate, since the Jew was not set up on its platform. Consequently it sunk deeper into the soft soil with each shot fired. Nevertheless Captain Du Toit kept on firing, about 16 or 18 shots, while the soldiers closed in on him.

Since at that time Du Toit had fewer than 40 shots left for the Jew, he decided that it would serve no purpose to attempt to escape with the gun. In addition, one of the officers whose burghers were supposed to protect the gun, Commandant Neethling, panicked and decided to surrender. Commandant De Villiers and Du Toit decided it was time to flee. However, before this could happen there was a very unpleasant task that had to be carried out.

The British were hardly two kilometres away when Du Toit ordered an artillery officer, the engineer Gustav Thiel, to destroy the Jew. Thiel told our correspondent that he forced as much dynamite as possible down the gun's muzzle before inserting a fuse and cap and compacting it with soil. He also placed a large measure of dynamite on the carriage above the axle. He then placed the remaining shells and the gunpowder that was still left over around the gun and attached fuses and caps to each measure of dynamite.

Thiel and Watch Master Maher ignited the fuses and ran for their lives. They had gone only about 200 metres when the first dynamite load exploded. This was the dynamite on the gun carriage, and the explosion broke the gun apart. Immediately afterwards two other explosions followed. Together these destroyed the barrel as well as the remaining ammunition. Parts of the barrel fell amongst the Boers, but fortunately nobody was hurt. It was a sad task to blow up the gun, Thiel said, but he was glad that the Khakis were unable to capture it. The latter indeed arrived on the scene moments after the explosions, but their only trophies are broken pieces of metal.

TWO WELL-KNOWN TRANSVAALERS DIE

31 May 1901 – Two well-known public figures who had recently made themselves rather unpopular died last month. The first is the former president, M.W. Pretorius. He was 82 years old and lived with friends in Potchefstroom. There he died on Sunday 19 May of influenza. He almost certainly contracted that disease when British soldiers woke him up a few nights earlier and interrogated him for more than two hours on the open verandah where it was bitterly cold. Next morning he complained that he did not feel well, and soon afterwards he collapsed. He was buried in the town.

Exactly a week later, on Sunday 26 May, General Hendrik Schoeman died in a freak accident in his house in Pretoria. His wife, one of his daughters and two guests, including the father of General Ben Viljoen, were talking in his lounge. Schoeman lighted his pipe and then dropped the match, which may still have been burning, into his ashtray – the shell of a British lyddite grenade that Schoeman had brought to Pretoria as a souvenir of the war. For some reason or other it exploded. Schoeman died on impact. His daughter as well as one of his guests died soon afterwards. The other guest and Mrs Schoeman were severely injured. Many Boers believe that Schoeman was a joiner. In their opinion the explosion was his punishment for his treason.

OUR MILITARY OFFICERS

General Jan Kemp

Jan Christoffel Greyling Kemp was born in 1872 in Amersfoort in the southern Transvaal. He is the son of Jurie Johannes Kemp and his wife Maria Aletta Greyling. Kemp attended school in the State Gymnasium in Pretoria. In 1889 he became a clerk in the education department of the South African Republic. Soon afterwards he was transferred to the office of the mine commissioner in Krugersdorp. By 1899 he was a chief clerk.

As for military experience, Kemp participated in the campaign against the black chief Magato in 1895. At the end of the same year he took part in the capture of Jameson and his freebooters. When this war broke out 20 months ago, Kemp joined the Krugersdorp Commando as an ordinary burgher. He participated in numerous battles on the Natal front. In November 1899 he was elected as assistant field cornet. Later on he served in the northern Transvaal under General Christiaan Beyers and was elected as a commandant. In December last year he played a leading role in the famous Boer victory at Nooitgedacht, where he was wounded in the arm.

In February this year Beyers appointed Kemp as fighting general and ordered him to make contact with General De la Rey in western Transvaal. Subsequently he has been active in the area south of the Magaliesberg range, where he almost managed to score a major victory last month at Vlakfontein. The young Kemp – he is not yet 30 years old – was certainly born to be in command.

General Jan Kemp

THE War Reporter
MONTHLY EDITION

Number 54 — In the Veld, South African Republic — 1 July 1901

WHAT IS REALLY HAPPENING IN THE CONCENTRATION CAMPS?
EYE-WITNESS REPORT BY A COURAGEOUS BOER WOMAN FROM STANDERTON

In the veld in the eastern Transvaal, 30 June – Here follows the first report that we have received directly from a concentration camp, written by Mrs Maria Fischer of Buhrmansvalei, near Ermelo. She insisted that her name be mentioned since she wants to reveal openly how harshly the British treat women and children. A burgher who had crept into the camp the night before yesterday and spent a few hours with his wife and children smuggled the report out. The report begins by describing her capture on the farm:

'When the English arrived on our farm, the officer told me and my sister to be ready to be taken away within half an hour. We refused and said he could burn down the house if he wanted to. His answer was that he was going to do it anyway. If we did not accompany him willingly, he would remove us by force. Then a man with the name of Snoeks arrived. He threatened that he would send blacks to throw us on a wagon if we did not co-operate.

'I was busy packing a few things into a small trunk, when Snoeks grabbed a packet of candles from my hand. His explanation was that I would not need it. Fortunately I had some others in my suitcase.

'Late that afternoon a whole British convoy arrived and camped at our house. They destroyed everything. In addition to the doors and the frames that they broke out, they even chopped down the trees. Then they looted my kitchen.

'Early the next morning the wagon was there to transport us. We were allowed to take two mattresses with cushions and blankets, a field table, a bath, a pot and a kettle. A handsupper who had to guard over us, threw the bucket and two chairs that I loaded onto the wagon off again.

'On 30 May we left the farm and the trek began. On 1 June the Khakis bombarded a house on the farm Vaalbank. Mrs Le Roux, the wife of Jan Hendrik le Roux, was wounded and two children, Daniel le Roux (10 years) and Anna Bloem (3 years) were fatally wounded. The two children died the next day and were buried in one grave – the one in a coffin and the other in a blanket. At the grave a handsupper said a prayer. For us it was horrible that that man had the audacity to pray at the grave of innocent children whom he had betrayed.

'While we were trekking past Blaauwkop on 3 June, the Boers fired on our guards. The infantry, the cavalry and even the British guns immediately took up a position in the midst of the wagons, which meant that the Boers could no longer attack since they might perhaps hit us. We reprimanded the British about their cowardice, but this made no difference.

'By 5 June we were close to Standerton. The Khakis were still busy demolishing all the houses as we trekked, chopping down the trees, slaughtering countless sheep and leaving everything behind just like that.

'On 6 June we reached the camp at Standerton. We were off-loaded on a heap of sand and told to immediately hand in our names to the Camp Commandant. When we encountered the Commandant we asked him for a tent. His answer was that we must move into the first tent. When we said there was no room, his answer was that we would have to remain outside, then. Late that afternoon we found room in a marcuee tent that was already full. There were already 37 people in the tent. An old man of 30 and his wife of 73, Nicolaas and Treina Fourie, slept at night in one corner of the tent and by day they sat outside.

'That first night in the camp I could not sleep. I think I was too tired to sleep and in addition the people coughed terribly. It was never silent for a minute throughout the night.

'For rations we receive flour, sugar, coffee and salt. Children under 12 receive half rations. Three times per week we receive meat – any type of meat that is available – slaughtered ram, ewe, lamb and also sheep that died of misery in the kraal. One day we had meat of a goat ram. It gave off such a terrible smell that we could not even approach the pot. One day a few women complained to the Commandant about the meat. For their impudence, having the audacity to complain about something given to them out of "mercy", those women had to go without meat for eight days.

'On 20 June a baby was born in our tent. Together with all the other people who had joined us in the meantime, we are now 61 inhabitants in the tent.

'Today Johanna Bührmann and I went to the town to the Dutch Reformed Church building. There total chaos rules. It is not a particularly big building, but 41 families have been forced into it. One family even lives on the pulpit. Everybody in the church building seem to be busy – one with somebody who is ill, another one with needlework, another one with crying children, with singing, reading, laughing, talking, resoling shoes, ironing and crushing cinnamon with a pestle. The children are playing hide and seek under the church pews. It is enough to make one mad. And this in a church, where God had earlier been served! But the English think nothing of using a church building as a jail.

'For us it is a terrible tribulation to be thus separated from everybody and everything that is dear to us. We had to leave our men, our boys, our fathers, our houses behind, and do not know what will happen to us. The women who have been in the camp for a long time say that death is better than the "protection" that the Khakis provide in these prisoner camps. But we are powerless, since we refuse to bow under the British yoke, so now we have decided to accept our harsh fate. My conscience will never allow me to contribute to us losing our country. I will give up everything to ensure our people's continued existence, since I believe that God will take note of our tribulations and will hear our prayers. He will inspire our men with the necessary courage and power to go on fighting to the end.'

Boer women and children being taken to a concentration camp

VICTORIES AND SETBACKS IN THE CAPE COLONY
Kritzinger re-enters the Colony with a huge force

Orange River, 25 June – Commandant Pieter Kritzinger and his burghers re-crossed the border into the eastern district of the Cape Colony on 22 May, and soon reached the Molteno district. Kritzinger's commando of 800–900 men was made up of Commandant Willem Fouchee's 250 burghers, Stoffel Myburgh and Piet Bester's Rebel commando of 100 men, Hans Lotter and Gert van Reenen's Rebel commando of 250 men and his own approximately 300 burghers. From Syferbult on the railway line they moved northwards with the aim of repulsing all Khakis from the Stormberg Mountains. However the weather was against them, since a heavy snowstorm from 26 to 28 May caused brutal coldness. In addition the white layer of snow that covered the ground made it impossible to move around undetected and there was insufficient pasture for their horses. In the end, they were forced to fall back again.

JAMESTOWN OCCUPIED – AND ABANDONED

Kritzinger and his men's first target at the beginning of June was the village of Jamestown, where they hoped to procure food, blankets and warm clothes – as well as ammunition, with luck. On 28 May they sent a message to Magistrate Kidwell to demand surrender, but Kidwell's answer was that if they wanted the town, they would have to conquer it. Four days later, in a surprise attack, Kritzinger dislodged the town guard from their station on a hill south of Jamestown. The next day the burghers moved into the village itself and forced the town guard to surrender after some sharp firing. One of them, Myburgh, was killed in the skirmish. It is said that he was wearing a British uniform coat for protection against the cold and that his own comrades, who thought he was a Khaki, shot him. The British loss was four men dead, five wounded and 130 captured.

After the British had surrendered unconditionally, Magistrate Kidwell, who acted as their commander, took the oath of neutrality to ensure that the Boers would not execute two blacks who had spied for the British. Kidwell's sense of honour ultimately cost him dearly, since when the British re-occupied the town after Kritzinger and his men left, he remained true to his oath and was stripped of his rank. As for Kritzinger's burghers, they took a huge quantity of loot with them when they retreated after receiving reports that a British force was on its way. A number of Boers remained behind in Jamestown, making free with the liquor in the local hotel. The next day they were captured by the British soldiers who re-occupied the town, but since the latter themselves also imbibed too much of the hotel's liquor, all but one of the Boers managed to escape again.

TOUGH GOING IN THE WINTER COLD

After the Jamestown episode the Boer commandos were forced to divide into small units to find pasture for their horses. The men were exhausted and almost numb with cold and needed a safe retreat. To add to their difficulties, Kritzinger's men were surprised by a British unit on the farm Wildefontein near Barkly East one night. Fortunately Kritzinger himself managed to escape, and his men fled in all directions, but in the process they lost many of their horses, saddles and most of their other supplies. The Boers then went towards Aliwal North, but since many were on foot and there were suddenly thousands of Khakis in the area, it was tough going. In the light of the poor condition of their remaining horses, Kritzinger finally decided to leave the area of the Stormberg Mountains.

On 13 June Kritzinger issued a proclamation in the Stormberg that the Boer annexation of those areas in November 1899 was still in force and that they regarded the area as part of the Orange Free State Republic. In the same proclamation he announced that the Boers would in future summarily execute black spies working for the British, should they capture them.

On 15 June Kritzinger and his burghers crossed the railway line near Syfergat in a southerly direction. They are still finding the going tough since the r horses are weak, and without a horse a Boer warrior is not worth much. Some evenings ago, at Ruitevlei, near the village of Maraisburg, a British unit surprised the Rebel commando of Gert van Reenen and captured 22 of them. Since then Kritzinger and his men have been in continual flight.

Commandant Fouchee and his men are still active in the Stormberg and are causing the British authorities endless headaches. According to reports from Graaff-Reinet, Commandant Malan and his men were resting in the Kamdeboo Mountains early in June.

From the northwestern Cape it is reported that the Kakamas Rebel Commando clashed with a Border Scout patrol at N'Rougas on 23 May. The Rebels were soundly beaten and suffered the loss of seven men killed and about 20 wounded.

Kritzinger's laager

Number 54 1 July 1901

FROM THE EDITOR

It is mid-winter and the elements are warring against the Boers – both the burghers in the field and the women and children in the camps. Readers who have never spent a few nights under the clear sky on a snow- or frost-covered field, wearing ragged clothing and with hardly enough food to silence the worst hunger pangs, cannot imagine what tribulations virtually our whole population has to suffer at the moment. That makes it all the more miraculous that their courage is not failing, and that they have remained full of confidence in their struggle for freedom against a ruthless enemy. Some Transvaal generals have wondered if the time is not ripe for a conditional peace, but in this issue we report that the two Republican governments have rejected such a possibility.

This month, for the first time, we are publishing a report by a Boer woman on conditions in a concentration camp where she herself is being held. Mrs Maria Fischer describes in detail the humiliation and poor treatment to which our women and children are subjected. The prayers of all true Republicans are that the sacrifices of these women and children will not be in vain.

REPUBLICAN GOVERNMENTS MEET AT WATERVAL

NO PEACE POSSIBLE AT THIS TIME

Waterval, 20 June – The governments and most important military commanders of both Republics met here for negotiations at Waterval, near Standerton in the southeastern Transvaal, yesterday and today. President Steyn and Generals De Wet and Hertzog represented the Free State, while Acting President Burger and Generals Botha, De la Rey, Viljoen and Jan Smuts attended the meeting on behalf of Transvaal. We have heard that they had received a telegram from President Kruger in which he encouraged them to continue with the war. Steyn furthermore castigated the Transvaalers for their one-sided decision in May to make peace. General Botha, supported by General Viljoen, warned that the Republican authorities might in the end be fighting without the support of the people. Eventually the entire meeting unanimously decided to keep on fighting and to issue a proclamation to that effect (see below).

Two other important decisions were taken here at Waterval. One was that General de la Rey should send a well-supplied commando led by General Smuts into the Cape Colony in an attempt to spread the war over an ever-increasing area and thus decrease the pressure on the Republics. The second was that all Republicans should celebrate 8 August as a Day of Thanksgiving and 9 August as a day of reconciliation and prayer. The Free State deputation returned to their Republic immediately after the close of the meeting.

THE WAR CONTINUES

The following general notice was issued today by the government of the South African Republic, immediately after the negotiations at Waterval:

'Since His Excellency State President Kruger and the deputation in Europe had heard nothing directly from our government since the conference between Commandant General Botha and Lord Kitchener in Middelburg, the government decided at the request of the Commandant-General and with the assistance of Lord Kitchener to send a secret telegram to President Kruger [through the assistance of the Dutch Consul] in which the general situation is fully explained and His Excellency's advice is requested.

'His Excellency answered to this that he and the deputation are still hoping for a positive result in our struggle and that we should continue the struggle.

'To discuss and consider His Excellency's answer, a conference of the governments of both Republics was held at which Chief Commandant C.R. de Wet, Commandant-General Louis Botha and Assistant Commandant-General J.H. de la Rey were present.

'After a detailed discussion of the military situation and of our position both governments unanimously took the following decision:

'The governments of the ZAR and the OFS, taking note of the immeasurable personal and material sacrifices that have already been made for our cause, which would all become worthless and futile if we made a peace in which the freedom of the Republics was abandoned; and taking note of the certainty that the loss of our independence after all the destruction that has occurred and the losses that have been suffered, would lead to the national and material demise of our whole people, and taking note of the spirit of uncompromising perseverance that is still present in the vast majority of our people, women and children as well as men, and in which we thankfully recognise the hand of the Almighty protector; have decided that no peace will be made and no peace conditions will be accepted whereby our independence and separate national existence, or the interests of our colonial brothers, will be surrendered; and that the war will be energetically continued with the adoption of all measures which are calculated to maintain that independence and those interests.'

OUR MILITARY OFFICERS

Commandant Wynand Viljoen

Wynand Viljoen is not nearly as well known as his older brother, Ben Viljoen, but he is certainly the latter's equal when it comes to valour, as he reaffirmed in the past month with his courageous actions in the battle at Wilmansrust and the crossing of the eastern railway line at Balmoral. (Events reported on in this issue.)

Viljoen was born in 1876 in the Cape Colony, but later moved to Johannesburg where he joined the South African Republic Mounted Police. At the beginning of the war he participated in the battles on the southern front near Colesberg, where he became a celebrated figure, and consequently at the end of last year he was, despite his young age, appointed as a commandant. It is men like him who contribute to the fact that the British authorities increasingly regret their folly in ever entering this costly war.

Wynand Viljoen

BRITISH FORCE SURPRISES WOMEN'S LAAGER

In the veld in the northern Free State, 30 June – There was only one noteworthy skirmish in the Orange Free State last month. At daybreak on 6 June a British force of about 600 men carried out a surprise attack on a women's laager at Graspan near Reitz. This laager was one of a number of similar laagers of women and children as well as elderly men fleeing to evade the Khakis. The women are afraid that they will be captured and forced into the so-called refugee camps. There, maltreatment, suffering and illness would be their destiny. Consequently they flee in the bitterly cold winter of the eastern Free State across the veld with wagons and carts loaded with furniture and food as well as huge flocks of livestock and horses.

It is not clear to us how big the women's laager at Graspan was when the British overran it, but it seems likely that the women had 120 wagons and carts with them and were accompanied by about 100 elderly men. The laager was easily captured, since the men were powerless and fled to escape being captured. The Khakis confiscated all the vehicles, and took a few of the men prisoner.

At that time, Generals De Wet and De la Rey, as well as President Steyn, were in the area of Verkykerskop, north of Reitz. They were on the point of departing to the Transvaal for negotiations with the government of the South African Republic. About an hour and a half after sunrise a burgher on horseback came galloping into their camp and informed them of the disaster at Graspan. De la Rey's reaction was that they should immediately rush to the women's assistance. Even though they had to save their own horses for the long journey that lay ahead, De la Rey, De Wet and Commandant Loffie Davel, with 55 men on horseback, rushed to Graspan. Former General Piet Fourie accompanied them.

That afternoon, the burghers commanded by Davel encountered the Khakis as they hauled the wagons of the women's laager away, and attacked them, driving the first line of soldiers back. Some of the Khakis found shelter between the wagons, which made it difficult for the burghers to keep on firing, for fear of hitting women or children. The burghers kept advancing on foot and captured many of the wagons and carts, while the British found shelter in the huts and a kraal of a black community. The British kept firing on the burghers as they began hauling the wagons away. Both sides suffered losses.

At three o'clock that afternoon a huge British unit reached the battlefield and began bombarding the burghers and the retreating wagons. De la Rey and De Wet decided a retreat was in order. As a result the Khakis recaptured the wagons and carts of the women's laager. Fourie got away with about 1 500 cattle, however.

The total losses of the Boer forces amounted to 17 men killed and 20 wounded, as well as about 40 taken prisoner of war. Captain Thuynsma was killed and Lieutenant H. Howell is one of the wounded. We have heard from a reliable source that 26 Khakis were killed and 25 wounded. Of the laager, one boy of 13 was killed and one woman and a girl slightly wounded.

After the battle Steyn, as well as De Wet and De la Rey and General Hertzog, moved off to the north for the negotiations with the Transvaal government.

BOERS REPULSE KHAKIS AT WILMANSRUST

Few battles in the eastern Transvaal

In the veld in the eastern Transvaal, 30 June – Last month there was hardly any military activity on this front. Only two noteworthy clashes between Boer and Brit took place. The first was on 12 June, when the burghers of General Chris Muller attacked a British unit of some 350 men at Wilmansrust on the Highveld between Middelburg and Ermelo and overpowered them in the dark. These Khakis were Australians of the 5th Victorian Mounted Rifles. Their commander in the battle was Major Morris.

From a distance Muller and his commando of 120 men kept a close watch on the British camp throughout the afternoon and noted that their guards were not well placed. Soon after dark Muller and his burghers attacked. A local farmer acted as guide. Muller and his men crept past the guards in the dark and then stormed and captured the camp. About 60 Khakis were wounded; 15 died. Virtually all the other Khakis were taken prisoner.

For the Boers the biggest bonus of the victory was a magnificent booty. It included two pom-pom rapid-fire guns with a huge supply of ammunition, as well as other weapons, food and very handy clothing. Unfortunately, for lack of facilities, General Muller had to let the prisoners of war free again before he proceeded. Only one of the captives was not released – a man named Drotsky, a Transvaal burgher. It is known that he joined the enemy and took up arms against his own brothers. He was charged with treason and the war council heard his case. The Council sentenced him to death and he was shot on 26 June.

Muller's victory at Wilmansrust was important for two reasons. In the first place it was an undoubted military success, lifting the morale of all the burghers who heard of it. In the second place the burghers are once again provided with luxuries such as blankets, coffee, sugar, fresh horses, clothing and other valuable articles. In all respects this victory is a blessing!

On 27 June General Ben Viljoen's commando in the eastern Transvaal carried out an attack on the British blockhouse line next to the eastern railway line between Balmoral and Brugspruit. In this area the blockhouses are about one kilometre apart along the railway line. Next to the railway line there are ground walls and trenches, which means that a commando cannot cross the railway line in a hurry. In addition numerous armoured trains pass by. Commandant Wynand Viljoen and his men overran one blockhouse, but the attack by Commandant Groenewald and his men failed. Nevertheless, a large section of Viljoen's commando crossed the railway line that same evening. At the northern side of the railway they came upon a deep trench which they had to fill up before they could proceed with their wagons. That took a long time. Only four wagons were through before an armoured train unexpectedly arrived, illuminating the burghers with its searchlights. All of them hurriedly looked for shelter and consequently not all the burghers managed to cross the railway line.

The next day the burghers who were still on the southern side of the railway line quickly moved eastwards and by evening reached the vicinity of Uitkyk Station. Soon after dark Captain Jack Hindon, one of Viljoen's scouts, placed a charge of dynamite under the railway line in the south and the burghers began crossing the line. The Khakis fired from the blockhouses in the vicinity, but no burgher was hit.

As was to be expected, a British armoured train arrived, but it was destroyed when it steamed over the dynamite charge, and failed to hinder the burghers. Viljoen, Muller and their men now have to restore a strong Republican presence north of the eastern railway line.

A British blockhouse in the Transvaal

THE War Reporter
MONTHLY EDITION

Number 55 | **In the Veld, South African Republic** | **1 August 1901**

SCORCHED EARTH IN WESTERN TRANSVAAL

Smuts's report on shocking deeds by the Khakis

In the veld in the western Transvaal, 25 July – General Jan Smuts recently sent a long report on the British destruction of Boer farms in the western Transvaal to President Steyn of the Orange Free State. The following extracts describe the shocking misdemeanours of the British forces in carrying out their policy of scorched earth:

'When I arrived in the district of Krugersdorp in the valley between the Magaliesberg and the Witwatersberg ranges in July 1900, the so-called *moot*, this was a fertile area and a feast for the eye with its fields, its gardens and its neat farmyards. But now – now it is a wasteland, since the British have laid waste to all the fields, the gardens and burnt down the houses. In many cases they were not satisfied with mere burning, but blew up the houses with dynamite, so that not one brick was left on another. Where there had recently been life and joy, death now reigns supreme.

'I do not believe that there has ever in history been a more horrible destruction that can be compared with the British actions. I often sat on the summit of the Magaliesberg Mountains and gazed down on the unbroken flame of burning fields, sheds, storerooms and dwellings. We could do little about it, since if we wanted to fight the British, they sheltered behind the houses where our women and our children dwelled. And if we wanted to bombard their camps, those camps were filled with our women and children. The troops are even driving elderly men with their one foot in the grave before them. In one case they had a grey old man of 75 years sent away as a prisoner of war, and in other cases little boys of 12 years old were made prisoners of war, since to the British officers they looked like fighting burghers.

'What is extremely alarming is the mentality of the British officers. In the pocket of an officer who was killed in action, we found a letter in which he wrote how he enjoyed carrying out his work of destruction. At one house he forced the women and children to listen how "God save the Queen" was played on their piano while the troops sang with the music, before he torched the house and everything in it. On another farm he ordered the women and children to carry out all they wanted to take with them within an hour, since then he would burn down the house. They placed everything on a neat pile, whereupon he set it alight. For him it was a big joke. This contempt, insult and barbaric roughness with which the British treat our women and children is totally incomprehensible.

'The ordinary Khakis and the blacks and Coloureds in their service, are acting in an even more brutal fashion towards our women and children. In some cases they physically assault the defenceless individuals, as happened with the elderly widow Coetzee of Elands River, Rustenburg. After the British left, I found her in a condition of pitiful maltreatment. That night after leaving the widow Coetzee, I undertook a reconnaissance trip along the Elands River. In the moonlight I passed by 12 or 14 farmhouses. All had been burned down or plundered and there was not a soul in sight. A month ago this was still a prosperous region, but now the British have turned it into a devastated, haunted world. I wondered what had happened to all the families who had lived in this region. To my surprise I saw them the next morning creeping like dassies from the hillocks in the area. The women and children prefer to live like wild animals in the veld rather than under the protection of Her Majesty Queen Victoria's flag.

'From the Elands River I proceeded eastwards to the Koster River, where I found the same destruction and pitiful conditions. Seven families consisting of women with small children are living under trees in the veld. Generals Plumer and Paget had destroyed their farms. On the farm Cyferfontein that belongs to Paul Grobler, everything has been burnt. His mother-in-law, a widow of over 70 years, had beforehand strapped all their money and a few valuable items under her skirt as a measure of security. The soldiers became aware of this, threw her to the ground and removed some of her clothing to rob everything. They then left her behind for dead.

'I see in the foreign newspapers that the mistreatment of the wives and children of the fighting burghers is causing some uproar. The foreigners hardly know what the real situation is. If the people in the outside world knew one hundredth of what the British forces are doing in the Republics, the whole Christendom would tear their clothes and a huge call would rise to heaven against this indescribable barbarity.

'What is to me the most amazing is the unshakable determination of the maltreated women. This determination is the result of a firm trust in God. The martyrs of the Middle Ages did not exhibit a stronger faith and tougher determination than the Boer women of today. The British believe they can subjugate us by famine. That would not help them at all, since our women and our fighting burghers would rather live on termites than abandon their holy rights on account of hunger.

'Another very disconcerting issue in this area is the way in which the British make use of black people to make life unbearable for the Boers. The British authorities have invited numerous black chiefs to cross the western border and to occupy the western districts of the Republic. These black people do not hesitate to carry out murders and other horrors which even the British soldiers back away from. As a result we have had to abandon large areas and to form women's laagers in the central area. We provided them with weapons, tents, food and clothing. Elderly men who are no longer fit for military duty, have been appointed to protect them. One would imagine that the British would leave these women's laagers in peace, but no. They attack these laagers, burn all the wagons, food and tents, take the elderly guards prisoner of war and bring about indescribable sorrow. And where the British cannot reach themselves, they send in blacks to carry out the work of destruction. After all the enemy raids the women are left in pitiful destitution, without a doctor, without medicine and virtually without clothing. But no suffering can break the spirit of these noble martyrs. With one voice they pleaded with me and my burghers to hold out until the end.'

BRITISH NEWSPAPERS CONFIRM SCORCHED EARTH

In the veld in Eastern Transvaal, 30 July – Commandant-General Louis Botha has just received a copy of the British daily *The Times* of 2 July. One of the reports in this newspaper includes a report by a British soldier on farm destructions. This confirms General Smuts's description of the British policy of scorched earth that is printed elsewhere in this issue of *War Herald*. The report by the British soldier reads as follows:

'We burn everything we come across, and are living like fighting-cocks. We think it a bad day if we haven't a couple of chickens and a suckling pig apiece. It's funny to see us with bayonets chasing the pigs round the farmyard. I have an appetite like a wolf. We went to Vrede next, and after a day's rest left that place in a shocking state. We killed thousands of sheep, and put a few carcasses in every house. The stench will be horrible in a week. It is to prevent the Boers from returning.'

FROM THE EDITOR

The British are attaching new meaning to the controversial old idiom that the end justifies the means. Their objective is the subjugation of the Boer Republics, and they obviously will not shrink from any method of breaking down the Republican resistance. Last month we reported on their onslaught on Boer women and children. This month we report on their destruction of the Republics: the burning down of harvests, of dwellings, of orchards and the wholesale slaughter of livestock. Thus they intend to douse the fighting spirit of the Republicans, and thus they doom virtually the whole next generation of Afrikaner children to poverty, even should the Republics eventually win the war.

On the military front neither side won any noteworthy victories this month. The British forces can claim that they were unlucky to miss capturing two major figures on the Republican side. As reported in this issue, both President Steyn and General Smuts barely managed to avoid falling into British hands. In some circles Steyn is regarded as the soul of the struggle. That the British failed to exploit their excellent opportunity to remove him as a factor in this war may cost them dearly in future.

All wars claim their victims. On the Republican side two highly respected figures passed away this month. We hereby honour the memory of the late Mrs Gezina Kruger, the wife of our President, and of General Cornelis Spruyt, for whom it was an honour to die for his fatherland.

MRS GEZINA KRUGER PASSES AWAY

Eyewitness report on her funeral

In the veld in Eastern Transvaal, 29 July – Today the mournful news reached us from Pretoria that Mrs Gezina Kruger, the wife of our President-in-exile, died on 20 July. After the President left for the eastern Transvaal and subsequently for Europe last May, she had been living in their residence in Church Street, where she was cared for by her daughter, Mrs Elsie Eloff.

The late Mrs Gezina Kruger with a daughter, granddaughter and great-granddaughter

Our correspondent in Pretoria sent us the following eyewitness report on the events surrounding Mrs Kruger's death as well as her funeral. It was written by Jacoba Lorentz, a Boer woman who lives in the British-occupied city:

'Mrs Kruger, the wife of the President, suffered terribly. She was so obese that she could hardly walk. In the last year or so the events of the war caused her a lot of sorrow. Her husband had been away for more than a year and a number of her children had been killed or captured. She was a simple, friendly woman, a true Christian, who remained attached to her old Boer customs in the midst of all the worldly goods that surrounded her. She steadfastly refused to meet the Governor or any senior British officers, claiming that she was a humble person and would not know how to behave towards such people. She was worshipped by her children and grandchildren, of whom there are about 80.

'Last week she contracted pneumonia, but she died of heart failure. The funeral took place on Sunday 21 July. I attended the ceremony that took place in the Reformed Church directly across the street from her house. The whole street (Church Street) was black with people and vehicles when we arrived. We had a hard time to get into the house since there were people everywhere. We found the coffin in a large room. It was covered with wreaths. It was a coffin of polished oak with her name and age, 67 years, engraved on a metal plate attached to it.

'When we failed to find the family members whom we were looking for, we made our way to the church. It was packed and we realised that there would be no room for us. Consequently we went to the vestry where there was more than enough room. I opened the door to enable us to follow the sermon. The Reverend H.S. Bosman, the only Afrikaans minister left in the occupied town, led the service. He read a chapter from the book of Revelations and took a text from the Book of Judges, 'A Mother in Israel'. He spoke with great feeling and referred to her as a mother both for her children and for her people.

'The funeral procession then made its way to the cemetery, followed by a large section of the public. And now Mrs Kruger is no more. A feeling of desolation came over us when we thought of her empty place, her empty house that was for a long time the hub around which everything centred that would otherwise have fallen apart.

'Two days after the funeral the family members of President Kruger who were still in Pretoria were ordered to leave the country.'

BATTLES IN THE CAPE COLONY

Eastern Cape, 29 July – In the eastern Cape there were only sporadic military confrontations last month. The British advantage in numbers and munitions served them well. Thus General French's Khakis managed to drive Commandant Scheepers' burghers from the Kamdeboo Mountains, while a British unit overran the laager of the Rebel commandant Stoffel Myburgh near Jamestown on 17 July. Commandant Willem Fouchee rushed to Myburgh's assistance, inflicting heavy casualties on the Khakis, but could not subdue them.

Since 18 July the British have launched large-scale military operations in the Cape Midlands. In the process they overwhelmed Commandant Hendrik Lategan's commando north of Graaff-Reinet. The Republicans also scored some successes. On 21 July Commandant Kritzinger's commando attacked a British unit near Cradock and stampeded its horses. On the same day a Boer commando captured a British supply train north of Beaufort West and set it alight.

FUNERAL IN A CONCENTRATION CAMP

EYEWITNESS REPORT FROM PRETORIA

In the veld, 30 July – Our correspondent in Pretoria sent us the following report by Jacoba Lorentz on the funeral of a young girl who died in the concentration camp in Pretoria. Hundreds of similar events take place in camps all over South Africa every month.

'On 23 July I visited the women's camp in Arcadia. In one of the tents I found a girl of 11 who was suffering from influenza. She appeared to be dying. Her mother, Mrs Coetzee, told me that they had recently been brought in from the Schurweberg area. The child had been complaining of a pain in her chest for months. On their journey here they had to sleep for three nights in the open winter air without shelter. The child caught a cold and has now been ill for more than a week. The doctor gave her medicine but the child reacted very negatively to it. Now nobody knows what to do. The mother sits in despair. I returned to the city and later heard that the child died that evening.

'On 25 July I visited the women's camp again. I went to Mrs Coetzee's tent. The funeral had not yet taken place, since the doctor had not yet written out the death certificate. While I was there the little hearse arrived. A small child was weeping bitterly. Two other children were sick in bed. A boy of 14 was dressed in new clothes and had a mourning band around his hat. He was to be the only mourner at the graveside.

'The hearse halted in front of the tent. A number of people quickly gathered. An old man requested us to sing Psalm 103:8, "Our brief life is like grass, Like a flower in the field." At first there was no one to intone. At last a young Boer woman and her friend began singing in a harsh, dragging tone, after which we all joined in.

'It was a motley gathering of men, women and children of various ages, all dressed in typical Boer clothing. After we had finished singing the verse, the old man said a prayer. He prayed for the mother who had had to give up her child, but who was consoled to know that the little girl had gone to Him who once said: "Suffer little children to come unto me."

'After ending the prayer he announced that the authorities allowed only 10 minutes for a funeral service. There was no time to read from the Bible or to make a speech. He only said that even if a mother holds her child to her heart and will not let it go, when death comes, we go alone. Nobody can accompany us. He requested us to sing again, Hymn 10:8 and 9, "When we enter the valley of death, All earthly friends forsake us" and "Come, let us set forth with new heart". A few young men then placed the coffin on the hearse, and the gathering dispersed. The hearse slowly made its way down the hill towards the river, with only one mourner following it: the 14-year-old brother of the girl that died.'

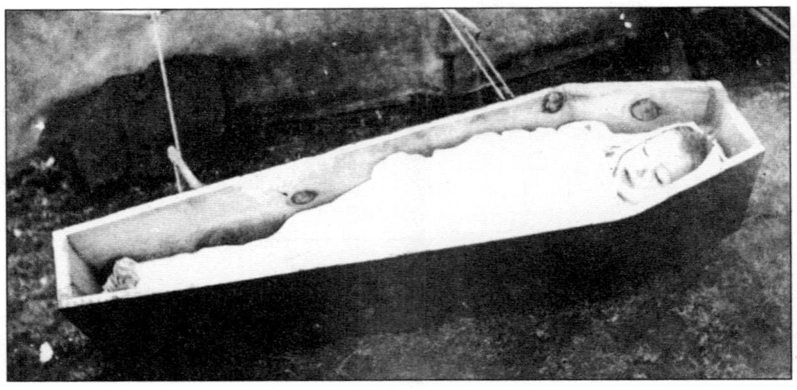

The corpse of a Boer baby in a concentration camp

MIXED FORTUNES IN TRANSVAAL

Disastrous attack on British train

In the veld in the eastern Transvaal, 31 July – In the past month there have been a number of clashes, but none of major interest. On 4 July Captain Jack Hindon's burghers derailed a military train south of Naboomspruit. One of the burghers who participated in this event, E.J. Weeber, told our correspondent what happened:

'We came to this area with the specific aim of attacking the military trains. We decided to use the long wire method. This method was devised by Carl Craemer, a burgher of German descent, who had also developed the method of detonating dynamite that is set underneath a railway line by means of the firing mechanism of a rifle, triggered by the weight of the train.

'Captain Hindon and Lieutenant Slegtkamp chose the place where the attempt to capture the train would be made.

'Since we wanted to ensure that we captured a train fully loaded with supplies, Craemer attached a long copper wire to the trigger of the rifle that had to detonate the dynamite. He then hid himself in the veld and waited for a suitable train. Our commando of about 40 men anxiously looked on from our hiding place in thorn bushes about 40 metres away.

'We have no doubt that the Khakis were aware of our plans. Nevertheless we managed to blow up the locomotive of a train that approached from the south. The remainder of the train shuddered to a halt directly in front of us. A heavy engagement followed. Suddenly a woman appeared in the train window and shouted at us to stop firing, since we were killing our own people. We did stop and some of us left our hiding places, upon which Khakis from an armoured train wagon fired on them. A few of our comrades, including Craemer, were killed in this incident.

'The battle now flared up again. It soon became clear to us that we would be overwhelmed. As a result those of us who were able ran for our lives. A large number of us were either killed or wounded. I barely managed to escape. Even though we had derailed the locomotive, the whole venture was a terrible disaster.'

Our correspondent subsequently established that seven burghers and nine Khakis were killed in the battle.

KEMP ACTIVE AGAINST KHAKIS

On 5 July General Jan Kemp's burghers carried out simultaneous attacks on a number of Witwatersrand towns. Kemp himself relates: 'Field Cornet Meyer meticulously spied on Roodepoort the previous day. We approached the farms outside the town stealthily, but found nobody there. We then moved on to the railway station, but it was deserted. We realised that the enemy had staged an ambush for us and it was indeed the case. When we moved towards the mines, a spattering of rifle fire welcomed us from the forts and from numerous houses. We had to abandon our plan to set alight the batteries at the mines and could only burn down the railway station.'

On 17 July Kemp and his commando were on the farm Bultfontein near Ventersdorp in the western Transvaal. There they drove off a number of Khakis who were looting cattle. One of the Khakis who was killed was Lieutenant Kimber, the son of the mayor of London.

FIGHTING IN THE EASTERN TRANSVAAL

A huge setback was suffered by the Transvaal forces on 20 July when the respected Heidelberg General, Cornelis Spruyt, was killed in action near Val Station. He was shot while he and his burghers were crossing the railway line with the objective of invading Natal. General Smuts had a very narrow escape on the same day in the area of Gatsrand in the southwestern Transvaal when he and a number of burghers were surprised while they were sleeping. Smuts escaped in the dark of night by shouting out orders in English, but Kleinbooi, his *agterryer*, or black attendant, was killed. The next day a British unit halted Smuts's plans to cross the Vaal River at Lindequesdrift. Smuts, Commandant T.F.J. Dreyer and their burghers consequently moved off to the west and crossed the Vaal west of Klerksdorp a week later. Their objective is to join Commandants Van Deventer, Kirsten and Ben Bouwer in the vicinity of Hoopstad.

On Sunday 21 July General Tobias Smuts arrived at Bremersdorp in Swaziland on orders of Commandant-General Botha to investigate complaints by the Swazi regent, Labotsibeni, that a British unit was molesting her subjects. Smuts's burghers encircled the British unit, who call themselves Steinaecker's Horse, in Bremersdorp and captured their position. Subsequently they burnt down the place. Altogether 41 men, including a few armed blacks, were taken prisoner of war. The joiners who were amongst the prisoners of war, as well as the armed blacks, were brought before a military court last Saturday and sentenced to death. Afterwards they were shot.

Since the day before yesterday a British army commanded by General Walter Kitchener has repeatedly attacked the burghers of Generals Ben Viljoen and Chris Muller near Middelburg, here in the eastern Transvaal. At times the burghers were under severe pressure, but fortunately they evaded the claws of the Khakis.

PRESIDENT STEYN ALMOST IN BRITISH HANDS

Free State government captured near Reitz

In the veld in the northern Free State, 28 July – A large measure of thanks must go to Jan Ruiter, the *agterryer* of President Steyn of the Free State, for the fact that Steyn was not made a prisoner of war with the rest of his government on 11 July. The President himself told our correspondent what had happened:

'The government and I and our escort commanded by Commandant Loffie Davel went to Reitz on 9 July where I planned to have a number of defective heliograph systems repaired at the local smith's store. Davel wanted to allow some members of his commando a few days of leave. Davel sent out scouts to ensure that British forces would not surprise us and they reported that there were no Khakis in the vicinity. Consequently we were not as careful as we normally are.

'We spread out over virtually the whole town. The burghers wanted to sleep in the houses, but I pitched my tent in front of the former dwelling of the justice of the peace, Rossouw. My horse was in a stable about 400 metres from my tent. Generals Andries Cronjé and Jan Wessels as well as my eldest brother, Pieter Steyn, slept with me in the tent.

'At about two o'clock in the morning I rose, as my custom is, to ensure that everything was in order. Although there were no guards to be seen, everything seemed quiet and I went back to sleep. My personal *agterryer*, Jan Ruiter, was busy making coffee just before daybreak when he heard a noise. His first thought was that it was cattle, but he soon realised that it was a British force and that they were already in the town! Ruiter plucked open the tent door and called softly to me: "Master, the English are here!"

'I wasted no time, but jumped up and saw the soldiers approaching on horseback in the half-light of dawn. They were about 300 or 400 metres from us. I was not sure where my horse was, but Ruiter fortunately knew and we both ran to the stable. Fortunately we had to go around a corner and were out of sight of the enemy. At the stable I intended jumping bareback on my horse, but a young Cape teacher, Curlewis, ran up with his saddle and insisted that I use it, which I did. The stirrups were rather short, but since there was no time I did not set them right.

'When Ruiter and I galloped from the stable on our horses, the whole town was full of Khakis. A Brit shouted on us to halt, but we kept on fleeing. A moment later a shot rang out. Ruiter jumped from his horse in the half-light. I thought he had been hit and only later heard to my relief that it was his objective to draw the attention of the British away from me. That made it possible for me to make my escape, even though my horse, old Dapper, was somewhat ancient and a bit stiff. Fortunately the Khakis did not pursue me immediately.

'With this flight my saddle, my hat and my coat remained behind. Fortunately I was wearing a warm nightcap. Later that day I commandeered a hat from a burgher who had an extra one, and the wife of burgher De Jager gave me her husband's wedding jacket. I did not want to take it, but she insisted. At that stage I was not dressed painfully correctly, like a Prussian general, but that is of no significance.

'My fortune at being able to escape from the Khakis is somewhat dampened by the loss of my letters and reports that were in the pockets of my coat and in my saddlebags. A bigger loss is of course that all the members of the Free State government fell into the hands of the enemy, namely State Secretary Brain, Generals Cronjé and Wessels, military commissioner Pieter Steyn (my brother), my secretaries and my personal guard, altogether 29 people. In addition the British captured £11 500 in notes and coins as well as all our government documents. I will now have to appoint new people to fill the vacancies.

'After the enemy left Reitz again, we sent scouts there. They established that the British took all the prisoners of war to Heilbron, and inflicted massive damage on the town. Fortunately they allowed Ruiter and all our other servants to go out on their own, according to Ruiter, since they were in a hurry. He then told me that he was not wounded, but jumped from his horse because he was afraid. The Brit who fired on us ran to him and asked who it was galloping away (referring to me). Ruiter answered: "That is just an old farmer." "Where is the President?" the officer wanted to know. "He sleeps in his tent," Ruiter answered. "Come show me," the officer ordered. And Ruiter walked from tent to tent to give me an opportunity to get away before reaching the correct tent. There the other members of the government confirmed that I slept there but I was no longer there.

'Ruiter is now in my service again, but with bigger prestige than ever, and he leaves none of the other *agterryers* in any doubt about that.'

OUR MILITARY OFFICERS

Fighting General Cornelis Spruyt

Cornelis Johannes Spruyt was born in 1857 in the Heidelberg district in the Transvaal. He was the son of Jan and Johanna Spruyt. He grew up on a farm and served as deacon and Sunday school teacher in the Dutch Reformed Church.

In February 1899 Spruyt was elected Field Cornet of the Heidelberg Town Commando; during the military operations on the Natal front in December of the same year he was appointed acting commandant. His commando participated in the battle of Platrand in January 1900, where Spruyt revealed outstanding leadership qualities. Soon afterwards he and the Heidelberg Commando were transferred to the front in the Orange Free State. Spruyt participated with Chief Commandant De Wet in the attempts to relieve General Cronjé's laager at Paardeberg, but was made prisoner of war on 20 February by British infantry troops with bayonets. He was sent in the baggage wagon of a goods train as a prisoner of war to Cape Town, but fortunately managed to jump from the moving train near De Aar in the northern Cape and escaped. After four days of walking he reached the Boer forces at Colesberg. In April last year he rejoined his commando after being incapacitated by a disease for a brief period.

In the Battle of Bergendal Spruyt acted as provisional fighting general and in October last year was promoted to Assistant Commandant-General. During the Battle at Chrissiesmeer he was a witness when his brothers, Ockert and Dolf, were both killed in action.

On 20 July Spruyt was fatally wounded when his commando attempted to cross the railway line between Val and Vlaklaagte Stations. Two days later he was buried at Wonderfontein, the farm of Abraham Pretorius. He is survived by his wife, Suzara Johanna Smith, and their four children.

General Cornelis Spruyt

THE War Reporter
MONTHLY EDITION

Number 56   In the Veld, South African Republic   1 September 1901

KITCHENER'S LATEST 'PAPER BOMB'
BOERS HAVE TO SURRENDER BEFORE 15 SEPTEMBER, OR …

In the veld, 31 August – On 7 August General Kitchener fired another paper bomb – this time a major one. (Paper bomb is the word used by the Boers to refer to threatening British proclamations.) We hesitate to provide any publicity to the desperate attempts of the Khakis to intimidate our people, but this latest proclamation is so dripping with half-truths, blunders and a lack of discretion that we feel forced to react to it.

The proclamation begins by honouring Kitchener himself, and then alleges that the vast majority of the civilian population is at present quietly living in the towns or camps under the control of the British forces. This is of course untrue: the British have destroyed most of the towns and the Boers in the so-called refugee camps are detained there against their will.

Second allegation: the burghers of the so-called late Republics who are still fighting are pitifully few in numbers, have lost virtually all their artillery pieces and war supplies and can no longer offer organised resistance against the British forces. Fact is, they are fewer in number, but there are no cowards left and the burghers who are still fighting are highly motivated and determined; the loss of their guns and vehicles has left them more mobile, which is a partial blessing since their tactics are much more effective than a year ago. By comparison, the gigantic British forces seem clumsy and over-organised.

The next allegation: the burghers who are still fighting destroy property and prevent the carrying out of agriculture and industry. Now this is a blatant distortion of the truth by the leader of the greatest destroyers of property that the world has ever seen. It is the British themselves who make the progress of agriculture and industries in the Republics impossible by their barbaric destruction of our farms and our towns.

After other questionable statements, Kitchener proceeds with a whole series of threats that are summarised in the following ultimatum:

'All Boer officers who are still fighting as well as all the members of the governments of the "former" Republics will, if they do not surrender before 15 September, be permanently banned from South Africa and the cost of the care of their dependents will be covered by selling their property.'

Most of the Boer officers attach so little value to the proclamation that they refuse to react to it. Chief Commandant De Wet sent a short answer to Kitchener. In this he acknowledges receipt of this proclamation and declares that he and his officers are fighting for only one purpose, namely their independence, and they cannot and will not abandon that. De Wet says bluntly that he has only contempt for this proclamation and that only children will fear its threats. There is a proverb that states: To instil fear does not mean to kill.

PRESIDENT STEYN'S ANSWER

President Steyn was so annoyed about the misstatements in the proclamation of 7 August that he answered at length on behalf of the government of the Orange Free State, both in Dutch and in English. In his answer he points out that the British had continuously interfered in the affairs of the Boer Republics since long before the outbreak of this war – specifically through their abysmal involvement in Jameson's traitorous raid in 1895–96. Furthermore he points out that a member of the British government has admitted that they would have sent an ultimatum to the Republics, had President Kruger not done so. This makes a joke of the continuous accusations that the Boers were the aggressors in this war. Indeed, the Boer Republics simply attempted to keep the British sword away from their throats and acted in all respects out of self-defence, which is one of the most holy rights in humanity.

In reaction to Kitchener's allegation that the Boers are in a hopeless position, Steyn answered that the Boers are indeed in a much better position than they were a year ago. There are commandos in the veld everywhere in the Cape Colony, and with the exception of the cities, the big towns and the railway lines, the remainder of the Republics are in the Boers' hands.

The threat of banning, the Free State president says, has no power to frighten men whose country, whose farms and whose houses have been destroyed, whose livestock has been killed, whose wives and children are locked up in prisons and are maltreated, and hundreds of whose loved ones have already paid the highest price for freedom. If self-defence is a crime, the British will have to satisfy themselves with the destruction of the property of others and the punishment of the wives and children of others. The Boers do not ask any magnanimity from the British – they purely demand justice!

MILITARY ACTIVITIES IN THE TRANSVAAL

In the veld, 31 August – This month hardly any military activities took place in the Transvaal. In the eastern Transvaal, General Chris Muller, Lieutenant Colonel Fanie Trichard and their men restored their reputation on 16 August by overwhelming a section of General Walter Kitchener's forces at Vrieskraal, near the Elands River, after three weeks of being under tremendous pressure. Five Khakis were killed in the skirmish and 26 taken prisoner. In addition the Boers captured a number of horses as well as a herd of cattle that had previously been taken from them by the British.

In a previous issue we reported on General Tobias Smuts's raid on the British robbers' nest at Bremersdorp in Swaziland. The reigning Swazi regent, Queen Labotsibeni, thanked Smuts afterwards during an audience for repulsing the British soldiers and their cronies, the notorious Steinacker's Horse. These Khakis fled to the north, and by the beginning of August were at Mpisaan's Fort in the Lowveld, east of Lydenburg. General Ben Viljoen's commando attacked them there early on the morning of 6 August. A fierce battle followed during which six burghers were killed and Commandant Moll of Lydenburg was seriously wounded. Eventually the whole complement of the fort surrendered. Among the British one officer and several soldiers were killed. In addition to 74 prisoners of war, the burghers captured important documents and a huge store of food and ammunition. After correspondence with General Walter Kitchener on the status of the members of the notorious Steinacker's Horse, Viljoen released all the white prisoners of war, but ordered all the blacks who had fought against the Boers to be shot.

In the meantime, the Executive Council of the South African Republic discussed General Smuts's treatment of the enemy during his attack on Bremersdorp. Finding that Smuts had probably overextended his authority and acted against the usages of civilised warfare, the council ordered Commandant-General Louis Botha to investigate the issue and to act against Smuts if necessary. Botha found that Smuts had indeed overreached and took his rank away from him. It is tragic that an experienced officer such as Tobias Smuts must now continue the struggle as an ordinary burgher, but Smuts accepted his fate and Commandant-General Botha probably had no other option but to restore the good name of the South African Republic.

On 20 August British soldiers unexpectedly attacked a campsite of about 200 Boers some distance south of Bronkhorstspruit. The surprised burghers initially found it difficult to defend themselves and were almost overwhelmed by the enemy. In the end, however, they found their feet, drove the Khakis back and even took a number of them prisoner. The price was high, since unconfirmed reports indicate that 23 burghers were killed and a large number wounded.

In the western Transvaal General Methuen's Khakis attacked the town Schweizer-Renecke on 4 August and destroyed everything but the church building.

The month ended with a huge success for the Transvaal forces. Yesterday a group of scouts led by the well-known train wrecker, Jack Hindon, derailed a British train between Waterval and Hammanskraal north of Pretoria, and forced the crew on board to surrender. One British officer, 12 soldiers and three civilians were killed and some 20 wounded. Of infinitely more value to Hindon and his burghers are all the war supplies, food and dynamite that they captured. The latter would enable them to destroy many more British trains.

Lieutenant Colonel Fanie Trichard

FROM THE EDITOR

The major news this month is Kitchener's latest paper bomb. Having finally realised that they will never win the struggle against us on the battlefield, now the Brits are trying psychological warfare. We have bad news for them: this attempt will not work either. The Boer officers still in the field are not men who are easily frightened, and it is unthinkable now that any officer or government member will suddenly lay down his arms. Kitchener seems to be very slow to realise the unavoidable – and in addition, quite incapable of formulating logical proclamations. President Steyn and State Secretary Reitz could not resist the temptation to reveal the weaknesses in his proclamation. The British commander will in the course of time realise that one cannot violate the truth and expect to force the Boers into surrendering by threats.

In the meantime, there have been numerous small skirmishes in which the Republican forces have managed to give a good account of themselves against the mass of Khaki forces. Even though there are still a few lame and lazy burghers, the flame of our people's hopes and their determination are reaching new heights and we believe with President Steyn that justice will in the final instance be victorious.

DAYS OF SUPPLICATION

In the veld, 30 August – In a previous issue we reported that the governments of the Orange Free State and the South African Republic decided during their meeting on 20 June to declare 8 and 9 August days of supplication and prayer. Most of the commandos found it virtually impossible to carry out this decision. General Beyers, in the northern Transvaal, believed that a state of true humility would be worth more than a glorious victory; nevertheless he could not provide an opportunity for all his burghers to spend those two days in thought and prayer. The problem was that one of his officers, Field Cornet De Villiers, and his wife chose that specific time to assist the British and attempted to lead Beyers's commando into an ambush. Fortunately the De Villiers couple failed, though Beyers and his burghers had to fight valiantly to escape from the traps set for them. It was only the burghers without horses in Beyers's laager who had the opportunity to humble themselves before God.

In the eastern Transvaal General Muller's and Lieutenant Colonel Trichard's commandos spent these days in serious speeches and prayers. Many burghers attended the joint event. Muller proposed that everyone should take a rock and place it on a cairn as a signal of their commitment to fight to the bitter end.

His hope is that if they should eventually achieve a victory, they should return to this place every year and erect a monument to commemorate their victory. Many of the burghers brought rocks and placed it on the cairn. A few days later, after the Boers had left again, the Khakis came and dumped all the rocks of the cairn in the river.

BATTLES IN THE FREE STATE

In the veld in the Free State, 28 August – The most important news from the Orange Free State in the past month has been the trek of General Jan Smuts and his commando through the Republic – and the futile attempts of the British to restrict the Republican forces. Smuts crossed the Vaal River from the western Transvaal into the Free State near Hoopstad about a month ago with a commando of about 340 men. On 1 August a British force surprised them at Grootvlei, east of Hoopstad. Apparently six of Smuts's burghers were killed in the skirmish that followed, and 12 were made prisoner of war.

Smuts realised that the British would do everything in their power to capture him and his men. Numerous reports certainly indicate that the Khakis gathered a huge force in the northwest Free State and launched a massive drive to corner the Boer commandos. However, our burghers were too wily to allow themselves to be captured that easily. The entire British attempt failed.

On 3 August Smuts divided his commando into two sections. One group moved southwards under Commandant Van Deventer and the second in the same direction under Smuts's own command. In effect they followed the British forces that were looking for them. On Koot Krause's farm they met with shocking scenes. The Khakis had filled a whole kraal with sheep and then thrown a dynamite candle in amongst them. Smuts and his men found many of the sheep mangled but still alive. On another farm, Smuts says, the British had bundled the sheep into camps and then set the veld on fire, so that the poor animals were burned alive.

He furthermore reports that virtually all the farm dams are filled with the corpses of dead animals, obviously in an attempt to poison the water so that the Boers cannot use it. The veld is covered with slaughtered sheep and goats, cattle and horses. It is indescribably shocking. The most tragic sight is that of the huge number of lambs, weak from hunger and thirst, stumbling around the carcasses of their dead and mangled mothers. Smuts said that he had never seen anything so pitiful and heard anything so tragic as the helpless bleating of the lambs in this death acre of destruction. It is incomprehensible that people can be so entirely unfeeling. The deeds of those who are guilty can in the end only lead to their own downfall.

Carcasses of horses shot by the Khakis to prevent the Boers using them

Khakis shooting Boer cattle in a kraal

The overwhelming numbers of British in the Free State often placed Smuts and his men under tremendous pressure. Yesterday the Khakis clamped down on the commandos near Reddersburg and took a total of 34 burghers prisoner of war. The combined commandos of Smuts and Van Deventer at present only consist of about 200 men and they are surrounded by thousands of Khakis.

Elsewhere in the Free State Commandant Alberts and his men destroyed a British blockhouse near Brand-fort on 7 August. Seven Khakis died in this battle and a large number were wounded. On 15 August Commandant Kritzinger's commando of 150 men broke through the blockhouse line south of Springfontein without any casualties.

CLASHES IN THE WESTERN CAPE

In the veld in the Cape Colony, 20 August – Here in the western Cape north of the Boland, Commandant Manie Maritz and about 160 men are keeping the British forces guessing on a large scale. This is the Boers' intention: as many Khakis as possible must be involved in pursuing the Republican forces across the vast stretches of the Cape Colony, since the pressure on the Republics themselves will be relieved in that way. At the end of last month Maritz and his men surprised a patrol consisting of 31 Khakis near Clanwilliam and captured them all. This led to panic in Clanwilliam itself, since everybody expected that the Boers would attack the town. However, Maritz and his men had other plans, since he had to shake off a large British force that was pursuing him.

Early in August the Khakis almost managed to corner Maritz and his commando against the Bokkeveld Mountains. They got away after dark and crossed the mountains. A number of horses tumbled down the steep mountain slope, but the commando was subsequently safe again and found shelter and rest in the thick bushes on the farm Grootdrift near Vanrhynsdorp. Maritz's scouts informed him of the exact layout of the town and the living quarters of the commander of the Western Province Mounted Rifles, Commandant Rosten. Maritz decided that it was time to attack. Before daybreak on 7 August he and his men advanced on the town. At four o'clock in the morning Maritz walked into the sleeping quarters of the snoring Rosten and captured him and his lieutenant. A skirmish followed but the Khakis hoisted the white flag after a few hours. Two British soldiers were killed and 29 made prisoner of war. Maritz's men suffered no casualties. Indeed, they captured a number of British vehicles, including three heavily loaded supply wagons and 65 horses, before leaving again. They heard that their pursuers only reached Vanrhynsdorp three days later.

Maritz and his men plan to remain in the western Cape, since their mere presence in that area generates panic in the ranks of the British military and civilian authorities in South Africa.

DEATH PENALTY FOR CAPE REBELS

Martial law strictly applied: even black newspapers prohibited

In the veld, 29 August – At least 11 Cape Rebels have been executed by the British in the past three months. The first was F.A. Marais, who was hanged at Middelburg in the Cape Colony on 10 June after being found guilty of treason and attempted murder. Two days later J.P. Coetzee was hung in Cradock and another week later, on 20 June, P.W. Kloppert was hung at Burgersdorp. In the northern Cape, H.L. Jacobs and A.C. Jooste were executed at Kenhardt on 24 July on accusations of treason. On the same day C. Claassen, a poor young man who was mentally retarded and who never really knew what was happening, was found guilty of treason in Somerset-East, sentenced to death and hanged. His crime was that he attended horses for a Boer commando.

On the day before Coetzee was executed, the following notice was put up at several places in the town: 'All Male Adults in the Township of Cradock are hereby ORDERED to attend in the Market Square TOMORROW MORNING at a quarter to eleven to witness the promulgation of the sentence of Death to be passed on Johannes Petrus Coetzee for High Treason and attempt to Murder. All places of business must be closed from half past ten till after the promulgation of the sentence.'

On 19 August three men, P.J. Fourie, J. van Rensburg and L.F.S. Pfeiffer died in Graaff-Reinet in front of a firing squad on charges of treason and the death of British soldiers. A week later Daniel Olewagen and Ignatius Nel were executed in the same way. Their crime was that they acted as horse guards for a Boer commando.

In an attempt to allay the fear of Cape Rebels in the veld that the Republics might leave them in the lurch, President Steyn issued a statement on 25 August that the Republics would not accept a peace agreement that made no provision for the interests of the Cape Rebels.

The British are not only acting against relatively unknown rebels. From 25 August armed soldiers held the well-known Cape politician, J.X. Merriman, under house arrest like a criminal on his farm near Stellenbosch. And on 27 August the British placed a ban, in terms of martial law regulations, on the Xhosa–English newspaper *Imvo Zabantsundu*. The reason: the editor of this paper, John Tengo Jabavu, who is a well-known black politician and leader, had dared to criticise the British military policy of scorched earth and the concentration camps.

Another report from Pretoria is that two Boers, N.T. Venter and P.R. Krause, were shot by a British firing squad on 11 June after being found guilty of attempted murder, breaking their oath of neutrality and illegal possession of weapons.

OUR MILITARY OFFICERS

Commandant Willem Fouchee

Willem Fouchee is an officer of whom hardly anything is known in the South African Republic. He is a Free Stater, the seventh of the nine children of Stephanus Phillippus Fouchee, who was a *bywoner* (sharecropper) on the farm Brandewynsgat, owned by Piet du Plessis, in the Rouxville district. Fouchee's father died when he was nine years old, whereupon Du Plessis adopted him.

Before the war broke out Fouchee, who was by then 25 years old, lived at Philippolis. He joined the Rouxville Commando and took part in the Battle of Stormberg in December 1899. After the fall of Bloemfontein he achieved fame as a scout and by the end of last year he was a captain. Commandant Kritzinger promoted him to the rank of commandant earlier this year. His commando consists mostly of Cape Rebels who are active in the Stormberg range.

Fouchee is a tall, well-built man with a youthful face. His strong leadership qualities and his legendary valour make him a popular figure, especially amongst the younger members of his commando. The members of his commando wear yellow hatbands and are known as the Yellow Hats. Some of the Stormberg people refer to them as the Yellow Cobras, since Fouchee's fighting method is to attack quickly like a snake and then withdraw again. The British certainly have great respect for him. In a local English newspaper he is referred to as the 'Notorious Fouchee' and a British information booklet that fell into our hands says of him that 'he is not likely to surrender'. For the first time we agree with the Khakis – the blood of a true 'Bitter-ender' flows in the veins of Commandant Willem Diederich Fouchee.

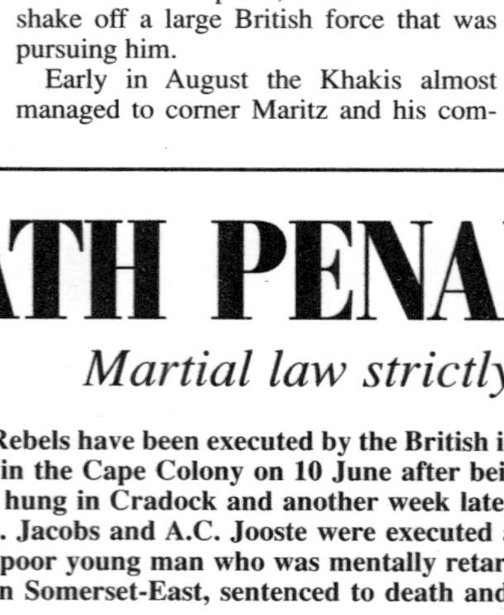

Commandant Willem Fouchee

THE PRISONERS OF WAR IN INDIA

A first-hand report by one of them

In the veld, 30 Juy – The following report was smuggled to South Africa from a prisoner-of-war camp in India. It was compiled by the Reverend D.J. Viljoen, who was until abduction by the Khakis a minister of the Dutch Reformed Church in Reitz in the northeastern Orange Free State:

'When we woke up on the morning of 23 April we could see Bombay in the distance. There was gratitude in our hearts that the Lord had led us to safety over the vast ocean, and we prayed that He would lead and protect us in the unfamiliar India. Towards one o'clock that afternoon we sailed into the harbour. It was very hot. A great number of spectators who were curious to see the Boer prisoners of war awaited us. The extent of their curiosity about our appearance was matched by their interest and sympathy with us. Not a word of contempt was heard and no sign of hate was visible. How different was this from Cape Town, where our poor prisoners of war were reviled in the streets as ugly and detestable.

'We were not allowed to enter the city but left Bombay by train that evening. Before we left the burghers sang the two republican anthems at the request of an English lady. It was striking to note the respect with which the spectators listened to the singing of our anthems.

'Our journey commenced in the moonlight. We passed through a mountainous area. Even though it was night, there were huge crowds of curious and interested spectators at all the stations. It was a pleasant journey since we were not accompanied by an armed guard. We only fell asleep late that night.

'We were disappointed when we woke the next morning (24 April) in a dry area. At seven o'clock that morning we arrived at Ahmednagar Station. We had to walk the six kilometres to our camp. After about an hour we arrived at the fort. When we saw the high walls we felt all but comfortable. Strangers in a strange land, and now we would be locked up in a prison! Once inside we were even more unhappy. Everything seemed dismal. Virtually no green leaves, unbearable heat, locked up between high walls, barbed wire and the ever-present armed guards. Our thoughts were that we would not be here long before a huge number of us would find our graves here.

'After our arrival we were counted and it was established that one of the prisoners, Grey, had escaped. We have no idea where he is. We then occupied bungalows or corrugated iron huts. We were all very tired and spent most of the day sleeping.'

THE
War Reporter
MONTHLY EDITION

Number 57 | In the Veld, South African Republic | 1 October 1901

REPUBLICAN FORCES IN THE CAPE COLONY

Success and adversity in widespread military actions

In the veld, 30 September – The Republican commandos active in the Cape Colony have achieved mixed success in the past months. After occupying Vanrhynsdorp in the western districts last month, Commandant Manie Maritz and his commando retreated east to Calvinia, where they are resting while a few burghers recuperate from measles. On the last day of August, a British force attacked them, but they escaped. Their casualties were three men wounded.

In the northeastern Cape, Comman-dants Myburgh and Fouchee led a British column into an ambush at Wolwekraal in the Stormberg Mountains early in September and inflicted heavy casualties on them. However, on 5 September a British force overwhelmed Commandant Hans Lötter and his commando near Cradock. The Khakis surprised the commando while they were sleeping in a shed one night, while it was raining outside. Lötter and his men fought back desperately but suffered heavy casualties and were eventually forced to surrender. Alto-gether 14 burghers were killed, and more than 50, including Lötter himself, were wounded. That means that by the end of the fight more than half of the men were either dead or wounded.

In the Southern Cape, a tragedy struck the commando of Commandant Piet van der Merwe on 10 September. A huge British force overwhelmed them at Driefontein at the foothills of the Swartberg. Van der Merwe, who was only 19 years old (as far as we know the youngest Boer commandant), was killed and his whole commando, with the exception of three men who escaped, were taken prisoner of war.

On the northern side of the Karoo, Commandant Wynand Malan's commando fared much better. On 16 September a British column attempted an attack on them, but the Boers led the attackers into an ambush and forced them to surrender. Four Khakis were killed in the process.

SMUTS'S EXPEDITION INTO THE CAPE

In spite of intensive British attempts to halt him, General Jan Smuts crossed the Orange River with about 250 men on 3 September, and entered the eastern Cape district Herschel. Three burghers were killed in fights with armed black men in an area that they did not know at all. On 5 September, Smuts and his commando reached the Stormberg Mountains. Smuts says that the local Afrikaners received them with open arms. On one farm, the woman and children literally cried with joy when the Boers off-saddled. Fodder is scarce in the area, however.

On 7 September a major calamity was narrowly averted. Smuts himself, accompanied by three scouts on horseback, was looking for a safe route for his commando near Dordrecht. When they entered a narrow ravine with the rather frightening name of Murderer's Poort, they were unexpectedly attacked by a number of Khakis. The three scouts were shot down at point blank range, and Smuts's horse was killed under him, but he escaped unharmed.

All the mountains in the eastern Cape were suddenly full of enemy soldiers, and Smuts looked desperately for a thoroughfare for his commando. From 9 to 13 September they were continuously surrounded by Khakis in the area of Penhoek Pass in the Stormberg. They had to fight desperately to prevent being overwhelmed. Smuts says that they went without sleep for three nights. To worsen matters, it rained continuously, and a strong wind blew. Men and animals were wet through, numb with cold, and ultimately exhausted to the point of death. Fortunately, they suffered few casualties (only one man killed in action), while inflicting heavy casualties on the Khakis. A Boer over whose farm they trekked gave them grain bags, old blankets and sheepskins from which they made coats to protect themselves against the cold.

Eventually they managed to slip out of the net. Deneys Reitz, son of State Secretary F.W. Reitz, told our correspondent that the Khakis had cornered them at a small farmhouse one evening and their speedy capture seemed certain. However, 'out of the house came a hunchbacked cripple, who said that he would lead us through the English troops to the edge of the tableland, by a way which was unlikely to be watched, for it ran through boggy soil. His offer was eagerly accepted and orders were given to mount at once. Six or seven men had been wounded during the day, two of them so badly that they had to be left behind, but the others chose to accompany us, and in a few minutes we were silently filing off into the darkness, the cripple crouching insecurely at our head. He took us along a squelching path that twisted for a mile or two so close to the investing troops that we could hear voices and the champing of bits, but at the end of an anxious hour, he had brought us undiscovered to the escarpment. From here the mountain-side fell sharply away into black depths below, how steeply we could not tell, but our guide warned us that it was very steep indeed. Dropping from his horse he plodded off into the night on his crutches, carrying with him our heartfelt thanks, for he had risked his life and goods on our behalf.

'We now began to descend what was probably the nearest approach to the vertical attempted by any mounted force during the war. I doubt whether we could have accomplished it by day, but horses are more tractable and surer-footed in the dark, so we pulled them over the edge and went slithering down.

'Somewhere on the plain before us ran the railway line on which we had looked down that morning, and many miles beyond that lay still another track, both of which had to be crossed before sunrise, if we did not wish to have the troop-trains hurrying up more men. So General Smuts implacably ordered us on, and, leading our horses, we tramped obediently but wearily forward.

'After crossing the rails, we went on mile after mile, days on end for want of rest. Whenever there was delay at a fence or a ditch, whole rows of men would fall asleep on their hands and knees before their horses like Mohammedans at prayer, and it was necessary to go round shaking them to their feet to prevent them being left behind.'

Commandant Piet van der Merwe

Unfortunately for Smuts and his men, their suffering was not over yet. They now entered the Bamboes Mountains. On the night of 15–16 September, it rained continuously, and became increasingly cold. Reitz reported thus to our correspondent:

'The night that followed was the most terrible of all. Our guide lost his way; we went floundering ankle-deep in mud and water, our poor weakened horses stumbling and slipping at every turn; the rain beat down on us, and the cold was awful. Towards midnight sleet began to fall. The grain-bag which I wore froze solid on my body, like a coat of mail, and I believe that if we had not kept moving every one of us would have died. We had known two years of war, but we came nearer to despair that night than I care to remember. Hour after hour we groped our way, with men groaning who had never before uttered a word of complaint, as the cold seared their ill-protected bodies.

'We also lost a large number of horses, and I remember stumbling at intervals over their carcasses. We went on till daybreak, dragging ourselves along. Then, providentially, came a deserted homestead. We staggered into shelter, standing huddled together in rooms, stables, and barns until dawn, still shivering, but gradually recovering from the dreadful ordeal. When it grew light, some 50 or 60 horses lay dead outside. My little roan mare was still alive, but both my uncle's horses died here, and he, with 30 or 40 more, was now a foot-soldier.'

Not only did they lose their horses, but Smuts discovered a British spy in his camp, and 12 of his men got lost. Later they did receive some good news. At that stage they thought the lost men had been taken prisoner by the Khakis, but in fact those men got away and acted as a loose commando, causing serious problems for the enemy.

On 17 September, Smuts and his commando were trudging along between Tarkastad and Cradock. Reitz reports: 'The sky was clear, and the sun warm and bright for the first time for weeks, so that the men were cheerful again, although there was little other cause for optimism.

'As a fighting force we were on our last legs. In front walked those who still had horses, dragging scarecrows behind them; then came a trail of footmen in twos and threes, their saddles slung across their shoulders, and in the rear rode the wounded in charge of their friends.

'When we got to where the valley widened into more open country, a Dutch farmer rushed from a cottage beside the road, and in a voice hoarse with excitement, told us that the English cavalry were waiting for us lower down. He said that they had mountain- and machine-guns, and he estimated their strength at 200 men, with over 300 horses and mules, all of which proved substantially correct.

'General Smuts immediately decided to attack, and I heard him say that if we did not get those horses and a supply of ammunition we were done for.'

The enemy initially fought back courageously, but suffered heavy losses and soon raised the white flag. The British casualties were 73 men dead and wounded and 51 unwounded men made prisoner of war. Smuts's loss was one man dead and seven wounded. They captured the two guns. Their most valuable booty, however, was the British horses, rifles, ammunition and food. They were once more a fighting force!

After destroying the two guns, so that the British would not be able to use those armaments on them again, and setting the tents and wagons on fire, Smuts and his men turned to the south and on 23 September crossed the Winterberg range. Three days later they were in the vicinity of Adelaide and on 27 September they crossed the Great Fish River. They achieved exactly what they intended with this expedition, namely to involve a growing number of British units in futile attempts to capture them.

FROM THE EDITOR

A blessed period for the Republican forces on the battlefield! Generals Louis Botha and Koos de la Rey proved in two separate clashes that the Boers are not a spent force. And General Smuts made significant progress with his expedition into the eastern districts of the Cape Colony, in spite of the tens of thousands of Khakis who are attempting to capture him. He has without doubt already achieved his aim of forcing the British military authorities to divert huge forces to the Colony. However, his other aim – to stimulate a general uprising of Cape Afrikaners – has produced nothing so far.

The unanimous rejection by Republican officers and burghers of Lord Kitchener's threatening proclamation of 7 August can only mean one thing: the burghers' reaction to the sufferings caused by the war is to shift their own interests to the background, and concentrate on their people's cause. That is a very positive development. The British seem to foster the illusion that they have already won the war. Indeed, the future looks increasingly bright for the Boer cause every single day.

DEMOLITION OF TRAINS AND RAILWAY LINES

WHAT IS CIVILISED AND WHAT IS UNCIVILISED WARFARE?

In the veld in the eastern Transvaal, 20 September – One of the Boers' most important objectives is to sabotage as many railway lines and trains as possible to hinder the British war effort. Such attacks have numerous advantages. In the first place, the burghers often capture valuable supplies, including food, ammunition, clothing and blankets. Secondly, they have psychological value for the Boers, since each time they demolish a train, they feel that they are still in a position to inflict damage on the enemy, despite the latter's huge advantage in manpower and supplies. Thirdly, the British army has to use tens of thousands of soldiers to guard the railway lines, since the next Boer attack may occur anywhere. Those railway guards can then not be used to act offensively against the commandos.

Boer attacks on the railway lines are a massive headache for the British authorities, who are employing all sorts of gimmicks to bring them to an end.

Early in September Lord Kitchener wrote to Commandant-General Botha threatening harsh action because the way in which the Boers were sabotaging railway lines and telegraphic communications was, according to him, outside the accepted practices of civilised warfare.

The Republican military authorities wondered what merciless actions Kitchener planned to implement. The secret was soon revealed. Only a day after his letter to Botha, Kitchener formally ordered that two prominent burghers of the 'former South African Republic' must accompany each train that transports civilians or British soldiers north of the Vaal River. Kitchener hopes that the fighting burghers will not attack trains if they know that well-known Transvaalers are on board.

The Republican authorities could hardly be blamed for asking if this is civilised warfare! Is it fair and just to use prominent members of a community against whom you are fighting, and who now find themselves under the protection of your flag, as living shields against attacks by their own people? We believe it most certainly is not.

Kitchener's use of human shields is not the only action we believe to be against the practices of civilised warfare. Many reports have reached us in the last few days of a unit known as the Bushveld Carbineers that is active in the northern Transvaal. The members of this unit seem to have the habit of shooting the Boer prisoners of war who fall into their hands.

BATTLES IN THE TRANSVAAL

BOTHA ACTIVE IN THE SOUTHEAST

In the veld, 30 September – In the eastern Transvaal, Commandant-General Louis Botha forced the enemy to show their heels last month. He moved into the Vryheid district with a force of more than 1 000 burghers, with the objective of spreading the war into Natal. On 17 September, Botha and his men reached the Bloedrivier's Poort west of Vryheid. A British unit of about 1 200 men under Colonel Gough spotted them and prepared to attack. Botha was aware of the British plan and executed a counter-attack. The Khakis were caught so unawares that they could offer no proper resistance and hoisted the white flag with 44 dead or wounded. Botha's men took almost 250 Khakis prisoner of war and took possession of all their weapons and ammunition, including two field guns. On the Boer side, only one burgher was killed and three wounded.

Soon after this illustrious victory, General Cheere Emmett, Botha's brother-in-law, joined the Commandant-General with his commando. Together they had approximately 2 000 burghers at their disposal for their invasion of Natal. Botha decided to eliminate the British garrisons of the forts on the boundaries before moving into Zululand. He sent General Chris Botha with the greater part of his commando to attack Fort Itala and General Emmett to attack Fort Prospect.

Fort Itala proved a tough nut to crack. General Chris Botha sent his men in soon after midnight on 25 September, but they failed to force the Khakis to capitulate. We have learned that both sides suffered heavy casualties.

At Fort Prospect the same happened. On 26 September, Emmett's burghers surrounded the fort and attacked just before daybreak. The Boers never came close to overwhelming the Khakis, who fought particularly valiantly and held out for the whole day. In the two battles at least 15 burghers were killed and 42 injured. According to a reliable source, the combined British casualties amounted to about 20 men dead and 70 wounded.

General Chris Botha and his men moved across the border into Natal immediately after their attacks on the forts.

General Louis Botha (standing, centre) with his staff and his son Louis in the veldt

THE BATTLE AT MOEDWIL

Western Transvaal, 30 September – The most important battle on this front in the past month took place today at Moedwil, a farm on the eastern bank of the Selons River, where the wagon road between Swartruggens and Rustenburg crosses that stream. General Kemp had been following a British army under the command of Colonel Kekewich for a long time with the objective of attacking them. Yesterday Kekewich pitched camp at Moedwil with about 1 200 men. He had three guns and a pom-pom at his disposal.

General de la Rey reached Kemp's laager yesterday evening. The two generals decided to attack the British camp from the west. The majority of the 300 burghers who were available for this venture would execute a frontal assault on the British camp, while smaller groups of burghers would outflank the British in the north and the south.

De la Rey's men were some three kilometres west of Moedwil by midnight yesterday evening. He addressed them in the moonlight, after which they all bowed their heads in prayer and then moved off in silence to their attack positions. They proceeded unnoticed to the low hills above the Selons River. Kemp had to lead the main force of fewer than 200 men across the Selons River and into the attack on the British camp.

Kemp's men crossed the river before daybreak and were approaching the hill to the east, where the British camp was, when a British guard post fired on them. Even though they easily took those sentries prisoner, all the other Khakis were now awake and Kemp and his men realised that they would have to hurry.

The Boer attack developed very rapidly. Even though the soldiers fired sharply on them from the hill in the east, they quickly crossed the open ground between the river and the hill and occupied the lowest Khaki entrenchments. The burghers also made good progress on the flanks, since the Boer attack on their camp caught the British force totally unprepared. After a while some Boers reached the summit of the hill and fired so effectively on the British gun emplacements that two of their three field guns and the pom-pom were silenced.

By six o'clock this morning Kekewich had managed to restore order in his camp, and even launched a counter-attack on the northern side. The burghers could find no weak spot anywhere in the British line and after a while their attacks stalled. Since they were running out of ammunition, and Kemp wanted to ensure that his men would not be encircled, he soon afterwards ordered them to retreat, bringing the battle to an end.

Even though the Boers did not achieve a victory, they came out of the encounter by far the best. According to a reliable source the British loss was 56 men killed and 131, including Kekewich himself, wounded. In addition, the more than 300 horses and hundreds of cattle that stampeded out of the British camp at the beginning of the battle, fell in the hands of the Boers. On the Boer side, nine men, including the brave Commandant Boshoff and C.J. Bodenstein, Kemp's adjutant, were killed, 33 men wounded and three made prisoner of war.

An incident that endlessly infuriated the Boers came to light early this evening. De la Rey sent his ambulance to the British camp to request the bodies of the four burghers who had been killed and had been left behind when the Boers retreated. The ambulance returned with the bodies of seven men. Amongst them was the body of Commandant Boshoff, who had been left behind with a stomach wound, and the bodies of two burghers who had been left behind with leg wounds only. The skulls of all three had been shattered by bullet wounds. There is only one possible conclusion as to the fate of these three unlucky prisoners. We have been told that De la Rey will officially complain about it to the British command.

General de la Rey (left) and his secretary

KITCHENER'S PAPER BOMB

Reaction of the burghers

In the veld, 30 September – Kitchener's paper bomb (in other words, his threatening proclamation of 7 August) was intended to explode on 15 September. The burghers widely speculated on the question if anybody would take the threats seriously. General Koos de la Rey decided that it would be wise to issue a counter-proclamation in which he declared: 'How can we subject ourselves to a people who do not know how to honour a convention, a holy treaty? The British not only contravened the conventions of 1852 and 1854, but also those of 1868 and 1881. Brothers, I cannot do that. I believe we have to keep ourselves strictly to the decision made by the governments of the Republic of South Africa and the Orange Free State at Waterval on 20 June this year and keep on fighting till the bitter end.'

Jan F.E. Celliers, the former city librarian of Pretoria, reports from the vicinity of Marikana in the northwest that the burghers laughed heartily at Kitchener's latest gimmick, and thought no more of it. They regard the proclamation as a last desperate attempt to trap the burghers like you trap old birds with chaff. How, they ask, can he ban people that he cannot even capture? Kitchener alleges that everything is lost for the burghers, since their ammunition is finished. Why doesn't he go on and subdue us, the burghers want to know. The answer to both questions is: He is incapable of doing it. There is at present such a strong confidence under the burghers that nothing can bring them down, Celliers reports. As one burgher stated: 'If somebody told me before the war that I would, after my house had been burned down, after by wife and children had been forced into a camp, after my livestock had been captured by the enemy with all else that I owned, that I would still resist the enemy, I would have answered: impossible. Here I stand alone in the world today with nothing but the rags on my body, but my weapons I would never surrender!'

In the northern Transvaal General Beyers held a meeting of all his officers on 7 September to discuss the proclamation. He asked everybody to talk openly and give free vent to their feelings. It seems as if the destruction of their property, the torching of their houses and especially the maltreatment of their wives are causing both officers and burghers great suffering. It embitters them against the enemy, and makes them all the more resolute to keep on fighting rather than filling them with fear. Therefore they unanimously decided to keep on fighting till the very end.

As 15 September approached, it became clear everywhere that the burghers were determined to keep on fighting. In the western Transvaal only 20 surrendered that day, under suspicious circumstances. In the northern Transvaal only the Reverend Van Rooyen surrendered. That was after he had asked General Beyers's leave to take that step, since he had heard that his wife was in a bad condition. From the Orange Free State the Reverend Kestell reported that he was aware of two cases of surrender in the districts of Vrede and Harrismith, and only a few in the rest of the Republic. Assistant Chief Commandant Georg Brand reported that about 20 men in his district joined the enemy. The proclamation had not achieved its goal at all.

State Secretary F.W. Reitz was so stimulated by the haughty nature of Kitchener's proclamation and by the defiant reaction of both the Republican authorities and the burghers, that he composed the following poem:

THE PROCLAMATION OR PAPER BOMB

I undersign'd *Lord Kitchener of Karthoum*
(For all my other titles there's no room)
In the King's name, at least we call it so,
But really meaning 'Chamberlain & Co.'
Hereby proclaim and solemnly declare,
And this is final – so let all Beware!

Whereas I with a quarter-million men,
Can't beat you, though you're only one to ten,
And flying columns answer just as well
Or just as little – as a lyddite shell,

Whereas by setting fields and homes a-flame
I have but added to my former shame,
And catching women really shows no true sense,
Since it has only proved a dreadful nuisance,

Whereas it's now more than a year ago,
Since we annexed you – Roberts did you know –
Yet, notwithstanding this illegal Fiction,
Where big guns fail there ends my jurisdiction.

Whereas Cape rebels still continue rising
In numbers both alarming and surprising
And Kritzinger with Scheepers and Fouché,
Are causing French so much anxiety,

Whereas the war-costs that we have to pay
Run to a quarter-million pounds per day
And things have now already gone so far
That even the Funds are falling below par,

Whereas my horses ridden to and fro
But serve to feed the vulture and the crow,
And that in spite of all my plans and schemes,
Ending the war is harder than it seems,

Whereas no other means I can conceive,
Than just to bluster and to make believe,
I have resolved this paper bomb to let off
To try if that perchance may make you 'get off'.

So I proclaim – that if there's any Judas
Who has no wish to go to the Bermudas
Let him lay down his arms – but then remember
The day I fix is Fifteenth of September.

Generals and Officers I hereby warn,
That if they treat these liberal terms with scorn,
Their goods will all be 'forfeit' to the state,
They'll bitterly repent it when too late,

Now therefore come up Burghers one and all
'Tis for the sake of Peace I make this call,
Oh! come to me and then you'll quickly feel
How a Boer's neck fits to a British heel.

Oh! come to me! oh! come and do surrender
Then Chamberlain's hard heart may yet grow
tender,
And p'rhaps he'll send you one of his old
shoes,
That you may kiss as often as you choose.

Then all men shall the Great Millenium see
Then Boer and Briton both shall equal be,
The British lion will no longer sham
For he will swallow th' Africander lamb.

Thus given under my own hand – and so
Long Live the King! and long live Pushful Joe!
Signed Kitchener – dated – and to be of use
To be sent under a *Private* flag of *Truce*!

OUR MILITARY OFFICERS

General Jan Smuts

Jan Christiaan Smuts was born in 1870 on the farm Bovenplaats near Riebeek West in the Cape Colony. His parents are Jacobus Abraham Smuts and his wife Catharina de Vries. Smuts spent his boyhood years on farms in the vicinity of Riebeek West and from his twelfth year attended school in the town. Four years later he enrolled at the Stellenbosch Gymnasium and subsequently at Victoria College and in 1891 was awarded a degree in literature and science at the University of the Cape of Good Hope.

Smuts then left for the University of Cambridge in England on scholarship and in 1894 completed his law studies with the highest honours. He was then admitted as a barrister in London.

In 1895 Smuts returned to South Africa and practised as an advocate in Cape Town. He soon entered politics and became a supporter of Jan Hofmeyr's Afrikaner Bond. At that stage he was also a supporter of the Cape premier, Cecil John Rhodes. Jameson's raid disillusioned him, however, and he became a staunch supporter of President Kruger. He is also a supporter of one united Afrikaner nation that should force British imperialism out of a united South Africa.

In 1897 Smuts moved to Johannesburg, where he practised as an advocate until 1898, when he became State Attorney of the South African Republic. As legal advisor of the Executive Council, he was intimately involved in the disputes between the Transvaal government and Britain. He realised that the British authorities aimed to bring an end to the independence of the Republics, but believed that the British would not start the war without a solid, formal reason. Therefore he advised the Transvaal government to introduce franchise reforms to make it difficult for the British to fabricate a good reason for war.

By the middle of 1899 Smuts had realised that war was virtually inevitable. Just before the war actually began, he coauthored a document on the century-long conflict between Boer and Brit. It was published by the Transvaal government under the title *A Century of Wrong*. Soon after the war broke out, he proceeded with his duties as State Attorney under Martial Law. We have often reported on his activities, especially his major role in getting everything in Pretoria ready before the British occupied the city in June last year.

Jan Smuts and his wife, Isie, who is at present living in Pietermaritzburg in Natal, have no children. They did have a little boy, but he recently died. The intellectually brilliant Smuts is a strict but respected commander. His unequalled knowledge of law and his capacity to confront the British on an equal footing in their own language are of immeasurable value to the Republics.

Jan Smuts as a student

THE
War Reporter
MONTHLY EDITION

Number 58 | In the Veld, South African Republic | 1 November 1901

MILITARY ACTIVITIES IN THE TRANSVAAL

Glorious victory for Botha at Bakenlaagte

In the veld, 31 October – Commandant-General Louis Botha has once again proved at the enemy's expense that he is a born military leader. The Transvaal forces under his command carried out a very successful attack on a large British column in the eastern Transvaal, capturing two field guns and a huge supply of war materials.

Less than a week ago Botha had a narrow escape when a British force surprised him on the farm Schimmelhoek, some distance east of Ermelo. Fortunately both Botha and the Transvaal government, who were in that area at that time, managed to escape in good time.

Botha soon got an opportunity to pay the Khakis back for the fright they had given him. On 29 October he was informed by Commandant H.S. Grobler that an enemy force had pitched camp at Swakfontein, about 20 kilometres west of Bethal. Grobler had been harassing this force, which had about 2 000 men and was well supplied with field guns, rapid-fire guns and a number of wagons, for the last week. These Khakis, under Lieutenant Colonel Benson, were notorious for their large-scale plundering and destruction of farms and for their abduction of hundreds of women and children to the concentration camps. Botha immediately decided to attack them with a combined force of at least six commandos.

Benson's soldiers were spread over a wide area early on the morning of 30 October when the burghers, led by Commandant Grobler, attacked them. Benson himself obviously underestimated the strength of the Boer attack in the beginning and did not immediately institute counter-measures. In the meantime it began raining and a strong wind brought the temperature down. Visibility became restricted. Benson's rearguard soon began to crumble in the face of the determined Boer attack.

The scale finally swung against the British when Commandant-General Louis Botha reached the battlefield at noon with 400 men. He, Grobler and the other Boer officers who were present quickly discussed tactics and decided to launch a coordinated attack. While two groups of burghers advanced respectively left and right around the British, at about two o'clock Botha launched the main attack on the British centre with about 800 burghers. The Khakis retreated in panic to a low hill where their guns were stationed. There they attempted to offer resistance but suffered heavy casualties. Benson himself was wounded twice. The burghers kept attacking valiantly and occupied the hill.

The guns were now in the hands of the Boers, who swung them around and fired on the British camp in the distance. Botha soon ordered the ceasefire, since it became known that there were Boer women and children in that camp and he did not want to take the risk of injuring them. Thus a golden opportunity to turn a glorious victory into a magnificent triumph was lost.

In this battle – Botha calls it the Battle of Bakenlaagte – the British suffered a loss of at least 66 men killed, 165 wounded and 120 made prisoner of war. Benson's wounds are so serious that he will probably not survive. The total Boer casualties were fewer than 100.

THE BATTLE AT KLEINFONTEIN

In the western Transvaal the burghers of Generals Koos de la Rey and Jan Kemp divided themselves into small groups after the battle of Moedwil at the end of September. In ravines and small valleys, they searched for suitable places to plough and sow to ensure a supply of food for the next winter. Fortunately good rain has fallen continuously after fine early rains. There has been little contact between the burghers and the British, who have also kept a low profile and seemed to be licking their wounds after Moedwil. Last week De la Rey and Kemp decided to attack a British convoy, since their own supplies were running low. The result was the Battle of Kleinfontein, on 24 October.

Kleinfontein farm, where the battle took place, is on the transport road between Swartruggens and Zeerust, a little distance west of the drift across the Groot Marico River. It is a rolling landscape with a series of heights and valleys. De la Rey's scouts reported that a British convoy of about 100 wagons was trekking along this road. It was escorted by a force of about 1 000 Khakis with two rapid-fire and five field guns commanded by Colonel Von Donop.

Commandant-General Louis Botha

On 23 October Kemp and De la Rey agreed that the burghers would attack the convoy as it crossed the high ground on Kleinfontein. There were more than 500 burghers available for this onslaught.

On the night of 23–24 October, while De la Rey was still on his way from the southeast, Kemp and the other officers set up their burghers on high ground a little distance south of Kleinfontein and finalised their arrangements for the attack. The Khakis were already on the move at the crack of dawn, and reached Kleinfontein by seven o'clock that morning. In terms of the plan the burghers then charged on horseback from the south through a clump of boekenhout trees and fell on the enemy over the whole length of the enemy convoy. The British centre was easily overrun and some of the burghers began hauling away the supply wagons. The other burghers swerved towards the British rear and captured the field guns. However they could not haul them away, since too many of the gun mules had already been killed. A third group of burghers pursued the fleeing British mounted troops.

A major victory was within the grasp of the Boers, but they let it slip. In the first place the burghers were in such a hurry that they did not ensure that all the Khakis who had surrendered were disarmed. When the British vanguard launched a counter-attack, these Khakis began firing again and caught the Boers unawares. Secondly General De la Rey's burghers were still too far away from the battlefield when the fight began and could not, as the original plan was, participate at all. Consequently Kemp had to pull his burghers out of the battle by nine o'clock rather than take the risk of suffering heavy casualties. The Khakis did not pursue the retreating burghers.

From reliable sources it seems that the British suffered a loss of about 30 men killed and 54 wounded. The Boer loss was 20 men dead and 31 wounded. Kemp believes that these casualties were far too heavy, if one considers the profit of the battle. The Boers captured only 15 of the approximately 100 wagons and some 300 horses and mules. Fortunately the captured wagons were fully loaded with supplies which are of great value to the burghers.

ACTIVITIES NORTH OF THE EASTERN RAILWAY LINE

In the eastern Transvaal there were only a few skirmishes of no particular military significance north of the eastern railway line. General Ben Viljoen and his burghers amused themselves by holding concerts in Pilgrim's Rest, a mining town in the Transvaal Drakensberg range. On 30 September Viljoen himself acted in a drama whose topic had to do with a real-life incident when he caught a number of prospective handsuppers in a trap. In this concert the actors sang a song with 28 verses composed and written by one of the commando members, Roland Schikkerling.

On 14 October a section of 75 burghers led by Commandant Malan left Pilgrim's Rest on horseback in a southeasterly direction on a secret mission.

It later became known that their task was to sabotage the eastern railway line near Komatipoort to make it unusable for the British. After a few days the expedition members found themselves in the bushveld in the Sabi Nature Reserve, where there are absolutely no roads. Two guides who know these parts well, Koekemoer and Stoltz, led them.

Commandant H.S. Grobler

There is lots of game in this area, including sable antelope and wildebeest, as well as warthogs. It is lion country and some of the men were rather alarmed when five lions suddenly appeared on a footpath in front of them. At night they had to mount guard fires and fasten their horses to protect them against the lions. All went well and after a few days they reached the Crocodile River. However, all their attempts to sabotage the railway line failed and they returned without having achieved their objective.

In the northern Transvaal, on the first day of October, General Beyers and his commando forced a British unit to surrender on the farm Pruisen, a little distance south of Potgietersrus. They captured a huge store of supplies. From Potgietersrus, Beyers and his burghers trekked in a northeasterly direction, down the escarpment, into the Lowveld. Beyers plans to reconnoitre the whole country eastwards right up to the Portuguese border.

FROM THE EDITOR

The war entered its third year last month, with yet again no end in sight. Generally speaking, this was another good month for the Republican forces. In the eastern Transvaal, Commandant-General Louis Botha achieved a significant victory at Bakenlaagte. Generals Kemp and De la Rey almost achieved similar successes in the western Transvaal. In the Cape Colony there was action on a wide front. This is excellent news, since by keeping the enemy busy from the Soutpansberg in the north virtually to the fringes of Cape Town in the southwest, our men are continuously enlarging the field of operations and increasingly confusing the enemy.

One aspect of the actions of our forces that is alarming to the Republican commanders is the tendency of some officers to take retaliatory action. Revenge is usually accompanied by a cold calculation that can hardly be approved of. This, unfortunately, has often been the case with the recent actions of Commandants Fouchee and Myburgh in the eastern Cape. Retaliation may vent pent-up anger, but it usually has unwelcome consequences. The fact is that Fouchee's reign of terror is frightening off many potential supporters of the Republican cause in the Stormberg.

Conditions in the concentration camps are still critical, and not only in those where Boer women and children are locked up like criminals. The enemy has also established separate camps for black people, and from what we hear, the death rate in those camps is probably even higher than in the camps for whites.

COMMANDANT SCHEEPERS IN BRITISH HANDS

ILL-HEALTH FORCES HIM TO ABANDON THE STRUGGLE

In the veld in the Karoo, 12 October – A huge setback hit the Republican forces in the Cape Colony yesterday when Commandant Gideon Scheepers was forced to allow himself to become a British prisoner of war. Scheepers and his commando were active in the Little Karoo between Calitzdorp and Riversdal at the beginning of the month, and involved in skirmishes with Khaki patrols virtually every day.

For Scheepers this was no easy time. He began feeling ill on 28 September and by 4 October was so weak that he could no longer travel on horseback. His burghers transported him in a cart. The next day the British led them into an ambush near Ladismith and they had to flee for their lives. Scheepers was forced to abandon the cart, and experienced terrible pain traversing the mountainous area on horseback. He managed to get another cart the next day, but on 8 October, when the commando had to cross the mountain range northwards in the direction of Laingsburg, he had to travel on horseback again. His health progressively worsened.

On the 10th they reached a farmhouse in the area of Prince Albert, at the foot of the Swartberg range. By that time Scheepers felt so weak that he could not go any further. His horse cart was already inspanned in front of the farmhouse early yesterday morning when he called his officers into the room where he lay on a bed. They wanted to bodily take him with them, but in the end honoured his request to leave him there. One by one his burghers said farewell to him with heavy hearts. The servants also came in and greeted him with a last handshake.

Lieutenant Pypers took over command. On Scheepers's request he sent a local farmer to Prince Albert to fetch a doctor. Just before sunrise Pypers and the other burghers left. This morning he was informed that a British unit had reached Scheepers by two o'clock yesterday afternoon. We trust that the Khakis will provide decent care for this courageous warrior. According to a reliable source they will send him to the hospital at Matjiesfontein for treatment.

Nobody knows what ailment Scheepers suffers from. A rumour is abroad that a traitor poisoned him.

GENERAL JAN SMUTS STILL HAS KHAKIS CONFUSED

In the veld, 30 October – For the past month General Jan Smuts and his commando have been carrying on with their expedition in the Cape Colony – and with great success. The British are so confused about his objectives and movements, that they are jumping around like cats on a hot tin roof in their efforts to capture him. It has not all been plain sailing for Smuts and his men. On the first day of the month about 70 of them, including the General himself, suffered indescribable agony when they ate poisonous wild fruits. While some of them thought they were wrestling with death, the Khakis attacked them. Smuts says that they barely managed to repulse the attack but afterwards lay like dead men on the battlefield and only began recovering the next day. Some burghers were so weak that they had to be tied to the backs of their horses before they could resume their expedition.

Having nearly reached Port Elizabeth, Smuts and his men turned to the west and travelled through the Addo Forest near Uitenhage. On 3 October they clashed with a British unit in the Zuurberg Mountains, but repulsed the enemy attack with ease. Scarcity of fodder forced Smuts to send Commandant Ben Bouwer with a small unit ahead towards the district of Graaff-Reinet the next day. As far as could be ascertained, Bouwer was often in conflict with British units in the course of the next few weeks, and just as often came out on top.

Smuts subsequently placed another group of his men under the command of Commandant Jaap van Deventer, with orders to act independently. On 13 October Van Deventer and Commandant J.R.F. Kirsten were involved in a skirmish with a British unit near Aberdeen and scored a huge victory. More than 200 Khakis fell into their hands and they captured more than 200 horses before they allowed the Khakis to leave on foot. Two days later Van Deventer repeated his success when he captured 157 mounted Khakis at Doornbosch in the same area. However, on 21 October they were at the receiving end when the British attacked them at daybreak on the banks of the Sunday's River. They had to flee for their lives, leaving behind one man dead, one wounded and ten who became prisoners of war.

Smuts and his commando moved through the Kamdeboo on 10 October. The next night they were in the mountains near Murraysburg, where they almost froze to death in an untimely snowstorm. They then swerved to the south and on 16 October met the commando of Commandant Schalk Pypers, who had previously succeeded Commandant Gideon Scheepers, near Klaarstroom (see this issue). The two commandos crossed the Swartberg range together, trekked through the mysterious Gamkaskloof, which is called The Hell by the local people, and from there proceeded to the west. They have just crossed the railway line that runs from Cape Town to the north with no difficulty, but Deneys Reitz reports that they saw the double-tiered blockhouses at the bridge over the Dwyka River in the distance.

COMMANDANT MARITZ TAKES THE WESTERN CAPE BY STORM

Calvinia district, 29 October – Commandant Manie Maritz and his burghers were particularly active here in the past month, forcing the British authorities to incur massive costs as they transform the Western Cape into a defensive area.

At the beginning of October they attacked Piketberg, then Malmesbury, Porterville and on 10 October Hopefield, where they locked up the government officials and destroyed the telegraph office. From there they proceeded to Saldanha Bay, where a British cruiser was anchored. A few of the burghers could not resist the temptation to fire on the cruiser with their rifles. The crew of the ship answered with a bombardment. Fortunately no one was injured.

On 12 October Maritz and his men were involved in a skirmish with a mounted British unit near Hoedjiesbaai. Three days later they attacked Moorreesburg. Another four days later they were at Vier-en-twintig Riviere, where they were involved in a clash with a huge British force. On 21 October they reached the village of Darling and were only about 60 kilometres from Cape Town. By this time Maritz was burdened with a number of wounded men as well as a huge booty. Consequently he decided to leave for the north to get out of reach of the enemy.

On 25 October, Maritz was on the farm Kloudskraal, here in the Calvinia area, where a number of Cape Rebel groups gathered for a combined war council meeting. The officers on this council decided to elect Maritz as their Provisional Assistant Chief Commandant. Each rebel group accepted responsibility for a separate operational area. Maritz at this time had a force of about 500 men, 356 of them armed. Today they captured a convoy of 20 British wagons on the road between Clanwilliam and Lambertsbaai.

Field Cornet Thys Boonzaaier (centre) and his scouts who fired on a British battleship in Saldanha Bay

RETALIATION IN THE NORTHEASTERN CAPE

In the veld in the Stormberg, 25 October – Here in the Stormberg range in the northeast of the Cape Colony, Commandants Willem Fouchee and Stoffel Myburgh have been concentrating for the past month on retaliatory action against loyalists and blacks who support the British forces. These servants of the enemy endlessly frustrate the Republican forces.

Fouchee's preparedness to take retaliatory steps is exacerbated by reports that have reached him of the execution of Cape Rebels, and especially the trial and fate of his colleague, Commandant Hans Lötter. Reports on maltreatment of women and children in the concentration camps also fill him with disgust.

Fouchee's revenge against Koos Botha, the Cape Member of Parliament for Aliwal North, has had everyone talking. Suspecting Botha of supporting the enemy, a few weeks ago Fouchee abducted him and his brother. In his laager they were each fined £200 by his war council and given a hiding with his sjambok. He then released them and warned them to have the money ready – he would come and collect it. On 4 October he was back and forced the two Bothas to pay him £400. Fouchee has also fined or assaulted other Cape Afrikaners whom he suspected of assisting the British forces.

A much worse fate is in store for black people who support the British war effort and fall into Fouchee's hands. He has them summarily executed.

BRITISH MERCILESS AGAINST REPUBLICAN SUPPORTERS
Executions of Cape Rebels, violators of martial law

In the veld, 31 October – The British authorities have continued in recent times with their merciless persecution of people who support the Boer Republics in any way, who contravene martial law regulations or who, according to the British, act outside the accepted practices of 'civilised' warfare. From Pretoria it is reported that R.C. Upton, found guilty on a charge of espionage, died in front of a firing squad in August.

In Johannesburg the Khakis executed a foreign civilian. He was the Dutchman Cornelius Broeksma. The British regarded him as a spy since he dispatched information on the cruel nature of the scorched earth policy and the British concentration camps in secret code to The Netherlands.

On 2 October Piet Schuil, a foreign volunteer, was executed by firing squad. The Khakis accused him of shooting British soldiers under cover of a white flag towards the end of the battle of Moedwil.

In the eastern Cape the British executed three of Smuts's scouts on 3 October, since they were wearing Khaki uniforms. Ten days later another member of Smuts's commando died in front of a firing squad in Aberdeen for the same reason.

Cape Rebels or presumed rebels who fall into the hands of the Khakis are treated particularly harshly. On 4 September three men, F. Troy (a Swede who lived in Johannesburg), H.J. Veenstra and J. van Vuuren died before a British firing squad in Colesberg.

On 7 October an 18-year-old Cape Rebel, J.H. Roux, was executed on a charge of treason by the British in Graaff-Reinet. Four days later J.W.G. Jansen and one Rautenbach were hanged in Vryburg in the northern Cape on charges that they stole horses from the British.

We mourn the death of each individual so inhumanely treated by the British, and extend our condolences to the next of kin of all the victims. The most damning executions to be carried out in the past month, from a military point of view, were those of Commandant Hans Lötter, his Field Cornets W. Kruger, J. Schoeman and D.C. Breedt, and his adjutant P.J. Wolfaardt. They were sentenced to death on 11 October by a military court in Middelburg in the Cape on charges of treason. Lötter was shot by a British firing squad on 12 October. The other four also died by firing squad.

WOMEN, YOUNG GIRLS AND TEENAGE BOYS VICTIMS OF MARTIAL LAW

It is not only adult men who are victims of the implementation of martial law in the Cape Colony. On 11 September a Mrs Brooks and nine young girls appeared in court in Maraisburg, a small town in the eastern Karoo. The charges against them were that they sang the Republican anthems during the brief occupation of the town by a Republican commando. Even worse, they kissed burghers who were not related to them! Two girls were released, but Mrs Brooks and the other seven, aged between 15 and 19 were sentenced to 30 days' imprisonment each.

On 12 September the military court in Graaff-Reinet sentenced five teenage Cape Rebels who were members of Commandant Lötter's commando to death. The youngest is only 14 years old. We have just heard that Lord Kitchener has shown clemency and commuted their sentences to life imprisonment with corporal punishment.

On 26 September there was a court action again against a teenage Cape Afrikaner. Rochelle de Villiers, the 16-year-old son of the mayor of Aberdeen, was sent to prison for one week after contravening Martial Law regulations by galloping down the main street of the town on horseback.

P.J. Wolfaardt

OUR MILITARY OFFICERS

Commandant Hans Lötter

Johannes Cornelius Lötter was born in 1875 on the farm Bouwersfontein in the Somerset East district of the Cape Colony. He was the son of Magiel Petrus Lötter and his wife Maria Catharina Buys. Not much is known about his childhood years. As a young man he spent a few years in the Free State from 1896. Shortly before the outbreak of this war, he was operating a trade establishment in Noupoort in the Cape Colony.

Soon after the outbreak of the war Lötter joined the Boer forces as an ordinary burgher. On one occasion he was wounded but recovered and became a dispatch rider. In December last year he was a member of Commandant Pieter Kritzinger's commando that invaded the Cape Colony. It was Kritzinger who promoted him to Commandant and placed him in charge of a commando.

Lötter invaded the Cape again in May this year and was especially active in the Stormberg. He was present at the occupation of Jamestown in June 1901, and subsequently was active in the eastern Karoo. On the night of 4–5 September a British force surprised his commando in a shed where they were sheltering from the rain. All of them fought valiantly, but Lötter was wounded and had to surrender.

During his trial on charges of high treason Lötter attempted to prove that he was a Free State burgher. The court found that he was a Cape citizen who had rebelled, and sentenced him to death. He was informed about his sentence on 11 October during a ceremony on the Market Square of Middelburg, and the sentence was carried out the same day by a firing squad outside the town.

Commandant Hans Lötter

THE War Reporter
MONTHLY EDITION

Number 59   In the Veld, South African Republic   1 December 1901

THE WAR IN THE CAPE COLONY
BRITISH KEPT BUSY OVER A LARGE AREA

Cape Colony, 30 November – The Republican commandos have been particularly active in the Cape Colony in the past month. Early in November Commandant Jan Theron's commando attacked Piketberg in the western Cape. The Khakis had earlier erected extensive fortifications around the town and managed to beat off the attack. Both sides suffered light casualties. A few days later Commandant Manie Maritz divided his commando into two units for simultaneous attacks on Moorreesburg and Porterville. He himself commanded the group that attacked Moorreesburg. They occupied the town with ease and destroyed the telegraph equipment. On 10 November they attacked the village of Darling. Two days later a group of Boer scouts clashed with a British unit a few kilometres east of Darling. Field Cornet Casparus Hildebrand was killed in this skirmish.

We have been informed from Cape Town that Maritz's activities so close to the Mother City forced the British authorities there to set up their guns and prepare for the defence of the city. In the light of his shortage of weapons and mules, and the massive troop presence in that area, Maritz decided that such an attack would be pure lunacy, however. He fell back across the Berg River and by the end of November had returned to the vicinity of Calvinia.

With this second invasion into the southwestern Cape, Maritz has once again achieved the Boer aim of making life for the British military authorities difficult over as large an area as possible. His success is confirmed by the fact that the British are erecting a blockhouse line from Lambert's Bay to Calvinia to keep the Boers out of the area.

In the Cape Midlands Commandants Van Deventer and Neser crossed the main railway line between Beaufort West and Kimberley near Victoria West at the beginning of November and repulsed the Khakis in that area in a number of skirmishes. On 9 November they attacked a British unit at Voëlfontein. We have heard that 16 Khakis were killed and 30 made prisoner of war without the Boers suffering noteworthy casualties. From there Van Deventer and his commando proceeded quickly westwards to Namaqualand.

General Jan Smuts and his men have also arrived in the western Cape, sporadically clashing with British units. On 1 November Smuts and Commandant Schalk Pypers and their men, who had by then been together for more than two weeks, were involved in a skirmish near the main railway line north of the Hex River Mountains. The enemy was put to flight and left a number of good horses behind. From there the commandos moved ever further westwards. On 4 November Pypers and his commando parted company with Smuts. On 23 November Smuts and Commandant Ben Bouwer reached Vanrhynsdorp and two days later Smuts was in Nieuwoudtville.

In the eastern Cape this past month the Khakis have put tremendous pressure on the Republican commandos in the Stormberg mountain range. In order to confuse the British columns, Commandant Willem Fouchee often divided his commandos into small units under himself, Commandant Stoffel Myburgh, Field Cornets Bezuidenhout and Odendaal and Captain Wessels, the leader of his scout corps. These small commandos were involved in clashes with the enemy virtually every day and were forced by the vast numbers of the British army to move northwards in the direction of the Drakensberg.

On 19 November Bezuidenhout and a unit of 53 burghers were involved in a fight with a Khaki column consisting mainly of black soldiers in the Maclear district. Bezuidenhout's casualties were six men and 40 horses. The Khaki commander, Captain Elliot, was killed in the encounter. A few days later the weather suddenly turned bad and it even began snowing, with the result that some of the most emaciated horses froze to death.

The biggest setback in the Stormberg for the Republican forces thus far followed when the Khakis cornered Commandant Stoffel Myburgh's men near the Basutoland border and captured most of them. It is said that the British authorities heard from a traitor where Myburgh's campsite was and that they totally surprised the Boers. Fortunately Myburgh himself got away, but his commando suffered heavy casualties. On 29 November the remnants of Myburgh's commando were involved in another tough battle.

The commander of the British units who is making life so difficult for the Boer commandos is Colonel Harry Scobell. He is known in the eastern Cape as the rebel hunter and is a thorn in the flesh of the Republican forces.

Boer occupation of Hopefield, 9 November 1901

FROM THE EDITOR

The best news of the past month is without doubt that the Republican forces, especially in the Cape Colony, are pursuing the struggle with undiminished enthusiasm, making life difficult for the massive British army in spite of their own limited numbers. British reaction to the presence of Commandant Manie Maritz's burghers close to Cape Town indicates panic over their inability to end the war: they seem to be transforming the whole Cape Peninsula into a defensive area.

Unfortunately, British forces are still molesting women and children. The Transvaal authorities officially complained about that last month, but experience tells us that the British will not bring an end to that dastardly practice. We have also suffered a few telling setbacks on the battlefield, notably the wounding and capture of the highly respected Commandant Fanie Buys of Heidelberg.

This month, for the first time in a long while, we bring news from the valley of the lower Orange River, where a strong group of Cape Rebels is still active. That these people are suffering terribly under British martial law is clearly reflected in the report. And lastly, we bring news from two prisoner-of-war camps, namely St Helena and – for the first time – Bermuda, that will be of interest to readers with family members or friends who are detained there.

Boer prisoners of war in Deadwood Camp, St Helena (see report on next page)

Boer prisoners of war in St Helena hunting fleas (see report on next page)

127

Number 59　　1 December 1901

NEWS FROM PRISONER-OF-WAR CAMPS
Harsh fate of burghers in Bermuda

In the veld, 29 November – This month we report for the first time on the conditions of the Boer prisoners of war in Bermuda. Our reporter is Candidate-Minister J.A. van Blerk, who has gone to that Caribbean island at the request of the Dutch Reformed Church of the Cape Colony to minister to the spiritual needs of the prisoners of war. He managed not only to send us an extensive report but also a few photographs that he himself took.

'I arrived in Hamilton, the capital of Bermuda, on 21 October 1901. On the very same day I met the Reverend and Mrs J.R. Albertyn, who render spiritual service in the prisoner-of-war camps. Soon afterwards I procured a pass that gives me access to all the camps. These are spread over five small islands, namely Burtt's, Darrell's, Morgan's, Tucker's and Hawkins Island. The hospital is on Port's Island and the cemetery on Long Island. There are at present 4 600 Boer prisoners of war in Bermuda.

'My first visit was to Burtt's Island, where 94 Boers are detained in a camp surrounded by a barbed wire fence. The prisoners of war are housed in round tents. I was shocked by their general appearance. Some prisoners were half-naked and only a few have proper shoes. They were still wearing the clothes in which they were captured in South Africa. Since the clothes are in shreds, they are using pieces of khaki blanket to cover up the biggest holes. A few are wearing trousers of 100 per cent khaki blanket. They seemed very glad to meet me.

'Subsequently I visited all the prisoner camps. After a week I moved to Morgan's Island. Initially my tent was pitched next to the fence of the camp on the outside, but after two days I was allowed to move into the camp. I have the privilege to enjoy my meals with the Boer officers who are detained in that camp, including General Andries Cronjé and Jan Wessels, as well as Pieter Steyn, the brother of President Steyn. The food is of a low quality, but adequate. There is a "dry canteen" in the camp where the prisoners can buy extra supplies.

'The prisoners include elderly burghers approaching their eighties as well as young boys who are only eight. There is a continuous shortage of fresh water, even though it often rains, and fleas and lice torment the prisoners. Most of them sleep on the wooden floor of their tents since mattresses are not provided to everybody. In spite of these inconveniences most of the prisoners are healthy and the death rate is not at all excessive.

'One group of prisoners is treated differently from the rest, namely the 250 Cape Rebels, who have been sentenced to hard labour. They were at first detained in the prison on St George Island, where they were treated like criminals. Their heads were shaven and they were given bandit clothing with a broad arrow on the back. Later on they were transferred to Hawkins Island, where they are accommodated in a special camp. An old battleship is anchored right next to the island and its floodlights shine on the camp throughout the night. On the other side of the island there are also floodlights, which are called Wells Lamps, and these ensure that it is never dark in that camp. Armed guards continuously patrol the fences of the camps.

'When the first Boer prisoners of war arrived here in Bermuda they were at a loss in their battle against boredom. The islands are small and there is nothing to do. However, they soon found ways to keep themselves busy. A very popular pastime is woodwork. There are many cedar trees on the islands and the prisoners began carving pieces of cedar wood into ornaments. At first they only used knives, but soon they began making saws, planes, chisels and even lathes from pieces of wood and scrap iron that they found on the islands. Some ornaments found their way to Hamilton and in due course a healthy trade in Boer curios developed. Especially American tourists, of whom large numbers visit these tropical islands, love to buy the ornaments made by the Boer prisoners. At present curio production is a full-time occupation for many Boers.

'The Rebels who are subjected to forced labour work under the supervision of armed guards every day from dawn to dusk. Sometimes they are used to transport heavy materials. On other occasions they have to cut sandstone into building blocks. Those who are physically disabled remain in the camp, where they are given menial tasks. Two burghers who are paralysed have to lie on their sides and break up stones with a hammer. The Rebels have all been sentenced to hard labour because they came from the Cape but took up arms against the British authorities.

'Prisoners of war who break the rules or complain about their treatment are often punished by being detained in special enclosures, called 'ram camps' by the Boers. The detainees are often handcuffed for long periods. One of the prisoners thus detained is Fritz Joubert du Quesne, who alleges that he is French, but speaks Afrikaans perfectly. He has often attempted to escape, but has failed thus far.'

Van Blerk also sent us a poem written by Joubert Reitz, one of State Secretary F.W. Reitz's sons, who is one of the Boer prisoners of war on Morgan's Island. The subject of the poem is the destruction by its own crew of the last Long Tom gun of the Transvaal State artillery, on which we reported on 1 June 1901:

The gun that once from Lombards Kop
Its shrieking missels sped
Will ne'er be heard to roar again,
Its usefulness has fled.
The foeman need not fear it now
For it has lost its sting
It ne'er will trouble them again
Nor consternation bring.

For now it's but a shattered wreck
A relic of the past
A mighty instrument of death
Brought to its end at last
It gained its masters many a field
Checked many an advance
Which in the History of the War
Its memory will enhance.

ST HELENA PRISONERS OF WAR STILL LOYAL TO REPUBLICS

We recently received news directly from the prisoner-of-war camp on St Helena

Cape Rebels in the gaol on St George Island, Bermuda

for the first time in many months. Our source, as before, is L.C. Ruijssenaers, a member of the Hollander Corps, who became a prisoner of war early on in the war, at Elandslaagte. We will of course not divulge how the message reached us. In addition to his report on conditions and events in the camp, it is interesting to read that even though some of the prisoners of war have given up hope, the vast majority are remaining steadfast in their loyalty to the Republics. Here is his report of events on the island from March this year:

'At the beginning of March there was a massive flea plague in our camp. It was as if each flea multiplied by thousands or tens of thousands each day. We suffered terribly and each day conceded huge amounts of blood to the fleas. Our attempts to wipe out this scourge were more or less futile.

'In addition to the fleas, many of the prisoners of war suffer from enteric fever and from beri-beri. Both are debilitating and deadly diseases. Those who contract beri-beri have a very small chance of survival, since the only remedy is a change of climate.

'In June some of the Boers began to feel that it was time to surrender and take an oath of allegiance to Britain. It was only a handful of prisoners of war who felt that way, and their leaders soon had reason to rue their decision. Since when Commandant Sarel Eloff heard of this, he was so angry that he burned down the houses of two of the leaders of the handsuppers that same evening. The British subsequently afforded new accommodation in a separate camp to these two, as well as to 60 other burghers who had decided to become disloyal. The prisoners of war who remain loyal refer to the handsuppers' camp as the Jam Camp, since the handsuppers receive jam with their food as a sign of gratitude from the British. For the loyal Boers the worst is that the handsuppers sing psalms and hymns with gusto every night. It is incomprehensible that the traitors' conscience allows them still to glorify the God in whose name they began the war now that they have stabbed their comrades in the back.

'On 11 August there was great excitement amongst the prisoners of war on St Helena island. The news spread that morning like wildfire through all the camps that two Hollanders had escaped. It subsequently became known that these two as well as four other prisoners of war had planned their escape attempt for months. Their objective was to sail in one of the two old sailing boats that were anchored in the harbour of Jamestown to the United States of America. These boats, which nowadays are used to take fresh water to visiting steam ships, were indeed earlier used for sea journeys to America.

'The conspirators gathered a huge supply of tinned food and water containers in a rocky hollow along the coast. After dark on the evening of 10 August De Haas and Mulder swam to one of the boats. They fortunately reached it and even managed to weigh the anchor. Their plan was to load up their friends and the food supplies, but nothing came of this since the wind and the streams were not favourable.

'The next morning the British saw the ship drifting some distance from the island and our friends were picked up in a steam vessel. Since the Geneva Convention recognises the right of prisoners of war to escape, De Haas and Mulder could not be punished for their deeds. However, the English Colonel was furious and ordered that the escapees should be accused of theft, since they stole one of the sailing boats. The civilian judge found them both guilty and fined each to six months' hard labour or a £6 fine. If the English Colonel thought that our friends would now sit in jail for six months, he totally misjudged the situation, since within an hour the £12 was paid. All of us who had a shilling or more contributed to our brothers-in-distress.'

The paralysed Burgher Greef and other Cape 'bandits' on Bermuda

Boer prisoners of war crossing the bridge to Long Island, Bermuda

Well-known prisoners of war on Bermuda. General Jan Wessels (third from left, standing), General Andries Cronjé (fourth from left, standing) and Pieter Steyn, brother of the president (sixth from left, standing)

Burgher Van Brakel (79) and two 8-year-old prisoners of war

Prisoners of war with a lathe that they manufactured

128

Number 59 1 December 1901

MALTREATMENT OF WOMEN AND CHILDREN
Letter of protest to British Premier by Burger and Reitz

On 21 November, Acting State President Schalk Burger and State Secretary F.W. Reitz sent the following letter of protest to the British Prime Minister, Lord Salisbury, in reaction to the shocking treatment by the British forces of a group of women and children:

'This removal took place in the most uncivilised and barbarous manner, while such action is … in conflict with all the heretofore acknowledged rules of civilised warfare. The families were put out of their houses under compulsion, and in many instances by means of force … [the houses] were destroyed and burnt with everything in them … and these families, among them many aged ones, pregnant women, and children of very tender years, were removed in open trolleys [exposed] for weeks to rain, severe cold wind and terrible heat, privations to which they were not accustomed, with the result that many of them became very ill, and some of them died shortly after their arrival in the women's camps … The persons removed were in many instances exposed to insults and ill-treatment by [blacks] in the service of your troops as well as by soldiers … British mounted troops have not hesitated to drive them for miles before their horses, old women, little children, and mothers with sucklings to their breasts …'

Reitz is so upset by the British concentration camp system that he has composed a poem to express his disgust. In this poem, as in others we have published, he lays into Lords Roberts and Kitchener and their arrogant stance in the midst of the misery that they have created:

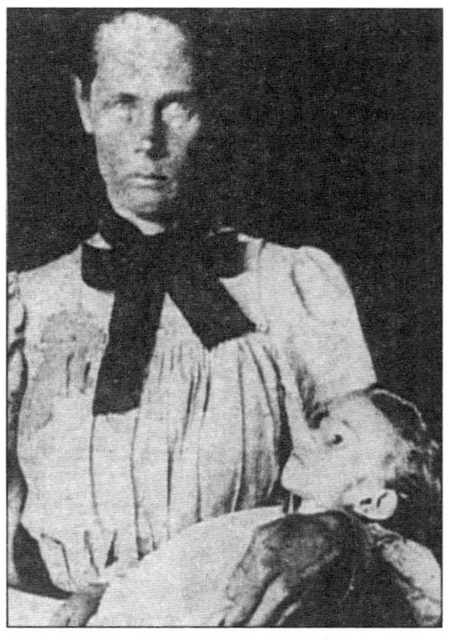

A mother with her dying daughter in a concentration camp

'THE REFUGEE CAMPS' (SO CALLED)

Lord Roberts he boasts that he stands at the head
Of all that is noble, and nice, and wellbred,
So we've got to believe it, it's only his due,
He says so himself – so it's bound to be true.

If against the "cowardly ignorant Boer"
In a barbarous manner he carries on war,
Why! What does it matter to me or to you,
He says so himself – so it's bound to be true.

The Boer has deserted his children and wife
For the purpose of leading a pleasanter life
Yes, "Such are those people, unnatural crew!"
Lord Kitchener says – so it's bound to be true.

If he harries weak women and children tender
It is *not* to induce the men to surrender,
Oh no! that's a thing he never would do,
He says so himself – so it's bound to be true.

If the women and orphans he drags away
In his pest-smitten camps are *willing* to stay
Let no one assert he the Innocents slew,
He says so himself – so it's bound to be true.

If, by thousands they die of disease and starvation
In those sweet health-resorts they call "concentration"
No matter! those people deserved it too,
He says so himself – so it's bound to be true.

Lord Kitchener persecutes woman and child
Because he was always exceedingly mild
And the more they objected the kinder he grew
He says so himself – so it's bound to be true.

Oh! he is so gentle; the Mahdi's head
He cut that off when his foe was dead;
In *uncivilized* warfare, that's nothing new
He says so himself – so it's bound to be true.

The wife gets a pass and may go away
To bring in the man; but the child must stay;
This, of course, Lord Kitchener never knew,
He says so himself – so it's bound to be true.

But Thanks to our wives, for they do not care
Whatever the hardships they have to bear,
They willingly suffer their woeful plight
If their husbands stand firm for God and the right.

By her noble example the Burgher's wife
Still gives him strength to continue the strife
And she cheers him on with all her might
To stand up firmly for God and the right.

O Africander! Be staunch and true
For that's what your wife is expecting from you
You will help her to make the burden light
By standing firm for God and the right.

A mother with her children in the Brandfort camp

Graveyard in a concentration camp

WAR IN THE LOWER ORANGE RIVER AREA
Cape Rebel women and children flee to German South West Africa

Kakamas, 20 November – The Upington–Kakamas area of the Orange River valley has undergone major disruptions as a result of the war in the past months. The last Rebel commando, that of Commandant Edwin Conroy, left Kenhardt on 17 June with the object of joining the Boer forces within the Republics. Some of the rebels refused to go with them, while others decided that they would first take their families to safety in German South West Africa. Everybody was afraid of the terror that the re-implementation of martial law by the British would entail.

Eventually between 30 and 60 families of the Rebels who had accompanied Conroy – between 200 and 400 souls – joined the flight to German South West Africa. Most of them were women and children. Only a few elderly men and a number of other men who refused to join Conroy accompanied them. It seems that the German authorities indicated they would be welcome, but added that they would have to stay in the German area until the end of the war.

The fleeing families trekked down the course of the Orange River on the southern bank. They loaded most of the belongings that they took with them on donkey carts. The loads included only a few pieces of furniture, consisting mostly of food such as wheat, maize and sweet potatoes. The daughters had to look after the livestock.

One group of refugees crossed the river at Byna-bo, while the rest moved further downstream to Skuitdrif. The crossing at Byna-bo was a virtually impossible task. It was incredibly difficult to get all the supplies, wagons and carts across the mountain. The men had to use thongs to ensure that the vehicles would not turn over. Nevertheless a Scots cart with its whole cargo crashed down when its draught-pole snapped. To worsen the situation even more an epidemic of diphtheria broke out and a number of girls died of this horrible disease.

At Skuitdrif one of the men built a float by means of which the refugees crossed the river. Here too some deaths occurred. In the end they all were on the northern bank of the river, and reached Jerusalem by the end of June. They remained there for four months and only returned to Kakamas in October.

While the refugees were in German South West Africa, the feared British occupation of Kakamas took place in July 1901.

On a specific day the British commander called all the women in the town together and warned them to report if there were Boers in the vicinity, or he would hang them. Mrs Martha Redman answered him that the Biblical figure Haman had similar plans with Mordechai, but eventually was hung on his own gallows!

REIGN OF TERROR IN THE CAPE COLONY

In the veld in the eastern Cape, 20 November – People here in Southern Africa who were under the impression that barbaric usages of the medieval period such as public executions were no longer practised by Europeans, must think again. The British forces still indulge in such activities. It seems to be a part of the British tactics to carry out a reign of terror through public pronouncements of judgement and public executions. Thus, by a figure of speech, they take a page from the book of Robespierre of French Revolution fame.

A good example was the pronouncement of sentence on 14 Cape Rebels at Aliwal North on 14 November. The public ceremony was held on the Market Square. There was even a stage erected for important people and seats for the civilian spectators. A military guard of honour took up position and the accused were marched in. Twelve of them were sentenced to death and the other two to life imprisonment. Thus ended the ceremony. Kitchener soon afterwards pardoned those who had been sentenced to death.

A noteworthy execution took place on 19 November. Piet Bester, a Rebel and former policeman, had been captured the previous day and summarily sentenced to death by a military court in Dordrecht. He was taken to a farmhouse, but in terms of martial law had to be executed in public. A midwife on the farm, Johanna Coetzer, angrily refused to allow any women to attend the execution.

The British then led Bester to a ravine and set up a firing squad. Bester refused to be blindfolded and looked the members of the squad in the eye. The poor soldiers could not find it in their hearts to fire at him. Bester was eventually bound to a chair, turned around and shot in the back.

Number 59 | 1 December 1901

THE WAR IN THE REPUBLICS
DECLINE IN MILITARY ACTIVITIES

In the veld, 30 November – British forces in the Orange Free State have proceeded with the destruction of farms in the past month – even though there is not much left to destroy. Tens of thousands of Khakis participate in massive drives, capturing thousands of cattle, but achieving very little military success. President Steyn issued a proclamation on 2 November that lowers to 14 the age at which boys become eligible for war service. This means that boys may be commandeered when they are 14 years old if their bodily strength and health allows it.

The Reverend J.D. Kestell told our reporter in the eastern Free State that he has been trekking with President Steyn's laager since the end of October. It often happens that women who have not been abducted from their farms invite the President for dinner. He usually accepts the dinner invitations, but never invitations to sleep in houses. He always sleeps in the veld, where the only roof over his head is the roof that stretches over the whole earth.

Commandant H. van Niekerk protects President Steyn's laager, which seldom remains in the same place for two consecutive nights. In order to be ready at all times for whatever may occur, the horses are caught at two o'clock every night, saddled up and fastened right next to the President and his guard. Steyn never takes off his boots in the evening and is ready at every moment to jump on the back of his horse.

Kestell says that even though they suffer great discomfort, there are more than enough pleasant factors to make up for it. That includes all the reading material in the laager. Newspapers that are picked up at abandoned British campsites reach them from all sides. On one of their horse carts they even have a small library that includes German translations of Tolstoy's *War and Peace* and *Anna Karenina*, a number of books of poetry, a book on physics, a history of the American War of Independence and some religious books.

The biggest clash in the Orange Free State in November took place on the 29th, on the farm Spytfontein, between Lindley and Reitz. General De Wet told our reporter that he received a message just after sunrise that morning from General Johannes Hattingh that a British column was attacking the women's laager on the farm Blydskap. De Wet immediately ordered all his officers to attack the Khakis. General Michael Prinsloo's burghers charged the British vanguard and Hattingh's burghers the rearguard. The Khaki reaction was to abandon their attack on the women's laager and carry out a counter-attack on the burghers.

According to De Wet, the British force, under the command of Colonel Rimington, consisted of about 1 000 mounted soldiers with three guns. De Wet was preparing his 600 burghers for a full-scale attack when a heavy hailstorm began. This went on until the sun set.

The Boer horses were still weak after the whole day's activity, and the burghers were wet to their skins, so De Wet ordered everybody to find shelter and to resume the attack the next day. Early in the morning, however, the scouts established that the Khakis had retreated in a northerly direction during the night. De Wet and his burghers then occupied the former town of Lindley. He explains that he calls it a 'former town' since the British have destroyed everything, including the church and the parsonage.

A QUIET MONTH IN THE TRANSVAAL

After a series of battles in October, things became very quiet in the Transvaal Republic during November, without any side gaining a significant advantage on the other. On 11 November the Khakis captured General Du Toit's laager at Doornhoek. Nine days later a British unit captured the highly respected Commandant Fanie Buys of the Heidelberg Commando. This was shortly after a successful attack by Buys and his men on a British guard post of 50 soldiers near Villiers.

A further setback for the Boers followed on 26 November when Commandant D. Joubert was captured in the eastern Transvaal. On the same day 80 burghers of Middelburg sent a petition to General Ben Viljoen in which they indicated that they refused to serve any longer under Lieutenant Colonel Fanie Trichard. Viljoen answered two days later that he respected Trichard's appointment and called on the burghers to stand together in fighting for their freedom.

Most of the burghers in the Transvaal are keeping themselves occupied with gathering food and storing surpluses in secret places. Burgher Frederik Rothmann told our correspondent that they are still full of confidence, having heard that the enemy despairs of ever catching all the burghers. Their attempts to starve out the Republics will never work, he says. The burghers are extremely glad about the war news that they receive from all over the country, and believe our tactics are the correct ones.

From the northern Transvaal it is reported that General Christiaan Beyers continued his expedition through the Lowveld during November. He and his burghers followed the course of the Letaba River all the way to the border with the Portuguese territory. Earlier on there had been Khakis guarding the border, but Beyers found nobody in that area. They moved up along the border to the Shingwedzi River and followed the course of that stream back to the west. One night two lions frightened their horses, but fortunately did not catch any. In the end Beyers and his party reached the Mission Station at Elim, south of the Soutpansberg, unharmed. There they heard gruesome details about the shooting of Boer prisoners of war and of a German missionary, the Reverend Heese, by officers of a British unit known as the Bushveld Carbineers. Since the British authorities themselves are conducting an investigation into these war crimes, we will provisionally refrain from commenting on the allegations.

While Beyers and his staff were busy enjoying dinner on a Boer farm near the village of Louis Trichardt one evening, the British garrison of Fort Hendrina, which they called Fort Edward, attacked them. Beyers managed to get away, but one burgher was taken prisoner. Beyers subsequently visited the missionary Hofmeyr at Mara, from where he rode around the western point of the Soutpansberg to the Salt Pan. About at that stage he began feeling ill. His strength quickly declined, since he is suffering from malaria. This is without doubt as a result of his visit to the Lowveld during the summer. His burghers are extremely concerned about his condition.

General C.F. Beyers

FARM DESTRUCTION

Eastern Transvaal, 30 November – The British are still busy destroying all the farms that they come across. Colonel John Blake, formerly of the Irish Brigade, told our correspondent quite bluntly: 'I do not believe that in the history of the world, one could find more acts of barbarity and brutality committed by any people in any land than by the English in the two little republics of the Transvaal and the Free State.' He recounted a specific incident that he witnessed earlier this month:

'There were about 15 of us near Dullstroom watching the movements of the English. A column about 500 strong rode up to a farmhouse occupied by a widow and her daughters. Soon we saw the girls pushing the organ out of the door and the smoke began to fill the windows and roof. The organ was pushed about 40 metres away and placed by a stone cattle kraal. The mother sat down and began to play and her girls collected about her. The house was now enveloped in flames, the soldiers were killing fowls, etc., while the officers were cracking jokes at the poor mother and her children.

'Of course, we thought that the old lady and her children were singing a hymn or psalm, because these are nearest to the Boer heart.

'The English, having completed their pleasant duty, rode off in search of other farms. We then went to the scene of destruction, because we knew that immediate help was necessary. On meeting them we asked the old lady how she could play and sing hymns while her home behind her back was burning and all her possessions were being destroyed. She replied, "We were not singing hymns or psalms, but our Boer War Song."'

Left and above: Khakis and their hangers-on looting Boer farms

OUR MILITARY OFFICERS

Commandant Fanie Buys

Stephanus Bernardus Buys was born in 1852 in the Marico district of the western Transvaal. He is the eldest son of Stephanus Bernardus Buys and his wife Sara Maria Snyman. Buys grew up on his parents' farm, Leeuspruit, south of Heidelberg in the southern Transvaal and later on farmed there himself. His first military experience was in the Transvaal War of Independence of 1880–81.

In 1882 Buys was elected field cornet of the Heidelberg-Roodekoppen Commando. Subsequently he was re-elected every year. In 1895–96 he and his commando were called up to keep an eye on the Uitlanders on the Witwatersrand at the time of the Jameson Raid.

With the outbreak of this war in October 1899, Buys was still a field cornet of the Heidelberg Commando. In that capacity he participated in numerous battles on the Natal front. In February 1900 he was elected provisional commandant of the Heidelbergers. He and his burghers were powerless to halt the British breakthrough on the Tugela front at the end of that month. They subsequently served in the Free State, and then Buys and his Heidelbergers were involved in the futile attempts to defend Pretoria against British occupation.

Early in June last year Buys succeeded J.D. Weilbach as commandant of the Heidelberg Commando. In that capacity he participated in the Battles of Donkerhoek and Bergendal. In September he was wounded near Machadodorp, but recovered and then led his commando in numerous engagements in the southern Transvaal.

Last month Buys and his commando were participating in a campaign along the Vaal River when he was wounded in his knee. Since he urgently needed medical attention, that courageous commander had to suffer the humiliation of surrendering to the British authorities a few days ago.

Buys is married to Catharina Johanna Susanna Labuschagne, who is at present in a concentration camp. They have two daughters and three sons, of whom the eldest was killed in action in October 1899 at Modderspruit.

Commandant Fanie Buys

THE War Reporter
MONTHLY EDITION

Number 60   In the Veld, South African Republic   1 January 1902

DE WET OVERRUNS KHAKIS ON GROENKOP
Glorious victory on Christmas Day

Eastern Free State, 30 December – The high point for the Republican forces in the Free State last month was on Christmas Day, when Chief Commandant Christiaan de Wet overwhelmed a Khaki camp on Groenkop, here in the eastern Free State. For some time, De Wet's scouts had been aware of a British construction team that was building blockhouses east of Bethlehem. An escort consisting of about 500 men commanded by Major Williams protected the builders from the vantage point of Groenkop, from where they had a good view over a large area. On 22 December De Wet and his commando captured a number of horses, and were fired on by Williams's gunners.

De Wet inspected Groenkop thoroughly and decided to attack. After dark on the night of 24 December he advanced on the low hill from the northwest with a force of about 1 000 burghers. The burghers left their horses and their only rapid-fire gun at the foot of the hill and climbed to the top as silently as possible. By two o'clock that morning they were virtually at the summit when a British sentry fired on them. De Wet then shouted at the top of his voice: 'Charge, burghers!' The burghers took up the shout and while the bullets were flying over their heads, they rushed to the summit, shouting in unison, 'Charge, charge!'

De Wet says that the slope was so steep that the burghers rather climbed than ran. Within minutes they were on top. By that time the Khakis, who were sleeping in tents, had of course woken up, and a sharp engagement followed. The burghers soon eliminated all the British gunners, but in the confusion in the dark many soldiers courageously resisted the onslaught. Within 15 to 20 minutes the die was cast and the camp was in the hands of the Boers. Most of the Khakis were captured, but a small number got away. The enemy's horses stampeded down the hill with a large number of soldiers in their nightdresses in pursuit. Some of the officers attempted to restore order, but it was in vain and they soon hoisted the white flag.

Before leaving again a few hours later, De Wet gave his burghers the opportunity to eat as much of the British food as they could as a Christmas meal. Since the booty included a wagon filled with liquor, those burghers who enjoyed a drink could slake their thirst! The Boers captured two guns and 20 wagons, some of which were loaded with rifle and artillery shells; also about 500 horses and mules. Altogether 57 Khakis and 25 of their black servants were killed, 84 wounded and about 200 made prisoner of war, including two scouts from another unit who arrived to investigate the firing. De Wet took the prisoners of war with him, and intends to release them on the other side of the border with Basutoland. Unfortunately there were also casualties on the Boer side. Altogether 14 men, including Commandant Olivier of Bethlehem, were killed and 30 wounded. It is notable that no British force attempted to pursue De Wet.

WAR NEWS FROM THE TRANSVAAL

Eastern Transvaal, 31 December – Early in December the Transvaal government, escorted by a bodyguard of about 200 burghers under the command of Commandant Joubert, crossed a blockhouse line. For security reasons we will not divulge where this took place. We can report that the garrisons of the blockhouses on both sides of the spot where the breakthrough took place, fired sharply on our men. Fortunately their only loss was two burghers wounded and 10 horses killed.

On 4 December Commandant-General Louis Botha had a narrow escape when a British army attacked his commando at Oshoek on the Swaziland border. A traitor, Lange, led the Khakis to the commando's retreat. Botha himself got away, but approximately 100 burghers as well as all their supplies fell into the hands of the enemy. The Khakis pursued Botha, but two days later he and his burghers carried out a counter-attack at Kalkoenkraal and dispersed his pursuers.

In the northwest Transvaal General Kemp's burghers undertook a punitive expedition against the Bakgatla of Chief Linchwe from 10 December. These Bakgatla had earlier attacked a women's laager at Holfontein. Two burghers who were protecting the laager were killed in the fight that followed, and a young girl was wounded. Linchwe furthermore announced the annexation of a part of the Transvaal from the western border up to the Elands River (at Swartruggens) and it was reported that his subjects looted large herds of livestock from the Rustenburgers.

The expedition was successful. Kemp and his burghers took about 7 000 cattle and 8 000 sheep and goats from the Bakgatla. On 16 December the commandos were back, and commemorated the Vow of Blood River with Reverend Roux on the banks of the Elands River. The next day the division of the booty followed. Kemp ensured that black chiefs whose subjects were still loyal to the ZAR got back all their livestock before the division of the rest of the animals among his burghers took place.

In the eastern Transvaal a setback was suffered by the Boer forces on 10 December when a British force of about 2 000 men attacked General Piet Viljoen's commando near Trichardtsfontein. Altogether 131 burghers were made prisoner of war, and part of Viljoen's supplies fell into enemy hands. Two days later the same British column attacked Viljoen's commando again, recapturing one of their field guns that Botha had earlier captured at Bakenlaagte. Altogether 16 burghers were killed and 70 made prisoner of war before the remainder escaped.

In the western Transvaal, Republican forces suffered two significant setbacks – on 13 December and again on 16 December – when General Methuen twice overran Commandant Potgieter's laagers near Makwassie. In the two skirmishes the Khakis took 36 burghers prisoner and captured a number of Potgieter's wagons.

On 19 December Commandant Coen Brits's commando lured a battalion of mounted soldiers into an ambush about 30 kilometres south of Ermelo in the eastern Transvaal and overpowered them. In the battle that followed 33 Khakis were killed or wounded and 117 made prisoner of war.

On the same day, the burghers of General Chris Muller and Lieutenant Colonel Fanie Trichard attacked a British camp at Elandspruit, near Dullstroom. Unfortunately there was a misunderstanding between them on the specific plan of action. Muller was under the impression that there was no actual decision to charge the British camp, but that his burghers would fire with their Maxim gun and rifles into the camp to inflict as much damage as possible. Trichard, believing that they were to capture the camp, ordered his men to charge. They actually overpowered a number of entrenchments, but could not reach the camp itself. At one stage Muller's gunners, unaware that there would be Boers within the entrenchments, fired on them with their Maxim gun. As might be expected, there was subsequently an argument between Trichard and Muller. The British casualties in this skirmish amounted to 37, while on the Republican side five men were killed and about 20 wounded.

In the western Transvaal General Celliers overpowered a British unit near Lichtenburg on 22 December. Altogether 33 Khakis were killed or wounded, while 40 were made prisoner of war. In the process the burghers captured about 100 horses and a supply of ammunition.

In the eastern Transvaal the first few days after Christmas were a tough time for the commando of Commandant Coen Brits, since British units encircled them twice. His burghers had to fight courageously to escape from the Khaki net on 28 December. Unfortunately, not all of them got away, since 31 burghers were made prisoner of war.

General Ben Viljoen and his burghers, on the contrary, had the luxury of a peaceful Christmas time in Pilgrim's Rest. Reverend H.J. Neethling conducted the formal part of the festivities while Viljoen himself made a speech. He told the 90 school children who were present how fortunate they were to go to a school under the *Vierkleur* flag while the poor children in the concentration camps were suffering terribly. In addition to formal activities, the burghers celebrated the festive season with races and athletics. As for the results: General Viljoen won the sprint for officers!

We have just heard that General Daniël Erasmus has been made prisoner of war by a British unit near Ermelo.

Commandant Coen Brits

Burghers of General Ben Viljoen's commando. Note the baboon with the rifle in the foreground

WAR NEWS FROM THE CAPE COLONY

In the veld, 30 December – Commandant Gideon Scheepers, who had to surrender himself to the British forces about two months ago on the grounds of poor health, was not sent to a prisoner-of-war camp after his recovery, but was taken from Beaufort West to prison in Graaff-Reinet. Scheepers is a Transvaal burgher, and has the right to demand prisoner-of-war status. However, the British authorities decided to accuse him of transgressing martial law in the Cape Colony. On 18 December his trial began. Three days later a member of the public who greeted Scheepers while he was transported between the jail and the courthouse was fined £5 or 14 days in prison.

In the light of the death penalty that was given to Commandant Hans Lötter, the general feeling even among sympathetically inclined people in Graaff-Reinet is that Scheepers' prospects are hopeless.

The Republican commandos in the Cape Colony suffered a major setback on 16 December when Commandant Pieter Kritzinger fell into British hands. Kritzinger had crossed the Orange River at Sanddrift three days earlier for his third invasion of the Cape Colony. British units pursued him. Since the sun was very hot and the horses in a weak state even before the crossing, Kritzinger's burghers found the going tough. In the end, they were cornered against the blockhouse line between Noupoort and De Aar, near Hannover Station, and were forced to cross this line, where the blockhouses are hardly 800 metres apart, in clear daylight. All the mounted burghers managed to cross safely despite heavy fire from both sides. Kritzinger was in the advance party, which first had to cut an opening in the barbed wire obstruction with their pliers. He was already through when he turned back to assist one of his burghers whose horse was shot under him. It was then that Kritzinger was hit in the chest. Even though it is a bad wound, he managed again to reach his men.

It was soon clear to Kritzinger's adjutants that he desperately needed medical treatment. They could not supply the necessary assistance, so they took him to a station close by, from where they sent a message to a British ambulance to request assistance. Thus the valiant Kritzinger became a prisoner of war. It is not known how he is doing, but his burghers are ex-

Continued overleaf

continued

tremely concerned about his condition.

Shocking news from Burgersdorp in the northeastern Cape is that drunken Khakis severely damaged the language monument in that town on Christmas Eve. This once beautiful monument commemorates the legislation passed in 1882 by the Cape Parliament in terms of which Dutch was given equal status with English.

In the western Cape the combined commandos of Commandant Wynand Malan, Jaap van Deventer and Manie Maritz launched an attack at the end of November on a British horse depot at Tontelboschkolk. The burghers' horses were in poor condition and they hoped to capture a good supply of fresh horses. The attack appears to have been poorly co-ordinated, however, and floundered on stiff resistance by the British guards at the depot. A few nights later Maritz targeted the depot again. Accompanied by a number of burghers, he crawled to the gate of the camp. A guard fired on them and hit Maritz in the side. The tough Commandant nevertheless managed to open the gate of the camp and the Boers captured approximately 400 horses. The burghers subsequently took Maritz to a farmhouse nearby, where he was treated for his wound. Fortunately he recovered quickly and was up and about again after a few days. In the meantime, the commandos abandoned their siege of Tontelboschkolk on 5 December.

General Smuts arrived in the Calvinia area at about that time. He reports that it is his considered opinion that there are thousands of Cape Afrikaners who would gladly join the Republican forces, but they have no horses – and in a big area like the Cape you are powerless if you have no horse.

A few days before Christmas two British columns left Clanwilliam for Calvinia and occupied the town before Smuts and his burghers were ready to confront them. However the Republican forces drove them back again to Clanwilliam after a heavy engagement. One burgher was killed. It is not known what the Khaki casualties were, but they left horses and wagons behind that the Boers captured.

On 19 December Smuts sent out general instructions from Nieuwoudtville to all the Republican commandos in the western districts, in his capacity as commander of the Republican forces in that part of the Cape Colony. The instructions were specifically to do with disciplinary issues – for example, all the inhabitants of the western districts, both white and Coloured, must be treated well and may not be molested, except if they actively support the enemy. Furthermore he instructs that the Boer military courts may not summarily sentence armed blacks that are made prisoner of war to death. The death penalty may only be given if there is absolute certainty that they were members of the British secret service or were acting as spies.

On 27 December Smuts gathered almost all the republican commandos active in the western half of the Cape Colony for a war council meeting at Soetwater, between Calvinia and Nieuwoudtville. Sixteen commandos, consisting of approximately 3 000 men, were represented. Smuts divided those 16, as well as three other commandos he was aware of in that area, into three groups, each under a fighting general. He himself would act as commander-in-chief, with Jaap van Deventer as fighting general for the southern districts, Manie Maritz as fighting general for Namaqualand, and Wynand Malan as fighting general for the Midland districts (Fraserburg, Victoria West, Carnarvon, Hopetown and Philipstown). At the moment there are no enemy forces on outposts in the western Cape.

In the Stormberg, the last month was relatively quiet. The British are vainly attempting to capture Commandant Willem Fouchee, but he is too wily for them. At the same time, he sporadically manages to capture British collaborators who are making life difficult for the Republican forces. One of those Khakis is a Captain Jelliman, a colonist from the Maclear district who knows that area very well. Jelliman previously played a big role in the virtual destruction of Commandant Stoffel Myburgh's commando, on which we reported earlier.

Fouchee regarded Jelliman as a traitor and ordered that he should be shot if he fell into Boer hands. One night a group of Khakis slept on the farm of a Scotsman named Mountjoy, a former member of Fouchee's commando, near Barkly East. Jelliman was one of them. A Boer commando overpowered them and prepared to shoot Jelliman, but Mountjoy pleaded for his life. When Fouchee arrived he wanted to shoot Jelliman immediately, but Mountjoy pleaded again. In the end Fouchee gave Jelliman an old, run-down mule and promised that if he could clear a low hill before the count of ten, he would be free. Fouchee secretly told his burghers to shoot to the side of the mule. The frightened Jelliman did his utmost, but it was only on the third attempt that he managed to drag the mule over the rise, while the shots rang out all around him. Since that incident nobody has heard anything of Jelliman!

FROM THE EDITOR

The war is now entering its fourth calendar year, and prospects seem much better now for the Republican forces than at any time since the fall of Bloemfontein in March 1900. The war has spread over the whole country and the enemy finds it increasingly difficult to fill all the gaps. Our commanders regularly overrun Khaki units, as the now legendary Chief Commandant Christiaan de Wet recently accomplished again on Christmas Day in the Orange Free State.

We do not claim that we can beat the British army on the battlefield. Their forces are simply too formidable. Our hope remains that some crisis or other erupting elsewhere in the world will relieve the pressure on the Republics by forcing Britain to send soldiers there on a large scale. We believe that our hope is their fear. That is why they are continuing to use brutal methods such as targeting our women and children and destroying our country in an attempt to break the fighting spirit of our burghers as quickly as possible.

In the meantime the destruction that the Khakis are bringing about – both morally and materially – is frightening. Many of our military officers state quite bluntly that they will fight till the bitter end. Let us hope that the bitter end is not too far away, since the alternative is that everything will be irreparably destroyed.

OTHER WAR NEWS FROM THE FREE STATE

In the veld, 30 December – The Khakis have resumed their attempts to corner the Boer commandos in the Free State during the past month. These attempts are futile – and Chief Commandant de Wet in particular is making a joke of them. On Sunday 8 December, for example, he escaped from the British net after a brief engagement with an enemy force near Lindley. On 16 December De Wet and his men commemorated the Vow of Blood River with President Steyn and a large number of Free State burghers near Lindley. Two days later De Wet's forces attacked a British unit at Tijgerkloof near Harrismith, but they encountered stiff resistance. Two burghers were killed and nine wounded in this attack.

The British forces too have had their moments of glory. On 15 December a unit captured Commandant Badenhorst. The next day the fearless Commandant Sarel Haasbroek was tragically killed during an attack on a British convoy near Senekal.

The Boer commandos are making life as difficult as possible for the British units erecting a line of blockhouses from Frankfort to Vrede. On 20 December General Wessel Wessels attacked one of the units protecting the builders at Tafelkop, with 300 burghers. The burghers overwhelmed the British force and captured two field guns, but since all the gun horses were killed and the burghers had none, they could not haul them away. Huge British forces soon arrived and recaptured the guns, as Wessels and his men retreated. Wessels's casualties amounted to 20 burghers. The British losses, according to reliable information, were 33 men killed and 45 wounded.

The 'War Song Book' recently published by Republicans in the Orange Free State

SALT AS VALUABLE AS GOLD

One of the burghers in General Ben Viljoen's commando, Frederik Rothmann, recently told our correspondent about the most valuable treasure he had found in years, namely about 30 kilograms of salt.

'On Friday 29 November I accompanied Field Cornet Swart's burghers. We were busy harvesting maize that had been left on the fields of the handsuppers along the Ohrigstad River for our maize meal. I walked a little distance from the wagons to look for tobacco leaves and on my way back crossed the farm of H. Haber, the brother-in-law of Abel Erasmus. They are both fighting against us now. On Haber's farm I heard that salt was buried somewhere. We have a great need for that product. To remain without salt for a long time is bad for the blood. Sores are beginning to appear on some burghers.

'In a big shed that is used to dry tobacco leaves, I noted a few places on the floor where somebody had previously been digging. I thought I would look there. I took a piece of wood and stamped on the floor to find a hollow sound. With the very first try it sounded to me as if the ground was not solid. I took a crowbar and dug a hole. With the first thrust I saw something white. It looked like salt. I tasted it – it was salt! I shoved the loose ground away with my hands and found that the crowbar had penetrated the lid of a tin. I lifted the lid. In front of my eyes I saw a huge expanse of salt …

'My heart almost stopped in ecstasy! A piece of gold would not have been as welcome at that moment. When I looked further I found altogether three tins – a total of 30 kilograms of salt as well as other luxuries. The news of the discovery of the salt very quickly spread. The demand for "a little bit of salt" continuously streams in. I am the hero of the day and I am congratulated all around.'

THE CONCENTRATION CAMPS

Kitchener's childish letter

It is clear that frustration is clouding the capacity of the British commander-in-chief to think realistically. The letter Kitchener dispatched to Acting President Burger of the ZAR, President Steyn of the OFS and Chief Commandant De Wet at the beginning of December would have been laughable had he not intended it to be serious. In this letter he informs the addressees that since they complain about the treatment of the women and children in the concentration camps, he accepts that the Boers would treat those women and children better. Therefore he offers to send all the families in the camps who are willing to the commandos as soon as he is informed where they should be delivered.

Our first reaction was that Burger, Steyn and De Wet should answer that Kitchener should send those women to about 10 000 farms in England, or at least as many farms as the British had destroyed in the Republics, and that the Boers would look after them there. Such an answer would sound as ridiculous to Kitchener as his offer sounds to us. However, President Steyn did not need our counsel. On 10 December he answered Kitchener in bitter words from the Free State:

'As if martyrdom is not enough for the women and children, Your Excellency is now making a proposal that would, if we accept it, make life impossible for those unfortunate victims. Since you know and the British government knows, or should know, that there is hardly a single house left in the Orange Free State that has not been burnt down or destroyed, that all the furniture and specifically the blankets and the clothing of the women and children has been burned or looted by British troops. If we were to take our women back, they would have to survive under the open sky. It is of no importance how glad each father or husband would be to have his wife and children with him, since for those reasons we must refuse your offer. I am convinced that you will now make it known all over the world that the Boers refuse to take their wives back. Consequently I expect from you as an honourable man to make the reasons why we refuse your offer public.'

Chief Commandant De Wet's answer to Kitchener was briefer than that of Steyn and more challenging:

'I refuse point blank to receive the families before the war has ended and we are in a position to state our claims for just compensation for the unlawful abduction and humiliation of our families and for compensations for the uncivilised action of England in taking our families away.'

Women collecting firewood in the Jacobs camp, Durban

OUR MILITARY OFFICERS

Commandant Sarel Haasbroek

Sarel Francois Haasbroek was born in 1849 in Swellendam in the Cape Colony, the son of Johannes Bernardus Haasbroek and his wife Maria Joubert. As a child he moved with his parents to Burgersdorp in the northeastern Cape, and as a young man to the Winburg district in the Orange Free State. In the 1870s he established his own farm at Grootboom, north of Winburg.

When the war broke out in October 1899 Haasbroek joined the Free State forces as an ordinary burgher. He was soon elected assistant field cornet and participated with distinction in numerous battles on the Natal front. After the start of the British offensive in February 1900, he was transferred with a part of his commando to the western Free State, where he participated in attempts to relieve Cronjé at Paardeberg. At this time he was promoted to the rank of field cornet.

Haasbroek subsequently participated in the futile attempts to halt the British offensive through the northern Free State. He was wounded but recovered. Soon afterwards he was appointed commandant of a volunteer unit that had to escort the Free State government. His courage and determination earned him the respect of his burghers and also of President Steyn and Chief Commandant de Wet. Later he became commandant of the Winburg Commando, which concentrated on breaking up British communication links.

Now Sarel Haasbroek is no more. His death on 16 December is a huge loss for the Republican forces. He leaves his wife, Adriana Myburgh, their five sons and three daughters. President Steyn wrote a letter of condolence to Mrs Haasbroek in which he noted: 'Our people have lost in him not only one of our most courageous heroes, but one of its most fair-minded front-line warriors.'

Commandant Sarel Haasbroek

THE War Reporter
MONTHLY EDITION

Number 61   In the Veld, South African Republic   1 February 1902

THE CASE OF GIDEON SCHEEPERS
Victim of British reign of terror

In the veld, 30 January – By this time everybody in South Africa, as well as thousands of our friends in the outside world, is aware that Commandant Gideon Scheepers was shot by a firing squad on 18 January. It is our objective to share with our readers as much information as possible on that tragic incident. In the first place, we managed to obtain through a friendly contact in Graaff-Reinet a report by Scheepers himself on his capture, his trial and his last days on earth. It is bloodcurdling reading matter:

'My commando left me behind near Prince Albert on 10 October at my own request, since it was too painful for me to accompany them any further. A few hours after my comrades left, a British unit arrived at the house where I was left behind. They treated me in a friendly way. The next morning a doctor took me to the railway station. I was taken by train to Matjiesfontein and felt tired and full of pain when I arrived there the next day. There I was placed in a dirty, unkempt hospital but was treated in a very friendly manner.

'On 19 October a train took me to Beaufort West, where I once again received excellent treatment. The British concern for me was notable: I was placed alone in a huge tent. A barbed wire fence with 24 wires was put up around the tent and guards with fixed bayonets watched over me.

'On 14 November I heard that I would, on the orders of General French, be taken to Graaff-Reinet. At that time I still suffered tremendous pain and felt weak. When we arrived by train at Noupoort, I was again put in the hospital. At that stage I did not know why I was being taken to Graaff-Reinet.

'On 18 November I got access to the latest newspaper in Noupoort. To my surprise I read in it that I would be executed in Graaff-Reinet the next week since there were serious charges against me. Three days later, four of the late Commandant Lötter's men were taken from the hospital. I was informed that they would be taken to Graaff-Reinet to be executed.

'From 8 December there were rather large changes in my circumstances. Soon after dark that evening I was told to dress immediately since I would be taken to Graaff-Reinet. I was ready soon and a doctor accompanied me to the train. I was transported in a first-class wagon and the next morning – my father's birthday – enjoyed looking through the train window at the green veld, the trees and the mountains.

'A huge crowd of people was gathered on the station and along the streets when I arrived here in Graaff-Reinet with my guards. However, those people did not welcome me. On the contrary – to me their glowing eyes seemed to gleam with contempt.

'Here in Graaff-Reinet I was led into the prison. It was a terrible feeling. I wished that the earth would open in front of me and swallow me. On my arrival I was searched before being locked into a hospital room. It is delightfully cool, but oh, the bars!

'On that very same day a certain Tennant, the British intelligence officer, came to see me. He looked down on me and wanted to know if I had witnesses to call up. When I asked what the charges were, he mentioned a few. The next day he handed me a list of the charges against me. There are 30 accusations of murder, seven of arson and some of rough treatment of prisoners of war and barbaric treatment of blacks. I pointed out to Tennant that my witnesses are in the veld and it would be impossible to recall them.

'My case was nevertheless heard from Wednesday 18 December. Numerous people gave evidence against me, and some, like John Momberg, a former Rebel and member of my commando, enjoyed telling the most infamous lies. This process went on until the Saturday, and was resumed on Monday.

'Christmas Day was a beautiful day. I was satisfied under the circumstances, since what I had done I had done for my country and for my people and for all that is dear to the Afrikaners. However, there was a feeling of longing in my heart to be with my relatives and friends on that festive day.

'After the quiet Christmas period my trial resumed on 27 December. I defended myself against all the accusations. The details can be seen in the court papers. The next day Tennant cross-examined me. That afternoon my agent, Auret, defended me well.

'Then it was Tennant's turn. He spoke like somebody delivering a funeral oration. It was notable that he called my actions "cowardly". I am not very courageous, but would enjoy challenging Tennant to a duel.

'I quickly realised what the outcome of my trial would be. It would take a miracle for me to get away alive. However, I was prepared for any punishment for my country, my beloved and noble people, for my brave President Steyn, for my beloved Chief Commandant De Wet and for the many valiant and noble men who have given their lives for the Afrikaner cause, such as General Kock, Commandant Theron, Colonel de Villabois-Mareuil and Commandant Haasbroek. It would be a pleasant feeling to be counted amongst those who were crucified for our dear country.

'A question that came to me was: how is it possible for me to defend myself against the false accusations and witnesses, while my own witnesses, documents and instructions are still in the field? Is it possible to reveal everything that my government has commissioned me to do while the war is still in progress and thus become a traitor to my country and my people? After the ending of the war a just trial would be possible, but it can never be this court in Graaff-Reinet. It seems to me as if our Afrikaner people will never receive justice from an Englishman.

'New Year's Day was a quiet day for me. I spent it in loneliness and in longing to be with my family circle. From then until 8 January nothing in particular happened. On that day Commandant Kritzinger was admitted here to the prison hospital. I would have enjoyed saying a few words to him, but it was not permitted. I have heard that Lord Kitchener must decide my fate

'Another few days of doing nothing in my condition of exile between prison walls and bars followed. The only way to shorten the time was to read newspapers. These are filled with lies, but I know how to understand them.

'This morning at about eight o'clock the warden informed me that they would fetch me at eleven o'clock to hear the verdict. They put me in an ambulance wagon and took me to the military square. Colonel Henniker read all the accusations and then announced that I had been found guilty on all but one of them and that I had been sentenced to death. Kitchener approved of the proceedings.

'Back in my cell I was informed that I would be shot tomorrow. I do not feel frightened at all. I am only sad for my dear mother, whose birthday it is today. My biggest consolation is that I am not guilty. I hope that all the commandants and officers who are still in the field will avenge this. Our God will bring about justice in the light of his justice. Save your people, dear God!'

Scheepers was shot by a British firing squad the next day. At his request all the members of the firing squad were British soldiers. He was not executed in front of a huge audience, but taken out of town. There in the veld he was bound to a chair and blindfolded before he was shot. His body was not put into a coffin, but placed in a grave without covering. Lime, which quickens the process of decomposition of a body, was sprinkled on his corpse. However, since the British authorities feared that the place of his funeral might become a martyr's grave, they dug up his body in secret that night and reburied it in an unmarked place in the stream of the Sunday's River.

Death sentence pronounced on Scheepers

Trial of Commandant Gideon Scheepers

Scheepers shot next to his grave

FROM THE EDITOR

The most newsworthy event of the past month was the execution of Commandant Gideon Scheepers on the orders of a British military court, and with Kitchener's specific blessing. When Commandant Hans Lötter died under similar circumstances three months ago, we were sad; but he was, strictly speaking, a Cape Rebel who had taken up arms against his own authorities. In the case of Scheepers, there is no possibility of extenuating circumstances for his murderers. He was a Republican officer who participated on the orders of an internationally recognised government in an officially declared war. It is no wonder that even the outside world reacted with shock and contempt with his murder. The British, however, do not take any notice of criticism.

On the war front the Republican forces, actively supported by thousands of Cape Rebels, are still making life difficult for the Khakis over a wide area. We report in this issue of a battle near Kakamas in the Orange River valley, where a commando of Rebels successfully defended themselves against the enemy. These Rebels are just as shocked as the inhabitants of the Republics (and the parliamentary opposition in Britain itself, as we report in this issue) about the inhuman treatment accorded to them by the Khaki authorities.

Against the background of the murder of Scheepers and the support that the Republics receive from the Cape Rebels, the activities of the traitors in our own midst – the joiners – become all the more detestable. Our only explanation is that they are acting purely in self-interest. The bitterness with which loyal Republicans refer to them is a clear indication that they will probably never be forgiven their betrayal.

Number 61 1 February 1902

NEWS FROM THE WAR FRONT

FIGHTING IN THE EASTERN TRANSVAAL

In the veld, 31 January – Early in January in the far eastern Transvaal, Republican commandos struck with success on two consecutive days at a British unit commanded by General Plumer, who was carrying out a drive in that area. On 3 January General Chris Botha's burghers captured most of the vanguard of Plumer's column, consisting of 28 Khakis from New Zealand. On 4 January General J.D. Opperman's burghers overpowered a much bigger section of Plumer's rearguard in an ambush at Bankkop, east of Ermelo. The Khakis attempted to offer resistance, but after their commander, Major Vallentin, was killed they hoisted the white flag. Altogether 20 Khakis were killed in the battle and 45 were wounded, while in addition the Boers took a further 70 soldiers prisoner of war, with numerous horses and a rapid-fire gun. The price of this victory was high, unfortunately, since one of the very few Boers who were killed in action by the enemy was General Opperman, one of the most able Transvaal officers.

On 10 January a British unit assisted by black guides carried out a successful night attack on a Boer laager north of Ermelo. Two well-known officers of the former State Artillery, Major Wolmarans and Captain Wolmarans, as well as 42 other burghers, became prisoners of war. Two evenings later, a similar British attack on another Boer laager in the same area led to 32 burghers being captured. On 18 January the Khakis took 27 burghers prisoner of war at Spitskop, some 40 kilometres southeast of Ermelo.

The enemy certainly was particularly successful with night attacks on a number of Boer commandos in the eastern Transvaal during January. There are burghers who speculate that joiners lead the British forces to our commandos, since they know where the burghers are inclined to look for shelter. The joiners know the veld and can find their way in the dark. They certainly pose a dangerous threat to us.

On 24 January a British unit captured 12 burghers at Boschmansfontein in a night attack. The next day the British captured a total of 64 burghers in the mountains northeast of Wakkerstroom, and on 26 January a further 87 burghers at Nelspan, some 10 kilometres west of Ermelo. In the last skirmish six burghers were killed.

SKIRMISHES IN THE WESTERN TRANSVAAL

After a quiet December, the Boer commandos in the western Transvaal were on the go early in the New Year. The first activity was a combined expedition in the vicinity of Mafeking. General De la Rey was in overall command. General Kemp and his burghers crossed the railway line near Kraaipan in a westerly direction and General Celliers and his burghers did the same near Mafeking. Field Cornet Meyer, who is called Old Mot by all and sundry, remained behind at the railway line with a few men to break it up if an armoured train should steam out of Mafeking. The commandos made good progress and a number of British patrols and handsuppers were put to flight. One group of burghers even visited the concentration camp at Mafeking.

By that evening both commandos returned with a combined booty of more than 6 000 head of livestock and 66 horses. Unfortunately Old Mot had not been able to carry out his assignment. Sur-prised by a British patrol, he put up stiff resistance but was killed in action. A number of burghers did manage to lure away the armoured train and the commandos safely crossed the railway line with their booty. The entire booty was divided amongst the burghers the next day.

A British force of about 250 men from Lichtenburg attempted to attack General De la Rey's field hospital at Leliesdal near Coligny on 20 January. However, General Celliers and Commandant Viljoen, a member of the Marico scouts, drove them off. The burghers pursued the fleeing Khakis and fired on them from the saddle. The result was a great victory, since about 80 Khakis were killed, wounded or made prisoner of war, and only one burgher was killed.

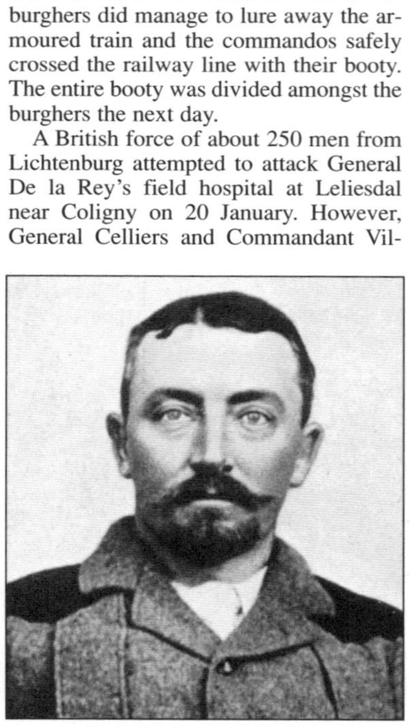

General Ben Viljoen

FIGHTING IN THE NORTHERN TRANSVAAL

In the far northern Transvaal, General Beyers recovered from his malaria and was back in action by the beginning of the year. On 22 January he and 300 burghers carried out a valiant night attack on Pietersburg and occupied the concentration camp southwest of the town. The defenders fled and the burghers captured the Superintendent and his personnel. By half past two in the morning they were in control of the camp. All the inhabitants had of course woken up as a result of the noise, and there was a mixture of applause and crying as seldom heard before.

Beyers invited all the burghers in the camp, excluding the elderly, to join his commando – but they had to hurry up. He wanted to leave before daybreak, since he believed that the British would fire on the camp with guns from the town. Some 150 burghers who had earlier surrendered to the British and been detained in the camp made use of the opportunity to rejoin the commando. They quickly gathered their clothing in bundles and took leave of their loved ones. At daybreak Beyers released his Khaki prisoners without doing them any harm, and the commando left again.

Four burghers who had left with them deserted again within a few hours and returned to a state of imprisonment. They could now, however, provide particulars about the commando to the Khakis. As a result, when Beyers attacked Pietersburg the next morning with 75 burghers, enemy troops were ready for them. The burghers only managed to capture some livestock before retreating. Three burghers were killed and seven wounded. Beyers had to send two of the wounded for treatment to Pietersburg, since he does not have the services of either a doctor or an ambulance. The departure of those wounded burghers was quite touching. When one of them, who believed that he would not survive his wounds, greeted Beyers, he declared in a faltering voice, 'Through you, General, I am prepared today to meet my God.'

BEN VILJOEN CAPTURED

In the eastern Transvaal, north of the eastern railway line, General Ben Viljoen's burghers attacked the British garrison in Lydenburg early in January. They failed to occupy the town, since the British fortifications were impenetrable. However, the major news from this front is not the attack, but Viljoen's capture. It is not clear to us exactly what happened. Information at our disposal indicates that Viljoen and his staff were on their way from Oshoek to Pilgrim's Rest on the night of 25–26 January. They rode into a British ambush near a spruit. Viljoen's horse was shot under him and a bullet hit his pocket book, but he was not wounded. Two of his lieutenants were killed in action and two other staff members who were with him were captured.

All sorts of rumours are being spread with regard to Viljoen's capture. We summarily reject the rumour that Viljoen himself informed the British where they could capture him. He is in favour of ending the war, but his whole career indicates that he is no traitor. Other rumours are that joiners betrayed him or that a black guide by the name of Wildebeest gave the British forces the information that led to Viljoen's capture. General Chris Muller took over command of that part of the front and Viljoen's brother, Wynand, took over the command of his commando.

FIGHTING IN THE CAPE COLONY

In the first battle in Griqualand West after a long time, the Republican forces came off by far the best. On 14 January Commandant Edwin Conroy's forces attacked a British unit at Doornfontein near Griquatown. According to reliable sources the British casualties amounted to 24 men killed, including their commander, Major Whitehead.

On the coast of Namaqualand, there was a naval encounter at Doornbaai. Earlier this month Commandant Ben Bouwer's men fired on a British battleship anchored in that bay. The crew of the ship fired back with their guns, raised anchor and sailed away. Now Bouwer wonders if he can claim a naval victory!

At the end of January, the fiery Fighting General Manie Maritz was involved in an unsavoury incident that almost cost him his life. He and eight of his men visited the Leliefontein mission station near Garies on 27 January. As they were explaining to the inhabitants that the Republican forces would leave them in peace as long as they remained neutral, they were suddenly attacked by a number of the inhabitants. Maritz and his men were not well armed and they had to fight with their bare hands to survive. Subsequently a very angry Maritz decided to punish the inhabitants of Leliefontein. The next day he and his men carried out a retaliatory attack on the mission station. Approximately 30 of the inhabitants, who were all Coloureds, were killed. The rest of the inhabitants were sent to Garies, where the British authorities will have to look after them. Maritz and his burghers captured hundreds of bags of maize meal, about 500 head of cattle and 3 000 sheep, and took all this along to Bushmanland.

In the Cape Midlands, Louis Wessels leads the surviving members of Commandant Pieter Kritzinger's commando. Last month they derailed a British supply train between Middelburg and Cradock, and burned its entire freight. There are some 50 men in Wessels's commando.

In the Stormberg the tussle between Commandant Willem Fouchee and the English Rebel-hunter, Colonel Scobell, continued last month. Fouchee's tactic is to divide his burghers into small groups of five to 10 men who take off in all directions when the commando is cornered. In that way the enemy is confused. Within a few days all the burghers unite again at a previously appointed place and time.

Since the main British aim seems to be to capture Fouchee himself, he usually only joins one of the groups at the very last minute, and the other groups do not know with which group he is before they unite again. In some cases one group of retreating burghers draws the attention of the British on purpose in order to give the others an opportunity to get away. Thus Fouchee keeps the enemy guessing. He usually does his own reconnaissance work and is legendary for his sharp sight. He never sleeps in a house and rises once or twice every night to ensure that all the guards are safe and at their posts. No wonder that his burghers have unlimited faith in and admiration for him!

On the last day of last year there was a noteworthy skirmish between Fouchee's burghers and Scobell, who was on their track near Roodenek. Fouchee was concerned that his burghers would not be able to stay ahead with their weak horses, so he decided to set an ambush for the Khakis. Scobell realised this too late, and the Khakis suffered heavy casualties in the battle that followed. A rumour subsequently spread that Scobell was one of the dead, but this is definitely not the case.

REBELS REPEL KHAKIS AT KAKAMAS

Kakamas, 30 January – By the beginning of the year the Rebels of Kakamas had openly been occupying the town for four months without the British forces ever challenging their position. They used this town on the Orange River as a base for numerous raids and the capturing of supplies from British patrols and convoys. At the same time they meticulously observed all the Khakis' movements. Early this month they noted that a British force was gathering at Kenhardt, and concluded that an attack was being planned. Scouts reported that a large number of empty wagons were arriving, which the Rebels concluded were to take their women and children to the concentration camps. That made them even more determined to offer resistance to the Khakis.

Smuts and his staff – Deneys Reitz far left in front

Burghers on duty with emaciated horses

The Kakamas commando of 81 men led by Commandant Jan Louw camped at Putsies. Louw had earlier heard that Commandant Manie Maritz was at Tontelboschkolk. He sent scouts there to report on their position and to request reinforcements. Even before assistance could arrive, Louw heard that the British force of 800 men had left Kenhardt on Friday 10 January and was on its way to Kakamas. The Rebels prepared for a confrontation.

Early on the morning of 11 January the first shots of the Battle of Kakamas were fired when Field Cornet Albert Stadler with 14 men confronted the British vanguard at Swartpad. The Rebels were soon forced back to Omkyk, where the rest of the commando entered the fight at about 10 o'clock that morning.

Louw positioned his rebels in such a way as to give the Khakis the impression that his force was much bigger than his mere 81 men. He placed them in groups of three or four in rocky outcrops over a line of approximately nine kilometres all along the Hartbees River, all the way from Omkyk to Letterkop.

The battle went on for the whole of Saturday. The Rebel line managed to hold their ground, often misleading the enemy by sticking hats up from behind rocks or bushes. The Khakis fired away every time, revealing their own positions as well as wasting ammunition. After dark that evening the Khakis almost managed to break through, but obviously did not realise that they had driven back one of the small Rebel groups.

The battle resumed on Sunday 12 January. At one stage a group of mounted Khakis charged a hillock near Omkyk. At the foot of the hillock they jumped from their horses and resumed the charge on foot. All of them were shot down by the Rebels and killed.

By Sunday evening the Rebels were dead tired after two days of continuous fighting and sentry duty during the night in between. They had enough food, since the women brought them supplies in wagons and carts. Some of the Rebels who came from other areas considered the option of falling back, but the Kakamas men refused. They were not prepared to let their women, children and property fall into British hands again. Consequently they manned their positions throughout the night and intended to go on fighting the next day.

On Monday morning everything was quiet. To the relief of the Rebels it was soon established that the British force had departed in the course of the night. Thus the Battle of Kakamas ended in a clear victory for the Rebels. At least 15 Khakis, including a number of officers, were killed, while on the Rebel side only three men were wounded.

General Jan Smuts arrived at Kakamas a few days later. The scouts who had gone to Commandant Maritz to request assistance for the Rebels had found him at Tontelboschkolk. Smuts had immediately left for Kakamas with 25 men. They went on horseback, resting by day and travelling during the night to escape the heat of the summer in that part of the world. Smuts held discussions with numerous rebel leaders in this vicinity. To his surprise he also met Willie Steyn, who had arrived three days earlier from German South West Africa. Our correspondent used the opportunity to talk to Steyn about the latter's experiences as an escaped prisoner of war (see separate report).

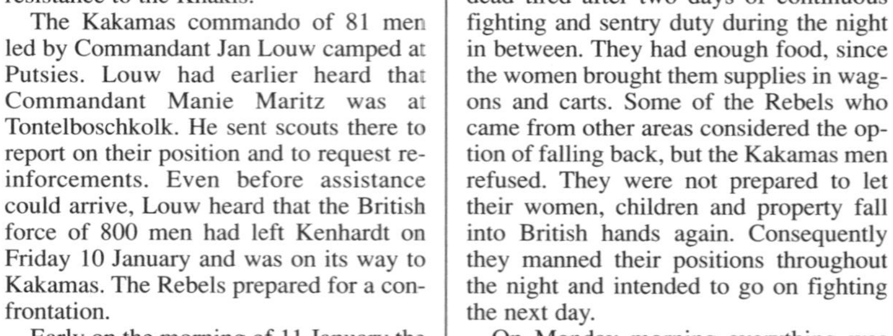

Maritz's commando in Namaqualand

THE ECSTASIES AND WOES OF COMMANDO LIFE
The latest informative report by Jan Celliers

Western Transvaal, 30 December – Jan F.E. Celliers, formerly of Pretoria and at present a member of a commando of foot soldiers in the western Transvaal, recently gave our correspondent a report on events in that part of the Republic. From this our readers will, as is always the case with Celliers's reports, learn a lot about conditions on commando for the ordinary burgher.

At the end of September Celliers and his comrades received an order from General Kemp to join him at Swartruggens. They immediately proceeded there. Since only a few of them had horses, they loaded their luggage on a wagon and began walking. During their trek they often came upon abandoned British campsites and searched those locations thoroughly. Celliers reports in this regard:

'Often we find at the spots where the British previously camped, newspapers with news of conditions in Europe and on England's problems. This helps to fill us with new courage and determination. The burghers sit around in small groups discussing the news.'

On 3 October Celliers and his group were peacefully walking in front of the wagon with no worries in this world when somebody suddenly shouted: 'Khaki! There they come!' Celliers writes that all the sleepy walkers were suddenly galvanised into action:

'Everybody ran back to our wagon, which immediately took a new direction. Our major obstacle was the large rocks. My breath was soon gone. We expected the boom-boom and the ka-ra-ka-ra-ka-rah of shots on us at any moment. Our wagon was heavy and it was uphill and the sand thick. The oxen stopped and we had to help by pushing the wagon. Mounted burghers arrived and told us to hurry up. We cut open some of the maize bags while on the move and shook them out to make the load somewhat less heavy. We carried blankets on our backs so that we could save them in a real emergency if we had to abandon the wagon. Somebody galloped up to us and said we had to change direction. In the end we stopped to catch our breath. In this commotion I lost my knife – a loyal servant made of the best German steel – a massive loss on commando. Fortunately we shook off the Khakis.'

On 16 October General Kemp visited them. Celliers writes about this: 'The burghers formed two rows with their rifles in their hands and waited for the General. A welcoming address was read out. Kemp responded and told us some news about conditions in the country. There is no immediate prospect of peace. We must remain steadfast in our trust in President Kruger's words that our cause is just.'

At this stage of the war the burghers are beginning to make their own saddles. Celliers describes the process: 'Two wooden elbows that form the front and back beam of the saddle are connected by two broad, flat planks to serve as saddle cushions. Since these cushions are rather hard, a thick blanket is first placed on the back of the horse. This skeleton of wood is then covered with a raw cowhide that is nailed onto the elbows and is then cut into the form of a regular saddle. A couple of thongs, each with a triangle of thick wire at one end, serve as stirrups. As a bridle, one simply uses a thick thong through the mouth of the horse.'

At the end of October a number of women and children who were fleeing from the Khakis joined their commando. On the farm Rustvoorbij, Celliers writes, a German teacher, Koch, told them how the Khakis had looted his house and took everything they wanted, including food and cutlery, and then plundered the rest:

'His library, consisting of German books, of which Khakis cannot understand one single word, was totally destroyed. All his books were carried out and torn. He pleaded with them to save his children's toys, including a small wooden wagon, but they broke everything into pieces.'

'At many of the burnt-down houses,' Celliers writes, 'the flat corrugated iron roofs of one or more of the back rooms did not tumble in since there were not enough wooden beams that could burn. In some of these burnt-out rooms women and children are now sheltering. They flee into the bushes when the enemy appears, but return later to the pitiful remains of their former houses. Semi-burnt and badly repaired furniture, a few pots, pans and cups are all that is to be seen. When it rains the mother squats in a dry corner with her little lambs around her. These barefoot children with their torn clothes have not, however, lost their lust for life and create amusement for themselves by playing in the black ruins with the remains of articles from their former houses. For subsistence the women and children are dependent on the nomadic Boer commandos.'

By the middle of November Celliers and his group were occupied with what he calls shifting movements. When they hear that the Khakis are moving to the west on the other side of the mountain, they shift to the east. When they hear that the Khakis are shifting to the east on the other side, they shift to the west. Thus it goes on. The objective is to keep Khaki guessing and make him war-weary.

Celliers writes that the burghers often talk about peace, which is an indication that they also are getting tired of the war. He writes:

'Peace, peace – that is the talk of the day. Yes, the Generals are gathering, cousin Hermanus saw them; they are very secretive, they say nothing, but just smile. There is something that is not generally known; uncle Gert heard it from somebody who heard it himself from somebody who actually talked with the general's adjutant. Uncle Fanie assures us that he will be back home before Christmas.

'Cousin Jan has heard of an old man who has prophesied a military event that actually occurred exactly as he predicted. Now this old man prophesies that in January a big man will arrive from Europe – a man wearing a large white hat – and this man will arrange an armistice and in February there will be peace. I laughed at uncle Fanie and expressed my disbelief in modern-day prophets, but what uncle Fanie does not know is that I love him because of his beliefs. The prophets and the man with the white hat are perhaps dream images, but for us they are beacons of light in our discussions on the war and peace prospects. And thus it goes from day to day. We are building our hope on castles in the air, even though these repeatedly and sorrowfully tumble. But when there is no hope left to rebuild these dream images with an iron patience – what will remain for us?'

On 16 December Celliers attended the Blood River Commemoration – a normal religious service in the morning followed by speeches at noon.

Celliers writes: 'I expected that the headmen would bring us encouraging news, but am disappointed, for in the end I experienced the whole ceremony as nothing more than continuous talking and singing.'

DESTRUCTION CONTINUES
Khakis intend destroying Afrikanerdom

In the veld near Lindley, 20 December – One of the most respected persons in Republican ranks here in the Free State is the Reverend J.D. Kestell. Today he gave our correspondent some information on his experiences of the British military policy of scorched earth:

'On 16 December a group of women near Lindley told me how a British unit treated them. They were not taken away but were driven out of their houses and had to look on while their houses were burnt down and totally destroyed in front of their eyes. Can brutality go any further? If the British do not want to eradicate us, what else do they mean by driving women and children from their houses and then destroying the latter. All the food that these families possessed was taken away and thrown out on the ground. It was only here and there that a good-hearted officer or a simple Tommy with some noble feelings left a bucket of flour behind for a woman.

'On the farm Windbult I heard from Mrs Van Niekerk what her fate had been. The Khakis arrived at about 10 o'clock on the morning of 10 December and immediately began breaking the doors, windowpanes and furniture with axes and hammers and destroying everything. When she attempted to save some of her belongings, these were grabbed from her hands and broken to pieces. All this happened while former General Piet de Wet, whom she had previously known well as her neighbour, looked on. She pointed out to De Wet that he was acting treacherously, but he answered that the country was lost and that it was a mistake for President Steyn to continue fighting.

'Mrs Van Niekerk's house was totally demolished. The middle wall was pushed over and the roof caved in. The poor woman then moved into a miserable hut that she had previously used to store dry cattle dung as fuel. However, the next morning the British ordered her to leave that as well. The enemy loaded her and her daughters on a wagon and later that afternoon off-loaded them at the house of Field Cornet Thys de Beer. That house was also in flames and Mrs De Beer stood with her children in the yard. That night the women and children slept under a shed that was fortunately not destroyed. After killing all the sheep, the Khakis left, taking all the remaining livestock with them.'

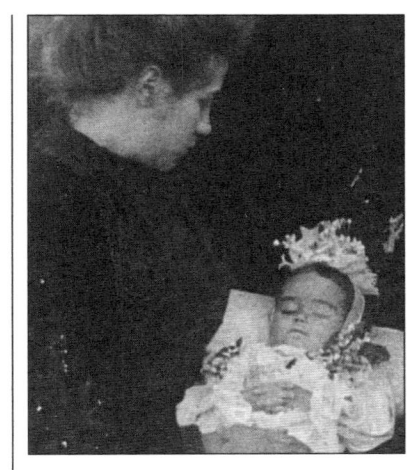

A young woman gazing at the corpse of her little sister in the Bloemfontein camp

Wash day in the Norvalspont concentration camp

Children fetching water in the Bloemfontein camp

ADVENTURES OF WILLIE STEYN

Swims to freedom from Ceylon

Kakamas, 28 January – Willie Steyn can boast that he and his comrades have had the most adventurous experiences in the war so far. He was made a prisoner of war last year and taken to Ceylon. When their ship, the *Catalonia*, anchored in the harbour of Colombo, Steyn and four other burghers escaped. They used a rope to lower themselves from the deck to the water level, and then swam to a large Russian ship, the *Gherson*, which was anchored some distance away. As our readers can imagine, they could not take anything with them. The Russians were delighted to welcome them on board. The *Gherson*'s captain, Vladimir Kissimoff, sailed off before dawn the next morning to ensure that the five swimmers would not be recaptured immediately. When they finally arrived in Russia they were accorded a heroes' welcome.

From Russia the 'five swimmers' eventually made their way to Holland, where they visited President Kruger, who gave them money to return to South Africa. A German ship transported them to Swakopmund, where they arrived in April last year. After a difficult overland passage across the driest parts of southern Africa, they eventually reached Commandant Manie Maritz in the Calvinia area.

Early this month, General Smuts sent Steyn and two other burghers to take reports to President Kruger in Europe via German South West Africa. When Steyn reached the southern border of that territory, somebody warned him that the Germans suspected him of arms smuggling and would arrest him. Consequently he did not cross the border but came here to Kakamas.

Steyn and his comrades with a well-wisher in Russia after their escape

TRIALS AND EXECUTIONS

In the veld, 31 January – On 12 January the British authorities hanged a Free Stater, Lieutenant I. Liebenberg, in Aliwal North. He had been found guilty and sentenced for the murder of Lieutenant L. Neumeyer in November 1900. Liebenberg's trial was a controversial affair. Two Cape Rebels who were themselves facing heavy sentences after being captured by the British gave evidence against him in return for their freedom. Frans Steenberg and Tobias du Plessis alleged that they saw Liebenberg shoot Neumeyer. Other witnesses alleged that it was Fanie Swanepoel, who had in the meantime died in action, who shot Neumeyer. Even though it is highly unlikely that either Steenberg or Du Plessis was present when the shooting of Neumeyer took place, their evidence was accepted and Liebenberg was sentenced to death.

From Pietersburg in the north we have heard that the British convened a military court in mid-January to hear numerous accusations against members of the Bushveld Carbineers. This unit consists mainly of Australian Khakis. The accusations were rather serious, and included the shooting of burghers who became prisoners of war. The three officers who were accused, Lieutenant H.H. (Breaker) Morant, P.J. Handcock and G.R. Witton, all Australians, were found guilty on 28 January and sentenced to death.

In Graaff-Reinet, Commandant Gideon Scheepers died on 18 January in front of a firing squad.

BRITISH ESTABLISH NATIONAL SCOUT CORPS

Piet de Wet and Andries Cronjé lead the traitors

In the veld in the Free State, 28 December – One of the biggest disgraces in this war is the establishment within the ranks of the British forces of military units that consist of former burghers (handsuppers). Examples are the Kroonstad Burgher Scouts of the Free State and the Lydenburg Volunteer Burgher Scouts in the Transvaal.

Last month the British began organising a National Scout Corps. It consists of joiners who explain their treacherous actions by arguing that they are actually saving the country by assisting the enemy to end the war as quickly as possible. The two foremost traitors in this Corps are both former generals of the Republics, namely Andries Cronjé in the Transvaal and Piet de Wet in the Free State. No loyal burghers have any sympathy with their actions. Their names are mentioned with the greatest possible contempt.

A few days ago the Reverend Kestell remarked to our correspondent that the assistance rendered by disloyal Afrikaners to the British is perhaps the most tragic aspect of the whole war. 'These Afrikaners,' Kestell declares, 'are making it possible for the British to cover long distances at night and since the joiners know the nature of the enemy to co-Afrikaners, they enable the enemy to capture the Boers and to steal their livestock, while the enemy would have found it difficult on their own to accomplish the same. How tragically are the noble feelings within those people dampened! It is unbelievable that they can remain sane while listening to the blasphemous language that the enemy uses in their camps when referring to the Afrikaners! Inexplicable how they can go from farm to farm and look on while women and children are molested – blood of their own blood and marrow of their own marrow.'

Chief Commandant Christiaan de Wet has no doubt that the joiners are of great value to the British war effort.

He stated bluntly to our correspondent: 'The Eng-lish are only now beginning to understand the art of scouting, and that with the assistance of the handsuppers. These joiners could bring about our demise.'

State Secretary F.W. Reitz's contempt for the joiners knows no bounds. As is his way, he took up his pen and composed the following satirical poem, in which he ridicules the speech that Lord Kitchener made to the 'National Burgher Corps' at Balmoral on 17 December last year:

KITCHENER'S SPEECH

Dear friends I've just come over here
To cheer up and admonish you,
'End of the War' is now so near
't Will really quite astonish you.

Three or Four hundred Boers a week
Are regularly taken,
If past my forts they try to sneak
They'll find themselves mistaken.

And ye – ex-Burghers of Transvaal
Who've shown such love for *Royalty*
I'll compensate you one and all
For your exceeding *Loyalty*,

To show the confidence I feel
We'll send you out unguarded,
Quite by yourselves to rob and steal
Thus will you be rewarded.

Now, Burghers of the *National* Corps,
I have come here to harangue you,
But my hope is if Brother Boer
Should catch you – he may hang you.

And as to that same Brother Boer,
To me it's very funny,
If he wants cash – who can want more –
It's England has the Money.

Why does the brute my Tommies shoot,
And can't he comprehend it
That I've my foot in the wrong boot,
And wish the war was ended.

I do believe this war would cease
If your Officers would let it,
And I too long for rest and peace,
If I could only get it.

So this advice I would suggest
And only wish they'd try it
Choose other leaders – that's the best
But do it '*on the quiet!*'

Surrender Botha and De Wet,
Your guns – and there's no telling
But what I'll let each Burgher get
Back to his burned-down dwelling.

His house is gone, and quite right too,
– For I and Roberts willed it –
But I'll do my best and promise you
To help him to rebuild it.

And as regards de Wet and Steyn,
It is my firm conviction
That all they're seeking for is gain,
The rest is just pure fiction.

They make the ignorant Boer believe
His freedom he'll be losing
If he submits – so they deceive,
It's really quite amusing.

I can't conceive how any man
Believes them – so doubt whether,
It isn't just a clever plan
Their own two nests to feather.

At all events I'm well aware
It is a big, big story,
That British Officers *don't* care
For anything but *glory*!

For did not Parliament bestow
On 'Bobs' a hundred thousand 'quid'
Just lately, – and I'd like to know
What that old fellow really did!

He to Pretoria in a gig
Behind his Tommies drove along,
And, like a bird upon a twig,
Left me to sing this doleful song.

But never mind it's all right now
Some day I too shall be anointed
And if they make it a hundred 'thou'
Why then I sha'nt be disappointed.

***

Now – do not think that what I've writ
Is mere imagination
No! for I've taken every bit
From Kitch'ners oration.

I've added here and there a word
With that you need not quarrel
't Was just to show you how absurd
He has been at Balmoral.

The 'handsuppers' they raised a cheer
And so this 'function' ended
And all that I would ask you here
Is – wasn't this now splendid?

NEWS FROM THE OUTSIDE WORLD

A few interesting news articles reached us in the past month from Europe. The British Parliament opened on 16 January. The leader of the Opposition, Sir Michael Campbell-Bannerman of the Liberal Party, immediately launched an attack on the British government for its conduct of the war in South Africa. He demanded an answer from the government on the following questions: Are farms still being burnt down? How many death penalties have been executed in terms of martial law in the Cape Colony? In how many cases were civilians forced to witness the execution of death penalties? And why has the next session of the Cape Parliament not yet started? In addition, he wanted to know what had been done in the name of England in South Africa, and the chances of a peace settlement in the near future.

The war in South Africa was discussed in the British Parliament again on 20 January. A.J. Balfour declared on behalf of the government that the farm burnings were still proceeding, as a military necessity. He added that if the situation demanded it, he hoped that British generals would not hesitate to undertake such actions, even if it seemed gruesome. Balfour then spelled out the British war objective: 'We do mean to subjugate the Boers. Subjugation means conquer. We do mean to conquer them. We do mean to annex them, we do mean to incorporate them within the Empire. The Boers say: We are not going to surrender our independence. We say: You are going to. That is the issue. And the war will go on until one of these parties is subjugated. We do not mean to be subjugated.'

This statement by Balfour makes it virtually impossible to reach a settlement. On 25 January, in an attempt to find a solution, the Dutch Prime Minster, Dr Abraham Kuyper, offered his services as an intermediary between Boer and Brit to the British Minister of Foreign Affairs, Lord Lansdowne. The latest news from London is that Lansdowne rejected the offer and wrote to the Dutch government that peace would be reached in the quickest and easiest way if the Boer leaders contacted the British commander-in-chief in South Africa directly.

It is also reported from London that the Senate of the United States of America had adopted a resolution calling on the British government to stop the execution of Commandant Gideon Scheepers. However, Scheepers had already been shot by the time that the resolution was unanimously adopted.

OUR MILITARY OFFICERS

Commandant Gideon Scheepers

Gideon Jacobus Scheepers was born in the Middelburg district in the Transvaal in 1878. He was the eldest son of Jacobus Johannes Scheepers and his wife Sophia Charlotte van der Merwe. Scheepers spent his boyhood years on the farms Grootlaagte and Roodepoort in the vicinity of Middelburg and received his basic education in farm schools. He was 17 years old when he joined the field telegraph section of the Transvaal State Artillery in 1895. After two years he was promoted to corporal and soon afterwards to guard master.

In 1898, when Scheepers was only 20, he was promoted to the rank of sergeant and was transferred to the Free State State Artillery in Bloemfontein on their request to establish a field telegraph service in that Republic. When the war broke out in October 1899 he was still in Bloemfontein. He proceeded to the western border with the Free State Artillery and was involved in the Battle of Magersfontein.

In February 1900, when the British offensive from the southwest began, Scheepers was a member of the forces of Chief Commandant Christiaan de Wet. De Wet appointed him as a scout and promoted him to the rank of captain in May 1900. He participated in the sabotage of British railway lines, including the famous capture of massive quantities of British supplies at Roodewal in June 1900. In that period he often campaigned with De Wet, joining him in his escape from the Brandwater Basin in July and in the epic crossing of the Magaliesberg in August 1900.

In December 1900 De Wet ordered Scheepers to accompany Commandant Pieter Kritzinger into the eastern Cape in an attempt to broaden the war theatre as widely as possible. Scheepers's activities made him a thorn in the flesh of the British military authorities, and thousands of soldiers were sent to that area. Numerous Cape Rebels joined his commando. In May 1901 he was promoted to the rank of Commandant. It is estimated that his commando took more than 1 300 Khakis prisoner of war.

Commandant Gideon Scheepers

THE
War Reporter
MONTHLY EDITION

Number 62 | In the Veld, South African Republic | 1 March 1902

CLASHES IN THE WESTERN TRANSVAAL

DE LA REY CAPTURES LARGE BRITISH SUPPLY COLUMN

The National Scouts or 'joiners' are without doubt a major acquisition for the British forces. On 5 February a huge British force that used joiners as guides executed a highly successful surprise attack on Commandant Sarel Alberts's burghers at Gruisfontein, east of Lichtenburg. The burghers fought back courageously, but the British encircled them and fired on them with guns, killing eight burghers and wounding at least ten. In the end Alberts had to surrender with more than 100 men. Only a few burghers managed to escape to bring the tragic news to General De la Rey. The British only suffered minor losses. In addition all the Boer horses stampeded. (This was actually very fortunate, since General Kemp's burghers collected them soon afterwards.) Kemp has about 1 000 burghers under his command who have no horses – and, as we all know, a burgher without a horse is not worth much on commando. A large number of Kemp's horseless burghers now have horses again, which almost makes up for the loss of Alberts's burghers. However, Alberts himself is irreplaceable, and his capture is a tremendous loss for the Republicans in the western Transvaal.

On 8 February, Commandant Potgieter's commando was attacked by Khakis near Wolmaransstad and 36 of his burghers were made prisoner of war. The British then continued with the destruction of farms in that area.

In the eastern Transvaal the burghers of Generals H.A. Alberts and Hans Grobler pretended to flee and led a British mounted unit into an ambush at Klip River on 12 February. Ten Khakis were killed and about 50 wounded. Six days later, on 18 February, the same two Boer generals led about 400 Khakis into an ambush at Kliptang, south of Nigel, using similar tactics. In this case the Khaki casualties were 10 men wounded and 50 captured. Unfortunately this was their last success, since the Khakis overpowered Grobler's commando at Chrissiesmeer on 22 February and took most of them prisoner of war.

THE BATTLE OF YZERSPRUIT

By the beginning of February General Koos de la Rey's burghers in the western Transvaal were experiencing a dire need of supplies, and he was on the lookout for a British convoy to attack. Throughout the month his scouts spied on the British garrison at Wolmaransstad, under the command of Lieutenant Colonel S.B. von Donop. Since there is no railway line to Wolmaransstad, Von Donop and his men were dependent on convoys to bring the necessary supplies to them from Klerksdorp, about 80 kilometres away. On 18 February the scouts reported that a huge supply column had reached Von Donop's camp; five days later they reported that the convoy had left Wolmaransstad and was moving back in an easterly direction.

De la Rey decided it was time to attack. He had about 700 burghers available, namely General Celliers's 250 men from Lichtenburg and Marico, General Liebenberg's 250 men from Klerksdorp and Potchefstroom and General Kemp's 200 men from Pretoria and Krugersdorp. The British convoy also consisted of about 700 men with about 160 supply wagons. Their commander was Colonel William Anderson.

Late on the afternoon of 24 February the Khakis pitched camp at Yzerspruit, about 20 kilometres west of Klerksdorp. About 80 mounted Khakis rode on to Klerksdorp, which meant that only about 620 Khakis remained. This was an indication that the Khakis did not expect an attack. De la Rey realised that he would not often be presented with an easier target and explained his plan of attack to his generals. By one o'clock the next morning all the Boers were ready in position at Jagdspruit.

The British rose early and the convoy resumed its journey at about half past four, just before daybreak. Since there had been a heavy downpour the previous evening, it was a foggy morning and visibility was limited. The British vanguard was only about 20 metres away when Liebenberg's burghers opened fire. The convoy immediately halted and a desperate battle followed. General Celliers's burghers failed to show up, which severely restricted the Boer firepower. Liebenberg and Kemp's men attacked courageously, but they were in open terrain, and the enemy defended the convoy with equal valour. Anderson extended his infantry in a full circle around the convoy and managed to bring all his field guns into action. A second attack by the burghers also failed and they seemed unwilling to go on with the engagement.

The outcome of the battle was in the balance until General Celliers's burghers suddenly arrived on the scene. Our correspondent reports that Celliers and his men charged the enemy rearguard at a full gallop and it seemed as if they were going to overrun them. At first they fired from the saddle, but when they were very close to the Khakis, they jumped from their horses and proceeded on foot. A number of Celliers's burghers galloped around the enemy and thus filled Kemp's cheering burghers with new courage. The whole British line suddenly began floundering. Liebenberg's burghers now also resumed their attack, overpowering the British guns. Khaki resistance collapsed, and less than 100 minutes after the first shot was fired, the battle ended in a total victory for the Boers. This time they immediately disarmed all the British soldiers and thus avoided the mistake that cost them a victory at Kleinfontein in October last year.

The Boers captured all the supply wagons, but about 100 mounted Khakis got away and fled in an easterly direction. They probably reported in Klerksdorp what had happened, since later that morning a force of about 250 mounted Khakis and joiners approached the battlefield from the east. Kemp's burghers easily repulsed them, and that was the end of the whole affair.

The British loss was 55 men dead and 270 (including 10 officers and the 130 wounded) made prisoner of war. The 156 wagons and carts of the convoy, 1 500 mules, 200 horses, 400 oxen, two guns, one pom-pom as well as 2 000 rifles and wagonloads of ammunition fell into Boer hands. Unfortunately most of the wagons were empty, but on the others there was a treasure of very necessary supplies. De la Rey's loss was 12 men dead and 42 wounded. This was the price the burghers had to pay for a victory that lifted their morale tremendously. De la Rey afterwards called all the burghers together and congratulated them expressing a special word of thanks to General Celliers's burghers. The burghers who were killed were then taken to Rietvlei, where they were buried.

As it is his custom, De la Rey ensured that the wounded on both sides were treated as soon as possible. A British ambulance was requested from Klerksdorp to treat the severely wounded Khakis and De la Rey gave them two wagons to transport their casualties back to Klerksdorp. The British field surgeon, Doctor Laing, handed some medical apparatus to De la Rey's field surgeon, Dr von Rennenkampf. The burghers took the other prisoners of war, including those who were lightly wounded and could easily walk, with them when they departed with their booty. The idea is to release them in Bechuanaland.

Generals Kemp, De la Rey, Celliers and Liebenberg with British guns captured at Yzerspruit

FIGHTING NORTH OF THE EASTERN RAILWAY LINE

In the eastern Transvaal, north of the eastern railway line, the commando of Lieutenant Colonel Fanie Trichard suffered a calamity on 20 February. A mixed force consisting of hundreds of Khakis, about 300 joiners and an unknown number of armed blacks surprised Trichard's camp at Botha's Mountain and took about 150 burghers prisoner of war. Two burghers were killed in action. Trichard has no doubt that traitors in his own midst who wanted him to be taken prisoner of war made the position of his camp known to his attackers.

He bases his allegations on the fact that his sentries did not report on the approach of the enemy, and that a large number of his burghers ignored his orders that morning. Neither did they all follow when he and 40 burghers charged through the enemy lines. The joiners certainly are a cancer that has to be wiped out before it destroys the Boer forces from the inside.

Trichard is furthermore very upset about the conduct of Chief Jafta Mahlangu of the Ndzundza Ndebele. Trichard told our correspondent that Jafta's subjects and the Boers had lived in peace until recently. One day, however, he heard that a number of joiners and Khaki officers had visited Jafta and threatened him that if he did not carry out some specified deed to prove his loyalty to the British authorities, they would imprison him. Soon afterwards Jafta's subjects attacked a small group of burghers who were harvesting grain for the commando and killed one of them with their spears.

Trichard wanted to launch a revenge attack on Jafta immediately, but General Muller refused. After a whole impi of armed blacks led by British officers soon afterwards overwhelmed a women's laager near Middelburg, molested the women and children and abducted them to a concentration camp, Trichard nevertheless decided to punish Jafta for what he regards as the Chief's disloyalty, treachery and murderous actions. He and his burghers attacked Jafta's subjects and shot 52 of them.

WAR NEWS FROM THE FREE STATE

The month of February began on a low note for the Republican forces in the Orange Free State. Commandant W. Mears and his men encountered a British unit at Roodekraal near Reitz on 3 February. In the clash that followed, Captain Muller and 13 other burghers, including artillerymen with two field guns and a rapid-fire gun that they had previously captured from the British, were captured by the enemy.

Soon afterwards the British began another drive with about 10 000 Khakis. They probably planned to corner Chief Commandant Christiaan de Wet, but he remains invincible.

In addition to soldiers, the Khakis employed several armoured trains against De Wet. The Chief Commandant was of course aware of the British movements and ensured in time that they would not be able to encircle him. In addition to his scouts, who continuously supply him with information, the Free Staters have by now established an extensive heliographic network through which they can rapidly send messages over long distances. Blockhouse lines cannot halt this communication. The only disadvantage is that messages can only be sent while the sun is shining.

On 7 February De Wet crossed the blockhouse line between Kroonstad and Lindley with 700 men east of Doornkloof. The British subsequently claimed that their drive led to the death, wounding or capturing of 286 Republicans. How many of this number are truly fighting burghers remains a question, since it is known that the captured Republicans include one boy of nine and one of twelve.

On 9 February De Wet broke through the British blockhouse line again, this time at Palmietfontein, west of Lindley. At that stage a large number of civilian refugees had begun trekking with De Wet's forces. A number of them, including small children, were caught in the crossfire while breaking through the British lines.

On 13 February the British launched another massive drive in the eastern Free State. At least 30 000 Khakis participated in this. Since they did not know exactly where De Wet was, the drive was a senseless action. The commandos of Commandants Wessel Wessels, Manie Botha and Alec Ross broke through the line on 21 February.

De Wet and President Steyn crossed the Wilge River in a northerly direction on the same day, pursued by a British unit.

De Wet remarked to our correspondent that the British masses were making it very difficult for him. In addition to the soldiers pursuing him and President Steyn, there was a closely linked cordon of tens of thousands of soldiers approaching from the northeast. On 22 February De Wet decided that it was high time for his burghers to shoot their way through the British cordon, since the net was drawing dangerously close. On 23 February he and the commandos who accompanied him charged the approaching British line at Langverwacht, which is also called Kalkkrans, and opened up a gap through which Steyn could escape. There was a high price for this breakthrough, however, since the British captured about 400 burghers, including De Wet's son, Kotie. In addition, 14 burghers were killed and 20 wounded. Khaki casualties were 23 men dead and 49 wounded.

This was not the only setback for the Republican forces in the Free State last month. A few days ago the British forced Commandant Jan Meyer to surrender at Tandjiesberg with 571 burghers of the Harrismith Commando. The British are doubtless satisfied with their military successes: Steyn and De Wet are still free, but the Khakis took more than 1 300 burghers prisoner of war and captured about 25 000 head of cattle from the commandos. This is the biggest British success in one month since Prinsloo's surrender 20 months ago.

Number 62 1 March 1902

WAR NEWS FROM THE CAPE

On 1 February Commandants Van Reenen and Smit attacked a British column under the command of Colonel Crabbe on the road between Beaufort West and Fraserburg in the Karoo, but their attack was repulsed. The next day Fighting General Wynand Malan led four commandos in an attack on the same column, inflicting heavy casualties. Malan allowed a British doctor to take the wounded Khakis to Fraserburg that same evening. These Khakis reported in what a fix Crabbe found himself and British units rushed from everywhere to his assistance.

Malan's scouts carried out very thorough reconnaissance. On 4 February they spotted the British units coming to Crabbe's assistance and retreated. On the same day they captured a British reconnaissance patrol of 25 men. The British had no idea of the location of Malan's commando, which had disappeared in all directions, and were charging up and down on their horses looking for the Boers. That afforded Malan and Smit the opportunity to capture a British supply column consisting of 100 donkey carts at Uitspanningsfontein, near Fraserburg. Malan's men took whatever they could carry off and burnt the rest. Crabbe rushed to the assistance of this column, but arrived too late and his men were almost encircled by Malan's burghers.

According to unconfirmed reports about 30 Khakis were killed, more than 50 were wounded and another 100 made prisoner of war in all these actions. On the Republican side there were hardly any losses.

Partly as a result of Malan's actions against the Khakis near Fraserburg, the Khakis from the area around Sutherland proceeded to the east on 5 February to assist their comrades. This afforded Fighting General Jaap van Deventer and 25 men the opportunity to attack a British convoy at Middelpos, on the road between Sutherland and Calvinia. Unfortunately Van Deventer's men were too few in number to capture the convoy, but on 6 February General Smuts arrived with his commando and overpowered the enemy.

Thus 130 wagons fell into Boer hands. Here also they took what they needed and torched the rest, including the wagons. In addition to the supplies, 400 horses and mules fell into the hands of the Boers. The British casualties were nine men dead and 22 wounded, while on the side of the burghers four men were killed and 10 wounded.

The Boers did not rest on their laurels. On 10 February Commandant Ben Bouwer attacked a convoy consisting of about 1 500 Khakis at Aties, on the road between Calvinia and Clanwilliam. The British had a desperate time warding off Bouwer's attack. Four nights later Bouwer and his men had an ugly experience when a British unit attacked them where they slept at Kranz near Vredendal. It soon became known that Lambert Colyn, who had deserted from Bouwer's commando the previous day, had led the British there. Altogether 17 burghers were killed or wounded in the fighting that night, and nine, including Bouwer's brother, was captured. Bouwer himself fortunately escaped. Colyn was captured by General Smuts's burghers two weeks later. Smuts immediately sentenced him to be executed. He was shot the same day.

In Griqualand West, Commandant H. Badenhorst's commando captured a British column near Wasberg on 17 February. On 21 February Fighting General Malan's burghers destroyed the railway line at Nobelsfontein with dynamite, thus forcing two armoured trains to a standstill.

On 25 February Smuts united five Boer commandos in the northwest for an attack on the Cape police camp at Windhoek, south of the village of Vredendal. They easily overpowered the camp and captured 100 horses and 25 wagons loaded with supplies. The British losses were one man dead, seven wounded and 18 made prisoner of war. It was a costly victory, since four Boer officers and eight burghers were killed, and 10 men, including Commandant Bouwer, wounded.

In the Stormberg range of the northeastern Cape, Commandant Willem Fouchee and his commando are still a thorn in the flesh of the Khakis. Fouchee himself was wounded in a skirmish with the enemy on 5 February. One of the members of his commando, P.J. du Plessis, told our correspondent that this unfortunate event occurred while they were involved in a skirmish with a group of Khakis in a rather hilly area. Fouchee remained behind to cover the retreat of his burghers when a bullet hit him in his buttocks. Assisted by a number of burghers, the brave Commandant remained in the saddle and managed to elude the enemy. Even though Fouchee's wound was extremely painful and there was a danger of infection, he refused to surrender himself to a British ambulance for treatment. There was no doctor in his commando – only a man who had been trained how to treat a wound by nurses in the Free State. His burghers took him to the farm Smoorfontein in the Bonthoeke, where he found shelter in an open cave. After about three weeks he had recovered his strength. He immediately joined his commando again and they decided to proceed to the Cape Midlands.

In the meantime, Commandant Edwin Conroy is active in the vicinity of Prieska and Britstown with a small commando of about 35 men. On 5 February they destroyed the post office and looted three shops at Vosburg.

FROM THE EDITOR

One of the most unfortunate aspects of this war is the involvement of blacks in the struggle between Boer and Brit. Most black South Africans would probably have elected to remain uncommitted and to proceed with their daily activities unhindered. They are, however, often forced – or tempted – to choose sides. In the process they invariably earn the anger of the side against which they choose. In most cases they take the side of the Khakis against the Boers. The one simple reason is that the Khakis pay for services rendered, while the Boers can only promise compensation. This issue reports the fate of the Ndebele Chief Jafta Mahlangu, forced by the British army to act against Boers who then claimed the right to revenge. In the end, everybody suffers, and in addition a spirit of bitterness is nurtured which will, for a long time after the conclusion of peace, if there will ever be peace, bedevil intergroup relations in South Africa.

Peaceful relations in a future South Africa are under threat from another quarter. Last month the highly respected Reverend J.D. Kestell warned, in reaction to the statements of numerous women on their maltreatment by the enemy (see reports in this issue), that such molestations will leave a legacy of racial hatred. We can only agree with his rhetorical question: 'Who can blame the Afrikaner of the future if he will not be able to forget what was done to his mother, his wife, his sister?'

On the military front, there have been both positive and negative developments. On the positive side, the Republican forces are still active and are making life difficult for the enemy on a wide front. On the negative side, there are no indications that the Khakis are losing their own determination. Their huge drives remain a problem and their massive numbers are tapping our strength. What is needed to boost the confidence of our burghers is significant victory on the battlefield.

THE CONCENTRATION CAMPS

The long-awaited report of the British Women's Commission on the concentration camps in South Africa was finally published in London last month. The Commission members visited numerous camps in South Africa last year. From the statements of individual members at the time we concluded that they would attempt to whitewash the inhuman camp system, but we were pleasantly surprised by the Commission's extremely critical findings, especially with regard to the pathetic administration of the camps.

The Commission does not recommend that the camps should be closed immediately. In their opinion it would be brutal to leave the approximately 100 000 people who are in the camps at present in the veld to care for themselves. It would be tantamount to sentencing them to starvation.

According to the Commission, even after peace is concluded Britain will have to keep on supplying necessities to the present camp inhabitants for many months. If these women and children were immediately returned to their former farms, which are of course totally devastated, it would be impossible to carry out that task.

A concentration camp

MALTREATMENT OF WOMEN

In the veld in the Free State, 20 February – Judge Hertzog, who has been included in the Executive Council by President Steyn and is now a member of the Orange Free State government, spent the last month taking sworn statements from women and burghers who suffered under the barbarity of British soldiers and blacks in service of the enemy. One is often tempted to become so angry about the shocking revelations of the horrible treatment of women and children in the concentration camps, that one forgets how terrible the fate of the women outside those camps often is. The statements of numerous women contain allegations of such brutalities committed against them that we feel fired up with fury and want to shout out to Heaven: 'Father, why did you allow such a conscienceless, cruel enemy to invade our country?'

Since the publication of the worst accounts of the deliberate maltreatment and dishonouring of women would only have negative effects, generating bitterness that would become a source of racial hatred between Boer and Brit in South Africa, we refrain from providing particulars. We choose to believe that many British officers are filled with disgust and reject the cruelties committed by their colleagues, and we trust that the British people themselves, when the extent of the cruelties become known to them, will bring an end to the excesses that do not fit a civilised nation.

NEWS FROM THE PRISONER-OF-WAR CAMPS

From St Helena it is reported that one of the prisoners of war almost managed to escape from the island in a very creative way. He is a Dutchman, Andries Smorenberg. It seems as if he was aware of the way in which the famous Dutch jurist, Hugo de Groot, escaped his pursuers in 1619 by hiding in a bookcase. Each month when the postal boat sails from St Helena to Britain, one of the large wooden trunks containing articles made by the prisoners of war goes with it. Somebody in London sells the products on behalf of the prisoners of war. The trunks have never been opened for inspection.

Smorenberg planned his escape well. He made a big trunk, hid in it, and had himself hoisted onto the postal boat. The trunk was designed in such a way that he could open it from inside, and he had packed enough rusks, tinned meat and fresh water for the ocean journey. All went well until Smorenberg climbed out to get some fresh air after two days, and a sailor sounded the alarm. Smorenberg was caught, and a few days later he was off-loaded on Ascension Island, from where another ship brought him back to St. Helena. Now he is with his fellow prisoners of war again, but it is sad, since he certainly deserves to be free.

Soon after Smorenberg's return, on 14 February, there was a tragedy when one of the prisoners of war, H.J. Bantjes, was shot by a British guard for allegedly attempting to escape. Three days later, on 17 February, J. Balderacchi, an Italian volunteer, swam to a Spanish ship, the *Nautilus*. According to unconfirmed reports the ship is taking him to Spain.

General Ben Viljoen arrived on St Helena as a prisoner of war on 25 February.

From Bermuda it is reported that the vast majority of burghers who are being imprisoned there, totally distance themselves from the British authorities.

In a newspaper that the Reverend Kestell procured somewhere, there is a report from a Reuter's correspondent that states: 'Many of the prisoners of war are irreconcilable and reveal their bitterness and enmity in various ways. Thus they reject the show of military respect for their dead that is usually accorded to a dead British soldier. The Boer chaplain, the Reverend J.R. Albertyn of Wellington in the Cape Colony, requested on behalf of the burghers that the coffins of deceased burghers who are buried should not be covered with the Union Jack and that the three salvoes that are usually fired over a soldiers' grave should be cancelled.'

OUR MILITARY OFFICERS

General Koot Opperman

In last month's issue we reported on the death of the able and courageous Transvaal general, Jacobus Daniel Opperman. He was born in 1861 in Cradock in the Cape Colony and was the son of Pieter Johannes Opperman and his wife Jacoba Frederika Beatrix Opperman. When he was 12 years old he moved with his parents to the Orange Free State, where they settled in the Harrismith district. Later on he moved to the eastern Transvaal.

Opperman enjoyed his first military experience in 1884 when he fought as a volunteer on the side of Crown Prince Dinizulu in the civil war in Zululand. Here he met the present Commandant-General, Louis Botha. In 1893 Opperman was appointed lieutenant in the Police and sent to Swaziland.

After the outbreak of this war in October 1899 Opperman initially served as field cornet of the Swaziland burghers on the Natal front. His value as an officer quickly became known and he was eventually promoted to the rank of general. He participated in numerous battles, including Colenso in December 1899 and Pietershoogte in February 1900. A few days before the British breakthrough on that front he suffered severe shell shock when a British lyddite grenade burst in the trench where he was sheltering.

Later on in the war Opperman distinguished himself in numerous battles in the eastern Transvaal. He was regarded as one of the most capable officers. He was wounded once, but recovered and kept fighting until he was killed in a skirmish with a British column at Bankkop near Ermelo on 4 January this year, when a bullet hit him in the forehead from a distance of about 20 metres.

Opperman is survived by his widow, Anna Catharina Badenhorst and four children.

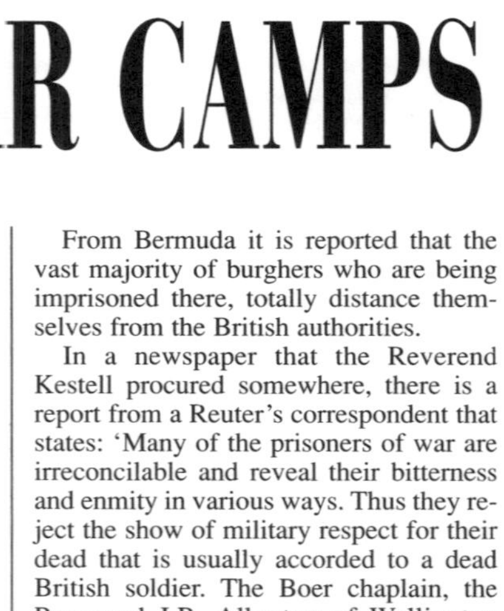

General J.D. Opperman

THE

War Reporter

MONTHLY EDITION

Number 63 | **In the Veld, South African Republic** | **1 April 1902**

DE LA REY SCORES MAGNIFICENT VICTORY

Methuen defeated, wounded and captured at Tweebosch

In the veld in western Transvaal, 31 March – There is no end to General Koos de la Rey's achievements! On 7 March he and his burghers scored one of the most magnificent victories of the whole war. His victim was once again his major opponent of the first few months of the war, namely General Methuen, whom he outwitted so magnificently at Magersfontein in December 1899. In this latest encounter Methuen himself was at the receiving end of a Boer bullet and fell into the hands of the burghers as a wounded man. This provided De la Rey with the opportunity to show a high-ranked Brit directly how a civilised combatant should treat his archenemy.

March began on a positive note for the Republican forces in the western Transvaal when General Kemp and Commandant Wolmarans liberated a women's laager from the claws of the enemy. De la Rey's scouts informed him a few days later that a huge Khaki column of about 1 500 men was approaching from the direction of Vryburg towards Lichtenburg. There were eight guns and two pom-poms in the column as well as 85 supply wagons. All unaware that Methuen was in command, De la Rey decided to attack this column. At the same time, another British force of about 1 500 men was approaching Lichtenburg from the direction of Klerksdorp. De la Rey sent a number of burghers to slow down their progress.

General Methuen

By 5 March Methuen and his column had reached Baberspan, from where they proceeded to the northeast. The next day they reached the junction of the Groot and the Klein Harts Rivers and pitched camp on the farm Tweebosch, belonging to the Schutte family. General Van Zyl's Griqualand West Rebel commando of about 100 men was involved in a skirmish with Methuen's rearguard on that day, but the result was inconclusive. A number of Methuen's soldiers, including 11 armed blacks, damaged the Schuttes' farm, molested the white women and prepared to burn down the farmhouse, but Methuen personally intervened and restored order.

De la Rey was informed about all these developments and prepared to attack Methuen's column the next morning, 7 March. He had about 750 burghers available for this purpose. General Celliers's commando spent the night southwest of Tweebosch, and Kemp and his commando rested on the opposite side of the farm. De la Rey dispatched three scouts to investigate the situation as close as possible to the British camp and report exactly what route the Khakis were taking as soon as they began moving the next morning.

One of De la Rey's burghers, Niklaas van Rensburg (who, according to many burghers, was born with a caul), has the nickname 'Seer'. That evening he revealed one of his visions to Kemp and his burghers. He said that he saw an angry red bull charging down a hill, but as the bull approached, he lowered his head and his horns sagged. Then the bull turned around with broken horns and walked away with a broken front leg. Niklaas himself has no explanation for what he 'sees'. According to the burghers' interpretation, the vision meant that they would become involved in a battle with the enemy and would win. The broken horns were an indication that the British would lose their laager, and the broken leg that a general would be wounded. De la Rey regarded this vision as a positive signal.

BEGINNING OF THE BATTLE

British participants in the battle afterwards revealed that Methuen had heard on the evening of 6 March that De la Rey was in the vicinity. Consequently he ordered his Khakis to get going very early the next morning. By three o'clock, long before daybreak, the first wagons of the convoy were already on the move. A strong escort accompanied them. An hour later the main force followed and soon afterwards the rearguard with the guns also began moving. By five o'clock the vanguard reached the Groot Harts River at De Klipdrift. The burghers, who were kept informed of enemy movements by the scouts, had taken up position in this area parallel to and a little distance away from the column.

The first shots of the battle, which the Boers refer to as the Battle of Tweebosch, were fired at first light by the burghers of General Van Zyl on the British rearguard. The Khaki gunners immediately swung around their guns and fired back, but most of the Khakis who formed the rearguard were totally inexperienced and reacted with panic. Methuen became concerned about the extent of the attack on his rearguard and brought his whole convoy to a standstill. Soon afterwards, at about six o'clock, De la Rey's main attack began when Kemp, Cilliers and Wolmarans ordered their burghers to charge the British right flank. The attack was carried out with precision and valour and Methuen's whole column was placed under pressure at the same time. Initially the major British resistance came from the gunners, but virtually all of them were soon shot down.

Kemp had a narrow escape during the battle when his horse was shot under him and fell on him. He told our correspondent afterwards that a Khaki aimed at him while he was struggling to escape from under his horse, but that another burgher fortunately shot that Khaki. De la Rey, who did not personally participate in the battle at the request of his officers, had a narrow escape at the laager when he was charged by a group of mounted Khakis who were fleeing. Fortunately his bodyguard forced them to surrender.

At half past nine that morning Methuen was wounded when a bullet hit his upper thigh. He dismounted, but moments later his horse was shot right next to him and partly fell on him, as a result of which his thighbone broke. The last action of the battle occurred when a large number of mounted Khakis fled. Kemp attempted to cut them off, but they were too quick for him and got away. At ten o'clock De la Rey ordered his gunners to set up one of the guns that they had captured from the British at Yzerspruit last month and fired on the Khakis who were sheltering behind a stone wall. When the first shot hit the stone wall, the Khakis put up a white flag and the battle ended.

The wounded Methuen taken to hospital in his own wagon

De la Rey scored a huge victory at Tweebosch. The price of this was eight burghers dead and 26 wounded. On the British side 68 men were killed, 121 wounded and 872, including the wounded Methuen, made prisoners of war. (This number does not include black wagon drivers who were captured.) All Methuen's supplies and equipment fell into De la Rey's hands. This includes 115 wagons and carts with the animals that haul them, more than 500 horses, four field guns, two pom-poms and a huge supply of ammunition, plus huge quantities of blankets and coats that can now be sent to the women and children who are hiding in the bushveld north of Swartruggens, to protect them against cold in the coming winter.

THE AFTERMATH OF THE BATTLE OF TWEEBOSCH

General de la Rey soon heard that Methuen had been wounded, and immediately went to his opponent to pay his respects. Communication was a problem since De la Rey cannot speak English. After introducing all his officers to the British general by means of an interpreter, he ensured that Methuen received good treatment. The other wounded warriors on both sides were also treated by both the British doctors and ambulances and the Boer doctor, Carl von Rennenkampf, as well as conditions in the veld allowed.

Our correspondent reports that he was struck by the almost unbelievable phenomenon that two groups of opponents who had moments before done their utmost to kill each other, immediately after the battle were assisting each other on the battlefield to help the wounded and carry away the dead, while smoking and talking together. It was especially the friendliness of the burghers towards the enemy, who had destroyed their country and had taken their loved ones to the concentration camps, that seemed almost irrational. Amongst the prisoners of war there are a large number that had been captured by the Boers before. There is no doubt that the war would have been a totally different affair if the Boers had had a safe place where they could have detained the thousands of Khakis whom they captured. However all they could do was to release the captured Khakis again.

Mrs Nonnie de la Rey, who has thus far managed to stay out of the clutches of the Khakis and survive in the veld with her young children in a tent and a wagon, arrived at Tweebosch on the day after the battle. She promptly prepared a meal of chicken for the wounded Methuen, who many months ago had personally ordered the destruction of her house. That evening the burghers held a thanksgiving service. The next day, Sunday 9 March, De la Rey consulted his generals and then sent Methuen to Klerksdorp for treatment of his wounds. A British military doctor as well as a small bodyguard accompanied Methuen on his journey in his own horsecart. De la Rey's burghers seriously complained about this and insisted that Methuen should remain a prisoner of war or should at least be exchanged for Boer officers who had earlier been captured by the British forces. Messengers were then dispatched and Methuen was halted at Oorbietjiesfontein. The next day De la Rey discussed the whole issue with his burghers in a meeting and convinced them that it was in everybody's best interest to let Methuen go. Messengers were sent out to inform Methuen of this. In addition De la Rey dispatched a telegram to Methuen's wife to inform her that he was concerned about the condition of the wounded British general.

Methuen was extremely thankful for the way he was treated. He sent his horse cart back to De la Rey, fully loaded with a supply of food, as well as two new rifles to replace the two with which his leg was set.

In the meantime it became known that, on the night before the Battle of Tweebosch, armed blacks had molested the women at the Schuttes' house, and that these blacks had now been captured by the Boers. They were taken to a neighbouring farm, forced to dig a hole that would serve as their mass grave, and summarily shot. It is clear that the Boers have no mercy for black people who serve the British in an armed capacity and then molest Boer women.

STEYN, DE WET VISIT DE LA REY

About 10 days after the Battle of Tweebosch, President Steyn and Chief Commandant De Wet visited De la Rey at his laager at Sendelingsfontein, southwest of Klerksdorp. The burghers were so glad when they heard that the Free Staters were on their way, that they drew up an address of welcome and formed a men's choir. A guard of honour awaited the vis-

Continued overleaf

FROM THE EDITOR

General Koos de la Rey exalted the name of the Republican forces last month by inflicting a defeat on Lord Methuen's Khakis at Tweebosch. With that victory he not only showed that the Republican commandos are far from a spent force, but through the magnanimous way in which he treated the wounded Methuen after the battle, he gave the Khakis a lesson in humanity and manliness that should force them to bow their heads in shame about the brutal mentality that they usually reveal towards the Boers.

The news that serious negotiations to bring an end to the war might take place was greeted with scepticism by many Boers, but at the same time it fills them with hope. Unfortunately there is no indication that the British have abandoned their overriding demand that the war can only end if the Republics cease to exist. The Boers are not prepared to bow to that demand: burghers have specifically sacrificed their lives and their property for freedom, and under the British yoke there cannot be any freedom. On the other hand, the fact that the British government has dispatched copies of the correspondence between it and the Dutch government on the possible termination of the war, and requested the Republics to state proposals on the possible conclusion of peace, is very encouraging. This means two things:

In the first place, as President Steyn points out, the British army and the British people are tired of this war. The troops no longer have the heart to go on fighting and Kitchener has had enough. The cost of the war is rising every day and it is becoming increasingly difficult to find recruits. Secondly, the requests to the Republican governments indicate that the British authorities are not demanding an unconditional surrender. The opportunity is there now to gain numerous concessions from the British by wise negotiations. Even though the chances seem minimal, there is a much better opportunity now than at any other time during the past year or two to negotiate from a position of strength, since even though they would want to conceal it, the fact that the British leaders have initiated these negotiations means that they are suddenly the embarrassed party. All is not lost.

continued

itors a little distance from the laager. After hearty, brotherly handshakes the choir sang the Transvaal Anthem and the address was read to Steyn. In this he was assured of the highest regard of the Transvaalers; that they trusted him as a true friend and that they thanked him for his forceful action when their own government became disheartened last year. Steyn referred in his inspiring answer to the faith and the courage of the Afrikaner women, whose bitter suffering was much worse than the burghers' discomfort; to the treason of the joiners, which was so horrible that he had no words to describe his contempt for them; and to the necessity that all the burghers should now remain steadfast in their trust in God and not in people. The choir then sang the Free State Anthem

Back in the laager at Sendelingsfontein, De Wet addressed the burghers and told them of his close encounters in the Free State. The burghers now also had the opportunity to meet the other visitors from the Free State, namely General Hertzog, State Secretary Brebner and the Reverend Kestell. In the midst of all these pleasantries with the Free Staters in their laager, however, the burghers were concerned: it was clear to everybody that President Steyn was suffering from an ailment. He is indeed so weak that he can no longer travel on horseback and finds it difficult even to get on his horse-cart. In addition there is something wrong with his eyes. Doctor von Rennenkampf closely examined him but could not establish the nature of the problem. De Wet returned to the Free State after three days.

CLASHES AT THE END OF MARCH

The British seem determined to avenge the humiliation of Tweebosch as quickly as possible and to repay De la Rey and his burghers in their own medicine. For that purpose a large number of Khakis were transferred to the western Transvaal from the eastern Transvaal and the Orange Free State. According to a reliable source, there are now about 16 000 mounted infantry soldiers as well as hundreds of foot soldiers and gunners in this part of the Republic.

On 24 March thousands of Khakis began a drive from Klerksdorp. De la Rey and President Steyn, who was still with him, easily evaded the Khaki nets, as did Kemp and his men. However, General Liebenberg and the burghers under his command had a tough time. The British found out where they sheltered and surrounded them. There was no possibility to fight – Liebenberg and his burghers had to flee for all their worth. They were eventually forced to abandon their wagons and field guns. It was only after dark that night, in heavy rain that made life extremely unpleasant for both pursuer and pursued, that Liebenberg and most of his men shook the Khakis off at Hartbeesfontein. In the drive as a whole, approximately eight burghers were killed and about 160 captured. We do not know if the British suffered any casualties.

On the last day of March, De la Rey again attacked the enemy. The result was the Battle of Boschbult. De la Rey's scouts kept him informed of British troop movements in the area between Klerksdorp and Lichtenburg. The experienced general chose his target after careful investigation. It was a British column of about 1 800 men with four field guns, moving along the Brakspruit. On 30 March De la Rey ordered an attack the next morning. Unfortunately there seems to have been a misunderstanding between the generals on the exact nature of the attack, but they did not realise it before the encounter.

President Steyn's reception at De la Rey's laager

The day began peacefully and the British, as usual, were on the move by daybreak. At ten o'clock a group of Boers confronted them. This time the British did not pursue them wildly, but halted and began digging themselves in thoroughly. By half past one that afternoon the burghers were ready and the men of Generals Kemp and Du Toit advanced on the British position. At the same time, the Boer gunners opened fire on the British camp with the guns they had captured in the previous engagements. The mules in the British camp stampeded and caused a measure of chaos. Kemp and Du Toit's burghers noted this and decided to exploit the confusion amongst the soldiers by attacking.

Their plan was to charge directly at the British camp in the hope that the enemy would flee to one or the other side. Kemp believes that fleeing Khakis are easier targets than Khakis who are surrounded from all sides and fight from defensive positions. However, the Khakis fought off the Boer attack that afternoon. De la Rey never sent General Lieben-berg's burghers into the battle. By five o'clock that afternoon Kemp and his men halted their attack, and with that the fight came to an end.

Kemp was very annoyed afterwards, but De la Rey explained that it was never his plan to charge the British camp. Kemp believes differently.

Whatever the case, we have learned from reliable sources that the British casualties here at Brakspruit amount to 27 men dead and about 70 wounded. The burghers took about 100 Khakis prisoner of war. On the Boer side, six burghers were killed and at least 16 wounded.

NEWS FROM BRITAIN

In the veld, 30 March – From London it is reported that the British Parliament met early in March to discuss the report of the British Women's Committee (the so-called Fawcett Report) on the concentration camps in South Africa. The committee attributes the high death rate in the camps to three causes: unsanitary conditions as a result of the war; some causes within the control of the women and the children; and causes that can be blamed on poor administration by the camp authorities. The opposition in the British Parliament hereupon tabled the following motion: 'This House deplores the great mortality in the concentration camps formed in the execution of the policy of clearing the country.'

The British Minister of Colonies and one of the major instigators of the war, Joseph Chamberlain, answered on behalf of his government. As can be expected, he attempted to defend the military authorities. What is shocking, however, is how shamelessly he distorted the truth in his speech. Claiming that the Boers forced the British to establish the camps, he alleges that the British had no option but to accept responsibility for the care of the women and children, since the Boers refused to look after them themselves. The Minister did of course not add that the British had systematically burned down all the farmhouses, destroyed the fields, gardens, orchards and all the food sources, killed all the livestock and farm animals, and forcibly abducted the women. Indeed, he claimed that the Boers were the first people in the history of the human species who exposed their women and children to death and starvation, suffering and illness in an attempt to play on the feelings of the enemy. And then he declared that there had never been a people who had done so much to alleviate the terror of war as the British were doing at present. The motion was rejected by 230 to 119 votes.

It makes the Boers sick to hear a British Minister reason in that way. The worst is that he seemed to believe his own lies. We feel tempted to answer quite bluntly that there has in the history of humankind never been a people who have plundered, robbed and destroyed the property and the heritage of so many other people and nations as the British, and especially the English, people have done. That is why it is so tragic that it is our fate to become their victims at this time in our history.

Other news from the British Parliamentary session is that David Lloyd George, a front bencher of the Liberal Party, stated in the House of Commons that the British army in South Africa contained about 30 000 blacks. That is more than the total Free State forces at the time of the outbreak of the war.

Further news from London is that Mrs Methuen received De la Rey's telegram with regard to the wounding of her husband when she arrived in Southampton harbour from South Africa. She immediately boarded another ship and is returning to South Africa to support her husband.

A last piece of news from the British capital is that both Miss Emily Hobhouse and the Aborigines Protection Society have expressed their shock that the Fawcett Report makes no mention of the hopeless conditions in the concentration camps for black people in South Africa. It is not known if the British Government has commented at all on that criticism.

NEWS FROM THE CAPE

Cape Colony, 31 March – Commandant Pieter Kritzinger, who was wounded earlier and fell into the hands of the British, was charged in a military court in Graaff-Reinet on 7 March. He is accused on four counts of murder of black people.

On 12 March Commandant Rudolph of General Wynand Malan's commando was seriously wounded in a skirmish near Richmond. His burghers left him behind in the hope that the British would treat his wounds. Malan appointed the 25-year-old Carel van Heerden to succeed Rudolph as commandant.

Generals Smuts, Van Deventer and Maritz and Commandant Bouwer are still active in the vicinity of Namaqualand. In the recent past they have only been in action against small British patrols.

The major news from the Cape in the past month is that Cecil John Rhodes died on 26 March. He was 49 years old and without doubt one of the richest people on earth. However, he was lonely since he never married and had no children. The cause of his death is not known to us; we have heard simply that he was ill and died in his house in Muizenberg. It is reported that Rhodes will be buried in the Matopos Hills south of Bulawayo in Matebeleland.

The news of Rhodes's death spread like wildfire through the Republican commandos. One would find it difficult to identify any burgher who mourns his passing away. Indeed, the general reaction amongst the Boers is that it is a pity that he did not pass away somewhat earlier.

This harsh sentiment is understandable if one considers that most Boers regard Rhodes, together with Milner and Chamberlain, as being jointly responsible for this disastrous war. We heard that one burgher yesterday evening at the time of the commando's religious service expressed his true feelings with regard to the instigators of the war when he addressed the Lord with the greatest piety as follows in his prayer: 'Dear God, we have been informed that you have gathered Mr Rhodes to you. We would like to remind you that Mr Milner is still here on earth.'

OUR MILITARY OFFICERS

General Pieter Kritzinger

Pieter Hendrik Kritzinger was born in 1870 on the farm Wildemanskraal in the Port Elizabeth district in the Cape Colony. He is the son of Wessel Kritzinger and his wife Magdalena Rudolph. As a child he moved with his parents to the Ladybrand district in the Orange Free State. When he was 17 he began his own farm in the Rouxville district.

When this war broke out in October 1899, Kritzinger participated as a burgher of the Rouxville commando in Chief Commandant Olivier's invasion of the Cape Colony. In December 1899 he took part in the Battle of Stormberg. After the start of the British offensive in the western Free State in February 1900, Kritzinger's commando hurriedly retreated from the northeastern Cape to Bloemfontein. He later on joined the forces of Chief Commandant Christiaan de Wet.

Kritzinger took part in the fight at Sannaspos in March, at Reddersburg in April and Lindley in May 1900. In August he participated in the Rouxville Commando's attack on Winburg, when Commandant Olivier was made prisoner of war. Kritzinger was elected commandant in his place.

In December 1900 Kritzinger invaded the Cape Colony with his commando on the orders of Chief Commandant De Wet. He criss-crossed the Colony and proceeded southwards all the way to Oudtshoorn in the Little Karoo before returning to the Free State in April 1901. Many Cape Afrikaners joined his commando and the British military authorities desperately but vainly instituted measures to corner him.

Soon after his return Kritzinger was rewarded with promotion to the rank of general. De Wet appointed him as assistant chief commandant of the Republican forces in the Cape Colony. In May 1901 Kritzinger again invaded the Cape, concentrating on a thorough organisation of all the Republican and rebel groups that were active there. The British reacted with a determined attempt to stamp out the Republican presence and in August Kritzinger returned to the Free State.

On 15 December Kritzinger's third invasion of the Cape began when he and his commando crossed the Orange River at Sanddrift. The enemy was on his heels and the next day he was wounded and became a prisoner of war.

General Pieter Kritzinger

TALKS ON PEACE AGAIN?

In the veld, 31 March – The possibility that serious negotiations on ending the war may take place at last seems realistic. The Dutch Prime Minister, Dr Abraham Kuyper, wrote to the British government in January to offer his services as mediator between the Boer Republics and Britain. According to Lord Kitchener, the British government answered that they could not accept the offer, since the best way to bring about peace would be through direct negotiations between the British commander-in-chief in South Africa and the Boer leaders. When Kitchener received copies of the correspondence between his government and Kuyper, he in turn decided to send copies to the government of the South African Republic (Transvaal). Kitchener included an invitation to Acting President Burger to submit proposals from the Republican side with regard to a possible ending of the war.

Burger regarded this development as so significant that on 21 March he requested, without first consulting President Steyn, a free passage from the British authorities to negotiate with the Free State government on this issue. Kitchener immediately agreed and two days later the Transvaal government arrived in Pretoria, from where they proceeded to Kroonstad. That was in the wrong direction, since President Steyn was actually in the Transvaal, in General De la Rey's laager. He was still there on 27 March when he received a letter from Burger. In this letter Burger informed the Free State President that he and the Transvaal government were in Kroonstad and that Kitchener had given them a free passage to go there to discuss the early ending of the war with the Free State government. Steyn reacted with anger, since he had no desire to negotiate with the British, but felt that he was now forced to condone the Transvaal government's action in order to keep up a united Republican front. It is expected that the two governments will meet soon.

THE War Reporter
MONTHLY EDITION

Number 64 — In the Veld, South African Republic — 1 May 1902

NEGOTIATIONS ON PEACE

In the veld, 30 April – Serious discussions between the representatives of the Boer Republics on the issue of possible negotiations with the British on the ending of the war became a reality this month. Last month we reported that President Steyn was furious when he received a letter from Acting President Burger on possible negotiations with the enemy. He nevertheless agreed to meet the Transvaal government in Klerksdorp. General Koos de la Rey was also invited to attend these discussions as a member of the Transvaal government. When he was informed about this, De la Rey's reaction was: 'To me it seems as if our government is making a mistake with this gathering.' General Kitchener provided free passage for De la Rey, Steyn and members of the Free State government.

The discussions in Klerksdorp between the two governments began on 9 April. The most important Transvaal deputies were Acting President Schalk Burger, State Secretary F.W. Reitz and Generals Louis Botha and Koos de la Rey. In addition to Steyn, the most important members of the Free State delegation were Chief Commandant Christiaan de Wet, Acting State Secretary Jack Brebner and Judge (General) J.B.M. Hertzog. The discussions were held in a tent next to the Schoonspruit in the middle of the town.

The most important issue discussed at this assembly was the possibility of peace negotiations with the British. The deputies agreed to make certain proposals to Lord Kitchener as a basis for negotiations. Kitchener agreed to meet them in Pretoria. Consequently the Republican leaders travelled there by train. Soon after arriving in Pretoria on 12 April, they met Kitchener. They offered the following proposals:
- That a treaty of everlasting friendship be concluded between the Republics and Britain and that arrangements with regard to customs, post and telegraph issues, the railway union and franchise should be agreed on.
- That the Republican forts at Johannesburg and Pretoria should be demolished, as Lord Milner had demanded even before the war.
- That arbitration would in future be used to solve differences.
- That Dutch and English would be accorded equal status as educational languages.
- Reciprocal amnesty.

In the discussion that followed, President Steyn assured Kitchener that the governments and the population of both Republics sincerely wish that peace should be restored. However, they also wish to see the issue for which they struggled and are still struggling realised. Kitchener reacted by asking with a gesture of surprise: 'Does that mean you want to keep your independence?' Steyn answered on behalf of the Republics: 'Yes, so that the people may not lose their self-respect.' Kitchener assured him that people who had fought so valiantly would not that easily lose their self-respect. He furthermore expressed his personal opinion that the British government would never agree to Republican independence. Nevertheless, he and the deputation agreed on the text of a telegram that was sent to London in which the proposals of the deputation were included. The meeting then adjourned.

On Monday 14 April Kitchener informed the Republican deputation that he had been informed by cable from London that the British government would not accept the continued independence of the Republics. Later that morning the negotiations resumed. Lord Milner was now also present on the British side. He initially addressed both President Steyn and Acting President Burger as 'mister', but soon began using their official titles. Shortly after the resumption of the discussions, the Republican deputation informed the two British representatives that they were not empowered to discuss the ending of the independence of the Republics. In terms of the stipulations of the constitutions of both Republics, only the people in each Republic could decide on that.

The next major point of discussion was: who constitutes 'the people'? The deputation of the Republics argued that the burghers who had accepted British proclamations and had taken an oath of neutrality, or those locked up in prisoner-of-war camps, were no longer participating in civil activities and could not be considered as burghers. Those who had signed an oath of allegiance to Britain had rejected their own citizenship and are now represented in the negotiations by Britain. The only people who could claim to represent 'the people' are the burghers who are still fighting and their legal authorities, namely the Republican governments. Since President Steyn believed that the fighting burghers would not accept peace without independence, he strongly stood on this point. To his surprise Kitchener and Milner accepted it.

The Republican representatives subsequently agreed with Kitchener that another telegraph should be sent in his name to the British government, in which the deputation indicated that it could only negotiate on the possible loss of independence with the permission of their burghers; that the British government would be requested to list conditions which it would offer to the burghers in return for their possible agreement to sacrifice their independence; and that the deputation would go to the people with those conditions.

The telegram was sent that Monday, but by Wednesday no answer had been received. The Boer officers became impatient, since they wanted to return to their commandos. The answer of the British government arrived at last by telegram on Thursday morning, 17 April. It indicated that the conditions Kitchener had proposed to Commandant-General Louis Botha in Middelburg in February 1901 could serve as a basis, but that the particulars should be agreed upon between the two parties.

The negotiations between Kitchener and the Republican deputation could now proceed, and culminated that same morning in a very important agreement, namely that 30 representatives of each Republic would meet at Vereeniging on the Vaal River in the second half of May to decide on the future of the war. With that the British representatives officially accepted that only the Republican governments would represent the people. The British representatives furthermore agreed that from 11 May no commando whose commander had gone to Vereeniging would be attacked, so long as it remained within its operational area. This meant an armistice, even though Kitchener refused to officially accept that an armistice would come into force.

Sketch by a British officer of General de Wet at the peace negotiations

The Republican leaders left Pretoria the next day (Friday 18 April) to sound out their burghers in the veld. President Steyn went away with them, even though numerous doctors requested him to stay in Pretoria for treatment. One doctor warned him that he would only live for three weeks if he returned to the front instead of resting. His answer was: 'I know, but I have to give my life for my people.' He argued that it would have a negative effect on the spirit of his burghers if they heard that he had remained behind in Pretoria, and for that reason he was prepared to put his life on the line.

CLASHES IN THE TRANSVAAL

In the veld, 30 April – On 1 April about 350 Khakis carried out a night attack on the commandos of Generals Piet Viljoen and J.J. Alberts, who were sleeping near Bosmanskop, some 30 kilometres southeast of Springs. A number of joiners acted as guides for the attackers. The Boers were taken totally by surprise, but quickly found their feet and launched a counter-attack. Consequently most of the burghers managed to escape, even though 30 of them were wounded. According to a reliable source British casualties amounted to 77 men killed in action or wounded.

General De la Rey left his commando on 7 April to accompany President Steyn to Klerksdorp for the discussions on peace negotiations. Before he left he appointed General Jan Kemp as commander of all the Republican commandos in the western Transvaal, and clearly ordered him to avoid contact with the Khakis. However, since the British went on with drives in the western Transvaal after De la Rey had left, Kemp had no choice in the matter.

On 11 April there was a major battle between Kemp's combined commandos and a British army at Roodewal, southwest of Lichtenburg. A British army of 11 000 Khakis under the command of Kitchener's Chief of Staff, General Ian Hamilton had formed a line that covered more than 40 kilometres. Kemp had to break through that drive line with his burghers to escape encirclement. Unfortunately, his scouts totally underestimated the extent of the British units who were participating in this drive in the Roodewal area. In addition, the opening in the British line that the scouts reported on 10 April had been closed up in the night that followed.

On the evidence of his scouts' reports, Kemp decided to attack in clear daylight on 11 April in order to open up an escape route. In an attempt to mislead the Khakis, he had carried out a mock attack on the Khaki line west of Roodewal the previous afternoon. In the course of that night he set up his 1 300 burghers in a long, continuous line. General Liebenberg and his men were on the right, followed by the burghers of Commandant Potgieter and General Celliers, and on the left flank Generals Lodewyk Lemmer and Du Toit. Soon after sunrise the commandos began moving. After a while they could see Khakis in front of them, but those soldiers did not fire on them, probably thinking that the burghers were a British unit. It was only when they were very close that the burghers began firing.

The Khakis on whom the first shots were aimed fled in confusion, and the burghers gained confidence. The Khakis not
Continued overleaf

The body of Commandant Potgieter at Roodewal

FROM THE EDITOR

The end of the war is in sight. A final agreement between Boer and Brit will probably be reached within weeks rather than months. In this regard there are of course extremely negative factors as well as major positive factors that have to be weighed against one another. On the positive side there are three outstanding issues:
- An early peace will bring an end to further destruction and loss of life.
- The British do not demand the unconditional surrender of the Republics, which means that the Boers can negotiate for as advantageous an agreement as is possible under these circumstances.
- The British accept that the Republican deputies at the peace negotiations will only consist of representatives of the burghers who are still fighting. This means that the joiners and other handsuppers who took the side of the British are summarily stabbed in the back by their new masters, in the same way that these handsuppers and joiners themselves stabbed their own people in the back. They will have no further say in the determination of the future of South Africa. This means that the Bitter-enders did not fight for nothing at all, since the harvest of all their sacrifices is that they alone on the Boer side will have a say in the future of their people.

On the negative side, one dark blot threatens to smother us. That is the price that the Republics will have to pay for an early peace will be the loss of their independence. No other peace condition can make up for this one. It will be the task of the representatives of the Bitter-enders at Vereeniging to determine if they are prepared to pay so high a price for an early peace.

continued

only began firing back with their field guns, but within a very short time a huge number became visible in the maize fields right in front of them, as well as on the low hills in the background. There were four times as many Khakis as burghers. Kemp realised that his burghers would either have to retreat, or would have to attack and hopefully repulse the Khakis. Since there was no possible way to inform everybody to retreat, Kemp had no alternative but to let the attack go on.

A major problem for the burghers in the centre of the Boer line was that the nature of the terrain forced them to charge in a bunch, thus making them easy targets. The impressive figure of Commandant F.J. Potgieter of Wolmaranstad was in the centre, where he urged the burghers on. In the end Potgieter, whose supporters dwindled as thousands of bullets and shells were fired on them, reached to within 60 metres of the British line before he himself was fatally wounded and tumbled from the back of his horse. With that the charge ended at about eight o'clock that morning, and those burghers who could, fled as fast as possible.

The only advantage for Kemp at that stage was that the British line was in such a shambles immediately after the battle that the Khakis could not immediately pursue the fleeing burghers. This does not mean that there were no pursuers whatsoever. Indeed, a large number of mounted British soldiers pursued groups of burghers for hours on end. The latter however built up a sufficient advantage and their good knowledge of the terrain enabled them to dodge the Khakis despite the very poor condition of their horses. It was a terrible flight, nevertheless, since the Khakis only ended their chase at half past two that afternoon, after a pursuit of about 30 kilometres. With that the catastrophe of Roodewal finally ended. The British not only managed to capture Kemp's guns, but the Boer casualties in this battle were the highest they had suffered in a long time. From all the available information it seems as if 43 men, including Commandant Potgieter, were killed and 50 wounded. Forty of the wounded as well as 36 other Boers were captured by the Khakis. The British casualties seem to have been only 12 men dead and 75 wounded.

The commander of the Khakis at Roodewal, General Ian Hamilton, who had participated as a young officer in the Battle of Majuba in 1881, and was wounded there, afterwards commented that Potgieter's charge had been impressive. Each rifle, each pom-pom and each field gun with which the British could aim, fired as rapidly as possible, but Potgieter, dressed in his clear blue shirt, came charging with the valiant burghers right behind him. The charge of the light brigade during the Crimean War at Balaclava was nothing in comparison to this, Hamilton said. When the British buried the Boer heroes after the battle, they did it with the honour they would have accorded their own comrades.

After the Battle of Roodewal, Kemp's burghers were dispersed all over the flats of that wide area and it took days to reassemble them again, all feeling extremely dejected about the loss they suffered.

Soon after the battle, a setback hit the British in western Transvaal when a military train collided with a goods train at Machavie near Klerksdorp. Twelve Khakis from New Zealand were killed by the impact of the collision.

MILITARY ACTIVITIES ELSEWHERE IN THE TRANSVAAL

In the veld, 31 March – There were only a few skirmishes in the eastern Transvaal this month. In the Vryheid district General Cheere Emmett was made prisoner of war on 15 March. M.W. Myburgh was appointed as a general in his place and succeeds him as commander of the Utrecht and Vryheid Commandos. The British army is making extensive use of armed blacks as soldiers in this area. Even the Zulu king, Dinizulu, who earlier on when he was in dire straits himself requested the Boers to assist him against usurpers supported by the British, was persuaded by the British forces to participate with 250 warriors in an expedition to loot Boer cattle in the Vryheid district. A minor chief, Sikhobobo, also participated in this raid. After three days they were back in Vryheid with thousands of cattle. In the raid they took one Boer prisoner of war and according to reports two Boers were killed in clashes with the robbers. King Dinizulu was given 100 head of cattle for his assistance. Chief Sikhobobo has refused to return to his kraal, since he expects revenge from the side of the burghers.

In the far northern Transvaal General Christiaan Beyers besieged the British garrison in Fort Hendrina, where the village of Louis Trichardt was measured out just before the war. The British had previously totally destroyed the village and renamed Fort Hendrina Fort Edward. Unfortunately Beyers and his men could not force the garrison to surrender before they themselves abandoned the siege on 28 March when a huge British force approached from the south.

In the far north of Transvaal a huge Khaki force assisted by black warriors attacked General Beyers's commando at Malepspoort, near Pietersburg, on 8 April. Beyers himself was wounded in the leg during the clash and Mauritz Dommisse and Commandant Hendrik Mentz took over the command from him. Mentz and his burghers could unfortunately not halt the Khakis and were forced to flee on 9 April after 20 men had been killed or wounded and 108 made prisoner of war. They disappeared into the mountains, the wounded Beyers getting away on the back of a mule.

On 15 April a British unit commanded by Colonel Colenbrander attacked Beyers's burghers in the Wolkberg mountain range in the same area. This time Beyers's burghers lured the enemy into an ambush and inflicted severe casualties without suffering any loss themselves. We have heard that 48 Khakis were killed or wounded in the clash. Furthermore the burghers took 60 Khakis prisoner, including a number of joiners, and captured 15 saddled horses. From the Wolkberg Beyers and his burghers returned to Malepspoort. The Khakis had in the meantime retreated.

In the eastern Transvaal, members of a black community murdered Commandant Groenewald on 8 April.

General Cheere Emmett

CLASHES IN THE CAPE COLONY

PARTIAL SUCCESS IN NAMAQUALAND

Outside Okiep, 30 April – In the northwestern Cape there was a lot of action at the beginning of April and the outcome was more or less in favour of the Republican forces. On 1 April Generals Jan Smuts, Manie Maritz and Jaap van Deventer attacked the mining town of Springbokfontein. The British garrison of about 220 Khakis was protected by three forts. One of these was on a mine dump, surrounded by barbed wire and well fitted out with loopholes. The second was situated on a hillock and the third on a high rock. It was decided that Smuts would lead the attack on the first, Van Deventer on the second and Maritz on the third fort. Since rifles, the only weapons the Boers had available, are not ideal to conquer forts, the burghers made hand bombs of dynamite compacted into jam tins.

The attacks on all three forts began simultaneously with nightfall on 1 April. Van Deventer's men soon occupied their fort when Van Rooyen managed to launch a dynamite bomb on the roof. Maritz's task was much more difficult due to the position of the third fort, but he and his men also forced its garrison to surrender. The toughest nut to crack was Smuts's fort. The attackers soon ran out of dynamite bombs and took over Maritz's unused ones. One of Smuts's burghers managed to shoot a hole in the fort's water tank, and eventually the garrison surrendered when their commander was killed. Some other Khakis were also killed, and on the Boer side one man died.

From Springbokfontein Generals Smuts, Van Deventer and Maritz proceeded to Nababeep on 3 April. To their surprise they found the town deserted. Van Deventer and his burghers remained behind to occupy Nababeep while Smuts, Maritz and Commandant Bouwer, who had by then joined up with them, left for Concordia. While observing that small mining town from a hillock some distance away on 4 April, Smuts decided on the spur of the moment to send a burgher under a white flag to demand the surrender of the town. A little while later the burgher was back with a letter in which the authorities of Concordia agreed to surrender if the Boers would respect all private property and would not interfere with mining activity. Smuts accepted this and the garrison of 250 men laid down their arms.

In addition to the boost to morale, the Republican forces enjoyed a huge material gain, namely loot consisting of a huge supply of munitions and six tons of dynamite!

Smuts subsequently also demanded the surrender of the nearby mining town of Okiep, but the commander of the British forces in Namaqualand, Colonel Shelton, rejected his demand. The Boers then began to besiege the town. To overwhelm it would not be an easy task, since even though Smuts had about 1 000 burghers in his combined commando, Shelton reportedly had a force of 900 men in Okiep. Most of those were members of the citizen force and not well-trained soldiers, but they had a large arsenal of weapons, a field gun, a machine gun and 15 blockhouses in a circle around the town to assist their defence.

Smuts's burghers determinedly attacked Okiep on 9 April. They conquered one blockhouse, but failed to break through to the town. On 10 April they made another attempt. This time the burghers launched dynamite bombs at the blockhouses, but still failed to gain the upper hand. Maritz in desperation tied three dynamite bombs together. With a well-aimed throw he severely damaged one of the blockhouses. Unfortunately its garrison escaped in the dark. Bouwer was wounded in the head during the attack. Since they had now run out of bombs, the Boers once again retreated.

On 11 April Smuts wrote to Colonel Shelton to advise him to send all the non-fighting inhabitants to a safe place south of the town. Shelton consulted the inhabitants on this issue and then reported back to Smuts that the non-fighting inhabitants would not leave the town. Smuts decided that he would not, under these circumstances, lessen his determination. The next day he again attacked the town, but still in vain.

By the middle of April Smuts heard that a relief force had landed in Port Nolloth and was rushing to Shelton's assistance. His reaction was to send General Van Deventer out in the direction of Steinkopf to halt the approaching Khakis. These Khakis indeed appeared on 27 April, but Van Deventer and his burghers confronted them and stopped them in their tracks. In all these clashes, six burghers were killed and 15 wounded, while the British loss was at least four dead and three wounded.

For the Republican forces at Okiep it was clear that their lack of heavy-calibre ammunition was their major weakness. Consequently Maritz and his men attempted to manufacture a gun. On 21 April they fired an experimental shot on Okiep, but the gun broke into pieces. This did not dampen their enthusiasm and they assembled it again, but this time strengthened it considerably. The next day they fired another experimental shot, but again the gun disintegrated.

On 23 April British messengers arrived in Okiep under a white flag with an official letter to General Smuts in which he was requested to attend the envisioned peace negotiations (see main report) as legal advisor. Smuts left by train for Port Nolloth on 25 April and proceeded from there by ship to Cape Town. His brother in law, Tottie Krige, and his secretary, Deneys Reitz, son of the State Secretary F.W. Reitz, accompanied him. In the meantime the Republican siege of Okiep continued. Smuts transferred his command to Maritz and warned him to keep up the pressure, since the war might go on for a long time.

Maritz certainly continued with the siege. On 28 April he sent a wounded British sergeant to the British garrison for treatment. This action led to attempts to organise a rugby match between the garrison and the besiegers. Maritz agreed to an armistice for this purpose and the British were ready, but then they heard of the fight at Steinkopf the previous day and cancelled their arrangements.

Today the Republicans launched a last futile attempt to enter Okiep. They loaded a whole train wagon full of dynamite, lighted the fuses and pushed the train into the town. However, the dynamite never exploded.

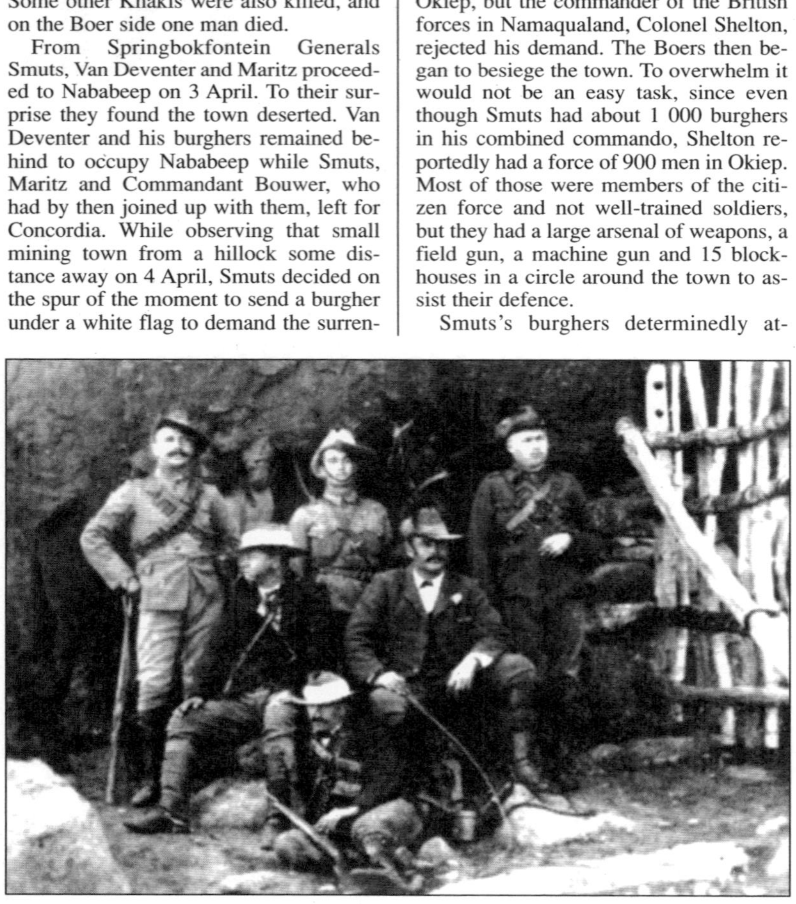

Generals Smuts (seated left), Maritz and their staff at Springbokfontein

MILITARY SITUATION IN THE LOWER ORANGE RIVER VALLEY

Kakamas, 30 April – Here in the valley of the Orange River and in an enormous area around us, there has been little action since February. The British seemed to be satisfied to allow the Rebels free rein in this area, with the exception of Kenhardt and Upington. British garrisons are stationed in those towns, but nowhere else. The British probably believe that this uninhabitable and isolated area is of no particular military value and that whatever happens here will have hardly any influence on the course of the war as a whole. For that reason they have limited their expenses by only sending a contingent of Border Scouts to this area.

For the Cape Rebels this is an excellent development. Commandant Jan Louw's Kakamas Commando has now been in continuous occupation of the town and numerous villages in the area for more than six months. There is little talk of fighting and campaigns. The last noteworthy expedition was undertaken in February by Field Cornet Stadler with 30 men of Louw's commando. They were accompanied by Willie Steyn, the burgher who earlier escaped from a prisoner-of-war ship in Ceylon.

Stadler's group proceeded northwards via Lutzputz to Rietfontein. At Middelpos they were involved in a skirmish with the local Coloured community. The leader of the Coloureds, Captain David Philander, was killed in the fight. At Rietfontein, supplies that came through German South West Africa awaited them. They included clothing, shoes, tobacco from Holland and two small but extremely heavy trunks from Germany. Stadler and his men loaded the supplies in a wagon and began their journey back. At Abeam, British soldiers sent from Upington lay in wait for them, and a skirmish followed, but the rebels suffered no casualties.

Back in Kakamas Stadler took the two heavy trunks, whose contents were a secret, and buried them. It is alleged that those trunks contain telegraphic apparatus. Stadler has however decided to wait for orders before revealing where the trunks are.

After this expedition Steyn left for Namaqualand to join General Smuts's forces. Soon afterwards, at the end of February, one of Commandant Louw's patrols was involved in a skirmish with the Border Scouts at Dreyersput. One of the Rebels, Johannes Jacobs, was wounded and the others had to flee for their lives. When they returned the next morning, they found Jacobs's dead body. It was naked and his face was mangled.

The Rebels' last attack was aimed at Keimoes. They attacked the town in the middle of the day and looted approximately 400 head of livestock. They now have enough meat to keep them going through the approaching winter.

Good news from elsewhere in the Cape Colony is that on 6 April the British military court that heard the case of Commandant Pieter Kritzinger found him not guilty on all charges. Since then he has been treated as an ordinary prisoner of war. From the Calvinia district, however, bad news is that Commandant Jan Theron, the brother of the legendary Commandant Danie Theron and his successor as commander of the Theron Scout Corps, died on 14 April from a stomach ailment.

EXECUTIONS

Executions of civilians in the Cape Colony in terms of martial law are still continuing. On 5 February F. du Rand was shot by a firing squad in Cradock. Lord Kitchener confirmed the death sentences of Lieutenants Morant and Handcock of the notorious Bushveld Carbineers in the past month, but commuted Lieutenant Witton's sentence to life-long imprisonment. Morant and Handcock were taken to Pretoria, where they were shot by a firing squad in the old prison building.

The Cape Rebel F. du Rand who was executed

NEWS FROM A CONCENTRATION CAMP

In the veld, 30 March – While the disruption and tribulations of commando life are still the fate of our loyal burghers, our wives and children are suffering an even worse fate in the concentration camps. Here is another report by Mrs Maria Fischer on camp life in the Merebank concentration camp near Durban:

'Early in December (1901) I went to the beach for the first time with a number of women. The ocean is huge, but I thought it would be somewhat different. Unfortunately it does not help one to escape from the sad realities of our horrible existence.

'From 18 December the camp was placed under quarantine for 15 days as a result of one or two outbreaks of diphtheria. We were carefully protected against infection. Women and children, old, young, ill or well, are off-loaded in heaps from the Free State and the Transvaal and bundled into small tents or wet, dirty rooms and then – thus we believe – are poisoned with coloured sugar or rather vitriol water – as a result of which dozens of emaciated corpses are carried to the cemetery every day.

'On New Year's Day the inhabitants of the camp held a procession in the midst of our suffering. The children sang the Transvaal Anthem and marched with the *Vierkleur*. In their excitement they tore a piece off an English flag that a woman had on her tent pole and trampled on it. In the meantime little children are continually dying in large numbers – today again two from the usual camp disease. Perhaps those who die are the fortunate ones, since they escape further suffering. Every now and then babies are born in the camp, including twins on 8 January. Those two little ones are the first illegitimate children that I am aware of.

'One morning at about nine o'clock all the men in the camp had to go to the office of the Commandant. A number of handsuppers turned up, as well as a few curious women. Everybody expected a serious announcement. In the end a black man was brought out and the men were told to study him carefully. He had a scar on his head and one on his arm. Then the order came: "If anybody spots this black man in the vicinity of one of the tents, they must capture him and bring him to the Commandant. If he resists, they have the right to shoot him." A woman inquired: "Commandant – with what?"

'In January all the news we heard in this camp from our burghers was negative. They allege there is no hope, but I cling to hope like a maniac. The mere thought that everything, everything was in vain, that my child would become a slave together with the thousands who suffered death and misery to remain free, is enough to make me mad. It embitters me in my soul. Is it a sin to have a heartfelt wish to see the women and children of England in similar misery one day?

'On 1 February sister Rachel and me were transferred from the tent to a sink house. Earlier the camp authorities had erected a bathhouse with eight rooms. It is open at the top and has a wooden floor below and the wind often blows through it. Unfortunately there is often neither water nor soap. The sink houses are more comfortable than the tents in which we lived. We have new neighbours whom we do not know; we wonder if they will become good friends.

'Generally speaking the women get along very well. One seldom hears of disputes or fighting. Here the high, low, rich, poor, good, bad, pretty and ugly from all the corners of the two Republics, women in the greatest misery and destitution, and who have no hope, are heaped together. Each one does her best to make her own circumstances as well as those of the others as bearable as possible.

'Early in February a few of us went to Durban harbour to visit relatives who are prisoners of war. Since we could provide their names, we were granted permission to talk to them for one hour. We stood on the quay next to the ship and talked to burghers who are prisoners of war on board the ship. They leaned over the ship's railing and talked until we were forbidden that. Later on the designated hour came and we talked to our relatives who are prisoners of war. This discussion made me very sad, since they say that our burghers are being captured one after another.

'A few days later a lady from Durban arrived with some things from Holland for the needy ones in our camp. If no help came from such sources, quite a number of us would by now have been in our birthday suits. To see girls of 16 and above barefoot is nothing new. Many women's footwear certainly no longer deserves the name of "shoe".

'We should be extremely thankful that there are people elsewhere who are thinking of us. If the opportunity should arise one day that we could give back something to Holland or Germany, what would our Afrikaners – if there are any Afrikaners left – do? God must ensure that we never forget that thousands of naked little ones were dressed from Dutch and German purses.

'At the end of February all the girls and women who gave private education to the children here in the camp were told that it is no longer permissible, probably to give the so-called government schools an opportunity. All the children are forced to go to those schools. That is well, since it keeps them busy. There are not yet benches and the children must sit on the sand.

'Rumours are making the rounds about battles. On 11 March, for example, we heard that the Boers captured a number of guns at Klipstapel. We will only find out later if that is true. In a camp like this there is lots of talk! One knows this, the other something else. A number of women claim that they saw gun smoke in the washhouses and heard rifle and gunshots. Now I wonder where that comes from?

'There are many people who do hand work and then sell it. In a little room near us an old lady from Irene lives with two children. She is busy from early morn till late in the evening making dogs, chickens, pots, mugs and lots of other things from clay, of which there is plenty available here, and selling this, and she makes a few neat shillings. It is a pity that the poor old soul herself looks like a piece of pot clay by now! I myself made a dog out of clay and called it Bousfield in honour of our camp commandant.

'To end this report: the women are trying their utmost to remain happy and peaceful. Even if we have to carry wood and water for another year or more, there are hardly any complaints.'

Sink houses in a concentration camp

Wood distributed in the Merebank concentration camp

Maria Fischer with her husband and son before the war

FIGHTING IN THE FREE STATE

In the veld, northern Free State, 30 April – Military activities in the Free State have come to a virtual standstill during the past month. At the beginning of April the Khakis were still busy with a drive in the northeast Free State. They claimed afterwards that they killed or captured 86 burghers and captured large herds of livestock.

On 8 April General C.C.J. Badenhorst overpowered and captured a British unit of about 200 Khakis who attacked him near Bultfontein. On the same day the Free Staters occupied two blockhouses at Steenkampskop, near Fouriesburg, and took the combined garrison of 21 men prisoner of war.

The joiner S.G. Vilonel and a group of so-called Orange River Colony Volunteers under his command attempted to trouble the Republican forces in the vicinity of Marquard in April. On 18 April they even managed to take a single burgher prisoner of war, but this burgher's comrades launched a counter-attack, killed two joiners and captured five. Three of the captured joiners were charged in a military court under the chairmanship of General Froneman, found guilty of treason and executed.

On 28 April Commandant K.D. Coetzee was killed in a skirmish with Coloured scouts at Rooikop, between Bloemfontein and Dewetsdorp.

OUR MILITARY OFFICERS

General Wynand Malan

Wynand Charl Malan was born in 1872 on the farm Beyersfontein, in the Murraysburg district of the Cape Colony. He is the eldest son of Jacobus Malan and his wife Margaretha Elizabeth Pienaar. As a child he attended a school in Franschhoek. When he was 17 he moved to Langlaagte in Johannesburg, where his father owned a dairy.

In 1898 Malan participated in the campaign against the Baverda of Chief Mphephu and thus earned citizenship of the South African Republic. Soon after the outbreak of this war in October 1899 he went to the Natal front as a member of the Fordsburg Commando. There he participated in numerous well-known battles.

After the British breakthrough in Natal at the end of 1900, Malan joined the Republican forces in the northern Free State. He was recognised for personal bravery and joined Commandant Danie Theron's Scout Corps. There he excelled in the risky business of capturing trains.

After Theron's death in September 1900, Malan was elected lieutenant and joined the forces of Chief Commandant De Wet. From February 1901 he acted on his own in the Cape Colony, giving the British headaches with his continuous attacks on isolated garrisons. His men elected him commandant.

When General Jan Smuts began his invasion of the Cape Colony in September 1901, Malan was placed under his authority. In January this year Smuts appointed him as fighting general over the commandos in the Cape Midland districts. A month later he was seriously wounded but he and his commando continued fighting in the area designated to him.

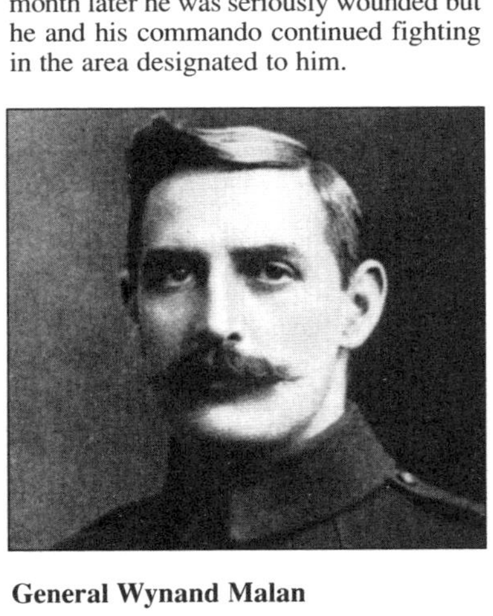

General Wynand Malan

NEWS FROM THE PRISONER-OF-WAR CAMPS

Cape Town, 30 April – Candidate-Minister J.A. van Blerk reports from Bermuda that the approximately 6 000 burghers who are detained there are still experiencing rather harsh conditions, but are full of confidence. One of the burghers, Joubert Reitz, managed to avoid the censors and to send a letter to a newspaper in Boston in the United States of America. In this letter, Reitz revealed the circumstances under which the prisoners of war were detained by the British authorities, pointing out that the prisoners were given neither sufficient food nor sufficient clothing.

The British authorities in Bermuda were furious when they heard of the publication of the letter. Reitz was imprisoned and Van Blerk and Mrs Albertyn, the wife of the Reverend J.R. Albertyn, were placed under severe restrictions. However, Reitz's letter became so celebrated in the United States that it stimulated an upsurge of sympathy for the Boers. As a result Americans are now sending massive stores of food and clothing to the prisoners of war. This is of course extremely welcome and highly appreciated by the burghers. In Boston an organisation called 'The Lend a Hand Society' was established to co-ordinate support for the prisoners of war. A delegate of the Society visited the prisoners of war early this year. Subsequently the restrictions on Van Blerk were lifted.

Ever since the beginning of this year the British authorities have attempted to lure the burghers to sign an oath of submission to the British king by promising early repatriation to those who do. A small number of burghers bowed to the temptation. In the process they earned the wrath of the patriotic burghers, who subsequently made the lives of the traitors particularly unpleasant. As a result the British authorities had to intervene to protect the traitors.

The Reverend Albertyn had earlier decided to have abridged Dutch hymn books that included only well-known psalms and hymns printed in America. When these books arrived in Bermuda, the censor decided that they could not be allowed in the prisoner-of-war camps, since the psalms of David included inflammatory language. Subsequently Albertyn and Van Blerk were severely restricted in their spiritual activities in the camps. Indeed, Albertyn and his wife left Bermuda early in March.

In some cases the decisions that the British authorities take with regard to the prisoners of war seem quite incomprehensible. Thus when a 12-year-old boy became critically ill his father, who was also a prisoner of war, was refused permission to visit him in hospital. Even when it became clear that the boy would probably die, no permission was given. Neither was the father allowed to attend the funeral. It was only afterwards that Burgher Moolman was allowed to visit his son's grave.

The Boer prisoners of war on the Bermuda islands include 200–300 boys under the age of 16. The youngest ones are only eight years old. Initially the children were not detained separately, but with the older prisoners of war. The latter included a number of teachers, who gathered some of the boys together and gave them school lessons. Catechism classes were also provided to the boys.

Since the British camp authorities in due course realised that they could perhaps influence the children by separating them from the adult prisoners and giving them school lessons by British-oriented teachers, they ordered that all children had to be transferred to Hinson's Island. The children on Hawkins Island initially refused to go, but relented when the camp authorities decreased the amount of food provided to all the prisoners detained on that island. When the children left by boat for their new destination, they sang the Transvaal anthem at the top of their voices for the benefit of the Camp Commandant, who was present and could understand Afrikaans.

Once on Hinson's Island and separated from the adults, the children remained rebellious. A prisoner of war who had recently become a joiner was appointed as teacher. Since he failed to control the children, he inflicted corporal punishment on them. The reaction of adult prisoners of war was to grab him one evening and to dip him in the ocean. He was only released when he agreed to sing the Transvaal anthem. At school the children sang the same anthem every time the teacher attempted to force English culture down their throats. A number of boys were consequently given severe corporal punishment, which left their backs blue and purple. However, they continued defying the teacher until he, as well as his successor, was replaced by a patriotic burgher, A.W. Bester. The latter won the confidence of the boys, but was also replaced by the authorities, since he refused to influence the children against the Republics.

A very tragic event took place on the evening of 27 April when 16-year-old Henkie Bosch, a prisoner of war whose parents live in Pretoria, was treacherously shot by a guard. Bosch was confined with the most irreconcilable prisoners of war in a special enclosure on Tucker's Island. One of the guards offered to assist them to escape in exchange for money. A secret agreement was made and the date and time of the proposed escape was set. The signal was that the guard would throw a stone on their tent. When the signal was given, Bosch rushed out, jumped the fence and ran. He had barely gone 25 paces when the guard shot him. He is the only prisoner thus far in Bermuda to die of unnatural causes.

News from Bellary in India is that a prisoner of war, W. Hoffman, was shot by guards when, allegedly, he attempted to escape from the hospital. The youngest member of the Republican forces to be imprisoned in India, eight-year-old David Matthys Jacobs of the Vrede district, died of measles in the same camp on 2 April.

Schoolmaster Bester and his two adopted sons

PRISONER OF WAR POEM

The poem that follows was written by Joubert Reitz, the prisoner of war on Bermuda who was responsible for smuggling out the letter that was subsequently published in the United States. Joubert is a son of State Secretary F.W. Reitz of the South African Republic, whose poems we have published before. In this poem one reads about the loneliness and longing for their fatherland that probably fill the hearts of all the Boer prisoners of war.

The Searchlight

When the searchlight from the gunboat
Throws its rays upon my tent,
Then I think of home and Comrades
And the happy days I spent
In the country where I come from
And where all I love are yet,
Then I think of things and places
And of scenes I'll ne'er forget.

Then a face comes up before me,
Which will haunt me to the last,
And I think of things that have been
And of happiness that's past.
And only then I realise
How much my freedom meant
When the searchlight from the gunboat
Throws its rays upon my tent.

Burgher Moolman at his son's grave on Bermuda

School pupils on Bermuda

Boer prisoners of war in front of their hut in Ceylon

Boer prisoners of war holding a sports meeting in Ceylon

THE War Reporter
MONTHLY EDITION

Number 65 | In the Veld, South African Republic | 1 June 1902

ZULUS MURDER 56 BURGHERS

Final military actions of the war?

Even though the peace negotiations got going early on in the past month, fighting continued to the bitter end. In one of the most shocking incidents of the whole war, a Zulu force led by Chief Sikhobobo killed and maimed 56 burghers on 6 May. These burghers were members of a commando of about 70 men led by Field Cornet J. Potgieter. They were sleeping in a cave at Holkrantz near Vryheid in the southeast of the Transvaal when the Zulus surprised them. The Zulus were armed with rifles as well as spears. The Boers fought back, killing altogether 52 Zulus and wounding 48.

This incident, which is a direct result of black involvement in the war due to the personal interests of the white participants, naturally generated widespread reaction. The Republican authorities have no doubt that the British authorities are at least partly to be blamed. The fact that A.J. Shepstone visited Chief Sikhobobo three days before the events contributes to that suspicion. Shepstone is the son of Sir Theophilus Shepstone, the man who in 1877 annexed the old South African Republic on behalf of Britain, and who revealed himself as an archenemy of the Boers. What A.J. Shepstone, who was accompanied by members of the British Military Intelligence department, discussed with Sikhobobo is not known, but the timing of that visit seems rather suspicious.

Another factor that probably partly contributed to the incident is the cycle of revenge and counter-revenge that unfortunately characterises relations between white and black in South Africa. It is known that Commandant-General Louis Botha ordered General M.W. Meyer on 23 April to torch Zulu kraals in the Vryheid district in retaliation for King Dinizulu and Chief Sikhobobo's raid on Boer livestock in March. On 1 May a Boer commando led by the late Field Cornet Potgieter burned down a number of Zulu kraals in carrying out the abovementioned order. They also looted grain and livestock and forced the frightened inhabitants of the kraals to flee for protection to the British garrison in Vryheid. It is highly likely that Sikhobobo's attack on Holkrantz was inspired by determination to avenge Potgieter's actions.

FIGHTING IN THE CAPE COLONY

The Republican siege of the British garrison in Okiep ended on 1 May. The burghers were short of food and fodder for their horses, so General Manie Maritz ordered them to retreat to Concordia. On 4 May a large British force arrived and entered the town unhindered. After about 10 days Maritz and his men also abandoned Springbokfontein and Concordia and moved off in a southerly direction with the objective of launching a third campaign in the Western Cape.

Commandant Carel van Heerden

In the Cape Midlands, Commandant Willem Fouchee attacked a British unit at the Willows near Middelburg with 40 burghers on the evening of 3 May. P.J. du Plessis, who participated in the attack, told our correspondent that General Wynand Malan was supposed to join the attack with 20 burghers, but the Khakis surrendered before he arrived. A number of Khakis were killed, with one Boer lightly wounded. Fouchee and his men took all the horses and as many supplies as they could carry before disappearing in the night.

About two weeks later, on Sunday 18 May, General Wynand Malan, Commandant Carel van Heerden and their burghers launched a night attack on Aberdeen with the objective of capturing horses from the enemy. P.J. du Plessis, who was present again, told our correspondent that this attack was a fiasco. The moon was shining brightly when they entered the town and the British garrison were ready for them. Van Heerden, who led the attack, was killed and a number of the burghers suffered a similar fate or were wounded. The rest got away with only 54 horses. According to an unconfirmed report, Van Heerden's naked body was exhibited publicly in Aberdeen, which is his hometown, the next day.

The last fight in the Cape Colony took place on 27 May when Malan and Fouchee attacked a British unit near Jansenville. Malan was wounded for the umpteenth time in a fight, but this time so seriously that his comrades had to leave him behind. Thus he became a prisoner of war.

FIGHTING IN THE TRANSVAAL

On the battlefront there was very little action in the Transvaal in May. In the western Transvaal the British executed a drive involving thousands of soldiers from 7 to 11 May, but without dramatic success. They did take 350 burghers prisoners of war, but few of them were true *Bittereinders*. In addition their loot consisted of wagons, carts and livestock. Probably the best-known prisoner of war was Acting General A.J.G. de la Rey, an elder brother of General Koos de la Rey who is popularly known as *Klein Adriaan* (Little Adriaan).

In the eastern Transvaal the British also undertook a last offensive before the 'armistice' of 11 May became operational. On 8 May a combined force of Khakis and armed blacks attempted to encircle General Chris Muller's commando near Belfast. The burghers beat off the attempt with the loss of one man. They regarded the attack as a mean action, since it was carried out while preparations for the peace conference were already under way.

FIGHTING IN THE FREE STATE

In the Orange Free State the British made a few last attempts, before the 'armistice' began on 11 May, to gain a military advantage over the Boers. On 6 May they undertook a drive southwards from Heilbron. Only a few dozen burghers were made prisoners of war. The only well-known burgher who suffered this unfortunate fate was Commandant Manie Botha, a cousin of General Louis Botha. He was captured in the Brandwater Basin on 10 May.

ELECTION OF DEPUTIES

Vereeniging, 15 May – The process of electing deputies to represent the burghers here at the peace conference began before the end of last month. Chief Commandant Christiaan de Wet says that he held eight meetings at commandos from 22 April onwards. Deputies to the peace negotiations were elected and the burghers unanimously voted that independence must be upheld. Judge Hertzog visited the other Free State commandos and oversaw the election of deputies. De Wet assured our correspondent that at these meetings too the burghers were unanimous in their decision that independence cannot be given up.

General Jan Kemp recounted this morning that he and General Celliers had to cross the British blockhouse line between Lichtenburg and Mafeking in a northerly direction before they could reach the place where the election of deputies for their commando would be held, namely the farm Rietvlei in the Marico district. The scouts recommended that they should cross the line in a valley between two blockhouses. A few burghers rode out ahead in the dark to cut the barbed wire fence. Kemp organised his carts and wagons into a convoy. When they charged through the line in clear moonlight, they fought for the last time. Fortunately nobody was killed; only three burghers were lightly wounded. They were hardly through, and still within sight of the blockhouses, when you could see matches everywhere as the burghers lighted up their pipes again. As can be expected, the enemy immediately fired a few shots in their direction.

On 11 May Acting President Burger and General de la Rey addressed the meeting of western Transvaal burghers at Rietvlei and asked them how they felt about negotiations with the British. One of the burghers expressed his dissatisfaction that the Transvaal government had corresponded with the British about a possible settlement without first consulting their ally, the Free State government. These burghers furthermore pointed out to Burger that many burghers in the western Transvaal had signed a petition requesting the transfer of the Transvaal government power to a military authority, and only abandoned that initiative when General de la Rey expressed himself strongly against it. Burger answered that it was especially at the request of Commandant-General Botha that the government had taken up the issue of a possible settlement with the British.

The discussion that followed clearly reflected the burghers' unanimous feeling that the Republics could make limited concessions to the British, but that their independence must remain untouched. If the British would not respect it, the Republics must go on fighting. The burghers of Krugersdorp then elected Kemp as their representative, the burghers of Pretoria and Johannesburg elected the field preacher J.F. Naude, and the Rustenburgers elected B.J. van Heerden. The deputies left for Vereeniging that same afternoon.

General Christiaan Beyers and Landdrost Stoffberg journeyed as deputies of the northern Transvaal burghers to Vereeniging. Beyers says that when they arrived at Malepspoort, after a battle with the British forces in the Wolkberg, he was surprised to find State Secretary Reitz and Acting State Attorney Jacobs waiting for them. The burghers were given an explanation of the latest developments and why the important visitors were there, and then clearly indicated that they were determined that their independence must not be touched in any negotiations. Before Beyers left in a southerly direction on 10 May, he undertook an expedition into Sekhukhuneland to demand livestock that the Bapedi allegedly stole from burghers. The campaign involved a few clashes, and in the end the burghers returned with 400 cattle.

From the eastern Transvaal our correspondent reports that approximately 1 000 burghers met at the beginning of May at Vanggatkoppie to discuss peace. The members of the government who addressed them were Executive Council members General Lukas Meyer and J.C. Krogh. General Meyer drew a dark picture of war conditions and stressed the necessity of a peace conference. Lieutenant Colonel Fanie Trichard declared that if independence could not be guaranteed, it was unnecessary to hold a peace conference at all, since the burghers had fought primarily for their independence and free existence as people, and he was prepared to fight a little longer for this. In the end the burghers elected General Muller as their representative.

General Jan Smuts travelled by train from Cape Town to Vereeniging for the conference. At Kroonstad he interrupted his journey for a meeting with Lord Kitchener. Smuts refused to divulge any particulars on their negotiations. He merely said that they talked straight and that both of them were now better informed on the state of affairs.

Here at Vereeniging all the deputies are accommodated in tents that the British pitched for them. The two camps of the Transvaal and the Free State deputations are about 60 metres apart. In addition to the 60 deputies and their secretaries or adjutants, the governments of the two Republics are present. Altogether there are about 150 Boers. There are two large marquees, one of which serves as dining hall and the second as meeting place.

The first meeting began this morning at half past eleven. A scene that was sobering to all of us immediately preceded it. Indeed, it virtually drove us to tears. President Steyn's health had deteriorated to such an extent that he, the symbol of strength and of firmness, had to be carried into the hall like a little child. The only news that we have up to now is that the 60 delegates have elected General Beyers as chairman of the meeting.

FROM THE EDITOR

The war has ended – and so has the existence of the Boer Republics. Peace has been declared, and the price is our independence. The loyal burghers were united in their determination to fight to the bitter end – and now the bitter end has arrived. The enemy did not destroy the Republican military power. It was the Republican leaders who decided: enough. We have given our best, but the force against us was too massive. The price we were paying day by day for our independence and freedom became too high. The destruction of our country by our ruthless enemy was simply too damaging; the death rate of our women and children was catastrophic. It would not have helped to go on fighting indefinitely while the deaths went on unchecked, since in the end there would have been no Afrikaners left to enjoy the fruits of our determination.

We believe that the Republican leaders had no alternative but to conclude peace the way they did.

Number 65 **1 June 1902**

THE PEACE NEGOTIATIONS

FIRST MEETING AT VEREENIGING

Vereeniging, 31 May – The Boer delegates who assembled at Vereeniging finally reached an agreement this afternoon. It was no easy accomplishment. It became clear immediately after the meeting began on 15 May that even though all agreed that the war could go on much longer, there was no unanimity on the question whether this would be a good thing. Chief Commandant Christiaan de Wet was very specific in his standpoint: 'We have to go on with the war.' General Kemp agreed: 'I will fight till I die.' Commandant-General Louis Botha, however, stated that the situation was hopeless and that the Republican forces became weaker every day. Acting President Schalk Burger expressed the strong opinion that it would be criminal to keep on fighting until everything was destroyed and everybody was dead, if there was agreement that the prospects seemed hopeless anyway. The words that impressed most were those uttered by General Koos de la Rey: 'There has been talk of fighting to the bitter end. But has the bitter end already come? Each man must answer that question for himself. You must remember that everything has been sacrificed – cattle, goods, money, wife and child. Our men are going about naked and our women have nothing but clothes made of skins to wear. Is not this the bitter end?'

The Reverend J.D. Kestell, who was elected as one of the secretaries when the meeting began, later told our correspondent that the delegates were divided into two camps at that stage. The one group was convinced that it was no longer possible to continue the war, while the second group believed that the bitter end had not yet arrived. With one or two exceptions, the Free State deputies supported the second conviction, while most of the Transvaal deputies supported the first viewpoint.

Since the majority of the deputies were not prepared to accept the loss of independence, a feeling emerged that they should try once more to convince the British government to accept peace with independence by making large-scale concessions on other issues. Following that trend, State Secretary F.W. Reitz of the Transvaal proposed that the Republics should offer to concede both the Witwatersrand and Swaziland, and even control over their foreign affairs to the British. The Republics could even concede to becoming British protectorates. In the end the deputies accepted two resolutions on 17 May. The first was that the Republican governments could agree to a peace settlement on the basis of Reitz's proposals. The second was that a negotiation commission should be formed. The delegates elected Generals Louis Botha, Koos de la Rey and Jan Smuts of the Transvaal and Chief Commandant Christiaan de Wet and General (Judge) Hertzog of the Free State. If this commission could reach an agreement with the British government, the text should be tabled for ratification by the full meeting of delegates.

NEGOTIATIONS IN PRETORIA

The negotiation commission left Vereeniging for Pretoria on 18 May to negotiate with Lords Kitchener and Milner. The next day they handed a written proposal to Milner. In this they offered to make the following concessions as a basis for negotiations with the objective of ending the war:

1 That the Republics would hand control over their foreign affairs to Britain.
2 That the Boers retain self-government under British control.
3 That the Republics concede part of their territory to Britain.

They added that particulars could be worked out later.

Kitchener and Milner immediately rejected those proposals, and indicated that the British government would not consider any proposals that entailed the continued independence of the Republics. Milner tabled a document in terms of which the Boers would recognise the annexation of the Republics in 1900. The negotiation commission rejected that out of hand. After a long discussion the negotiation commission and the British representatives agreed that a sub-committee of the commission, consisting of General Smuts and Judge Hertzog, would draft a concept proposal with Milner.

The sub-committee made rapid progress. They convinced Milner to accept the principle that both parties would sign the eventual agreement, and not only the Boers. Furthermore, they agreed on a preamble to the agreement. The British representatives recognised that the Boer deputies represented the governments of the Republics and that the document would reflect this. From their side, the commission accepted that it could be written that the burghers accepted King Edward VII as their king. On 21 May the negotiators went on formulating the conditions of the peace agreement. They again made good progress and by that afternoon the conditions were telegraphed to Britain. The British cabinet discussed the document in the course of the next few days and seems to have been satisfied.

On 27 May the British cabinet agreed to the final document and it was telegraphed to Kitchener and Milner. Milner presented the document to the Republican negotiation commission the next day. He informed them that this would be the final document and that the British government would not accept any changes. The Boers would have to accept and sign it by midnight on 31 May or reject it. Smuts immediately crossed out the words 'Act of Surrender' on the title page of the document and replaced it by the words 'Act of Peace'. The British representatives did not react to this, thus indicating that they accepted the change.

CONDITIONS OF THE PEACE AGREEMENT

The ten conditions of the peace agreement are the following:

1 The burgher forces will lay down their arms and will recognise King Edward VII as their lawful sovereign.
2 Burghers in the field outside the Transvaal and the Orange Free State and all prisoners of war will be returned on making the same acknowledgement.
3 Burghers who lay down arms will not be deprived of their personal liberty or property.
4 No proceedings will be taken against burghers except specific cases for war crimes.
5 Dutch will be taught at schools where parents desire it and will be admitted in courts of law.
6 Burghers will be permitted to possess licensed rifles for their personal protection.
7 Military administration in the former Republics will at the earliest possible date be succeeded by civil, and subsequently by self-government.
8 The issue of 'Native Franchise' will not be decided until after the introduction of self-government.
9 There is to be no special war tax.
10 Commissions will be set up in each district to assist resettlement and supply necessities such as food, seed, farm implements and livestock lost in the war and to honour Republican bank or promissory notes. For this purpose, a free gift of £3 million is to be provided by the British government, as well as loans free of interest for a specific period.

General Jan Smuts

General Hertzog

The negotiation commission wanted absolute clarity on the issue of amnesty. The British representatives indicated that all burghers would receive amnesty except three specific cases where war crimes might have been committed. The cases had to do with a Field Cornet Salmon van As, Barend Cilliers and one Muller, who was not known to the Boer leaders. As for the Cape Rebels, they would lose their franchise. The Rebel leaders would probably be tried in court, but none would receive the death penalty.

FINAL MEETING AT VEREENIGING

At nine o'clock on the evening of 28 May the negotiation commission left Pretoria by train for Vereeniging, where they submitted the conditions to the full meeting of the Republican deputies the next day. President Steyn, whose health further deteriorated, finally withdrew from the meeting at that time. At his request Chief Commandant de Wet subsequently took over as Acting President of the Orange Free State. The Transvaal government immediately handed a sum of money to the Free State government to cover the cost of Steyn's treatment as well as his personal expenses. The Free State deputies contributed from their own pockets to this fund. It was a very touching scene. The weakened President then left in the company of Dr W.J. van der Merwe for treatment in Krugersdorp.

The deputies at Vereeniging had to decide between three possibilities – reject the proposals and surrender unconditionally; decide to go on fighting; or accept the conditions. It soon became clear that the majority of the Transvaalers supported the third option, but that the Free Staters wanted to go on fighting. The question was whether the Republics would be able to keep up a united front.

Early this morning Generals Botha and De la Rey visited Chief Commandant de Wet in his tent. Kestell told our correspondent this evening that the two Transvaal generals pointed out to De Wet that after all was said and done, they could not go on with the war. Up to now the Republics have been absolutely united. It would be wrong if there were division.

De Wet agreed with them. The three military leaders then arranged that De Wet would meet the Free State deputies alone, while Botha and De la Rey would meet with the Transvaal deputies, and that they would all attempt to achieve unanimity. When the morning session of all the deputies resumed soon afterwards, De Wet proposed that a committee should be appointed to formulate a proposal that would be acceptable to everybody. The deputies agreed to this proposal and elected Smuts and Hertzog as the committee. The meeting then adjourned while the committee carried out its task.

While the Transvaal deputies remained behind in the assembly tent, the Free Staters went to De Wet's tent. He then informed them that it was his conviction that it would be futile to go on with the war. For the sake of unity, it would be best if they could vote unanimously for one proposal. The bitter end had arrived.

Later all of them returned to the tent of assembly. The statement drafted by Hertzog and Smuts was then read to the deputies. The deputies then had to vote on whether they accepted the statement, which would mean accepting the peace proposals, or not. The statement was accepted by 54 votes against six. Three Transvaalers, namely General Kemp, Commandant J.J. Alberts and Burgher J.F. Naude, and three Free Staters, namely General C.C.J. Badenhorst and Commandants A.J. Bester and C.A. van Niekerk, rejected it.

After the decision of the meeting became known, there was absolute silence. Then Acting President Burger spoke: 'Here we stand at the grave of the two Republics. Much yet remains to be done, although we can no longer do so in the official capacities which we have heretofore held. Let us not draw our hands back from doing what is our duty. Let us pray God to guide us, and to show us how we can keep our people together. That part of our people which has proved unfaithful we must not reject. We must learn to forgive and to forget.'

A deputation of 10 men has just left by train for Pretoria. Later this evening, they will sign the peace treaty. Acting President Schalk Burger, State Secretary F.W. Reitz, and Generals Louis Botha, Koos de la Rey, Lucas Meyer and J.C. Krogh will sign on behalf of the South African Republic, and Acting President Christiaan de Wet, State Secretary Jack Brebner and Generals J.B.M. Hertzog and J.H. Olivier will sign on behalf of the Republic of the Orange Free State. Lords Kitchener and Milner will sign on behalf of the British government. The war will then, after 963 days, come to an end, and the two Boer Republics will cease to exist.

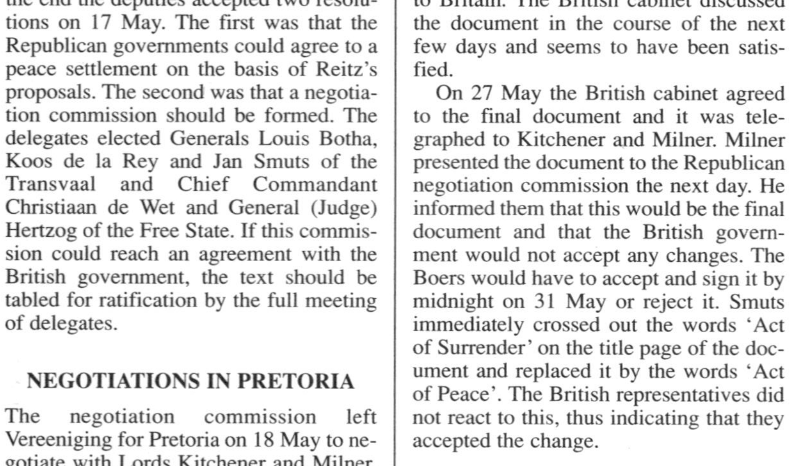

Six burghers at the Vereeniging peace conference (from left to right): M.J Dommisse, F.S. van Manen, Hendrik Mentz, General Christiaan Beyers, Captain Heinrich du Toit and Commandant T.S. Stoffberg

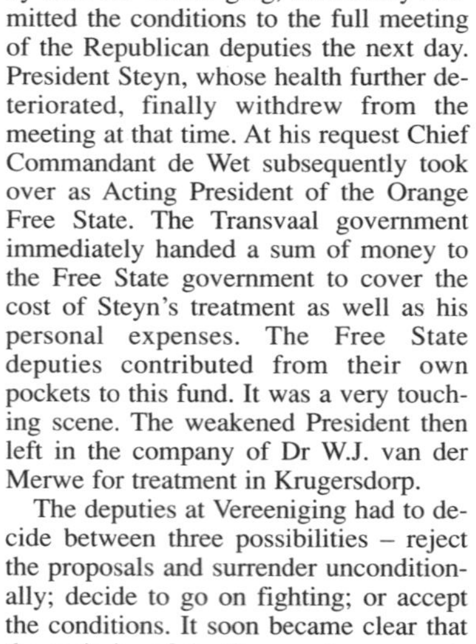

General de la Rey

OUR MILITARY OFFICERS

General Christiaan Beyers

Christiaan Frederik Beyers was born in 1869 in the Stellenbosch district of the Cape Colony, the third son of Christiaan Frederik Beyers and his wife Anna Maria van der Bijl. He attended the Stellenbosch Gymnasium as well as the Victoria College in that town. At the end of 1888 he settled in Pretoria where he worked as a lawyer's clerk and in 1894 completed his lawyer's examination. Beyers then moved to Boksburg, where he began his own practice. In 1897 he was given full citizenship on the grounds of his membership of the military forces of the South African Republic at the time of the Jameson Raid of 1895–96.

After the outbreak of this war in 1899, Beyers joined the Republican forces again. He participated in all the more important battles on the Natal front. In March 1900 Beyers was elected as an assistant field cornet. His valour and determined action during the field battles east of Pretoria in the months that followed even drew the attention of Commandant-General Louis Botha. In September 1900 Botha appointed him assistant general of the districts Waterberg and Soutpansberg. At the end of that year he participated with distinction in the Battle of Nooitgedacht.

From the beginning of last year Beyers and his men were involved in a continuous battle with the enemy in the far north of the Transvaal. When the meeting of Boer deputies began their negotiations here at Vereeniging on 15 May, he was elected chairman of the meeting. That is a good indication of the stature that Beyers enjoys in the Boer ranks.

General C.F. Beyers

THE

War Reporter

MONTHLY EDITION

Number 66 | **Pretoria, Transvaal Colony** | **1 July 1902**

THE BITTER SURRENDER

Pretoria, 30 June – The 10 Republican deputies arrived in Pretoria late on the evening of 31 May to sign the peace treaty. They immediately proceeded to Lord Kitchener's headquarters, Melrose House, where they met both Kitchener and Lord Milner. In the dining room, starting at five past eleven, one by one they made their signatures on the two copies of the peace treaty. Milner was the last to sign, and Kitchener afterwards declared: 'We are good friends now!' His remark was ignored by the Boers.

Chief Commandant Christiaan de Wet told our reporter that it was bitter to sign the treaty, but they could do nothing else. It had been even more bitter when they decided earlier that afternoon that the document had to be signed, but neither could they do anything else then. 'The way to keep on fighting,' De Wet said, 'would lead to a pitch dark night. To go on with the struggle, after everything is said and done, could not be considered, since our women and children will be decimated.'

Later this month, De Wet told our correspondent in Bloemfontein that the surrender of the burghers was even more bitter to him than signing the peace treaty. He had been accompanied by a British general to various places to receive the burghers' weapons: 'On 5 June the first commando laid down their arms near Vredefort. It was a bitter moment for me and for each burgher to give our valuable independence away like that. I have often stood at the deathbed or at the funeral of people who had been dear to me; my father, my mother, friend – but never had I experienced the pain that can be compared to what I had to witness at the funeral of my people.'

Most of the Bitter-enders proceeded to designated places all across the former Republics and the Cape Colony for organised ceremonies to lay down their arms. These were always touching events. General Kemp says that the western Transvaal burghers gathered on a hillock behind the burnt-out house on the farm Doornkom, at an old stone kraal. 'They had already heard that there was peace, but now they had to hear the painful news that independence had to be given away. It was shattering news. Tears ran down the sunburnt cheeks of many a burgher and indescribable sadness took hold of every heart. Ancient grey beards and youngsters with beardless faces sobbed and cried when they had to put their weapons down at the foot of the hillock at the request of General De la Rey. When General Walter Kitchener arrived there the next day, General De la Rey gave him an order: 'Here are my burghers who loyally served their country and their people up to the end. Today they are orphans and as such I hand them over to you.'

In the eastern Transvaal the burghers of General Muller's commando gathered near Middelburg. They were still hoping that everything had gone well, since they had heard that there was peace. When Muller arrived, they could immediately see on his face that something was wrong. It was Muller's task to inform them that independence had been lost. There were tears in the eyes of many a burgher when they were told to lay down their arms. Many broke their rifles against rocks and threw their cartridges into the air. Of course, not all the burghers had to hand in their arms, since the farmers in the border districts could apply for permits and keep their rifles for self-defence.

Melrose House, where the peace treaty was signed

After General Muller's commando laid down their arms, it was the turn of Lieutenant Colonel Trichard's commando. Trichard assured the Khaki officer who was present that there was now peace between Boer and Brit, but requested him to keep all joiners and handsuppers out of their way, since there might be a murder if any of them were to arrive. The officer promised to arrange matters in that way. The Khakis in the meantime made tents available in which the Bitter-enders could temporarily find shelter.

The next day the ladies of Middelburg treated them to a splendid dinner. For the Bitter-enders it was wonderful to sit back and enjoy a hearty meal that was stylishly prepared. Trichard thanked the ladies on behalf of his men and at the same time declared that if there was a handsupper present, he had better go, since they did not want any dissonance at their festive dinner. There actually was a joiner present, who decided to ignore Trichard. The burghers quickly removed him, and he can be glad that he got away without any physical injury. The joiner immediately went to the Khaki officer to complain about his treatment, but found no sympathy there. It is notable that the ladies of Middelburg have only respect for the Bitter-enders, and even treat the wives of the handsuppers with contempt.

In the Cape midlands, Commandant Fouchee was still active when he was called to Cradock by General Smuts on 2 June to be informed about the peace. From that town Fouchee returned to his commando to inform them that they had to lay down their arms. His reception was stormy and he was accused of treason. Fouchee, who had not yet completely recovered after he was wounded in February, reacted by baring his chest and challenging anyone who believed that he was a traitor to shoot him.

On 4 June, Fouchee led his commando under Khaki escort into Cradock for the surrender of arms. After formally placing their rifles on the ground, the burghers formed two rows. On the one side there were 30 Free Staters, who were allowed to each take a horse, a saddle and stirrups with them as they walked away as free men. On the other side there were 73 Cape Rebels, who were marched away to the jail through the streets of Cradock under a strong escort. There they were locked up.

Four days later, on Sunday 8 June, Fouchee was in Aliwal North, where the rest of his commando officially surrendered. Commandants Odendaal and Bezuidenhout led the commando to the market square for the ceremony. Here too the Free Staters, 25 of them, and the Cape Rebels, 107 of them, formed separate rows. It was a sombre ceremony. Here also the Free Staters were allowed to keep their horses, saddles and stirrups, while the rebels were locked up in jail.

Many burghers are not sure what they should do, now that they have surrendered their arms. Some are immediately returning to their destroyed farms. Others whose loved ones are in the concentration camps, hasten to be reunited with them.

The reunification has so far been a wonderful experience for those who could actually find their family members, but often tempered by sad news about loved ones who are no longer alive. In a few cases, burghers have arrived at the camps to find that there were no loved ones left to greet them. All that was left to show to them was the graves – hundreds, if not thousands of them at each concentration camp. And on most of the graves a tombstone consisting of a piece of slate on which the next of kin scraped the name, birth date and day of death of the wretched victims of a war they did not want.

FROM THE EDITOR

This will be our last issue, since the war, mercifully, has ended. It is to be hoped that the destruction brought about by the Khakis and their henchmen, including tens of thousands of black South Africans and a few thousand former burghers, will now end. Looking back at the traumatic events of the past 32 months, one might ask if President Kruger and his government were wrong when they entered this war against Britain in October 1899. After all, despite all their sacrifices, the Boers have lost both the war and their freedom. Statistics on the destruction that accompanied this war are published elsewhere in this issue.

A much higher price than the loss of property that both the farmers and the town-dwellers suffered is the terrible loss of life – especially of women and children in the concentration camps. There is hardly a single Boer family that did not lose at least one member as a direct result of the war.

To blame President Kruger for this national disaster would be unjust. Nobody could, when the war broke out, predict that the British would use barbaric war tactics. Kruger's presidential oath of inauguration made it his duty to uphold his country's sovereignty. He would have failed in his duty if he had accepted British supremacy over his Republic at that time. He and his government were left with no option but to take up arms.

The farmers of the former Republics are on their way back to their homesteads – or at least to the ruins of their houses and the wreckage of their former farms. Most of them will have to start all over again to rebuild an existence. Many towns will have to be re-erected from ground level. An even bigger challenge facing the Boers is to re-establish their self-respect after the humiliation of surrendering. The character of a people is determined by the way in which people react to crises. Will the Afrikaner people be derailed by this crisis and be shunted to the rubbish heap of history? Or will the Afrikaner people take up the challenge and re-assert themselves? Only the future will tell.

There are many Boers and Cape Afrikaners who refuse to accept that British supremacy has triumphed in South Africa. They believe there is no future for them or their children in this beautiful country, and plan to move to greener pastures elsewhere in the world. We have news for them: an Afrikaner can only be and remain an Afrikaner in South Africa. By leaving these shores you would be turning your back on your fellow Afrikaners. Moreover you would thereby be playing directly into the hands of Lord Milner and his henchmen, whose outspoken objective it is to destroy Afrikanerdom. Stay here and do your duty.

This war has united Afrikaners all over South Africa to an unequalled degree. That is one of the strongest, most positive results of the war. The thousands of children, women and burghers who perished in this war did not die to support the destructive aims of Milner and his cronies; they sacrificed their lives for the future of the Afrikaner community. It is our duty to honour the memory of those Boer heroes and heroines by jointly building up a new, strong and positive Afrikaner community in this southland where the Master of the fate of nations gave us a home.

REACTION TO THE PEACE TREATY

President Steyn was in Krugersdorp under doctor's treatment when the peace treaty was signed. Jack Brebner, the State Secretary of the (now former) Republic of the Orange Free State, had the bitter task of informing Steyn about the signing. The President's reaction was, as Brebner afterwards related, a bitter exclamation: 'Jack! Oh no, Jack! You have sold the people for three million.' He was, of course, referring to the £3 million that the British government had promised to cover the cost of reconstruction.

Brebner did not want to say more to our correspondent than that the only aspect of the whole peace process that Steyn felt thankful about was that he did not have to sign the treaty. Having promised his burghers at the beginning of the war that he would never place his hand on a piece of paper that would destroy the independence of the Republic of the Orange Free State, he was glad that he received the grace to remain true to his word. As far as he was concerned, the peace treaty was a damnation: he believed that the struggle should have continued.

Lieutenant Colonel Fanie Trichard shared that opinion. He declared quite bluntly that the women and children had suffered poverty, hunger and maltreatment in vain. The burghers in the veld withstood all sorts of difficulties for three years, only to see the sun of their freedom sink below the horizon. Now they would have to return as defeated men to their torched dwellings and their destroyed farms, where they would cry about the lost legacy of their forefathers. The poor prisoners of war who had been waiting so long in distant places for a positive result would probably weep many tears for the loss of the greatest gift that a people can possess, namely their freedom.

Jan F.E Celiers, a member of General Kemp's commando of foot-soldiers, related that he was busy cocking porridge in their laager on the morning of 5 June, when their field cornet suddenly came galloping towards them with a white scarf around his neck. He briefly informed them that peace had been concluded and that they should proceed to Doornkom immediately.

That same afternoon they inspanned their oxen and started their journey. Many burghers fired off a festive salute – blissfully unaware of the terrible news waiting for them. When somebody suggested that evening at the campfire that they were going to Doornkom to surrender, everybody laughed at his 'joke'. It was only when they arrived at their destination the next day that they learned the devastating truth. Celliers says that he was rocked to silence by the news. His head suddenly pained as though he had been hit by a thunderclap.

The commandos in Namaqualand heard on 2 June that peace had been declared, but had to wait until the 14th for General Jan Smuts to arrive there to explain the peace conditions to them. For all of them, both the Republican and Rebel officers, the burghers and the Rebels, the announcement was 'like thunder from a cloudless heaven' as one of them explained.

It was as if the men were all of a sudden paralysed. Many a fellow who had never been afraid of an enemy bullet, began crying like a little child. It was like a message of death in the family. Some just walked into the veld to think on their own and to weep alone.

KRUGER STAYS IN EUROPE, DEVASTATED ABOUT PEACE CONDITIONS

No plans to return to Africa; refuses to accept King Edward as his sovereign

Pretoria, 30 June – President Kruger's private secretary, Manie Bredell, reports that our former president (that is what his official position is) was filled with disbelief when he was informed about the peace conditions. Kruger believes that there must be secret promises that have not been made public and that will make the outcome much better than it seems to be. It is clear that he was shocked that the independence of the Republics has come to an end, but his reaction as a deeply religious person is: 'The Lord will rise in His time. He will neither abandon nor forsake us.'

Kruger clearly stated in February, when the Dutch Prime Minister offered his services as mediator, that the independence of the Republics is not negotiable. However, he was plagued by anxiety about the situation in the Republics themselves. What especially concerned him was that joiners such as the former general Andries Cronjé had begun fighting against their own people. As for the concentration camps, the President asked indignantly: 'How can one regard it in any other way than that the concentration camps were established with the sole purpose of exterminating our nation?' On another occasion Kruger remarked that he never thought that the British would conduct the war in such a barbarous way.

On 11 March Kruger was delighted when he heard the news that General De la Rey had defeated Lord Methuen at Tweebosch. Bredell reports that the President was already in bed when the telegrams arrived that evening. He woke Kruger up and read the telegrams to him. His delight about De la Rey's glorious victory was written in large letters on Kruger's face, Bredell relates.

Early in April the Republican messengers visited Kruger in Utrecht and brought him encouraging news. The messengers, Commandant F.S. Alleman, Mining Commissioner J.L. van der Merwe, and Lieutenants D. Malan and De Klerk, reached Europe via German South West Africa. They intended to take military and medical supplies back with them by the same route, but nothing came of their plans. Their visit cheered up the President, however.

In the middle of April the newspapers in Holland published news of the peace negotiations at Klerksdorp on a daily basis.

Kruger discussed these developments with the Republican deputation of Messrs Fischer, Wessels and Wolmarans, as well as with Dr Leyds, but they did not attempt to intervene in the process. The President felt that he would be satisfied with a peace that guaranteed our independence, even if we had to concede some sort of suzerainty to Britain, as was done in the Convention of Pretoria in 1881.

In mid-May Kruger remarked that it was possible that the Republican deputies to the peace negotiations would concede our independence if there was a real possibility that our freedom would soon be restored. However he would prefer a peace that guaranteed our independence. Bredell reports that Kruger was greatly disappointed that the Republican deputies never contacted him. In addition, he was utterly in the dark with regard to the progress made with the negotiations at Vereeniging.

Bredell read the stipulations of the peace treaty to Kruger early on the morning of 3 June. He writes that the President listened attentively and every so often uttered a sigh of despondency. His first words were that he could not understand how our people could accept such conditions. It was clear that he was filled with great suffering. The next day he told Bredell that he had no plans to return to Africa, since he could not accept King Edward VII as his sovereign. On 5 June the Mayor of Utrecht, Dr Reiger, visited the President to convey his sympathies. When Reiger enquired how he was, Kruger answered despondently: 'Yes, let me answer as Job did at the time of his great suffering: The Lord gave and the Lord hath taken away, blessed be the name of the Lord.'

THE REACTION OF A BRAVE BOER WOMAN

MRS MARIA FISCHER WRITES FROM A CONCENTRATION CAMP

Vice-President Burger (at the gate) addresses the women in Merebank Camp

Pretoria, 23 June – It is not only the burghers who have mixed feelings with regard to the peace treaty. In the concentration camps women like Mrs Maria Fischer of the Ermelo district are delighted that there is at last peace, but feel that the loss of the independence of both Republics is too high a price. She handed our correspondent in Durban the following extensive report on her response to the peace process as a whole:

'By the end of March numerous rumours regarding peace were making their rounds in the Merebank camp, where I was detained. It was alleged, for example, that General Schalk Burger had concluded an unconditional peace with the enemy. The more I heard of these rumours, the more anxious my heart became. God protect us against surrender, I pleaded. Generally speaking, the women had no appetite for an unfavourable peace.

'The peace rumours and discussions about peace continued unabatedly in April. One rumour was that there would be arbitration. At our religious services the Reverend Van Belkum prayed fervently for peace. By the end of April we heard that an unconditional peace had been concluded. All the rumours of peace left me beside myself. The prospect of peace without freedom was a nightmare.

'At the beginning of May we heard that our vice-president and generals had been in Pretoria to hear what the conditions are. We became increasingly agitated, since nobody could predict what the outcome would be. By the middle of the month we heard that everything was lost for the future. I refused to continue going to the prayer-hour, since it seemed to me as if God was no longer interested about what happened on earth. It became difficult for me to say: *Thy will be done*.

'On 19 May we heard that 30 of our people had been killed by blacks near Vryheid. Two days later even worse news was confirmed. It was 54 men who had been killed by order from on high by blacks and National Scouts. Another two days later a list of the names of the murdered burghers was pinned up in our camp.

'On 25 May people who came to the camp told us that peace had been signed, but nobody knew the terms. We went to see Miss Burger, the daughter of Vice-President Burger, in block 9. She said everything was dark and hopeless. The next day the terrible rumour caused uproar in the camp. It was said that there were armed blacks in the camp and that a commando of black warriors were ready to overrun the women's camp if the Boers refused to make peace. There was fear reflected in the faces of many women and children. A group of women even requested protection from the Commandant. I did not believe that it could be true.

'By the end of May we had no doubt that all was lost. It was however only on 1 June, at seven o'clock in the morning, that Commandant Bousfield informed us officially that peace had been made. I was shocked. What a peace? Victory for England, struggle and slavery for us and for our descendants. I would have chosen the deprivation of the camp with all its terror above such a peace. We are doomed to an existence without hope, without confidence, an impossible future.

'I do not want to see anything, to hear anything. Away, away with everything that reminds me of the past. Everything in me is dead, with no feeling left. Are the words "My God, my God, why hast thou forsaken me?" applicable to us and our children?

'Some of the women refused to accept the peace announcement. They said it was a pack of lies concocted by the English to terrorise us. They are now mocking us about all our prayers and pleading and our faith in a definite salvation. 'Where is your God in whom you trusted?', they ask. We are now in the power of a detestable, lowly enemy who would not hesitate to use black people to reach their objectives. A complete silence has descended on our camp, similar to the silence after a devastating hail storm.'

FAREWELL TO THE VIERKLEUR

Poem by F.W. Reitz, Vereeniging, 31 May 1902

No longer may our Standard wave
And flaunt its colours to the sky,
'Tis buried with our heroes brave
Who on the field of Glory lie.

Oh! happier far were they who fell
Ere yet its tints began to fade
Than we, who loved its passing well,
Yet in the dust have seen it laid

For it there bides no glad to-morrow,
And this Farewell must be our last,
Stained with a Nation's tears of sorrow
We consecrate it to the Past.

To those who bore our flag on high
And dared the haughty foe to face
And who, when death was drawing nigh
Clung to it with a last embrace.

Forever be their story told
As long as there are men at all,
Until the very heavens grow old
And Earth shall totter to her fall!

THE FINAL TOLL: WAR STATISTICS

Not counting some former burghers and Cape Rebels who refuse to recognise the British king as their monarch and who have not surrendered yet, a total of more than 20 000 burghers and 3 000 Colonial Rebels have already laid down their arms. Of those burghers, approximately 11 000 surrendered in the Transvaal, 6 400 in the Free State and 3 600 in the Cape Colony.

As far as we could establish, approximately 4 000 burghers were killed in action in this futile struggle for freedom. A further more than 2 000 burghers died on commando or as prisoners of war as a result of disease or accidents.

There is as yet no reliable list of all the women and children who died in the concentration camps. On trustworthy information, we calculate that more than 27 000 people – the vast majority of them women and children – died in those camps.

As for the burghers who were sent away as prisoners of war, there are at present also no reliable statistics. At this stage we estimate that at the most 26 600 suffered that fate.

To calculate the destruction that occurred as a result of the war is no easy task. It is estimated that approximately 30 000 houses were burnt down. Nobody knows how many smaller buildings suffered the same fate, nor how many sheep, cattle, pigs, horses and other farm animals were killed.

On the Khaki side the early estimates indicate that at least 8 000 men were killed in action and 22 000 died of other war-related causes.

In addition it is estimated that more than 14 000 black people died in concentration camps set up by the British for them.

ACT OF SURRENDER

In terms of the peace agreement all the burghers of the former Republics have to recognise the British King as their monarch.

The British drew up the following statement, which has been signed by most of the former Bitter-enders and some prisoners of war already:

'I … adhere to the terms of the agreement signed at Pretoria on 31 May 1902, between my late Government and the representatives of His Majesty's Government. I acknowledge myself to be a subject of King Edward VII and I promise to own allegiance to him, his heirs, and successors according to law.'

WILL BITTER-ENDERS LEAVE THE COUNTRY?

Since the conclusion of peace, many burghers have indicated that they would rather leave the country than accept the British king as their sovereign, after fighting for such a long time against the Khakis.

One of the people who feel that way is Lieutenant Colonel Trichard. He is no longer a young man, but having served his country all his life, he is convinced that he cannot now accept a new dispensation.

He plans to proceed as quickly as possible to Durban, where his wife is in the concentration camp, and from there to Madagascar. It is a French colony and he hopes that it will be suitable for habitation by Afrikaner Boers.

In the Cape a number of former Boer leaders, including Generals Manie Maritz and Pieter Kritzinger, Commandants Willem Fouchee and Hendrik Lategan, as well as Andries de Wet and the Marquis de Kersauson, refuse to take the oath. According to reports they are on their way to German South West Africa.

Jack Brebner, C.R. de Wet and J.B.M. Hertzog at Vereeniging after the declaration of peace

OUR MILITARY OFFICERS

The Bitter-enders

In addition to the Republican military officers whose careers have already been highlighted in this column in the course of the war, there are dozens of other officers who did their duty up to the bitter end, but who have not really been introduced to our readers. Those who have since died in action or have been incapacitated for whatever reason, except of course voluntary surrender, also deserve our highest praise. Unfortunately, due to lack of space, we can only give attention to the most prominent of those officers in this final edition.

General Jaap van Deventer

Jacob Louis van Deventer was born in Ficksburg in the Orange Free State in 1874. His parents were Christoffel and Johanna van Deventer. He moved to the South African Republic as a young man and joined the State Artillery as a gunner in 1896. He soon rose to the rank of adjutant-officer.

When this war broke out in October 1899, Van Deventer proceeded to the western frontier as a battery commander. He participated in the first battle of the war at Kraaipan and subsequently in the battles on the western border of the Free State from November 1899.

After the British occupation of the Republican capitals, Van Deventer fought under General Christiaan Beyers in the Transvaal. In March 1901 he was promoted to the rank of commandant. A few months later he joined General Smuts's commando for the proposed invasion of the Cape Colony.

After sweeping southwards through the eastern Cape and then up the west coast, he and his men operated mainly in the western Cape, north of Sutherland. He was wounded at least once. At the beginning of this year Smuts promoted him to the rank of fighting general. When the war ended he and his men were still in the veld.

General Chris Muller

Christiaan Hendrik Muller was born at Adelaide in the Cape Colony in 1865, the second son of Thomas Ignatius Muller and his wife Agatha Catharina Ferreira. His parents were farmers. He received some school education, but it was often interrupted when his parents moved, first to the Orange Free State in 1874 and later to the Transvaal.

Soon after the discovery of the main gold reef in 1886, Muller moved to Elsburg on the Witwatersrand. He served on the Elsburg school committee for a lengthy period. His first military campaign was against the freebooters of Jameson in 1896. Two years later he participated in the campaign of the South African Republic against the Venda.

When this war broke out in October 1899, Muller proceeded as an ordinary burgher to the Natal front with the Boksburg Commando. He was soon elected as chief corporal and took part in the battles at Modderspruit, Colenso and Spioenkop. In May 1900 he was elected as field cornet.

Back in the Transvaal, Muller took part in the battles of Donkerhoek and Bergendal, amongst others. In October 1900 he was elected as commandant and two months later as assistant fighting general. In December he achieved instant fame when he led the Boer forces that captured a huge British naval gun known as the Lady Roberts.

After the capture of General Ben Viljoen in January 1902, Muller was appointed Assistant Commandant-General. He was one of the Boer representatives at Vereeniging, where he voted in favour of peace.

General Jan Celliers

Johannes Gerhardus Celliers was born in Fraserburg in the Cape Colony in 1861. He is the son of Jacob Daniël Celliers and his wife Johanna Elizabeth Kruger. As a young man he settled in Zeerust in the western Transvaal, where he became a clerk. In 1880–81 he participated in the Transvaal War of Independence. Immediately afterwards he became involved in the establishment of the Republic Land Goosen. After the collapse of that venture he farmed in the Marico district. After the discovery of the gold reef in 1886 he moved to the Witwatersrand.

When this war broke out in October 1899, Celliers proceeded to the Natal front with the Krugersdorp Police. After participating in fighting on the Natal front, he served in the northern Cape. After the start of the British invasion of the Republics, he became well known for his leadership abilities. When General Manie Lemmer was killed in December 1900, Celliers succeeded him as commander of the Lichtenburg and Marico Commandos.

Celliers and his burghers spent the last 17 months of the war fighting under the overall command of General Koos de la Rey. He played a leading role in the battles of Yzerspruit, Tweebosch and Roodewal. He was present at the peace negotiations at Vereeniging, and pleaded for continuation of the war, but in the end voted in favour of peace.

General Manie Maritz

Solomon Gerhardus Maritz was born in Kimberley in the Cape Colony in 1876. He is the eldest son of Johannes Stephanus Maritz and his wife Anna Coetzee and is a direct descendant of the Voortrekker leader Gerrit Maritz. Soon after moving to Johannesburg, he was awarded citizenship of the South African

Republic as a reward for his voluntary service in the campaign against Jameson's freebooters. He subsequently joined the South African Republic Police (ZARPs) and served in Johannesburg and Boksburg.

After the outbreak of the war in October 1899, he served as burgher on various fronts. Early in 1901 he was a member of Chief Commandant De Wet's commando that invaded the Cape Colony. He subsequently served there under Commandant Wynand Malan, who sent him to the northwestern Cape in March 1901 to assist the Cape Rebels to organise an uprising.

In May 1901 he was elected commandant of all the Republican forces in that area.

In January 1902 General Smuts promoted him to the rank of general. He subsequently campaigned with Smuts and was involved in the siege of Okiep. He and his men were busy moving towards the southwestern Cape again when they heard that the war had ended.

General Wessel Wessels

Wessel Jacobus Wessels was born in about 1865 in the Orange Free State and grew up in the Harrismith district. His parents were Hermanus Nicolaas Wessels and his wife Johanna Wilhelmina Elizabeth Catharina Wessels.

When the war broke out in October 1899, Wessels proceeded to the Natal front with the Harrismith Commando as an ordinary burgher. Later on he fought under Chief Commandant Prinsloo in the Orange Free State, but when Prinsloo surrendered to the enemy in the Brandwater Basin in July 1900, he managed to escape.

Wessels was soon afterwards appointed as Commandant of the Harrismith Commando. In February 1901 he took part in Chief Commandant De Wet's attempt to invade the Cape Colony. A month later De Wet appointed him as one of the seven assistant chief commandants of the Orange Free State, specifically for the Vrede district.

In the course of the last year of the war Wessels was involved in numerous clashes with the enemy forces. He raided enemy units on a number of occasions, and successfully avoided the massive British drive movements of February 1902. Guerrilla warfare seemed to bring out the best in his military talents and he became one of De Wet's stalwarts.

Wessels attended the peace conference at Vereeniging in May 1902, and voted in favour of peace.

General Stoffel Badenhorst

Christoffel Cornelius Jacobus Badenhorst was born at Biesjesfontein in the Boshof district of the Orange Free State in 1871. His parents were Hendrik Johannes Badenhorst and his wife Magdalena Petronella Susanna Catharina van der Merwe. He received basic education at a farm school. From 1893 he farmed with cattle on his father's farm, but he lost virtually all his stock in the rinderpest epidemic of 1896.

At the outbreak of this war in October 1899 Badenhorst joined the Boshof Commando. He participated in the siege of Kimberley and subsequently in all the major battles on the western border of the Orange Free State in November and December. By March 1900 he had been promoted to the rank of field cornet.

After the British occupation of Boshof, Badenhorst joined the forces of Chief Commandant de Wet. He escaped with De Wet from the Brandwater Basin in July 1900, and joined him on his epic journey through the Transvaal. De Wet appointed him as commandant at about this time.

In April 1901 he was promoted to the rank of assistant chief commandant of the northeast Free State. He remained active in that area until the bitter end.

Badenhorst attended the peace conference at Vereeniging as a Free State deputy. He was one of the six burghers who voted against the peace.

Badenhorst is married to Catharina Maria Magdalena du Plessis.

War Reporter has no photograph of this able officer.

General Georg Brand

Georg Alfred Brand was born in Bloemfontein in 1875. He was the youngest son of the celebrated Orange Free State President, Johannes Henricus Brand, and his wife Johanna Sibella Zastron. He was educated in Bloemfontein at Grey College and in Cape Town at the South African College.

He joined the Civil Service of the Orange Free State and when the war broke out in October 1899 he was the public prosecutor in Frankfort. He joined the Frankfort–Vrede Commando and served on the Natal front. After the battle of Spioenkop he was transferred to the western front.

In December 1900 Brand participated in General Hertzog's invasion of the Cape Colony. He subsequently participated with distinction in a number of engagements, including Chief Commandant Christiaan de Wet's successful attack on a British unit at Groenkop in December 1901. Last month he attended the peace conference at Vereeniging. He was against the prolongation of the war.

Brand is not married.

General Lodewyk Lemmer

Lodewikus Arnoldus Stabbert Lemmer was born in 1864 on the farm Buffelshoek in the Klein Marico ward of the Marico district in the Western Transvaal. His father was Petrus Johannes Lemmer, who was killed in action near Zeerust in November 1900.

Lemmer himself studied at Stellenbosch in the Cape Colony before the war. After his return he became a teacher, but soon resigned to become the magistrate and collector of revenue of the Marico districts. He was 35 when the war broke

out and immediately joined the Marico Commando. He participated in the siege of Mafeking. Subsequently he took part in the Battle of Donkerhoek on 11 and 12 June as well as the Battle of Silkaatsnek a month later.

In January 1901 the Marico burghers elected Lemmer to the position of assistant fighting general.

He participated in the battles of Yzerspruit, Tweebosch and Roodewal as leader of the Marico horse commando. He gained the reputation of being a fearless leader who always accompanied his burghers into action.

General Hans Grobler

Johannes Nicolaas H. Grobler was born in the Lydenburg district in 1864. He moved to the Ermelo district with his parents. In 1891 he was elected as assistant field cornet, three years later as field cornet, and in 1899 as commandant of the Ermelo district.

When this war broke out later that same year, Grobler promptly led his men into Natal. He participated with his men in the battles of Talana, Modderspruit, Colenso, Spioenkop and the Upper Tugela, between October 1899 and February 1900, and gained the reputation of being a trustworthy officer.

After the British breakthrough in Natal, Grobler and his commando were transferred to the Orange Free State, where they participated in the attempts to halt the British offensive. After the British occupation of Pretoria he participated in the Battle of Donkerhoek and later on in the Battle of Bergendal (Dalmanutha). In November 1900 he was wounded in the battle at Witkloof. Fortunately he soon recovered.

Grobler and his men participated in Commandant General Louis Botha's second invasion of Natal in September 1901. In October 1901 he was appointed as fighting general. In the last few months of the war Grobler and his commando were involved in numerous skirmishes with the enemy. He himself was a deputy at the peace negotiations at Vereeniging, and voted in favour of acceptance of the treaty.

General Sarel du Toit

Sarel Petrus du Toit was born at Prince Albert in the Cape Colony in 1864. His parents were Sarel Petrus du Toit and his wife Lydia Magdalena Smit. He moved to the Transvaal, where he became a farmer in the Wolmaransstad district. In 1896 he was elected to the First Volksraad of the

South African Republic.

When this war broke out in October 1899, General Piet Cronjé appointed Du Toit as assistant general for the districts Wolmaransstad, Bloemhof and Lichtenburg. He participated in the siege of Kimberley, where he was at one stage in command of the Republican forces.

After the British relief of Kimberley in February 1900, Du Toit was placed in command of the Republican forces guarding the Vaal River crossing at Veertienstrome. Early in May, his forces were driven back by the British forces. Immediately after the British occupation of Pretoria he was present at the war council meeting that decided to go on with the war.

Du Toit subsequently took part in the Battle of Donkerhoek. After the battle, when the whole Transvaal military establishment was reorganised at the war council meeting at Balmoral, he lost his general command. However, he was soon reinstated by General De la Rey and became active in the western Transvaal.

Du Toit attended the Vereeniging peace conference in May as a deputy, and voted in favour of acceptance of the peace treaty.

Du Toit is married to Louisa Hosen and they have a number of children.

General Piet Viljoen

Piet Retief Viljoen is a grandson of the famous Great Trek leader whose name he inherited. He was born in 1853. We have no information with regard to his childhood and youth. He took part in the Transvaal War of Independence of 1880–81 as the adjutant of Commandant-General Piet Joubert. In addition he served in a number of campaigns of the South African Republic against rebellious black communities.

Viljoen was appointed as mining commissioner in Heidelberg in 1887, and kept that position up to the outbreak of this war in 1899. When the war started he was ordered to Natal to serve on the staff of the Commandant-General once again. After Joubert's death he was appointed as magistrate of Potchefstroom. Soon afterwards he was appointed to the rank of fighting general.

When General Andries Cronjé surrendered Potchefstroom to the British forces in June 1900, Viljoen managed to slip away with about 30 Cape Rebels. He eventually reached Heidelberg, where he was unanimously elected as fighting general of the Heidelberg Commando. This famous commando was involved in numerous skirmishes with the enemy under Viljoen's leadership.

Soon after the Battle of Bergendal (Dalmanutha), Viljoen was appointed as chairman of the military court in Barberton. When that area was occupied by British forces, he slipped away and returned to Heidelberg, where he quickly gathered a new commando of about 300 men. He served under General Spruyt at that time. He was wounded in the clash at Chrissiesmeer in February 1901 but recovered and was sworn in as a member of the Executive Council of the Transvaal Republic. He succeeded the late General Spruyt as commanding general of the Heidelbergers and participated in the Vereeniging Peace Conference in that capacity. He voted in favour of peace.

Commandant Hendrik Lategan

Hendrik Willem Lategan was born in 1858 in the Colesberg district in the Cape Colony. His parents were Jan Stefanus Lategan and his wife Hester Maria Catharina Oosthuizen. He became a respected and wealthy farmer in the Colesberg district before the outbreak of the war.

When this war broke out in October 1899, Lategan's sympathy was with the Republics. When the Free State forces invaded the northeastern Cape in November 1899, Lategan joined them. He soon gathered a commando of about 400 Cape Rebels, and was elected by them as their Commandant. They fought in numerous encounters with the British forces, and later on fell back with the Boer forces when the enemy invaded the Republics.

Lategan participated in De Wet's invasion of the Cape Colony, but subsequently acted independently with his rebel commando. They continuously clashed with British units in the Colesberg, Philipstown, Richmond, Graaff-Reinet and Beaufort-West districts and managed to hold out until the end of the war.

Commandant Ben Bouwer

Barend Daniël Bouwer was born in 1875 in Damaraland – a territory that Germany annexed as German South West Africa in 1884. His parents are Barend Daniël Bouwer, an elephant hunter, and his wife Hester. They later moved to the Portuguese colony of Angola, where Bouwer attended school at Moçamedes. After moving with his parents to the South African Republic, he attended school in Pretoria.

Bouwer subsequently became a clerk in the office of the Commandant-General in Pretoria. He participated in a number of campaigns against black communities and also in the capture of Jameson and his freebooters early in 1896. He gave evidence against Jameson during the latter's trial in London in 1897. After his return to the Transvaal he joined the office of the State Attorney as a clerk.

Bouwer was stationed in Ermelo in the southeastern Transvaal when the war broke out in October 1899. He joined the Ermelo Commando and took part in the Boer invasion of Natal, participating in numerous battles on that front. Later on he fought in the Orange Free State and in the Transvaal.

After being promoted to the rank of commandant, he participated in General Jan Smuts's invasion of the Cape Colony from September 1901. He was involved in numerous clashes, including the siege of Okiep in April this year. He was wounded several times, but recovered and was still in the veld when the war ended.

Commandant Pieter Steenekamp

Pieter Stefanus Steenekamp was born in the Potchefstroom district in 1845. His parents were Jacobus Christoffel Steenekamp and his wife Fransina Magdalena Johanna Basson, who eventually settled on the farm Naauwpoort, in the Rustenburg district. He still lives on that farm. He is married to Maria Elizabeth Dorothea Breitenbach. They do not have children.

Steenekamp became a well-known figure in the Rustenburg district. In 1890 he was elected field cornet of the Hoogeveld ward. When the war broke out in October 1899, he accompanied the Rustenburg Commando to the western frontier, where they participated in the siege of Mafeking. At this stage he was promoted to the rank of commandant. He served in that capacity for the remainder of the war and stayed in the veld till the bitter end.

His commanders, Generals De la Rey and Kemp, could always rely on this trusted officer.

Commandant Chris van Niekerk

Christiaan Andries van Niekerk was born in the Heilbron district of the Orange Free State in 1874. His parents are Adriaan Erasmus van Niekerk and his wife Margaretha Wilhelmina Smit. He grew up on a farm but received a thorough education. When he was 18 he went to the Cape Colony to further his studies, first in Wellington and then in Stellenbosch, but his ambition to become a minister in the church was disrupted by the outbreak of the war in October 1899.

Van Niekerk immediately returned to the Free State and joined the Kroonstad Commando. He and his fellow burghers proceeded to the Natal front, where he was wounded in the clash at Rietfontein on 24 October. After his recovery he returned to the front where he participated in numerous military operations and battles, including the Battle of Sannaspos and the raid on Roodewal. In April 1900 he became the acting commandant and in January 1901 the commandant of the Vredefort Commando. He served with distinction in that capacity up to the end of hostilities.

Van Niekerk attended the peace negotiations at Vereeniging. He was one of the six deputies who voted against the acceptance of the peace treaty.

Commandant Edwin Conroy

Edwin Alfred Conroy was born in 1879 in Hanover in the Cape Colony, the fourth child of James Conroy and his wife Johanna Carolina Stahl. He received little formal schooling and as a child worked in his father's shop in Britstown, which is also in the Cape Colony.

In 1895 he temporarily moved to Johannesburg where he worked in various capacities. By the time the war broke out in 1899 he was back in Britstown. He was known as an outspoken supporter of the Boer Republics.

In December 1900, when General Hertzog's Free State commando temporarily occupied Britstown, he joined their forces. He accompanied them all the way to Lambert's Bay on the western Cape coast and was there promoted to the rank of corporal. Two months later he was promoted yet again, this time to the rank of field cornet.

Hertzog's commando returned to the Free State in February last year. Conroy was then appointed to President Steyn's bodyguard. Subsequently Chief Commandant De Wet promoted him to the rank of commandant and appointed him as the leader of the Cape Rebel forces at Kakamas.

Conroy became famous for his fearless attacks on British forces wherever he encountered them.

He is a sturdily built and powerful young man of only 22. His unequalled bravery and commitment served as an inspiration for many Cape Afrikaners to become active supporters of the Republican cause.

Captain Jack Hindon

Oliver John Hindon was born in Scotland in 1874. We do not know who his parents were. He joined the British army at a young age and came to South Africa to serve in Zululand, but soon deserted and made his way to the South African Republic, where he became a bricklayer.

After participating in the campaign against Jameson's freebooters in 1895–96, Hindon was granted citizenship of the Republic. Soon afterwards he joined the South African Republic Police in Middelburg. When the war broke out in October 1899, he accompanied the Police to the Natal front. He participated in a number of battles and gained considerable fame when he, Henri Slegtkamp and Hans de Roos hoisted a Republican flag in defiance of an enemy attack at Tabanyama in January 1900.

In the course of the next year Hindon became a well-known scout, initially in Commandant Danie Theron's corps. In October 1900 he was promoted to the rank of Captain and organised his own corps, which concentrated on sabotaging railway lines and capturing enemy trains. His successes in this regard severely disrupted the British war effort. However, his own participation in these activities was ended when he contracted fever shortly before peace was concluded. He was never caught and can truly be regarded as a Bitter-ender.

Captain J.J. Naudé

The only noteworthy Boer officer on whom we never reported is Jacobus Johannes Naudé. The reason why we did not reveal his activities was that he was a Boer spy who often undertook secret operations. Our readers will appreciate that it would have been lunacy to reveal any information on him.

Naudé was born at Smithfield in the Orange Free State in 1876. His parents were Burgert Adriaan Naudé and his wife Hester Cecilia van den Berg. He moved with his parents as a young boy first to Johannesburg and subsequently to Rustenburg. He received basic school education but became a farmer.

Naudé gained some military experience before the war in the campaign of the South African Republic against the Hananwa in 1894 and in the actions against Jameson's freebooters at the end of 1895. He subsequently moved to Pretoria where he worked and furthered his studies.

When the war broke out in 1899 Naudé went to the Natal front, where he worked in the ambulance section. He missed the first few engagements, but later on fought in the clash at Willow Grange and in the Battle of Colenso in November–December 1899. He later on served in the Orange Free State.

On the eve of the British occupation of Pretoria in June 1900, General Louis Botha requested Naudé to become a spy in Pretoria. He regularly smuggled information such as railway timetables from the city and was assisted in his endeavours by a circle of mainly Afrikaner women, including Mrs Hendrina Joubert, the wife of our late Commandant-General, and Miss Johanna van Warmelo. It was an extremely dangerous occupation, especially after the names of some of the members of the ring were revealed to the British by traitors. Naudé moreover often wore a British officer's uniform, even though he can hardly speak English. Fortunately he was never captured, even though the British authorities offered a sum of £2 000 for information leading to his arrest.

Naudé is married to Isabella Fredericka Scholtz.

Bibliography

The numbers in brackets which appear at the end of each entry refer to the issues of *The War Reporter* in which they were utilised.

Amery, L.S., *The Times History of the War in South Africa, 1899–1902.* 7 volumes. London: Sampson Low, 1900-1909. (1-66)

Andriessen, W.F., *Gedenkboek van den Oorlog in Zuid-Afrika.* HAUM, Amsterdam & Cape Town, 1904. (1-11, 13, 14, 16, 18-23, 25, 26, 30, 32, 35, 36, 40, 41, 43-45, 47-50, 53-58, 60-66)

Badenhorst, A., *Tant Alie van Transvaal. Die Dagboek van Alie Badenhorst.* Translated from the original Dutch by M.E. Rothmann. Nasionale Pers, Cape Town, Bloemfontein & Port Elizabeth, 1939. Translated into English as *Tant' Alie of the Transvaal, Her Diary 1880–1902*, by Emily Hobhouse. London: George Allen and Unwin, 1923. (12, 17, 29, 41)

Bakkes, C.M., *Die Britse Deurbraak aan die Benede-Tugela op Majubadag 1900.* Pretoria: Government Printer, 1973. (17, 21)

Barnard, C.J., *Generaal Louis Botha op die Natalse Front, 1899-1900.* Cape Town: A.A. Balkema, 1970. (2, 4-11, 15, 16, 18-22, 25-27)

Barnard, C.J., Grepe uit die Krygskuns van die Boeregeneraals, *Historia* 19/1, May 1974, 2-19. (36, 48)

Barnard, C.J., *Die Vyf Swemmers. Die Ontsnapping van Willie Steyn en Vier Medekrygsgevangenes uit Ceylon 1901.* Cape Town: Tafelberg, 1988. (61)

Basson, J.L., Die Slag van Paardeberg. Unpublished M.A. dissertation, University of Pretoria, 1971. (18, 19, 20, 21)

Benbow, C.H., *Boer Prisoners of War in Bermuda.* Bermuda: Hamilton, 1962. (59)

Blake, J.Y.F., *A West Pointer with the Boers.* Boston: Angel Guardian Press, 1903. (12, 31, 59)

Blom, C.J., Die Wedervaringe van 'n Oud-onderwyser Tydens die Tweede Vryheidsoorlog, 1899-1902, III, *Historia* 8/4, December 1963, 293-97. (16)

Botha, H.J., Die Moord op Derdepoort, 25 November 1899, Nie-Blankes in Oorlogsdiens, *Militaria* 1/2, 1969, 2-98. (8,12)

Botha, J.P., Die Beleg van Mafeking Tydens die Anglo-Boereoorlog. Unpublished D. Litt et Phil thesis, Unisa, 1967. (1, 2, 3, 5, 12, 27, 32)

Brandt, J., *Die Kappie Kommando of Boerevrouwen in Geheime Dienst.* 2nd ed. Hollandsch-Afrikaansche Uitgevers-Maatschappij, Cape Town, 1915. Translated into English as *The Petticoat Commando, or Boer Women in Secret Service.* London: Mills and Boon, 1913. (35)

Bredell, H.C., *Dagboek van H.C. Bredell, 1900-1904.* Edited and annotated by A.G. Oberholster. Pretoria: HSRC, 1972. (47, 52, 66)

Breytenbach, J.H., *Die Geskiedenis van die Tweede Vryheidsoorlog in Suid-Afrika, 1899-1902.* 6 volumes. Pretoria: Government Printer, 1969-1983. (1-44)

Breytenbach, J.H., Die Oorgawe van Generaal P. A. Cronjé, *Historiese Studies*, 3/1, January 1942, 42-44. (21)

Breytenbach, J.H. (ed.), *Gedenkalbum van die Tweede Vryheidsoorlog,* Cape Town: Nasionale Pers, 1949. (1-4, 10, 13, 15, 17, 19-21, 24, 26, 33, 36, 38, 40, 44, 45, 47-51, 53, 56-59, 61-66)

Brink, J.N., *Recollections of a Boer Prisoner-of-War at Ceylon.* Amsterdam & Cape Town: Hollandsch-Afrikaansche Uitgevers-Maatschappij, 1904. (49, 61)

Brits, J.P., Die Slag van Doornkraal – toe De Wet se Manskappe nie wou Veg nie, *Historia* 15/3, September 1970, 192-96. (47)

Buitengewone Staatscourant der Zuid-Afrikaansche Republiek, Machadodorp 7 Juni – Nelspruit 5 September 1900 (Deel XX, no1121-1147) benevens de Ambtelijke Oorlogsberichten, Telegrammen, Circulaire-telegrammen, Gouvernements-kennisgevingen, Proclamatien enz. uitgevaardigd tusschen 9 Juni 1900 en 10 September 1900. (36-44)

Burger, S.J., *Oorlogsjoernaal van S.J. Burger 1899-1902.* Edited and annotated by T. van Rensburg. Pretoria: HSRC, 1977. (13, 33)

Buys, M.H., Militêre Regering in Transvaal, 1900-1902. Unpublished D.Phil thesis, University of Pretoria, 1972. (34, 35, 38, 40, 41, 44, 46, 49)

Carver, Lord, *The National Army Museum Book of the Boer War.* London: Sidgwick & Jackson, in association with the National Army Museum, 1999. (21)

Celliers, J.F.E., *Oorlogsdagboek van Jan F.E. Celliers 1899-1902.* Edited and annotated by A.G. Oberholster. Pretoria: HSRC, 1978. (19, 23, 24, 29, 46, 57, 60, 66)

Changuion, L., *Uncle Sam, Oom Paul en John Bull. Amerika en die Anglo-Boereoorlog 1899-1902.* Pretoria: Protea Book House, 2001. (33, 39, 61)

Changuion, L., *Silence of the Guns. The History of the Long Toms of the Anglo-Boer War.* Pretoria: Protea Book House, 2001. (1, 3-6, 9, 10, 12, 14, 18, 21, 32-37, 44, 45, 52, 53, 59)

Cilliers, J.H., *Die Slag van Spioenkop (24 Januarie 1900).* Archives Year Book of South African History 23/2. Elsies River: Government Printer, 1960. (16)

Cloete, B, *Die Lewe van Senator F.S. Malan (President van die Senaat).* Johannesburg: Afrikaanse Pers-Boekhandel, 1946. (48)

Cloete, P.G., *The Anglo-Boer War: A Chronology.* Pretoria: J.P. van der Walt, 2000. (1-66)

Coetzer, A. *et al, Generaal Hertzog in Beeld*, Johannesburg-Cape Town: Perskor, 1991. (46)

Coetzer, O., *Fire in the Sky. The Destruction of the Orange Free State 1899-1902.* Weltevreden Park: Covos-Day Books, 2000. (1, 14, 47, 49, 51, 53, 55, 59, 60)

Conradie, F.D., *Met Cronjé aan die Wesfront (1899-1902) en Waarom het die Boere die Oorlog Verloor*? Cape Town: Nasionale Pers, 1943. (1, 10, 18, 19, 21, 28)

Davey, A. (ed.), *Breaker Morant and the Bushveldt Carbineers.* Cape Town: Van Riebeeck Society Series, 1987. (59, 61, 62)

Davidson, A. & Filatova, I., The Russian Boer General, *Historia* 40/2, November 1995, 20-38. (30)

De Jager, M.J., *Gedenkboek van M.J. de Jager. Boerekryger, Staatsartilleris en Militêr.* Edited, translated and annotated by A.P. Smit. Pretoria: Protea Book House, 2000. (36)

De Jong, C., Die Teregstelling van Piet Schuil, *Historia* 22/1, May 1977, 47-52. (58)

De Jong, C., Lotgevallen van drie broers Douwes Dekker in de Anglo-Boerenoorlog, III: Guido M.G. Douwes Dekker, 1883-1959, *Historia* 28/2, September 1983, 14-26. (44)

De Kersauson de Pennendreff, R., *Ek en die Vierkleur.* Johannesburg-Cape Town: Afrikaanse Pers-Boekhandel, n.d. (47-50, 52, 64-66)

De la Rey, J.E., *Mijne Omzwervingen en Beproevingen Gedurende den Oorlog. Herinneringe van Mevrouw de la Rey,* Amsterdam: Höveker & Wormser, 1903. (Translated into English and published as *A Woman's Wanderings and Trials during the Anglo-Boer War,* London, 1903). (63)

De la Rey, J.H. *et al., Ambtelijke Verslagen van Generaal J.H. de la Rey en Generaal J.C. Smuts, Alsook Andere Stukken Betreffende den Oorlog in Zuid Afrika, Kort Geleden Ontvangen door de Boerenvertegenwoordigers in Europa, en met hun Toestemming Openbaar Gemaakt.* Uitgegeven door Algemeen Nederlandsch Verbond No 7. Amsterdam: J.H. de Bussy, n.d. (56, 57, 58)

De Oorlog in Zuid-Afrika. N.J. Boon, Amsterdam (periodical publication), 1899, 1900, 1901. (3, 10, 16, 19, 21, 26, 48)

De Wet, Christiaan Rudolf, *De Strijd tusschen Boer en Brit.* Amsterdam: Höveker & Wormser, 1902. (Translated into English and published as *Three Years' War.* New York, Scribner's Sons, 1902; translated into Afrikaans as *Die Stryd tussen Boer en Brit. Die Herinneringe van die Boere-Generaal C.R. de Wet,* and annotated by M.C.E. van Schoor. Cape Town: Tafelberg, 1999. (1, 3, 4, 18-24, 26, 27, 29–51, 53, 54, 56, 59, 60, 62-66)

Dominy, G., 'Spoiling his paint': A Chronicle of Anglo-Boer Naval Clashes, 1901-1902, *Historia* 37/1, May 1992, 55-75. (49, 58, 61)

Douwes Dekker, E., Selekats-nek. Episode uit den Vrijheidsoorlog in Zuid-Afrika, *Historia* 24/2, September 1979, 40-43. (40)

Doyle, A.C., *The Great Boer War.* London: Smith, Elder, 1900. (1-4, 7, 8, 10, 14, 16, 18, 19, 24, 32, 35, 44, 45)

Du Pisani, J.A., Oorsake van die Anglo-Boereoorlog: is ons al Nader aan 'n Antwoord? *Tydskrif vir Geesteswetenskappe* 39/3 & 4, September & December 1999, 205-215. (63)

Du Plessis, Ph.J., *Oomblikke van Spanning.* Cape Town, Bloemfontein and Port Elizabeth: Nasionale Pers, 1938. (62, 65)

Du Preez, S., Vredespogings Gedurende die Anglo-Boereoorlog tot Maart 1901. Unpublished M.A. dissertation, University of Pretoria, 1976. (24, 29, 34, 35, 46, 50, 51)

Du Toit, P.J., *Diary of a National Scout: P.J. du Toit, 1900-1902.* Edited and annotated by J.P. Brits. Pretoria: Institute for Historical Research, Source Publication 2, 1974. (42, 46)

Ehlers, A., Die Anglo-Boereoorlog as Stimulus vir die Stigting van Afrikaanse Plattelandse Trustmaatskappye en Eksekuteurskamers, *Historia* 45/1, May 2000, 177-198. (34)

Eloff, M., *Die President en Ek. (Herinneringe soos vertel aan Gezina du Plessis).* Cape Town & Johannesburg: Tafelberg, 1971. (34, 46, 47)

Engelenburg, F.V.. *Genl Louis Botha*, Pretoria: J.L. van Schaik, 1928. (9, 10, 11, 16, 36, 50, 63-66)

Engelenburg, F.V. & Preller, G.S., *Onze Krijgs-Officieren. Album van Portretten met Levens-schetsen der Transvaalse Generaals en Kommandanten e.a. Uitgegeven ten* Pretoria: 'Volksstem' Kantore, 1904. (1, 2, 4, 5, 7-9, 11, 13, 16-18, 21, 24-26, 31, 33, 35, 36, 40-43, 45, 47, 48, 51-55, 57, 59, 61, 62, 65, 66)

Ferreira, O.J.O., Boeregeïnterneerdes in Portugal tydens die Anglo-Boereoorlog (1899-1902) en hulle Tydverdrywe, *Historia* 42/2, November 1997, 33-56. (53)

Ferreira, O.J.O., *Viva Os Boers.* Pretoria: O.J.O. Ferreira, 1994. (53)

Ferreira, O.J.O., Portugal en die Anglo-Boereoorlog, *Tydskrif vir Geesteswetenskappe* 39/3 & 4, September & December 1999, 343-363. (45, 46, 53)

Fischer, M.A., *Tant Miem Fischer se Kampdagboek Mei 1901-Augustus 1902.* Tafelberg, 1964. (54, 63, 66)

Fourie, L.M., Die Militêre Loopbaan van Manie Maritz tot aan die Einde van die Anglo-Boereoorlog. Unpublished M.A. dissertation, Potchefstroom University, 1975. (50, 52, 56-61, 63-65)

Greeff, I., Two Victoria Crosses near Krugersdorp, *Historia* 36/2, November 1991, 17-30. (40)

Grobler, J.C.H., Enkele Gedagtes oor die Boere-ultimatum van Oktober 1899, *Tydskrif vir Geesteswetenskappe* 39/3 & 4, September & December 1999, 216-226. (1)

Grobler, M.J., *Met die Vrystaters Onder die Wapen. Generaal Prinsloo en die Bethlehem-Kommando.* Bloemfontein: Nasionale Pers, n.d. (39, 44, 48)

Groenewald, C., *Bannelinge oor die Oseaan: Boerekrygsgevangenes 1899-1902.* Pretoria: J.P. van der Walt, 1992. (39, 49, 51, 53, 59, 62, 64)

Gronum, M.A., *Die Engelse Oorlog 1899-1902. Die Gevegsmetodes Waarmee die Boere-Republieke Verower Is.* Cape Town & Johannesburg: Tafelberg, 1972. (46-48, 51)

Grundlingh, A.M., *Die 'Hendsoppers' en 'Joiners'. Die Rasionaal en Verskynsel van Verraad.* Pretoria: Protea Book House, 1999. (29, 35, 37, 40, 42, 43, 45, 48, 49, 57, 64)

Hale, F., The Scandinavian Corps in the Second Anglo-Boer War, *Historia* 45/1, May 2000, 220-237. (10)

Hancock, W.K. & J. van der Poel (eds), *Selections from the Smuts Papers. Volume I June 1886-May 1902.* Cambridge: Cambridge University Press, 1966. (25, 30, 37, 48, 49, 53, 54, 56, 57, 58, 65, 66)

Hancock, W. K., *Smuts: The Sanguine Years 1870-1919.* Cambridge: Cambridge University Press, 1962. (34, 35, 48, 49, 53-66)

Hattingh, J.L., Die Geval van Meyer de Kock en die Ontstaan van die Konsentrasiekampe Tydens die Anglo-Boereoorlog, 1899-1902, *Historia* 18/3, September 1973, 163-85. (48, 49)

Headlam, C. (ed.), *The Milner Papers. Vol II. South Africa 1899-1905.* London: Cassell, 1933. (1, 24, 32, 37, 48, 49, 50, 64-66)

Heath, I., *Die Rooi Bul van Krugersdorp, Veggeneraal S.F. Oosthuizen, Sy Aandeel in die Verloop van die Anglo-Boere-Oorlog 1899-1900.* Centurion: Isak Heath, 1999. (6, 7, 11, 21, 40)

Hiley, Alan, and Hassel, John A., *The Mobile Boer.* New York: Grafton Press, 1902. (16, 42, 45)

Hillegas, H.C., *With the Boer Forces.* London: Methuen, 1900. (7, 8, 19, 26)

Hobhouse, Emily, *The Brunt of the War and Where it Fell.* London: Methuen, 1902. (49, 51, 53, 63)

Hofmeyr, N., *Zes Maanden by de Commando's.* 's-Gravenhage: W.P. van Stockum & Zoon, 1903. (1, 9, 15, 17, 19)

Hopkins, H.C., *Maar én Soos Hy. Die Lewe van Kommandant C.A. van Niekerk.* Cape Town: Tafelberg, 1963. (1, 3, 26, 31, 36, 40, 65)

Hugo, M., Die Kruger-ultimatum (Vier Maande van Spanning), *Historiese Studies* 4/3 & 4, October-December 1943, 117-208. (1)

Izedinova, S., *A Few Months with the Boers. The War Reminiscences of a Russian Nursing Sister.* Translated and edited by C. Moody. Johannesburg: Perskor Publishers, 1977. (26, 30, 32, 40)

Jacobs, D.S., *Abraham Fischer in sy Tydperk (1850-1913).* Archives Year Book for South African History 28/2, Cape Town: Government Printer, 1965. (22, 29, 31, 33, 39, 43, 47, 52, 66)

Jacobs, J., Die Britse Besetting van Pietersburg en die Operasies in Noordoos-Transvaal in April 1901, *Tydskrif vir Geesteswetenskappe* 39/3 & 4, September and December 1999, 263-86. (52)

Jordaan, G., *Hoe Zij Stierven. Mededelingen Aangaande het Einde*

Dergenen, aan wie Gedurende de Oorlog 1899-1902, in de Kaap-kolonie het Doodvonnis Voltrokken is. 2nd ed. Cape Town: HAUM, 1917. (51, 56, 58, 61, 62)
Kandyba-Foxcroft, E., *Russia and the Anglo-Boer War 1899-1902*. Roodepoort: CUM Books, 1981. (30, 47)

Kemp, J.C.G., *Vir Vryheid en vir Reg.* Cape Town, Bloemfontein & Port Elizabeth: Nasionale Pers, 1941. (1-4, 6, 8, 10, 11, 14, 16, 18, 20, 21, 36, 44, 48, 51, 53, 55-58, 60-66)

Kepper, G.L., *De Zuid-Afrikaansche Oorlog. Historisch Gedenkboek.* Leiden: Sijthoff, c.1901. (1-11, 13, 15-27, 37, 39, 43, 45-47)

Kestell, J.D. & D.E. van Velden, *De Vredesonderhandelingen tusschen de Reegeringen der twee Zuid-Afrikaansche Republieken en de Vertegenwoordigers der Britsche Regeering, welke uitlieepen op den Vrede, op 31 Mei 1902 te Vereeniging gesloten.* Pretoria & Amsterdam: J.H. de Bussy, 1909. (63-66)

Kestell, J.D., *Through Shot and Flame.* London, 1903. (In Afrikaans: *Met die Boerekommando's*. Translated by D.P.M. Botes. Pretoria: Protea Book House, 1999. (1, 14, 17, 27, 57, 59, 60, 62, 63, 65, 66)

Kotzé, H.N. & Kotzé, D.A., *Oorlog Sonder Oorwinning: Die Anglo-Boereoorlog in die Omgewing van Kakamas, Kenhardt, Keimoes and Upington.* Hermanus: Pastelle, 1999. (28, 37, 52, 54, 59, 61)

Krige, J., *American Sympathy in the Boer War. A Plain Tale of Commando Life in the Boer War 1899-1900 and Subsequent Adventures in the United States of America.* Johannesburg: Automatic Printing Press, 1933. (34, 41)

Kruger, R., *Good-Bye Dolly Gray: A History of the Boer War.* London: The New English Library Limited, 1964. (1-6, 8, 10, 11, 14, 16, 18-26, 30-36, 41-44)

Kruger, S.J.P., *Gedenkschriften van Paul Kruger.* Dictated to H.C. Bredell & Piet Grobler. Amsterdam: J. Funke, 1902. (34, 39, 45-47, 52)

Lemmer, G., *Lemmers in die Anglo-Boereoorlog. Die Verhaal van Generaal H.R. (Manie) Lemmer en sy Familie se Bydrae tot die Anglo-Boereoorlog.* Outjo: I.G. Lemmer, 2000. (22-25, 34, 37-39, 42, 44, 48, 51, 66)

Lunderstedst, Steve (ed.), *Summer of 1899. The Siege of Kimberley 14 October 1899 to 15 February 1900.* Kimberley: Kimberley Africana Library, 1999. (5, 9, 13)

Mangold, W., *Vir Vaderland, Vryheid en Eer. Oorlogsherinneringe van Wilhelm Mangold 1899-1902.* Edited and annotated by T. van Rensburg. Pretoria: HSRC, 1988. (7, 11, 15, 18, 24, 33, 35, 37, 38, 43, 45, 49)

Maphalala, S.J., The Murder at Holkrantz (Mthashana) 6th May 1902, *Historia* 22/1, May 1977, 41-6. (52, 63, 65)

Maritz, M., *My Lewe en Strewe.* Johannesburg: Manie Maritz, 1939. (50, 52, 56, 58-61, 64-66)

May, Henry John, *Music of the Guns. Based on Two Journals of the Boer War.* Johannesburg: Hutchinson, 1970. (49)

McLeod, A., Generaal Christiaan de Wet en Jan Smuts: Hoe Hulle die Anglo-Boereorlog Ervaar het, *Tydskrif vir Geesteswetenskappe* 39/3 & 4, September & December 1999, 293-313. (19, 57)

Meijer, J.W., Ben Viljoen se Rol as Kommandant van die Johannesburgkommando, 1899-1900, *Tydskrif vir Geesteswetenskappe* 39/3 & 4, September & December 1999, 243-62. (3, 18, 34)

Meijer, J.W., *Generaal Ben Viljoen 1868–1917.* Pretoria: Protea Book House, 2000. (1, 3, 5, 11, 18, 34-36, 41, 45, 47-49, 52-56, 58-62)

Meintjies, J., *Stormberg, A Lost Opportunity.* Cape Town: Nasionale Boekhandel, 1969. (6, 9, 10, 56, 63)

Meintjies, J., *Sword in the Sand. The Life and Death of Gideon Scheepers.* Cape Town: Tafelberg, 1969. (36, 42, 48, 58, 60, 61)

Meintjies, J., *The Commandant-General. The Life and Times of Petrus Jacobus Joubert of the South African Republic 1831-1900.* Cape Town & Johannesburg: Tafelberg, 1971. (1, 11, 25)
Meyer, I.A., *Die Ervarings van 'n Veldkornet in die Engelse Oorlog 1899-1902.* Ladybrand: privately published, c.1952. (20, 34)

Meyer, J.H., *Kommando-jare. 'n Oudstryder se Persoonlike Relaas van die Tweede Vryheidsoorlog.* Cape Town & Pretoria: Human & Rousseau, 1971. (1, 8, 10, 19-23, 26, 34, 36, 44, 46, 51, 56-59, 62-64)

Meyer, M.J., 'De Brandwacht'. 'n Oorlogsherinnering. *Die Nuwe Brandwag* 1/4, November 1929, 245–51. (60)

Mocke, H.A., Die Slag van Colenso, 15 Desember 1899. Unpublished M.A. thesis, University of Pretoria, 1966. (11)

Mouton, J.A., *Genl Piet Joubert in die Transvaalse Geskiedenis.* Archives Year Book, Twentieth Year – Volume I. Cape Town: Government Printer, 1957. (1-6, 9, 11, 14, 17, 22, 24, 25, 26)

Muller, C.H., *Oorlogsherinneringe.* Cape Town, Bloemfontein & Pretoria: Nasionale Pers, 1936. (47-49, 52, 54, 56, 60-62, 65, 66)

Neethling, E., *Mag ons vergeet?* Cape Town, Bloemfontein & Port Elizabeth: Nasionale Pers, 1938. (49, 51, 55, 59, 60, 62, 65)

Odendaal, R.F., *Swartes en die Tweede Boere-Vryheidsoorlog 1899-1902.* Nylstroom: privately published, c.1999. (8, 65)

Oosthuizen, A.V., *Rebelle van die Stormberge.* Pretoria: J.P. van der Walt, 1994. (52, 54–62, 65, 66)

Oosthuizen, J., Die Eerste Slag van die Tweede Vryheidsoorlog – Kraaipan, *Historiese Studies* 3/2, May 1942, 68-86. (1)

Pelletier, J., France and the Boer War I, *Historia* 33/1, May 1988, 19-30. (26)

Pelletier, J., France and the Boer War II, *Historia* 34/1, May 1989, 52-63. (47)

Penning, L., *Verdedigers en Verdrukkers der Afrikaansche Vrijheid. Karakterschetsen van Mannen van Beteekenis uit den Engelsch-Zuid-Afrikaanschen Oorlog 1899-1902.*'s-Gravenhage: J.N. Voorhoeve, 1902. (1, 7-9, 14, 18, 19, 21)

Pienaar, Philip, *With Steyn and De Wet.* London: Methuen, 1902. (Published in Afrikaans as *Op kommando met Steyn en De Wet. Oorlogsherinneringe van lt. kol. F.F. Pienaar,* Pretoria: Protea Boek House, 2000). (21, 42, 53)

Pieterse, H.J.C., *Oorlogsavonture van Genl. Wynand Malan.* 2nd ed. Cape Town, Bloemfontein & Port Elizabeth: Nasionale Pers, 1946. (44, 47, 50, 51, 52, 54, 57, 60, 62, 63, 65)

Plokhooy, C., *Met den Mauser. Persoonlijke Ervaringen in den Zuid-Afrikaansche Oorlog.* Gorinchem: F. Duym, 1901. (1, 3, 31)

Preller, G.S., *Oorlogsoormag en Ander Sketse en Verhale.* Cape Town, Bloemfontein & Port Elizabeth: Nasionale Pers, 1923. (34)

Preller, G.S. (ed), *Scheepers se Dagboek en die Stryd in Kaapland (1 Okt. 1901-18 Jan. 1902).* Cape Town, Bloemfontein & Port Elizabeth: Nasionale Pers, 1938. (28, 48, 49, 50, 57, 58, 60, 61, 64, 66)

Preller, G.S., *Talana: Die Driegeneraalslag by Dundee met Lewenskets van Genl. Daniël Erasmus.* Cape Town: Nasionale Pers, 1942. (1-4, 43, 60)

Pretorius, E.E., Oorlogskorrespondensie van Jan Floris van der Wateren, 1900-1902, *Historia* 34/2, November 1989, 83-93. (30, 33)

Pretorius, F., Danie Theron Buit 'n Trein op Holfontein 3 Augustus 1900, *Historia* 21/1, May 1976, 55-65. (44)

Pretorius, F., *Die Anglo-Boereoorlog 1899-1902.* Kaapstad: Struik, 1998. (11, 26, 48, 60, 65)

Pretorius, F., *Kommandolewe tydens die Anglo-Boereoorlog, 1899-1902.* Cape Town: Human & Rousseau, 1991. (Translated into English as *Life on Commando during the Anglo-Boer War 1899-1902.* Cape Town: Human & Rousseau, 1999). (32, 65, 66)

Pretorius, F., *The Great Escape of the Boer Pimpernel. Christiaan de Wet. The Making of a Legend.* Pietermaritzburg: University of Natal Press, 2001. (19, 36, 41-44)

Pretorius, F. (ed.), *Verskroeide aarde.* Cape Town: Human & Rousseau, 2001. (37, 40, 59, 60, 62, 66)

Rabie, J.E., *Generaal C.R. de Wet se Krygsleiding by Sannaspos en Groenkop.* Pretoria: Documentation Service, SADF, 1980. (26, 60)

Rabie-Van der Merwe, H., *Onthou! In die Skaduwee van die Galg.* Bloemfontein: Nasionale Pers, 1940. (46)

Rademeyer, J.I., Die Slag van Bakenlaagte, *Historia* 3/3, September 1958, 179-81. (58)

Reichmann, C., Personal Reminiscences from the Campaign in the Orange Free State in March 1900, *Journal of the Military Service Institution of the United States,* XXIX, July-November 1901, 56-73. (26)

Reitz, D., *Commando. A Boer Journal of the Boer War.* London: Faber & Faber, 1933. (16, 46-49, 57, 64)

Reitz, F.W., *Oorlogs en Andere Gedichten.* Potchefstroom: Unie Lees- en Studie-Bibliotheek, 1910. (48, 57, 59, 60, 64, 66)

Reitz, F.W., *Outobiografie met sy Twee en Sestig Uitgesogte Afrikaanse Gedigte.* Edited by J.C. Moll & C.J.S.C. Burger. Cape Town: Tafelberg, 1978. (35, 45, 66)

Rompel, F., *Heroes of the Boer War.* London: 'Review of Reviews' Office, 1903. (1, 7-9, 13, 18, 21, 46, 57, 61, 63, 66)

Ross, E., *Diary of the Siege of Mafeking October 1899 to May 1900.* Edited by Brian P. Willan. Cape Town: Van Riebeeck Society, Second Series 11, 1980. (12, 32)

Rothmann, F.L., *Oorlogsdagboek van 'n Transvaalse Burger te Velde 1900-1901.* Introduced and annotated by M.E.R. Cape Town: Tafelberg, 1976. (35, 48, 52, 59, 60)

Ruijssenaers, L.C., *Krijgsgevangenschap van L.C. Ruijssenaers 1899-1902.* Edited and annotated by O.J.O. Ferreira. Pretoria: HSRC, 1977. (12, 39, 51, 59, 62)

Scheepers Strydom, C.J., *Kaapland en die Tweede Vryheidsoorlog.* Cape Town, Bloemfontein & Port Elizabeth: Nasionale Pers, 1943. (3, 7, 8, 28, 33, 34, 38, 48, 58)

Scheepers Strydom, C.J., *Spieëlbeeld Oorlog 1899-1902* (Part II of the series *Die Afrikaner en sy kultuur,* ed. P.W. Grobbelaar). Cape Town & Johannesburg: Tafelberg, 1974. (6, 49)

Schikkerling, R.W., *Commando Courageous.* Johannesburg: Hugh Keartland, 1964. (36, 52, 55)

Schoeman, J., *Generaal Hendrik Schoeman – was hy 'n Verraaier?* Pretoria: privately published, 1950. (6, 9, 13, 15, 17, 19, 22, 43, 48, 53)

Schoeman, K., *Witnesses to War – Personal Documents of the Anglo-Boer War (1899-1902) from the Collection of the South African Library.* Cape Town: Human & Rousseau, 1998. (34, 53, 55, 61)

Scholtz, G.D., *Europa en die Tweede Vryheidsoorlog 1899-1902.* Johannesburg & Pretoria: Voortrekkerpers, 1939. (29, 31, 33, 39, 43, 45-47, 52, 61, 66)

Scholtz, G.D., *Generaal Christiaan Frederik Beyers 1869-1914.* Johannesburg & Pretoria: Voortrekkerpers, 1941. (36, 41, 48, 52, 58, 59, 61, 63, 64, 65)

Scholtz, G.D., *In Doodsgevaar. Die Oorlogervarings van Kapt. J.J. Naudé.* Johannesburg & Pretoria: Voortrekkerpers, 1940. (66)

Scholtz, L., Die Slag van Tweebosch, 7 Maart 1902, *Historia* 24/2, September 1979, 44-55. (63)

Scholtz, L., Die Slag van Bakenlaagte, 30 Oktober 1901, *Historia* 19/1, May 1974, 60-74. (58)

Scholtz, L. (ed.), *Beroemde Suid-Afrikaanse Krygsmanne.* Cape Town: Rubicon-Pers, 1984. (1, 7, 8, 9, 19, 21)
Schulenburg, C.A.R., Boerekrygsgevangenes van Bermuda, II, Begraafplaas op Eiland, *Historia* 24/1, May 1979, 20-41. (64)

Schulenburg, C.A.R., Die 'Bushveldt Carbineers'. 'n Greep uit die Anglo-Boereoorlog, *Historia* 26/1, May 1981, 37-58. (57, 61, 62)

Schultz, B.G., Die Slag van Bergendal (Dalmanutha). Unpublished M.A. dissertation, University of Pretoria, 1974. (41, 42, 43, 44)

Smail, T. L., *Monuments and Battlefields of the Transvaal War 1881 and the South African War 1899.* Cape Town: Howard Timmins, 1966. (2-4, 6-8, 10, 11, 13-16, 18, 20, 21, 26, 27, 29, 34, 36, 42, 50, 57, 58, 60, 64)

Smith, J.A., *Ek Rebelleer.* Cape Town: Nasionale Pers, 1946. (57-60, 62, 65)

Spies, S.B., *Methods of Barbarism? Roberts and Kitchener and Civilians in the Boer Republics January 1900-May 1902.* Cape Town & Pretoria: Human & Rousseau, 1978. (24, 37, 41, 46-51, 53, 56-65)

Spies, S.B. and Nattrass, G. (eds), *Jan Smuts, Memoirs of the Boer War.* Johannesburg: Jonathan Ball, 1999. (7, 15, 37, 44, 48, 49, 51-55, 64-66)

Stafleu, A., *Die Beleg van Mafeking. Dagboek van Abraham Stafleu.* Edited by A.P. Smit & L. Maré. Pretoria: HSRC, 1985. (1, 2, 3, 5, 12, 16, 25, 27, 32)

Steevens, G. W., *From Capetown to Ladysmith.* Edinburgh: William Blackwood, 1900. (3, 4)

Stemme uit die Vrouekampe. Gedurende die Tweede Vryheids Oorlog Tussen Boer en Brit van 1899 tot 1902. Potchefstroom: privately published, 1925. (62)

Steyn, M.T., *'n Bittereinder aan die woord. Geskrifte en toesprake van Marthinus Theunis Steyn.* Collected, translated and annotated by M.C.E. van Schoor. Bloemfontein: Oorlogsmuseum van die Boererepublieke, 1997. (1, 24, 28, 36, 44, 45, 53, 55, 56, 63-65)

Suid-Afrikaanse Biografiese Woordeboek, volumes 1-5, Pretoria: HSRC, 1968–1987. (1-15, 17-33, 35-40, 42-43, 46-47, 49, 51, 53, 55-66)

Trichard, S.P.E., *Geschiedenis Werken en Streven van S.P.E. Trichard, Luitenant Kolonel der vroegere Staats-artillerie ZAR door hemzelve beschreven.* Edited and annotated by O.J.O Ferreira. Pretoria: HSRC, 1975. (1, 2, 4, 24, 48, 52, 56, 60, 62, 65, 66)

Uddgren, H.E., *Die Helde van Magersfontein. 'n Beskrywing van die lotgevalle en avonture van die Skandinawiese Korps en Ambulans.* Tranlated from the original Swedish into Afrikaans by R. Germann. Uddevalla: Hallman se Boekdrukkery A.G., 1925. (5, 10)

Van Blerk, J.A., *Op die Bermudas Beland. My Herineringe uit die Tweede Vryheidsoorlog.* Cape Town & Amsterdam: A.A. Balkema, 1949. (59, 64)

Van Dalsen, J., Die Hollander-Korps Tydens die Tweede Vryheidsoorlog. *Historiese Studies* 4/2, June 1943, 63-107. (2, 3)

Van den Bergh, G., *24 Veldslae en Slagvelde van die Noordwes Provinsie.* Potchefstroom: privately published, 1996. (1, 3, 8, 12, 21, 32, 42, 44-46, 48, 49, 51, 53, 57, 58, 62-65)

Van den Heever, C.M., *Generaal J.B.M. Hertzog.* Johannesburg: Die A.P.-Boekhandel, 1948. (37, 44, 46, 48, 49, 50, 54, 62, 63-65)

Van der Walt, H.R., Amerika en die Anglo-Boereoorlog, *Historia* 12/4, December 1967, 218-24. (33)

Van Heerden, A.J., Kommandant Carl Petrus van Heerden. Sy Karakter Soos Blyk Uit Vertellinge van sy Strydmakkers, *Historiese Studies* 7/4, December 1946, 164-71. (65)

Van Heerden, P., *Kerssnuitsels.* Cape Town: Tafelberg, 1962. (15)

Van Helsdingen, J., *Vrouwenleed. Persoonlijke Ondervindingen in den Boerenoorlog,* Amsterdam & Cape Town: Hollandsch-Afrikaansche Uitgevers-Maatschappij, c.1903. (49, 54, 56)

Van Jaarsveld, F.A., Dr Otto Gottlob Schnitter: Van Skeeps- en Mynarts tot Boeredokter. *Historia* 40/1, August 1995, 3-29. (59)

Van Loggerenberg, J., Schalk Willem Burger as Boeregeneraal, 1899–1900, *Historia* 37/1, May 1992, 33-43. (14, 16, 18)

Van Reenen, R. (ed.), *Emily Hobhouse Boer War Letters.* Cape Town & Pretoria: Human & Rousseau, 1984. (49, 51, 53)

Van Warmelo, D.S., *Mijn Commando en Guerilla Commando-leven.* Amsterdam: A. Versluys, 1901. (10, 35, 40, 44, 46, 48)

Van Warmelo, J., War Diary (7 volumes, unpublished). Pretoria: Archives of the Nederduitsch Hervormde Kerk. (38)

Van Zyl, P.H.S., *Die Helde-album. Verhaal en Foto's van Aanvoerders en Helde uit ons Vryheidstryd.* Johannesburg: Afrikaanse Pers Boekhandel, 1944. (1-12, 14, 16, 18, 20, 21, 23, 26-28)

Venter, C., Jotham Joubert: Profiel van 'n Kaapse rebel, *Tydskrif vir Geesteswetenskappe* 39/3 & 4, September & December 1999, 329-42. (7, 38)

Viljoen, B.J., *My Reminiscences of the Anglo-Boer War.* Cape Town: Struik, 1973. (18)

Visagie, L.A., *Terug na Kommando. Avonture van Willie Steyn en Vier Ander Krygsgevangenes.* Cape Town: Nasionale Pers, 1932. (61, 65)

Wassermann, J. & Kearney, B. (eds), *A Warrior's Gateway. Durban and the Anglo-Boer War 1899-1902.* Pretoria: Protea Book House, 2002.[numbers 1, 6, 8, 12, 40]

Weeber, E.J., *Op die Natalse Front (1 Oktober 1899-31 Mei 1900).* Cape Town, Bloemfontein & Port Elizabeth: Nasionale Pers, 1940. (2, 4, 6, 11, 15, 16, 20, 21)

Weeber, E.J., *Op die Transvaalse Front, 1 Junie 1900-31 Oktober 1900.* Bloemfontein, Cape Town & Port Elizabeth: Nasionale Pers, 1942. (35, 45, 48, 55)

Wessels, A., Die Boere se Strategie aan die Begin van die Anglo-Boereorlog, *Tydskrif vir Geesteswetenskappe* 39/3 & 4, September & December 1999, 227-42. (1)

Wormser, J.A., *Het Leven van Petrus Jacobus Joubert.* 2nd ed. Amsterdam & Cape Town: J.H. de Bussy, 1916. (1, 25, 26)

Index of Place Names

Abeam 142
Aberdeen 111, 114, 126, 145
Abrahamskraal 47, 49-51, 55
Addo Forest 126
Adelaide 123
Agtertang 14
Ahmednagar Station (India) 122
Albert Junction 14
Alexanderfontein (Kimberley) 14, 41
Alexandria 96
Aliwal North 14, 20, 22, 49, 61, 104, 112, 117, 126, 129, 136, 143, 147
Allemans Nek 78
Aloe Hill (Spioenkop) 34
America Siding 82
Amersfoort 83, 90, 91, 93, 116
Arundel Station 14, 20, 28, 41, 47
Ascension Island 138
Aties 138

Baberspan 139
Bainsvlei 50
Bakenlaagte 125, 131
Balmoral 79, 80, 82, 83, 85, 90, 92, 99, 118, 136
Bamboes Mountains 123
Bankkop 134, 138
Bank Station 88
Bapsfontein 86
Barberton 93, 96, 104
Barkly East 20, 117, 132
Barkly West 27
Bastersnek (Colesberg) 37
Baviaansberg Mountains 65
Beaufort West 2, 59, 119, 127, 131, 133, 138
Begin-der-Lyn 75
Belfast 93, 104, 107, 113, 114, 145
Bellary 144
Belmont Station 6, 13, 15-18, 27
Benaauwdheidsfontein (Kimberley) 12
Bergendal 93, 94, 96
Berg Plaats 116
Berg River 127
Bermuda 127, 128, 138, 144
Berlin (Germany) 74, 100
Bester Station 6, 8
Bethal 125
Bethany railway halt 61
Bethlehem 77, 83, 86, 87, 89, 131
Bethulie 14, 49, 103
Bezuidenhout's Pass 3
Biddulphsberg 71, 72, 80
Biggarsberg Mountains 45, 48, 58, 68
Birmingham (England) 70
Blaauwkop 110, 117
Blesbokfontein (OFS) 89
Blikkiesdorp (St Helena) 112
Blinkwater 114
Bloedrivier's Poort 124
Bloemfontein 2, 7, 12, 14, 21, 28, 32, 40, 41, 43, 44, 47-52, 54, 55, 57, 59, 61-64, 66, 70, 71, 73, 81, 82, 84, 98, 100, 103, 105-107, 112, 115, 135, 136, 143, 147
Bloemhof 63
Bloubank (Ladysmith) 14
Bloubank (OFS) 41
Bloukrans River 42
Blydskap 130
Boesmankop (OFS) 61
Boesmansfontein 63
Bokfontein 94
Bokkeveld Mountains 122
Boksburg 72, 146
Bombay (India) 122
Bontehoeke 138
Boschbult 140
Boschfontein 101
Boschmansfontein 134
Boshof 56, 63, 64
Boskop (Poplar Grove) 47
Bosmanskop 141
Bosrand (Kroonstad) 67
Boston (USA) 71, 84, 144
Botha's Mountain 93, 107, 137
Botha's Pass 4, 78
Bothaville 97, 99, 100

Bothwell 109
Brakfontein (Swartruggens) 94
Brakfontein (Tugela River) 39
Brak River 110
Brakspruit (Western Transvaal) 140
Brandfort 49, 51, 54, 55, 61, 63-66, 70, 122, 129
Brandvlei 114
Brandwater Basin 86, 87, 89, 91, 145
Bremersdorp (Swaziland) 120, 121
Bronkhorstspruit 73, 76, 79, 88, 99, 121
Brugspruit 118
Buffalo (USA) 84
Buffalo River 4
Buffelshoek 44
Buffelspoort 102
Buhrmansvalei 117
Bulawayo 52, 54
Bultfontein (near Mafeking) 3
Bultfontein (near Ventersdorp) 120
Bultfontein (OFS) 143
Bulwana Hill (Ladysmith) 12, 14, 29, 37, 38
Burgersdorp 14, 20, 22, 122, 132
Burtt's Island, Bermuda 128
Byna-bo 129

Caeser's Camp (Ladysmith) 29
Caldas da Rainha (Portugal) 116
Caledon River 57, 87, 103
Calitzdorp 125
Calvinia 106, 123, 126, 127, 132, 136, 138, 142
Cape Town 2, 6, 11, 13, 18, 20, 25, 26, 29, 32, 60, 62, 70, 83, 103, 105, 106, 108, 112, 115, 122, 124, 125, 127, 142, 146
Carolina 92, 93, 99
Carter's Ridge (Kimberley) 19
Cayingubo Hill 9
Ceylon 98, 108, 136
Charlestown 4, 6
Chicago (USA) 14, 84
Chieveley 13, 23, 24, 86
Chrissiesmeer 109, 110, 137
Christiana 63, 64, 67, 70
Cingolo 42, 44
Clanwilliam 122, 126, 132, 138
Clocolan 67
Colenso 4, 12, 13, 15, 16, 18, 19, 21, 23-25, 31, 39, 42, 44, 46, 80, 92
Colesberg 14, 16, 20, 21, 28, 32, 37, 39, 40, 41, 47, 48, 52, 53, 62, 84, 90, 96, 118, 120, 126
Cole's Kop 28, 32, 41
Coligny 134
Colombo 108, 136
Commando Nek (Brandwater Basin) 87, 89
Concordia 142, 145
Cradock 111, 114, 119, 122, 123, 134, 138, 142, 147
Crocodile Pools 12, 54
Crocodile River (eastern Transvaal) 96, 125
Crocodile River (western Transvaal) 85, 94
Cyferfontein 107, 119

Dalmanutha 93
Damvlei (OFS) 50
Darling 126, 127
Darrell's Island (Bermuda) 128, 144
Daspoort (OFS) 57
Daspoortrand, Fort 71
De Aar 14, 59, 103, 110, 111, 115, 120, 131
De Beer's Pass 3, 58
Deadwood Camp (St Helena) 84, 112
De Emigratie 115
De Klipdrift 139
Derdepoort 17-19, 25, 54, 68
Dewetsdorp 42, 52, 53, 56, 61, 62, 99, 100, 103, 114, 143
Diekels Drift (Riet River) 41
Dinokana 54
Diyatalawa (Ceylon) 108
Donkerhoek (Diamond Hill) 77, 79, 82, 86, 90, 96
Donkerpoort Station (OFS) 50
Doornbaai 134
Doornberg 111
Doornbosch 126
Doornfontein (Griqualand West) 134
Doornfontein (near Donkerhoek) 77
Doornhoek 130
Doornhoek (near Greylingstad) 88
Doornkloof (OFS) 137
Doornkom 147
Doornkop (near Krugersdorp) 16, 71, 72
Doornkraal (Bothaville) 100
Doorn River (OFS) 66
Doornspruit (OFS) 89
Dordrecht 20, 28, 32, 49, 123, 129
Doringberg 107
Doringkloof 91
Douglas 27, 80
Drakensberg Mountains 33, 48, 58, 68, 75, 78, 127
Dreyersput 142
Driefontein (Karoo) 123
Driefontein (OFS) 50
Dronfeld station (Kimberley) 7
Dullstroom 98, 113, 114, 130, 131
Dundee 4-8, 38, 68, 80
Durban 2, 13, 18, 26, 86, 132, 143, 148
Dwars River 113
Dwarsvlei 85, 86, 111
Dwyka River 126

Edenburg 41, 97, 115
Edward, Fort (Fort Hendrina) 130, 142
Eerste Fabrieken 71, 77
Eerste Geluk (Brandwater Basin) 91
Eikenhof 95
Elandsfontein 72, 82, 96
Elandsfontein (OFS) 83
Elandslaagte 6-8, 10, 20, 26, 40, 58, 68
Elandspruit 131
Elands River (eastern Transvaal) 91, 121
Elands River (western Transvaal) 94, 119, 131
Elim 130
Enslin Station 22, 41
Ermelo 53, 90, 93, 109, 115, 117, 118, 125, 131, 133, 138, 148
Estcourt 4, 13, 15, 18

Fabersput 80
Fauresmith 97
Feeskop 116
Ficksburg 52, 53, 89, 97, 108
Florida 68, 71
Fouriesburg 86, 87, 89, 143
Frankfort 69, 132
Fraserburg 118
Fraserdrift (Modder River) 40
Frederikstad 91, 93, 97
Frere Station 13, 39
Frierdale 60
Frischgewaagd 93
Frogmore (UK) 105

Gaborone 12, 52
Game Tree Hill (Mafeking) 26
Gamkaskloof 126
Gannapan 63
Gansvlei Kop 78
Garies 134
Gatsrand 93, 95
Geduld 111
Geluk 93
Gelukspoort 110
Germiston 72
Glen 52, 54
Glencoe 8, 21, 45, 58, 68
Goede Hoop 103
Goedvertrouwen 116
Goedvooruitzicht 114
Golden Gate 89, 91
Graaff-Reinet 10, 71, 81, 114, 117, 119, 122, 126, 131, 133, 136, 140
Grahamstown 100
Graskop (Colesberg) 32
Graskop (SE Transvaal) 90
Graspan (near Reitz) 118
Graspan Station 15, 17, 18, 22

Great Fish River 123
Green Point 62, 70, 105
Greylingstad 82, 83, 88, 92
Griquatown 27, 59, 60, 134
Groenkop (OFS) 131
Groenkop (Tugela River) 39, 42, 44
Grootdrift 122
Groot Harts River 139
Groot Marico 94
Groot Marico River 125
Grootvlei 122
Gruisfontein 137
Gun Hill (Mafeking) 11

Haenertsburg 116
Hamelsfontein 110
Hamilton (Bermuda) 128
Hammanskraal 121
Hannover Station 131
Harrismith 3, 8, 124, 132
Hartbeesfontein 78, 88, 104, 111, 140
Hartbees River 134
Hartebeespoort 32, 85
Hart's Hill 46
Hawkins Island (Bermuda) 128, 144
Hectorspruit 95, 96
Hedge Hill 46
Heidelberg (ZAR) 25, 40, 50, 70, 76, 80, 82, 83, 88, 104, 110, 120, 130
Heilbron 67, 69, 70, 77, 80, 86, 89, 90, 107, 120, 145
Hekpoort 101, 102, 116
Hell, The 126
Helpmekaar 8
Helvetia (eastern Transvaal) 93, 102, 114
Helvetia (OFS) 103
Hendrina, Fort (Fort Edward) 130, 142
Hennops River 73, 76
Hermannsburg 12
Herschel 123
Heuningneskloof 13
Heuningspruit Siding 82
Hex River (western Transvaal) 94
Hex River Mountains 127
Hilversum (Netherlands) 113
Hinson's Island (Bermuda) 144
Hlangwane Hill 23, 24, 42, 44, 46
Hoedjiesbaai 126
Holfontein (OFS) 93
Holfontein (western Transvaal) 131
Holkrantz 145
Hoopstad 56, 63, 67, 120, 122
Hopefield 126
Hopetown 6, 72, 80, 82, 90
Horseshoe Hill 46
Houtboschdorp 116
Houtkraal 103
Houtnek (Thaba Nchu) 63-65
Houwater 59, 60, 103
Hussar Hill 42

Impati Hill 5
Ingogo River 69, 75
Irene 73, 143
Israel's Farm 68
Itala, Fort 124

Jacobsdal 17, 18, 41, 97
Jagdspruit 137
Jagersfontein 97, 110
Jam Camp (St Helena) 128
Jamestown 20, 49, 117, 119, 126
Jamestown (St Helena) 84, 128
Jammersbergsdrif 52, 57, 61, 62, 64
Jan Massibi's village 68
Jansenville 111, 145
Jericho Mission Station 85
Jerusalem (GSWA) 129
Johannesburg 2, 6, 28, 32, 40, 47, 63, 67, 69, 71-73, 75, 76, 82, 90, 107, 118, 124, 126, 141, 143

Kaap Muiden 80, 96
Kafferskraal 111
Kakamas 60, 129, 133, 134, 136, 142
Kalahari Desert 16
Kalkkrans 137
Kalkoenkraal 131
Kamdeboo Mountains 117, 119, 126

Kamfer's Dam (Kimberley) 15
Kareefontein 103
Kareepan (OFS) 56
Karee Station 54
Karmel 103
Kaspersnek 96
Katbosch 82
Keeromsberg (near Brandfort) 64
Keeromspruit (near Brandfort) 64
Keimoes 60, 142
Kenhardt 59, 60, 80, 122, 129, 134, 142
Khartoum (Sudan) 25
Kheis 80
Kimberley 6-8, 11, 12, 14-20, 27, 28, 33, 36, 39, 41, 47, 56, 63, 98, 103, 110, 115, 127
Kissie Hill (Stormberg) 21
Klaarstroom 126
Klapperkop, Fort 71, 74
Kleinfontein 125, 137
Klein Harts River 139
Klein Marico 3, 99
Klein Zonderhout 77
Klerksdorp 64, 76, 78, 88, 90, 104, 114, 120, 137, 139-142, 148
Klipdam 114
Klip Drift (Modder River) 41
Klipkraaldrif 41, 43
Klip River (eastern Transvaal) 137
Klip River (Johannesburg) 72, 95
Klip River (Ladysmith) 15, 37, 39, 46
Klip River Station 95
Klipriviersberg 72, 88
Klipstapel 143
Kliptang (south of Nigel) 137
Kloudskraal 126
Koedoesberg 39, 40
Koedoes Drift 43
Koedoesrand (near Mafeking) 68
Koesberg 103
Koffiefontein 41, 97
Komatipoort 80, 96, 125
Kommandonek 85, 91
Kommissiebrug 103
Kommissie Drift 49
Koornspruit 55
Koranaberg Mountain 64
Koster 116
Koster River 119
Kraaipan 1, 7, 8, 18, 68, 90, 134
Kraal Station 92
Kranz 138
Krokodilpoort (western Transvaal) 98
Kromdraai 116
Kromspruit 107
Kroonstad 3, 49-51, 53, 56, 59, 62, 64, 66, 67, 69, 70, 77, 82, 85, 86, 87, 89-91, 93, 106, 114, 115, 136
Krugersdorp 40, 46, 64, 68, 79, 80, 82, 85, 86, 95, 107, 116, 119, 140, 145-147
Kuruman 16, 32
Kwaggafontein (western Transvaal) 96
Kwaggas Poort 73

Labuschagne's Nek (near Dordrecht) 28, 49
Ladismith 125
Ladybrand 8, 26, 52, 53, 55, 67, 96, 100, 108
Lady Grey 20
Ladysmith 4, 6-10, 12, 13, 14, 16, 19-21, 23-26, 28-30, 32, 33, 36-40, 46, 48, 50, 55, 68, 70, 84, 116
Laingsburg 70, 125
Laing's Nek 4, 26, 58, 67-70, 75, 78
Lambertsbaai 106, 126, 127
Langeberg (Magersfontein) 22
Langverwacht 137
Lapfontein 104
Leeukop (near Bloemfontein) 61
Leeu River (OFS) 53
Leeuspruit 80
Le Havre (France) 91
Leliefontein (OFS) 82
Leliefontein (near Garies) 134
Leliesdal 134
Lennox Hill 5
Letaba River 130

153

Letterkop 134
Lichtenburg 3, 18, 72, 78, 88, 102, 107, 111, 112, 131, 134, 137, 139, 140, 141, 145
Limpopo River 10, 14
Lindequesdrift 69, 120
Lindley62, 67, 71, 72, 77, 82-84, 87, 89, 107, 130, 132, 135, 136
Lisbon (Portugal)116
Lobatse12, 58
Lombard's Hill (Ladysmith) 20
London (England) 2, 24, 70, 74, 105, 106, 115, 120, 124, 136, 138, 140, 141
Long Hill (Ladysmith) 9
Long Island (Bermuda) 128
Longwood (St Helena) 84, 112
Loogkop (Poplar Grove) 47
Louis Trichardt 130, 142
Lourenco Marques 61, 86, 95, 96, 116
Luckhoff 97
Lutzputz 142
Lydenburg 28, 78, 96, 100, 102, 113, 114, 121, 134

Machadodorp 71, 73, 74, 78, 80, 82, 92, 93, 96, 102, 107, 114, 130
Machavie 142
Maclear 127, 131
Madibogo Pan 1
Mafeking 1, 3, 5, 8, 11, 13, 14, 16, 17, 25, 26, 28, 32, 33, 36, 39, 41, 54, 57, 58, 62, 67, 68, 70, 84, 90, 94, 106, 115, 134, 145
Magaliesberg Mountains 83, 85, 91, 94, 98, 101, 102, 107, 116, 119
Magersfontein 18, 19, 22, 25-27, 32, 37, 38, 40, 41, 43, 59, 60, 88, 139
Mahemsfontein 92
Mahem Spruit 89
Majuba Hill 2, 4, 9, 26, 29, 34, 58, 68, 69
Makwassie 131
Maleoskop 114
Malepspoort 142, 145
Malmesbury 126
Mapochsgronden 98
Mara 130
Marabastad 52
Maraisburg (eastern Cape) 68, 117, 126
Marico 3, 102, 145
Marico River 18
Mariepskop 75
Marikana 124
Marquard 143
Marseilles (France) 100
Matjiesfontein 125, 133
Matlabas River 10, 14
Mauch's Hill 96
Merebank 143
Middelburg (ZAR) 87, 90, 91, 103, 109, 112, 114, 118, 120, 130, 136, 137, 141, 147
Middelburg (Cape) 122, 126, 134, 145
Middelfontein (western Transvaal)107
Middelpos (near Sutherland) 138
Middelpos (near Lutzputs) 142
Milan (Italy) 61
Mochudi18
Modderfontein (Gatsrand district) 107
Modderfontein (west of Ventersdorp) 93
Modderpoort (OFS) 52, 53
Modder River 17, 18, 22, 25, 27, 32, 37, 40, 41, 43, 45, 47, 50, 52, 54, 55, 61, 62, 70, 97, 100
Modder River Poort 47
Modder River Station 6
Moddersspruit 9, 10, 16, 38, 80
Moddersspruit Station 16, 20, 25, 33
Moedwil 124-126
Mogol River 14
Mogosane River 5
Molopo River 3, 67, 68, 96
Mol's Kop 4, 69, 75
Molteno 21, 32, 114, 117
Monte Christo 42, 44
Mooiplaas 105
Mooi River (Natal) 15
Moolman's Heights 80
Moolman's Nek 89
Moorreesburg 126, 127
Morgan's Island (Bermuda) 128
Moshette's village 1
Moss Drift (Modder River) 22
Mossel Bay 114
Mostertshoek 56, 57, 62
Mpisaan's Fort 121
Muizenberg 140
Muller's Pass 3
Murderer's Poort 123
Murraysburg 114, 126, 145

Nababeep 142
Naboomspruit 120
Naples (Italy) 61
Natal Spruit 72
Nelspan133
Nelspoort 89
Nelspruit 80, 93, 95, 96
Newberry's Mill 53
Newcastle 4, 6, 68, 75, 78, 80
New York (USA) 69, 71, 84
Ngotwane River 54
Nicholson's Nek 9, 10, 76
Nieuwoudtville 127, 131
Nigel 82, 137
Nobelsfontein 138
Nooitgedacht (eastern Transvaal) 80, 93, 107
Nooitgedacht (Magaliesberg) 101, 102
Norvalspont 14, 37, 47-50, 62, 103, 110, 112, 135
Noupoort 14, 20, 47, 103, 126, 131, 133
Noupoort Nek (Brandwater Basin) 87, 89
Nqutu 69
N'Rougas 117
Nylstroom 104, 114

Ohrigstad 96, 114
Ohrigstad River 132
Okiep 142
Old Viljoensdrift 69
Olifantsfontein (Kimberley) 7
Olifantsfontein (Pretoria) 88, 105
Olifants Nek 83, 94, 107
Olifants River 90, 114
Oliviershoek Pass 3, 58
Omdraaivlei 59
Omkyk 134
O'Neill's Farm 69, 75
Onderstepoort 85
Ongers River 59
Oorbietjiesfontein 139
Orange River 6, 8, 13-16, 18, 22, 28, 32, 37, 47-50, 59, 62, 80, 103, 110, 123, 127, 129, 131, 133, 134, 142
Orange River Station 13, 110
Oshoek 131, 134
Oskoppies 43
Ottoshoop 94
Oudtshoorn 114, 140

Paardeberg 43-48, 60, 70, 80
Paardekop 83, 88, 90
Paardekraal (Krugersdorp) 2, 16, 76, 95
Paardekraal (OFS) 80, 82
Paardeplaats 87
Paarl 81
Palala River 10, 14
Palmietfontein 114, 137
Pan 107
Paris (France) 92, 112
Parys 69, 97, 114
Pearston 114
Penhoek Pass 123
Pepworth's Hill (Ladysmith) 9, 14, 20
Perdebergs Drift 42
Petrus Steyn 87
Petrusville 103
Philadelphia (USA) 71, 84
Philippolis 14, 97, 110, 111, 122
Philipstown 103, 110
Pienaarspoort 87
Pienaars River Station 96
Pietermaritzburg13, 19, 26, 32, 106, 124
Pietersburg 10, 12, 96, 104, 114, 116, 134, 136, 142
Pieter's Hill 46
Pieters Station (Natal) 12
Piketberg 126, 127
Pilgrim's Rest 96, 125, 131, 134
Pitsani 58
Platberg114
Platboomfort (near Mafeking) 26
Platkop (Tugela River) 42
Platrand (Ladysmith) 29, 30
Platrand Station 88
Plessisdam 63
Plessispoort (Colesberg) 37
Polfontein (near Mafeking) 3
Poortjiesnek 99
Pootjiesnek 114
Poplar Grove 47, 48, 50, 55
Port Elizabeth 2, 97, 106, 126
Porterville 126, 127
Port Nolloth 142
Port Said (Egypt) 61
Port's Island (Bermuda) 128
Postmasburg 60
Potchefstroom 5, 10, 16, 50, 76, 78, 91, 93, 94, 97, 106, 107, 116
Potgietersdrift (Tugela River) 23, 31
Potgietersrus 116, 125
Poupan 110
Pretoria 1-6, 8, 10-13, 16, 18-25, 27, 28, 32, 33, 38, 39, 43, 45, 47, 48, 51-53, 56, 60-63, 66-68, 70, 71, 73-88, 90, 92, 94, 95, 98, 101, 102, 104-107, 109, 114, 116, 119, 120, 122, 124, 126, 136, 140-142, 146-148
Prieska 59, 60, 81, 90, 103, 110, 138
Prince Albert 125, 133
Prospect, Fort 124
Pruisen (near Potgietersrus) 125
Pyramid Station 85
Pudimoe 6
Putsies 134

Railway Hill (Tugela) 46
Ragama (Ceylon) 108
Ramatlabama 3, 5, 58
Ramdam 15, 41
Ramotswa 54
Ratelpoort (Colesberg) 37
Reddersburg 56, 100, 122
Reitz 3, 78, 114, 115, 118, 120, 130, 137
Reitzburg 93
Remhoogte 94
Renosterkop 99
Renosterpoort 94
Renoster River 67, 69, 70, 77, 79, 97
Renostersspruit 89
Rensburgsdrif 97
Rensburg Station (Colesberg) 41
Retief's Nek 86, 87, 89
Rhenosterpoort 116
Rhodes 20
Rhodes Drift 10
Richmond 140
Riebeek West 124
Rietfontein (Colesberg) 47
Rietfontein (Kenhardt) 60, 142
Rietfontein (Lydenburg) 114
Rietfontein (Mafeking) 68
Rietfontein (Natal) 8
Rietfontein (west of Pretoria) 85
Riet River 17, 41
Rietvlei (Pretoria) 88
Rietvlei (western Transvaal) 137
Rietvlei (Marico district) 145
Riversdal 30
Riverton 6, 7
Robben Island 70
Rondawels Drift (Modder River) 41
Rondebult 116
Roodeheuvel (near Brandfort) 64
Roodekop (OFS) 61
Roodekraal (OFS) 137
Roodenek 134
Roodepoort (Witwatersrand) 71, 120
Roodepoort (OFS) 77, 79
Roodewal (western Transvaal) 141, 142
Roodewal Station 67, 77, 81
Rooidam (near Warrenton) 70, 90
Rooigrond 58
Rooikop (OFS) 143
Rooikop (Tugela River) 46
Rooikoppies 90
Rooikrans 114
Roossenekal 98, 107, 114
Rossmead village (Ritchie) 17
Rotterdam (Netherlands) 66, 69
Rouxville 14, 104, 122, 140
Ruitevlei (near Maraisburg) 117
Rustenburg 68, 78, 79, 82, 83, 85, 88, 94, 102, 107, 116, 119, 124
Rustfontein 56
Rustvoorbij 135

Sabi Nature Reserve 96, 125
Saldanha Bay 126
Salt Pan 130
Sanddrift 103, 110, 131
Sand River 6, 49, 51, 65-68
Sand River Railway Bridge 49, 51, 53, 54, 65, 80
Sandspruit Railway Station 4, 16, 32, 83, 88, 92
Sannaspos 55-57, 61, 62, 103
Schanskop, Fort 71, 74
Scheepersnek 69
Schimmelhoek 125
Schoemansdrift 93
Scholtz Nek 22
Schoonspruit 141
Schuinshoogte (Natal) 26, 69
Schuinshoogte (OFS) 64
Schurweberg 120
Schweizer-Renecke 121
Sebastopol (OFS) 89
Sekhukhuneland 80, 145
Selati Railway Line 75, 96
Selons River 124
Sendelingsfontein 139, 140
Senekal 72, 82, 86, 108, 111, 132
Serfontein Siding 82, 89
Seven Hills (Poplar Grove) 47
Sewefontein (Cradock) 111
Shingwedzi River 130
Signal Hill (Mafeking) 5
Signal Hills (NW of Pretoria) 98
Silkaatsnek 85, 91, 114
Simonstown 26, 32, 62, 70, 83
Skoonpoort 113
Skuitdrif 60, 129
Slaapkrans (Brandwater Basin) 91
Slabbert's Nek (Brandwater Basin) 87, 89
Slagkraal (Poplar Grove) 47
Slingerfontein (Colesberg) 32, 41, 76
Slypklip 6
Smaldeel Station 54, 65, 66, 107
Smithfield 3, 49, 57, 61, 103
Smitsdrif 116
Smoorfontein 138
Soetwater 132
Somerset-East 104, 122, 126
Southampton (UK) 6, 140
Soutpan (northwest of Pretoria) 94
Soutpan (Soutpansberg) 14
Soutpansberg Mountains 14, 125, 130
Spioenkop 31, 33-36, 38, 39, 80, 100
Spitskop (eastern Transvaal) 134
Spitskop (western Transvaal) 116
Spitskrans (Spitskop) 89
Springbokfontein (Springbok) 50, 142, 145
Springfield (USA) 84
Springfontein 110, 115
Springs 105, 141
Sprinkaansnek 64, 100, 103
Spytfontein 6, 22, 130
Standerton 80, 82, 88, 92, 117, 118
Steenkampsberg Mountains 98
Steenkampskop (near Fouriesburg) 143
Steinkopf 142
Stellenbosch 3, 53, 70, 82, 98, 122, 124, 146
Sterkfontein (near Krugersdorp) 86
St George Island (Bermuda) 128
St. Helena 62, 83, 98, 112, 127, 138
Stormberg Mountains 14, 28, 39, 114, 117, 122, 123, 125-127, 132, 134, 138, 143
Stormberg Railway Junction 14, 20-22, 25, 28, 32, 53, 86, 94
St. Petersburg (Russia) 64, 100
Strydenburg 110
Strydkraal Hills 90
Suikerbos 88
Suikerbosrand River 92
Sunday's River (Cape) 126, 133
Sundays River (Natal) 68
Sutherland 138
Swakfontein 125
Swakopmund 136
Swartberg Mountains 123, 125, 126
Swartkoppiesfontein 63
Swartlapberg Mountain 64, 65
Swartpad 134
Swartruggens 93, 94, 124, 125, 131, 135, 139
Swawelkrans 77
Swellendam 132
Swemkuil 59
Syferbult 117
Syfergat 117

Taaibosch 111
Tabaksberg Mountain 65, 107
Tabanyama 31, 33, 34, 36, 38
Tafelkop (OFS) 103, 132
Talana Hill 5, 8
Tandjiesberg 137
Tarentaalrand (Kimberley) 12
Tarkastad 114, 123
Taung 6-8
Tautesberg 114
Terrace Hill 46
Thaba Nchu 52-55, 61, 63-66, 100, 103, 107
The Hague (Netherlands) 66, 113
Tijgerfontein (near Parys) 93
Tijgerkloof (near Harrismith) 132
Tijgerpoort (Pretoria) 86, 88
Tintinyoni 8
Tintwa Pass 3
Toba Mountain 63, 64
Tontelboschkolk132, 134
Transvaal Drakensberg Mountains 116, 125
Trichardsdrif (Tugela River) 31
Trichardtsfontein 131
Tucker's Island (Bermuda) 128, 144
Tugela River 12, 13, 18, 19, 21, 23, 24, 28, 31-35, 37-40, 42, 44, 46, 48
Tulbagh 46
Tuli, Fort 10, 14, 32, 52
Tweebosch 139, 140, 148
Twin Peaks (Spioenkop) 35

Uitenhage 126
Uitkyk Station 103, 118
Uitspanningsfontein 138
Umtata 40
Upington 60, 80, 129, 142
Utrecht (ZAR) 6, 75, 83
Utrecht (Netherlands) 113, 148
Vaalbank 117
Vaalkop (Colesberg) 28
Vaalkop (Hekpoort) 101, 102
Vaalkop (Ladysmith) 21, 24
Vaalkrans 39, 40
Vaal River 7, 27, 56, 63, 64, 69-72, 78, 84, 89, 91, 97, 114, 120, 122, 123
Val Station 83, 120
Vals River 62, 67, 100
Van der Merwe Station 77, 87, 89, 90
Vanggatkoppie 145
Van Kolderskop 92
Van Reenen's Pass 3, 6, 9
Vanrhynsdorp 106, 110, 122, 123, 127
Van Vuuren's Kloof 93
Van Wykskop 78
Van Wyksrust 72
Vanwyksvlei 60
Van Zyl (Colesberg) 14
Vatican 113
Veertien Strome 6, 7, 47, 63, 64, 70
Vendusie Drift 43
Ventersburg 72, 82, 90, 111
Ventersburg Railway Station 66
Ventersdorp 78, 88, 93, 97, 107, 111, 116, 120
Venterskroon 93, 94
Venterstad 114
Vereeniging 69, 72, 106, 107, 131, 145, 146, 148
Verkykerskop 118
Vet River 51, 64-66
Victoria West 70, 127
Vier-en-twintig Riviere 126
Viljoen's Drift (Vaal River) 40, 77
Villiers 82, 130
Vlakfontein (Marico) 102
Vlakfontein (SE Transvaal) 72, 88, 92
Vlakfontein (western Transvaal) 116
Vlaklaagte 83, 120
Voëlfontein 127
Volksrust 4, 19-21, 53, 56, 78, 80, 82
Volstruispoort 93
Vosburg 103, 138
Vrede (OFS) 48, 69, 119, 124, 132
Vredefort 82, 89, 114, 147
Vredefort Road 80
Vredefort Road Station 77
Vredendal 138
Vrieskraal 121
Vroupan 110
Vryburg 1, 5, 6, 8, 12, 16, 32, 126, 139
Vryheid 6, 46, 69, 124, 142, 145, 148

Waaikraal 93
Wagon Hill (Ladysmith) 29
Wakkerstroom 2, 53, 80, 109, 115, 134
Warmbaths 96
Warrenton 6, 56, 64, 70, 115
Wasbank 21, 69
Wasberg 138
Washington DC 49, 69
Waterval (SE Transvaal) 83, 118, 124
Waterval (POW camp) 27, 48, 71, 75, 83, 121
Waterval (western Transvaal) 98, 116
Waterval Boven 83, 93, 103
Waterval Onder 83, 93
Watervals Drift (Riet River) 41
Watervals River 113, 114
Wellington 70
Wepener 52, 57, 61
Wesselton (Kimberley) 11, 12
Wildefontein (near Barkly East) 117
Wildfontein 107, 111
Wilge River (eastern Transvaal) 99
Wilge River (OFS) 137
Wilge River Station (Eastern Transvaal) 99
Willow Grange 15, 18
Willowmore 114
Willows (near Middelburg) 145
Wilmansrust 118
Winburg 3, 51, 54, 64-66, 82, 100, 107, 132
Windsorton 70
Windhoek (Cape) 138
Winterberg Mountains 123
Witbank 114
Witklip 87
Witkloof (Carolina) 99
Witnek 87, 89
Witpoort 88, 98
Witpoortdrif 88
Witpoortjie (near Mafeking) 58
Witsieshoek 87
Witteputs Station 15
Witwatersberg 119
Witwatersrand 2, 6, 68, 120, 130, 146
Wodehouse 40
Wolhuterskop (Bethlehem) 86
Wolhuterskop (Transvaal) 94
Wolkberg Mountains 142, 145
Wolmaranstad 64, 137
Wolwehoek 97
Wolwekraal 43, 123
Wolwekuil 110
Wonderboompoort 85
Wonderboompoort, Fort 71
Wonderfontein (eastern Transvaal) 107, 120
Wonderfontein (western Transvaal) 16
Wonderwaterdrift 72
Worcester 70, 104
Wynne's Hill 46

Ysterberg 116
Ysternek (west of Thaba Nchu) 61
Yzerspruit 137, 139

Zastron22, 103
Zeekoegat 114
Zeerust 3, 91, 94, 125
Zoetmelksvlei 111
Zuurberg Mountains 126
Zwingelpan 110

Index of Names

Ackerman, D.P. 56
Adye, Colonel 60, 80
Albert, Prince 105
Alberts, Commandant 122
Alberts, J.J. 141, 146
Alberts, S. 137
Alberts, H.A. 137
Albertyn, Mrs 128, 144
Albertyn, J.R. 128, 138, 144
Albrecht, F.W.R. 15, 17, 22, 40, 41, 43-45
Alheit, Reverend   70
Alleman, F.S. 148
Anderson, W. 137
Apthorpe, J.K. 112
Aucamp, Commandant 88
Auret 133

Badenhorst, A. 25, 38, 62, 88
Badenhorst, Commandant 132
Badenhorst, C.C.J. 101, 107, 143, 146, 149
Badenhorst, C.P.S. 98
Badenhorst, Field Cornet 34
Badenhorst, Field Cornet 87
Badenhorst, F. 25, 38, 62
Badenhorst, H. 138
Badenhorst, Hans 87
Badenhorst, J. 38
Badenhorst, K. 62
Baden-Powell, R.S.S. 1, 5, 8, 11, 25, 36, 58, 67, 83, 94, 106
Balderacchi, J. 138
Balfour, A.J. 136
Bam, Field Cornet 72
Bantjes, H.J. 138
Bantjes, J.G. 28
Barnard, G. 28
Barton, General 82, 97
Benson, Lieutenant Colonel 125
Bester, A.J. 146
Bester, A.W. 144
Bester, P. 117, 129
Beukes, Field Cornet 54
Beyers, A.M. (née Van der Bijl) 146
Beyers, C.F. 77, 88, 96, 101, 114, 121, 124, 125, 130, 134, 142, 145, 146
Beyers, C.F. (senior) 146
Bezuidenhout, Field Cornet/Commandant 127, 147
Biccard, J. 76, 96, 109
Bierens de Haan, Doctor 109
Blake, J.Y.F. 9, 12, 14, 25, 64, 66, 67, 70, 130
Blignaut, Field Cornet 111
Blignaut, B. 89
Blignaut, J.S.F. 69, 88
Blignaut, P. 88
Bloem, A. 117
Blumlein 81
Bodenstein, C.J. 124
Bonaparte, Napoleon 62, 83, 84, 91, 112
Boonzaaier, T. 126
Borrius, Field Cornet 60
Bosch, F.H. 144
Boshoff, F.J. 102, 124
Boshoff, H.C. 104
Boshoff, K. 85, 94
Bosman, M.S. 23, 24, 119
Botha, A. 20, 109
Botha, C. 23, 44, 68-70, 75, 78, 80, 87, 88, 90, 114, 115, 124, 137
Botha, J.D.L. 3, 54, 58, 68
Botha, J.D.L. (Junior) 99
Botha, K. 126
Botha, L. 9, 12-14, 16, 19-21, 23, 24, 31, 33-35, 39, 42-44, 46, 48, 53, 56, 58, 64, 66-68, 70-73, 75, 77, 79, 80, 82, 83, 86-88, 90, 93, 95, 96, 98, 100, 104, 105, 107, 109, 110-112, 114, 115, 118-121, 123-125, 131, 136, 138, 145, 146
Botha, L. (Junior) 124
Botha, L. (Senior) 20, 48, 70
Botha, M. 137, 145
Botha, M.M. (née Wessels) 48
Botha, Mrs 112
Botha, P. 7
Botha, P.R. 45, 47-49, 54, 61, 64, 65, 67, 77, 100, 107, 111
Botha, S.A. (née Van Rooyen) 20, 48, 70
Bothma, L. 34
Bottomly, Colonel 114
Boyle, C. 107
Bousfield, Commandant 143, 148
Bouwer, B.D. 120, 126, 127, 134, 140, 142, 150
Bouwer, (B.D. Bouwer's brother) 138
Bracht, M.J. 15, 18
Brain, T. 120
Brand, Georg 110, 124, 149
Brand, J.H. 93
Brebner, J. 140, 141, 146, 147, 148
Bredell, M. 148
Breedt, D.C. 126
Bresler, Commandant 114
Breytenbach, J.J.M. 60
Briel, A.Z.A. 10, 23
Brink, J. 108
Brits, C. 131
Brits, Commandant 45
Broadwood, General 55, 87, 90
Broeksma, C. 126
Broers, F. 25
Bronkhorst, Corporal 92
Brooks, Mrs 126
Bruce, R. 26
Brullbeck, A. 29
Bührmann, J. 117
Buller, R.H. 6, 11, 13, 18, 23, 25, 26, 29, 31-33, 36, 38, 39, 41, 42, 44, 46, 48, 68, 75, 78, 80, 92, 93, 100, 102
Bullock, Colonel 24
Burger, A.P. 5
Burger, J.J. (Kootjie) 28
Burger, Miss 148
Burger, S. 27, 70
Burger, S.W. 1, 9, 19, 21, 23, 25, 28, 29, 31, 34, 39, 71, 82, 95, 109, 118, 129, 132, 140, 141, 145, 146, 148
Burgers, T.F. 2
Buys, C.J.S. (née Labuschagne) 130
Buys, S.B. 23, 79, 92, 127, 130
Buys, S.B. (Senior) 130
Buys, S.M. (née Snyman) 130

Campbell-Bannerman, H. 43, 136
Carleton, F.R.C. 9, 10
Carrington, F. 91, 94
Cartwright, A. 81
Celliers, J.F.E. 42, 50, 52, 62, 98, 124, 135, 147
Celliers, J. 42
Celliers, J.G. 111, 131, 134, 137, 139, 141, 146, 149
Cetshwayo, King 20
Chamberlain, J. 70, 102, 124, 140
Churchill, W. 13, 24, 75, 86
Cilliers, B. 146
Cilliers, Field Cornet 30
Cilliers, S. 97
Cilliers, S.A. 97
Claassen, C. 123
Claassens, Commandant 116
Clements, General 41, 82, 101, 102
Cloete 87
Coetzee, Commandant 85
Coetzee, Field Cornet 91
Coetzee, J.C. 1
Coetzee, J.P. 122
Coetzee, K.D. 143
Coetzee, Mrs 120
Coetzee, Widow 119
Coetzer, Field Cornet 20
Coetzer, J. 129
Coleman, W. 56
Colenbrander, Colonel 142
Colley, G. 9, 26, 29, 34, 68, 69
Colvile, H.E. 72, 80
Colyn, L. 138
Conroy, E.A. 129, 134, 138, 150
Conyngham Greene, W. 1, 2, 81
Cronwright-Schreiner, S.C. 104
Coster, H.J. 7
Cotton, Major 102
Crabbe, Colonel 138
Craemer, C. 120
Cray, R.B. 112
Cronjé, A.P. (Father of P.A. Cronjé) 16
Cronjé, A.P. (General) 8, 23, 30, 31, 45, 49, 55, 65, 120, 128
Cronjé, A.P.J. 16, 40, 45, 63, 64, 70, 78, 88, 104, 136, 148
Cronjé, D.J.G.W. (née Rahl) 30
Cronjé, Field Cornet 60
Cronjé, H.S. (née Visser) 16, 84
Cronjé, J.C. (née Geldenhuis) 16
Cronjé, J.D. 30
Cronjé, P. 70
Cronjé, P.A. 1-3, 5-8, 12, 14, 16-18, 22, 27, 28, 32, 37, 39-41, 43-47, 50, 55-60, 62, 83, 84, 88, 90, 91, 120, 132
Crowther, J. 53, 65, 87, 89, 91, 108
Curlewis 120

Dagety, Colonel 57
Daniels, Field Cornet 56, 63
Davel, L. 118, 120
De Beaufort 66
De Beer, J.A.B. 104
De Beer, J. du P. 10
De Beer, J.J. 50
De Beer, Mrs 135
De Beer, Thys 135
De Beer, Tollie 6, 41, 43, 85, 96
De Breda, P. 56
De Bruin, J.M. 61
De Bruin, P.C. 104
De Haas, H. 128
De Hart, P.C. van N. 37, 50
De Jager, M.J. 77
De Jager, Mrs 120
De Jager, Z. 30
De Kersauson, R. 110, 114, 148
De Klerk, Lieutenant 148
De Kock 60
De Kock, M. 104, 107
De la Rey, A. (Adaan) 18
De la Rey, A.G. 18
De la Rey, A.J.G. (Klein Adriaan) 17, 64, 145
De la Rey, A.W. (née Van Rooyen) 18
De la Rey, J.A. (née Greeff) 18, 139
De la Rey, J.H. 1-3, 7, 8, 12, 14-18, 22, 32, 37, 41, 47-50, 54, 62, 64-66, 68, 72, 73, 76-80, 82, 83, 85, 86, 88, 90, 91, 93, 94, 96, 101-104, 107, 111, 114, 115, 118, 123-125, 134, 137, 139, 140, 141, 145-148
Delport, G. 72
Delport, Mrs 25
De Meillon, K. 26
Dercksen, A.J. 23, 42, 86, 88
De Roos, H. 33
De Souza, L. 71
De Villebois-Mareuil, G. 29, 47, 48, 55, 56, 63, 64, 132
De Villiers, A.I. 56, 65, 71, 72, 80
De Villiers, A.I. (Senior) 80
De Villiers, C.J. 12, 13, 29, 30, 37, 87, 89
De Villiers, Commandant 116
De Villiers, Field Cornet 121
De Villiers, J. 30
De Villiers, Jacob (Cape) 81
De Villiers, Jacob (OFS) 100
De Villiers, L. 35
De Villiers, P.H. 65
De Villiers, P.I.F. 80
De Villiers, P.J. 80
De Villiers, R. 126
De Villiers, S.M. (née De Klerk) 80
De Vos, P.W. 77, 100, 110
De Vos, W. 35
De Waal 81
De Wet, A. 20, 59, 60, 148
De Wet, A.S.M. (née Strydom) 42
De Wet, C. (son of C.R.) 42
De Wet, C.M. (née Kruger) 42
De Wet, C.R 2, 9, 10, 28, 39-45, 47, 49-51, 53-58, 60-62, 64-67, 69, 73, 77-83, 86-91, 93, 95-100, 103, 106-108, 110, 111, 115, 118, 120, 121, 130-133, 136, 137, 139-141, 143, 145-148
De Wet, G. 49
De Wet, G. 104
De Wet, I. (son of C.R.) 42
De Wet, J. (Kotie – son of C.R.) 42, 137
De Wet, J. 60
De Wet, J.I. 42
De Wet, N.J. 109
De Wet, P.D. 28, 37, 41, 47, 49, 55, 61, 62, 66, 71, 72, 83, 89, 91, 104, 112, 135, 136
De Wet, P.J. 28, 81
De Wet, S.M. 62
De Wit Hamer, Captain V. 84
De Wit, J. 103
Diederichs, A.P.J 26
Diederichs, C.A. (née Van Wijk) 26
Diederichs, J.H. 26
Diederichs, M.M.M. (née Wolmarans) 26
Diedericks, Commandant 63, 64
Dinizulu, King 6, 20, 114, 138, 142, 145
Dixon, General 116
Doeleman, Kootjie 112
Dommisse, Mauritz 142, 146
Dönges, T. 29
Douthwaite, C.M. 77
Drake, S. 57
Dreyer, T.F.J. 120
Drotsky 118
Du Plat Taylor, Captain 112
Du Plessis, Assistant-Commandant 12
Du Plessis, C. 79, 82
Du Plessis, C.N.J. 50
Du Plessis, Commandant (Free State) 6
Du Plessis, J. 56
Du Plessis, P. 122
Du Plessis, P.J. 138, 145
Du Plessis, T. 136
Du Plooy, Commandant 20
Du Plooy, F.J. 40, 77
Du Preez, D. 80
Du Preez, I.W. 12, 27
Du Preez, J. 40
Du Quesne, F.J. 128
Du Rand, F. 142
Du Toit, H. 116, 146
Du Toit, S.P. 19, 41, 56, 63, 64, 70, 130, 140, 141, 149, 150

Edward VII, King 105, 146, 148
Elliot, Captain 127
Eloff, E.E. (née Kruger) 68, 119
Eloff, F.C. 68
Eloff, J.I. 58
Eloff, S.J. 10, 14, 67, 68, 128
Emmett, C. 124, 142
Enslin, B. 54
Erasmus, A. 132
Erasmus, A.S.D. 114
Erasmus, D.E. 92
Erasmus, D.J.E. 4-6, 8, 9, 14, 21, 31, 69, 75, 82, 91, 92, 131
Erasmus, M.M. 92
Erasmus, P.E. 72
Erasmus, S.M. (née Jacobs) 92
Erasmus, S.M.A. (née Schabort) 92
Esau, A. 106

Fawkes, G. 63
Ferreira, I.S. 41, 44
Fischer, A. 32, 45, 47, 58, 61, 66, 69, 84, 91, 100, 113, 148
Fischer, M. 117, 118, 143, 148
Flygare, Captain 11, 22
Fouchee, W. 114, 117, 119, 122-127, 132, 134, 138, 145, 147, 148
Fourie, A.E. (née De Clercq) 100
Fourie, C. (née Espach) 100
Fourie, C.E. 24, 44, 77, 78
Fourie, C.E. (senior) 100
Fourie, Field Cornet 58
Fourie, J. 78, 82, 91, 93, 99, 100
Fourie, L.J. 107
Fourie, M.M. (née Pieterse) 107
Fourie, N. 117
Fourie, P.J. (General) 17, 41, 55, 61, 77, 86, 91, 96, 103, 107, 110, 111, 118
Fourie, P.J. (Cape Rebel) 22
Fourie, T. 117
Fraser, J.G. 49

Fraser, G. 98
French, J. 7, 20, 28, 32, 37, 41, 43, 52-54, 93, 103-105, 119, 124, 133
Froneman, C.C. 40, 41, 43, 45, 49, 55-58, 61, 77, 80, 82, 91, 97, 100, 107, 110, 142

Garstin, F.C. 60
Gatacre, W. 21, 28
Geyser, Field Cornet 40
Gough, Colonel 124
Gouws, E.M. 2
Gravett, Gert 72, 88, 96, 98
Gravett, P. (née Oosthuizen) 96
Gravett, R. 96
Greef (paralysed POW) 128
Greeff, H.A. 18
Grenfeld, Colonel 82
Grey (POW) 122
Greyling 87
Greyling, Field Cornet 88
Greyling, J.J.C. 41
Grobler, A. (née Snyman) 14
Grobler, A. 91
Grobler, E.N. 14
Grobler, E.R. 14, 18, 20, 21, 28, 62
Grobler, F.A. 10, 14, 28, 32, 37, 41, 47-49, 52, 53, 61, 64, 65, 72, 77, 82, 85
Grobler, H. 3
Grobler, H.S. 125
Grobler, J.N.H. 23, 64, 82, 99, 137, 149
Grobler, P. 119
Groenewald, Commandant 118, 142
Grunberg 63

Haasbroek, A. (née Myburgh) 132
Haasbroek, J.B. 132
Haasbroek, M. (née Joubert) 132
Haasbroek, S.F. 89, 103, 110, 132, 133
Haber, H. 132
Haldane, J.A.L. 13
Hamilton, B. 99
Hamilton, I. 65, 72, 76, 90, 141, 142
Handcock, P.J. 136, 142
Hart, General 46
Hattingh, F.J.W.J. 58, 82, 87, 89, 107, 130
Hassell, J. 34, 90, 95
Haveman, Commandant 28, 72
Havenga, K. 106
Hay, J. 69
Heese, J. 29
Heese, Reverend 130
Henniker, Colonel 132
Hertzog, A. 98
Hertzog, J.A.M. 98
Hertzog, J.B.M. 27, 80, 91, 94, 97, 98, 103, 105-107, 110, 111, 118, 138, 140, 141, 145, 146, 148
Hertzog, S.M.J. (née Hamman) 98
Hertzog, W.J. (née Neethling) 97, 98
Hildebrand, C. 127
Hiley, A. 34, 90, 95
Hillegas, H. 55
Hindon, O.J. 33, 118, 120, 121, 150
Hoare, Colonel 67
Hobhouse, E. 105, 106, 111, 112, 115, 140
Hobbs, Major 15
Hoffman, Dr 81
Hoffman, W. 144
Hofmeyr, J.H. 124
Hofmeyr (missionary) 130
Hofmeyr, N. 2, 20, 24, 31, 38, 42
Höhls, A. (née Mucklenbroek) 12
Höhls, C. 12
Höhls, J.O. 9, 12
Höhls, M. (née Gewes) 12
Hore, C. 94
Howard, General 90
Howell, H. 118
Hunter, General 70, 90, 91, 97

Jabavu, J.T. 120
Jacobs, Acting State Attorney 145
Jacobs, D.M. 144
Jacobs, H.L. 122
Jacobs, J. 142

155

Jameson, L.S. 3, 16, 18, 38, 42, 58, 68, 71, 86, 114, 116, 121
Jansen, J.W.G. 126
Jelliman, Captain 132
Jeppe, C. 35
Jooste, A.C. 122
Jooste, J.P. 59, 60
Jooste, J.P. (senior) 60
Jooste, M.E.C. (née Swanevelder) 60
Jooste, T. 76, 96
Jordaan, J.J. 27
Joubert, Commandant 131
Joubert, D. 130
Joubert, G. 107
Joubert, Gys 62
Joubert, H.J.S. (neé Botha) 2, 20, 53, 150
Joubert, Jotham 81
Joubert, Jozua 23, 24
Joubert, J.F. 2
Joubert, J.J. 101
Joubert, P.J. 1-4, 6-16, 18-23, 28-30, 32, 37-39, 42, 45, 46, 48, 49, 51-53, 55, 56, 58, 71, 101
Joubert, W.F. 28
Judelewitz, H. 60, 80

Kekewich, R.G. 6, 12, 124
Kellner, B.O. 49
Kemp, J.C.G. 88, 101, 111, 116, 120, 124, 131, 134, 135, 137, 139, 140, 141, 142, 145-147
Kemp, J.J. 116
Kemp, M.A. (née Greyling) 116
Kestell, J.D. 3, 29, 30, 38, 58, 124, 130, 135, 136, 138, 140, 146
Kestell, Mrs 3
Kgama, Chief 14, 18
Kidwell, Magistrate 117
Kimber, Lieutenant 120
Kipling, R. 28
Kirstein, Acting Commandant 18
Kirsten, J.R.F. 120, 126
Kirsten (Scout) 85
Kissimoff, V. 136
Kitchener, H.H. 25, 29, 76, 81, 99, 102-107, 110-112, 114, 115, 118, 121, 123, 124, 126, 129, 132, 133, 136, 140-143, 145-147
Kitchener, W. 120, 121, 147
Klein, Sargeant 58
Kleinbooi 120
Kloppert, P.W. 122
Knox, General 91
Koch 135
Kock, C.C.S. (née Schoeman) 10
Kock, E.M. (née Smit) 10
Kock, J. 10
Kock, J.H.M. 1, 4, 6-8, 10, 20, 28, 40, 133
Kolbe, W.J. 41, 45, 49, 54, 64, 65, 91
Koekemoer 125
Krause (burgher) 37
Krause, F.E.T. 71
Krause, K. 122
Krause, L.E. 101
Krause, P.R. 122
Krige, (burgher) 37
Krige, Tottie 142
Kritzinger, M. (née Rudolph) 140
Kritzinger, P.H. 103, 114, 117, 119, 122, 124, 126, 131, 133, 134, 136, 140, 142, 148
Kritzinger, W. 140
Krogh, J.C. 145, 146
Kruger, A. 116
Kruger, H. 62
Kruger, G. (Mrs) 78, 119
Kruger, S.J.P. 1, 2, 6-8, 14, 18-21, 23, 28, 29, 32, 33, 36, 37, 40, 42, 45, 47, 48, 50, 51, 53, 56, 57, 60, 62, 64, 66-74, 76, 78, 79, 83, 86, 90, 92, 95-100, 105, 113, 115, 118, 119, 121, 124, 135, 136, 147, 148
Kruger, W. 126
Kunze, Commandant 109
Kuyper, A. 136, 140

Labotsibeni 120, 121
Laing, Colonel 107
Laing, Doctor 137
Lambart, Captain 78
Lange (traitor) 131
Lansdowne, Lord 136
Lategan, H. 100, 119, 148, 150
Lee, C.J. 85
Le Gallais, M.L. 100
Lemmer, H.J.R. 58
Lemmer, H.S. 42, 47-49, 52, 53, 61, 65, 72, 79, 82, 83, 94, 99, 102, 104
Lemmer, L.A.S. 99, 111, 141, 149
Lemmer, M. 38
Lemmer, P. 54, 99
Lemmer, S. 38
Leo XIII, Pope 113
Leon (Engineer) 53
Leopold, Lieutenant 114
Le Roux, D. 117
Le Roux, J.H. 117
Le Roux, K. 85
Le Roux, Mrs 117
Leyds, W.J. 56, 61, 66, 91, 100, 148
Liebenberg, C.J. 90
Liebenberg, C.P. (née Van der Westhuizen) 90
Liebenberg, I. 136
Liebenberg, P.J. 58, 60, 68, 90, 93, 95, 97, 105, 107, 111, 137, 140, 141
Linchwe, Chief 18, 25, 54, 131
Lloyd George, D. 140

Lombard, H.S. 10
Lombard, J. 3
Lorentz, J. 75, 119, 120
Lorenz, Commandant 64
Lötter, J.C. 117, 123, 126, 131, 132
Lötter, M.C. (née Buys) 126
Lötter, M.P. 126
Loubert, President 113
Louw, A. 60
Louw, A.J. 15
Louw, J. 11
Louw, J. (Commandant) 134, 142
Louw, J.M. 114
Loxton, J. 60
Lubbe, D. S. 14, 15, 17, 27, 65
Ludick, W. 58
Lynch, G. 19
Lyon, J. 12

Machado, A.J. 95, 96
Magato, Chief 116
Maher, Watch Master 116
Mahlangu, Chief J. 137, 138
Mahon, Colonel 68
Malan, A. 65, 66, 88
Malan, Commandant 125
Malan, D. 148
Malan, Field Cornet 54
Malan, F.S. 104
Malan, J. 143
Malan, K. 79
Malan, M.E. (née Pienaar) 143
Malan, W.C. 110, 111, 114, 117, 123, 132, 138, 140, 143, 145
Malherbe, J. 83
Malopi, A. 104
Mangold, L. (née Niesewand) 110
Mangold, W.F.C. 16, 25, 31, 40, 51, 70, 76, 80, 82, 92, 96, 109, 110
Marais, Commandant 101
Marais, D. 32
Marais, F.A. 122
Maritz, G. 55, 68
Maritz, S.G. (Manie) 110, 114, 122, 123, 126, 127, 132, 134, 136, 140, 142, 145, 148, 149
Massey, Major 100
Maximov, E.I. 56, 64
Maxwell, Major General 81
McKinley, President 66, 69, 84
McWhinnie, W.J. 56
Mears, W. 137
Meijer, I.Z. 6
Meijer, M.M.E. (née Landman) 6
Meintjies, L. 57
Meiring, Reverend 42
Menning, C. 29
Mentz, Field Cornet 31
Mentz, H. 142, 146
Merriman, J.X. 81, 122
Methuen, Lord 13, 15, 17-19, 22, 40, 41, 77, 88, 91, 96, 99, 121, 131, 139, 140, 148
Methuen, Mrs 140
Meyer, Field Cornet 120
Meyer, Field Cornet Mot 134
Meyer, G. 40
Meyer, J. (Commandant) 137
Meyer, J.H. 56
Meyer, L.J. 4-6, 8, 9, 12, 20, 31, 41, 42, 44, 46, 68, 69, 71, 72, 82, 145, 146
Meyer, M.W. 145
Meyer, O. 92
Milner, A. 2, 25, 42, 44, 51, 81, 82, 93, 101, 104, 106, 111, 112, 115, 140, 141, 146, 147
Minnaar, P. 103
Minny, P. 30
Mitchell, W.F. 19
Moilwa, M. 54
Molala, Chief 7
Moll, Commandant 121
Molteno, C. 81
Momberg, J. 133
Moneypenny, W.F. 46
Mooiroos 77
Moolman 44
Morant, H.H. (Breaker) 136, 142
Morgendaal, J.J. 107
Morris, Major 118
Morris, Reverend 81
Moshette, Captain 104
Moshweshwe, King 8, 15, 18, 22, 26, 50, 58, 107
Motsewakhumo, Chief M. 36
Mountjoy 132
Mphephu, Chief 24, 36, 38, 53, 143
Mulder, A. 128
Muller (mentioned in peace negotiations) 146
Muller, Captain 137
Muller, C.H. 99, 102, 114, 118, 120, 121, 131, 134, 137, 145, 147, 149
Muller, H.P.N. 61
Muller, J.A. 23
Muller, Sargeant 21
Mussman, Adjutant 84
Myburgh (a burgher) 117
Myburgh, M.W. 142
Myburgh, S. 117, 119, 123, 125-127, 132, 142

Naude, J.F. 145, 146
Naudé, J.J. 150
Neethling, Commandant 116
Neethling, C. 72
Neethling, H. 95
Neethling, H.J. 131
Nel, C. 3, 14, 55, 77

Nel, E. 60
Nel, I. 122
Nel, M. 68
Nesbit, Lieutenant 1
Neser, Commandant 127
Neumeyer, L. 136
Nicholas II, Tsar 100
Nienaber, K. 111
Nienaber, P. 111
Nieuwoudt, C. 103, 106
Nieuwoudt, J. 111
Nyabela, Chief 114

Oberholzer, A.G. 3, 58
Odendaal, Field Cornet/Commandant 127, 147
Odendaal, K. 30
Olewagen, D. 122
Olivier, Commandant 131
Olivier, General 108
Olivier, J.H. 14, 20, 21, 22, 28, 49, 52, 53, 55, 61, 64, 65, 82, 83, 86, 91, 140, 146
Oosthuizen, A.S. 86
Oosthuizen, Commandant 116
Oosthuizen, D.J. 86
Oosthuizen, I. 85
Oosthuizen, Lieutenant 86
Oosthuizen, P.R. 88, 93, 94
Oosthuizen, S.C.H.J. (née Alberts) 86
Oosthuizen, Sergeant 89
Oosthuizen, S.F. 13, 15, 23, 46, 58, 72, 79, 82, 85, 94
Opperman, A.C. (née Badenhorst) 138
Opperman, D.J. 36
Opperman, D.J.E. 31, 34-36
Opperman, J.D. (Koot) 44, 96, 134, 138
Opperman, J.F.B. 138
Opperman, L.C. (née Erasmus) 36
Opperman, P.E. 36
Opperman, P.J. 138
Otto, H.J. 19

Paget, General 99, 119
Parsons, Colonel 60
Papenfus, Magistrate 49
Pauliat, Senator 91
Pepworth 9
Pfeiffer, L.F.S. 122
Philander, D. 142
Pienaar, A. 102
Pienaar, Commandant 88
Pienaar, F. 45, 90, 116
Pienaar, J. 102
Pierce, C.D. 84
Pierson (Dutch Prime Minister) 66
Pieterse, Commandant 65
Pilcher, T.D. 27, 53
Plokhooy, C. 7, 66
Plumer, H. 10, 32, 52, 54, 58, 67, 68, 114, 116, 119, 134
Pohlman, W.F. 93, 94
Postma, Reverend 8
Potgieter, A.H. 68
Potgieter, J. 145
Potgieter, M. 30
Potgieter, F.J. (Commandant, Wolmaranstad Commando) 3, 43, 56, 107, 131, 137, 141, 142
Potgieter, F.J. (Commandant, Krugersdorp Commando) 9
Potgieter, J.F. 65
Potgieter, P.J. 71, 74
Preller, Commandant 47, 48
Pretorius, A.W.J. 55
Pretorius, C. 99
Pretorius, C.M. (née Bouwer) 24
Pretorius, H.P.N. 24
Pretorius, J.L. 5, 23, 24, 73
Pretorius, M.W. 10, 107, 116
Prinsloo, A.M. 72, 83, 84, 107, 110, 130
Prinsloo, H.F. 34, 36, 68, 99
Prinsloo, I. (née Rautenbach) 84
Prinsloo, J. 6, 15, 17, 22
Prinsloo, K. 114
Prinsloo, M. 3, 8, 14, 29, 37, 48, 58, 83, 89, 91, 137
Prinsloo, N.F. 8, 84
Pypers, S. 125-127

Rademeyer, A. 109
Ramapula, Chief 114
Rampolla, Cardinal 113
Ramsbottom, Doctor 103
Raubenheimer, N. 107
Rautenbach, P. 72
Redelinghuys, H. 60
Redman, Mrs Martha 129
Reiger, Dr 148
Reinecke, R. 35
Reitz, D. 35, 98, 101, 105, 123, 126, 134, 142
Reitz, F.W. 1, 25, 60, 73, 76, 78, 86, 95, 98, 101, 102, 115, 121, 123, 124, 128, 129, 136, 141, 142, 144-146, 148
Reitz, J. 128, 144
Retief, P. 55, 68
Rhodes, C.J. 6, 12, 16, 42, 81, 124, 140
Ricchiardi, Captain 68
Rimington, Colonel 130
Roberts, F. Lieutenant 25
Roberts, F., Lord 25, 26, 29, 39, 41, 43-45, 47, 49, 50-53, 59, 61, 62, 64, 66, 67, 69, 71, 73-75, 77-79, 81, 86-90, 93-96, 98, 99, 102, 105, 106, 124, 129, 136
Roberts, H.R. 84
Roberts, Lady 74
Roberts, Mr 19

Roos family (Kimberley) 12
Roos, J. 23
Roos, K. 96
Roos, P. 98
Ross, A. 137
Rossouw 81
Rosten, Commandant 122
Rothmann, F. 102, 113, 130, 132
Roux, D.H.D. 82
Roux, F.J. (née Wiid) 82
Roux, H.H. (née Eksteen) 82
Roux, J.H. 126
Roux, P.H. 65, 80, 82, 83, 87, 89, 91, 108
Roux, Reverend 131
Rudolph, Commandant 140
Ruijssenaers, L.C. 26, 83, 84, 112, 128
Ruiter, J. 120
Rundle, L. 72

Salisbury, Lord 29, 43, 48, 51, 52, 98, 129
Sandberg, C. 73
Scheepers, J. 77, 89, 96, 97, 103, 111, 114, 119, 124, 125, 131, 132, 136
Scheepers, J.J. 136
Scheepers, S.C. (née Van der Merwe) 136
Schiel, A. 4, 7
Schikkerling, R. 77, 113, 125
Schoeman, D. 113, 114
Schoeman, G.J. (née Schutte) 32
Schoeman, H. 10, 14, 18, 20, 21, 28, 32, 37, 41, 47, 48, 76, 91, 92, 104, 116
Schoeman, J. 126
Schoeman, Miss 116
Schoeman, Mrs 116
Schoeman, S. 10, 32, 92
Scholtz, J. 27
Schreiner, O. 81, 104
Schreiner, W.P. 70, 81, 82
Schröder, C.W.H. 60, 81
Schuil, P. 126
Schutte, B.J. 59
Schutte family 139
Schutte, P. 43
Scobell, H. 127, 134
Sechele 18
Sekhukhune 18, 28
Sekota 104
Serfontein, Commandant 15
Shelton, Colonel 142
Shepstone, A.J. 145
Shepstone, T. 145
Sikhobobo, Chief 142, 145
Slegtkamp, H. 33, 120
Smeer, F. 59
Smit, Acting Commandant (Waterberg) 64
Smit, Commandant 138
Smit, J. 64
Smit, N. 69
Smith, C. 112
Smith, H. 30
Smith, Jimmy 71, 76
Smith (POW) 26
Smith, T. 53
Smith-Dorien, General 99
Smorenburg, A. 138
Smorenburg, Commandant 56
Smuts, A. 53
Smuts, C. (née De Vries) 124
Smuts, I. (née Krige) 124
Smuts, J.A. 124
Smuts, J.C. 6, 21, 29, 73, 86, 101, 102, 104, 107, 111, 114, 115, 118-120, 122-124, 126, 127, 132, 134, 136, 138, 140, 142, 143, 145-147
Smuts, J.J. (née Buhrmann) 53
Smuts, R. 143
Smuts, R.M. (née Joubert) 53
Smuts, T. 23, 31, 39, 53, 54, 58, 64, 72, 77, 88, 90, 120, 121
Snoeks 117
Snyman, H. 3, 11, 54, 58
Snyman, J.P. 8, 12, 25, 36, 54, 57, 58, 67, 68, 77
Snyman, P.S. 24
Solomon, R. 70, 81
Spragge, Colonel 72
Sprigg, G. 81
Spruyt, C. 44, 96, 119, 120
Spruyt, D. 40, 109, 120
Spruyt, Jan 120
Spruyt, Johanna 120
Spruyt, John 76, 82, 92
Spruyt, M. 20
Spruyt, O. 120
Spruyt, S.J.G. (née Smith) 120
Stadler, A. 134, 142
Stafleu, A. 3, 25, 54, 57
Stead, W.T. 24, 30
Steenberg, G. 57
Steenekamp, Commandant (Free State) 9, 10
Steenekamp, P.S. 3, 94, 150
Steenkamp, L. (Cape Rebel) 59, 60
Steenkamp, L. (Heilbron Commando) 77, 86
Steenkamp, Mrs 113
Steenkamp, P. 20
Steevens, G.W. 7, 10
Steyn, M.T. 2, 6, 7, 13-15, 18-22, 28, 32, 33, 37, 40, 42, 45, 47-49, 51-54, 57, 59, 61, 66, 67, 69, 71, 73, 77, 78, 80, 82, 83, 86, 87, 89, 90, 91, 94, 98, 100, 103, 106, 107, 110, 111, 115, 118-122, 128, 130, 132, 133, 135-141, 145-147
Steyn, P.G. 120, 128
Steyn, T. (née Fraser) 59
Steyn, W. 134, 142

Stoffberg, T.S. 146
Stoltz 125
Stowe, Colonel 93
Swanepoel, F. 136
Swanepoel, J. 14, 20, 57
Swart, Field Cornet 132
Swart, P.D. 12, 54
Symons, W.P. 4, 5, 6, 8

Taute, Commandant 114
Tennant 132
Te Water, T.N.G. 70, 81
Theron, D. 8, 23, 45, 46, 48, 51-54, 59, 60, 63, 73, 87, 89, 93, 95, 133, 142, 143
Theron, J. 95, 110, 127, 142
Theron, T.P. 81
Theunissen, Commandant (Bloemhof) 63
Theunissen, H. 45
Thiel, G. 116
Thomas, Captain 90
Thuynsma, Lieutenant 77, 118
Trichard, Carolus 114
Trichard, Carolus 114
Trichard, Louis 114
Trichard, S.P.E. 4, 6, 9, 46, 51, 54, 65, 77, 103, 114, 121, 130, 131, 137, 145-148
Trichardt, P.F. 23, 86
Turner (Engineer) 52
Turner, H.S. 19
Tuynsma, Sargeant 27

Upton, R.C. 126
Uys, D. 55
Uys, P. 55, 68

Vallentin, Major 134
Van Aardt, F. 86
Van Alphen, Mrs 81
Van As, L. 103
Van As, S. 146
Van Belkum, Reverend 148
Van Blerk, J.A. 128, 144
Van Brakel (POW) 128
Van Dam, C.D. (née Kroep) 76
Van Dam, G.M.J. 9, 12, 28, 41, 66, 76
Van Dam, G.C.A. 76
Van Dam, M.M. (née Steyn) 76
Van den Berg, Field Cornet (Vryheid) 58
Van der Lingen, Reverend 3
Van der Merwe, G. 13, 15
Van der Merwe, J.L. 148
Van der Merwe, K. 85
Van der Merwe, P. 123
Van der Merwe, W.J. 146
Van der Walt, I.J. 81
Van der Werf, A. 88
Van der Westhuizen, J. 59
Van Deventer, J.L. 116, 120, 122, 126, 127, 132, 138, 140, 142, 149
Van Heerden, B.J. 145
Van Heerden, C. 140, 145
Van Heerden, H. 111
Van Lier, S. 93, 94
Van Manen, F.S. 146
Van Niekerk, C.A. 3, 146, 150
Van Niekerk, H. 130
Van Niekerk, Mrs 135
Van Reenen, G. 114, 117, 138
Van Rensburg, H.C.J. 10, 14, 23, 44
Van Rensburg, J. 122
Van Rensburg, N. 139
Van Rensburg, W.C.J. 25, 54
Van Rooyen 142
Van Rooyen, Reverend 124
Van Staden, G. 57
Van Staden, M.P. 101
Van Tonder, A. 110
Van Velden, D. 109
Van Vuuren, F. 32
Van Vuuren, J. 126
Van Warmelo, J. 75, 81, 150
Van Zijl, E.L. 24
Van Zyl, General 139
Veenstra, H.J. 126
Venter, Commandant 80
Venter, N.T. 122
Vermaas, H.C.W. 3, 85, 96, 107, 111, 112
Victoria, Queen 25, 30, 48, 70, 71, 105, 106, 119
Viljoen, B.J. 4, 7, 12, 14, 23, 39, 40, 71-73, 77, 85, 86, 96, 99, 102, 107, 114-116, 118, 120, 121, 125, 130, 131, 132, 134, 138
Viljoen, Commandant (Marico) 134
Viljoen, D.J. 122
Viljoen, H.B. (née Els) 40
Viljoen, J. 25
Viljoen, J.W. 25
Viljoen, Field Cornet Jan (OFS) 100
Viljoen, Johannes 84
Viljoen, P. 25, 26
Viljoen, P.R. 80, 82, 131, 141, 150
Viljoen, Reverend 3
Viljoen, S.M. (née Storm) 40
Viljoen, W. 102, 114, 118, 134
Viljoen, W.J. 40
Vilonel, S.G. 86, 91, 143
Visser, P.H. 8, 16, 32, 40, 85
Von Dalwig, Captain 54, 58, 72, 77, 92, 93
Von Donop, S.B. 125, 137
Von Lossberg, O. 73, 77, 85
Von Rangel, F. 64
Von Rennenkampf, C.W. 137, 139, 140
Von Wichmann, Lieutenant 75
Vorster, B. 14
Vorster, Commandant 80